Thinking Critically

JOHN CHAFFEE, PhD

Director, Center for Philosophy and Critical Thinking,
City University of New York

CENGAGE
Learning·

Australia • Brazil • Japan • Korea • Mexico • Singapore • Spain • United Kingdom • United States

Thinking Critically, Eleventh Edition
John Chaffee

Product Director: Monica Eckman

Product Manager: Margaret Leslie

Senior Content Developer: Leslie Taggart

Development Editor: Craig Leonard

Content Coordinator: Sarah Turner

Product Assistant: Cailin Barrett-Bressack

Media Developer: Janine Tangney

Marketing Brand Manager: Lydia LeStar

Senior Content Project Manager:
Aimee Chevrette Bear

Art Director: Hannah Wellman

Manufacturing Planner: Betsy Donaghey

Rights Acquisition Specialist: Ann Hoffman

Production Service: Tania Andrabi,
Cenveo® Publisher Services

Text Designer: Liz Harasymczuk

Cover Designer: Sarah Bishins

Cover Image: Antonio M. Rosario/
The Image Bank/Getty Images

Compositor: Cenveo Publisher Services

For product information and technology assistance, contact us at
Cengage Learning Customer & Sales Support, 1-800-354-9706

For permission to use material from this text or product,
submit all requests online at **www.cengage.com/permissions.**
Further permissions questions can be emailed to
permissionrequest@cengage.com.

Library of Congress Control Number: 2013941787

ISBN-13: 978-1-285-43011-9

ISBN-10: 1-285-43011-5

Cengage Learning
200 First Stamford Place, 4th Floor
Stamford, CT 06902
USA

Cengage Learning is a leading provider of customized learning solutions with office locations around the globe, including Singapore, the United Kingdom, Australia, Mexico, Brazil and Japan. Locate your local office at **international.cengage.com/region.**

Cengage Learning products are represented in Canada by Nelson Education, Ltd.

For your course and learning solutions, visit **www.cengage.com.**

Purchase any of our products at your local college store or at our preferred online store **www.cengagebrain.com.**

Instructors: Please visit **login.cengage.com** and log in to access instructor-specific resources.

Printed in the United States of America
1 2 3 4 5 6 7 17 16 15 14 13

Brief Contents

For Jessie and Joshua

Contents

Dan McCoy–Rainbow/Science Faction/Corbis

Thinking Critically About Visuals
Learn to think critically about what you see on pages 5, 6, 16, 33, and 38.

Thinking Critically About New Media
Learn to think critically about new media on page 34.

© The Metropolitan Museum of Art, New York, NY, U.S.A./Art Resource, NY

Thinking Critically About Visuals
Learn to think critically about what you see on pages 56, 64, 68, 74, 82, and 89.

Thinking Critically About New Media
Learn to think critically about new media on page 80.

Justin Sullivan/Getty Images

Thinking Critically About Visuals Learn to think critically about what you see on pages 110, 117, 118, 121, and 126.

Thinking Critically About New Media Learn to think critically about new media on page 128.

CHAPTER 3   Solving Problems   105

CHAPTER 4   Perceiving and Believing   143

Radius Images/Jupiter Images

Thinking Critically About Visuals Learn to think critically about what you see on pages 149, 155, 158, 166, and 190.

Thinking Critically About New Media
Learn to think critically about new media on page 178.

CHAPTER 5   Constructing Knowledge   197

AP Photo/Susan Sterner

Thinking Critically About Visuals
Learn to think critically about what you see on pages 208, 209, 212, 225, 227, and 237.

Thinking Critically About New Media
Learn to think critically about new media on page 222.

CHAPTER 6   Language and Thought   251

Thinking Critically About Visuals
Learn to think critically about what you see on pages 268, 270, and 280.

Reuters/Ahmed Jadallah/CORBIS

Thinking Critically About New Media
Learn to think critically about new media on page 290.

CHAPTER 7 Forming and Applying Concepts 309

Thinking Critically About Visuals
Learn to think critically about what you see on pages 318, 331, 333, 334, and 339.

Thinking Critically About New Media
Learn to think critically about new media on page 342.

AP Photo/Peter Kramer

CHAPTER 8 Relating and Organizing 349

Thinking Critically About Visuals
Learn to think critically about what you see on pages 368, 374, and 379.

Abid Katib/Getty Images

Thinking Critically About New Media
Learn to think critically about new media on page 366.

CHAPTER 9   Thinking Critically About Moral Issues   387

David Silverman/Getty Images News/Getty Images

Thinking Critically About Visuals
Learn to think critically about what you see on pages 397, 402, 408, and 416.

Thinking Critically About New Media
Learn to think critically about new media on page 418.

CHAPTER 10   Constructing Arguments   437

LondonPhotos-Homer Sykes/Alamy

Thinking Critically About Visuals
Learn to think critically about what you see on pages 439, 452, and 457.

Thinking Critically About New Media
Learn to think critically about new media on page 460.

CHAPTER 11   Reasoning Critically   473

Courtesy, Do It Now Foundation

Thinking Critically About Visuals
Learn to think critically about what you see on pages 498, 501, 509, 517, and 523.

Thinking Critically About New Media
Learn to think critically about new media on page 504.

CHAPTER 12   Thinking Critically, Living Creatively   531

AP Photo/Peter R. Barber/The Daily Gazette

**Thinking Critically
About Visuals**
Learn to think
critically about what
you see on pages
540, 561, and 563.

Readings

Preface

Critical thinking is the cornerstone of higher education, the hallmark of an educated person, and teaching a course in critical thinking is one of the most inspiring and rewarding experiences that a teacher can have. Because the thinking process is such an integral part of who we are as people, the prospect of expanding students' thinking implies expanding who they are as human beings—the perspective from which they view the world, the concepts and values they use to guide their choices, and the impact they have on the world as a result of those choices. Teaching students to become critical thinkers does not mean simply equipping them with certain intellectual tools; it involves their personal transformation and its commensurate impact on the quality of their lives and the lives of those around them. This is truly education at its most inspiring!

Thinking Critically, Eleventh Edition, is a comprehensive introduction to the cognitive process and helps students develop the higher-order thinking abilities needed for academic study and career success. Based on a nationally recognized interdisciplinary program in Critical Thinking established in 1979 at LaGuardia College (The City University of New York) and involving more than two thousand students annually, *Thinking Critically* integrates various perspectives on the thinking process drawn from a variety of disciplines such as philosophy, cognitive psychology, linguistics, and the language arts (English, reading, and oral communication).

Thinking Critically addresses a crucial need in higher education by introducing students to critical thinking and fostering sophisticated intellectual and language abilities. Students apply their evolving thinking abilities to a variety of subjects drawn from academic disciplines, contemporary issues, and their life experiences. *Thinking Critically* is based on the assumption, supported by research, that learning to think more effectively is a synthesizing process, knitting critical thinking abilities together with academic content and the fabric of students' experiences. Thinking learned in this way becomes a constitutive part of who students are.

Features

This book has a number of distinctive characteristics that make it an effective tool for both instructors and students. *Thinking Critically*

- *teaches the fundamental thinking, reasoning, and language abilities that students need for academic success.* By focusing on the major thinking and language abilities needed in all disciplines, and by including a wide variety of readings, the text helps students perform more successfully in other courses.

- *stimulates and guides students to think clearly about complex, controversial issues.* The many diverse readings provide in-depth perspectives on significant social issues. More important, the text helps students develop the thinking and language abilities necessary to understand and discuss intelligently these complex issues.

- *presents foundational thinking, reasoning, and language abilities in a developmentally sequenced way.* The text begins with basic abilities and then carefully progresses to more sophisticated thinking and reasoning skills. Cognitive maps open each chapter to help students understand the thinking process as well as the interrelationship of ideas within that chapter.

- *engages students in the active process of thinking.* Exercises, discussion topics, readings, and writing assignments encourage active participation, stimulating students to critically examine their own and others' thinking and to sharpen and improve their abilities. The text provides structured opportunities for students to develop their thinking processes in a progressive, reflective way.

- *provides context by continually relating critical-thinking abilities to students' daily lives.* Once students learn to apply critical-thinking skills to situations in their own experiences, they then apply these skills to more abstract, academic contexts. Additionally, by asking students to think critically about themselves and their experiences, the text fosters their personal development as mature, responsible, critical thinkers.

- *integrates the development of thinking abilities with the four language skills so crucial to success in college and careers: reading, writing, speaking, and listening.* The abundant writing assignments (short answer, paragraph, and essay), challenging readings, and discussion exercises serve to improve students' language skills.

- *provides a design for a visual culture.* The four-color design supports visual learning styles, prompts students to think critically about the way print media messages are shaped, and helps clarify distinctions between the many different features and elements of the book's pedagogy—text, readings, and other elements.

- *includes coverage of analyzing visual information.* A section in Chapter 1, "Images, Decision Making, and Thinking About Visual Information," discusses and models the ways in which the medium shapes the message, and introduces concepts for critical evaluation of visual information. Each chapter also includes a feature, "Thinking Critically About Visuals," that engages students in comparing and evaluating images drawn from current events and popular culture.

- *includes substantive treatment of creative thinking.* Chapters 1 and 12 begin and end the book by linking critical thinking to creative thinking. Chapter 1 analyzes the creative process and develops creative-thinking abilities, providing a template for approaching issues and problems both critically and creatively throughout the text. Chapter 12, "Thinking Critically, Living Creatively," reinforces these connections and encourages students to create a life philosophy through moral choices.

- *includes a chapter on ethics.* Chapter 9, "Thinking Critically About Moral Issues," was developed at the suggestion of reviewers who noted the deep engagement many students have with the moral and ethical choices our complex and interconnected society requires them to make.
- *includes a section on constructing extended arguments.* Chapter 10, "Constructing Arguments," includes a section, "Constructing Extended Arguments," that presents a clear model for researching and writing argumentative essays.
- *includes a critical-thinking test.* "Tom Randall's Halloween Party," or the Test of Critical Thinking Abilities, developed by the author, is included in the Instructor's Resource Manual and in interactive form on the student website, and provides for a comprehensive evaluation of student thinking and language abilities. Using a court case format arising from a fatal student drinking incident, the test challenges students to gather and weigh evidence, ask relevant questions, construct informed beliefs, evaluate expert testimony and summation arguments, reach a verdict, and then view the entire case from a problem-solving perspective.

New to the Eleventh Edition

The eleventh edition gives students a method for integrating self-assessment throughout the course; provides new readings, films, and visuals for students to analyze and critique; and takes a casebook approach to give students a richer context in which to read individual perspectives on current issues.

A **new "Assessing Your Strategies and Creating New Goals" at the end of each chapter helps students monitor their own progress.** Self-assessment ratings provide an ongoing opportunity for students to evaluate their critical- and creative-thinking abilities, as well as how thoughtful and enlightened their choices are. Strategies are then suggested that students can methodically apply to improve their thinking abilities and, thus, their lives.

New readings increase the emphasis on important social issues. Twenty new readings have been added on such topics as the Casey Anthony trial, gun control and school shootings, climate change, genetically modified foods, and the changing notion of what constitutes a family. These timely and provocative readings have been written by a variety of noteworthy authors and journalists:

"Worse Than O.J.!" by Marcia Clark
"Casey Anthony: The System Worked" by Alan M. Dershowitz
"Casey Anthony Juror: 'Sick to Our Stomachs' Over Not Guilty Verdict" by Mary Kate Burke, Jessica Hopper, Enjoli Francis, and Lauren Effron
"Connecticut School Shooting 'An Attack On America'" by Ted Anthony
"The Price of Gun Control" by Dan Baum
Edited text of remarks delivered by NRA CEO Wayne La Pierre
"Why Gun 'Control' Is Not Enough" by Jeff McMahan
"The (Terrifying) Transformative Potential of Technology" by Lisa Wade
Comments by Joe Scarborough on *Morning Joe*
"The Great Climate Experiment" by Ken Caldeira

"Global Warming: Hoax of the Century" by Patrick J. Buchanan
"Why Media Tell Climate Story Poorly" by Tyler Hamilton
An analysis of the crash of Avianca Airlines flight 052, by Malcolm Gladwell
"New 'Non-Traditional' American Families" by Kate Rice
"We Are Family" by Bob Morris
"Three Grown-Ups and a Baby" by Lisa Belkin
"What Makes a Family? Children, Say Many Americans" by John Berman
"The Rise of Post-Familialism: Humanity's Future?" by Joel Kotkin
"Do Seed Companies Control GM Crop Research?" by the Editors of *Scientific American*

In addition to the new readings, we have also kept those readings that have earned consistently high praise from users of the book, including the following:

"Critical Thinking and Obedience to Authority" by John Sabini and Maury Silver
"The Disparity Between Intellect and Character" by Robert Coles
"Accounts of the Assassination of Malcolm X"

A casebook approach to readings reveals multiple perspectives on the important events of the day and enriches students' understanding of the larger context of each issue. For easy reference, all the readings in the book are now listed after the detailed table of contents.

Expanded lists of "Suggested Films" help students explore the chapter's topics through the medium of film. A description of each of the sixty suggested films helps students and instructors decide which are most interesting and relevant to their current study.

New photos in "Thinking Critically About Visuals" features and throughout the chapters give students material for critical thinking and evaluation. Each chapter features new photographs in the "Thinking Critically About Visuals" boxes and elsewhere. These twenty-eight new photographs, along with the many others in the book, challenge students to think critically about the role of images in viewers' perceptions and about their own responses to them.

Supplements for Instructors and Students

ENHANCED INSITE FOR *THINKING CRITICALLY*, 11e*

Easily create, assign, and grade writing assignments with Enhanced InSite™ for *Thinking Critically, 11e*. From a single, easy-to-navigate site, you and your students can manage the flow of papers online, check for originality, and conduct peer reviews. Access a fully customizable, interactive and true-to-page eBook (YouBook), writing prompts for each chapter, private tutoring options, and resources for

*Access card required. Instructors may contact their local representative for packaging information. Students may purchase instant access to **Enhanced InSite™ for John Chaffee's Thinking Critically**, Eleventh Edition, at CengageBrain.com, our preferred online store.*

writers that include anti-plagiarism tutorials and downloadable grammar podcasts. Enhanced InSite™ provides the tools and resources you and your students need plus the training and support you want. Learn more at http://www.cengage.com/insite.

APLIA FOR *THINKING CRITICALLY*

Aplia is a learning solution that increases student effort and engagement, enabling instructors to concentrate on the important work of teaching and interacting with students. Features include customizable, auto-graded homework assignments with randomized questions; assessment analytics that track student participation, progress, and performance in real-time graphical reports; flexible gradebook tools compatible with other learning management systems; convenient course communication resources, offering a discussion board, email, document uploads, and more; and an industry-leading support team.

ONLINE INSTRUCTOR'S MANUAL

Available for download on the book's companion site, the Instructor's Manual is designed to help instructors tailor *Thinking Critically* to their own courses. The manual includes both a comprehensive bibliography of critical- and creative-thinking resources and a bibliography of suggested fiction, nonfiction readings, and films relating to the themes of the text.

QUICK COACH GUIDE TO CRITICAL THINKING

Part of the *Quick Coach Guide* series, this is a brief paperback intended to help students focus on key concepts in critical thinking, with explanations, practice exercises, and cases to help students develop their critical-thinking skills. (Instructors may contact their local sales representative for information about bundling options.)

Acknowledgments

Many persons from a variety of disciplines have contributed to this book at various stages of its development over the past editions, and I thank my colleagues for their thorough scrutiny of the manuscript and their incisive and creative comments. In addition, I offer my deepest gratitude to the faculty members at LaGuardia who have participated with such dedication and enthusiasm in the Critical Thinking program, and to the countless students whose commitment to learning is the soul of this text.

The following reviewers also provided evaluations that were of great help in preparing the Eleventh edition:

Sabine Winter, Eastfield College
Sunita Lanka, Hartnell College
James Barnes, James Madison University
Karen Zempel, Bryant and Stratton College
Joanne Richmond, Western Technical College
Kirsten Hanson, Indian Hills Community College

Jen Hirt, Penn State Harrisburg
Todd Spellman, Lincoln College
Glenda Yount, Alamance Community College
Jennifer Caseldine-Bracht, Indiana University-Purdue University
Shannon Sanchez, Cerritos College
Anissa Harris, Harding University

I have been privileged to work with a stellar team of people at Cengage who are exemplary professionals and also valued friends. Monica Eckman, Product Director, has been steadfast in her personal and professional support of *Thinking Critically* in its various editions, and I am deeply grateful. Margaret Leslie, Product Manager, provided wise guidance and crucial decisions in overseeing this and the previous revisions of *Thinking Critically*; her steady hand at the helm and insightful suggestions at key junctures were essential. My heartfelt thanks go to Leslie Taggart who, in her role as Senior Content Developer, provided the comprehensive direction and creative vision for this splendid edition, as she did for previous editions; that will be crucial for the book's continued success. My ongoing friendship with the "two Leslies" has been a unique joy which I treasure. It was a special pleasure working with the Development Editor, Craig Leonard, who was instrumental in shaping this new edition with a conscientious attention to detail and unwavering commitment to excellence. His talented eye for striking visuals was particularly valued. I am appreciative of the excellent support provided by the Assistant Editor, Sarah Turner, and also the Editorial Assistant, Cailin Barrett-Bressack. Aimee Bear, Senior Content Project Manager, was assiduous in making sure the production process moved ahead flawlessly, and my thanks are also extended to the Senior Production Manager Samantha Ross Miller for her expert oversight. I am indebted to Hannah Wellman, who as Art Director oversaw the stunning new design of this edition, and my thanks go also to the Media Editor, Janine Tangney. Ann Hoffman was unusually conscientious in her role as Rights Acquisition Specialist, and I am grateful for the expert work of the Manufacturing Planner, Betsy Donaghey. I would like to extend my appreciation to the Marketing staff for their talented and innovative efforts on behalf of *Thinking Critically*: Marketing Director Stacey Purviance, Marketing Manager Lydia LeStar, and Marketing Development Manager Erin Parkins.

Finally, I thank my wife, Heide, and my children, Jessie and Joshua, for their complete and ongoing love, support, and inspiration. It is these closest relationships that make life most worth living. And I wish to remember my parents, Charlotte Hess and Hubert Chaffee, who taught me lasting lessons about the most important things in life. They will always be with me.

Although this is a published book, it continues to be a work in progress. In this spirit, I invite you to share your experiences with the text by sending me your comments. I hope that this book serves as an effective vehicle for your own critical thinking explorations in living an examined life. You can contact me online at **JCthink@aol.com**; my mailing address is LaGuardia College, City University of New York, Humanities Department, 31-10 Thomson Avenue, Long Island City, NY 11101.

John Chaffee

ELEVENTH EDITION

Thinking Critically

Chuck Thomas Close (born July 5, 1940, Monroe, Washington) is an American painter and photographer who achieved fame as a photorealist through his massive-scale portraits. Though a catastrophic spinal artery collapse in 1988 left him severely paralyzed, he has continued to paint and produce work that remains sought after by museums and collectors. What life lessons can we learn from the way he has responded to adversity?

Thinking

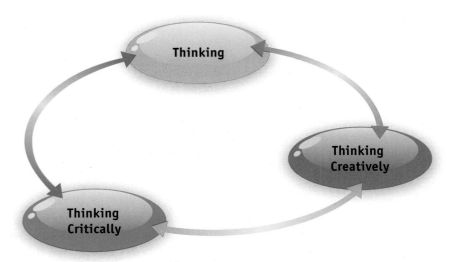

Thinking can be developed and improved by

- **becoming aware of** the thinking process.
- carefully **examining** the thinking process.
- **practicing** the thinking process.

Thinking is the extraordinary process we use every waking moment to make sense of our world and our lives. Successful thinking enables us to solve the problems we are continually confronted with, to make intelligent decisions, and to achieve the goals that give our lives purpose and fulfillment. It is an activity that is crucial for living in a meaningful way.

This book is designed to help you understand the complex, incredible process of thinking. You might think of this text as a map to guide you in exploring the way your mind operates. This book is also founded on the conviction that you can improve your thinking abilities by carefully examining your thinking process and working systematically through challenging activities. Thinking is an active process, and you learn to do it better by becoming aware of and actually using the thought process, not simply by reading about it. By participating in the thinking activities contained in the text and applying these ideas to your own experiences, you will find that your thinking—and language—abilities become sharper and more powerful.

College provides you with a unique opportunity to develop your mind in the fullest sense. Entering college initiates you into a community of people dedicated to learning, and each discipline, or subject area, represents an organized effort to understand some significant dimension of human experience. As you are introduced to various disciplines, you learn new ways to understand the world, and you elevate your consciousness as a result. This book, in conjunction with the other courses in your college experience, will help you become an "educated thinker," expanding your mind and developing your sensibilities.

thinking critically Carefully exploring the thinking process to clarify our understanding and make more intelligent decisions.

Achieving the goal of becoming an educated thinker involves two core processes that are the mainsprings of our thoughts and actions: **thinking critically** and **thinking creatively**. The process of *thinking critically* involves thinking for ourselves by carefully examining the way that we make sense of the world. Taking this approach to living is one of the most satisfying aspects of being a mature human being.

thinking creatively Using our thinking process to develop ideas that are unique, useful, and worthy of further elaboration.

We are able to think critically because of our natural human ability to *reflect*—to think back on what we are thinking, doing, or feeling. By carefully thinking back on our thinking, we are able to figure out the way that our thinking operates and thus learn to do it more effectively. In this book we will be systematically exploring the many dimensions of the way our minds work, providing the opportunity to deepen our understanding of the thinking process and stimulating us to become more effective thinkers.

Of course, carefully examining the ideas produced by the thinking process assumes that there are ideas that are worth examining. We produce such ideas by thinking creatively, an activity we can define as follows.

Living an "Examined" Life

Over 2,500 years ago, the Greek philosopher Socrates cautioned, "The unexamined life is not worth living," underscoring the insight that when we don't make use of our distinctive human capacity to think deeply and act

Thinking Critically About Visuals

The Mystery of the Mind

Why is thinking a difficult process to understand? Why does improving our thinking involve sharing ideas with other people? Why does each person think in unique ways?

Using functional magnetic resonance imaging (or fMRI), researchers can observe changes in blood flow in the brain. In this way, they can see which parts of the brain are most active when a person is engaged in different mental processes. In the fMRI images (right), the red areas indicate the most blood flow or activity. What can we learn about the thinking process by examining the brain states that are correlated with different experiences as depicted by these different fMRI images?

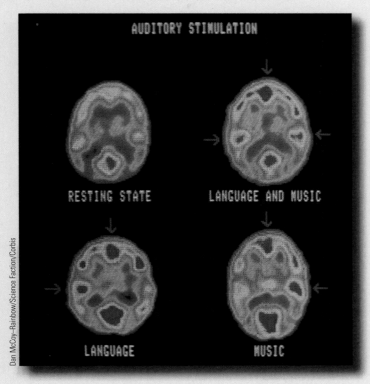

Dan McCoy–Rainbow/Science Faction/Corbis

intelligently, our lives have diminished meaning. In a warning that is at least as relevant today as it was when he first spoke it, Socrates cautioned his fellow citizens of Athens:

"You, my friend—a citizen of the great and mighty and wise city of Athens—are you not ashamed of heaping up the greatest amount of money and honor and reputation, and caring so little about wisdom and truth and the greatest improvement of the soul, which you never regard or heed at all?"

Thinking Critically About Visuals

You Are the Artist of Your Life

In what ways does this metaphor help you understand your personal development? In what ways does it highlight the role of personal responsibility in your life?

Adam Crowley/Photodisc/Getty Images

Today's world is a complex and challenging place in which to live. The accelerated pace at which many people live often makes them feel as though they are rushing from deadline to deadline, skating on the surface of life instead of exploring its deeper meanings. What is the purpose of your life? Who are you, and who do you want to become? These are essential questions that form the core of life, and yet the velocity of our lives discourages us from even posing these questions, much less trying to answer them.

We all have our own unique challenges to meet in order to find our life path, just as the painter Chuck Close (pictured below) has overcome physical disability to achieve great success. What choices will you have to make in order to reach your full potential as a person?

AP Photo/Mark Lennihan

Your efforts to become thoughtful and reflective, to explore the nature of your self and the meaning of your life, are made even more difficult by the unthinking world in which we live. Consider all of the foolish opinions, thoughtless decisions, confused communication, destructive behavior, and self-absorbed, thoughtless people whom you have to deal with each day. Reflect on the number of times you have scratched your head and wondered, "What was that person thinking?" And how many times have you asked yourself, "What was I thinking?" The disturbing truth is that many people don't think very well; they are not making use of their potential to think clearly and effectively.

Every day you encounter a series of choices, forks in your life path that have the cumulative effect of defining you as a person. In thinking about these choices, you may discover that there are habitual patterns in your life that rarely change. If you find that your life is composed of a collection of similar activities and routines, don't despair; this is typical, not unusual. However, it may be an indication that you are not living your life in the most thoughtful fashion possible, that your choices have become automatic, and that your experiences are fixed in certain "ruts." If this is the case, it may be time to reflect on your life, reevaluate the choices you are making, and consider living your life in a more reflective and creative fashion.

You are an artist, creating your life portrait, and your paints and brush strokes are the choices you make each day of your life. This metaphor provides you with a way to think about your personal development and underscores your responsibility for making the most intelligent decisions possible.

You have the capacity to create a richly fulfilling life, but you must develop and make full use of your thinking potential to do so. By becoming a true educated thinker, you will have the tools to unlock the mysteries of yourself and meet the challenges of the world.

A Roadmap to Your Mind

This book is designed to help you become an educated thinker by providing you with many opportunities to use your mind in ways that will strengthen and elevate your thinking abilities. Many of these abilities—such as working toward your goals, solving problems, or making intelligent decisions—will already be familiar to you. Others, such as understanding the conceptualizing process or constructing rigorous extended arguments, will be less so. But whatever your degree of familiarity, and no matter what your level of expertise, you can always improve your thinking abilities, and doing so will enrich your life in countless ways. Here is a brief preview of the thinking abilities you will be studying—the very same abilities that you will be *using to think with* as you study them! (The numbers following the abilities refer to the chapters that deal with them.)

- Establishing and achieving your goals (1)
- Becoming an intelligent and effective **decision maker** (1)
- Becoming a confident and productive **creative thinker** (1)
- Becoming an independent, informed, and open-minded **critical thinker** (2)
- Learning to analyze and discuss complex, controversial ideas in an organized fashion (2)
- Becoming a powerful and successful **problem solver** (3)

- Becoming familiar with the perceptual "lenses" through which you view the world, and understanding the way these lenses shape and influence your entire experience (4)
- Learning to develop informed, well-supported beliefs and achieve authentic knowledge of important issues (5)
- Learning to critically analyze information and images presented in the media, the Internet, and popular culture (5)
- Developing your ability to understand and use **language** in an effective way in order to express your ideas clearly and coherently (6)
- Learning to form and apply concepts in order to understand the world in a clear, sophisticated way (7)
- Developing your ability to relate and organize concepts in complex thinking patterns (8)
- Learning to think critically about ethical issues and moral beliefs (9)
- Learning to construct logically valid and compelling arguments to support your point of view (10)
- Learning to evaluate the soundness of deductive and inductive arguments and detect illogical ways of thinking ("fallacies") (10, 11)
- Developing your ability to make enlightened choices and work toward creating a meaningful and fulfilling life (12)

Of course, these abilities do not operate in isolation from one another; instead, they work together in complex patterns and relationships. So, for example, in the remainder of this first chapter, we're going to explore three core areas that are central to being an accomplished thinker and living a successful, fulfilling life:

- Establishing and achieving your goals
- Becoming an intelligent and effective decision maker
- Becoming a confident and productive creative thinker

Achieving your full potential in these areas involves *all* of the other thinking abilities that you will be studying in this book. In this chapter you will be laying the foundation for achieving your goals, making effective decisions, and learning to think creatively. However, your abilities in these areas will continue to grow as you develop and practice the full range of your thinking capabilities included in this text.

Working Toward Goals

"Ah, but a man's reach should exceed his grasp, / Or what's a heaven for?"

—Robert Browning

My future career goal is to become a professional photographer, working for *National Geographic Magazine* and traveling around the world. I originally had different dreams, but gradually drifted away from them and lost interest. Then I enrolled in a photography course and loved it. I couldn't wait until the weekend was over to attend class on Monday or to begin my next class project—reactions that were really quite unusual for me! Not everyone is certain at my age about what they would like to become, and I think it is important to discover a career you will enjoy because you are going to spend the rest of your life doing it. I have many doubts, as I think everyone does. Am I good enough? The main thing I fear is rejection, people not liking my work, a possibility that is unavoidable in life. There is so much competition in this world that sometimes when you see some-one better at what you do, you can feel inadequate. These problems and obstacles that interfere with my goals will have to be overcome. Rejection will have to be accepted and looked at as a learning experience, and competition will have to be used as an incentive for me to work at my highest level. But through it all, if you don't have any fears, then what do you have? Lacking competition and the pos-sibility of rejection, there is no challenge to life.

As revealed in this student passage, goals play extremely important functions in your life by organizing your thinking and giving your life order and direction. Whether you are preparing food, preparing for an exam, or preparing for a career, goals suggest courses of action, and influence your decisions. By performing these functions, goals contribute meaning to your life. They give you something to aim for and lead to a sense of accomplishment when you reach them, like the satisfaction you may have received when you graduated from high school or entered college. Your thinking abilities enable you first to identify what your goals are and then to plan how to reach these goals.

Most of your behavior has a purpose or purposes, a goal or goals, that you are trying to reach. You can begin to discover the goals of your actions by asking the question "Why?" about what you are doing or thinking. For example, answer the following question as specifically as you can:

Why did you enroll in college?

This question may have stimulated any number of responses:

- Because I want to pursue a fulfilling career.
- Because all of my friends enrolled in college.
- Because my parents insisted that I go to college in order to get a good job.

Whatever your response, it reveals at least one of your goals in attending college.

Using your response to the question "Why did you enroll in college?" as a starting point, try to discover part of your goal pattern by asking a series of "Why" questions. After each response, ask "Why?" again. (For example: Why did you enroll in college? "Because I want to pursue a fulfilling career." Why do you want to pursue a fulfilling career? "Because. . . .") Try to give thoughtful and specific answers.

As you may have found in completing the activity, this "child's game" of repeatedly asking "Why?" begins to reveal the network of goals that struc-ture your experience and leads you to progressively more profound questions regarding your basic goals in life, such as "Why do I want to be successful?" or "Why do I want a happy and fulfilling life?" These are complex issues that require thorough and ongoing exploration. A first step in this direction is to examine the way your mind works to achieve your goals, which is the "goal" of this section. If you can understand the way your mind functions when you think effectively, then you can use this knowledge to improve your thinking abilities. This in turn will enable you to deal more effectively with new situations you encounter. To begin this process, think about an important goal you have achieved in your life, and then complete Thinking Activity 1.1. Thinking Activities are designed to stimulate your thinking process and provide the opportunity to express your ideas about important topics. By sharing these ideas with your teacher and other members of the class, you are not only expanding your own thinking, but also expanding theirs. Each student in the class has a wealth of experiences and insights to offer to the class community.

Thinking Activity 1.1

ANALYZING A GOAL THAT YOU ACHIEVED

1. Describe an important goal that you recently achieved.
2. Identify the steps you had to take to achieve this goal in the order in which they were taken, and estimate the amount of time each step took.
3. Describe how you felt when you achieved your goal.

ACHIEVING SHORT-TERM GOALS

By examining your responses to Thinking Activity 1.1, you can see that thinking effectively plays a crucial role in helping you to achieve your goals by enabling you to perform two distinct, interrelated activities:

1. Identifying the appropriate goals
2. Devising effective plans and strategies to achieve your goals

You are involved in this goal-seeking process in every aspect of your daily life. Some of the goals you seek to achieve are more immediate (short-term) than others, such as planning your activities for the day or organizing your activities for an upcoming test.

Although achieving these short-term goals seems as though it ought to be a manageable process, the truth is your efforts probably meet with varying degrees of success. You may not always achieve your goals for the day, and you might *occasionally* find yourself inadequately prepared for a test. By improving your mastery of the goal-seeking process, you should be able to improve the quality of every area of your life. Let's explore how to do this.

Identify five short-term goals you would like to achieve in the next week. Now rank these goals in order of importance, ranging from the goals that are most essential for you to achieve to those that are less significant.

Once this process of identifying and ranking your goals is complete, you can then focus on devising effective plans and strategies to achieve your goals. In order to complete this stage of the goal-seeking process, select the goal that you ranked 1 or 2, and then *list all of the steps* in the order in which they need to be taken to achieve your goal successfully. After completing this list, estimate how much time each step will take and plan the step in your daily/weekly schedule. For example, if your goal is to prepare for a quiz in biology, your steps might include the following:

Goal: Prepare for biology quiz in 2 days

Steps to be taken	*Time involved*	*Schedule*
1. Photocopy the notes for the class I missed last week	20 minutes	after next class
2. Review reading assignments and class notes	2 hours	tonight
3. Make a summary review sheet	1 hour	tomorrow night
4. Study the review sheet	30 minutes	right before quiz

Although this method may seem a little mechanical the first few times you use it, it will soon integrate into your thinking processes and become a natural and automatic approach to achieving the goals in your daily life. Much of our failure to achieve our short-term goals is due to the fact that we skip one or more of the steps in this process. Common thinking errors in seeking our goals include the following:

- We neglect to explicitly identify important goals.
- We concentrate on less important goals first, leaving insufficient time to work on more important goals.
- We don't identify all of the steps required to achieve our goals, or we approach them in the wrong order.
- We underestimate the time each step will take and/or fail to plan the steps in our schedule.

Method for Achieving Short-Term Goals

Step 1: Identify the goals.

Identify the short-term goals.
Rank the goals in order of importance.
Select the most important goal(s) to focus on.

Step 2: Devise effective plans to achieve your goals.

　List all of the steps in the order in which they should be taken.
　Estimate how much time each step will take.
　Plan the steps in your daily/weekly schedule.

ACHIEVING LONG-TERM GOALS

Identifying immediate or "short-term" goals tends to be a fairly simple procedure. Identifying the appropriate "long-term" goals is a much more complex and challenging process: career aims, plans for marriage, paying for children's college, goals for personal development. Think, for example, about the people you know who have full-time jobs. How many of these people get up in the morning excited and looking forward to going to work that day? Probably not that high a number. The unfortunate fact is that many people have not been successful in identifying the most appropriate career goals for themselves, goals that reflect their true interests and talents.

How do you identify the most appropriate long-term goals for yourself? To begin with, you need to develop an in-depth understanding of yourself: your talents, your interests, the things that stimulate you and bring you satisfaction. You also need to discover what your possibilities are, either through research or actual experience. Of course, your goals do not necessarily remain the same throughout your life. It is unlikely that the goals you had as an eight-year-old are the ones you have now. As you grow and mature, it is natural for your goals to change and evolve as well. The key point is that you should keep examining your goals to make sure that they reflect your own thinking and current interests.

Research studies have shown that high-achieving people are able to envision a detailed, three-dimensional picture of their future in which their goals and aspirations are clearly inscribed. In addition, they are able to construct a mental plan that includes the sequence of steps they will have to take, the amount of time each step will involve, and strategies for overcoming the obstacles they will likely encounter. Such realistic and compelling concepts of the future enable these people to make sacrifices in the present to achieve their long-term goals. Of course, they may modify these goals as circumstances change and they acquire more information, but they retain a well-defined, flexible plan that charts their life course.

Research also reveals that people who are low achievers tend to live in the present and the past. Their concepts of the future are vague and ill defined: "I want to be happy" or "I want a high-paying job." This unclear concept of the future makes it difficult for them to identify the most appropriate goals for themselves, to devise effective strategies for achieving these goals, and to make the necessary sacrifices in the present that will ensure that the future becomes a reality. For example, imagine that you are faced with the choice of studying for an exam or participating in a social activity. What would you do? If you are focusing mainly on the present rather than the future, then the temptation to go out with your friends may be too strong. But if you see this exam as connected to a future that is real and extremely important to you, then you are better equipped to sacrifice a momentary pleasant time for your future happiness.

Thinking Activity 1.2

ANALYZING AN IMPORTANT FUTURE GOAL

Apply some of the insights we have been examining about working toward goals to a situation in your own life.

1. Describe as specifically as possible an important longer-term goal that you want to achieve in your life. Your goal can be academic, professional, or personal.

2. Explain the reasons that led you to select the goal that you did and why you believe that your goal makes sense.

3. Identify both the major and minor steps you will have to take to achieve your goal. List your steps in the order in which they need to be taken and indicate how much time you think each step will take. Make your responses as specific and precise as possible.

4. Identify some of the sacrifices that you may have to make in the present in order to achieve your future goal.

Images, Decision Making, and Thinking About Visual Information

Journalists, scientists, website creators, lawyers, advertisers—the variety of professionals who rely on visuals to communicate is staggering. From college and military recruitment brochures to consumer advertising to a company's annual reports, images work in both subtle and overt ways to persuade us to do, believe, or buy something. As a critical thinker, you must pay attention to the ways in which images can inspire, support, and reflect your beliefs and your goals.

Each chapter of *Thinking Critically* includes a feature that challenges you to apply new thinking strategies to pairs of images that provoke the viewer into finding connections, confronting beliefs, and questioning evidence. This feature is called "Thinking Critically About Visuals."

IMAGES, PERCEIVING, AND THINKING

Whether they are recording events as they happen or reflecting imaginatively on their personal experiences, visual artists in all media (painters, cartoonists, graphic artists, photographers, and others) are fundamentally aware that they are *communicating*—that, even without words, their images will tell a story, make an argument, show a process, or provide information. In order for you to think critically about the many kinds of information you encounter in your personal, academic, and professional life, you need to understand how these images are created and the purposes they serve.

Images and Learning In college, you will often be asked to present information in a visual manner. Classes in the sciences and social sciences require you to present numerical data in the form of charts, graphs, and maps. In the visual arts and humanities, you may be asked to analyze a painting's message and style or to describe a film director's approach to setting a scene. As you read your textbooks, study your instructor's PowerPoint slides, and conduct your own research, be sure that you understand the point of visual information and how it complements written information. In addition, be sure to ask your instructor for each of your classes how to locate, correctly cite, and usefully include images in your own essays and research papers.

Images, Creative Thinking, and Problem Solving Creative thinking teaches us that there are many different ways of experiencing and communicating information. When you use any of the creative or critical approaches to problem solving discussed in this book, try to incorporate visual as well as verbal descriptions and information. You could collect images from magazines, books, and online sources and print them out or scan them electronically to create a kind of visual "mind map." Or you could look online at sites such as The National Archives, Flickr.com, and Google Images, all of which allow you to search for images using key words related to your task.

Images and "Reading" As you come across visual images to use in your essays, reports, and arguments, remember that the content of an image—just like the content of a text—is composed of elements that work together to convey a message. Some of these elements are similar to those you consider when evaluating a piece of writing: setting, point of view, the relationship between characters, and an objective or subjective perspective. Other elements are specifically visual: how color is used, how images are manipulated in a graphics editor such as Photoshop, how images are cropped (or cut), and how images are arranged on a page or screen. Also important, of course, is how the text that accompanies images describes and contextualizes what you are seeing; this text, called a *caption*, should also be a part of your critical interpretation of visual evidence.

Images and Evaluation When you have gathered images that relate to your topic, you can use questions of fact, interpretation, analysis, synthesis, evaluation, and application (pages 59–60) to help you sort through the visuals and select those that best support your purpose in writing. For example, a witty or satirical editorial cartoon about the federal response to Hurricane Sandy might be appropriate for an argument essay in which you analyze the political impact of that disaster, but for a paper about the storm's long-term environmental effects, you would be better served by a map showing the loss of land or a satellite photograph showing the extent of flood damage.

The Thinking Critically About Visuals activity on pages 16–17 contains two photographs of a very different kind of human disaster—the tragedy of human trafficking. Both types of disasters have devastating consequences for innocent people caught up in these events.

Thinking Critically About Visuals

"Human Sex Trafficking"

Human trafficking for sexual purposes is an international evil involving an estimated 25 million women and children a year, a $35 billion industry that reaches to every corner of the world. Nor is the United States immune to this evil: an estimated 45,000–50,000 women and children are caught in the snare of human trafficking

AP Photos/New Mexico Attorney General's Office

every year. Of those victims who are found and released, 83% of them are American citizens. So the idea that sex trafficking "only happens in other countries" is not accurate. Consider this photograph: what approach is being used to dramatize to the public the evil of human trafficking? What makes this photograph arresting? Do you find this approach effective? Why or why not? If you were asked to create an ad to dramatize human trafficking how would you go about it?

This photograph of young girls lined up and dressed in the same outfits tells the story of human trafficking in a different way. From what perspective is this photograph taken? What makes this perspective especially compelling? In what ways, and in what contexts, can visual images tell stories from the perspective of someone other than the photographer? What story does this photograph tell to you? How does this image compare to the image on the previous page? Does the combined message and effect of these two images influence your thinking about human trafficking? In what way?

Sean Sprague/Age fotostock

Thinking Passage

THE AUTOBIOGRAPHY OF MALCOLM X

Born May 19, 1925 as Malcolm Little in Omaha, Nebraska, the son of an activist Baptist preacher, Malcolm X saw racial injustice and violence from a very young age. His father, Earl Little, was outspoken in his support for Black Nationalist leader Marcus Garvey; as a result, the family was the target of harassment and was forced to move frequently. In 1931, Earl Little's body was found on the town's trolley tracks. Although the local police dismissed it as an accident, Earl Little's death was believed to have been a murder committed by white supremacists. Malcolm dropped out of high school after a teacher's contemptuous discouragement of his ambitions to become a lawyer. For the next several years, he moved between Boston and New York, becoming profitably involved in various criminal activities. After a conviction for burglary in Boston, he was sentenced to prison. There he began writing letters to former friends as well as to various government officials. His frustration in trying to express his ideas led him to a course of self-education, described in the following excerpt from *The Autobiography of Malcolm X*. After his release from prison, Malcolm converted to Islam and rose to prominence in the Nation of Islam. A pilgrimage that he made to Saudi Arabia led him to begin working toward healing and reconciliation for Americans of all races. Unfortunately, the enemies he had made and the fears he had provoked did not leave Malcolm X much time to share this message. Three assassins gunned him down as he spoke at the Audubon Ballroom in Harlem on February 15, 1965.

From The Autobiography of Malcolm X

by Malcolm X with Alex Haley

Many who today hear me somewhere in person, or on television, or those who read something I've said, will think I went to school far beyond the eighth grade. This impression is due entirely to my prison studies.

It had really begun back in the Charlestown Prison, when Bimbi first made me feel envy of his stock of knowledge. Bimbi had always taken charge of any conversation he was in, and I had tried to emulate him. But every book I picked up had few sentences which didn't contain anywhere from one to nearly all of the words that might as well have been in Chinese. When I just skipped those words, of course, I really ended up with little idea of what the book said. So I had come to the Norfolk

Prison Colony still going through only book-reading motions. Pretty soon, I would have quit even these motions, unless I had received the motivation that I did.

I saw that the best thing I could do was get hold of a dictionary—to study, to learn some words. I was lucky enough to reason also that I should try to improve my penmanship. It was sad. I couldn't even write in a straight line. It was both ideas together that moved me to request a dictionary along with some tablets and pencils from the Norfolk Prison Colony school.

I spent two days just riffling uncertainly through the dictionary's pages. I'd never realized so many words existed! I didn't know which words I needed to learn. Finally, just to start some kind of action, I began copying. In my slow, painstaking, ragged handwriting, I copied into my tablet everything printed on that first page, down to the punctuation marks. I believe it took me a day. Then, aloud, I read back, to myself, everything I'd written on the tablet. Over and over, aloud, to myself, I read my own handwriting.

I woke up the next morning, thinking about those words—immensely proud to realize that not only had I written so much at one time, but I'd written words that I never knew were in the world. Moreover, with a little effort, I also could remember what many of these words meant. I reviewed the words whose meanings I didn't remember. . . .

I was so fascinated that I went on—I copied the dictionary's next page. And the same experience came when I studied that. With every succeeding page, I also learned of people and places and events from history. . . . That was the way I started copying what eventually became the entire dictionary. . . . Between what I wrote in my tablet, and writing letters, during the rest of my time in prison I would guess I wrote a million words. I suppose it was inevitable that as my word-base broadened, I could for the first time pick up a book and read and now begin to understand what the book was saying. . . .

QUESTIONS FOR ANALYSIS

In describing how he worked toward the goals of becoming literate and knowledgeable, Malcolm X touches on a variety of important issues related to developing thinking and language abilities. We can analyze some of the issues raised by answering the following questions:

1. Malcolm X describes the process of how learning words from a dictionary sparked a hunger for learning that lead to his being able to "pick up a book and read and now begin to understand what the book was saying." Explain the importance of his hunger for knowledge in terms of how it impacted his life.

2. Malcolm X envied one of the other inmates, Bimbi, because his stock of knowledge enabled him to take charge of any conversation he was in. Explain why knowledge—and our ability to use it—leads to power in our dealings with others. Describe a situation from your own experience in which having

expert knowledge about a subject enabled you to influence the thinking of other people.

3. Malcolm X also states about pursuing his studies in prison that "up to then, I never had been so truly free in my life." Explain what you think he means by this statement.

An Organized Approach to Making Decisions

Identifying and reaching the goals in our lives involves making informed, intelligent decisions. Many of the decisions we make are sound and thoughtful, but we may also find that some of the decisions we make turn out poorly, undermining our efforts to achieve the things we most want in life. Many of our poor decisions involve relatively minor issues—for example, selecting an unappealing dish in a restaurant, agreeing to go out on a blind date, taking a course that does not meet our expectations. Although these decisions may result in unpleasant consequences, the discomfort is neither life-threatening nor long-lasting (although a disappointing course may seem to last forever!). However, there are many more significant decisions in our lives in which poor choices can result in considerably more damaging and far-reaching consequences. For example, one reason that the current divorce rate in the United States stands at approximately 50 percent (for first marriages) is the poor decisions people make before or after the vows "till death do us part." Similarly, the fact that many employed adults wake up in the morning unhappy about going to their jobs, anxiously waiting for the end of the day and the conclusion of the week so they are free to do what they really want to do, suggests that somewhere along the line they made poor career decisions, or they felt trapped by circumstances they couldn't control. Our jobs should be much more than a way to earn a paycheck—they should be vehicles for using our professional skills, opportunities for expressing our creative talents, stimulants to our personal growth and intellectual development, and experiences that provide us with feelings of fulfillment and self-esteem. In the final analysis, our careers are central elements of our lives and important dimensions of our life-portraits. Our career decision is one that we'd better try to get right!

An important part of becoming an educated thinker is learning to make effective decisions. Let's explore the process of making effective decisions.

Thinking Activity 1.3

ANALYZING A PREVIOUS DECISION

1. Think back on an important decision that you made that turned out well, and describe the experience as specifically as possible.

2. Reconstruct the reasoning process that you used to make your decision. Did you:

- Clearly define the decision to be made and the related issues?

- Consider various choices and anticipate the consequences of these various choices?

- Gather additional information to help in your analysis?

- Evaluate the various pros and cons of different courses of action?

- Use a chart or diagram to aid in your deliberations?

- Create a specific plan of action to implement your ideas?

- Periodically review your decision to make necessary adjustments?

As you reflected on the successful decision you were writing about in Thinking Activity 1.3, you probably noticed your mind working in a more or less systematic way as you thought your way through the decision situation. Of course, we often make important decisions with less thoughtful analysis by acting impulsively or relying on our "intuition." Sometimes these decisions work out well, but often they don't, and we are forced to live with the consequences of these mistaken choices. People who approach decision situations thoughtfully and analytically tend to be more successful decision makers than people who don't. Naturally, there are no guarantees that a careful analysis will lead to a successful result—there are often too many unknown elements and factors beyond our control. But we can certainly improve our success rate as well as our speed by becoming more knowledgeable about the decision-making process. Expert decision makers can typically make quick, accurate decisions based on intuitions that are informed, not merely impulsive. However, as with most complex abilities in life, we need to learn to "walk" before we can "run," so let's explore a versatile and effective approach for making decisions.

The decision-making approach we will be using consists of five steps. As you gradually master these steps, they will become integrated into your way of thinking, and you will be able to apply them in a natural and flexible way.

Step 1: Define the Decision Clearly This seems like an obvious step, but a lot of decision making goes wrong at the starting point. For example, imagine that you decide that you want to have a "more active social life." The problem with this characterization of your decision is it defines the situation too generally and therefore doesn't give any clear direction for your analysis. Do you want to develop an intimate, romantic relationship? Do you want to cultivate more close friendships? Do you want to engage in more social activities? Do you want to meet new people? In short, there are many ways to define more clearly the decision to have a "more active social life." The more specific your definition of the decision to be made, the clearer will be your analysis and the greater the likelihood of success.

STRATEGY: Write a one-page analysis that articulates your decision-making situation as clearly and specifically as possible.

Step 2: Consider All the Possible Choices Successful decision makers explore all of the possible choices in their situation, not simply the obvious ones. In fact, the less obvious choices often turn out to be the most effective ones. For example, a student in a recent class of mine couldn't decide whether he should major in accounting or business management. In discussing his situation with other members of the class, he revealed that his real interest was in the area of graphic design and illustration. Although he was very talented, he considered this area to be only a hobby, not a possible career choice. Class members pointed out to him that this might turn out to be his best career choice, but he needed first to see it as a possibility.

STRATEGY: List as many possible choices for your situation as you can, both obvious and not obvious. Ask other people for additional suggestions, and don't censor or prejudge any ideas.

Step 3: Gather All Relevant Information and Evaluate the Pros and Cons of Each Possible Choice In many cases you may lack sufficient information to make an informed choice regarding a challenging, complex decision. Unfortunately, this doesn't prevent people from plunging ahead anyway, making a decision that is often more a gamble than an informed choice. Instead of this questionable approach, it makes a lot more sense to seek out the information you need in order to determine which of the choices you identified has the best chance for success. For example, in the case of the student mentioned in Step 2, there is important information he would need to have before determining whether he should consider a career in graphic design and illustration, including asking: What are the specific careers within this general field? What sort of academic preparation and experience are required for the various careers? What are the prospects for employment in these areas, and how well do they pay?

STRATEGY: For each possible choice that you identified, create questions regarding information you need to find out, and then locate that information.

In addition to locating all relevant information, each of the possible choices you identified has certain advantages and disadvantages, and it is essential that you analyze these pros and cons in an organized fashion. For example, in the case of the student described earlier, the choice of pursuing a career in accounting may have advantages such as ready employment opportunities, the flexibility of working in many different situations and geographical locations, moderate to high income expectations, and job security. On the other hand, disadvantages might include the fact that accounting may not reflect a deep and abiding interest for the student, he might lose interest over time, or the career might not result in the personal challenge and fulfillment that he seeks.

STRATEGY: Using a format similar to the one outlined in the following worksheet, analyze the pros and cons of each of your possible choices.

Define the decision:

Possible choices	Information needed	Pros	Cons
1.			
2.			

(and so on)

Step 4: Select the Choice That Seems to Best Meet the Needs of the Situation The first three steps of this approach are designed to help you analyze your decision situation: to clearly define the decision, generate possible choices, gather relevant information, and evaluate the pros and cons of the choices you identified. In this fourth step, you must attempt to synthesize all that you have learned, weaving together all of the various threads into a conclusion that you believe to be your "best" choice. How do you do this? There is no one simple way to identify your "best" choice, but there are some useful strategies for guiding your deliberations.

STRATEGY: Identify and prioritize the goals of your decision situation and determine which of your choices best meets these goals. This process will probably involve reviewing and perhaps refining your definition of the decision situation. For example, in the case of the student whom we have been considering, some goals might include choosing a career that will

a. provide financial security.

b. provide personal fulfillment.

c. make use of special talents.

d. offer plentiful opportunities and job security.

Once identified, the goals can be ranked in order of their priority, which will then suggest what the "best" choice will be. For example, if the student ranks goals (a) and (d) at the top of the list, then a choice of accounting or business administration might make sense. On the other hand, if the student ranks goals (b) and (c) at the top, then pursuing a career in graphic design and illustration might be the best selection.

STRATEGY: Anticipate the consequences of each choice by "preliving" the choices. Another helpful strategy for deciding on the best choice is to project yourself into the future, imagining as realistically as you can the consequences of each possible choice. As with previous strategies, this process is aided by writing your thoughts down and discussing them with others.

Step 5: Implement a Plan of Action and Then Monitor the Results, Making Necessary Adjustments Once you have selected what you consider your best choice, you need to develop and implement a specific, concrete plan of action. As was noted in the section on short-term goals, the more specific and concrete your plan of action, the greater is the likelihood of success. For example, if the student in the case we have been considering decides to pursue a career in graphic design and illustration, his plan should include reviewing the major that best meets his needs, discussing his situation with students and faculty in that department, planning the courses he will be taking, and perhaps speaking to people in the field.

Method for Making Decisions

Step 1: Define the decision clearly.

Step 2: Consider all the possible choices.

Step 3: Gather all relevant information and evaluate the pros and cons of each possible choice.

Step 4: Select the choice that seems to best meet the needs of the situation.

Step 5: Implement a plan of action and then monitor the results, making necessary adjustments.

STRATEGY: Create a schedule that details the steps you will be taking to implement your decision and a timeline for taking these steps.

Of course, your plan is merely a starting point for implementing your decision. As you actually begin taking the steps in your plan, you will likely discover that changes and adjustments need to be made. In some cases, you may find that, based on new information, the choice you selected appears to be the wrong one. For example, as the student we have been discussing takes courses in graphic design and illustration, he may find that his interest in the field is not as serious as he thought and that, although he likes this area as a hobby, he does not want it to be his life work. In this case, he should return to considering his other choices and perhaps add additional choices that he did not consider before.

STRATEGY: After implementing your choice, evaluate its success by identifying what's working and what isn't, and make the necessary adjustments to improve the situation.

Thinking Activity 1.4

ANALYZING A FUTURE DECISION

1. Describe an important decision in your academic or personal life that you will have to make in the near future.

2. Using the five-step decision-making approach we just described, analyze your decision and conclude with your "best" choice.

Share your analysis with other members of the class and listen carefully to the feedback they give you.

Living Creatively

Sometimes students become discouraged about their lives, concluding that their destinies are shaped by forces beyond their control. Although difficult circumstances *do* hamper our striving for success, this fatalistic sentiment can also reflect a passivity that is the opposite of thinking critically. As a critical thinker, you should be confident that you can shape the person that you want to become through insightful understanding and intelligent choices.

In working with this book, you will develop the abilities and attitudes needed to become an educated thinker and a successful person. You will also integrate these goals into a larger context, exploring how to live a life that is creative, professionally successful, and personally fulfilling. By using both your creative and your critical thinking abilities, you can develop informed beliefs and an enlightened life philosophy. In the final analysis, the person who looks back at you in the mirror is the person you have created.

Thinking Activity 1.5

DESCRIBING YOUR CURRENT AND FUTURE SELF

1. Describe a portrait of yourself as a person. What sort of person are you? What are your strengths and weaknesses? In what areas do you feel you are creative?

2. Describe some of the ways you would like to change yourself.

"CAN I BE CREATIVE?"

The first day of my course Creative Thinking: Theory and Practice, I always ask the students in the class if they think they are creative. Typically fewer than half of the class members raise their hands. One reason for this is that people often confuse being "creative" with being "artistic"—skilled at art, music, poetry, creative writing, drama, dance. Although artistic people are certainly creative, there are an infinite number of ways to be creative that are *not* artistic. This is a mental trap that I fell into growing up. In school I always dreaded art class because I was so inept. My pathetic drawings and art projects were always good for a laugh for my friends, and I felt no overwhelming urges to write poetry, paint, or compose music. I was certain that I had simply been born "uncreative" and accepted this "fact" as my destiny. It wasn't until I graduated from college that I began to change this view of myself. I was working as a custom woodworker to support myself, designing and creating specialized furniture for people, when it suddenly struck me: I was being creative! I then began to see other areas of my life in which I was creative: playing sports, decorating my apartment, even writing research papers. I finally understood that being creative was a state of mind and a way of life. As writer Eric Gill expresses it, "The artist is not a different kind of person, but each one of us is a different kind of artist."

Are you creative? Yes! Think of all of the activities that you enjoy doing: cooking, creating a wardrobe, raising children, playing sports, cutting or braiding hair, dancing, playing music. Whenever you are investing your own personal ideas, putting on your own personal stamp, you are being creative. For example, imagine that you are cooking your favorite dish. To the extent that you are expressing your unique ideas developed through inspiration and experimentation, you are being creative. Of course, if you are simply following someone else's recipe without significant modification, your dish may be tasty—but it is not creative. Similarly, if your moves on the dance floor or the basketball court express your distinctive personality, you are being creative, as you are when you stimulate the original thinking of your children or make your friends laugh with your unique brand of humor.

Living your life creatively means bringing your unique perspective and creative talents to all of the dimensions of your life. The following passages are written by students about creative areas in their lives. After reading the passages, complete Thinking Activity 1.6, which gives you the opportunity to describe a creative area from your own life.

One of the most creative aspects of my life is my diet. I have been a vegetarian for the past five years, while the rest of my family has continued to eat meat. I had to overcome many obstacles to make this lifestyle work for me, including family dissension. The solution was simple: I had to learn how to cook creatively. I have come to realize that my diet is an ongoing learning process. The more I learn about and experiment with different foods, the healthier and happier I become. I feel like an explorer setting out on my own to discover new things about food and nutrition. I slowly evolved from a person who could cook food only if it came from a can into someone who could make bread from scratch and grow yogurt cultures. I find learning new things about nutrition and cooking healthful foods very relaxing and rewarding. I like being alone in my house baking bread; there is something very comforting about the aroma. Most of all I like to experiment with different ways to prepare foods, because the ideas are my own. Even when an effort is less than successful, I find pleasure in the knowledge that I gained from the experience. I discovered recently, for example, that eggplant is terrible in soup! Making mistakes seems to be a natural way to increase creativity, and I now firmly believe that people who say that they do not like vegetables simply have not been properly introduced to them!

As any parent knows, children have an abundance of energy to spend, and toys or television does not always meet their needs. In response, I create activities to stimulate their creativity and preserve my sanity. For example, I involve them in the process of cooking, giving them the skin from peeled vegetables and a pot so they can make their own "soup." Using catalogs, we cut out pictures of furniture, rugs, and curtains, and they paste them onto cartons to create their own interior decors: vibrant living rooms, plush bedrooms, colorful family rooms. I make beautiful boats from aluminum foil, and my children spend hours in the bathtub playing with them. We "go bowling" with empty soda cans and a ball, and they star in "track meets" by running an obstacle course we set up. When it comes to raising children, creativity is a way of survival!

After quitting the government agency I was working at because of too much bureaucracy, I was hired as a carpenter at a construction site, although I had little knowledge of this profession. I learned to handle a hammer and other tools by watching other coworkers, and within a matter of weeks I was skilled enough to organize my own group of workers for projects. Most of my fellow workers used the old-fashioned method of construction carpentry, building panels with inefficient and poorly made bracings. I redesigned the panels in order to save construction time and materials. My supervisor and site engineer were thrilled with my creative ideas, and I was assigned progressively more challenging projects, including the construction of an office building that was completed in record time.

Thinking Activity 1.6

DESCRIBING A CREATIVE AREA

1. Describe a creative area of your life in which you are able to express your unique personality and talents. Be specific and give examples.

2. Analyze your creative area by answering the following questions:

   - Why do you feel that this activity is creative? Give examples.
   - How would you describe the experience of being engaged in this activity? Where do your creative ideas come from? How do they develop?
   - What strategies do you use to increase your creativity? What obstacles block your creative efforts? How do you try to overcome these blocks?

BECOMING MORE CREATIVE

Although we each have nearly limitless potential to live creatively, most people use only a small percentage of their creative gifts. In fact, there is research to suggest that people typically achieve their highest creative point as young children, after which there is a long, steady decline into progressive uncreativity. Why? Well, to begin with, young children are immersed in the excitement of exploration and discovery. They are eager to try out new things, act on their impulses, and make unusual connections between disparate ideas. They are not afraid to take risks in trying out untested solutions, and they are not compelled to identify the socially acceptable "correct answer." Children are willing to play with ideas, creating improbable scenarios and imaginative ways of thinking without fear of being ridiculed.

All of this tends to change as we get older. The weight of "reality" begins to smother our imagination, and we increasingly focus our attention on the nuts and bolts of living rather than on playing with possibilities. The social pressure to conform to group expectations increases dramatically. Whether the group is our friends, classmates, or fellow employees, there are clearly defined "rules" for dressing, behaving, speaking, and thinking. When we deviate from these rules, we risk social disapproval, rejection, or ridicule. Most groups have little tolerance for individuals who want to think independently and creatively. As we become older, we also become more reluctant to pursue untested courses of action because we become increasingly afraid of failure. Pursuing creativity inevitably involves failure because we are trying to break out of established ruts and go beyond traditional methods. For example, going beyond the safety of a proven recipe to create an innovative dish may involve some disasters, but it's the only way to create something genuinely unique. The history of creative discoveries is littered with failures, a fact we tend to forget when we are debating whether we should risk an untested idea. Those people who are courageous enough to risk failure while expressing their creative impulses are rewarded with unique achievements and an enriched life.

Thinking Activity 1.7

IDENTIFYING CREATIVE BLOCKS

Reflect on your own creative development, and describe some of the fears and pressures that inhibit your own creativity. For example, have you ever been penalized for trying out a new idea that didn't work out? Have you ever suffered the wrath of the group for daring to be different and violating the group's unspoken rules? Do you feel that your life is so filled with responsibilities and the demands of reality that you don't have time to be creative?

Although the forces that discourage us from being creative are powerful, they can nevertheless be overcome with the right approaches. We are going to explore four productive strategies:

- Understand and trust the creative process.
- Eliminate the "voice of criticism."
- Establish a creative environment.
- Make creativity a priority.

Understand and Trust the Creative Process Discovering your creative talents requires that you understand how the creative process operates and then have confidence in the results it produces. There are no fixed procedures or formulas for generating creative ideas because creative ideas *by definition* go beyond established ways of thinking to the unknown and the innovative. As the ancient Greek philosopher Heraclitus once said, "You must expect the unexpected, because it cannot be found by search or trail."

Although there is no fixed path to creative ideas, there are activities you can pursue that make the birth of creative ideas possible. In this respect, generating creative ideas is similar to gardening. You need to prepare the soil; plant the seeds; ensure proper water, light, and food; and then be patient until the ideas begin to sprout. Here are some steps for cultivating your creative garden:

- *Absorb yourself in the task.* Creative ideas don't occur in a vacuum. They emerge after a great deal of work, study, and practice. For example, if you want to come up with creative ideas in the kitchen, you need to become knowledgeable about the art of cooking. The more knowledgeable you are, the better prepared you are to create valuable and innovative dishes. Similarly, if you are trying to develop a creative perspective for a research paper in college, you need to immerse yourself in the subject, developing an in-depth understanding of the central concepts and issues. Absorbing yourself in the task "prepares the soil" for your creative ideas.

- *Allow time for ideas to incubate.* After absorbing yourself in the task or problem, the next stage in the creative process is to *stop* working on the task or problem. Even when your conscious mind has stopped actively working on the task, the unconscious dimension of your mind continues working—processing, organizing, and ultimately generating innovative ideas and solutions. This process is known as *incubation* because it mirrors the process in which baby chicks gradually evolve inside the egg until the moment comes when they break out through the shell. In the same way, your creative mind is at work while you are going about your business until the moment of *illumination*, when the incubating idea finally erupts to the surface of your conscious mind. People report that these illuminating moments—when their mental lightbulbs go on—often occur when they are engaged in activities completely unrelated to the task. One of the most famous cases was that of the Greek thinker Archimedes, whose moment of illumination came while he was taking a bath, causing him to run naked through the streets of Athens shouting "Eureka" ("I have found it").

- *Seize on the ideas when they emerge and follow them through.* Generating creative ideas is of little use unless you recognize them when they appear and then act on them. Too often people don't pay much attention to these ideas when they occur, or they dismiss them as too impractical. You must have confidence in the ideas you create, even if they seem wacky or far-out. Many of the most valuable inventions in our history started as improbable ideas, ridiculed by popular wisdom. For example, the idea of Velcro started with burrs covering the pants of the inventor as he walked through a field, and Post-it Notes resulted from the accidental invention of an adhesive that was weaker than normal. In other words, thinking effectively means thinking creatively *and* thinking critically. After you use your creative thinking abilities to generate innovative ideas, you then must employ your critical thinking abilities to evaluate and refine the ideas and design a practical plan for implementing them.

Eliminate the "Voice of Criticism" The biggest threat to our creativity lies within ourselves, the negative "voice of criticism" (VOC). This VOC can undermine your confidence in every area of your life, including your creative activities, with statements like:

> This is a stupid idea and no one will like it.
>
> Even if I could pull this idea off, it probably won't amount to much.
>
> Although I was successful the last time I tried something like this, I was lucky and I won't be able to do it again.

These statements, and countless others like them, have the ongoing effect of making us doubt ourselves and the quality of our creative thinking. As we lose confidence, we become more timid, more reluctant to follow through on ideas and present them to others. After a while our cumulative insecurity discourages us from even generating ideas in the first place, and we end up simply conforming to established ways of thinking and the expectations of others. In doing so we surrender an important part of ourselves, the vital and dynamic creative core of our personality that defines our unique perspective on the world.

Where do these negative voices come from? Often they originate in the negative judgments we experienced while growing up, destructive criticisms that become internalized as a part of ourselves. In the same way that praising children helps make them feel confident and secure, consistently criticizing them does the opposite. Although parents, teachers, and acquaintances often don't intend these negative consequences with their critical judgments and lack of positive praise, the unfortunate result is still the same: a "voice of criticism" that keeps hammering away at the value of ourselves, our ideas, and our creations. As a teacher, I see this VOC evident when students present their creative projects to the class with apologies like "This isn't very good, and it probably doesn't make sense."

How do we eliminate this unwelcome and destructive voice within ourselves? There are a number of effective strategies you can use, although you should be aware that the fight, while worth the effort, will not be easy.

- *Become aware of the VOC.* You have probably been listening to the negative messages of the VOC for so long that you may not even be consciously aware of them. To conquer the VOC, you need to first recognize when it speaks. In addition, it is helpful to analyze the negative messages, try to figure out how and why they developed, and then create strategies to overcome them. A good strategy is to keep a VOC journal, described in Thinking Activity 1.8.

- *Restate the judgment in a more accurate or constructive way.* Sometimes there is an element of truth in our self-judgments, but we have blown the reality out of proportion. For example, if you fail a test, your VOC may translate this as "I'm a failure." Or if you ask someone for a date and get turned down, your VOC may conclude "I'm a social misfit with emotional bad breath!" In these instances, you need to translate the reality accurately: "I failed this test—I wonder what went wrong and how I can improve my performance in the future," and "This person turned me down for a date—I guess I'm not his or her type, or maybe he or she just doesn't know me well enough."

- *Get tough with the VOC.* You can't be a coward if you hope to overcome the VOC. Instead, you have to be strong and determined, telling yourself as soon as the VOC appears, "I'm throwing you out and not letting you back in!" This attack might feel peculiar at first, but it will soon become an automatic response when those negative judgments appear. Don't give in to the judgments, even a little bit, by saying, "Well, maybe I'm just a little bit of a jerk." Get rid of the VOC entirely, and good riddance to it!

- *Create positive voices and visualizations.* The best way to destroy the VOC for good is to replace it with positive encouragements. As soon as you have stomped on the judgment "I'm a jerk," you should replace it with "I'm an intelligent, valuable person with many positive qualities and talents." Similarly, you should make extensive use of positive visualization, by "seeing" yourself performing well on your examinations, being entertaining and insightful with other people, and succeeding gloriously in the sport or dramatic production in which you are involved. If you make the effort to create these positive voices and images, they will eventually become a natural part of your thinking. And because positive thinking leads to positive results, your efforts will become self-fulfilling prophecies.

- *Use other people for independent confirmation.* The negative judgments coming from the VOC are usually irrational, but until they are dragged out into the light of day for examination, they can be very powerful. Sharing our VOC with others we trust is an effective strategy because they can provide an objective perspective that reveals to us the irrationality and destructiveness of these negative judgments. This sort of "reality testing" strips the judgments of their power, a process that is enhanced by the positive support of concerned friends with whom we have developed relationships over a period of time.

Thinking Activity 1.8

COMBATING THE "VOICE OF CRITICISM"

1. Take a small notebook or pad with you one day, and record every self-defeating criticism that you make about yourself. At the end of the day classify your self-criticisms by category, such as negative self-criticism about your physical appearance, your popularity with others, or your academic ability.

2. Analyze the self-criticisms in each of the categories and try to determine where they came from and how they developed.

3. Use the strategies described in this section, and others of your own creation, to start fighting these self-criticisms when they occur.

....

Establish a Creative Environment An important part of eliminating the negative voices in our minds is to establish environments in which our creative resources can flourish. This means finding or developing physical environments conducive to creative expression as well as supportive social environments. Sometimes working with other people is stimulating and energizing to our creative juices; at other times we require a private place where we can work without distraction. For example, I have a specific location in which I do much of my writing: sitting at my desk, with a calm, pleasing view of the Hudson River, music on the iPod, a cold drink, and a supply of roasted almonds and Jelly Bellies. I'm ready for creativity to strike me, although I sometimes have to wait for some time! Different environments work for different people. You have to find the environment(s) best suited to your own creative process and then make a special effort to do your work there.

The people in our lives who form our social environment play an even more influential role in encouraging or inhibiting our creative process. When we are surrounded by people who are positive and supportive, they increase our confidence and encourage us to take the risk to express our creative vision. They can stimulate our creativity by providing us with fresh ideas and new perspectives. By engaging in *brainstorming* (described on page 117), they can work with us to generate ideas and then later help us figure out how to refine and implement the most valuable ones.

However, when the people around us tend to be negative, critical, or belittling, then the opposite happens: We lose confidence and are reluctant to express ourselves creatively. Eventually, we begin to internalize these negative criticisms, incorporating them into our own VOC. When this occurs, we have the choice of telling people that we will not tolerate this sort of destructive behavior or, if they can't improve their behavior, moving them out of our lives. Of course, sometimes this is difficult because we work with them or they are related to us. In this case we have to work at diminishing their negative influence and spending more time with those who support us.

Make Creativity a Priority Having diminished the voice of negative judgment in your mind, established a creative environment, and committed yourself to trusting your creative gifts, you are now in a position to live more creatively. How do you actually do this? Start small. Identify some habitual patterns in your life and break out of them. Choose new experiences whenever possible—for example, ordering unfamiliar items on a menu or getting to know people outside your circle of friends—and strive to develop fresh perspectives in your life. Resist falling back into the ruts you were previously in by remembering that living things are supposed to be continually growing, changing, and evolving, not acting in repetitive patterns like machines.

Thinking Critically About Visuals

"You Must Expect the Unexpected"—Heraclitus

Can you think of a time when a creative inspiration enabled you to see a solution to a problem that no one else could see? What can you do to increase these creative breakthroughs in your life? What strategies can you use to "expect the unexpected"?

Radioactive Cats © 1980 Sandy Skoglund

Thinking Activity 1.9

BECOMING MORE CREATIVE

Select an area of your life in which you would like to be more creative. It can be in school, on your job, in an activity you enjoy, or in your relationship with someone. Make a special effort to inject a fresh perspective and new ideas into this area, and keep a journal recording your efforts and their results. Be sure to allow yourself sufficient time to break out of your ruts and establish new patterns of thinking, feeling, and behaving. Focus on your creative antennae as you "expect the unexpected," and pounce on new ideas when they emerge from the depths of your creative resource.

THINKING CRITICALLY ABOUT NEW MEDIA

Creative Applications

The world is changing at warp speed, and many of these changes have to do with what is popularly termed the "new media," forms of information and communication technologies that were made possible by the creation of the Internet, wireless phones, and text communication devices. Virtually every aspect of our lives has been affected by the development and use of these technologies, including the way we think and write, communicate with one another, research and gather information, develop and sustain relationships, create our sense of self-identity, and construct "virtual" realities that have complex connections to the space-and-time world in which we go about the business of living. For example, it used to be that communicating with someone else involved speaking in person, writing a letter, or talking on a landline telephone. We can now speak by cell phone directly to almost anyone on the planet from wherever we are whenever we want. What's more, we can use the technologies of email, texting or tweeting to stay socially connected to a large number of people on a continual basis. And through the development of social networking sites like Facebook, YouTube, and LinkedIn, people have been able to create "virtual communities." These virtual communities transcend geographical boundaries, and as the new media critic and writer Howard Rheingold explains, these globalized societies are self-defined networks, which resemble what we do in real life. "People in virtual communities use words on screens to exchange pleasantries and argue, engage in intellectual discourse, conduct commerce, make plans, brainstorm, gossip, feud, fall in love, create a little high art and a lot of idle talk."

However, accompanying this new universe of possibilities are many risks and challenges that, more than ever, make it necessary to develop and apply our critical thinking abilities as we navigate our way through this digital universe. To this end, I have included a number of readings in this edition that address various aspects of new media. In addition, each chapter contains a section on "Thinking Critically About New Media." It's essential that we have the strategies and insight to make sure that these powerful new vehicles of communication are used to enhance our lives, not complicate and damage them.

One of the themes of this chapter has been creative thinking, and new media offer an unprecedented opportunity to roam far and wide in our search for information that will enrich our creative endeavors. But new media also afford us the chance to gather many different perspectives on our projects, with others' ideas serving as catalysts to our creative imaginations. For example, the columnist David Pogue suggests that companies should use what he calls "crowdsourcing" to generate new ideas. To try this out, he asked his Twitter followers for their best tech-product enhancement ideas. He reports that "They responded wittily, passionately—and immediately (this is Twitter, after all)." Ideas that were tweeted back included:

- Cell phone batteries that recharge through kinetic motion as you walk around
- Technology that lets you use your hand as a TV remote control (the TV recognizes your gestures)
- A camera warning that responds to voice commands and also tells you if your thumb is in the way of the lens
- Laptop computers with built-in solar panels for charging batteries
- Music players that can be shifted to "Karaoke mode"

The column with its complete list of creative ideas can be found at www.nytimes .com/2009/09/10/technology/personaltech/10pogue.html?emc=eta1.

Thinking Activity 1.10

CREATIVE "CROWDSOURCING"

Following up on David Pogue's ingenious use of "crowdsourcing" to generate creative ideas, try some crowdsourcing of your own to generate innovative ideas to improve the quality of your life. Send several queries out to your network of friends asking them for their creative ideas, then compile these into a master list that you share with everyone (be sure to give credit!). Here are some possible topics:

- Ideas for organizing the many activities in your life more efficiently
- Ideas for making studying more entertaining *and* effective
- Ideas for having a party with a totally unique theme

Thinking Passages

NURTURING CREATIVITY

The process of creating yourself through your choices is a lifelong one that involves all the creative and critical thinking abilities that we will be exploring in this book. The processes of creative thinking and critical thinking are related to one another in complex, interactive ways. We use the creative thinking process to develop ideas that are unique, useful, and worthy of further elaboration, and we use the critical thinking process to analyze, evaluate, and refine these ideas. Creative thinking and critical thinking work as partners, enabling us to lead fulfilling lives. The first of the following articles, "Original Spin" by Lesley Dormen and Peter Edidin, provides a useful introduction to creative thinking and suggests strategies for increasing your creative abilities. In the second article, "Revenge of the Right Brain," the author Daniel Pink contends that the creative thinking abilities associated with the right half of our brains are increasingly essential to succeeding in the new "Conceptual Age." After reading the articles and reflecting on their ideas, answer the questions that follow.

Original Spin

by Lesley Dormen and Peter Edidin

Creativity, somebody once wrote, is the search for the elusive "Aha," that moment of insight when one sees the world, or a problem, or an idea, in a new way. Traditionally, whether the discovery results in a cubist painting or an improved carburetor, we have viewed the creative instant as serendipitous and rare—the product of genius, the property of the elect.

Unfortunately, this attitude has had a number of adverse consequences. It encourages us to accept the myth that the creative energy society requires to address its own problems will never be present in sufficient supply. Beyond that, we have come to believe that "ordinary" people like ourselves can never be truly creative. As John Briggs, author of *Fire in the Crucible: The Alchemy of Creative Genius*, said, "The way we talk about creativity tends to reinforce the notion that it is some kind of arbitrary gift. It's amazing the way 'not having it' becomes wedded to people's self-image. They invariably work up a whole series of rationalizations about why they 'aren't creative,' as if they were damaged goods of some kind." Today, however, researchers are looking at creativity, not as an advantage of the human elite, but as a basic human endowment. As Ruth Richards, a psychiatrist and creativity researcher at McLean Hospital in Belmont, MA, says, "You were being creative when you learned how to walk. And if you are looking for something in the fridge, you're being creative because you have to figure out for yourself where it is." Creativity, in Richards' view, is simply fundamental to getting about in the world. It is "our ability to adapt to change. It is the very essence of human survival."

In an age of rampant social and technological change, such an adaptive capability becomes yet more crucial to the individual's effort to maintain balance in a constantly shifting environment. "People need to recognize that what Alvin Toffler called future shock is our daily reality," says Ellen McGrath, a clinical psychologist who teaches creativity courses at New York University. "Instability is an intrinsic part of our lives, and to deal with it every one of us will need to find new, creative solutions to the challenges of everyday life."

. . .

But can you really become more creative? If the word creative smacks too much of Picasso at his canvas, then rephrase the question in a less intimidating way: Do you believe you could deal with the challenges of life in a more effective, inventive, and fulfilling manner? If the answer is yes, then the question becomes, "What's stopping you?"

Defining Yourself as a Creative Person

People often hesitate to recognize the breakthroughs in their own lives as creative. But who has not felt the elation and surprise that come with the sudden, seemingly inexplicable discovery of a solution to a stubborn problem? In that instant, in "going beyond the information given," as psychologist Jerome Bruner has said, to a solution that was the product of your own mind, you were expressing your creativity.

This impulse to "go beyond" to a new idea is not the preserve of genius, stresses David Henry Feldman, a developmental psychologist at Tufts University and the author of *Nature's Gambit*, a study of child prodigies. "Not everybody can be Beethoven," he says, "but it is true that all humans, by virtue of being dreamers and fantasizers, have a tendency to take liberties with the world as it exists. Humans are always transforming their inner and outer worlds. It's what I call the 'transformational imperative.'"

The desire to play with reality, however, is highly responsive to social control, and many of us are taught early on to repress the impulse. As Mark Runco, associate professor of psychology at California State University at Fullerton and the founder of the new *Creativity Research Journal*, says, "We put children in groups and make them sit in desks and raise their hands before they talk. We put all the emphasis on conformity and order, then we wonder why they aren't being spontaneous and creative."

Adults too are expected to conform in any number of ways and in a variety of settings. Conformity, after all, creates a sense of order and offers the reassurance of the familiar. But to free one's natural creative impulses, it is necessary, to some extent, to resist the pressure to march in step with the world. Begin small, suggests Richards. "Virtually nothing you do can't be done in a slightly different, slightly better way. This has nothing to do with so-called creative pursuits but simply with breaking with your own mindsets and trying an original way of doing some habitual task. Simply defer judgment on yourself for a little while and try something new. Remember, the essence of life is not getting things right, but taking risks, making mistakes, getting things wrong."

Avoiding the Myths

David Perkins, co-director of Project Zero at the Harvard Graduate School of Education, asks in *The Mind's Best Work*, "When you have it—creativity, that is—what do you have?" The very impalpability of the subject means that often creativity can be known only by its products. Indeed, the most common way the researchers define creativity is

Thinking Critically About Visuals

"Express Yourself!"

Our creative talents can be expressed in almost every area of our lives. How is the woman in the photo expressing herself creatively? What are some of your favorite activities in which you are able to express your unique personality in innovative ways?

Jeff Greenberg/Alamy

by saying it is whatever produces something that is: a. original; b. adaptive (i.e., useful); c. meaningful to others. But because we don't understand its genesis, we're often blocked or intimidated by the myths that surround and distort this mercurial subject.

One of these myths is, in Perkins's words, that creativity is "a kind of 'stuff' that the creative person has and uses to do creative things, never mind other factors." This bit of folk wisdom, that creativity is a sort of intangible psychic organ—happily present in some and absent in others—so annoys Perkins that he would like to abolish the word itself.

Another prevalent myth about creativity is that it is restricted to those who are "geniuses"—that is, people with inordinately high IQs. Ironically, this has been discredited by a study begun by Stanford psychologist Lewis Terman, the man who adapted the original French IQ test for America. In the early 1920s, Terman had California schoolteachers choose 1,528 "genius" schoolchildren (those with an IQ above 135), whose lives were then tracked year after year. After six decades, researchers found that the putative geniuses, by and large, did well in life. They entered the professions in large numbers and led stable, prosperous lives. But very few made notable creative contributions to society, and none did extraordinarily creative work.

According to Dean Simonton, professor of psychology at the University of California at Davis and the author of *Genius, Creativity and Leadership* and *Scientific Genius*, "There just isn't any correlation between creativity and IQ. The average college graduate has an IQ of about 120, and this is high enough to write novels, do scientific research, or any other kind of creative work."

A third myth, voiced eons ago by Socrates, lifts creativity out of our own lives altogether into a mystical realm that makes it all but unapproachable. In this view, the creative individual is a kind of oracle, the passive conduit or channel chosen by God, or the tribal ancestors, or the muse, to communicate sacred knowledge.

Although there *are* extraordinary examples of creativity, for which the only explanation seems to be supernatural intervention (Mozart, the story goes, wrote the overture to *Don Giovanni* in only a few hours, after a virtually sleepless night and without revision), by and large, creativity begins with a long and intensive apprenticeship.

Psychologist Howard Gruber believes that it takes at least 10 years of immersion in a given domain before an eminent creator is likely to be able to make a distinctive mark. Einstein, for example, who is popularly thought to have doodled out the theory of relativity at age 26 in his spare time, was in fact compulsively engaged in thinking about the problem at least from the age of 16.

Finally, many who despair of ever being creative do so because they tried once and failed, as though the truly creative always succeed. In fact, just the opposite is true, says Dean Simonton. He sees genius, in a sense, as inseparable from failure. "Great geniuses make tons of mistakes," he says. "They generate lots of ideas and they accept being wrong. They have a kind of internal fortress that allows them to fail and just keep going. Look at Edison. He held over 1,000 patents, but most of them are not only forgotten, they weren't worth much to begin with."

Mindlessness Versus Mindfulness

"Each of us desires to share with others our vision of the world, only most of us have been taught that it's wrong to do things differently or look at things differently," says John Briggs. "We lose confidence in ourselves and begin to look at reality only in terms of the categories by which society orders it."

This is the state of routinized conformity and passive learning that Harvard professor of psychology Ellen Langer calls, appropriately enough, mindlessness. For it is the state of denying the perceptions and promptings of our own minds, our individual selves. Langer and her colleagues' extensive research over the past 15 years has shown that when we act mindlessly, we behave automatically and limit our capacity for creative response. Mired down in a numbing daily routine, we may virtually relinquish our capacity for independent thought and action.

By contrast, Langer refers to a life in which we use our affective, responsive, perceptive faculties as "mindful." When we are mindful, her research has shown, we avoid rigid, reflexive behavior in favor of a more improvisational and intuitive response to life. We notice and feel the world around us and then act in accordance with our feelings. "Many, if not all, of the qualities that make up a mindful attitude are characteristic of creative people," Langer writes in her new book, *Mindfulness*. "Those who can free themselves of mindsets, open themselves to new information and surprise, play with perspective and context, and focus on process rather than outcome are likely to be creative, whether they are scientists, artists, or cooks."

Much of Langer's research has demonstrated the vital relationship between creativity and uncertainty, or conditionality. For instance, in one experiment, Langer and Alison Piper introduced a collection of objects to one group of people by saying, "This is a hair dryer," and "This is a dog's chew toy," and so on. Another group was told, "This *could be* a hair dryer," and "This *could be* a dog's chew toy." Later, the experimenters for both groups invented a need for an eraser, but only those people who had been conditionally introduced to the objects thought to use the dog's toy in this new way.

The intuitive understanding that a single thing is, or could be, many things, depending on how you look at it, is at the heart of the attitude Langer calls mindfulness. But can such an amorphous state be cultivated? Langer believes that it can, by consciously discarding the idea that any given moment of your day is fixed in its form. "I teach people to 'componentize' their lives into smaller pieces," she says. "In the morning, instead of mindlessly downing your orange juice, *taste it*. Is it what you want? Try something else if it isn't. When you walk to work, turn left instead of right. You'll notice the street you're on, the buildings and the weather. Mindfulness, like creativity, is nothing more than a return to who you are. By minding your responses to the world, you will come to know yourself again. How you feel. What you want. What you want to do."

Creating the Right Atmosphere

Understanding the genesis of creativity, going beyond the myths to understand your creative potential, and recognizing your ability to break free of old ways of thinking are the three initial steps to a more creative life. The fourth is finding ways to work that encourage personal commitment and expressiveness.

Letting employees learn what they want to do has never been a very high priority in the workplace. There, the dominant regulation has always been, "Do what you are told."

Today, however, economic realities are providing a new impetus for change. The pressure on American businesses to become more productive and innovative has made creative thinking a hot commodity in the business community. But innovation, business is now learning, is likely to be found wherever bright and eager people *think* they can find it. And some people are looking in curious places.

Financier Wayne Silby, for example, founded the Calvert Group of Funds, which today manages billions of dollars in assets. Silby, whose business card at one point read Chief Daydreamer, occasionally retreats for inspiration to a sensory deprivation tank, where he floats in warm water sealed off from light and sound. "I went into the tank during a time when the government was changing money-market deposit regulations, and I needed to think how to compete with banks. Floating in the tank I got the idea of joining them instead. We wound up creating an $800-million program. Often we already have answers to our problems, but we don't quiet ourselves enough to see the solutions bubbling just below the surface." Those solutions will stay submerged, he says, "unless you create a culture that encourages creative approaches, where it's OK to have bad ideas."

. . .

The Payoff

In *The Courage to Create*, Rollo May wrote that for much of [the twentieth] century, researchers had avoided the subject of creativity because they perceived it as "unscientific, mysterious, disturbing and too corruptive of the scientific training of graduate students." But today researchers are coming to see that creativity, at once fugitive and ubiquitous, is the mark of human nature itself.

Whether in business or the arts, politics, or personal relationships, creativity involves "going beyond the information given" to create or reveal something new in the world. And almost invariably, when the mind exercises its creative muscle, it also generates a sense of pleasure. The feeling may be powerfully mystical, as it is for New York artist Rhonda Zwillinger, whose embellished artwork appeared in the film *Slaves of New York*. Zwillinger reports, "There are times when I'm working and it is almost as though I'm a vessel and there is a force operating through me. It is the closest I come to having a religious experience." The creative experience may also be quiet and full of wonder, as it was for Isaac Newton, who compared his lifetime of creative effort to "a boy playing on the seashore and diverting himself and then finding a smoother pebble or prettier shell than ordinary, while the greater ocean of truth lay all undiscovered before me."

But whatever the specific sensation, creativity always carries with it a powerful sense of the mind working at the peak of its ability. Creativity truly is, as David Perkins calls it, the mind's best work, its finest effort. We may never know exactly how the brain does it, but we can feel that it is exactly what the brain was meant to do.

Aha!

QUESTIONS FOR ANALYSIS

1. According to the authors, "Creativity . . . is the search for the elusive 'Aha,' that moment of insight when one sees the world, or a problem, or an idea, in a new way." Describe an "aha" moment that you have had recently, detailing the origin of your innovative idea and how you implemented it.

2. Identify some of the influences in your life that have inhibited your creative development, including the "myths" about creativity that are described in the article.

3. Using the ideas contained in this chapter and in this article, identify some of the strategies that you intend to use in order to become more creative in your life—for example, becoming more mindful, destroying the "voice of criticism," and creating an atmosphere more conducive to creativity.

Revenge of the Right Brain

by Daniel H. Pink

When I was a kid growing up in a middle-class family, in the middle of America, in the middle of the 1970s—parents dished out a familiar plate of advice to their children: Get good grades, go to college, and pursue a profession that offers a decent standard of living and perhaps a dollop of prestige. If you were good at math and science, become a doctor. If you were better at English and history, become a lawyer. If blood grossed you out and your verbal skills needed work, become an accountant. Later, as computers appeared on desktops and CEOs on magazine covers, the youngsters who were really good at math and science chose high tech, while others flocked to business school, thinking that success was spelled MBA.

Tax attorneys. Radiologists. Financial analysts. Software engineers. Management guru Peter Drucker gave this cadre of professionals an enduring, if somewhat wonky, name: knowledge workers. These are, he wrote, "people who get paid for putting to work what one learns in school rather than for their physical strength or manual skill." What distinguished members of this group and enabled them to reap society's greatest rewards, was their "ability to acquire and to apply theoretical and analytic knowledge." And any of us could join their ranks. All we had to do was study hard and play by the rules of the meritocratic regime. That was the path to professional success and personal fulfillment.

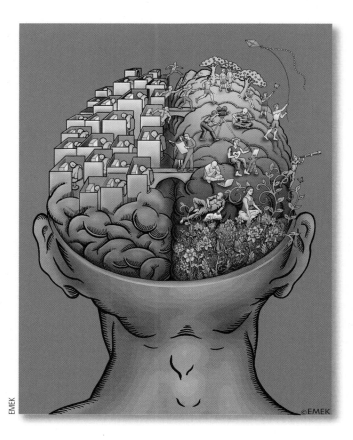

Source: "Revenge of the Right Brain–Wired Magazine 2/2005," from *A Whole New Mind* by Daniel Pink, copyright © 2005, 2006 by Daniel H. Pink. Used by permission of Riverhead Books, an imprint of Penguin Group (USA) Inc.

But a funny thing happened while we were pressing our noses to the grindstone: The world changed. The future no longer belongs to people who can reason with computer-like logic, speed, and precision. It belongs to a different kind of person with a different kind of mind. Today—amid the uncertainties of an economy that has gone from boom to bust to blah—there's a metaphor that explains what's going on. And it's right inside our heads.

Scientists have long known that a neurological Mason-Dixon line cleaves our brains into two regions—the left and right hemispheres. But in the last 10 years, thanks in part to advances in functional magnetic resonance imaging, researchers have begun to identify more precisely how the two sides divide responsibilities. The left hemisphere handles sequence, literalness, and analysis. The right hemisphere, meanwhile, takes care of context, emotional expression, and synthesis. Of course, the human brain, with its 100 billion cells forging 1 quadrillion connections, is breathtakingly complex. The two hemispheres work in concert, and we enlist both sides for nearly everything we do. But the structure of our brains can help explain the contours of our times.

Until recently, the abilities that led to success in school, work, and business were characteristic of the left hemisphere. They were the sorts of linear, logical, analytical talents measured by SATs and deployed by CPAs. Today, those capabilities are still necessary. But they're no longer sufficient. In a world upended by outsourcing, deluged with data, and choked with choices, the abilities that matter most are now closer in spirit to the specialties of the right hemisphere—artistry, empathy, seeing the big picture, and pursuing the transcendent.

Beneath the nervous clatter of our half-completed decade stirs a slow but seismic shift. The Information Age we all prepared for is ending. Rising in its place is what I call the Conceptual Age, an era in which mastery of abilities that we've often overlooked and undervalued marks the fault line between who gets ahead and who falls behind.

To some of you, this shift—from an economy built on the logical, sequential abilities of the Information Age to an economy built on the inventive, empathic abilities of the Conceptual Age—sounds delightful. "You had me at hello!" I can hear the painters and nurses exulting. But to others, this sounds like a crock. "Prove it!" I hear the programmers and lawyers demanding.

OK. To convince you, I'll explain the reasons for this shift, using the mechanistic language of cause and effect.

The effect: the scales tilting in favor of right brain-style thinking. The causes: Asia, automation, and abundance.

Asia

Few issues today spark more controversy than outsourcing. Those squadrons of white-collar workers in India, the Philippines, and China are scaring the bejesus out of software jockeys across North America and Europe. According to Forrester Research, 1 in 9 jobs in the US information technology industry will move overseas by 2010. And it's not just tech work. Visit India's office parks and you'll see chartered accountants preparing American tax returns, lawyers researching American lawsuits, and radiologists reading CAT scans for US hospitals.

The reality behind the alarm is this: Outsourcing to Asia is overhyped in the short term, but underhyped in the long term. We're not all going to lose our jobs tomorrow. (The total number of jobs lost to offshoring so far represents less than 1 percent of the US labor force.) But as the cost of communicating with the other side of the globe falls essentially to zero, as India becomes (by 2010) the country with the most English speakers in the world, and as developing nations continue to mint millions of extremely capable knowledge workers, the professional lives of people in the West will change dramatically. If number crunching, chart reading, and code writing can be done for a lot less overseas and delivered to clients instantly via fiber-optic cable, that's where the work will go.

But these gusts of comparative advantage are blowing away only certain kinds of white-collar jobs—those that can be reduced to a set of rules, routines, and instructions. That's why narrow left-brain work such as basic computer coding, accounting, legal research, and financial analysis is migrating across the oceans. But that's also why plenty of opportunities remain for people and companies doing less routine work—programmers who can design entire systems, accountants who serve as life planners, and bankers expert less in the intricacies of Excel than in the art of the deal. Now that foreigners can do left-brain work cheaper, we in the US must do right-brain work better.

Automation

Last century, machines proved they could replace human muscle. This century, technologies are proving they can outperform human left brains—they can execute sequential, reductive, computational work better, faster, and more accurately than even those with the highest IQs. (Just ask chess grandmaster Garry Kasparov.)

Consider jobs in financial services. Stockbrokers who merely execute transactions are history. Online trading services and market makers do such work far more efficiently. The brokers who survived have morphed from routine order-takers to less easily replicated advisers, who can understand a client's broader financial objectives and even the client's emotions and dreams.

Or take lawyers. Dozens of inexpensive information and advice services are reshaping law practice. At CompleteCase.com, you can get an uncontested divorce for $249, less than a 10th of the cost of a divorce lawyer. Meanwhile, the Web is cracking the information monopoly that has long been the source of many lawyers' high incomes and professional mystique. Go to USlegalforms.com and you can download— for the price of two movie tickets—fill-in-the-blank wills, contracts, and articles of incorporation that used to reside exclusively on lawyers' hard drives. Instead of hiring a lawyer for 10 hours to craft a contract, consumers can fill out the form themselves and hire a lawyer for one hour to look it over. Consequently, legal abilities that can't be digitized—convincing a jury or understanding the subtleties of a negotiation— become more valuable.

Even computer programmers may feel the pinch. "In the old days," legendary computer scientist Vernor Vinge has said, "anybody with even routine skills could get a job as a programmer. That isn't true anymore. The routine functions are increasingly being turned over to machines." The result: As the scut work gets offloaded, engineers will have to master different aptitudes, relying more on creativity than competence.

Any job that can be reduced to a set of rules is at risk. If a $500-a-month accountant in India doesn't swipe your accounting job, TurboTax will. Now that computers can emulate left-hemisphere skills, we'll have to rely ever more on our right hemispheres.

Abundance

Our left brains have made us rich. Powered by armies of Drucker's knowledge workers, the information economy has produced a standard of living that would have been unfathomable in our grandparents' youth. Their lives were defined by scarcity. Ours are shaped by abundance. Want evidence? Spend five minutes at Best Buy. Or look in your garage. Owning a car used to be a grand American aspiration. Today, there are more automobiles in the US than there are licensed drivers—which means that, on average, everybody who can drive has a car of their own. And if your garage is also piled with excess consumer goods, you're not alone. Self-storage—a business devoted to housing our extra crap—is now a $17 billion annual industry in the US, nearly double Hollywood's yearly box office take.

But abundance has produced an ironic result. The Information Age has unleashed a prosperity that in turn places a premium on less rational sensibilities—beauty, spirituality, emotion. For companies and entrepreneurs, it's no longer enough to create a product, a service, or an experience that's reasonably priced and adequately functional. In an age of abundance, consumers demand something more. Check out your bathroom. If you're like a few million Americans, you've got a Michael Graves toilet brush or a Karim Rashid trash can that you bought at Target. Try explaining a designer garbage pail to the left side of your brain! Or consider illumination. Electric lighting was rare a century ago, but now it's commonplace. Yet in the US, candles are a $2 billion a year business—for reasons that stretch beyond the logical need for luminosity to a prosperous country's more inchoate desire for pleasure and transcendence.

Liberated by this prosperity but not fulfilled by it, more people are searching for meaning. From the mainstream embrace of such once-exotic practices as yoga and meditation to the rise of spirituality in the workplace to the influence of evangelism in pop culture and politics, the quest for meaning and purpose has become an integral part of everyday life. And that will only intensify as the first children of abundance, the baby boomers, realize that they have more of their lives behind them than ahead. In both business and personal life, now that our left-brain needs have largely been sated, our right-brain yearnings will demand to be fed.

As the forces of Asia, automation, and abundance strengthen and accelerate, the curtain is rising on a new era, the Conceptual Age. If the Industrial Age was built on people's backs, and the Information Age on people's left hemispheres, the Conceptual Age is being built on people's right hemispheres. We've progressed from a society of farmers to a society of factory workers to a society of knowledge workers. And now we're progressing yet again—to a society of creators and empathizers, pattern recognizers, and meaning makers.

But let me be clear: The future is not some Manichaean landscape in which individuals are either left-brained and extinct or right-brained and ecstatic—a land in which millionare yoga instructors drive BMWs and programmers scrub counters at Chick-fil-A. Logical, linear, analytic thinking remains indispensable. But it's no longer enough.

To flourish in this age, we'll need to supplement our well-developed high tech abilities with aptitudes that are "high concept" and "high touch." High concept involves the ability to create artistic and emotional beauty, to detect patterns and opportunities, to craft a satisfying narrative, and to come up with inventions the world didn't know it was missing. High touch involves the capacity to empathize, to understand the subtleties of human interaction, to find joy in one's self and to elicit it in others, and to stretch beyond the quotidian in pursuit of purpose and meaning.

Developing these high concept, high touch abilities won't be easy for everyone. For some, the prospect seems unattainable. Fear not (or at least fear less). The sorts of abilities that now matter most are fundamentally human attributes. After all, back on the savannah, our caveperson ancestors weren't plugging numbers into spreadsheets or debugging code. But they were telling stories, demonstrating empathy, and designing innovations. These abilities have always been part of what it means to be human. It's just that after a few generations in the Information Age, many of our high concept, high touch muscles have atrophied. The challenge is to work them back into shape.

Want to get ahead today? Forget what your parents told you. Instead, do something foreigners can't do cheaper. Something computers can't do faster. And something that fills one of the nonmaterial, transcendent desires of an abundant age. In other words, go right, young man and woman, go right.

QUESTIONS FOR ANALYSIS

1. Explain the differences between what the author characterizes as the Industrial Age, the Information Age, and the Conceptual Age. Why does he feel that being a "knowledge worker" will no longer be sufficient for achieving success in the new Conceptual Age?

2. Identify and describe the social forces that the author believes are responsible for moving us from the Information Age to the Conceptual Age.

3. According to the author, the thinking abilities associated with the left brain are linear, logical, and analytic, while the thinking abilities associated with the right brain involve artistry, empathy, inventiveness, and seeing the big picture. Using examples, explain how being able to think in both of these ways is advantageous for most careers.

Thinking Ahead

The first line of this chapter stated, "Thinking is the extraordinary process we use every waking moment to make sense of our world and our lives." Throughout this chapter we have explored the different ways our thinking enables us to make sense of the world by working toward goals, making decisions, and living creatively. Of course, our thinking helps us make sense of the world in other ways as well. When we attend a concert, listen to a lecture, or try to understand someone's behavior, it is our thinking that enables us to figure out what is happening. In fact, these attempts to make sense of what is happening are going on all the time in our lives, and they represent the heart of the thinking process.

If we review the different ways of thinking we have explored in this chapter, we can reach several conclusions about thinking:

- Thinking is directed toward a purpose. When we think, it is usually for a purpose—to reach a goal, make a decision, or analyze an issue.
- Thinking is an organized process. When we think effectively, there is usually an order or organization to our thinking. For each of the thinking activities we explored, we saw that there are certain steps or approaches to take that help us reach goals, make decisions, and live creatively.

We can put together these conclusions about thinking to form a working definition of the term.

Thinking is a purposeful, organized cognitive process that we use to understand the world and make informed decisions. It develops with use over a lifetime, and we can improve our thinking in an organized and systematic way by following these steps:

thinking A purposeful, organized cognitive process that we use to understand the world and make informed decisions.

- Carefully examining our thinking process and the thinking process of others. In this chapter we have explored various ways in which our thinking works. By focusing our attention on these (and other) thinking approaches and strategies, we can learn to think more effectively.
- Practicing our thinking abilities. To improve our thinking, we actually have to think for ourselves, to explore and make sense of situations by using our thinking abilities. Although it is important to read about thinking and learn how other people think, there is no substitute for actually doing it ourselves.

Examining critical thinking and creative thinking is a rich and complex enterprise. These two dimensions of the thinking process are so tightly interwoven that both must be addressed together in order to understand them individually. For example, you can use your creative thinking abilities to visualize your ideal future. With this idea as a starting point, you can then use your critical thinking abilities to refine your idea and research existing opportunities.

Once a clear goal is established, you can use your creative thinking abilities to generate possible ideas for achieving this goal, while your critical thinking abilities can help you evaluate your various options and devise a practical, organized plan.

It is apparent that creative thinking and critical thinking work as partners to produce productive and effective thinking, thus enabling us to make informed decisions and lead successful lives. As this text unfolds, you will be given the opportunity to become familiar with both of these powerful forms of thought as you develop your abilities to think both critically and creatively.

CHAPTER 1 | Reviewing and Viewing

Summary

- Living an *examined life* means painting your life portrait with reflective understanding and informed choices.

- *Thinking critically* involves carefully exploring the thinking process to clarify our understanding and make more intelligent decisions.

- *Thinking creatively* involves using our thinking process to develop ideas that are unique, useful, and worthy of further elaboration.

- Achieving your goals involves identifying the "right" goals and then developing an effective plan of action.

- We can make more intelligent decisions by using an organized five-step approach to guide our analysis.

- Living your life creatively means bringing your unique perspective and creative talents to all of the dimensions of your life.

- Creative thinking and critical thinking work as partners to produce productive and effective thinking, thus enabling us to make informed decisions and lead successful lives.

Assessing Your Strategies and Creating New Goals

How Much of a Creative Thinker Am I?

Critical thinking and creative thinking are partners; in order to become an expert thinker, we need to develop our abilities in both of these areas. Described below are key personal attributes that are correlated with becoming a powerful creative thinker. Evaluate your position regarding each of these attributes, and use this self-evaluation to guide your choices as you shape the creative thinker that you want to become.

Make Creative Thinking a Priority

I believe that creativity is important.	I believe that creativity is overrated.
5 4 3 2 1	

Research demonstrates that creative people typically consider creativity to be more important than things like wealth and power, and they take pleasure in being imaginative, curious, and creatively expressive. The author Khalil Gibran wrote: "*For the self is a sea, boundless and measureless.*" For many people that sea remains largely undiscovered.

Strategy: Make creativity a conscious priority in your life by putting reminders in prominent places (a mirror, the refrigerator door, next to your phone at the office) and by evaluating your daily progress in your Thinking Notebook at the conclusion of the day. Habit and conformity are powerful forces that must be consciously struggled against in order to reshape your life.

Take Creative Risks

I am willing to take creative risks.	I tend to avoid taking creative risks.
5 4 3 2 1	

According to the French proverb, "*Only he who does nothing makes a mistake.*" Most people avoid mistakes like bats flee light, but it's difficult to be creative if you aren't willing to risk failure. If you consistently take what the Danish philosopher Søren Kierkegaard characterized as a "*leap of faith*" toward your creative potential, the luminosity of your successes will far outshine the momentary disappointment of experiments gone awry.

Strategy: Take some genuinely risky creative actions, and if failures occur, view them as badges of courage, symbols of your own self-confidence and independent thinking. Your failure is a healthy indication that you are sufficiently alive to keep learning and growing as a unique, valuable individual.

Nurture Your Imagination

I make time to use my imagination.	I don't make time to use my imagination.
5 4 3 2 1	

In one of his most memorable statements, Albert Einstein asserted, "*Imagination is more important than knowledge.*" Caught up in "reality," we fail to see what *might* exist, a terrible loss, for as the philosopher Jean-Jacques Rousseau observed, "*The world of reality has its limits; the world of imagination is boundless.*"

Strategy: Practice using your imagination to alter reality—playing with possibilities, creating new scenarios. Indulge your fantasies, challenge conventional ways of doing and thinking, try to come up with many ideas when you are making decisions or solving problems. Don't censor ideas, no matter how outlandish. Record your results and evaluate your progress in your **Thinking Notebook***.*

Strive for Independence

My actions reflect my own ideas.	My actions are influenced by the ideas of others.
5 4 3 2 1	

The journey toward increased creativity travels the same path as the journey toward independent thinking and action. When we subordinate ourselves to others at the expense of our own thinking and personalities, we are being "other-directed," surrendering control of our lives to external forces. To live creatively, we have to be "inner-directed," maintaining our own personal vision of the world and making confident choices based on what *we* think. As the author Robert Louis Stevenson observed, "*To know what you prefer instead of humbly saying Amen to what the world tells you you ought to prefer, is to have kept your soul alive.*"

Strategy: *Record in your* **Thinking Notebook** *the ideas you express that are directed toward pleasing or impressing others. Also record the ideas that you did* **not** *express because you were concerned that others would not appreciate or approve of them. After a few days you should be able to discern "inner-directed" and "other-directed" patterns in your life. If you conclude that the scales are tipped toward "other-directed," start making the appropriate adjustments and evaluate your daily progress.*

Cultivate Curiosity, Avoid Judgment

I approach life with a questioning attitude.	I often make quick, final judgments about things in my life.
5 4 3 2 1	

"*I like it.*" "*I don't like it.*" "*She's nice.*" "*He's a fool.*" The problem with automatic judgments like these is that they close minds, cutting off lines of inquiry and paths of exploration, the heart of creativity. Instead of dismissing someone's creation with "*I don't like it,*" asking yourself "*What ideas is she trying to express?*" stimulates you to reflect and opens you to the possibility of new ideas. By asking questions instead of passing judgments, you are discovering significant things about yourself and the world, and you are training your mind to think productively and creatively.

Strategy: *Try playing different roles in order to increase your curiosity. For example, when you are speaking to others, adopt the role of a* **psychologist** *in your mind: What are they really trying to say, and are there deeper motivations at work? Why am I responding the way that I am? When you are examining someone's work, adopt the* *role of an **investigator**: What is the goal of this project? What specific suggestions can I make for improving its effectiveness? Record particularly effective questions and the new insights you discover in your **Thinking Notebook**.*

Suggested Films

Amelie (2001)

A discovery inspires a solitary young French woman to creatively reimagine her own life and to bring creativity and wonder to the lives of others. The film is a celebration of life, and our ability to change our lives by shifting our perspectives.

American Beauty (1999)

What are the dangers of "sleepwalking through life"? Lester Burnham lives a seemingly perfect life in suburbia with his high-powered wife and adolescent daughter. But he is depressed with his mundane existence until he develops a crush on his daughter's friend. His actions in the wake of this fantasy have powerful effects on himself and all those around him.

Examined Life (2008)

Filmmaker Astra Taylor interviews leading contemporary philosophers in an effort to examine the application of philosophy in the world today. Her conversations with Cornel West, Peter Singer, Michael Hardt, Martha Nussbaum, and others illuminate the vital importance of critical and creative thinking in the modern world.

Life Is Beautiful (1997)

Is it possible to create meaning in desperate circumstances? A charismatic and playful Jewish bookkeeper refuses to lose hope or give up when he, his wife, and his young son are sent to a Nazi concentration camp. Instead, he finds ways to communicate with his family and, through humor and playacting, attempts to convince his son that the camp is an elaborate game.

The Visitor (2007)

A widowed professor connects with an immigrant couple that has been living illegally in his apartment. His friendship with them allows for his own creative growth and significantly changes his perspective on himself and the world.

During a prodemocracy protest, a student stands up for what he believes by blocking the way of a line of Communist military tanks in Tiananmen Square in China in 1989. Stated beliefs and actions based on sound critical thinking have sometimes led people to make difficult or unpopular decisions, or, as in this case, have even put their lives at risk. Have you ever made a difficult or unpopular decision based on your critical thinking? Would you do it again? (To read more about the event at Tiananmen Square, see Thinking Activity 5.5.)

Thinking Critically

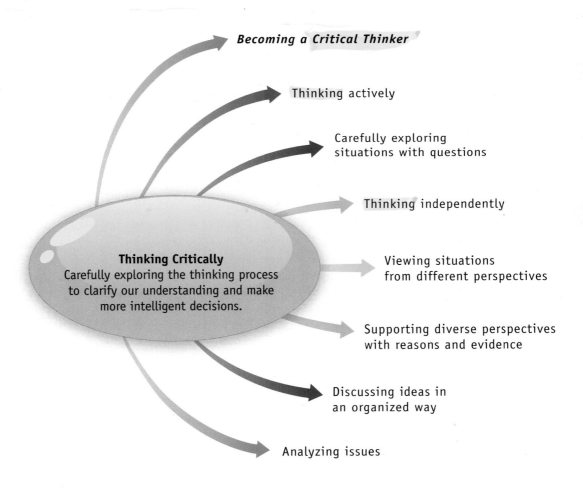

Becoming a Critical Thinker

Thinking actively

Carefully exploring
situations with questions

Thinking independently

Thinking Critically
Carefully exploring the thinking process
to clarify our understanding and make
more intelligent decisions.

Viewing situations
from different perspectives

Supporting diverse perspectives
with reasons and evidence

Discussing ideas in
an organized way

Analyzing issues

In ancient Greece, most advanced students studied philosophy in order to achieve "wisdom." (The term *philosophy* in Greek means "lover of wisdom.") In today's world, many college students are hoping, through their studies, to become the modern-day equivalent: informed, *critical thinkers*. A critical thinker is someone who has developed a knowledgeable understanding of our complex world, a thoughtful perspective on important ideas and timely issues, the capacity for penetrating insight and intelligent judgment, and sophisticated thinking and language abilities.

The word *critical* comes from the Greek word for "critic" (*kritikos*), which means "to question, to make sense of, to be able to analyze." It is by questioning, making sense of situations, and analyzing issues that we examine our thinking and the thinking of others. These critical activities aid us in reaching the best possible conclusions and decisions. The word *critical* is also related to the word *criticize*, which means "to question and evaluate." Unfortunately, the ability to criticize is often used only destructively, to tear down someone else's thinking. Criticism, however, can also be *constructive*—analyzing for the purpose of developing a better understanding of what is going on. We will engage in constructive criticism as we develop our ability to think critically.

Thinking is the way you make sense of the world; thinking critically is thinking about your thinking so that you can clarify and improve it. In this chapter you will explore ways to examine your thinking so that you can develop it to the fullest extent possible. That is, you will discover how to *think critically*.

Becoming a critical thinker transforms you in positive ways by enabling you to become an expert learner, view the world clearly, and make productive choices as you shape your life. Critical thinking is not simply one way of thinking; it is a total approach to understanding how you make sense of a world that includes many parts.

The best way to develop a clear and concrete idea of the critical thinker you want to become is to think about people you have known who can serve as critical-thinking models. They appear throughout humanity. The Greek philosopher Socrates was in many ways the original critical thinker for whom we have a historical record, and the depth and clarity of his thinking are immortalized in the *Dialogues* recorded by Plato, his student. As a renowned teacher in his native city of Athens, Socrates had created his own school and spent decades teaching young people how to analyze important issues through dialectical questioning—an approach that became known as the **Socratic method**. At the age of seventy, he was deemed a dangerous troublemaker by some of the ruling politicians. Based on his teachings, students were asking embarrassing questions; in particular, they were questioning the politicians' authority and threatening their political careers. Those publicly accusing him gave Socrates an ultimatum: Either leave the city where he had spent his entire life, never to return, or be put to death. Rather than leave his beloved Athens and the life he had created, Socrates chose death. Surrounded by his family and friends, he calmly drank a cup of hemlock-laced tea. He reasoned that leaving Athens would violate the intellectual integrity upon which he had built his life and that he had taught his students to uphold. Instead of sacrificing his beliefs, he ended his life, concluding with these words: "Now it is time for us to part, I to die and you to live. Whether life or death is better is known to God, and to God only."

Socratic method
A method of inquiry that uses a dynamic approach of questioning and intellectual analysis in order to explore the essential nature of concepts.

Today especially, we all need to think like philosophers, to develop a philosophical framework. Critical thinking is a modern reworking of a philosophical perspective.

Whom would *you* identify as expert critical thinkers? To qualify, the people you identify should have lively, energetic minds. Specifically, they should be

- **Open-minded:** In discussions they listen carefully to every viewpoint, evaluating each perspective carefully and fairly.
- **Knowledgeable:** When they offer an opinion, it's always based on facts or evidence. On the other hand, if they lack knowledge of the subject, they acknowledge this.
- **Mentally active:** They take initiative and actively use their intelligence to confront problems and meet challenges instead of simply responding passively to events.
- **Curious:** They explore situations with probing questions that penetrate beneath the surface of issues instead of being satisfied with superficial explanations.
- **Independent thinkers:** They are not afraid to disagree with the group opinion. They develop well-supported beliefs through thoughtful analysis instead of uncritically "borrowing" the beliefs of others or simply going along with the crowd.
- **Skilled discussants:** They are able to discuss ideas in an organized and intelligent way. Even when the issues are controversial, they listen carefully to opposing viewpoints and respond thoughtfully.
- **Insightful:** They are able to get to the heart of the issue or problem. While others may be distracted by details, they are able to zero in on the essence, seeing the "forest" as well as the "trees."
- **Self-aware:** They are aware of their own biases and are quick to point them out and take them into consideration when analyzing a situation.
- **Creative:** They can break out of established patterns of thinking and approach situations from innovative directions.
- **Passionate:** They have a passion for understanding and are always striving to see issues and problems with more clarity.

Thinking Activity 2.1

WHO IS A CRITICAL THINKER?

Think about people you know whom you admire as expert thinkers, and list some of the qualities these people exhibit that you believe qualify them as "critical thinkers." For each critical-thinking quality, write down a brief example involving the person. Identifying such people will help you visualize the kind of people you'd like to emulate. As you think your way through this book, you will be creating a *portrait* of the kind of critical thinker you are striving to become, a *blueprint* you can use to direct your development and chart your progress.

This chapter explores some of the cognitive abilities and attitudes that characterize critical thinkers, including the following:

- Thinking actively
- Carefully exploring situations with questions
- Thinking independently
- Viewing situations from different perspectives
- Supporting diverse perspectives with reasons and evidence
- Discussing ideas in an organized way

The remaining chapters in the book examine additional thinking abilities that you will need to develop in order to become a fully mature critical thinker.

Thinking Critically About Visuals

"Now It Is Time for Us to Part, I to Die and You to Live...."

What can you tell about Socrates' reaction to his impending death based on this painting by Jacques-Louis David? What is the reaction of his family and friends? If you were a close friend of Socrates, what would be your reaction? Why?

Thinking Actively

When you think critically, you are actively using your intelligence, knowledge, and abilities to deal effectively with life's situations. When you think actively, you are:

- Getting involved in potentially useful projects and activities instead of remaining disengaged.
- Taking initiative in making decisions on your own instead of waiting passively to be told what to think or do.
- Following through on your commitments instead of giving up when you encounter difficulties.
- Taking responsibility for the consequences of your decisions rather than unjustifiably blaming others or events "beyond your control."

When you think actively, you are not just waiting for something to happen. You are engaged in the process of achieving goals, making decisions, and solving problems. When you react passively, you let events control you or permit others to do your thinking for you. Thinking critically requires that you think actively—not react passively—to deal effectively with life's situations.

INFLUENCES ON YOUR THINKING

As our minds grow and develop, we are exposed to influences that encourage us to think actively. We also have many experiences, however, that encourage us to think passively. For example, some analysts believe that when people, especially children, spend much of their time watching television, they are being influenced to think passively, thus inhibiting their intellectual growth. Listed here are some of the influences we experience in our lives, along with space for you to add your own influences. As you read through the list, place an *A* next to those items you believe in general influence you to think *actively* and a *P* next to those you consider to be generally *passive* influences.

Activities	*People*
Reading books A /P	Family members A/P
Text messaging P	Friends A/P
Watching television A/P	Employers P
Dancing A	Advertisers P
Using Facebook P	School/college teachers A/P
Playing video games P	Police officers A/P
Playing sports A /P	Religious leaders P
Listening to music P	Politicians P

Thinking Activity 2.2

INFLUENCES ON OUR THINKING

All of us are subject to powerful influences on our thinking, influences that we are often unaware of. For example, advertisers spend billions of dollars to manipulate our thinking in ways that are complex and subtle. For this exercise, choose one of the following tasks.

1. Watch some commercials, with several other class members if possible, and discuss the techniques each advertiser is using to shape your thinking. Analyze with the other viewers how each of the elements in a commercial—images, language, music—affects an audience. Pay particular attention to the symbolic associations of various images and words, and identify the powerful emotions that these associations elicit. Why are the commercials effective? What influential roles do commercials play in our culture as a whole? New DVR technologies, such as TiVo, enable us to watch favorite shows without commercials. If we never had to watch commercials, would we lose a valuable part of the cultural experience—for example, those commercials that everyone talks about?

2. Select a commercial website and do an in-depth analysis of it. Explain how each of the site's elements—design, content, use of music or video, and links—works to influence our thinking.

Of course, in many cases people and activities can act as both active and passive influences, depending on the situations and our individual responses. For example, consider employers. If we are performing a routine, repetitive job, work tends to encourage passive, uncreative thinking. We are also influenced to think passively if our employer gives us detailed instructions for performing every task, instructions that permit no exception or deviation. On the other hand, when our employer gives us general areas of responsibility within which we are expected to make thoughtful and creative decisions, then we are being stimulated to think actively and independently.

BECOMING AN ACTIVE LEARNER

Active thinking is one of the keys to effective learning. Each of us has our own knowledge framework that we use to make sense of the world, a framework that incorporates all that we have learned in our lives. When we learn something new, we have to find ways to integrate this new information or skill into our existing knowledge framework. For example, if one of your professors is presenting material on Sigmund Freud's concept of the unconscious or the role of Heisenberg's uncertainty principle in the theory of quantum mechanics, you need to find ways to relate these new ideas to things you already know in order to make this new information "your own." How do you do this? By actively using your mind to integrate new information into your existing knowledge framework, thereby expanding the framework to include this new information.

For instance, when your professor provides a detailed analysis of Freud's concept of the unconscious, you use your mind to call up what you know about Freud's theory of personality and what you know of the concept of the unconscious. You then try to connect this new information to what you already know, integrating it into your expanding knowledge framework. In a way, learning is analogous to the activity of eating: "You ingest food (*information*) in one form, actively transform it through digestion (*mental processing*), and then integrate the result into the ongoing functioning of your body.

Carefully Exploring Situations with Questions

Thinking critically involves actively using your thinking abilities to attack problems, meet challenges, and analyze issues. An important dimension of thinking actively is the ability to ask appropriate and penetrating questions. Active learners explore the learning situations they are involved in with questions that enable them to understand the material or task at hand and then integrate this new understanding into their knowledge framework. In contrast, passive learners rarely ask questions. Instead, they try to absorb information like sponges, memorizing what is expected and then regurgitating what they memorized on tests and quizzes.

Questions can be classified in terms of the ways that people organize and interpret information. We can identify six categories of questions, a schema that was first suggested by the educator Benjamin Bloom:

1. Fact
2. Interpretation
3. Analysis
4. Synthesis
5. Evaluation
6. Application

Active learners are able to ask appropriate questions from all of these categories. These various types of questions are closely interrelated, and an effective thinker is able to use them productively in relation to one another. These categories of questions are also very general and at times overlap. This means that a given question may fall into more than one of the six categories. Following is a summary of the six categories of questions with some sample questions for each category.

1. **Questions of Fact:** Questions of fact seek to determine basic information about a situation. These questions seek information that is relatively straightforward and objective. *Who, what, when, where, how*? *Describe*
   _____ .

2. **Questions of Interpretation:** Questions of interpretation seek to select and organize facts and ideas, discovering the relationships among them. Examples of such relationships include the following:

   Chronological relationships: What is the *time sequence* relating the various events?

Process relationships: What are the steps in the *process of growth* or *development* in _____?

Comparison/contrast relationships: How are things similar or different? How would you *compare and contrast* _____?

Causal relationships: Which events are responsible for bringing about other events? What was the *cause/effect* of _____?

3. ***Questions of Analysis:*** Questions of analysis seek to separate an entire process or situation into its component parts and to understand the relation of these parts to the whole. These questions seek to classify various elements, outline component structures, articulate various possibilities, and clarify the reasoning being presented.

What are the *parts or features* of _____? *Classify* according to _____.

Outline/diagram/web _____. What *evidence* can you present to support _____?

What are the *possible alternatives* for _____? Explain the *reasons why* you think _____.

4. ***Questions of Synthesis:*** Questions of synthesis combine ideas to form a new whole or come to a conclusion, make inferences about future events, create solutions, and design plans of action.

What would you *predict/infer* from _____? What ideas can you *add to* _____?

How would you *create/design* a new _____? What might happen if you *combined* _____ with _____? What *solutions/decisions* would you suggest for _____?

5. ***Questions of Evaluation:*** The aim of evaluation questions is to help us make informed judgments and decisions by determining the relative value, truth, or reliability of things. The process of evaluation involves identifying the criteria or standards we are using and then determining to what extent the things in common meet those standards.

How would you *evaluate* _____? What standards would you use?

Do you agree with _____? Why or why not?

How would you *decide* about _____? What *criteria* would you use to assess _____?

6. ***Questions of Application:*** The aim of application questions is to help us take the knowledge or concepts we have gained in one situation and apply them to other situations.

How is _____ *an example of* _____? How would you *apply* this rule/principle to _____?

Mastering these forms of questions and using them appropriately will serve as powerful tools in your learning process.

Becoming an expert questioner is an ongoing project. When you are talking to people about even everyday topics, get in the habit of asking questions from all of the different categories. Similarly, when you are attending class, taking notes, or reading assignments, make a practice of asking—and trying to answer—appropriate questions.

As children, we were natural questioners, but this questioning attitude was often discouraged when we entered the school system. Often we were given the message, in subtle and not so subtle ways, that "schools have the questions; your job is to learn the answers." The educator Neil Postman has said, "Children enter schools as question marks and they leave as periods." In order for us to become critical thinkers and effective learners, we have to become question marks again.

Thinking Activity 2.3

ANALYZING A COMPLEX ISSUE

Review the following decision-making situation (based on an incident that happened in Springfield, Missouri), and then critically examine it by posing questions from each of the six categories we have considered in this section:

1. Fact	4. Synthesis
2. Interpretation	5. Evaluation
3. Analysis	6. Application

Imagine that you are a member of a student group at your college that has decided to stage the controversial play *The Normal Heart* by Larry Kramer. The play is based on the lives of real people and dramatizes their experiences in the early stages of the AIDS epidemic. It focuses on their efforts to publicize the horrific nature of this disease and to secure funding from a reluctant federal government to find a cure. The play is considered controversial because of its exclusive focus on the subject of AIDS, its explicit homosexual themes, and the large amount of profanity contained in the script. After lengthy discussion, however, your student group has decided that the educational and moral benefits of the play render it a valuable contribution to the life of the college.

While the play is in rehearsal, a local politician seizes upon it as an issue and mounts a political and public relations campaign against it. She distributes selected excerpts of the play to newspapers, religious groups, and civic organizations. She also introduces a bill in the state legislature to withdraw state funding for the college if the play is performed. The play creates a firestorm of controversy, replete with local and national news reports, editorials, and impassioned speeches for and against it. Everyone associated with the play is subjected to verbal harassment, threats, crank phone calls, and hate mail. The firestorm explodes when the house of one of the key spokespersons for the play is burned to the ground. The director and actors go into hiding for their safety, rehearsing in secret and moving from hotel to hotel.

Your student group has just convened to decide what course of action to take. Analyze the situation using the six types of questions listed previously and then conclude with your decision and the reasons that support your decision.

Thinking Independently

Answer the following questions with *yes, no,* or *not sure,* based on what you believe to be true.

1. Is the earth flat? N 0
2. Is there a God? Yes / No
3. Is abortion wrong? Yes
4. Have alien life forms visited the earth? N 0
5. Should men be the breadwinners and women the homemakers? No

Your responses to these questions reveal aspects of the way your mind works. How did you arrive at these conclusions? Your views on these and many other issues probably had their beginnings with your family. As we grow up, we learn how to think, feel, and behave in various situations. In addition to our parents, our "teachers" include our brothers and sisters, friends, religious leaders, schoolteachers, books, television, and the Internet. Most of what we learn we absorb without even being aware of the process. Many of your ideas about the issues raised in the preceding questions were most likely shaped by the experiences you had growing up.

As a result of our ongoing experiences, however, our minds—and our thinking—continue to mature. Instead of simply accepting the views of others, we use this standard to make our decisions: Are there good reasons or evidence that support this thinking? If there are good reasons, we can actively decide to adopt these ideas. If they do not make sense, we can modify or reject them.

How do you know when you have examined and adopted ideas yourself instead of simply borrowing them from others? One indication of having thought through your ideas is being able to explain *why* you believe them, explaining the reasons that led you to these conclusions.

For each of the views you expressed at the beginning of this section, explain how you arrived at it and give the reasons and evidence that you believe support it.

EXAMPLE: Is the earth flat?

EXPLANATION: I was taught by my parents and in school that the earth was round.

REASONS/EVIDENCE:

a. *Authorities:* My parents and teachers taught me this.

b. *References:* I read about this in science textbooks.

c. *Factual evidence:* I have seen a sequence of photographs taken from outer space that show the earth as a globe.

d. *Personal experience:* When I flew across the country, I could see the horizon line changing.

Of course, not all reasons and evidence are equally strong or accurate. For example, before the fifteenth century some people believed that the earth was flat. This belief was supported by the following reasons and evidence:

- *Authorities:* Educational and religious authorities taught people the earth was flat.
- *References:* The written opinions of scientific experts supported the belief that the earth was flat.
- *Factual evidence:* No person had ever circumnavigated the earth.
- *Personal experience:* From a normal vantage point, the earth looks flat.

Many considerations go into evaluating the strengths and accuracy of reasons and evidence. Let's examine some basic questions that critical thinkers automatically consider when evaluating reasons and evidence by completing Thinking Activity 2.4.

Thinking Activity 2.4

EVALUATING YOUR BELIEFS

Evaluate the strengths and accuracy of the reasons and evidence you identified to support your beliefs on the five issues by addressing questions such as the following:

- **Authorities:** Are the authorities knowledgeable in this area? Are they reliable? Have they ever given inaccurate information? Do other authorities disagree with them?
- **References:** What are the credentials of the authors? Are there other authors who disagree with their opinions? On what reasons and evidence do the authors base their opinions?
- **Factual evidence:** What are the source and foundation of the evidence? Can the evidence be interpreted differently? Does the evidence support the conclusion?
- **Personal experience:** What were the circumstances under which the experiences took place? Were distortions or mistakes in perception possible? Have other people had either similar or conflicting experiences? Are there other explanations for the experience?

In critically evaluating beliefs, it makes sense to accept traditional beliefs if they enrich and sharpen our thinking. If they don't stand up to critical scrutiny, then we need to have the courage to think for ourselves, even if it means rejecting "conventional wisdom."

Thinking for yourself doesn't always mean doing exactly what you want to; it may mean becoming aware of the social guidelines and expectations of a given situation— for example, a dress code at the office where you work—and then making an informed decision about what is in your best interests. Thinking for yourself often involves balancing your view of things against those of others, integrating yourself into social structures without sacrificing your independence or personal autonomy.

Viewing Situations from Different Perspectives

Although it is important to think for yourself, others may have good ideas from which you can learn and benefit. Critical thinkers realize that their viewpoints are limited and that their perspective is only one of many. If we are going to learn and develop, we must try to understand and appreciate the viewpoints of others. For example, consider the following situation.

Imagine that you have been employed at a new job for the past six months. Although you enjoy the challenge of your responsibilities and you are performing well, you find that you simply cannot complete all your work during office hours. To keep up, you have to work late, take work home, and even occasionally work on

Thinking Critically About Visuals

Thinking Independently

Leonardo da Vinci was an astonishingly independent thinker. For example, he depicted this idea of a helicopter centuries before anyone else conceived of it. But many people are not independent thinkers. What are the reasons that people too often get locked into passive, dependent ways of thinking? What strategies can we use to overcome these forces and think independently? Describe a time when you took an independent, and unpopular, stand on an issue. What was the experience like?

Gianni Dagli Orti/Corbis

weekends. When you explain this to your employer, she says that, although she is sorry that the job interferes with your personal life, it has to be done. She suggests that you view these sacrifices as an investment in your future and that you should try to work more efficiently. She reminds you that there are many people who would be happy to have your position.

1. Describe this situation from your employer's standpoint, identifying reasons that might support her views.

2. Describe some different approaches that you and your employer might take to help resolve this situation.

For most of the important issues and problems in your life, one viewpoint is simply not adequate to provide a full and satisfactory understanding. To increase and deepen your knowledge, you must seek *other perspectives* on the situations you are trying to understand. You can sometimes accomplish this by using your imagination to visualize other viewpoints. Usually, however, you need to actively seek (and *listen* to) the viewpoints of others. It is often very difficult for people to see things from points of view other than their own, and if you are not careful, you can make the mistake of thinking that the way you see things is the way things really are. In addition to identifying with perspectives other than your own, you also have to work to understand the *reasons* that support these alternate viewpoints. This approach deepens your understanding of the issues and also stimulates you to critically evaluate your beliefs.

Thinking Activity 2.5

ANALYZING A BELIEF FROM DIFFERENT PERSPECTIVES

Describe a belief of yours about which you feel very strongly. Then explain the reasons or experiences that led you to this belief. Next, describe a point of view that *conflicts* with your belief. Identify some of the reasons why someone might hold this belief.

A Belief That I Feel Strongly About

I used to think that we should always try everything in our power to keep a person alive.

But now I strongly believe that a person has a right to die in peace and with dignity. The reason why I believe this now is because of my father's illness and death.

It all started on Christmas Day, December 25, when my father was admitted to the hospital. The doctors diagnosed his condition as a heart attack. Following this episode, he was readmitted and discharged from several different hospitals. On June 18, he was hospitalized for what was initially thought to be pneumonia but which turned out to be lung cancer. He began chemotherapy treatments. When complications occurred, he had to be placed on a respirator. At first he couldn't speak or eat. But then they operated on him and placed the tube from the machine in his throat instead of his mouth. He was then able to eat and move his mouth. He underwent radiation therapy when they discovered he had three tumors in his head and that the cancer had spread all over his body. We had to sign a paper that asked us to indicate, if he should stop breathing, whether we would want the hospital to try to revive him or just let him go.

We decided to let him go because the doctors couldn't guarantee that he wouldn't become brain-dead. At first they said that there was a forty percent chance that he would get off the machine. But instead of that happening, the percentage went down. It was hard seeing him like that since I was so close to him. But it was even harder when he didn't want to see me. He said that by seeing me suffer, his suffering was greater. So I had to cut down on seeing him. Everybody that visited him said that he had changed dramatically. They couldn't even recognize him. The last two days of his life were the worst. I prayed that God would relieve him of his misery. I had come very close to taking him off the machine in order for him not to suffer, but I didn't. Finally he passed away on November 22, with not the least bit of peace or dignity. The loss was great then and still is, but at least he's not suffering. That's why I believe that when people have terminal diseases with no hope of recovery, they shouldn't place them on machines to prolong their lives of suffering, but instead they should be permitted to die with as much peace and dignity as possible.

Somebody else might believe very strongly that we should try everything in our power to keep people alive. It doesn't matter what kind of illness or disease the people have. What's important is that they are kept alive, especially if they are loved ones. Some people want to keep their loved ones alive with them as long as they can, even if it's by a machine. They also believe it is up to God and medical science to determine whether people should live or die. Sometimes doctors give them hope that their loved ones will recover, and many people wish for a miracle to happen. With these hopes and wishes in mind, they wait and try everything in order to prolong a life, even if the doctors tell them that there is nothing that can be done.

Being open to new ideas and different viewpoints means being *flexible* enough to modify your ideas in the light of new information or better insight. Each of us has a tendency to cling to the beliefs we have been brought up with and the conclusions we have arrived at. If we are going to continue to grow and develop as thinkers, we have to modify our beliefs when evidence suggests that we should. As critical thinkers, we have to be *open* to receiving this new evidence and *flexible* enough to change and modify our ideas on the basis of it.

In contrast to open and flexible thinking, *uncritical thinking* tends to be one-sided and closed-minded. People who think this way are convinced that they alone see things as they really are and that everyone who disagrees with them is wrong. The words we use to describe this type of thinking include "subjective," "egocentric," and "dogmatic." It is very difficult for such people to step outside their own viewpoints in order to see things from other people's perspectives.

Thinking Activity 2.6

WRITING FROM INTERACTIVE PERSPECTIVES*

Think of a well-known person, either historical (e.g., Socrates) or contemporary (e.g., Oprah Winfrey), and identify different perspectives from which that person can be viewed. For example, consider viewing Oprah Winfrey as:

- a pop culture icon.
- a black activist.
- a wealthy celebrity.
- a self-help guru.
- an actress.

Next, select two perspectives from the ones you identified and, using research, provide an explanatory background for each perspective. Then, through investigative analysis, describe the interactive relationship between the two perspectives—the basis on which they interact and the ways in which each supports the other. Finally, in a summary conclusion to your findings, assess the significance of the two perspectives for contemporary thought.

Supporting Diverse Perspectives with Reasons and Evidence

When you are thinking critically, you can give sound and relevant reasons to back up your ideas. It is not enough simply to take a position on an issue or make a claim; we have to *back up our views* with other information that we believe supports our position. There is an important distinction as well as a relationship between *what* you believe and *why* you believe it.

If someone questions why you see an issue the way you do, you probably respond by giving reasons or arguments you believe support your point of view. For example, consider the issue of whether using a cell phone while driving should be prohibited. As a critical thinker trying to make sense of this issue, you should attempt to identify not just the reasons that support your view but also the reasons that support other views. The following are reasons that support each view of this issue.

Issue:

Cell phone use while driving should be prohibited.	Cell phone use while driving should be permitted.
Supporting reasons	*Supporting reasons*
1. Studies show that using cell phones while driving increases accidents.	1. Many people feel that cell phones are no more distracting than other common activities in cars.

*This activity was developed by Frank Juszcyk.

Thinking Critically About Visuals

"You Leave—I Was Here First!"

Critical thinkers actively try to view issues from different perspectives. Why would someone take the position "Let's get rid of illegal immigrants in America"? How would Native Americans view the person making that statement? What is your perspective on illegal immigrants in this country? Why?

Steve Kelly/ The Times-Picayune

Now see if you can identify additional supporting reasons for each of these views on cell phone use while driving.

Supporting reasons	Supporting reasons
2.	2.
3.	3.
4.	4.

Seeing all sides of an issue combines two critical-thinking abilities:

- Viewing issues from different perspectives
- Supporting diverse viewpoints with reasons and evidence

Combining these two abilities enables you not only to understand other sides of an issue but also to understand *why* these views are held.

Thinking Activity 2.7

ANALYZING DIFFERENT SIDES OF AN ISSUE

For each of the following issues, identify reasons that support each side of the issue.

Issue:

1. Multiple-choice and true/false exams should be given in college-level courses.	Multiple-choice and true/false exams should not be given in college-level courses.

Issue:

2. Immigration quotas should be reduced.	Immigration quotas should be increased.

Issue:

3. The best way to deal with crime is to give long prison sentences.	Long prison sentences will not reduce crime.

Issue:

4. When a couple divorces, the children should choose the parent with whom they wish to live.	When a couple divorces, the court should decide all custody issues regarding the children.

Thinking Activity 2.8

ANALYZING DIFFERENT PERSPECTIVES

Working to see different perspectives is crucial in helping you get a more complete understanding of the ideas being expressed in the passages you are reading. Read each of the following passages and then do the following:

1. Identify the main idea of the passage.
2. List the reasons that support the main idea.
3. Develop another view of the main issue.
4. List the reasons that support the other view.

1. In a letter that has stunned many leading fertility specialists, the acting head of their professional society's ethics committee says it is sometimes acceptable for couples to choose the sex of their children by selecting either male or female embryos and discarding the rest. The group, the American Society of Reproductive Medicine, establishes positions on ethical issues, and most clinics say they abide by them. One fertility specialist, Dr. Norbet Gleicher, whose group has nine centers and who had asked for the opinion, was quick to act on it. "We will offer it immediately," Dr. Gleicher said of the sex-selection method. "Frankly, we have a list of patients who asked for it." Couples would have to undergo *in vitro* fertilization, and then their embryos would be examined in the first few days when they consisted of just eight cells. Other leading fertility specialists said they were taken aback by the new letter and could hardly believe its message. "What's the next step?" asked Dr. William Schoolcraft. "As we learn more about genetics, do we reject kids who do not have superior intelligence or who don't have the right color hair or eyes?" (*New York Times,* September 28, 2001).

2. When Dr. Hassan Abbass, a Veterans Affairs Department surgeon, and his wife arrived at the airport to leave for vacation last May 24, they were pulled aside and forced to submit to a careful search before boarding the plane. They are among the thousands of Americans of Middle Eastern heritage who have complained that a secretive and wide-scale "profiling" system sponsored by the government and aimed at preventing air terrorism has caused them to be unfairly selected for extra scrutiny at airports. "Profiling" of this type is being used more frequently in many areas of law enforcement, raising fundamental questions of how a free society balances security fears with civil liberties and the desire to avoid offensive stereotyping (*New York Times,* August 11, 1997).

Discussing Ideas in an Organized Way

Thinking critically often takes place in a social context. Although every person has his or her own perspective on the world, no single viewpoint is adequate for making sense of complex issues, situations, or even people. As we will see in the chapters ahead, we each have our own "lenses" through which we view the world—filters that shape, influence, and often distort the way we see things. The best way to expand our thinking and compensate for the bias that we all have is to be open to the viewpoints of others and willing to listen and to exchange ideas with them. This process of give and take, of advancing our views and considering those of others, is known as discussion. When we participate in a *discussion*, we are not simply talking; we are exchanging and exploring our ideas in an organized way.

Unfortunately, our conversations with other people about important topics are too often not productive exchanges. They often degenerate into name calling, shouting matches, or worse. Consider the following dialogue.

PERSON A: A friend of mine sent a humorous email in which he wrote about "killing the president." He wasn't serious, of course, but two days later the FBI showed up on his doorstep! This is no longer a free society—it's a fascist regime!

PERSON B: Your friend's an idiot and unpatriotic as well. You don't kid about killing the president. Your friend is lucky he didn't wind up in jail, where he deserves to be!

PERSON A: Since when is kidding around treason? With the way our freedoms are being stolen, we might as well be living in a dictatorship!

PERSON B: Your friend isn't the only idiot—you're an idiot, too! You don't deserve to live in America. It's attitudes like yours that make terrorist attacks possible, like those against the World Trade Center and the Pentagon.

PERSON A: You're calling me a terrorist? I can't talk to a fascist like you!

PERSON B: And I can't talk to an unpatriotic traitor like you. America: Love it or leave it! Good-bye and good riddance!

If we examine the dynamics of this dialogue, we can see that the two people here are not really

- listening to each other.
- supporting their views with reasons and evidence.
- responding to the points being made.
- asking—and trying to answer—important questions.
- trying to increase their understanding rather than simply winning the argument.

In short, the people in this exchange are not *discussing* their views; they are simply *expressing* them, and each is trying to influence the other person into agreeing.

Contrast this first dialogue with the following one. Although it begins the same way, it quickly takes a different direction.

PERSON A: A friend of mine sent a humorous email in which he wrote about "killing the president." He wasn't serious, of course, but two days later the FBI showed up on his doorstep! This is no longer a free society—it's a fascist regime!

PERSON B: Your friend's an idiot and unpatriotic as well. You don't kid about killing the president. Your friend is lucky he didn't wind up in jail, where he deserves to be!

PERSON A: Since when is kidding around treason? With the way our freedoms are being stolen, we're living in a repressive dictatorship!

PERSON B: Don't you think it's inappropriate to be talking about killing the president, even if you are kidding? And why do you think we're living in a repressive dictatorship?

PERSON A: Well, you're probably right that emailing a message like this isn't very intelligent, particularly considering the leaders who have been assassinated—John Kennedy, Robert Kennedy, and Martin Luther King, for example—and the terrorist attacks that we have suffered. But the only way FBI agents could have known about the email is if they are monitoring our private emails on an ongoing basis.

Doesn't that concern you? It's like Big Brother is watching our every move and pouncing when we do something they think is wrong.

PERSON B: You're making a good point. It is a little unnerving to realize that our private conversations on the Internet may be monitored by the government. But doesn't it have to take measures like this in order to ensure we're safe? After all, remember the catastrophic attacks that destroyed the World Trade towers and part of the Pentagon, and the Oklahoma City bombing. If the government has to play the role of Big Brother to make sure we're safe, I think it's worth it.

PERSON A: I see what you're saying. But I think that the government has a tendency to go overboard if it's not held in check. Just consider the gigantic file the FBI compiled on Martin Luther King and other peaceful leaders, based on illegal wiretaps and covert surveillance.

PERSON B: I certainly don't agree with those types of activities against peaceful citizens. But what about people who are genuine threats? Don't we have to let the government do whatever's necessary to identify and arrest them? After all, threatening to kill the president is like telling airport personnel that you have a bomb in your suitcase—it's not funny, even if you're not serious.

PERSON A: You're right: It's important for the government to do what's necessary to make sure we're as safe as possible from terrorist threats. But we can't give it a blank check to read our email, tap our phones, and infringe on our personal freedoms in other ways. After all, it's those freedoms that make America what it is.

PERSON B: Yes, I guess the goal is to strike the right balance between security and personal freedoms. How do we do that?

PERSON A: That's a very complicated question. Let's keep talking about it. Right now, though, I better get to class before my professor sends Big Brother to look for me!

Naturally, discussions are not always quite this organized and direct. Nevertheless, this second dialogue does provide a good model for what can take place in our everyday lives when we carefully explore an issue or a situation with someone else. Let us take a closer look at this discussion process.

LISTENING CAREFULLY

Review the second dialogue and notice how each person in the discussion listens carefully to what the other person is saying and then tries to comment directly on what has just been said. When you are working hard at listening to others, you are trying to understand the point they are making and the reasons for it. This enables you to imagine yourself in their position and see things as they see them. Listening in this way often brings to your attention new ideas and different ways of viewing the situation that might never have occurred to you. An effective dialogue in this sense is like a game of tennis—you hit the ball to me, I return the ball to you, you return my return, and so on. The "ball" the discussants keep hitting back and forth is the subject they are gradually analyzing and exploring.

SUPPORTING VIEWS WITH REASONS AND EVIDENCE

Critical thinkers support their points of view with evidence and reasons and also develop an in-depth understanding of the evidence and reasons that support other viewpoints. Review the second dialogue and identify some of the reasons used by the participants to support their points of view. For example, Person B expresses the view that the government may have to be proactive in terms of identifying terrorists and ensuring our security, citing as a reason the horrific consequences of terrorist attacks. Person A responds with the concern that the government sometimes goes overboard in situations like this, citing as a reason the FBI's extensive surveillance of Martin Luther King.

RESPONDING TO THE POINTS BEING MADE

When people engage in effective dialogue, they listen carefully to the other person and then respond directly to the points being made instead of simply trying to make their own points. In the second dialogue, Person B responds to Person A's concern that "Big Brother is watching our every move" with the acknowledgment that "It is a little unnerving to realize that our private conversations on the Internet may be monitored by the government" and also with the question "But doesn't it have to take measures like this in order to ensure we're safe?" When you respond directly to other people's views, and they to yours, you extend and deepen the exploration into the issues, creating an ongoing, interactive discussion. Although people involved in the discussion may not ultimately agree, they should develop a more insightful under-standing of the important issues and a greater appreciation of other viewpoints.

ASKING QUESTIONS

Asking questions is one of the driving forces in your discussions with others. You can explore a subject first by raising important questions and then by trying to answer them together. This questioning process gradually reveals the various reasons and evidence that support each of the different viewpoints involved. For example, although the two dialogues begin the same way, the second dialogue moves in a completely different direction when Person B poses the question "[W]hy do you think we're living in a repressive dictatorship?" Asking this question directs the discussion toward a mutual exploration of the issues and away from angry confrontation. Identify some of the other key questions that are posed in the dialogue.

A guide to the various types of questions that can be posed in exploring issues and situations begins on page 59 of this chapter.

INCREASING UNDERSTANDING

When we discuss subjects with others, we often begin by disagreeing. In an effective discussion, however, our main purpose should be to develop our understanding—not to prove ourselves right at any cost. If we are determined to prove that we are

Thinking Critically About Visuals

Complex Issues, Challenging Images

Hurricane "Sandy" ripped into the Eastern United States leaving a path of destruction and personal devastation. It cost the lives of 285 people in 7 countries and was the second deadliest storm in United States history with property damage estimated at over $75 billion. Large sections of ocean front communities on the East coast were simply swept away, and for the first time in modern history, a record-high storm surge inundated New York City, flooding streets, tunnels, and subway lines and cutting power to large sections of the city for days and weeks in some cases.

Jana Shea/iStockphoto.com

Photography is typically a powerful medium to communicate the reality and emotional power of events. Examine these post-Sandy photographs carefully and evaluate the meaning they are expressing. What is your reaction to the iconic image of the destroyed roller-coaster in Seaside Heights, New Jersey? What emotions does it evoke? For example, do you find that it calls up memories of carefree summer vacations that contrast sharply with the bleak and twisted wreckage of the storm's aftermath?

Now examine the photograph of the submerged taxi cabs lined up in orderly rows pointing towards the New York City skyline. What is your emotional reaction to this image? In what ways does it communicate nature's awesome power which can wreak havoc on even the most impressive of human creations? If you were to add a third or fourth photo to these two in order to communicate the reality and significance of this devastating event, which ones would you select? Why?

WANG CHENGYUN/Xinhua/Landov

right, then we are not likely to be open to the ideas of others and to viewpoints that differ from our own. A much more productive approach is for all of the individuals involved to acknowledge that they are trying to achieve a clear and well-supported understanding of the subject being discussed, wherever their mutual analysis leads them.

Imagine that instead of ending, the second dialogue had continued for a while. Create responses that expand the exploration of the ideas being examined. Be sure to keep the guidelines for effective discussions in mind as you continue the dialogue.

PERSON B: Yes, I guess the goal is to strike the right balance between security and personal freedoms. But how do we do that? (and so on)

Thinking Activity 2.9

CREATING A DIALOGUE

Select an important social issue and write a dialogue that analyzes the issue from two different perspectives. As you write your dialogue, keep in mind the qualities of effective discussion: listening carefully to the other person and trying to comment directly on what has been said, asking and trying to answer important questions about the subject, and trying to develop a fuller understanding of the subject instead of simply trying to prove yourself right.

After completing your dialogue, read it to the class (with a classmate as a partner). Analyze the class members' dialogues by using the criteria for effective discussions that we have examined.

Reading Critically

A crucial aspect of being an effective critical thinker in the world is learning to read critically. As a critical reader, you will analyze the text and evaluate its ideas and methods of presenting them. You will think of other subjects or issues to which the text might be connected. One of the most powerful tools in reading critically is asking the right questions.

ASKING QUESTIONS

Asking questions will help you read critically. One set of useful questions is based on the basic components of writing: purpose, audience, subject, writer, and context.

- What is the *purpose* of the selection, and how is the author trying to achieve it?
- Who is the intended *audience*, and what assumption is the writer making about it?

- What is the *subject* of the selection, and how would you evaluate its cogency and reliability?
- Who is the *writer*, and what perspective does she bring to the writing selection?
- What is the larger *context* in which this selection appears? Is the writer responding to a particular event or participating in an ongoing debate?

The questions that we explored earlier in this chapter are often used to generate writing and can also help with critical reading.

Questions of Interpretation: Questions of interpretation probe for relationships among ideas.

- Is a *time sequence* given in this text? If so, what is its importance?
- Is a *process of growth or development* explained in this text? If so, what is its importance?
- What is *compared or contrasted* in this text? What are the purposes of any comparisons?
- What is the *context* of the selection, and what contextual components might be significant? (For example, the time of its writing, characteristics of that time, the relationship to other works by the same author, whether or not it is a translation)
- Are *causes* discussed in this text? If so, what is suggested about those causes and their effects?

Questions of Analysis: Questions of analysis look at parts of a text and the relationship of those parts to the whole, and at the reasoning being presented.

- Is this text divided into identifiable *sections?* What are they? Are sections arranged logically?
- What *evidence* or *examples* support the ideas presented in the text?
- Does the text give *alternatives* to the ideas presented?

Questions of Evaluation: Questions of evaluation establish the truth, reliability, applicability—the value of the text. They usually address the effectiveness of the writing as well.

- What is the *significance* of the ideas in this text?
- What is the apparent level of *truth* in this text? What criteria for truth does it meet?
- What are the sources of information in this text? Are they *reliable?* Why?

- Can the ideas in this text be *applied* to other situations?
- What is *effective* about the writing in this text? Clarity? The right tone? Appropriate—or imaginative—word choices? Organization?

Of course, you are not likely to ask all these questions about everything you read, and you will find other questions to ask as well.

USING A PROBLEM-SOLVING APPROACH

Successful readers often approach difficult reading passages with a problem-solving approach, similar to the method we will be exploring in Chapter 3. Here's how a critical thinker might apply this approach to reading a difficult work.

Step 1: *What is the problem?* What don't I understand about this passage? Are there terms or concepts that are unfamiliar? Are the logical connections between the concepts confusing? Do some things just not make sense?

Step 2: *What are the alternatives?* What are some possible meanings of the terms or concepts? What are some potential interpretations of the central meaning of this passage?

Step 3: *What is the evaluation of the possible alternatives?* What are the "clues" in the passage, and what alternative meanings do they support? What reasons or evidence support these interpretations?

Step 4: *What is the solution?* Judging from my evaluation and what I know of this subject, which interpretation is most likely? Why?

Step 5: *How well is the solution working?* Does my interpretation still make sense as I continue my reading, or do I need to revise my conclusion?

Of course, expert readers go through this process very quickly, much faster than it takes to explain it. Although this approach may seem a little cumbersome at first, the more you use it, the more natural and efficient it will become. Let's begin by applying it to a sample passage. Carefully read the following passage from the French philosopher Jean-Paul Sartre's "Existentialism Is Humanism," and use the problem-solving approach to determine the correct meanings of the italicized concepts and the overall meaning of the passage.

Existentialism, of which I am a representative, declares with greater consistency that if God does not exist there is at least one being whose existence comes before its essence, a being which exists before it can be defined by any conception of it. That being is man or, as Heidegger has it, the human reality. What do we mean by saying that *existence precedes essence*? We mean that man first of all exists, encounters himself, surges up in the world—and defines himself afterwards. If man as the existentialist sees himself as not definable, it is because to begin with he is nothing. He will not be anything until later, and then he will be what he makes of himself. Thus, there is no human nature, because there is no God to have a conception of it. Man simply is. Not that he is simply what he conceives himself to be, but he is what he wills, and as he conceives existence. Man is nothing else but that which he makes of himself. This is the first principle of existentialism. . . . If, however, it is true that existence is prior to essence, man is responsible for what he is. Thus, the first effect of existentialism is that it puts every man in possession of himself as he is, and places the entire responsibility for his existence squarely upon his own shoulders. . . . That is what I mean when I say that man is *condemned to be free*. Condemned, because he did not create himself, yet is nevertheless at liberty, and from the moment that he is thrown into this world he is *responsible for everything he does*. . . . In life, a man commits himself, draws his own portrait and there is nothing but that portrait.

Thinking Activity 2.10

A PROBLEM-SOLVING APPROACH TO READING

Step 1: What parts (if any) of this passage do you find confusing?

Step 2: What are some possible definitions of the italicized words, and what are some potential interpretations of this passage?

> *Existentialism:*
>
> *Existence precedes essence:*
>
> *Condemned to be free:*
>
> *Responsible for everything he does:*
>
> Overall meaning:

Step 3: What contextual clues can you use to help you define these concepts and determine the overall meaning? What knowledge of this subject do you have, and how can this knowledge help you understand this passage?

Step 4: Judging from your evaluation in Step 3, which of the possible definitions and interpretations do you think are most likely? Why?

Step 5: How do your conclusions compare with those of the other students in the class? Should you revise your definitions or interpretation?

Select a challenging passage from a course textbook and apply the preceding problem-solving approach.

THINKING CRITICALLY ABOUT NEW MEDIA

Issues with Communication

New media have created a rapidly expanding universe of possibilities, and with this expansion comes the need to expand our critical thinking abilities to successfully navigate our way through unfamiliar terrain.

In this section we are going to briefly consider the way new media have affected our relationships with others. As is obvious, online communication has greatly expanded the frequency of our contact with others as well as the number of people with whom we are in touch. But with this ease of communication have come new challenges as well. For example, how many times have you regretted impulsively pressing the "send" button on a message written in the heat of the moment? For most of us, this is an all-too-frequent occurrence. As a rule of thumb, it's often a good idea to delay sending our composed message until we've had an opportunity to let things settle and review it with fresh vision. This goes for all important messages we send, professional or otherwise. We can almost always improve the content and clarity of our message by giving ourselves time to think about it for a while. It's helpful to recognize also that emailing and text messaging can sometimes encourage a weakening of our inhibitions or internal censors, emboldening us to write things that we would probably not say in person. Again, making a practice of revisiting our message before sending it will doubtless save us from those next-day "How could I?" moments. Finally, we should always remind ourselves that email and text messages are usually stripped down to the essentials, lacking the rich context that is provided when we are speaking to someone. Without our tone of voice, body language, or detailed articulation, the words and tone are often ambiguous, a situation that can easily lead to misunderstandings. Just because *we* know what we intend to say doesn't mean that the other person will interpret it in the same way. So, when sending significant communications via new media, the watchword is "Handle with care." Make the time and effort to say precisely what you intend in a way that leaves minimal chance that the recipient will take it any other way.

Analogously, social networking sites like Facebook and MySpace have opened up a Pandora's box of trouble. These sites provide the unprecedented opportunity for individuals to create a "virtual self," building records of their social identities via descriptions, comments, photographs, and music. In addition to serving as powerful models of social communication, such public displays of private information play to the twin human impulses of showmanship and voyeurism. But problems arise when the "wrong" people visit our site and learn things about us we would never want them to know. For example, 30 percent of today's employers are using Facebook to check out potential employees prior to hiring! There are a number of ways to protect yourself from embarrassment, whether it's an employer, your parent, or your romantic partner. To begin with, you can think carefully about what you post on the site and also exercise care in choosing whom you invite to have access. Too often items are posted or people are invited without any consideration of future consequences and complications. Additionally, you can create lists of people in different categories—for example, professional, family, close friends, casual friends—and then regulate who gets to see what through the site's settings. It may seem like a bother, but in the long run you will likely be thankful you took the time to take these basic precautions.

Thinking Activity 2.11

FACEBOOK TROUBLESHOOTING

Sometimes it's easier to detect problems that others face than to view our own potential problems. With this in mind, work with a group of friends to identify potential trouble spots, such as inappropriate disclosures or incriminating photographs (see the Thinking Critically About Visuals box on the next page). Once you have pinpointed the areas of concern, devise strategies for erasing the problems and avoiding similar difficulties in the future. In this regard, you might develop a list of criteria or "ground rules" to guide you in your posting and strategies for organizing your page to head off problems before they occur.

Analyzing Issues

We live in a complex world filled with challenging and often perplexing issues that we are expected to make sense of. For example, the media inform us every day of issues related to AIDS, animal experimentation, budget priorities, child custody, crime and punishment, drugs, environmental pollution, global warming, genetic engineering, human rights, individual rights, international conflicts, moral values, pornography, poverty, racism, reproductive technology, the right to die, sex education, terrorism, the economy, and many others. Often these broad social issues intrude into our own personal lives, taking them from the level of abstract

Thinking Critically About Visuals

Social Networking Disclosure Dangers

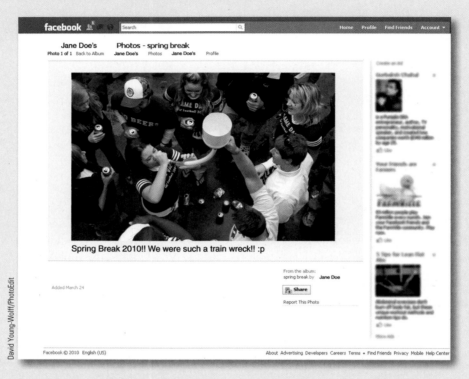

David Young-Wolff/PhotoEdit

Many teenagers and young adults like to have fun with their friends and share pictures with those friends on Facebook or other social networking sites. However, sometimes those photos and other information that has been shared may have unintended viewers, such as colleagues, employers, or potential employers. What impression might this photo leave on a potential employer?

discussion into our immediate experience. As effective thinkers, we have an obligation to develop informed, intelligent opinions about these issues so that we can function as responsible citizens and also make appropriate decisions when confronted with these issues in our lives.

Almost everyone has opinions about these and other issues. Some opinions, however, are more informed and well supported than others. To make sense of complex issues, we need to bring to them a certain amount of background knowledge and an integrated set of thinking and language abilities.

WHAT IS THE ISSUE?

Many social issues are explored, analyzed, and evaluated through our judicial system. Imagine that you have been called for jury duty and subsequently impaneled on a jury that is asked to render a verdict on the following situation. (*Note:* This fictional case is based on an actual case that was tried in May 1990 in Minneapolis, Minnesota.)

> On January 23, the defendant, Mary Barnett, left Chicago to visit her fiancé in San Francisco. She left her six-month-old daughter, Alison, unattended in the apartment. Seven days later, Mary Barnett returned home to discover that her baby had died of dehydration. She called the police and initially told them that she had left the child with a babysitter. She later stated that she knew she had left the baby behind, that she did not intend to come back, and that she knew Alison would die in a day or two. She has been charged with the crime of second-degree murder: intentional murder without premeditation. If convicted, she could face up to eighteen years in prison.

As a member of the jury, your role is to hear and weigh the evidence, evaluate the credibility of the witnesses, analyze the arguments presented by the prosecution and defense, determine whether the law applies specifically to this situation, and render a verdict on the guilt or innocence of the defendant. To perform these tasks with clarity and fairness, you will have to use a variety of sophisticated thinking and language abilities. To begin with, describe your initial assessment of whether the defendant is innocent or guilty and explain your reasons for thinking so.

As part of the jury selection process, you are asked by the prosecutor and defense attorney whether you will be able to set aside your initial reactions or preconceptions to render an impartial verdict. Identify any ideas or feelings related to this case that might make it difficult for you to view it objectively. Are you a parent? Have you ever had any experiences related to the issues in this case? Do you have any preconceived views concerning individual responsibility in situations like this? Then evaluate whether you will be able to go beyond your initial reactions to see the situation objectively, and explain how you intend to accomplish this.

WHAT IS THE EVIDENCE?

The evidence at judicial trials is presented through the testimony of witnesses called by the prosecution and the defense. As a juror, your job is to absorb the information being presented, evaluate its accuracy, and assess the reliability of the individuals giving the testimony. The following are excerpts of testimony from some of the witnesses at the trial. Witnesses for the prosecution are presented first, followed by witnesses for the defense.

CAROLINE HOSPERS: On the evening of January 30, I was in the hallway when Mary Barnett entered the building. She looked distraught and didn't have her baby Alison with her. A little while later the police arrived and I discovered that she had left poor little Alison all alone to die. I'm not surprised this happened. I always thought that Ms. Barnett was a disgrace—I mean, she didn't have a husband. In fact, she didn't even have a steady man after that sailor left for California. She had lots of wild parties in her apartment, and that baby wasn't taken care of properly. Her garbage was always filled with empty whiskey and wine bottles. I'm sure that she went to California just to party and have a good time, and didn't give a damn about little Alison. She was thinking only of herself. It's obvious that she is entirely irresponsible and was not a fit mother.

OFFICER MITCHELL: We were called to the defendant's apartment at 11 P.M. on January 30 by the defendant, Mary Barnett. Upon entering the apartment, we found the defendant holding the deceased child in her arms. She was sobbing and was obviously extremely upset. She stated that she had left the deceased with a babysitter one week before when she went to California and had just returned to discover the deceased alone in the apartment. When I asked the defendant to explain in detail what had happened before she left, she stated: "I remember making airline reservations for my trip. Then I tried to find a babysitter, but I couldn't. I knew that I was leaving Alison alone and that I wouldn't be back for a while, but I had to get to California at all costs. I visited my mother and then left." An autopsy was later performed that determined that the deceased had died of dehydration several days earlier. There were no other marks or bruises on the deceased.

DR. PARKER: I am a professional psychiatrist who has been involved in many judicial hearings on whether a defendant is mentally competent to stand trial, and I am familiar with these legal tests. At the request of the district attorney's office, I interviewed the defendant four times during the last three months. Ms. Barnett is suffering from depression and anxiety, possibly induced by the guilt she feels for what she did. These symptoms can be controlled with proper medication. Based on my interview, I believe that Ms. Barnett is competent to stand trial. She understands the charges against her, and the roles of her attorney, the prosecutor, the judge and jury, and can participate in her own defense. Further, I believe that she was mentally competent on January 23, when she left her child unattended. In my opinion she knew what she was doing and what the consequences of her actions would be. She was aware that she was leaving her child unattended and that the child would be in great danger. I think that she feels guilty for the decisions she made and that this remorse accounts for her current emotional problems.

To be effective critical thinkers, we need to try to determine the accuracy of the information and evaluate the credibility of the people providing the information. Evaluate the credibility of the prosecution witnesses by identifying those factors that led you to believe their testimony and those factors that raised questions in your mind about the accuracy of the information presented. Use these questions to guide your evaluation:

- What information is the witness providing?
- Is the information relevant to the charges?
- Is the witness credible? What biases might influence the witness's testimony?
- To what extent is the testimony accurate?

Based on the testimony you have heard up to this point, do you think the defendant is innocent or guilty of intentional murder without premeditation? Explain the reasons for your conclusion.

Now let's review testimony from the witnesses for the defense.

ALICE JONES: I have known the defendant, Mary Barnett, for over eight years. She is a very sweet and decent woman, and a wonderful mother. Being a single parent isn't easy, and Mary has done as good a job as she could. But shortly after Alison's birth, Mary got depressed. Then her fiancé, Tim Stewart, was transferred to California. He's a navy engine mechanic. She started drinking to overcome her depression, but this just made things worse. She began to feel trapped in her apartment with little help raising the baby and few contacts with her family or friends. As her depression deepened, she clung more closely to Tim, who as a result became more distant and put off their wedding, which caused her to feel increasingly anxious and desperate. She felt that she had to go to California to get things straightened out, and by the time she reached that point I think she had lost touch with reality. I honestly don't think she realized that she was leaving Alison unattended. She loved her so much.

DR. BLOOM: Although I have not been involved in judicial hearings of this type, Mary Barnett has been my patient, twice a week for the last four months, beginning two months after she returned from California and was arrested. In my professional opinion, she is mentally ill and not capable of standing trial. Further, she was clearly not aware of what she was doing when she left Alison unattended and should not be held responsible for her action. Ms. Barnett's problems began after the birth of Alison. She became caught in the grip of the medical condition known as postpartum depression, a syndrome that affects many women after the birth of their children, some more severely than others. Women feel a loss of purpose, a sense of hopelessness, and a deep depression. The extreme pressures of caring for an infant create additional anxiety. When Ms. Barnett's fiancé left for California, she felt completely overwhelmed by her circumstances. She turned to alcohol to raise her spirits, but this just exacerbated her condition. Depressed, desperate, anxious, and alcoholic, she lapsed into a serious neurotic state and became obsessed with the idea of reaching her fiancé in California. This single hope was the only thing she could focus on, and when she acted on it she was completely unaware that she was putting her daughter in danger. Since the trial has begun, she has suffered two anxiety attacks, the more severe resulting in a near-catatonic state necessitating her hospitalization for several days. This woman is emotionally disturbed. She needs professional help, not punishment.

MARY BARNETT: I don't remember leaving Alison alone. I would never have done that if I had realized what I was doing. I don't remember saying any of the things that they said I said, about knowing I was leaving her. I have tried to put the pieces together through the entire investigation, and I just can't do it. I was anxious, and I was real frightened. I didn't feel like I was in control, and it felt like it was getting worse. The world was closing in on me, and I had nowhere to turn. I knew that I had to get to Tim, in California, and that he would be able to fix everything. He was always the one I went to, because I trusted him. I must have assumed that someone was taking care of Alison, my sweet baby. When I was in California, I knew something wasn't right. I just didn't know what it was.

Based on this new testimony, do you think that the defendant is innocent or guilty of intentional murder without premeditation? Have your views changed? Explain the reasons for your current conclusion. Evaluate the credibility of the defense witnesses by identifying those factors that led you to believe their testimony and those factors that raised questions in your mind about the accuracy of the information being presented. Use the questions on page 85 as a guide.

WHAT ARE THE ARGUMENTS?

After the various witnesses present their testimony through examination and cross-examination questioning, the prosecution and defense then present their final arguments and summations. The purpose of this phase of the trial is to tie together—or raise doubts about—the evidence that has been presented in order to persuade the jury that the defendant is guilty or innocent. Included here are excerpts from these final arguments.

PROSECUTION ARGUMENTS: Child abuse and neglect are a national tragedy. Every day thousands of innocent children are neglected, abused, and even killed. The parents responsible for these crimes are rarely brought to justice because their victims are usually not able to speak on their own behalf. In some sense, all of these abusers are emotionally disturbed because it takes emotionally disturbed people to torture, maim, and kill innocent children. But these people are also responsible for their actions, and they should be punished accordingly. They don't have to hurt these children. No one is forcing them to hurt these children. They can choose not to hurt these children. If they have emotional problems, they can choose to seek professional help. Saying you hurt a child because you have "emotional problems" is the worst kind of excuse.

The defendant, Mary Barnett, claims that she left her child unattended, to die, because she has "emotional problems" and that she is not responsible for what she did. This is absurd. Mary Barnett is a self-centered, irresponsible, manipulative, deceitful mother who abandoned her six-month-old daughter to die so that she could fly to San Francisco to party all week with her fiancé. She was conscious, she was thinking, she knew exactly what she was doing, and that's exactly what she told the police when she returned from her little pleasure trip. Now she claims that she can't remember making these admissions to the police, nor can she remember leaving little Alison alone to die. How convenient!

You have heard testimony from her neighbor, Caroline Hospers, that she was considerably less than an ideal mother: a chronic drinker who liked to party rather than devoting herself to her child. You have also heard the testimony of Dr. Parker, who stated that Mary Barnett was aware of what she was doing on the fateful day in January and that any emotional disturbance is the result of her feelings of guilt over the terrible thing she did, and her fear of being punished for it.

Mary Barnett is guilty of murder, pure and simple, and it is imperative that you find her so. We need to let society know that it is no longer open season on our children.

After reviewing the prosecution's arguments, describe those points you find most persuasive and those you find least persuasive, and then review the defense arguments that follow.

DEFENSE ARGUMENTS: The district attorney is certainly correct—child abuse is a national tragedy. Mary Barnett, however, is not a child abuser. You heard the police testify that the hospital found no marks, bruises, or other indications of an abused child. You also heard her friend Alice Jones testify that Mary was a kind and loving mother who adored her child. But if Mary Barnett was not a child abuser, then how could she have left her child unattended? Because she had snapped psychologically. The combination of postpartum depression, alcoholism, the pressures of being a single parent, and the loss of her fiancé were too much for her to bear. She simply broke under the weight of all that despair and took off blindly for California, hoping to find a way out of her personal hell. How could she leave Alison unattended? Because she was completely unaware that she was doing so. She had lost touch with reality and had no idea what was happening around her.

You have heard the in-depth testimony of Dr. Bloom, who has explained to you the medical condition of postpartum depression and how this led to Mary's emotional breakdown. You are aware that Mary has had two severe anxiety attacks while this trial has taken place, one resulting in her hospitalization. And you have seen her desperate sobbing whenever her daughter Alison has been mentioned in testimony.

Alison Barnett is a victim. But she is not a victim of intentional malice from the mother who loves her. She is the victim of Mary's mental illness, of her emotional breakdown. And in this sense Mary is a victim also. In this enlightened society we should not punish someone who has fallen victim to mental illness. To do so would make us no better than those societies that used to torture and burn mentally ill people whom they thought were possessed by the devil. Mary needs treatment, not blind vengeance.

After reviewing the arguments presented by the defense, identify those points you find most persuasive and those you find least persuasive.

WHAT IS THE VERDICT?

Following the final arguments and summations, the judge sometimes gives the jury specific instructions to clarify the issues to be considered. In this case the judge reminds the jury that they must focus on the boundaries of the law and determine whether the case falls within these boundaries or outside them. The jury then retires to deliberate the case and render a verdict.

For a defendant to be found guilty of second-degree murder, the prosecution must prove that he or she intended to kill someone, made a conscious decision to do so at that moment (without premeditation), and was aware of the consequences of his or her actions. In your discussion with the other jurors, you must determine whether the evidence indicates, beyond a reasonable doubt, that the defendant's conduct in this case meets these conditions. What does the qualification "beyond a reasonable doubt" mean? A principle like this is always difficult to define in specific terms, but in general the principle means that it would not make good sense for thoughtful men and women to conclude otherwise.

Based on your analysis of the evidence and arguments presented in this case, describe what you think the verdict ought to be and explain your reasons for thinking so.

Verdict: Guilty _____   Not Guilty _____

Thinking Activity 2.12

ANALYZING YOUR VERDICT

Exploring this activity has given you the opportunity to analyze the key dimensions of a complex court case. Synthesize your thoughts regarding this case in a three- to five-page paper in which you explain the reasons and evidence that influenced your verdict. Be sure to discuss the important testimony and your evaluation of the credibility of the various witnesses.

Thinking Passages

JURORS' REASONING PROCESSES

The first of the following articles, "Jurors Hear Evidence and Turn It into Stories," by Daniel Goleman, author of the best-selling book *Emotional Intelligence*, describes recent research that gives us insight into the way jurors think and reason during the process of reaching a verdict. As you read this article, reflect on the reasoning process you engaged in while thinking about the Mary Barnett case, and then answer the questions found at the end of the article.

Thinking Critically About Visuals

"Tell the Truth, the Whole Truth, and Nothing But the Truth...."

Courtroom dramas, like that explored in the Mary Barnett and Casey Anthony trials in this chapter, provide rich contexts for sophisticated critical thinking. Imagine yourself as a member of the jury in the Casey Anthony trial. What is your reaction to this photograph? Can you tell anything about Casey Anthony by the way she presents herself? Why is her attorney standing next to her? Why are defendants typically handcuffed when they are being moved between locations even though they pose no risk of escape? Casey Anthony declined to take the stand in her defense: would that have influenced your judgment on her guilt or innocence (even though it's not supposed to)? Why or why not?

Red Huber/Orlando Sentinel/MCT/Getty Images

Jurors Hear Evidence and Turn It into Stories

by Daniel Goleman

Studies Show They Arrange Details to Reflect Their Beliefs

Despite the furor over the verdict in the Rodney G. King beating case, scientists who study juries say the system is by and large sound. Many also believe that it is susceptible to manipulation and bias, and could be improved in various specific ways suggested by their research findings.

If there is any lesson to be learned from the research findings, it is that juries are susceptible to influence at virtually every point, from the moment members are selected to final deliberation.

Much of the newest research on the mind of the juror focuses on the stories that jurors tell themselves to understand the mounds of disconnected evidence, often presented in a confusing order. The research suggests that jurors' unspoken assumptions about human nature play a powerful role in their verdicts.

"People don't listen to all the evidence and then weigh it at the end," said Dr. Nancy Pennington, a psychologist at the University of Colorado. "They process it as they go along, composing a continuing story throughout the trial that makes sense of what they're hearing."

That task is made difficult by the way evidence is presented in most trials, in an order dictated for legal reasons rather than logical ones. Thus, in a murder trial, the first witness is often a coroner, who establishes that a death occurred.

"Jurors have little or nothing to tie such facts to, unless an attorney suggested an interpretation in the opening statement," in the form of a story line to follow, Dr. Pennington said.

In an article in the November 1991 issue of *Cardozo Law Review,* Dr. Pennington, with Dr. Reid Hastie, also a psychologist at the University of Colorado, reported a series of experiments that show just how important jurors' stories are in determining the verdict they come to. In the studies, people called for jury duty but not involved in a trial were recruited for a simulation in which they were to act as jurors for a murder trial realistically reenacted on film.

In the case, the defendant, Frank Johnson, had quarreled in a bar with the victim, Alan Caldwell, who threatened him with a razor. Later that evening they went outside, got into a fight, and Johnson knifed Caldwell, who died. Disputed points included whether or not Caldwell was a bully who had started the first quarrel when his girlfriend had asked Johnson for a ride to the racetrack, whether Johnson had stabbed Caldwell or merely held his knife out to protect himself, and whether Johnson had gone home to get a knife.

In detailed interviews of the jurors, Dr. Pennington found that in explaining how they had reached their verdicts, 45 percent of the references they made were to events that had not been included in the courtroom testimony. These included inferences about the men's motives and psychological states, and assumptions the jurors themselves brought to the story from their own experience.

The stories that jurors told themselves pieced together the evidence in ways that could lead to opposite verdicts. One common story among the jurors, which led to a verdict of first-degree murder, was that the threat with the razor by Caldwell had so enraged Johnson that he went home to get his knife—a point that was in dispute— with the intention of picking a fight, during which he stabbed him to death.

By contrast, just as many jurors told themselves a story that led them to a verdict of not guilty: Caldwell started the fight with Johnson and threatened him with a razor, and Caldwell ran into the knife that Johnson was using to protect himself.

Role of Jurors' Backgrounds

The study found that jurors' backgrounds could lead to crucial differences in the assumptions they brought to their explanatory stories. Middle-class jurors were more likely to find the defendant guilty than were working-class jurors. The difference mainly hinged on how they interpreted the fact that Johnson had a knife with him during the struggle.

Middle-class jurors constructed stories that saw Johnson's having a knife as strong evidence that he planned a murderous assault on Caldwell in their second confrontation. But working-class jurors said it was likely that a man like Johnson would be in the habit of carrying a knife with him for protection, and so they saw nothing incriminating about his having the knife.

"Winning the battle of stories in the opening statements may help determine what evidence is attended to, how it is interpreted, and what is recalled both during and after the trial," Dr. Richard Lempert, a psychologist at the University of Michigan Law School, wrote in commenting on Dr. Pennington's article.

Verdicts that do not correspond to one's own "story" of a case are shocking. In the King case, "We didn't hear the defense story of what was going on, but only saw the strongest piece of the prosecution's evidence, the videotape," said Dr. Stephen Penrod, a psychologist at the University of Minnesota Law School. "If we had heard the defense theory, we may not have been so astonished by the verdict."

In the contest among jurors to recruit fellow members to one or another version of what happened, strong voices play a disproportionate role. Most juries include some people who virtually never speak up, and a small number who dominate the discussion, typically jurors of higher social status, according to studies reviewed in *Judging the Jury* (Plenum Press, 1986) by two psychologists, Dr. Valerie Hans of the University of Delaware and Dr. Neil Vidmar of Duke University.

The research also reveals that "juries are more often merciful to criminal defendants" than judges in the same cases would be, said Dr. Hans.

Blaming the Victim

In recent research, Dr. Hans interviewed 269 jurors in civil cases and found that many tended to focus on the ability of victims to have avoided being injured. "You see the same kind of blaming the victim in rape cases, too, especially among female jurors," Dr. Hans said. "Blaming the victim is reassuring to jurors because if victims are responsible for the harm that befell them, then you don't have to worry about becoming a victim yourself because you know what to do to avoid it."

That tendency may have been at work among the King jurors, Dr. Hans said, "when the jurors said King was in control and that if he stopped moving the police would have stopped beating him."

"Of course, the more they saw King as responsible for what happened, the less the officers were to blame in their minds," Dr. Hans said.

Perhaps the most intensive research has focused on the selection of a jury. Since lawyers can reject a certain number of prospective jurors during jury selection without having to give a specific reason, the contest to win the mind of the jury begins with the battle to determine who is and is not on the jury.

The scientific selection of juries began in the early 1970s when social scientists volunteered their services for the defense in a series of political trials, including proceedings arising from the 1971 Attica prison uprising in upstate New York. One method used was to poll the community where the trial was to be held to search for clues to attitudes that might work against the defendant, which the defense lawyers could then use to eliminate jurors.

For example, several studies have shown that people who favor the death penalty are generally pro-prosecution in criminal cases, and so more likely to convict a defendant. Defense lawyers can ask prospective jurors their views on the death penalty, and eliminate those who favor it.

On the basis of such a community survey for a trial in Miami, Dr. Elizabeth Loftus, a psychologist at the University of California at Irvine, found that as a group, whites trust the honesty and fairness of the police far more than blacks. "If you knew nothing else, you'd use that demographic variable in picking a jury in the King case," she said. "But in Ventura County, there's a jury pool with almost no blacks. It was a gift to the defense, in retrospect."

Over the last two decades, such methods have been refined to the point that 300 or more consulting groups now advise lawyers on jury selection.

QUESTIONS FOR ANALYSIS

1. Reflect on your own deliberations in the Mary Barnett case and describe the reasoning process you used to reach a verdict. Did you find that you were composing a continuing story to explain the testimony you were reading? If so, was this story changed or modified as you learned more information or discussed the case with your classmates?

2. Explain how factors from your own personal experience (age, gender, experience with children, and so on) may have influenced your verdict and the reasoning process that led up to it.

3. Explain how your beliefs about human nature may have influenced your analysis of Mary Barnett's motives and behavior.

4. Explain whether you believe that the research strategies lawyers are using to select the "right" jury for their cases are undermining the fairness of the justice system.

CASEBOOK: THE CASEY ANTHONY TRIAL

The Casey Anthony trial, which took place from May to July 2011, was infamous both because of its sensational content and because of the controversial nature of the jury's verdict. Casey was a young mother living in Orlando, Florida, with her parents, George and Cindy, and her two-year-old daughter, Caylee. On July 15, 2008, Casey's mother called 911 to report that Caylee was missing, that she had not been seen for thirty-one days, and that the trunk of Casey's car smelled as if a dead body had been in it. When confronted by the authorities, Casey gave various stories to explain Caylee's absence, including alleging that Caylee had been kidnapped by a nanny, Zenaida Fernandez-Gonzalez. This explanation, as well as others offered by Casey, turned out to be untrue. On December 11, 2008, Caylee's skeletal remains were found in a plastic bag in a wooded area near the family home. There was duct tape on the mouth of the skull. The cause of death was listed as homicide by "undetermined means." During the trial the prosecution claimed that Casey had killed her daughter by administering chloroform (which had been researched on Casey's computer) and then applying duct tape to suffocate her. They contended her motive was to free herself of parental responsibilities and live an active social life, which she continued to do even during the period of time that Caylee was missing.

The defense claimed that Caylee had died accidentally in the family's swimming pool and that Casey's father had disposed of the body. There was no evidence that this explanation was accurate; Casey never offered a persuasive explanation as to why she had never reported Caylee missing; and Casey declined to take the witness stand to answer the many unanswered questions.

On July 5, after a six-week trial, the jury found Casey innocent of the murder and manslaughter charges, and guilty only of providing false information to law enforcement officers. With credit for time served, she was released on July 17. The response of the general public to the verdict was mainly outrage, although some people, such as legal expert Allan Dershowitz, contended that the prosecution may not have proved the case "beyond a reasonable doubt."

The following articles provide a variety of perspectives on this case. As you read them, be aware of your own reasoning process as you work to discover what really happened to Caylee and who ought to be held responsible for her death.

Worse Than O.J.!

by Marcia Clark

Sick, shaken, in disbelief. As I listened to the verdicts in the Casey Anthony case, acquitting her of the homicide of her baby girl, I relived what I felt back when court clerk Deirdre Robertson read the verdicts in the Simpson case.

But this case is different. The verdict is far more shocking. Why?

Because Casey Anthony was no celebrity. She never wowed the nation with her athletic prowess, shilled in countless car commercials, or entertained in film comedies. There were no racial issues, no violent Rodney King citywide riot just two years earlier.

Because of those factors, many predicted from the very start in the Simpson case—in fact, long before we even began to pick a jury—that it would be impossible to secure a conviction.

There was no such foreshadowing here, and few who predicted that a jury might completely acquit Casey Anthony of the killing of her daughter.

The trial itself, despite bumps and turns, never introduced any unexpected bombshells that blew up in the prosecution's face (à la detective Mark Fuhrman's racially charged interview tapes with a novelist). All things considered, it went pretty smoothly. Judge Belvin Perry was fantastic—a model of even-tempered, no-nonsense control who kept the flow of evidence orderly and succinct, and who never let the lawyers run amok. He even jailed and fined a spectator for acting up in court.

Source: © 2013 The Newsweek/Daily Beast Company LLC (http://www.thedailybeast.com/articles/2011/07/05/casey-anthony-trial-marcia-clark-says-the-verdict-was-worse-than-the-o-j-simpson-case.html).

As a matter of fact, the coverage we *did* see of the Casey Anthony case leaned heavily in favor of conviction. The photographs of a half-clothed Casey dancing in a Hot Body contest days after her daughter died, getting tattooed with the words "La Bella Vida" (Beautiful Life), Casey's apparent celebration of freedom now that her baby was dead, the videotape of her spitting fury at her parents while in custody, and most important, her endless lies for a solid month about what had happened to her daughter.

Those lies were—most people agreed (myself included)—the proverbial noose around her neck. What mother sees that her child has drowned in the pool and not only fails to call 911, but then duct tapes her mouth and nose, hides the body in the trunk for days, and then dumps it in the woods? And *then* goes out to party *and* lies for a whopping 31 days about where the baby is? Who but a killer mother does that?

The defense had to come up with a plausible reason for that behavior. One that would persuade the jury that the death was accidental. One that would show the lies were not evidence that Casey was a psychopathic killer but would instead show that they were merely the irrational behavior of a troubled but ultimately innocent mother.

And so her lawyer, Jose Baez, came up with a shocker—the twist that ensured this case a primetime spot on cable, and occasionally network, television: He claimed that Casey Anthony's despicably callous behavior in the wake of her baby's death could be explained by the fact that she'd been molested by both her father and her brother.

I'm not so sure the logic follows. Even if it did, I never saw one shred of proof to back up the claim. Zilch.

We got a bit of innuendo in one brief reference to the fact that the FBI gave paternity tests to both brother and father—the intended point being that Casey had made the molestation claims early on. But with no evidence as to *when* those tests were performed, the intended implication was all but lost. Certainly, it was too weak to support Baez's claim.

In the end, after all the incendiary bluster of his opening statement, Baez never even tried to sell that story in any real way. (And there was a chance he could have: If the judge allows it, an attorney can put on a psychologist to give a general discussion of child abuse accommodation syndrome, even if he doesn't claim the defendant on trial suffers from the syndrome.)

Nor did the defense make any serious inroads on the prosecution's physical evidence.

But then again, it didn't need to. Because this case wasn't really about the physical evidence. Caylee's body was too decomposed to offer much information. Cause of death was undetermined. All the coroner could say was that it was a homicide, but that conclusion wasn't based on science so much as logic: The body was found wrapped in plastic bags and dumped in the woods. In fact, the most compelling aspect of the medical examiner's testimony (who was, by the way, a great witness) was not medical but merely logical: that when a baby drowns—and she said that's a common cause of death for babies—the mother or father calls 911 *every single time*; and if the baby had merely died accidentally, then why put duct tape over the baby's face?

So it was a circumstantial case. Most cases are. But the circumstances were compelling. Maybe not sufficient to prove premeditated murder—and I never believed the jury would approve the death penalty—but certainly enough to find Casey Anthony guilty of manslaughter at the very least.

Why didn't they? My guess, since I'm writing this before the inevitable juror cameos, is that the jury didn't necessarily believe Casey was innocent but weren't convinced enough of her guilt to bring in a conviction. The thinking goes something like this: Sure, Casey's behavior after her daughter's death looks bad—dancing, partying, lying—but that doesn't mean she killed the baby. Sure, that duct tape was weird, but that could've been done after the baby was already dead—no way to know who or when that tape was put on the baby's face. Sure, the chloroform computer search seems damning, but that may not even have been done by Casey (her mom took the fall for that one).

And so, every bit of evidence presented by the prosecution could've been tinged with doubt. At the end of the day, the jury might have found that they just couldn't convict her based on evidence that was reconcilable with an innocent explanation—even if the weight of logic favored the guilty one.

Jury instructions are so numerous and complex, it's a wonder jurors ever wade through them. And so it should come as no surprise that they can sometimes get stuck along the way. The instruction on circumstantial evidence is confusing even to lawyers. And reasonable doubt? That's the hardest, most elusive one of all. And I think it's where even the most fair-minded jurors can get derailed.

How? By confusing reasonable doubt with a reason *to* doubt. Some believe that thinking was in play in the Simpson case. After the verdict was read in the Simpson case, as the jury was leaving, one of them, I was later told, said: "We think he probably did it. We just didn't think they proved it beyond a reasonable doubt." In every case, a defense attorney will do his or her best to give the jury a reason to doubt. "Some other dude did it," or "some other dude threatened him." But those *reasons* don't necessarily equate with a *reasonable doubt*. A reason does not equal *reasonable*. Sometimes, that distinction can get lost.

In Scotland, they have three verdicts: guilty, not guilty, and not proven. It's one way of showing that even if the jury didn't believe the evidence amounted to proof beyond a reasonable doubt, it didn't find the defendant innocent either. There's a difference. And maybe that's what today's not-guilty verdict really meant. Not innocent. Just not proven. The jurors will eventually speak out and tell us.

Meanwhile, although I must accept their verdict, I don't have to agree with it. Because I did follow this case, and I have to be honest: If I'd been in that jury room, the vote would've been 11 to 1. Forever.

Marcia Clark is a former Los Angeles deputy district attorney who was the lead prosecutor in the O.J. Simpson murder case.

Casey Anthony: The System Worked

by Alan M. Dershowitz

"This case [is] about seeking justice for Caylee . . ." So argued the prosecutor in the Casey Anthony murder case. He was wrong, and the jury understood that.

Source: © 2013 Dow Jones & Company, Inc. (http://online.wsj.com/article/SB10001424052702303544 604576429783247016492.html).

A criminal trial is never about seeking justice for the victim. If it were, there could be only one verdict: guilty. That's because only one person is on trial in a criminal case, and if that one person is acquitted, then by definition there can be no justice for the victim in that trial.

A criminal trial is neither a whodunit nor a multiple choice test. It is not even a criminal investigation to determine who among various possible suspects might be responsible for a terrible tragedy. In a murder trial, the state, with all of its power, accuses an individual of being the perpetrator of a dastardly act against a victim. The state must prove that accusation by admissible evidence and beyond a reasonable doubt.

Even if it is "likely" or "probable" that a defendant committed the murder, he must be acquitted, because neither likely nor probable satisfies the daunting standard of proof beyond a reasonable doubt. Accordingly, a legally proper result—acquittal in such a case—may not be the same as a morally just result. In such a case, justice has not been done to the victim, but the law has prevailed.

For thousands of years, Western society has insisted that it is better for 10 guilty defendants to go free than for one innocent defendant to be wrongly convicted. This daunting standard finds its roots in the biblical story of Abraham's argument with God about the sinners of Sodom.

Abraham admonishes God for planning to sweep away the innocent along with the guilty and asks Him whether it would be right to condemn the sinners of Sodom if there were 10 or more righteous people among them. God agrees and reassures Abraham that he would spare the city if there were 10 righteous. From this compelling account, the legal standard has emerged.

That is why a criminal trial is not a search for truth. Scientists search for truth. Philosophers search for morality. A criminal trial searches for only one result: proof beyond a reasonable doubt.

A civil trial, on the other hand, seeks justice for the victim. In such a case, the victim sues the alleged perpetrator and need only prove liability by a preponderance of the evidence. In other words, if it is more likely than not that a defendant was the killer, he is found liable, though he cannot be found guilty on that lesser standard.

That is why it was perfectly rational, though difficult for many to understand, for a civil jury to have found O.J. Simpson liable to his alleged victim, after a criminal jury had found him not guilty of his murder. It is certainly possible that if the estate of Caylee Anthony were to sue Casey Anthony civilly, a Florida jury might find liability.

Casey Anthony was not found innocent of her daughter's murder, as many commentators seem to believe. She was found "not guilty." And therein lies much of the misunderstanding about the Anthony verdict.

This misunderstanding is exacerbated by the pervasiveness of TV shows about criminal cases. On television and in the movies, crimes are always solved. Nothing is left uncertain. By the end, the viewer knows whodunit. In real life, on the other hand, many murders remain unsolved, and even some that are "solved" to the satisfaction of the police and prosecutors lack sufficient evidence to result in a conviction. The Scottish verdict "not proven" reflects this reality more accurately than its American counterpart, "not guilty."

Because many American murder cases, such as the Casey Anthony trial, are shown on television, they sometimes appear to the public as if they were reality television shows. There is great disappointment, therefore, when the result is a verdict of not guilty. On the old Perry Mason show, the fictional defense lawyer would not only get his client acquitted but he would prove who actually committed the murder. Not so in real life.

The verdict in the Casey Anthony case reflected the lack of forensic evidence and heavy reliance on circumstantial inferences. There was no evidence of a cause of death, the time of death, or the circumstances surrounding the actual death of this young girl. There was sufficient circumstantial evidence from which the jury could have inferred homicide. But a reasonable jury could also have rejected that conclusion, as this jury apparently did. There are hundreds of defendants now in prison, some even on death row, based on less persuasive evidence than was presented in this case.

Juries are not computers. They are composed of human beings who evaluate evidence differently. The prosecutors in this case did the best they could with the evidence they had, though I believe they made a serious mistake in charging Casey Anthony with capital murder and introducing questionable evidence, such as that relating to the "smell of death" inside the trunk of Casey Anthony's car.

The defense also made mistakes, particularly by accusing Ms. Anthony's father of sexually abusing her. Although they leveled this unfounded accusation in an effort to explain why Casey had lied, it sounded like the kind of abuse excuse offered to justify a crime of violence. But a criminal trial is not about who is the better lawyer. It is about the evidence, and the evidence in this case left a reasonable doubt in the mind of all of the jurors. The system worked.

Mr. Dershowitz is a law professor at Harvard.

Casey Anthony Juror: 'Sick to Our Stomachs' Over Not Guilty Verdict

by Mary Kate Burke, Jessica Hopper, Enjoli Francis, and Lauren Effron

Casey Anthony juror Jennifer Ford said that she and the other jurors cried and were "sick to our stomachs" after voting to acquit Casey Anthony of charges that she killed her 2-year-old daughter Caylee.

"I did not say she was innocent," said Ford, who had previously only been identified as juror No. 3. "I just said there was not enough evidence. If you cannot prove what the crime was, you cannot determine what the punishment should be."

Ford, a 32-year-old nursing student at St. Petersburg College, praised the jurors, but said when deliberations began there were "a lot of conflicting ideas." At first, people came down on both sides of whether Casey Anthony killed her daughter, Ford said, and the first vote was 10-2 for "not guilty."

Source: © 2013 ABC News (http://abcnews.go.com/US/casey_anthony_trial/casey-anthony-juror-jury-sick-stomach-guilty-verdict/story?id=14005609).

"I toggled on manslaughter and not guilty," Ford told "Nightline" anchor Terry Moran in an exclusive TV interview. "It doesn't feel good. It was a horrible decision to have to make."

The jury's jaw-dropping not guilty verdict shocked court observers, but it was also a difficult moment for the panel, Ford said in her exclusive interviews with ABC News. No one from the jury was willing to come out and talk to the media in the hours after the verdict.

"Everyone wonders why we didn't speak to the media right away," Ford said. "It was because we were sick to our stomach to get that verdict. We were crying, and not just the women. It was emotional and we weren't ready. We wanted to do it with integrity and not contribute to the sensationalism of the trial."

Ford told Moran she thought Casey Anthony's claim that her 2-year-old daughter accidentally drowned and she lied for three years was more believable than the evidence the prosecution presented.

"I'm not saying I believe the defense," she said. "Obviously, it wasn't proven so I'm not taking that and speculating at all. But it's easier for me logically to get from point A to point B" via the defense argument.

Ford said that she couldn't make out "logically" the prosecution's argument because there were too many unanswered questions about how Caylee died, including how Casey Anthony would have used chloroform to smother her 2-year-old daughter, then put her in the trunk of her car without anyone seeing her.

"If there was a dead child in that trunk, does that prove how she died? No idea, still no idea." Ford told Moran. "If you're going to charge someone with murder, don't you have to know how they killed someone or why they might have killed someone, or have something where, when, why, how? Those are important questions. They were not answered."

Instead of murder, Casey Anthony, 25, was found guilty of four counts of lying to law enforcement and could be released from jail as early as Thursday. Ford agreed that Anthony was a "pathological liar" but said "bad behavior is not enough to prove a crime" and her actions could be blamed on her family dynamic.

"The family she comes from and the family that made her what she is had some influence," she said. "What do they say? You're as sick as your secrets? I mean, the family seemed to have a little something going on."

She added that she thought Casey Anthony's father, George Anthony, was "dishonest."

"I don't know if he had anything to do with it, but I think that he was there," she said. "He and Casey have something."

Earlier today, the prosecutor and an alternate juror agreed on why the jury refused to convict Anthony: They couldn't prove how Caylee Anthony died.

"It all came down to the evidence," said Florida state attorney Jeff Ashton on "The View." "I think ultimately it all came down to -- at least from what the one alternate said -- it came down to the cause of death."

Russell Huekler, one of five alternate jurors who were present for all the testimony and sequestered along with the 12 other jurors, said today that he would have delivered the same verdict and that he was shocked by the public outrage over the trial's outcome.

"The prosecution failed to prove their case and there was reasonable doubt," Huekler said. "Again, they didn't show us how Caylee died. They didn't show us a motive. I'm sorry people feel that way. . . . These were 17 total jurors. They really listened to this case and kept an open mind."

QUESTIONS FOR ANALYSIS

1. After reading the initial description of the Casey Anthony trial, would you have found her "guilty" or "not guilty" had you been a member of the jury? Explain your reasoning process that would have led you to that conclusion.

2. In her article "Worse Than O.J.!" Marcia Clark, the prosecutor in the O.J. Simpson trial, argues that the jury reached the wrong verdict because they failed to accurately understand the concept of "reasonable doubt." Explain the reason that the author reaches this conclusion. Do you agree or disagree with her?

3. After reading his article "Casey Anthony: The System Worked," explain why the well-known lawyer Alan Dershowitz believes the jury was justified in reaching the verdict that it did. At the same time, Dershowitz states, "There was sufficient circumstantial evidence from which the jury could have inferred homicide. But a reasonable jury could also have rejected that conclusion, as this jury apparently did." Do you find this statement to be problematic? Why or why not?

4. In the article about juror Jennifer Ford, why does she say that she and her fellow jurors were "Sick to Our Stomachs" after voting to acquit Casey Anthony of charges that she killed her two-year-old daughter Caylee? Do you agree with the reasoning that led her and the others to reach this verdict? Why or why not?

5. Goleman identifies a number of errors in reasoning that can lead jurors to illogical or unsubstantiated conclusions in their deliberations. Explain which of the following errors in reasoning might have been committed by the Casey Anthony jurors:

   - **Story telling:** Instead of listening to all of the evidence and then weighing it at the end, many jurors compose a story early on in the trial that makes sense of what they are hearing. The problem is that this may lead to "confirmation bias"—looking for information that supports their story and disregarding information that conflicts with their story.

   - **Filling in the blanks:** Often jurors inject information, inferences, and assumptions that were not included in the trial testimony because they—perhaps unconsciously—want to fill out their story in a way that is consistent with the conclusion they have already reached.

   - **Backgrounds:** Often jurors' background can lead to crucial differences in the assumptions they bring to their explanatory stories, which might in turn be illogical, unsubstantiated, or in contradiction with the known facts.

6. Explain whether you believe that the research strategies lawyers are using to select the "right" juries for their cases are undermining the fairness of the justice system.

7. In what way have reading and reflecting on these articles influenced your original conclusion regarding whether Casey Anthony should have been found "guilty" or "not guilty"?

CHAPTER 2   Reviewing and Viewing

Summary

Becoming a *critical thinker* involves

- Thinking actively
- Exploring situations with questions
- Thinking independently
- Viewing situations from different perspectives
- Supporting perspectives with reasons and evidence
- Discussing ideas in an organized way
- Analyzing issues thoughtfully

Becoming a sophisticated critical thinker is a lifelong process that requires ongoing analysis, reflection, and practice. Critical thinkers are better equipped to deal with the difficult challenges that life poses: to solve problems, establish and achieve goals, and analyze complex situations.

Assessing Your Strategies and Creating New Goals

How Effective a Critical Thinker Am I?

Described below are key thinking abilities and personal attributes that are correlated with thinking critically. Evaluate your position regarding each of these abilities and attributes, and use this self-evaluation to guide your efforts to become a critical thinker.

Make Critical Thinking a Priority

I live as though critical thinking is important in all areas of my life.	I don't always live as though critical thinking is a priority.
5 4 3 2 1	

The process of becoming a more powerful, sophisticated critical thinker begins with deciding that you *want* to become this kind of person.

Strategy: Having completed your portrait of a "critical thinker" earlier in this chapter, review your portrait regularly so that you can plan your thinking goals and evaluate your progress. Becoming a critical thinker is a long-term process that involves explicit goals, sustained effort, and ongoing self-evaluation.

Develop Well-Reasoned Beliefs

I strive to form the most well-reasoned beliefs possible.	I have not carefully examined many of my beliefs.
5 4 3 2 1	

The beliefs of a critical thinker form a coherent philosophy, a dynamic system in which all of the beliefs are organically related. Because their beliefs are the result of thoughtful reflection, critical thinkers are able to explain the rationale for their views, and they are open to productive discussions with conflicting perspectives.

Strategy: Develop the habit of critically examining your beliefs: What do I believe, and why do I believe it? Where did these beliefs originate, and what are the reasons that support them? What are other viewpoints that I haven't considered? Are my beliefs consistent with one another? If not, why not?

Support Your Beliefs with Thoughtful Reasons and Compelling Evidence

I always try to support my beliefs with reasons and evidence.	I often just accept my beliefs without supporting them.
5 4 3 2 1	

Critical thinkers recognize that it is not sufficient to have beliefs, it is necessary to provide *support* for your beliefs with thoughtful reasons and compelling evidence.

*Strategy: Every time you say (or think) "I believe . . ." or "I think . . .," develop the habit of explaining **why** you believe or think what you do. Similarly, when others offer their opinions, ask them "**Why** do you believe that?" This way you will be improving their critical thinking abilities as well as your own.*

Strive to Be Open-Minded

I am very open-minded and view situations from many different perspectives.	I see things mainly from my own point of view and I can be fairly dogmatic.
5 4 3 2 1	

Critical thinkers actively try to get outside of their own viewpoints and see issues and situations from alternate perspectives, particularly those that disagree with them. This perspective-taking helps you develop the strongest beliefs and broadest knowledge, and it contributes to productive relationships with other people.

Strategy: Seek out perspectives different from yours, particularly those that disagree with you. Listen openly and respectfully to the arguments they are making and strive to reach thoughtful conclusions that take all the perspectives into account.

Emulate Your Critical Thinking Portrait

I am an insightful, powerful, and confident critical thinker.	I am not as strong a thinker as I could be.
5 4 3 2 1	

This chapter has given you the opportunity to create a more detailed portrait of a *critical thinker* that can serve as your paradigm as you seek to elevate your intellectual abilities and enhance your reflective insight.

Strategy: Describe your portrait of a critical thinker on an index card that you can easily refer to, identifying the specific qualities that you would like to develop. Compare yourself to your portrait on a regular basis, noting the progress that you have made as well as the areas that need more attention.

Suggested Films

12 Angry Men (1957)

A jury decides the fate of a young man accused of murdering his father. A guilty verdict will result in a mandatory death sentence. The case appears to be open and shut until one juror challenges the others to move beyond their prejudices and presumptions and think critically about the facts before arriving at a decision.

Chinatown (1974)

Is a free and ethical existence possible? In Roman Polanski's neo-noir film, a private detective is hired by a woman to spy on her husband, then finds himself at the center of a complex conspiracy in which he quickly becomes a pawn. As the detective attempts to uncover the truth, he encounters pervasive corruption, dishonesty, and evil.

Good Night, and Good Luck (2005)

Based on a true story, this film depicts the conflict between journalist Edward R. Murrow and Senator Joseph McCarthy during the anticommunist committee hearings of the 1950s—hearings that destroyed the careers of many people and created national hysteria. In spite of pressure to remain silent, Murrow exhibited clarity of thought and profound moral fortitude when he openly criticized and exposed the scare tactics employed by the committee.

Guns, Germs, and Steel (2005)

In this National Geographic documentary based on his best-selling book, author Jarred Diamond explores the geographic and historical roots of global inequality. The author's ability to think critically and bring a new lens to history makes for an intelligent and compelling argument.

Malcolm X (1992)

How can one find meaning in an unjust world? Based on the autobiography, this film follows the life of the famous African American leader. After his father is killed by the Ku Klux Klan, Malcolm Little becomes a gangster before discovering the Nation of Islam while in prison. He subsequently becomes a militant political activist fighting for the rights of African Americans, advocating black pride, black power, identity politics, and economic self-reliance. When he is assassinated, he becomes a martyr for human rights and equality.

What's my next move? Our success in life—and sometimes our survival—depends on developing the ability to solve challenging problems in organized and creative ways. How can we learn to be effective problem solvers?

CHAPTER 3

Solving Problems

An Organized Approach to Analyzing Difficult Problems

Step 1: What is the problem?

What do I know about the situation?
What results am I aiming for?
How can I define the problem?

Step 2: What are the alternatives?

What are the boundaries?
What are the possible alternatives?

Step 3: What are the advantages and/or disadvantages of each alternative?

What are the advantages?
What are the disadvantages?
What additional information do I need?

Step 4: What is the solution?

Which alternatives will I pursue?
What steps can I take?

Step 5: How well is the solution working?

What is my evaluation?
What adjustments are necessary?

Critical thinking can help creatively *and* constructively *solve problems.*

105

Thinking Critically About Problems

Throughout your life, you are continually solving problems, including the many minor problems that you solve each day: negotiating a construction delay on the road, working through an unexpected difficulty at your job, helping an upset child deal with a disappointment. As a student, you are faced with a steady stream of academic assignments, quizzes, exams, and papers. Relatively simple problems like these do not require a systematic or complex analysis. For example, to do well on an exam, you need to *define* the problem (what areas will the exam cover, and what will be the format?), identify and evaluate various *alternatives* (what are possible study approaches?), and then put all these factors together to reach a *solution* (what will be your study plan and schedule?). But the difficult and complicated problems in life require more attention.

Problems are the crucibles that forge the strength of our characters. When you are tested by life—forced to overcome adversity and think your way through the most challenging situations—you will emerge a more intelligent, resourceful, and resilient person. However, if you lead a sheltered existence that insulates you from life's trials, or if you flee from situations at the first sign of trouble, then you are likely to be weak and unable to cope with the eruptions and explosions that are bound to occur. Adversity reveals the person you have become, the character you have created. As the Roman philosopher and poet Lucretius explained, "So it is more useful to watch a man in times of peril, and in adversity to discern what kind of man he is; for then, at last, words of truth are drawn from the depths of his heart, and the mask is torn off, reality remains."

The quality of your life can be traced in large measure to your competency as a problem solver. The fact that some people are consistently superior problem solvers is largely due to their ability to approach problems in an informed and organized way. Less competent problem solvers just muddle through when it comes to confronting adversity, using hit-or-miss strategies that rarely provide the best results. How would you rate yourself as a problem solver? Do you generally approach difficulties confidently, analyze them clearly, and reach productive solutions? Or do you find that you often get "lost" and confused in such situations, unable to understand the problem clearly and to break out of mental ruts? Of course, you may find that you are very adept at solving problems in one area of your life—such as your job—and miserable at solving problems in other areas, such as your love life or your relationships with your children.

Becoming an expert problem solver is, for the most part, a learned skill that you can develop by practicing and applying the principles described in this chapter. You can learn to view problems as *challenges*, opportunities for growth instead of obstacles or burdens. You can become a person who attacks adversity with confidence and enthusiasm.

Introduction to Solving Problems

Consider the following problem:

> My best friend is addicted to drugs, but he won't admit it. Jack always liked to drink, but I never thought too much about it. After all, a lot of people like to drink socially, get relaxed, and have a good time. But over the last few years he's started using other drugs as well as alcohol, and it's ruining his life. He's stopped taking classes at the college and will soon lose his job if he doesn't change. Last week I told him that I was really worried about him, but he told me that he has no drug problem and that in any case it really isn't any of my business. I just don't know what to do. I've known Jack since we were in grammar school together and he's a wonderful person. It's as if he's in the grip of some terrible force and I'm powerless to help him.

In working through this problem, the student who wrote this will have to think carefully and systematically in order to reach a solution. To think effectively in situations like this, we usually ask ourselves a series of questions:

1. What is the *problem*?
2. What are the *alternatives*?
3. What are the *advantages* and/or *disadvantages* of each alternative?
4. What is the *solution*?
5. How well is the solution *working*?

Let's explore these questions further—and the thinking process that they represent—by applying them to the problem described here.

What Is the Problem? There are a variety of ways to define the problem facing this student. Describe as specifically as possible what *you* think the problem is.

What Are the Alternatives? In dealing with this problem, you have a wide variety of possible actions to consider before selecting the best choices. Identify some of the alternatives you might consider. One possibility is listed already.

1. Speak to my friend in a candid and forceful way to convince him that he has a serious problem.
2.

   and so on.

What Are the Advantages and/or Disadvantages of Each Alternative? Evaluate the strengths and weaknesses of each of the possibilities you identified so you can weigh your choices and decide on the best course of action.

1. Speak to my friend in a candid and forceful way to convince him that he has a serious problem.

   Advantage: He may respond to my direct emotional appeal, acknowledge that he has a problem, and seek help.

   Disadvantage: He may react angrily, further alienating me from him and making it more difficult for me to have any influence on him.

2.

   Advantage:

   Disadvantage:

   and so on.

What Is the Solution? After evaluating the various alternatives, select what you think is the most effective alternative for solving the problem and describe the sequence of steps you would take to act on the alternative.

How Well Is the Solution Working? The final step in the process is to review the solution and decide whether it is working. If it is not, you must be able to modify your solution. Describe what results would inform you that the alternative you had selected to pursue was working well or poorly. If you concluded that your alternative was working poorly, describe what your next action would be.

In this situation, trying to figure out the best way to help your friend recognize his problem and seek treatment requires making a series of decisions. If we understand the way our minds operate when we are thinking effectively, then we can apply this understanding to improve our thinking in new, challenging situations. In the remainder of this chapter, we will explore a more sophisticated version of this problem-solving approach and apply it to a variety of complex problems.

Thinking Activity 3.1

ANALYZING A PROBLEM YOU SOLVED

1. Describe in specific detail an important problem you have solved recently.

2. Explain how you went about solving the problem. What were the steps, strategies, and approaches you used to understand the problem and make an informed decision?

3. Analyze the organization exhibited in your thinking process by completing the five-step problem-solving method we have been exploring.

4. Share your problem with other members of the class and have them try to analyze and solve it. Then explain the solution you arrived at.

Solving Complex Problems

Imagine yourself in the following situations. What would your next move be, and what are your reasons for it?

Procrastination

I am a procrastinator. Whenever I have something important to do, especially if it's difficult or unpleasant, I tend to put it off. Though this chronic delaying bothers me, I try to suppress my concern and instead work on more trivial things. It doesn't matter how much time I allow for certain responsibilities, I always end up waiting until the last minute to really focus and get things done, or I overschedule too many things for the time available. I usually meet my deadlines, but not always, and I don't enjoy working under this kind of pressure. In many cases I know that I'm not producing my best work. To make matters worse, the feeling that I'm always behind causes me to feel really stressed out and undermines my confidence. I've tried every kind of schedule and technique, but my best intentions simply don't last, and I end up slipping into my old habits. I must learn to get my priorities in order and act on them in an organized way so that I can lead a well-balanced and happier life.

Losing Weight

My problem is the unwelcome weight that has attached itself to me. I was always in pretty good physical shape when I was younger, and if I gained a few extra pounds, they were easy to lose if I adjusted my diet slightly or exercised a little more. As I've gotten older, however, it seems easier to add the weight and more difficult to take it off. I'm eating healthier than I ever have before and getting just as much exercise, but the pounds just keep on coming. My clothes are tight, I'm feeling slow and heavy, and my self-esteem is suffering. How can I lose this excess poundage?

Smoking

One problem in my life that has remained unsolved for about twelve years is my inability to stop smoking. I know it is dangerous for my health, and I tell my children that they should not smoke. They then tell me that I should stop, and I explain to them that it is very hard to do. I have tried to stop many times without success. The only times I previously was able to stop were during my two pregnancies because I didn't want to endanger my children's health. But after their births, I went back to smoking, although I realize that secondhand smoke can also pose a health hazard. I want to stop smoking because it's dangerous, but I also enjoy it. Why do I continue, knowing it can only damage me and my children?

Loss of Financial Aid

I'm just about to begin my second year of college, following a very successful first year. To this point, I have financed my education through a combination

Thinking Critically About Visuals

"Eureka! I have created something never seen before!"

Justin Sullivan/Getty Images

This photograph of Steve Jobs introducing the iPad to the world for the first time is a stunning image. In what ways was the iPad a completely unique creation? Studying the photograph, how do you think Steve Jobs feels at this moment? Why do people usually settle for conventional alternatives when trying to solve problems, rather than pushing for truly innovative ideas? Describe a time when you were able to solve a difficult problem by using a genuinely creative solution. How did this experience make you feel?

of savings, financial aid, and a part-time job (sixteen hours per week) at a local store. However, I just received a letter from my college stating that it was reducing my financial aid package by half due to budgetary problems. The letter concludes, "We hope this aid reduction will not prove to be too great an inconvenience." From my perspective, this reduction in aid isn't an inconvenience—it's a disaster! My budget last year was already tight, and with my job, I had barely enough time to study, participate in a few college activities, and have a modest (but essential) social life. To make matters worse, my mother has been ill, a condition that has reduced her income and created financial problems at home. I'm feeling panicked! What in the world am I going to do?

When we first approach a difficult problem, it often seems a confused tangle of information, feelings, alternatives, opinions, considerations, and risks. The problem of the college student just described is a complicated situation that does not seem to offer a single simple solution. Without the benefit of a systematic approach, our thoughts might wander through the tangle of issues like this:

> I want to stay in school . . . but I'm not going to have enough money . . . I could work more hours at my job . . . but I might not have enough time to study and get top grades . . . and if all I'm doing is working and studying, what about my social life? . . . and what about Mom and the kids? . . . They might need my help . . . I could drop out of school for a while . . . but if I don't stay in school, what kind of future do I have? . . .

Very often when we are faced with difficult problems like this, we simply do not know where to begin trying to solve them. Frustrated by not knowing where to take the first step, we often give up trying to understand the problem. Instead, we may

1. *Act impulsively* without thought or consideration (e.g., "I'll just quit school").
2. *Do what someone else suggests* without seriously evaluating the suggestion (e.g., "Tell me what I should do—I'm tired of thinking about this").
3. *Do nothing* as we wait for events to make the decision for us (e.g., "I'll just wait and see what happens before doing anything").

None of these approaches is likely to succeed in the long run, and they can gradually reduce our confidence in dealing with complex problems. An alternative to these reactions is to *think critically* about the problem, analyzing it with an organized approach based on the five-step method described earlier.

Although we will be using an organized method for working through difficult problems and arriving at thoughtful conclusions, the fact is that our minds do not always work in such a logical, step-by-step fashion. Effective problem solvers typically pass through all the steps we will be examining, but they don't always do so in the sequence we will be describing. Instead, the best problem solvers have an integrated and flexible approach to the process in which they deploy a repertoire of problem-solving strategies as needed. Sometimes exploring the various alternatives helps them go back and redefine the original problem; similarly, seeking to implement the solution can often suggest new alternatives.

The key point is that, although the problem-solving steps are presented in a logical sequence here, you are not locked into following these steps in a mechanical and unimaginative way. At the same time, in learning a problem-solving method like this, it is generally not wise to skip steps because each step deals with an important aspect of the problem. As you become more proficient in using the method, you will find that you can apply its concepts and strategies to problem solving in an increasingly flexible and natural fashion, just as learning the basics of an activity like driving a car gradually gives way to a more organic and integrated performance of the skills involved.

Before applying a method like the one just outlined above to your problem, however, you first need to prepare yourself by *accepting* the problem.

ACCEPTING THE PROBLEM

To solve a problem, you must first be willing to *accept* the problem by *acknowledging* that the problem exists, *identifying* the problem, and *committing* yourself to trying to solve it.

Successful problem solvers are highly motivated and willing to persevere through the many challenges and frustrations of the problem-solving process. How do you find the motivation and commitment that prepare you to enter the problem-solving process? There are no simple answers, but a number of strategies may be useful to you:

1. ***List the benefits.*** Make a detailed list of the benefits you will derive from successfully dealing with the problem. Such a process helps you clarify why you might want to tackle the problem, motivates you to get started, and serves as a source of encouragement when you encounter difficulties or lose momentum.

2. ***Formalize your acceptance.*** When you formalize your acceptance of a problem, you are "going on record," either by preparing a signed declaration

Problem-Solving Method (Advanced)

Step 1: What is the problem?
   a. What do I know about the situation?
   b. What results am I aiming for in this situation?
   c. How can I define the problem?

Step 2: What are the alternatives?
   a. What are the boundaries of the problem situation?
   b. What alternatives are possible within these boundaries?

Step 3: What are the advantages and/or disadvantages of each alternative?
   a. What are the advantages of each alternative?
   b. What are the disadvantages of each alternative?
   c. What additional information do I need to evaluate each alternative?

Step 4: What is the solution?
   a. Which alternative(s) will I pursue?
   b. What steps can I take to act on the alternative(s) chosen?

Step 5: How well is the solution working?
   a. What is my evaluation?
   b. What adjustments are necessary?

or by signing a "contract" with someone else. This formal commitment serves as an explicit statement of your original intentions that you can refer to if your resolve weakens.

3. ***Accept responsibility for your life.*** Each of us has the potential to control the direction of our lives, but to do so we must accept our freedom to choose and the responsibility that goes with it. As you saw in the last chapter, critical thinkers actively work to take charge of their lives rather than letting themselves be passively controlled by external forces.

4. ***Create a "worst-case" scenario.*** Some problems persist because you are able to ignore their possible implications. When you use this strategy, you remind yourself, as graphically as possible, of the potentially disastrous consequences of your actions. For example, using vivid color photographs and research conclusions, you can remind yourself that excessive smoking, drinking, or eating can lead to myriad health problems and social and psychological difficulties as well as an early demise.

5. ***Identify what's holding you back.*** If you are having difficulty accepting a problem, it is usually because something is holding you back. Whatever the constraints, using this strategy involves identifying and describing all of the factors that are preventing you from attacking the problem and then addressing these factors one at a time.

STEP 1: WHAT IS THE PROBLEM?

Once you have accepted the problem, the first step in solving a problem is to determine exactly what the central issues of the problem are. If you do not clearly understand what the problem really is, then your chances of solving it are considerably reduced. For example, consider the different formulations of the following problems.

"School is boring."	versus	"I feel bored in school."
"I'm a failure."	versus	"I just failed an exam."

In each of these cases, a very general conclusion (left column) has been replaced by a more specific characterization of the problem (right column). The general conclusions (e.g., "I'm a failure") do not suggest productive ways of resolving the difficulties. On the other hand, the more specific descriptions of the problem situation (e.g., "I just failed an exam") *do* permit us to attack the problem with useful strategies. Correct identification of a problem is essential if you are going to perform a successful analysis and reach an appropriate conclusion.

Let us return to the college finances problem we encountered on pages 109–110 and analyze it using our problem-solving method. (*Note:* As you work through this problem-solving approach, apply the steps and strategies to an unsolved problem in your own life. You will have an opportunity to write your analysis when you complete Thinking Activity 3.2 on page 124.) To complete the first major step of this problem-solving approach—"What is the problem?"—address these three questions:

1. What do I know about the situation?
2. What results am I aiming for in this situation?
3. How can I define the problem?

Step 1A: What Do I Know About the Situation? Solving a problem begins with determining what information you *know* to be the case and what information you *think* might be the case. You need to have a clear idea of the details of your beginning circumstances to explore the problem successfully.

You can identify and organize what you know about the problem situation by using *key questions.* In Chapter 2, we examined six types of questions that can be used to explore situations and issues: *fact, interpretation, analysis, synthesis, evaluation,* and *application.* By asking—and trying to answer—questions of fact, you are establishing a sound foundation for the exploration of your problem. Answer the following questions of fact—who, what, where, when, how, why—about the problem described at the beginning of the chapter on page 107.

1. *Who* are the people involved in this situation?

   Who will benefit from solving this problem?

   Who can help me solve this problem?

2. *What* are the various parts or dimensions of the problem?

   What are my strengths and resources for solving this problem?

   What additional information do I need to solve this problem?

3. *Where* can I find people or additional information to help me solve the problem?

4. *When* did the problem begin?

   When should the problem be resolved?

5. *How* did the problem develop or come into being?

6. *Why* is solving this problem important to me?

   Why is this problem difficult to solve?

7. Additional questions:

Step 1B: What Results Am I Aiming for in This Situation? The second part of answering the question "What is the problem?" consists of identifying the specific *results* or goals you are trying to achieve, encouraging you to look ahead to the future. The results are those goals whose achievement will eliminate the problem. In this respect, it is similar to the process of establishing and working toward your goals that you examined in Chapter 1. To identify your results, ask yourself: "What are the objectives that, once achieved, will solve this problem?" For instance, one of the results or objectives in the sample problem is having enough money to pay for college. Describe additional results you might be trying to achieve in this situation.

Step 1C: How Can I Define the Problem? Conclude Step 1 by defining the problem as clearly and specifically as possible. Defining the problem is a crucial task in the entire problem-solving process because this definition determines the direction of the analysis. To define the problem, you need to identify its central issue(s). Sometimes defining the problem is relatively straightforward, such as: "Trying to find enough time to exercise." Often, however, identifying the central issue of a problem is a complex process. In fact, you may only begin to develop a clear idea of the problem as you engage in the process of trying to solve it. For example, you might begin by believing that your problem is, say, not having the *ability* to succeed, and end by concluding that the problem is really a *fear* of success.

Although there are no simple formulas for defining challenging problems, you can pursue several strategies in identifying the central issue most effectively:

1. ***View the problem from different perspectives.*** As you saw in Chapter 2, perspective-taking is a key ingredient of thinking critically, and it can help you zero in on many problems as well. In the college finances problem, how would you describe the following perspectives?

   Your perspective:

   The college's perspective:

   Your parents' perspective:

2. ***Identify component problems.*** Larger problems are often composed of component problems. To define the larger problem, it is often necessary to identify and describe the subproblems that comprise it. For example, poor performance at school might be the result of a number of factors, such as ineffective study habits, inefficient time management, and preoccupation with a personal problem. Defining, and dealing effectively with, the larger problem means defining and dealing with the subproblems first. Identify possible subproblems in the sample problem:

   Subproblem a:

   Subproblem b:

3. ***State the problem clearly and specifically.*** A third defining strategy is to state the problem as clearly and specifically as possible, based on an examination of the results that need to be achieved to solve the problem. If you state the problem in very *general* terms, you won't have a clear idea of how best to proceed in dealing with it. But if you can describe your problem in more *specific* terms, then your description will begin to suggest actions you can take to solve the problem. Examine the differences between the statements of the following problem:

   General: "My problem is money."

   More specific: "My problem is budgeting my money so that I won't always run out near the end of the month."

   Most specific: "My problem is developing the habit and the discipline to budget my money so that I won't always run out near the end of the month."

Review your analysis of the sample problem and then define the problem as clearly and specifically as possible.

STEP 2: WHAT ARE THE ALTERNATIVES?

Once you have identified your problem clearly and specifically, your next move is to examine the possible actions that might help you solve the problem. Before you list the alternatives, determine first which actions are possible and which are impossible. You can do this by exploring the *boundaries* of the problem situation.

Step 2A: What Are the Boundaries of the Problem Situation? Boundaries are the limits in the problem situation that you cannot change. They are part of the problem, and they must be accepted and dealt with. At the same time, you must be careful not to identify as boundaries circumstances that can actually be changed. For instance, in the sample problem, you might assume that your problem must be solved in your current location without realizing that relocating to another, less expensive college is one of your options. Identify additional boundaries that might be part of the sample situation and some of the questions you would want to answer regarding these boundaries.

Step 2B: What Alternatives Are Possible Within These Boundaries? After you have established a general idea of the boundaries of the problem situation, identify the courses of action possible within these boundaries. Of course, identifying all the possible alternatives is not always easy; in fact, it may be part of your problem. Often we do not see a way out of a problem because our thinking is fixed in certain perspectives. This is an opportunity for you to make use of your creative thinking abilities. When people approach problems, they generally focus on the two or three obvious possibilities and then keep churning these around. Instead, a much more productive approach is to try to come up with ten, fifteen, or twenty alternatives, encouraging yourself to go beyond the obvious. In truth, the most inventive and insightful alternative is much more likely to be alternative number 17 or number 26 than it is number 2 or number 4. You can use several strategies to help you break out of conventional patterns of thought and encourage you to generate a full range of innovative possibilities:

1. *Discuss the problem with other people.* Discussing possible alternatives with others uses a number of the aspects of critical thinking you explored in Chapter 2, such as being open to seeing situations from different viewpoints and discussing your ideas with others in an organized way. As critical thinkers we live—and solve problems—in a community. Other people can often suggest possible alternatives that we haven't thought of, in part because they are outside the situation and thus have a more objective perspective, and in part because they view the world differently than we do, based on their past experiences and their personalities. In addition, discussions are often creative experiences that generate ideas. The dynamics of these interactions

often lead to ideas and solutions that are greater than the individual "sum" of those involved.

2. *Brainstorm ideas.* Brainstorming builds on the strengths of working with other people to generate ideas and solve problems. In a typical brainstorming session, a group of people work together to generate as many ideas as possible in a specific period of time. Ideas are not judged or evaluated because this tends to inhibit the free flow of ideas and discourages people from making suggestions. Evaluation is deferred until a later stage. A useful visual adjunct to brainstorming is creating mind maps, a process described in Chapter 7, "Forming and Applying Concepts."

3. *Change your location.* Your perspective on a problem is often tied to its location. Sometimes you need a fresh perspective; getting away from the location of the problem situation lets you view it with more clarity.

Using these strategies, identify alternatives to help solve the sample problem.

Thinking Critically About Visuals

"Necessity Is the Mother of Invention"

This photo is of a windmill designed and built by William Kamkwamba in 2003 in Masitala, a village in Malawi, Africa, for the purpose of generating power for his parents' home. At the time, Kamkwamba was just a teenager, and he researched and taught himself how to build the windmill all on his own using local scrap materials that he could find.

Lucas Oleniuk/The Toronto Star/zReportage.com/ZUMApress

This vividly illustrates the point that creative problem solving is both innovative and useful in a practical way, and that it often makes use of available materials—whatever they are—thus underscoring the wisdom of the statement "Necessity is the mother of invention." What other examples of creative innovation have you run into in the course of everyday life?

STEP 3: WHAT ARE THE ADVANTAGES AND/OR DISADVANTAGES OF EACH ALTERNATIVE?

Once you have identified the various alternatives, your next step is to *evaluate* them by using the evaluation questions described in Chapter 2. Each possible course of action has certain advantages, in the sense that if you select that alternative, there will be some positive results. At the same time, each of the possible courses of action likely has disadvantages, because selecting that alternative may involve a cost or a risk of negative results. Examine the potential advantages and/or disadvantages in order to determine how helpful each course of action would be.

Thinking Critically About Visuals

"I Have a Creative Idea!"

Most problems have more than one possible solution, and to discover the most creative ideas, we need to go beyond the obvious. Imagine that you are faced with the challenge of designing an enclosure that would protect an egg from breaking when dropped from a three-story building; then describe your own creative solution for this challenge. Where did your creative idea come from? How does it compare with the solutions of other students in your class?

AP Photo/The Murray Ledger & Times, Greg Travis

Step 3A: What Are the Advantages of Each Alternative? One alternative you may have listed in Step 2 for the sample problem might include the following advantages:

Alternative	Advantages
Attend college part-time	This would remove some of the immediate time and money pressures I am experiencing while still allowing me to prepare for the future. I would have more time to focus on the courses that I am taking and to work additional hours.

Identify the advantages of each of the alternatives that you listed in Step 2. Be sure that your responses are thoughtful and specific.

Step 3B: What Are the Disadvantages of Each Alternative? You also need to consider the disadvantages of each alternative. The alternative you listed for the sample problem might include the following disadvantages:

Alternatives	Disadvantages
Attend college part-time	It would take me much longer to complete my schooling, thus delaying my progress toward my goals. Also, I might lose motivation and drop out before completing school because the process would be taking so long. Being a part-time student might even threaten my eligibility for financial aid.

Now identify the disadvantages of each of the alternatives that you listed. Be sure that your responses are thoughtful and specific.

Step 3C: What Additional Information Do I Need to Evaluate Each Alternative? Determine what you must know (*information needed*) to evaluate and compare the alternatives. In addition, you need to figure out the best places to get this information (*sources*).

To identify the information you need, ask yourself the question "*What if* I select this alternative?" For instance, one alternative in the sample problem was "Attend college part-time." When you ask yourself the question "*What if* I attend college part-time?" you are trying to predict what will occur if you select this course of action. To make these predictions, you must find the information to answer certain questions:

- How long will it take me to complete my schooling?
- How long can I continue in school without losing interest and dropping out?
- Will I threaten my eligibility for financial aid if I become a part-time student?

Possible sources for this information include the following: myself, other part-time students, school counselors, the financial aid office.

Identify the information needed and the sources of this information for each of the alternatives that you identified. Be sure that your responses are thoughtful and specific.

STEP 4: WHAT IS THE SOLUTION?

The purpose of Steps 1 through 3 is to analyze your problem in a systematic and detailed fashion—to work through the problem in order to become thoroughly familiar with it and the possible solutions to it. Once the problem is broken down in this way, the final step should be to try to put the pieces back together—that is, to decide on a thoughtful course of action based on your increased understanding. Even though this sort of problem analysis does not guarantee finding a specific solution to the problem, it should *deepen your understanding* of exactly what the problem is about. And in locating and evaluating your alternatives, it should give you some very good ideas about the general direction you should move in and the immediate steps you should take.

Step 4A: Which Alternative(s) Will I Pursue? There is no simple formula or recipe to tell you which alternatives to select. As you work through the different courses of action that are possible, you may find that you can immediately rule some out. For example, in the sample problem, you may know with certainty that you do not want to attend college part-time (alternative 1) because you will forfeit your remaining financial aid. However, it may not be so simple to select which of the other alternatives you wish to pursue. How do you decide?

The decisions we make usually depend on what we believe to be most important to us. These beliefs regarding what is most important to us are known as *values*. Our values are the starting points of our actions and strongly influence our decisions. Our values help us *set priorities* in life. We might decide that, for the present, going to school is more important than having an active social life. In this case, going to school is a higher priority than having an active social life. Unfortunately, our values are not always consistent with each other—we may have to choose *either* to go to school or to have an active social life. Both activities may be important to us; they are simply not compatible with each other. Very often the *conflicts* between our values constitute the problem. Let's examine some strategies for selecting alternatives that might help us solve the problem.

1. *Evaluate and compare alternatives.* Although each alternative may have certain advantages and disadvantages, not all advantages are equally desirable

Thinking Critically About Visuals

"Why Didn't I Think of That?"

Many creative ideas—like Post-it Notes—seem obvious *after* they have been invented. The essence of creativity is thinking of innovative ideas *before* others do. Recall a time in your life when you were able to use your thinking abilities to come up with a creative solution to a problem, and share your creative solution with your classmates. Where do you think your creative idea came from?

Big Cheese Photo/Jupiter Images

or potentially effective. Thus it makes sense to evaluate and rank the various alternatives based on how effective they are likely to be and how they match up with your value system. A good place to begin is the "Results" stage, Step 1B. Examine each of the alternatives and evaluate how well it will contribute to achieving the results you are aiming for. Rank the alternatives or develop your own rating system to assess their relative effectiveness.

After evaluating the alternatives in terms of their anticipated *effectiveness*, the next step is to evaluate them in terms of their *desirability*, based on your needs, interests, and value system. After completing these two separate evaluations, select the alternative(s) that seem most appropriate. Review the alternatives you identified in the sample problem and then rank or rate them according to their potential effectiveness and desirability.

2. ***Combine alternatives.*** After reviewing and evaluating the alternatives, you may develop a new alternative that combines the best qualities of several options while avoiding their disadvantages. In the sample problem, you might combine attending college part-time during the academic year with attending school during the summer session so that progress toward your degree won't be impeded. Examine the alternatives you identified and develop a new option that combines their best elements.

3. ***Try out each alternative in your imagination.*** Focus on each alternative and try to imagine, as concretely as possible, what it would be like if you actually selected it. Visualize what impact your choice would have on your problem and what the implications would be for your life as a whole. By trying out the alternative in your imagination, you can sometimes avoid unpleasant results or unexpected consequences. As a variation of this strategy, you can sometimes test alternatives on a very limited basis in a practice situation. For example, if you are trying to overcome your fear of speaking in groups, you can practice various speaking techniques with your friends or family until you find an approach you are comfortable with.

After trying out these strategies on the sample problem, select the alternative(s) you think would be most effective and desirable.

Step 4B: What Steps Can I Take to Act on the Alternative(s) Chosen? Once you have decided on the correct alternative(s) to pursue, your next move is to *take action* by planning specific steps. In the sample problem, for example, imagine that one of the alternatives you have selected is "Find additional sources of income that will enable me to work part-time and go to school full-time." The specific steps you could take might include the following:

1. Contact the financial aid office at the school to see what other forms of financial aid are available and what you have to do to apply for them.
2. Contact some of the local banks to see what sorts of student loans are available.
3. Look for a higher-paying job so that you can earn more money without working additional hours.
4. Discuss the problem with students in similar circumstances in order to generate new ideas.

Identify the steps you would have to take in pursuing the alternative(s) you identified on pages 120–122.

Once you know what actions you have to take, you need to commit yourself to taking the necessary steps. This is where many people stumble in the problem-solving process, paralyzed by inertia or fear. Sometimes, to overcome these blocks and inhibitions, you need to reexamine your original acceptance of the problem, perhaps making use of some of the strategies you explored on pages 112–113. Once you get started, the rewards of actively attacking your problem are often enough incentive to keep you focused and motivated.

STEP 5: HOW WELL IS THE SOLUTION WORKING?

Any analysis of a problem situation, no matter how careful and systematic, is ultimately limited. You simply cannot anticipate or predict everything that is going to happen in the future. As a result, every decision you make is provisional, in the sense that your ongoing experience will inform you if your decisions are working out or if they need to be changed and modified. As you saw in Chapter 2, this is precisely the attitude of the critical thinker—someone who is *receptive* to new ideas and experiences and *flexible* enough to change or modify beliefs based on new information. Critical thinking is not a compulsion to find the "right" answer or make the "correct" decision; it is an ongoing process of exploration and discovery.

Step 5A: What Is My Evaluation? In many cases the relative effectiveness of your efforts will be apparent. In other cases it will be helpful to pursue a more systematic evaluation.

1. ***Compare the results with the goals.*** Compare the anticipated results of the alternative(s) you selected. To what extent will your choice(s) meet your goals? Are there goals that are not likely to be met by your alternative(s)? Which ones? Could they be addressed by other alternatives? Asking these and other questions will help you clarify the success of your efforts and provide a foundation for future decisions.

2. ***Get other perspectives.*** As you have seen throughout the problem-solving process, getting the opinions of others is a productive strategy at almost every stage, and this is certainly true for evaluation. It is not always easy to receive the evaluations of others, but maintaining open-mindedness toward outside opinions will stimulate and guide you to produce your best efforts.

   To receive specific, practical feedback from others, ask specific, practical questions that will elicit this information. General questions ("What do you think of this?") typically result in overly general, unhelpful responses ("It sounds okay to me"). Be focused in soliciting feedback, and remember: You do have the right to ask people to be *constructive* in their comments, providing suggestions for improvement rather than flatly expressing what they think is wrong.

Step 5B: What Adjustments Are Necessary? As a result of your review, you may discover that the alternative you selected is not feasible or is not leading to satisfactory results. At other times you may find that the alternative you selected is working out fairly well but still requires some adjustments as you continue to work toward your desired outcomes. In fact, this is a typical situation. Even when things initially appear to be working reasonably well, an active thinker continues to ask questions such as "What might I have overlooked?" and "How could I have done this differently?" Of course, asking—and trying to answer—questions like these is even more essential if solutions are hard to come by (as they usually are in real-world problems) and if you are to retain the flexibility and optimism you will need to tackle a new option.

Thinking Activity 3.2

ANALYZING AN UNSOLVED PROBLEM

Select a problem from your own life. It should be one that you are currently grappling with and have not yet been able to solve. After selecting the problem you want to work on, strengthen your acceptance of the problem by using one or more of the strategies described on pages 112–113 and describing your efforts. Then analyze your problem using the problem-solving method described in this chapter. Discuss your problem with other class members to generate fresh perspectives and unusual alternatives that might not have occurred to you. Write your analysis in outline style, giving specific responses to the questions in each step of the problem-solving method. Although you might not reach a "guaranteed" solution to your problem, you should deepen your understanding of the problem and develop a concrete plan of action that will help you move in the right direction. Implement your plan of action and then monitor the results.

Thinking Activity 3.3

ANALYZING COLLEGE PROBLEMS

Analyze the following problems using the problem-solving approach presented in this chapter.

Problem 1: Declaring a Major

The most important unsolved problem that exists for me is my inability to make that crucial decision of what to major in. I want to be secure with respect to both money and happiness when I make a career for myself, and I don't want to make a mistake in choosing a field of study. I want to make this decision before beginning the next semester so that I can start immediately in my career. I've been thinking about managerial studies. However, I often wonder if I have the capacity to make executive decisions when I can't even decide on what I want to do with my life.

Problem 2: Taking Tests

One of my problems is my difficulty in taking tests. It's not that I don't study. What happens is that when I get the test, I become nervous and my mind goes blank. For example, in my art history class, the teacher told the class a week in advance about an upcoming test. That afternoon I went home and began studying for the test. By the day of the test I thought I knew all of the material, but when the teacher began the test by showing slides of art pieces we were to identify, I became nervous and my mind went blank. I ended up failing it.

Problem 3: Learning English

One of the serious problems in my life is learning English as a second language. It is not so easy to learn a second language, especially when you live in an environment where only your native language is spoken. When I came to this country three years ago, I could speak almost no English. I have learned a lot, but my lack of fluency is getting in the way of my studies and my ability to do as well as I am capable of doing.

Solving Nonpersonal Problems

The problems we have analyzed up to this point have been "personal" problems in the sense that they represent individual challenges encountered by us as we live our lives. We also face problems as members of a community, a society, and the world. As with personal problems, we need to approach these kinds of problems in an organized and thoughtful way in order to explore the issues, develop a clear understanding, and decide on an informed plan of action.

Making sense of a complex, challenging situation is not a simple process. Although the problem-solving method we have been using in this chapter is a powerful approach, its successful application depends on having sufficient information about the situation we are trying to solve. As a result, it is often necessary for us to research articles and other sources of information to develop informed opinions.

The famous newspaper journalist H. L. Mencken once said, "To every complex question there is a simple answer—and it's clever, neat, and wrong!" Complex problems do not admit simple solutions, whether they concern personal problems in our lives or larger social problems like racial prejudice or world hunger. However, we should have the confidence that by working through these complex problems thoughtfully and systematically, we can achieve a deeper understanding of their many interacting elements as well as develop strategies for solving them.

Becoming an effective problem solver does not merely involve applying a problem-solving method in a mechanical fashion any more than becoming a mature critical thinker involves mastering a set of thinking skills. Rather, solving problems, like thinking critically, reflects a total approach to making sense of experience. When we think like problem solvers, we have the courage to meet difficult problems head-on and the determination to work through them. Instead of acting impulsively or relying exclusively on the advice of others, we are able to make sense of complex problems in an organized way and develop practical solutions and initiatives.

A sophisticated problem solver employs all of the critical-thinking abilities that we have examined so far and those we will explore in the chapters ahead. And while we might agree with H. L. Mencken's evaluation of simple answers to complex questions, we might endorse a rephrased version: "To many complex questions there are complex answers—and these are worth pursuing!"

Thinking Activity 3.4

ANALYZING SOCIAL PROBLEMS

Identify an important local, national, or international problem that needs to be solved. Locate two or more articles that provide background information and analysis of the problem. Using these articles as a resource, analyze the problem using the problem-solving method developed in this chapter.

Thinking Critically About Visuals

Advertising to Change Behavior

These ads are part of a campaign to eradicate the increasingly serious problem of people texting while they drive, a practice that often leads to accidents and sometimes fatalities. What is your reaction to each of these ads: do you think they would be effective in discouraging people to text while driving? The first ad makes the arresting claim that texting is equivalent to murder and is accompanied with a graphic photo. Do you agree with this claim? Why or why not? What is the flaw in people's thinking that enables them to engage in dangerous or self-destructive behaviors while ignoring the potential consequences of these actions?

texting and driving...

... it's really murder

Ian Shewan/Alamy

Examine the second ad carefully. In what ways is the approach it takes different than that of the first ad? Do you find it to be more or less effective? Why? The approach of this ad is to replicate the often random and unfocused thinking process that often precedes an accident. Do you think this is an accurate portrayal of what actually takes place in people's minds when they are texting and driving?

We can analyze texting and driving as a problem to be solved. Go back to the five steps (page 107) for thinking effectively about a problem. At which step would ads like these be helpful, and why? Conversely, would these ads perhaps not be effective in solving this problem? Why not? Imagine that you are a member of an advertising company hired to create an ad to attack this problem. What kind of ad would you create? Why? If time permits, your teacher may give you and your classmates an opportunity to work in small groups to actually create such an ad.

Bausmith KRT/Newscom

THINKING CRITICALLY ABOUT NEW MEDIA

Surfing Dangers and Addictions

Using the power and opportunities afforded by new media is intoxicating—but it is also potentially problematic. In the last chapter we explored the difficulties we can encounter when dealing with others on the Net. But you may encounter threats and challenges just by virtue of spending a lot of time online. These threats and challenges can be dealt with effectively if we take an informed, problem-solving approach, but we first have to be aware of what the dangers are.

To begin with, using the various aspects of new media can be addictive in the same way that watching television can be addictive. For example, have you ever found yourself "hypnotized" by the television, watching shows that you're not even that interested in? There are a variety of visual and psychological reasons why it's so difficult to stop watching television, many of which apply to the computer screen as well. Unlike real life, where we take in a tiny part of the visual panorama around us with the fovea (the sharp-focusing part of the eye), when we watch television we take in the entire frame of the image with our sharp foveal vision, making the experience more visually fascinating. Similarly, again in contrast to real life, the images on the screen are dynamic and almost always moving, creating an attention-grabbing bond that is difficult to tear ourselves away from. This continual eye movement as we watch activity on screens also causes the eye to defocus slightly, a physiological activity that typically accompanies various fantasy, daydreaming, and drug-induced states. As Marie Winn, in her seminal work *The Plug-In Drug*, observes: "This may very well be a reason for the trancelike nature of so many viewers' television experience, and may help to explain why the television image has so strong and hypnotic a fascination."

These same factors are at work whether we are watching a television screen or a computer screen. The difference is that new media are *interactive*: we can roam around the Net at will, follow an infinite succession of links and websites, and communicate with as many people as we wish to. It's no wonder that once we start our fingertips moving on the computer or communication device we're using, it's very difficult to get those fingers to stop. Although a certain amount of the time we spend engaged with new media is productive, much of it is not particularly useful, and it prevents us from engaging in other activities that *would* be more enriching and productive.

As with any addiction, seeking a solution involves recognizing that there *is* a problem and then using a problem-solving methodology like the one introduced in this chapter. Certainly a good place to begin is by strictly scheduling and limiting the time we spend "surfing" online or engaged in social exchanges. This is particularly true when it comes to email and text messaging. And if we're engaged in a real-world activity, it's useful to discipline ourselves by checking for messages every hour or so rather than reading and responding to them as they come in. Research has shown that leaving and then returning to the activity in which you were engaged is a tremendous time-waster.

A more subtle threat to our well-being is described in the article on page 130, "Is Google Making Us Stupid?" in which the author, Nicholas Carr, explores whether our immersion in new media is restructuring the way we think and process information, making it more difficult for us to concentrate on activities like reading for a lengthy period of time, spending time in quiet contemplation of important issues, or thinking in deep and complex ways. As Carr, a writer, explains: "Once I was a scuba diver in the sea of words. Now I zip along the surface like a guy on a Jet Ski."

Thinking Activity 3.5

READING PRINT VS. READING ONLINE

In anticipation of reading the following article, "Is Google Making Us Stupid?" perform the following reading "experiment" to explore the differences between print and online reading. Select a news source that has both a print version and an online version such as *The New York Times, Washington Post, Chicago Tribune,* or *The Los Angeles Times.*

First read the online version, selecting and reading the articles of interest as you normally would. Then read the print version of the same publication but on a different date. What differences did you find between the two experiences? For example, did you find that

- you spent more time reading one of the versions?
- one version provided you with the more detailed and developed information?
- one version exposed you to a greater variety of topics and stories?
- one version more deeply engaged you in the process of reading and thinking?
- One version resulted in a greater recall of what you had read?

After responding to these questions, analyze what factors accounted for the different experiences.

Thinking Passage

THE INFLUENCE OF NEW MEDIA

In the following provocative article, "Is Google Making Us Stupid?" the writer Nicholas Carr wonders if the culture's pervasive use of the Web-based new media is restructuring the way that we think, making it more difficult for us to concentrate, contemplate, and read lengthy, complex books and articles. The author's concern is that using the Web encourages us to jump quickly from link to link, spending little time at any one particular place to think deeply and analytically about the ideas we are considering. Is this a problem about which we ought to be concerned? After carefully reading and thinking about the article, answer the questions that follow.

Is Google Making Us Stupid?

by Nicholas Carr

"Dave, stop. Stop, will you? Stop, Dave. Will you stop, Dave?" So the supercomputer HAL pleads with the implacable astronaut Dave Bowman in a famous and weirdly poignant scene toward the end of Stanley Kubrick's *2001: A Space Odyssey.* Bowman, having nearly been sent to a deep-space death by the malfunctioning machine, is calmly, coldly disconnecting the memory circuits that control its artificial "brain." "Dave, my mind is going," HAL says, forlornly. "I can feel it. I can feel it."

I can feel it, too. Over the past few years I've had an uncomfortable sense that someone, or something, has been tinkering with my brain, remapping the neural circuitry, reprogramming the memory. My mind isn't going—so far as I can tell—but it's changing. I'm not thinking the way I used to think. I can feel it most strongly when I'm reading. Immersing myself in a book or a lengthy article used to be easy. My mind would get caught up in the narrative or the turns of the argument, and I'd spend hours strolling through long stretches of prose. That's rarely the case anymore. Now my concentration often starts to drift after two or three pages. I get fidgety, lose the thread, begin looking for something else to do. I feel as if I'm always dragging my wayward brain back to the text. The deep reading that used to come naturally has become a struggle.

I think I know what's going on. For more than a decade now, I've been spending a lot of time online, searching and surfing and sometimes adding to the great databases of the Internet. The Web has been a godsend to me as a writer. Research that once required days in the stacks or periodical rooms of libraries can now be done in minutes. A few Google searches, some quick clicks on hyperlinks, and I've got the telltale fact or pithy quote I was after. Even when I'm not working, I'm as likely as not to be foraging in the Web's info-thickets reading and writing e-mails, scanning headlines and blog posts, watching videos and listening to podcasts, or just tripping from link to link to link. (Unlike footnotes, to which they're sometimes likened, hyperlinks don't merely point to related works; they propel you toward them.)

Source: "Is Google Making Us Stupid?" by Nicholas Carr, *The Atlantic,* July/August 2008. Reprinted by permission of the author.

For me, as for others, the Net is becoming a universal medium, the conduit for most of the information that flows through my eyes and ears and into my mind. The advantages of having immediate access to such an incredibly rich store of information are many, and they've been widely described and duly applauded. "The perfect recall of silicon memory," *Wired's* Clive Thompson has written, "can be an enormous boon to thinking." But that boon comes at a price. As the media theorist Marshall McLuhan pointed out in the 1960s, media are not just passive channels of information. They supply the stuff of thought, but they also shape the process of thought. And what the Net seems to be doing is chipping away my capacity for concentration and contemplation. My mind now expects to take in information the way the Net distributes it: in a swiftly moving stream of particles. Once I was a scuba diver in the sea of words. Now I zip along the surface like a guy on a Jet Ski.

I'm not the only one. When I mention my troubles with reading to friends and acquaintances—literary types, most of them—many say they're having similar experiences. The more they use the Web, the more they have to fight to stay focused on long pieces of writing. Some of the bloggers I follow have also begun mentioning the phenomenon. Scott Karp, who writes a blog about online media, recently confessed that he has stopped reading books altogether. "I was a lit major in college, and used to be [a] voracious book reader," he wrote. "What happened?" He speculates on the answer: "What if I do all my reading on the web not so much because the way I read has changed, i.e., I'm just seeking convenience, but because the way I THINK has changed?"

. . .

Anecdotes alone don't prove much. And we still await the long-term neurological and psychological experiments that will provide a definitive picture of how Internet use affects cognition. But a recently published study of online research habits, conducted by scholars from University College London, suggests that we may well be in the midst of a sea change in the way we read and think. . . . They found that people using the sites exhibited "a form of skimming activity," hopping from one source to another and rarely returning to any source they'd already visited. They typically read no more than one or two pages of an article or book before they would "bounce" out to another site. Sometimes they'd save a long article, but there's no evidence that they ever went back and actually read it. The authors of the study report:

> It is clear that users are not reading online in the traditional sense; indeed there are signs that new forms of "reading" are emerging as users "power browse" horizontally through titles, contents pages and abstracts going for quick wins. It almost seems that they go online to avoid reading in the traditional sense.

Thanks to the ubiquity of text on the Internet, not to mention the popularity of text-messaging on cell phones, we may well be reading more today than we did in the 1970s or 1980s, when television was our medium of choice. But it's a different kind of reading, and behind it lies a different kind of thinking—perhaps even a new sense of the self. "We are not only what we read," says Maryanne Wolf, a developmental psychologist at Tufts University and the author of *Proust and the Squid: The Story and Science of the Reading Brain*. "We are how we read." Wolf worries that the style of reading promoted by the Net, a style that puts "efficiency" and "immediacy" above all else, may be weakening our capacity for the kind of deep reading that emerged when an earlier technology, the printing press, made long and complex works of prose commonplace. When we read online, she says, we tend to become "mere decoders of information." Our ability to interpret text, to make the rich mental connections that form when we read deeply and without distraction, remains largely disengaged.

Reading, explains Wolf, is not an instinctive skill for human beings. It's not etched into our genes the way speech is. We have to teach our minds how to translate the symbolic characters we see into the language we understand. And the media or other technologies we use in learning and practicing the craft of reading play an important part in shaping the neural circuits inside our brains. Experiments demonstrate that readers of ideograms, such as the Chinese, develop a mental circuitry for reading that is very different from the circuitry found in those of us whose written language employs an alphabet. The variations extend across many regions of the brain, including those that govern such essential cognitive functions as memory and the interpretation of visual and auditory stimuli. We can expect as well that the circuits woven by our use of the Net will be different from those woven by our reading of books and other printed works.

Sometime in 1882, Friedrich Nietzsche bought a typewriter—a Malling-Hansen Writing Ball, to be precise. His vision was failing, and keeping his eyes focused on a page had become exhausting and painful, often bringing on crushing headaches. He had been forced to curtail his writing, and he feared that he would soon have to give it up. The typewriter rescued him, at least for a time. Once he had mastered touch-typing, he was able to write with his eyes closed, using only the tips of his fingers. Words could once again flow from his mind to the page.

But the machine had a subtle effect on his work. One of Nietzsche's friends, a composer, noticed a change in the style of his writing. His already terse prose had become even tighter, more telegraphic. "Perhaps you will through this instrument even take to a new idiom," the friend wrote in a letter, noting that, in his own work, his "'thoughts' in music and language often depend on the quality of pen and paper."

"You are right," Nietzsche replied, "our writing equipment takes part in the forming of our thoughts." Under the sway of the machine, writes the German media scholar Friedrich A. Kittler, Nietzsche's prose "changed from arguments to aphorisms, from thoughts to puns, from rhetoric to telegram style."

The human brain is almost infinitely malleable. People used to think that our mental meshwork, the dense connections formed among the 100 billion or so neurons inside our skulls, was largely fixed by the time we reached adulthood. But brain researchers have discovered that that's not the case. James Olds, a professor of neuroscience who directs the Krasnow Institute for Advanced Study at George Mason University, says that even the adult mind "is very plastic." Nerve cells routinely break old connections and form new ones. "The brain," according to Olds, "has the ability to reprogram itself on the fly, altering the way it functions."

As we use what the sociologist Daniel Bell has called our "intellectual technologies"—the tools that extend our mental rather than our physical capacities— we inevitably begin to take on the qualities of those technologies. The mechanical clock, which came into common use in the 14th century, provides a compelling example. In Technics and Civilization, the historian and cultural critic Lewis Mumford described how the clock "disassociated time from human events and helped create the belief in an independent world of mathematically measurable sequences." The "abstract framework of divided time" became "the point of reference for both action and thought."

The clock's methodical ticking helped bring into being the scientific mind and the scientific man. But it also took something away. As the late MIT computer scientist

Joseph Weizenbaum observed in his 1976 book, *Computer Power and Human Reason: From Judgment to Calculation*, the conception of the world that emerged from the widespread use of timekeeping instruments "remains an impoverished version of the older one, for it rests on a rejection of those direct experiences that formed the basis for, and indeed constituted, the old reality." In deciding when to eat, to work, to sleep, to rise, we stopped listening to our senses and started obeying the clock.

The process of adapting to new intellectual technologies is reflected in the changing metaphors we use to explain ourselves to ourselves. When the mechanical clock arrived, people began thinking of their brains as operating "like clockwork." Today, in the age of software, we have come to think of them as operating "like computers." But the changes, neuroscience tells us, go much deeper than metaphor. Thanks to our brain's plasticity, the adaptation occurs also at a biological level.

The Internet promises to have particularly far-reaching effects on cognition. In a paper published in 1936, the British mathematician Alan Turing proved that a digital computer, which at the time existed only as a theoretical machine, could be programmed to perform the function of any other information-processing device. And that's what we're seeing today. The Internet, an immeasurably powerful computing system, is subsuming most of our other intellectual technologies. It's becoming our map and our clock, our printing press and our typewriter, our calculator and our telephone, and our radio and TV.

When the Net absorbs a medium, that medium is re-created in the Net's image. It injects the medium's content with hyperlinks, blinking ads, and other digital gewgaws, and it surrounds the content with the content of all the other media it has absorbed. A new e-mail message, for instance, may announce its arrival as we're glancing over the latest headlines at a newspaper's site. The result is to scatter our attention and diffuse our concentration.

The Net's influence doesn't end at the edges of a computer screen. . . . As people's minds become attuned to the crazy quilt of Internet media, traditional media have to adapt to the audience's expectations. Television programs add text crawls and pop-up ads, and magazines and newspapers shorten their articles, introduce capsule summaries, and crowd their pages with easy-to-browse info-snippets. When, in March of this year, *The New York Times* decided to devote the second and third pages of every edition to article abstracts, its design director, Tom Bodkin, explained that the "shortcuts" would give harried readers a quick "taste" of the day's news, sparing them the "less efficient" method of actually turning the pages and reading the articles. Old media have little choice but to play by the new-media rules.

Never has a communications system played so many roles in our lives—or exerted such broad influence over our thoughts—as the Internet does today. Yet, for all that's been written about the Net, there's been little consideration of how, exactly, it's reprogramming us. The Net's intellectual ethic remains obscure.

About the same time that Nietzsche started using his typewriter, an earnest young man named Frederick Winslow Taylor carried a stopwatch into the Midvale Steel plant in Philadelphia and began a historic series of experiments aimed at improving the efficiency of the plant's machinists.

· · ·

Once his system was applied to all acts of manual labor, Taylor assured his followers, it would bring about a restructuring not only of industry but of society, creating a utopia of perfect efficiency. "In the past the man has been first," he declared; "in the future the system must be first."

Taylor's system is still very much with us; it remains the ethic of industrial manufacturing. And now, thanks to the growing power that computer engineers and software coders wield over our intellectual lives, Taylor's ethic is beginning to govern the realm of the mind as well. The Internet is a machine designed for the efficient and automated collection, transmission, and manipulation of information, and its legions of programmers are intent on finding the "one best method"—the perfect algorithm—to carry out every mental movement of what we've come to describe as "knowledge work."

. . .

Google has declared that its mission is "to organize the world's information and make it universally accessible and useful." It seeks to develop "the perfect search engine," which it defines as something that "understands exactly what you mean and gives you back exactly what you want." In Google's view, information is a kind of commodity, a utilitarian resource that can be mined and processed with industrial efficiency. The more pieces of information we can "access" and the faster we can extract their gist, the more productive we become as thinkers.

Where does it end? Sergey Brin and Larry Page, the gifted young men who founded Google while pursuing doctoral degrees in computer science at Stanford, speak frequently of their desire to turn their search engine into an artificial intelligence, a HAL-like machine that might be connected directly to our brains. "The ultimate search engine is something as smart as people—or smarter," Page said in a speech a few years back. "For us, working on search is a way to work on artificial intelligence." In a 2004 interview with *Newsweek*, Brin said, "Certainly if you had all the world's information directly attached to your brain, or an artificial brain that was smarter than your brain, you'd be better off." Last year, Page told a convention of scientists that Google is "really trying to build artificial intelligence and to do it on a large scale."

Such an ambition is a natural one, even an admirable one, for a pair of math whizzes with vast quantities of cash at their disposal and a small army of computer scientists in their employ. A fundamentally scientific enterprise, Google is motivated by a desire to use technology, in Eric Schmidt's words, "to solve problems that have never been solved before," and artificial intelligence is the hardest problem out there. Why wouldn't Brin and Page want to be the ones to crack it?

Still, their easy assumption that we'd all "be better off" if our brains were supplemented, or even replaced, by an artificial intelligence is unsettling. It suggests a belief that intelligence is the output of a mechanical process, a series of discrete steps that can be isolated, measured, and optimized. In Google's world, the world we enter when we go online, there's little place for the fuzziness of contemplation. Ambiguity is not an opening for insight but a bug to be fixed. The human brain is just an outdated computer that needs a faster processor and a bigger hard drive.

The idea that our minds should operate as high-speed data-processing machines is not only built into the workings of the Internet, it is the network's reigning business model as well. The faster we surf across the Web—the more links we click and pages we view—the more opportunities Google and other companies gain to collect information about us and to feed us advertisements. Most of the proprietors of the commercial Internet have a financial stake in collecting the crumbs of data we leave behind as we flit from link to link—the more crumbs, the better. The last thing these companies want is to encourage leisurely reading or slow, concentrated thought. It's in their economic interest to drive us to distraction.

Roz Chast/The New Yorker Collection/www.cartoonbank.com

Maybe I'm just a worrywart. Just as there's a tendency to glorify technological progress, there's a countertendency to expect the worst of every new tool or machine. In Plato's *Phaedrus*, Socrates bemoaned the development of writing. He feared that, as people came to rely on the written word as a substitute for the knowledge they used to carry inside their heads, they would, in the words of one of the dialogue's characters, "cease to exercise their memory and become forgetful." And because they would be able to "receive a quantity of information without proper instruction," they would "be thought very knowledgeable when they are for the most part quite ignorant." They would be "filled with the conceit of wisdom instead of real wisdom." Socrates wasn't wrong—the new technology did often have the effects he feared—but he was shortsighted. He couldn't foresee the many ways that writing and reading would serve to spread information, spur fresh ideas, and expand human knowledge (if not wisdom).

The arrival of Gutenberg's printing press, in the 15th century, set off another round of teeth gnashing. The Italian humanist Hieronimo Squarciafico worried that the easy availability of books would lead to intellectual laziness, making men "less studious" and weakening their minds. Others argued that cheaply printed books and broadsheets would undermine religious authority, demean the work of scholars and scribes, and spread sedition and debauchery. As New York University professor Clay Shirky notes, "Most of the arguments made against the printing press were correct, even prescient." But, again, the doomsayers were unable to imagine the myriad blessings that the printed word would deliver.

So, yes, you should be skeptical of my skepticism. Perhaps those who dismiss critics of the Internet as Luddites or nostalgists will be proved correct, and from our hyperactive, data-stoked minds will spring a golden age of intellectual discovery and universal wisdom. Then again, the Net isn't the alphabet, and although it may replace the printing press, it produces something altogether different. The kind of deep reading that a sequence of printed pages promotes is valuable not just for the knowledge we acquire from the author's words but for the intellectual vibrations those words set off within our own minds. In the quiet spaces opened up by the sustained, undistracted reading of a book, or by any other act of contemplation, for that matter, we make our own associations, draw our own inferences and analogies, foster our own ideas. Deep reading, as Maryanne Wolf argues, is indistinguishable from deep thinking.

If we lose those quiet spaces, or fill them up with "content," we will sacrifice something important not only in our selves but in our culture. In a recent essay, the playwright Richard Foreman eloquently described what's at stake:

> I come from a tradition of Western culture, in which the ideal (my ideal) was the complex, dense, and "cathedral-like" structure of the highly educated and articulate personality— a man or woman who carried inside themselves a personally constructed and unique version of the entire heritage of the West. [But now] I see within us all (myself included) the replacement of complex inner density with a new kind of self—evolving under the pressure of information overload and the technology of the "instantly available."

As we are drained of our "inner repertory of dense cultural inheritance," Foreman concluded, we risk turning into "'pancake people'—spread wide and thin as we connect with that vast network of information accessed by the mere touch of a button."

I'm haunted by that scene in *2001*. What makes it so poignant, and so weird, is the computer's emotional response to the disassembly of its mind: its despair as one circuit after another goes dark, its childlike pleading with the astronaut—"I can feel it. I can feel it. I'm afraid"—and its final reversion to what can only be called a state of innocence. HAL's outpouring of feeling contrasts with the emotionlessness that characterizes the human figures in the film, who go about their business with an almost robotic efficiency. Their thoughts and actions feel scripted, as if they're following the steps of an algorithm. In the world of *2001*, people have become so machinelike that the most human character turns out to be a machine. That's the essence of Kubrick's dark prophecy: as we come to rely on computers to mediate our understanding of the world, it is our own intelligence that flattens into artificial intelligence.

QUESTIONS FOR ANALYSIS

1. Have you noticed in your own life that it's easier for you to move quickly around the Web than to spend concentrated time reading a book or lengthy article? Writing an extended essay or letter? Concentrating on an issue or problem for an extended period of time? Describe your experiences with both surfing the Web and reading books and lengthy articles in this regard.

2. The author notes that "The Web has been a godsend to me as a writer. Research that once required days in the stacks or periodical rooms of libraries can now be done in minutes." Do the powerful advantages of using the Internet necessarily mean that we have to sacrifice our ability to read deeply and think reflectively?

3. The author acknowledges that "the Net is becoming a universal medium, the conduit for most of the information that flows through my eyes and ears and into my mind" and that this puts him at risk for being a "mere decoder of information" rather than a deep thinker *about* information. Would you say that this is true for you as well? Why or why not?

4. Imagine that you are the president of your college and that you want students to use the full power of the Internet in their education but you also wish them to develop their abilities to think deeply, concentrate, and contemplate. Using the problem-solving method in this chapter, analyze this problem and develop some practical solutions for dealing with this challenge.

Reviewing and Viewing

Summary

We can become more effective *problem solvers* by approaching complex problems in an organized way:

- Have I accepted the problem and committed myself to solving it?
- Step 1: What is the problem?
- Step 2: What are the alternatives?
- Step 3: What are the advantages and/or disadvantages of each alternative?
- Step 4: What is the solution?
- Step 5: How well is the solution working?

This approach to solving problems is effective not only for problems that we experience personally but also for problems that we face as citizens of a community, a society, and the world.

Assessing Your Strategies and Creating New Goals

How Expert a Problem Solver Am I?

Described below are key personal attributes that are correlated with being an expert problem solver. Evaluate your position regarding each of these attributes, and use this self-evaluation to guide your choices as you shape the type of problem solver that you want to become.

Accept the Problem

I willingly acknowledge my problems and commit myself to solving them.	I often evade my problems and fail to follow through in solving them.
5　　4　　3　　2　　1	

"Accepting" a problem means saying honestly, and without excuse, *"Yes, I have a problem, and I am committed to do what it takes to solve it."* It's amazing how resistant people are to making this simple, courageous statement.

Strategy: Using the list of problems that you developed in the first question, create a timetable for solving each one. If you find that you are having particular difficulty in acknowledging or committing yourself to one or another problem, review the strategies for Accepting the Problem described on pages 112–113 to ignite your determination.

Define the Problem Clearly

I get to the "heart" of problems and define them clearly.	I often get confused trying to identify the "real" problem.
5 4 3 2 1	

Many people end up going round and round on problems because they are unable to penetrate beneath the surface to the "real" problems. They skate on the surface, mistaking the *symptoms* for the problem itself. As a critical thinker, you should distrust the simplest explanation of a problem, always asking yourself *"What are some underlying causes of the problem?" "What are some issues that I might be overlooking?" "Are there ways of looking at this that I haven't considered?"*

Strategy: By developing your abilities as a critical thinker, you will naturally learn to look beyond the superficial explanations to a more sophisticated understanding. You can also use the strategies described in Step 1: What Is the Problem? on pages 113–116, including specifying the results, identifying component problems, and viewing the problem from multiple perspectives.

Generate Many Alternatives

I usually come up with many diverse alternatives for solving a problem.	I generally focus on just two or three alternatives in solving a problem.
5 4 3 2 1	

Expert problem solvers have lively, fertile minds that identify many different options for solving a problem. Rather than stopping at the obvious alternatives, they push themselves to think of many additional possibilities, using their creative talents to generate inventive and unique options. They also view other people as resources for helping them think of alternatives they might not have come up with on their own.

Strategy: When analyzing a problem, set a goal of generating ten, fifteen, or twenty alternatives, forcing yourself to break out of fixed mental ruts and go beyond the obvious to identify unusual possibilities. The section on Becoming More Creative in Chapter 1, pages 27–32, will help you unleash your creative potential in every area of life.

Evaluate the Alternatives Thoughtfully

I evaluate alternatives in an organized way.	I use my intuition to pick the best alternative.
5 4 3 2 1	

While *creative thinking* plays the main role in generating many diverse alternatives, your *critical thinking* abilities come into play in evaluating the viability of these alternatives: advantages, disadvantages, further information needed. If you start evaluating too early, when you are still generating possibilities, you run the risk of shutting off the creative flow. However, having generated the potential alternatives, if you *fail* to evaluate them in a rigorous and organized way, then you have no basis on which to reach an informed solution. Intuitions are only reliable when they are based on a great deal of thoughtful reflection and analysis.

Strategy: *It is essential to evaluate these alternatives in a disciplined and organized way in order to reach an intelligent conclusion. This rigorous analysis is the mark of an expert problem solver as much as the ability to create inventive possibilities.*

Reach Intelligent Solutions

I am skilled at finding solutions for my problems.	I consistently have difficulty in reaching solutions.
5 4 3 2 1	

While many people are perfectly willing to perform a thoughtful analysis of their problems, they often seem paralyzed when it comes time to synthesize their ideas and commit themselves to a course of action. Why? Perhaps they lack confidence in their own thinking abilities or are reluctant to take the risks that come with taking action. Whatever the reason, a chronic inability to forge a solution and commit yourself to a plan of action is a serious disability, virtually guaranteeing a life of frustration, regret, and unfulfilled dreams.

Strategy: *If you have difficulty in reaching solutions and taking action to implement your plan, treat this chronic inability as a problem and use the problem-solving method to analyze it: What is the problem? Is it lack of confidence, lack of clarity, or lack of will? What are your alternatives? And so on.*

Make Necessary Adjustments

I take a flexible approach to making adjustments and trying new alternatives.	I tend to stick with my original plans, even when they run into difficulties.
5 4 3 2 1	

As important as it is to commit yourself to a solution with determination, it is equally important to keep an open and critical mind as you implement your ideas. In most cases your solution will need adjustments, which you should willingly make.

Strategy: *Commit yourself to your solutions wholeheartedly, but begin monitoring the results of your plan immediately. Make the necessary adjustments to adapt to* *unforeseen circumstances. If it becomes clear that your solution is not working, move quickly and decisively to implement a new solution, informed by what you have learned. Solving problems is a process, and the important thing is to keep moving forward in a positive direction, not stubbornly reenacting the Charge of the Light Brigade.*

Suggested Films

Gandhi (1982)

In the face of unjust laws, how can one effectively protest? Is it possible to achieve justice without the use of force? This film portrays the life of Mahatma Gandhi, who successfully addressed the problem of gaining human rights without violence when he used peaceful means to free India from British colonial rule in the first half of the twentieth century.

Hotel Rwanda (2004)

What happens when a government fails to protect its people? What responsibility do individuals have to involve themselves in issues of social justice, and what is the appropriate way to do so? In this historical film, a single man uses his social position, charisma, and intelligence to save thousands of people from the Rwandan genocide. He displays the far-reaching effects an individual can have when thinking critically to solve complex social problems.

Lord of the Flies (1963 and 1990)

Are humans fundamentally predisposed to selfishness, destruction, and a kind of crude "state of nature"? Based on the allegorical novel by William Golding, these two film versions chronicle the events that occur when a group of military students are stranded on an island after a plane crash.

Slumdog Millionaire (2008)

Is it possible to obtain freedom in spite of economic, social, and physical constraints? Jamal Malik, a teenager growing up in the slums of Mumbai, is one question away from winning India's equivalent of *"Who Wants to Be a Millionaire?"* when he is accused of cheating. Jamal recounts his life story to his interrogators in an attempt to prove that he has, in fact, acquired the knowledge necessary to be successful in spite of a challenging background, limited education, and limited resources. The story Jamal tells is one of tremendous hardship in which his ability to innovatively problem solve enables him to not only survive but, ultimately, triumph.

Welcome to Sarajevo (1997)

Does a country ever have an ethical right and/or responsibility to intercede in the affairs of another country? A British journalist travels to Sarajevo at the beginning of the Bosnian War, where he encounters firsthand the suffering of the people there. He also discovers an orphanage near the front line and attempts to rescue one of the children by taking her back to England with him.

Things aren't always what they seem! This "Mae West Room" in the Salvador Dali museum illustrates the complex and surprising nature of the process of perceiving and making sense of our world. How do we develop clear and accurate perceptions of the world that are not biased or slanted toward one perspective?

Perceiving and Believing

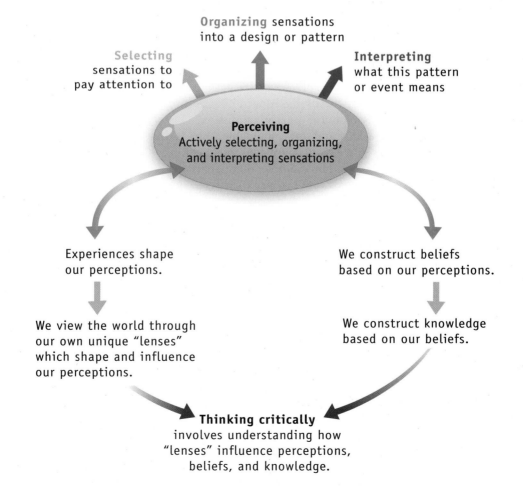

Organizing sensations
into a design or pattern

Selecting
sensations to
pay attention to

Interpreting
what this pattern
or event means

Perceiving
Actively selecting, organizing,
and interpreting sensations

Experiences shape
our perceptions.

We construct beliefs
based on our perceptions.

We view the world through
our own unique "lenses"
which shape and influence
our perceptions.

We construct knowledge
based on our beliefs.

Thinking critically
involves understanding how
"lenses" influence perceptions,
beliefs, and knowledge.

Thinking is the way you make sense of the world. By thinking in an active, purposeful, and organized way, you are able to solve problems, work toward your goals, analyze issues, and make decisions. Your experience of the world comes to you by means of your *senses*: sight, hearing, smell, touch, and taste. These senses are your bridges to the world, making you aware of what occurs outside you; the process of becoming aware of your world through your senses is known as *perceiving*.

In this chapter you will explore the way your perceiving process operates, how your perceptions lead to the construction of your beliefs about the world, and how both your perceptions and your beliefs relate to your ability to think effectively. In particular, you will discover the way you shape your personal experience by actively selecting, organizing, and interpreting the sensations provided by the senses. In a way, each of us views the world through a pair of individual "eyeglasses" or "contact lenses" that reflect our past experiences and unique personalities. As a critical thinker, you want to become aware of the nature of your own "lenses" to help eliminate any bias or distortion they may be causing. You also want to become aware of the "lenses" of others so that you can better understand why they view things the way they do.

At almost every waking moment of your life, your senses are being bombarded by a tremendous number of stimuli: images to see, noises to hear, odors to smell, textures to feel, and flavors to taste. The experience of all these sensations happening at once creates what the nineteenth-century American philosopher William James called "a bloomin' buzzin' confusion." Yet for us, the world usually seems much more orderly and understandable. Why is this so?

In the first place, your sense equipment can receive sensations only within certain limited ranges. For example, there are many sounds and smells that animals can detect but you cannot because their sense organs have broader ranges in these areas than yours do.

A second reason you can handle this sensory bombardment is that from the stimulation available, you *select* only a small amount on which to focus your attention. To demonstrate this, try the following exercise. Concentrate on what you can *see*, ignoring your other senses for the moment. Focus on sensations that you were not previously aware of and then answer the first question. Concentrate on each of your other senses in turn, following the same procedure.

1. What can you *see*? (e.g., the shape of the letters on the page, the design of the clothing on your arm)

2. What can you *hear*? (e.g., the hum of the air conditioner, the rustling of a page)

3. What can you *feel*? (e.g., the pressure of the clothes against your skin, the texture of the page, the keyboard on your fingers)

4. What can you *smell*? (e.g., the perfume or cologne someone is wearing, the odor of stale cigarette smoke)

5. What can you *taste*? (e.g., the aftereffects of your last meal)

Compare your responses with those of the other students in the class. Do your classmates perceive sensations that differ from the ones you perceived? If so, how do you explain these differences?

As you practice this simple exercise, it should become clear that for every sensation that you focus your attention on, there are countless other sensations that you are simply ignoring. If you were aware of *everything* that is happening at every moment, you would be completely overwhelmed. By selecting certain sensations, you are able to make sense of your world in a relatively orderly way. The activity of using your senses to experience and make sense of your world is known as **perceiving**.

> **perceiving**
> Actively selecting, organizing, and interpreting what is experienced by your senses.

Actively Selecting, Organizing, and Interpreting Sensations

It is tempting to think that your senses simply record what is happening out in the world as if you were a human camera or tape recorder. You are not, however, a passive receiver of information, a "container" into which sense experience is poured. Instead, you are an *active participant* who is always trying to understand the sensations you are encountering. As you perceive your world, your experience is the result of combining the sensations you are having with the way you understand these sensations. For example, examine the following collection of markings. What do you see?

Copyright © Cengage Learning

If all you see is a collection of black spots, try looking at the group sideways. After a while, you will probably perceive a familiar animal.

From this example you can see that when you perceive the world, you are doing more than simply recording what your senses experience. Besides experiencing sensations, you are also *actively making sense* of these sensations. That is why this collection of black spots suddenly became the figure of an animal—because you were able to actively organize these spots into a pattern you recognized.

When you actively perceive the sensations you are experiencing, you are engaged in three distinct activities:

1. *Selecting* certain sensations to pay attention to
2. *Organizing* these sensations into a design or pattern
3. *Interpreting* what this design or pattern means to you

In the case of the figure on page 145, you were able to perceive an animal because you *selected* certain of the markings to concentrate on, *organized* these markings into a pattern, and *interpreted* this pattern as representing a familiar animal.

Of course, when you perceive, these three operations of selecting, organizing, and interpreting are usually performed quickly, automatically, and often simultaneously. Also, you are normally unaware that you are performing these operations because they are so rapid and automatic. This chapter is designed to help you slow down this normally automatic process of perceiving so that you can understand how the process works.

Let's explore more examples that illustrate how you actively select, organize, and interpret your perceptions of the world. Carefully examine the following figure.

Mary Evans Picture Library

Do you see both the young woman and the old woman? If you do, try switching back and forth between the two images. As you switch back and forth, notice how, for each image, you are

- *Selecting* certain lines, shapes, and shadings on which to focus your attention.
- *Organizing* these lines, shapes, and shadings into different patterns.
- *Interpreting* these patterns as representing things that you are able to recognize— a hat, a nose, a chin.

Another way for you to become aware of your active participation in perceiving your world is to consider how you see objects. Examine the illustration that follows. Do you perceive different-sized people or the same-sized people at different distances?

When you see someone who is far away, you usually do not perceive a tiny person. Instead, you perceive a normal-sized person who is far away from you. Your experience in the world has enabled you to discover that the farther things are from you, the smaller they look. The moon in the night sky appears about the size of a quarter, yet you perceive it as being considerably larger. As you look down a long stretch of railroad tracks or gaze up at a tall building, the boundary lines seem to come together. Even though these images are what your eyes "see," however, you do not usually perceive the tracks meeting or the building coming to a point. Instead, your mind actively organizes and interprets a world composed of constant shapes and sizes, even though the images you actually see usually vary, depending on how far you are from them and the angle from which you are looking at them.

In short, your mind actively participates in the way you perceive the world. By combining the sensations you are receiving with the way your mind selects, organizes, and interprets these sensations, you perceive a world of things that is stable and familiar, a world that usually makes sense to you.

The process of perceiving takes place at a variety of different levels. At the most basic level, the concept of "perceiving" refers to the selection, organization, and interpretation of sensations—for example, being able to perceive the various objects in your experience, such as a basketball. However, you also perceive larger patterns of meaning at more complex levels, as when you are watching the action of a group of people engaged in a basketball game. Although these are very different contexts, both engage you in the process of actively selecting, organizing, and interpreting what is experienced by your senses—in other words, "perceiving."

PEOPLE'S PERCEPTIONS DIFFER

Your *active participation* in perceiving your world is something you are not usually aware of. You normally assume that what you are perceiving is what is actually taking place. Only when you find that your perception of the same event differs from the perceptions of others are you forced to examine the manner in which you are selecting, organizing, and interpreting the events in your world.

In most cases, people in a group will have a variety of perceptions about what is taking place in the picture in Thinking Activity 4.1. Some may see the couple having a serious conversation, perhaps relating to the baby behind them. Others may view them as being in the middle of an angry argument. Still others may see them as dealing with some very bad news they have just received. In each case, the perception depends on how the person is actively using his or her mind to organize and interpret what is taking place. Since the situation pictured is by its nature somewhat puzzling, different people perceive it in different ways.

Thinking Activity 4.1

ANALYZING PERCEPTIONS

Carefully examine this picture of a couple sitting on a bed with a baby. What do you think is happening in this picture?

© Radius Images/Jupiter Images

VIEWING THE WORLD THROUGH "LENSES"

To understand how various people can be exposed to the same stimuli or events and yet have different perceptions, it helps to imagine that each of us views the world through our own pair of "contact lenses." Of course, we are not usually aware of the lenses we are wearing. Instead, our lenses act as filters that select and shape what we perceive without our realizing it.

Thinking Critically About Visuals

The Investigation

Explain why each witness describes the suspect differently. Have you ever been involved in a situation in which people described an individual or event in contrasting or conflicting ways? What is the artist saying about people's perceptions?

To understand the way people perceive the world, you have to understand their individual lenses, which influence how they actively select, organize, and interpret the events in their experience. A diagram of the process might look like this:

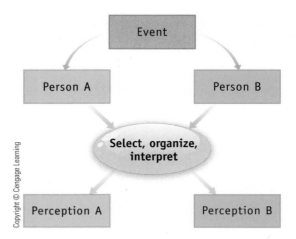

Consider the following pairs of statements. In each of these cases, both people are being exposed to the same basic *stimulus* or event, yet each has a totally different *perception* of the experience. Explain how you think the various perceptions might have developed.

1. a. That chili was much too spicy to eat.

   Explanation:

   b. That chili needed more hot peppers and chili powder to spice it up a little.

   Explanation:

2. a. People who wear lots of makeup and jewelry are very sophisticated.

   Explanation:

   b. People who wear lots of makeup and jewelry are overdressed.

   Explanation:

3. a. The music that young people enjoy listening to is a very creative cultural expression.

   Explanation:

   b. The music that young people enjoy listening to is obnoxious noise.

   Explanation:

To become an effective critical thinker, you have to become aware of the lenses that you—and others—are wearing. These lenses aid you in actively selecting, organizing, and interpreting the sensations in your experience. If you are unaware of the nature of your own lenses, you can often mistake your own perceptions for objective truth without bothering to examine either the facts or others' perceptions on a given issue.

WHAT FACTORS SHAPE PERCEPTIONS?

Your perceptions of the world are dramatically influenced by your past experiences: the way you were brought up, the relationships you have had, and your training and education. Every dimension of "who" you are is reflected in your perceiving lenses. It takes critical reflection to become aware of these powerful influences on our perceptions of the world and the beliefs we construct based on them.

Your special interests and areas of expertise also affect how you see the world. Consider the case of two people who are watching a football game. One person, who has very little understanding of football, sees merely a bunch of grown men hitting each other for no apparent reason. The other person, who loves football, sees complex play patterns, daring coaching strategies, effective blocking and tackling techniques, and zone defenses with "seams" that the receivers are trying to "split." Both have their eyes focused on the same event, but they are perceiving two entirely different situations. Their perceptions differ because each person is actively selecting, organizing, and interpreting the available stimuli in different ways. The same is true of any situation in which you are perceiving something about which you have special knowledge or expertise. The following are examples:

- A builder examining the construction of a new house
- A music lover attending a concert
- A naturalist experiencing the outdoors
- A cook tasting a dish just prepared
- A lawyer examining a contract
- An art lover visiting a museum

Think about a special area of interest or expertise that you have and how your perceptions of that area differ from those of people who don't share your knowledge. Ask other class members about their areas of expertise. Notice how their perceptions of that area differ from your own because of their greater knowledge and experience.

In all these cases, the perceptions of the knowledgeable person differ substantially from the perceptions of the person who lacks knowledge of that area. Of course, you do not have to be an expert to have more fully developed perceptions. It is a matter of degree.

Thinking Activity 4.2

THINKING CRITICALLY ABOUT MY PERCEIVING LENSES

This is an opportunity for you to think about the unique "prescription" of your perceiving lenses. Reflect on the elements in yourself and your personal history that you believe exert the strongest influence on the way that you view the world. These factors will likely include the following categories:

- Demographics (age, gender, race/ethnicity, religion, geographical location)
- Tastes in fashion, music, leisure activities
- Special knowledge, talents, expertise
- Significant experiences in your life, either positive or negative
- Values, goals, aspirations

Create a visual representation of the prescription for your perceiving lenses, highlighting the unique factors that have contributed to your distinctive perspective on the world. Then, compare your "prescription" to those of other students in your class, and discuss the ways in which your lenses result in perceptions and beliefs that are different from those produced by other prescriptions.

Thinking Activity 4.3

ANALYZING DIFFERENT ACCOUNTS OF THE ASSASSINATION OF MALCOLM X

Let's examine a situation in which a number of different people had somewhat different perceptions about an event they were describing—in this case, the assassination of Malcolm X as he was speaking at a meeting in Harlem. The following are five different accounts of what took place on that day. As you read through the various accounts, pay particular attention to the different perceptions each one presents of this event. After you have finished reading the accounts, analyze some of the differences in these perceptions by answering the questions that follow.

Five Accounts of the Assassination of Malcolm X

The *New York Times* (February 22, 1965)

Malcolm X, the 39-year-old leader of a militant Black Nationalist movement, was shot to death yesterday afternoon at a rally of his followers in a ballroom in Washington Heights. The bearded Negro extremist had said only a few words of greeting when a fusillade rang out. The bullets knocked him over backwards.

Source: (1) From *The New York Times*, February 22, 1965. © 1965 The New York Times. All rights reserved. Used by permission and protected by the Copyright Laws of the United States. The printing, copying, redistribution, or retransmission of this Content without express written permission is prohibited. (2) "On Death and Transfiguration," *Life* magazine, March 5, 1965. Copyright Time Inc. Reprinted/ translated by permission. Time is a registered trademark of Time Inc. All rights reserved. (3) Excerpt from the *New York Post*, February 22, 1965. Reprinted by permission. (4) Associated Press. (5) The *Amsterdam News*, February 27, 1965. Reprinted by permission of N.Y. Amsterdam News.

A 22-year-old Negro, Thomas Hagan, was charged with the killing. The police rescued him from the ballroom crowd after he had been shot and beaten.

Pandemonium broke out among the 400 Negroes in the Audubon Ballroom at 160th Street and Broadway. As men, women and children ducked under tables and flattened themselves on the floor, more shots were fired. The police said seven bullets struck Malcolm. Three other Negroes were shot. Witnesses reported that as many as 30 shots had been fired. About two hours later the police said the shooting had apparently been a result of a feud between followers of Malcolm and members of the extremist group he broke with last year, the Black Muslims.

. . .

Life (March 5, 1965)

His life oozing out through a half dozen or more gunshot wounds in his chest, Malcolm X, once the shrillest voice of black supremacy, lay dying on the stage of a Manhattan auditorium. Moments before, he had stepped up to the lectern and 400 of the faithful had settled down expectantly to hear the sort of speech for which he was famous—flaying the hated white man. Then a scuffle broke out in the hall and Malcolm's bodyguards bolted from his side to break it up—only to discover that they had been faked out. At least two men with pistols rose from the audience and pumped bullets into the speaker, while a third cut loose at close range with both barrels of a sawed-off shotgun. In the confusion the pistol man got away. The shotgunner lunged through the crowd and out the door, but not before the guards came to their wits and shot him in the leg. Outside he was swiftly overtaken by other supporters of Malcolm and very likely would have been stomped to death if the police hadn't saved him. Most shocking of all to the residents of Harlem was the fact that Malcolm had been killed not by "whitey" but by members of his own race.

The *New York Post* (February 22, 1965)

They came early to the Audubon Ballroom, perhaps drawn by the expectation that Malcolm X would name the men who firebombed his home last Sunday. . . . I sat at the left in the 12th row and, as we waited, the man next to me spoke of Malcolm and his followers: "Malcolm is our only hope. You can depend on him to tell it like it is and to give Whitey hell."

. . .

There was a prolonged ovation as Malcolm walked to the rostrum. Malcolm looked up and said, "A salaam aleikum (Peace be unto you)," and the audience replied, "We aleikum salaam (And unto you, peace)."

Bespectacled and dapper in a dark suit, sandy hair glinting in the light, Malcolm said: "Brothers and sisters. . . ." He was interrupted by two men in the center of the ballroom, who rose and, arguing with each other, moved forward. Then there was a scuffle at the back of the room. I heard Malcolm X say his last words: "Now, brothers, break it up," he said softly. "Be cool, be calm."

Then all hell broke loose. There was a muffled sound of shots and Malcolm, blood on his face and chest, fell limply back over the chairs behind him. The two men who had approached him ran to the exit on my side of the room, shooting wildly behind them as they ran. I heard people screaming, "Don't let them kill him." "Kill those bastards." At an exit I saw some of Malcolm's men beating with all their strength on two men. I saw a half dozen of Malcolm's followers bending over his inert body on the stage. Their clothes were stained with their leader's blood.

Four policemen took the stretcher and carried Malcolm through the crowd and some of the women came out of their shock and one said: "I hope he doesn't die, but I don't think he's going to make it."

Associated Press (February 22, 1965)

A week after being bombed out of his Queens home, Black Nationalist leader Malcolm X was shot to death shortly after 3 [P.M.] yesterday at a Washington Heights rally of 400 of his devoted followers. Early today, police brass ordered a homicide charge placed against a 22-year-old man they rescued from a savage beating by Malcolm X supporters after the shooting. The suspect, Thomas Hagan, had been shot in the left leg by one of Malcolm's bodyguards as, police said, Hagan and another assassin fled when pandemonium erupted. Two other men were wounded in the wild burst of firing from at least three weapons. The firearms were a .38, a .45 automatic and a sawed-off shotgun. Hagan allegedly shot Malcolm X with the shotgun, a double-barreled sawed-off weapon on which the stock also had been shortened, possibly to facilitate concealment. Cops charged Reuben Frances, of 871 E. 179th St., Bronx, with felonious assault in the shooting of Hagan, and with Sullivan Law violation—possession of the .45. Police recovered the shotgun and the .45.

The *Amsterdam News* (February 27, 1965)

"We interrupt this program to bring you a special newscast . . .," the announcer said as the Sunday afternoon movie on the TV set was halted temporarily. "Malcolm X was shot four times while addressing a crowd at the Audubon Ballroom on 166th Street." "Oh no!" That was my first reaction to the shocking event that followed one week after the slender, articulate leader of the Afro-American Unity was routed from his East Elmhurst home by a bomb explosion. Minutes later we alighted from a cab at the corner of Broadway and 166th St. just a short 15 blocks from where I live on Broadway. About 200 men and women, neatly dressed, were milling around, some with expressions of awe and disbelief. Others were in small clusters talking loudly and with deep emotion in their voices. Mostly they were screaming for vengeance. One woman, small, dressed in a light gray coat and her eyes flaming with indignation, argued with a cop at the St. Nicholas corner of the block. "This is not the end of it. What they were going to do to the Statue of Liberty will be small in comparison. We black people are tired of being shoved around." Standing across the street near the memorial park one of Malcolm's close associates commented: "It's a shame." Later he added that "if it's war they want, they'll get it." He would not say whether Elijah Muhammed's followers had anything to do with the assassination. About 3:30 P.M. Malcolm X's wife, Betty, was escorted by three men and a woman from the Columbia Presbyterian Hospital. Tears streamed down her face. She was screaming, "They killed him!" Malcolm X had no last words. . . . The bombing and burning of the No. 7 Mosque early Tuesday morning was the first blow by those who are seeking revenge for the cold-blooded murder of a man who at 39 might have grown to the stature of respectable leadership.

Thinking Critically About Visuals

Witnessing a Martyrdom

Have you ever been a witness to an event that other people present described in contrasting or conflicting ways? Why do you think this happens? What are the responsibilities of bearing witness?

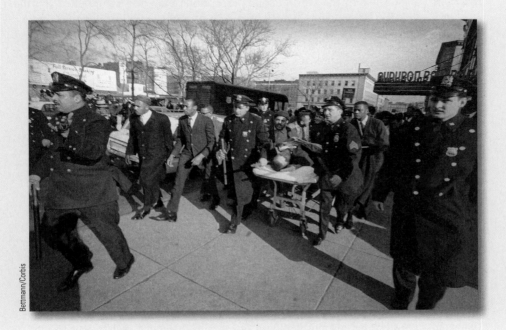

Bettmann/Corbis

QUESTIONS FOR ANALYSIS

1. What details of the events has each writer *selected* to focus on?

2. How has each writer *organized* the details that have been selected? Bear in mind that most news organizations present what they consider the most important information first and the least important information last.

3. How does each writer *interpret* Malcolm X, his followers, the gunmen, and the significance of the assassination?

4. How has each writer used *language* to express his or her perspective and to influence the thinking of the reader? Which language styles do you find most effective?

Thinking Passage

EXPERIENCES SHAPE YOUR PERCEPTIONS

Your ways of viewing the world are developed over a long period of time through the experiences you have and your thinking about these experiences. As you think critically about your perceptions, you learn more from your experiences and about how you make sense of the world. Your perceptions may be strengthened by this understanding, or they may be changed by it. For example, read the following student passage and consider the way the writer's experiences—and his reflection on these experiences—contributed to shaping his perspective on the world.

by Luis Feliz

I shuffle through a pile of photos on my desk and draw out one of my father. In this picture, he looks like Tito Rojas—thick mustachio, not one hair out of place, boyish and expectant eyes with wrinkles sprouting from the sides, gentle smile with big, square Chiclet white teeth overwhelming the brown earth of his face. He wears a yellow, black, and red striped turtleneck with long sleeves. The zipper of his black jeans has faded slightly. He is putting all his body weight on his left leg. He doesn't look much different in this photograph than he does today.

Sun up, he sleeps. Sun down, he works. He is a taxi-driver. He fades into the shadows. He becomes shadowy, no mark left behind, itinerant. The residue that remains is his absence. I recall the award ceremony he didn't attend because he was sleeping, the Christmas party cut short because he had to work. The fast stream of the highway allows two modes of existence: forward and backward. His foot is always pressed against the gas pedal. The taxi-cab roves. Forward. Reverse. Life rushes forward and recedes simultaneously. It's not that the driver doesn't pull to a curb to rest or park the car and get out to stretch or talk with friends. He claws out of the cab with a limp spine, but his mind remains belted in the seat his body occupied. He walks into relationships mentally immobilized. When I see my father, I see a man trapped behind a steering wheel.

Sleep and work triumph over family. When I was 7-years-old, I was reunited with my father after five years of separation. It was difficult to overcome the awkwardness of being separated for so long. So whenever I found him sleeping, I edged into the room and peered down at his toes. He lay wrapped up in blankets as if he were in a sack and his curled toes jutted out through a small tear.

Then, at 6 P.M., when he awoke, we sat down to eat. I never met his gaze at the dinner table. My eyes scoured the words on the magnets on the refrigerator door. I shuffled my feet. My moist hands clutched the toy in my pocket. I wanted to bolt out of there. Instead, I curled my toes into hooks and firmly latched myself to the floor. When the food was brought, I sucked my stomach in. I hated the food, and I would drop the fork to delay eating. The brown beans smelled like rotten eggs. The yellow rice filled with

Source: by Luis Feliz, student essay

meat looked like gnarled flesh. I pleaded with my eyes. O, Papi por favor. Dinner was the hardest part of living with strange people. I couldn't venture into their intimacy.

My step-mother approached. I bent down and snuck under the table. I prayed. Overhead, the conversation abruptly ended. My father yelled. I rose. I leaned over the table and looked at my father. He terrified me when he looked me in the eye. Without me realizing it, he had shamed me into eating; he began to tell of the hardships of his yola trip from the Dominican Republic to Puerto Rico.

In front of me I have a picture of him and Mami dancing at a family party after they got back together. He wears a white shirt with light gray stripes, top button undone, and those pointy white shoes that Mami always gives him hell about. The ring on his right hand gleams as light strikes its fake diamonds. He raises the Corona bottle to his lips before he gets up to dance. His hair is jet black and gelled up. He is well-groomed, unlike me. He wears blue H&M pants.

I recall how after they finish dancing he withdraws into his inner-cellar and the boyish dark almond eyes dim. A man's eyes hold not only the mountains he has climbed, but also the ditches into which he has fallen. My father's aspirations sag—the unfinished house in the Dominican Republic, the denied loan for a house here in New York, the incessant calls from bill collectors—his dreams wilt.

I remember his story of leaving for Puerto Rico on a yola again: "The morning before I leave I get a bill from the doctor. I owe 3,000 pesos. My son's health doesn't improve. I can't afford the bills anymore. The night before I depart a gentle breeze scatters some leaves into my room. I bend down and throw them out. I kiss my wife on the forehead. She moves, but doesn't rise. No one knows that I am leaving. In the center of town, I get into a van and then a man puts me into a boat. I lean over the wooden side of the turquoise blue boat and look up at the sky. I see so many stars. Below the water stirs. The boat sways from side to side. The men to my side are young like me. They are scared too. A woman wrinkles her forehead as the boat pulls away from the shore. She doesn't want to cry in the company of men. Shortly after, the men fall asleep. Just the woman and me remain awake. The silence of the sea terrifies me. I am alone, and although I don't know it yet, I will never be the same person, and I will never accept it; today I have scraped off the rust marks of security."

My father's words bind us to each other. He drenches me in the music of his voice. The bare language allows me a glimpse of his pain: "We had nothing to eat for weeks and weeks." I gazed at my father as he retold his hardships, and I loved him. I wanted to reach with outstretch arms and embrace him. An onrush of guilt propelled me forward. I attempted to rise from the chair, yet I slipped back. I guess that is the intent. Immigrant parents propagate the lie that the world is ours for the taking, and sometimes, the children believe it. I am here at Amherst College because I believed that lie. Graduating from high school at nineteen didn't stop me from pursuing my dreams. Having an accent does not prevent me from shouting my opinions in a crowded room.

I am here at Amherst College because my imperfect father taught me through his struggle to pursue my crooked path. The obstacles he braved for me to sit here and share his story and mine jolt me forward and sustain my hopes in days when I fear that I might tumble down and break a few bones.

I didn't want to understand my father's optimism because I saw him as a failure; someone to set up as a foil to a "successful" person. I grasped the lesson from the

Thinking Critically About Visuals

The Roots of Violence

In the wake of the horrific massacre of first-grade children and six adults in Newtown, Connecticut, there have been renewed efforts to understand the roots of gun violence so that we can better limit or even eradicate it from our lives. Although research studies have not yet established a definitive link between violent movies and video games, many people believe that these graphically violent experiences do in fact contribute to creating a culture of violence. Examine carefully these two photographs depicting images from violent video games. What elements do you find particularly disturbing? Do you think that repeated exposure to games like this, particularly in young children, contributes to "numbing" them to violence,

D. Hurst/Alamy

or helps make violence more socially acceptable? Or do you believe that these sorts of games provide harmless entertainment that in no way contributes to making people more violent? Adam Lanza, the Newtown murderer spent untold hours playing violent video games—does this fact influence your opinion regarding the potential threat of violent video games? Why or why not? If you were in a position to dictate public policy on video games for children, what policies would you recommend? For example, like movies, do you think that video games should be given ratings that prevent young children from playing the most graphically violent games? Why or why not?

Joe Klamar/AFP/Getty Images

stories about his hardships. Through the concept of *nosostros,* we, I started to see my father. Like Richard Rodriguez, I see *nosostros* as the horizontal and the communal vantage point. My father fell, got up, and shook it off, because it was never about him. He subsumed the individual into the collective. It was always about us, his family. If the bedrock of his dreams was solely his own progress, he would have quit the struggle long ago. Then, a naive child, I overlooked the power of my father's story, his effort to spin struggle into wisdom, his desire to share his most profound perceptions. I knew that my father had struggled, but it wasn't until later that I realized that he was the bearer of all his family's dreams. Once I realized this, I began to plumb the depths of his sorrow. I started to really understand the nature of his pain and struggle. Just as my father's dreams were fueled by love for us, so too I am fueled by the love I have for the people in my community. I meet a new daybreak with the voices and stories of a multitude. I am because of we.

Thinking Activity 4.4

DESCRIBING A SHAPING EXPERIENCE

Think of an experience that has shaped your life. Write an essay describing the experience and the ways it changed your life and how you perceive the world. (The essay by Luis Feliz that starts on page 156 is an example of a response to this activity.) After writing, analyze your experience by answering the following questions:

1. What were your *initial* perceptions of the situation? As you began the experience, you brought into the situation certain perceptions about the experience and the people involved.

2. What previous experiences had you undergone? Identify some of the influences that helped to shape these perceptions. Describe the actions that you either took or thought about taking.

3. As you became involved in the situation, what experiences in the situation influenced you to question or doubt your initial perceptions?

4. In what new ways did you view the situation that would better explain what was taking place? Identify the revised perceptions that you began to form about the experience.

Perceiving and Believing

As should be clear by now, perceiving is an essential part of your thinking process and your efforts to make sense of the world. However, your perceptions, by themselves, do not provide a reliable foundation for your understanding of the world. Your perceptions are often incomplete, distorted, and inaccurate. They are shaped and influenced by your perceiving "lenses," which reflect your own individual personality, experiences, biases, assumptions, and ways of viewing things. To clarify and validate your perceptions, you must critically examine and evaluate these perceptions.

Thinking critically about your perceptions results in the formation of your beliefs and ultimately in the construction of your knowledge about the world. For example, consider the following statements and answer *yes, no,* or *not sure* to each.

1. Humans need to eat to stay alive.
2. Smoking marijuana is a harmless good time.
3. Every human life is valuable.
4. Developing your mind is as important as taking care of your body.
5. People should care about other people, not just about themselves.

Your responses to these statements reflect certain beliefs you have, and these beliefs help you explain why the world is the way it is and how you ought to behave. In fact, beliefs are the main tools you use to make sense of the world and guide your actions. The total collection of your beliefs represents your view of the world, your philosophy of life.

What exactly are "beliefs"? **Beliefs** represent an interpretation, evaluation, conclusion, or prediction about the nature of the world. For example, this statement—"I believe that the whale in the book *Moby Dick* by Herman Melville symbolizes a primal, natural force that men are trying to destroy"—represents an *interpretation* of that novel. To say, "I believe that watching 'reality shows' is unhealthy because they focus almost exclusively on the least attractive qualities of people" is to express an *evaluation* of reality shows. The statement "I believe that one of the main reasons two out of three people in the world go to bed hungry each night is that industrially advanced nations have not done a satisfactory job of sharing their knowledge" expresses a *conclusion* about the problem of world hunger. To say, "If drastic environmental measures are not undertaken to slow the global warming trend, then I believe that the polar ice caps will melt and the earth will be flooded" is to make a *prediction* about events that will occur in the future.

Besides expressing an interpretation, evaluation, conclusion, or prediction about the world, beliefs also express an *endorsement* of the accuracy of the beliefs by the speaker or author. In the preceding statements, the speakers are not simply expressing interpretations, evaluations, conclusions, and predictions; they are also indicating that they believe these views are true. In other words, the speakers are saying that they have adopted these beliefs as their own because they are convinced that they represent accurate viewpoints based on some sort of evidence. This "endorsement" by the speaker is a necessary dimension of beliefs, and we assume it to be the case even if the speaker doesn't directly say, "I believe." For example,

beliefs
Interpretations, evaluations, conclusions, or predictions about the world that we endorse as true.

the statement "Astrological predictions are meaningless because there is no persuasive reason to believe that the position of the stars and planets has any effect on human affairs" expresses a belief, even though it doesn't specifically include the words "I believe."

Describe beliefs you have that fall into each of these categories (interpretation, evaluation, conclusion, prediction) and then explain the reason(s) you have for endorsing the beliefs.

1. **Interpretation** (an explanation or analysis of the meaning or significance of something)

   My interpretation is that . . .

   Supporting reason(s):

2. **Evaluation** (a judgment of the value or quality of something, based on certain standards)

   My evaluation is that . . .

   Supporting reason(s):

3. **Conclusion** (a decision made or an opinion formed after consideration of the relevant facts or evidence)

   My conclusion is that . . .

   Supporting reason(s):

4. **Prediction** (a statement about what will happen in the future)

   My prediction is that . . .

   Supporting reason(s):

Believing and Perceiving

The relationship between the activities of believing and perceiving is complex and interactive. On the one hand, your perceptions form the foundation of many of your beliefs about the world. On the other hand, your beliefs about the world shape and influence your perceptions of it. Let's explore this interactive relationship by examining a variety of beliefs, including:

1. *Interpretations* ("Poetry enables humans to communicate deep, complex emotions and ideas that resist simple expression.")

2. *Evaluations* ("Children today spend too much time on the Internet and too little time reading books.")

3. *Conclusions* ("An effective college education provides not only mastery of information and skills, but also evolving insight and maturing judgment.")

4. *Predictions* ("With the shrinking and integration of the global community, there will be an increasing need in the future for Americans to speak a second language.")

These beliefs, for people who endorse them, are likely to be based in large measure on a variety of perceptual experiences: events that people have seen and heard. The perceptual experiences by themselves, however, do not result in beliefs—they are simply experiences. For them to become beliefs, *you must think about* your perceptual experiences and then organize them into a belief structure. This thinking process of constructing beliefs is known as *cognition*, and it forms the basis of your understanding of the world. What are some of the perceptual experiences that might have led to the construction of the beliefs just described?

EXAMPLE: Many times I have seen that I can best express my feelings toward someone I care deeply about through a poem.

As we noted earlier in this chapter, your perceptual experiences not only contribute to the formation of your beliefs; the beliefs you have formed also have a powerful influence on the perceptions you *select* to focus on, how you *organize* these perceptions, and the manner in which you *interpret* them. For example, if you come across a poem in a magazine, your perception of the poem is likely to be affected by your beliefs about poetry. These beliefs may influence whether you *select* the poem as something to read, the manner in which you *organize* and *relate* the poem to other aspects of your experience, and your *interpretation* of the poem's meaning. This interactive relationship holds true for most beliefs. Assume that you endorse the four beliefs previously listed. How might holding these beliefs influence your perceptions?

EXAMPLE: When I find a poem I like, I often spend a lot of time trying to understand how the author has used language and symbols to create and communicate meaning.

The belief systems you have developed to understand your world help you correct inaccurate perceptions. When you watch a magician perform seemingly impossible tricks, your beliefs about the way the world operates inform you that what you are seeing is really a misperception, an illusion. In this context, you expect to be tricked, and your question is naturally "How did he or she do that?" Potential problems arise, however, in those situations in which it is not apparent that your perceptions are providing you with inaccurate information and you use these experiences to form mistaken beliefs. For example, you may view advertisements linking youthful, attractive, fun-loving people with cigarette smoking and form the inaccurate belief that smoking cigarettes is an integral part of being youthful, attractive, and fun loving. As a critical thinker, you have a responsibility to continually monitor and evaluate both aspects of this interactive process—your beliefs and your perceptions—so that you can develop the most informed perspective on the world.

Thinking Activity 4.5

ANALYZING A FALSE PERCEPTION

Describe an experience of a perception you had that later turned out to be false based on subsequent experiences or reflection. Answer the following questions.

1. What qualities of the perception led you to believe it was true?
2. How did this perception influence your beliefs about the world?
3. Describe the process that led you to conclude that the perception was false.

Types of Beliefs: Reports, Inferences, Judgments

All beliefs are not the same. In fact, beliefs differ from one another in many kinds of ways, including their accuracy. The belief "The earth is surrounded by stars and planets" is considerably more certain than the belief "The positions of the stars and planets determine our personalities and destinies."

Beliefs differ in other respects besides accuracy. Review the following beliefs, and then describe some of their differences.

1. I believe that I have hair on my head.
2. I believe that the sun will rise tomorrow.
3. I believe that there is some form of life after death.
4. I believe that dancing is more fun than jogging and that jogging is preferable to going to the dentist.
5. I believe that you should always act toward others in ways that you would like to have them act toward you.

In this section you will be thinking critically about three basic types of beliefs you use to make sense of the world:

- Reports
- Inferences
- Judgments

These beliefs are expressed in both your thinking and your use of language, as illustrated in the following sentences:

1. My bus was late today.
   Type of belief: reporting

2. My bus will probably be late tomorrow.

   Type of belief: inferring

3. The bus system is unreliable.

   Type of belief: judging

Now try the activity with a different set of statements.

1. Each modern atomic warhead has more than 100 times the explosive power of the bomb dropped on Hiroshima.

   Type of belief:

2. With all of the billions of planets in the universe, the odds are that there are other forms of life in the cosmos.

   Type of belief:

3. In the long run, the energy needs of the world will best be met by solar energy technology rather than nuclear energy or fossil fuels.

   Type of belief:

As you examine these statements, you can see that they provide you with different types of information about the world. The first statement in each list reports aspects of the world that you can verify—that is, check for accuracy. By doing the appropriate sort of investigating, you can determine whether the bus was actually late today and whether modern atomic warheads really have the power attributed to them. When you describe the world in ways that can be verified through investigation, you are said to be **reporting factual information** about the world.

> **reporting factual information** Describing the world in ways that can be verified through investigation.

Looking at the second statement in each list, you can see immediately that each provides a different sort of information from the first one. These statements cannot be verified. There is no way to investigate and determine with certainty whether the bus will indeed be late tomorrow or whether there is in fact life on other planets. Although these conclusions may be based on factual information, they go beyond factual information to make statements about what is not currently known. When you describe the world in ways that are based on factual information yet go beyond this information to make statements regarding what is not currently known, you are said to be **inferring** conclusions about the world.

> **inferring** Describing the world in ways that are based on factual information yet going beyond this information to make statements about what is not currently known.

Finally, as you examine the third statement in both lists, it is apparent that these statements are different from both factual reports and inferences. They describe the world in ways that express the speaker's evaluation—of the bus service and of energy sources. These evaluations are based on certain standards (criteria) that the speaker is using to judge the bus service as unreliable and solar energy as more promising than nuclear energy or fossil fuels. When you describe the world in ways that express your evaluation based on certain criteria, you are said to be **judging**.

> **judging** Describing the world in ways that express an evaluation based on certain criteria.

You continually use these various ways of describing and organizing your world—reporting, inferring, judging—to make sense of your experience. In most cases, you are not aware that you are actually performing these activities, nor are you usually aware of the differences among them. Yet these three activities work together to help you see the world as a complete picture.

Thinking Critically About Visuals

Observing a Street Scene

Marvin Newman/Tips Images

Carefully examine this photograph of a street scene. Then write five statements based on your observations of the scene. Identify each statement as reporting, inferring, or judging, and explain why you classify each one as such.

Thinking Activity 4.6

IDENTIFYING REPORTS, INFERENCES, AND JUDGMENTS

1. Compose six sentences that embody these three types of beliefs: two reports, two inferences, and two evaluations.

2. Locate a short article from a newspaper or magazine (either in print or online) and identify the reports, inferences, and judgments it contains.

Reporting Factual Information

The statements that result from the activity of reporting express the most accurate beliefs you have about the world. Factual beliefs have earned this distinction because they are verifiable, usually with one or more of your senses. For example, consider the following factual statement:

That young woman is wearing a brown hat in the rain.

This statement about an event in the world is considered to be factual because it can be verified by your immediate sense experience—what you can (in principle or in theory) see, hear, touch, feel, or smell. It is important to say *in principle* or *in theory* because you often do not use all of your relevant senses to check out what you are experiencing. Look again at your example of a factual statement: You would normally be satisfied to *see* this event, without insisting on touching the hat or giving the person a physical examination. If necessary, however, you could perform these additional actions—in principle or in theory.

You use the same reasoning when you believe factual statements from other people that you are not in a position to check out immediately. For instance:

- The Great Wall of China is more than 1,500 miles long.
- There are large mountains and craters on the moon.
- Your skin is covered with germs.

You consider these to be factual statements because, even though you cannot verify them with your senses at the moment, you could in principle or in theory verify them with your senses *if* you were flown to China, *if* you were rocketed to the moon, or *if* you were to examine your skin with a powerful microscope. The process of verifying factual statements involves *identifying* the sources of information on which they are based and *evaluating* the reliability of these sources, topics that we will be examining in the next chapter, "Constructing Knowledge."

You communicate factual information to others by means of reports. A *report* is a description of something experienced that is communicated in as accurate and complete a way as possible. Through reports you can share your sense experiences with other people, and this mutual sharing enables you to learn much more about the world than if you were confined to knowing only what you experience. The recording (making records) of factual reports also makes possible the accumulation of knowledge learned by previous generations.

Because factual reports play such an important role in our exchange and accumulation of information about the world, it is important that they be as accurate and complete as possible. This brings us to a problem. We have already seen in previous chapters that our perceptions and observations are often *not* accurate or complete. What this means is that often when we think we are making true, factual reports, our reports are actually inaccurate or incomplete. For instance, consider our earlier "factual statement":

That young woman is wearing a brown hat in the rain.

Here are some questions you could ask concerning the accuracy of the statement:

- Is the woman really young, or does she merely look young?
- Is the woman really a woman, or a man disguised as a woman?
- Is that really a hat the woman/man is wearing or something else (e.g., a paper bag)?

Of course, there are methods you could use to clear up these questions with more detailed observations. Can you describe some of these methods?

Besides difficulties with observations, the "facts" that you see in the world actually depend on more general *beliefs* that you have about how the world operates. Consider the question "Why did the man's body fall from the top of the building to the sidewalk?" Having had some general science courses, you might say something like "The body was simply obeying the law of gravity," and you would consider this to be a "factual statement." But how did people account for this sort of event before Newton formulated the law of gravity? Some popular responses might have included the following:

- Things always fall down, not up.
- The spirit in the body wanted to join with the spirit of the earth.

When people made statements like these and others, such as "Humans can't fly," they thought that they were making "factual statements." Increased knowledge and understanding have since shown these "factual beliefs" to be inaccurate, and so they have been replaced by "better" beliefs. These "better beliefs" are able to explain the world in a way that is more accurate and predictable. Will many of the beliefs you now consider to be factually accurate also be replaced in the future by beliefs that are *more* accurate and predictable? If history is any indication, this will most certainly happen. (Already Newton's formulations have been replaced by Einstein's, based on the latter's theory of relativity. And Einstein's have been refined and modified as well and may be replaced someday.)

Thinking Activity 4.7

EVALUATING FACTUAL INFORMATION

1. Locate and carefully read an article that deals with an important social issue.
2. Summarize the main theme and key points of the article.
3. Describe the factual statements that are used to support the major theme.
4. Evaluate the accuracy of the factual information.
5. Evaluate the reliability of the sources of the factual information.

Thinking Activity 4.8

"REAL" AND MANIPULATED IMAGES IN FILM

Earlier in this chapter we examined the process of perceiving, so we know that the cliché "Seeing is believing" is not always true. The increasing popularity and affordability of digital photography and image-enhancement software have

© Universal/Courtesy Everett Collection

© Universal/Courtesy Everett Collection

directly demonstrated to many people the degree to which images can be manipulated to create pictures of people and events with no counterpart in "real" life, as illustrated in the "before and after" photos on page 169 taken from the movie "King Kong."

Special effects in movies were much easier to identify as "unreal" before recent advances in computer modeling. The success of full-length animated feature films led some motion picture industry experts to predict that films would soon feature animated "synthetic actors." That prediction is now our reality. With the sophisticated motion-capture technology that was created for James Cameron's movie *Avatar*, audiences are now truly challenged to distinguish "real" from "synthetic" actors.

Inferring

Imagine yourself in the following situations:

1. Your roommate has just learned that she passed a math exam for which she had done absolutely no studying. Humming the song "I Did It My Way," she comes bouncing over to you with a huge grin on her face and says, "Let me buy you dinner to celebrate!" What do you conclude about how she is feeling?

2. It is midnight and the library is about to close. As you head for the door, you spy your roommate shuffling along in an awkward waddle. His coat bulges out in front like he's pregnant. When you ask, "What's going on?" he gives you a glare and hisses, "Shhh!" Just before he reaches the door, a pile of books slides from under his coat and crashes to the floor. What do you conclude?

In these examples, it would be reasonable to make the following conclusions:

1. Your roommate is happy.
2. Your roommate is stealing library books.

Although these conclusions are reasonable, they are not factual reports; they are *inferences*. You have not directly experienced your roommate's "happiness" or "stealing." Instead, you have inferred it based on your roommate's behavior and the circumstances. What are the clues in these situations that might lead to these conclusions?

One way of understanding the inferential nature of these views is to ask yourself the following questions:

1. Have you ever pretended to be happy when you weren't? Could other people tell?
2. Have you ever been accused of stealing something when you were perfectly innocent? How did this happen?

From these examples you can see that whereas factual beliefs can in principle be verified by direct observation, *inferential beliefs* go beyond what can be directly observed. For instance, in the examples given, your observation of certain of your roommate's actions led you to infer things that you were *not* observing directly— "She's happy"; "He's stealing books." Making such simple inferences is something you do all the time. It is so automatic that usually you are not even aware that you are going beyond your immediate observations, and you may have difficulty drawing a sharp line between what you *observe* and what you *infer*. Making such inferences enables you to see the world as a complete picture, to fill in the blanks and round out the fragmentary sensations being presented to your senses. In a way, you become an artist, painting a picture of the world that is consistent, coherent, and predictable.

Your picture also includes *predictions* of what will be taking place in the near future. These predictions and expectations are also inferences because you attempt to determine what is currently unknown from what is already known.

Of course, your inferences may be mistaken, and in fact they frequently are. You may infer that the woman sitting next to you is wearing two earrings and then discover that she has only one. Or you may expect the class to end at noon and find that the teacher lets you go early—or late. In the last section we concluded that not even factual beliefs are ever absolutely certain. Comparatively speaking, inferential beliefs are a great deal more uncertain than factual beliefs, and it is important to distinguish between the two.

Consider the following situations, analyzing each one by asking these questions: Is the action based on a factual belief or an inference? In what ways might the inference be mistaken? What is the degree of risk involved?

- Placing your hand in a closing elevator door to reopen it
- Taking an unknown drug at a party
- Jumping out of an airplane with a parachute on
- Riding on the back of a motorcycle
- Taking a drug prescribed by your doctor

Having an accurate picture of the world depends on your being able to evaluate how *certain* your beliefs are. Therefore, it is crucial that you *distinguish* inferences from factual beliefs and then *evaluate* how certain or uncertain your inferences are. This is known as "calculating the risks," and it is very important to solving problems successfully and deciding what steps to take.

The distinction between what is observed and what is inferred is given particular attention in courtroom settings, where defense lawyers usually want witnesses to describe only what they *observed*—not what they *inferred*—as part of the observation. When a witness includes an inference such as "I saw him steal it," the lawyer may object that the statement represents a "conclusion of the witness" and move to have the observation "stricken from the record." For example, imagine that you are a defense attorney listening to the following testimony. At what points would you make the objection "This is a conclusion of the witness"?

> I saw Harvey running down the street, right after he knocked the old lady down. He had her purse in his hand and was trying to escape as fast as he could. He was really scared. I wasn't surprised because Harvey has always taken advantage of others. It's not the first time that he's stolen either, I can tell you that. Just last summer he robbed the poor box at St. Anthony's. He was bragging about it for weeks.

Finally, you should be aware that even though in *theory* facts and inferences can be distinguished, in *practice* it is almost impossible to communicate with others by sticking only to factual observations. A reasonable approach is to state your inference along with the observable evidence on which the inference is based (e.g., John *seemed* happy because . . .). Our language has an entire collection of terms (*seems, appears, is likely*, and so on) that signal when we are making an inference and not expressing an observable fact.

Many of the predictions that you make are inferences based on your past experiences and on the information that you presently have. Even when there appear to be sound reasons to support these inferences, they are often wrong due to incomplete information or unanticipated events. The fact that even people considered by society to be "experts" regularly make inaccurate predictions with absolute certainty should encourage you to exercise caution when making your own inferences. Following are some examples of "expert predictions":

- "So many centuries after the Creation, it is unlikely that anyone could find hitherto unknown lands of any value."—the advisory committee to King Ferdinand and Queen Isabella of Spain, before Columbus's voyage in 1492

- "The energy produced by the breaking down of the atom is a very poor kind of thing. Anyone who expects a source of power from the transformation of the atom is talking moonshine."—Lord Rutherford, Nobel laureate, after the first experimental splitting of the atom, 1933

- "What use could the company make of an electrical toy?"—Western Union's rejection of the telephone in 1878

- "The actual building of roads devoted to motor cars is not for the near future in spite of many rumors to that effect."—a 1902 article in *Harper's Weekly*

- "The [atom] bomb will never go off, and I speak as an expert in explosives."—Vannevar Bush, presidential adviser, 1945

- "Space travel is utter bilge."—British astronomer Dr. R. Woolsey, 1958

- "Among the really difficult problems of the world, [the Arab-Israeli conflict is] one of the simplest and most manageable."—Walter Lippmann, newspaper columnist, 1948

- "You ain't goin' nowhere, son. You ought to go back to driving a truck." Denny, Grand Ole Opry manager, firing Elvis Presley after one performance, 1954

Examine the following list of statements, noting which statements are *factual beliefs* (based on observations) and which are *inferential beliefs* (conclusions that go beyond observations). For each factual statement, describe how you might go about verifying the information. For each inferential statement, describe a factual observation on which the inference could be based. (*Note:* Some statements may contain both factual beliefs and inferential beliefs.)

- When my leg starts to ache, that means snow is on the way.
- The grass is wet—it must have rained last night.
- I think that it's pretty clear from the length of the skid marks that the accident was caused by that person's driving too fast.
- Fifty men lost their lives in the construction of the Queensboro Bridge.
- Nancy said she wasn't feeling well yesterday—I'll bet that she's out sick today.

Now consider the following situations. What inferences might you be inclined to make based on what you are observing? How could you investigate the accuracy of your inference?

- A student in your class is consistently late for class.
- You see a friend of yours driving a new car.
- A teacher asks the same student to stay after class several times.
- You don't receive any birthday cards.

So far we have been exploring relatively simple inferences. Many of the inferences people make, however, are much more complicated. In fact, much of our knowledge about the world rests on our ability to make complicated inferences in a systematic and logical way. However, just because an inference is more complicated does not mean that it is more accurate; in fact, the opposite is often the case. One of the masters of inference is the legendary Sherlock Holmes. In the following passage, Holmes makes an astonishing number of inferences upon meeting Dr. Watson. Study carefully the conclusions he comes to. Are they reasonable? Can you explain how he reaches these conclusions?

"You appeared to be surprised when I told you, on our first meeting, that you had come from Afghanistan."

"You were told, no doubt."

"Nothing of the sort. I *knew* you came from Afghanistan. From long habit the train of thoughts ran so swiftly through my mind that I arrived at the conclusion without being conscious of intermediate steps. There were such steps, however. The train of reasoning ran, 'Here is a gentleman of a medical type, but with the air of a military man. Clearly an army doctor, then. He is just come from the tropics, for his face is dark, and that is not the natural tint of his skin, for his wrists are fair. He has undergone hardship and sickness, as his haggard face says clearly.

His left arm has been injured. He holds it in a stiff and unnatural manner. Where in the tropics could an English army doctor have seen much hardship and got his arm wounded? Clearly in Afghanistan.' The whole train of thought did not occupy a second. I then remarked that you came from Afghanistan, and you were astonished."

—Sir Arthur Conan Doyle, *A Study in Scarlet*

Thinking Activity 4.9

ANALYZING AN INCORRECT INFERENCE

Describe an experience in which you made an *in*correct inference that resulted in serious consequences. For example, it might have been a situation in which you mistakenly accused someone, you were in an accident because of a miscalculation, or you made a poor decision based on an inaccurate prediction. Analyze that experience by answering the following questions:

1. What was (were) your mistaken inference(s)?

2. What was the factual evidence on which you based your inference(s)?

3. Looking back, what could you have done to avoid the erroneous inference(s)?

Judging

Identify and describe a friend you have, a course you have taken, and the college you attend. Be sure your descriptions are specific and include *what you think* about the friend, the course, and the college.

1. _____ is a friend.

   He or she is . . . .

2. _____ is a course I have taken.

   It was . . . .

3. _____ is the college I attend.

   It is . . . .

Now review your responses. Do they include factual descriptions? For each response, note any factual information that can be verified.

In addition to factual reports, your descriptions may contain inferences based on factual information. Can you identify any inferences? In addition to inferences, your descriptions may include judgments about the person, course, and school—descriptions that express your evaluation based on certain criteria. Facts and inferences are designed to help you figure out what is actually happening (or will happen); the purpose of judgments is to express your evaluation about what is happening (or will happen). For example:

- My new car has broken down three times in the first six months. *(Factual report)*

- My new car will probably continue to have difficulties. *(Inference)*

- My new car is a lemon. *(Judgment)*

When you pronounce your new car a "lemon," you are making a judgment based on certain criteria you have in mind. For instance, a "lemon" is usually a newly purchased item—generally an automobile—with which you have repeated problems.

To take another example of judging, consider the following statements:

- Carla always does her work thoroughly and completes it on time. *(Factual report)*

- Carla will probably continue to do her work in this fashion. *(Inference)*

- Carla is a very responsible person. *(Judgment)*

By judging Carla to be responsible, you are evaluating her on the basis of the criteria or standards that you believe indicate a responsible person. One such criterion is completing assigned work on time. Can you identify additional criteria for judging someone to be responsible?

Review your previous descriptions of a friend, a course, and your college. Can you identify any judgments in your descriptions?

When we judge, we are often expressing our feelings of approval or disapproval. Sometimes, however, we make judgments that conflict with what we personally approve of. For example:

- I think a woman should be able to have an abortion if she chooses to, although I don't believe abortion is right.

- I can see why you think that person is beautiful, even though she is not the type that appeals to me.

In fact, at times it is essential to disregard your personal feelings of approval or disapproval when you judge. For instance, a judge in a courtroom should render evaluations based on the law, not on his or her personal preferences.

DIFFERENCES IN JUDGMENTS

Many of our disagreements with other people focus on differences in judgments. As a critical thinker, you need to approach such differences in judgments intelligently. You can do so by following these guidelines:

- Make explicit the criteria or standards used as a basis for the judgment.
- Try to establish the reasons that justify these criteria.

For instance, if I make the judgment "Professor Andrews is an excellent teacher," I am basing my judgment on certain criteria of teaching excellence. Once these standards are made explicit, we can discuss whether they make sense and what the justification is for them. Identify some of your standards for teaching excellence.

Of course, your idea of what makes an excellent teacher may be different from someone else's, a conclusion you can test by comparing your criteria with those of other class members. When these disagreements occur, your only hope for resolution is to use the two steps previously identified:

- Make explicit the standards you are using.
- Give reasons that justify these standards.

For example, "Professor Andrews really gets my mind working, forcing me to think through issues on my own and then defend my conclusions. I earn what I learn, and that makes it really 'mine.'"

In short, not all judgments are equally good or equally poor. The credibility of a judgment depends on the criteria used to make the judgment and the evidence or reasons that support these criteria. For example, there may be legitimate disagreements about judgments on the following points.

- Who was the greatest U.S. president?
- Which movie deserves the Oscar this year?
- Who should win *American Idol* or *Dancing with the Stars?*
- Which is the best baseball team this year?
- Which music is best for dancing?

However, in these and countless other cases, the quality of your judgments depends on your identifying the criteria used for the competing judgments and then demonstrating that your candidate best meets those criteria by providing supporting evidence and reasons. With this approach, you can often engage in intelligent discussion and establish which judgments are best supported by the evidence.

Understanding how judgments function also encourages you to continue thinking critically about a situation. For instance, the judgment "This course is worthless!" does not encourage further exploration and critical analysis. In fact, it may prevent such analysis by discouraging further exploration. Because judgments are sometimes made before you have a clear and complete understanding of the situation, they can serve to prevent you from seeing the situation as clearly and completely as you might. However, if you understand that all judgments are based on criteria that may or may not be adequately justified, you can explore these judgments further by making the criteria explicit and examining the reasons that justify them.

Thinking Activity 4.10

ANALYZING JUDGMENTS

Review the following passages, which illustrate various judgments. For each passage:

1. Identify the evaluative criteria on which the judgments are based.

2. Describe the reasons or evidence the author uses to support the criteria.

3. Explain whether you agree or disagree with the judgments and give your rationale.

> One widely held misconception concerning pizza should be laid to rest. Although it may be characterized as fast food, pizza is *not* junk food. Especially when it is made with fresh ingredients, pizza fulfills our basic nutritional requirements. The crust provides carbohydrates; from the cheese and meat or fish comes protein; and the tomatoes, herbs, onions, and garlic supply vitamins and minerals.
>
> —Louis Philip Salamone, "Pizza: Fast Food, Not Junk Food"

> Let us return to the question of food. Responsible agronomists report that before the end of the year millions of people, if unaided, might starve to death. Half a billion deaths by starvation is not an uncommon estimate. Even though the United States has done more than any other nation to feed the hungry, our relative affluence makes us morally vulnerable in the eyes of other nations and in our own eyes. Garrett Hardin, who has argued for a "lifeboat" ethic of survival (if you take all the passengers aboard, everybody drowns), admits that the decision *not* to feed all the hungry requires of us "a very hard psychological adjustment." Indeed it would. It has been estimated that the 3.5 million tons of fertilizer spread on American golf courses and lawns could provide up to 30 million tons of food in overseas agricultural production. The nightmarish thought intrudes itself. If we as a nation allow people to starve while we could, through some sacrifice, make more food available to them, what hope can any person have for the future of international relations? If we cannot agree on this most basic of values—feed the hungry—what hopes for the future can we entertain?
>
> —James R. Kelly, "The Limits of Reason"*

*Source: © 2013 Commonweal Foundation, reprinted with permission. For more information, visit www.commonwealmagazine.org.

THINKING CRITICALLY ABOUT NEW MEDIA

Distinguishing Perception from Reality

Sure, the Internet is full of information, but much of this information is based on perceptions that are incomplete, biased, and outright false. How do we tell the difference between beliefs that are relatively accurate, objective, and factual and those that aren't? The short answer is that we need to come armed with our full array of critical thinking abilities combined with a healthy dose of skepticism. Consider these examples:

Phony Journalism

"One could say my life itself has been one long soundtrack. Music was my life, music brought me to life, and music is how I will be remembered long after I leave this life. When I die there will be a final waltz playing in my head that only I can hear." When Dublin university student Shane Fitzgerald posted this poetic but phony quote on the Wikipedia obituary for the French composer Maurice Jarre, he said he was testing how our globalized, increasingly Internet-dependent media was upholding accuracy and accountability in an age of instant news. His report card: Wikipedia passed; journalism flunked. Although Wikipedia administrators quickly detected and removed the bogus quote, it wasn't quick enough to prevent journalists around the world from cutting and pasting it to dozens of blogs and newspaper websites. And the offending quote continued its viral spread until, after a full month went by, Fitzgerald blew the whistle on his editorial fraud. His analysis? "I am 100 percent convinced that if I hadn't come forward, that quote would have gone down in history as something Maurice Jarre said, instead of something I made up. It would have become another example where, once anything is printed enough times in the media without challenge, it becomes fact."

Phony Degrees

Want a college degree—or even a Ph.D.—in engineering, medicine, philosophy, or virtually any subject you choose, without having to attend all of those classes and pay all of that tuition? No problem! Your options range from having to take a limited number of online courses to simply coming up with the right cash payment, and an official looking diploma will be on its way before you can say *summa cum laude*! Phony degrees are nothing new: black markets in fake diplomas are known to have existed as far back as fourteenth-century Europe. But today's new media have raised the scam to a high art, with modern diploma mills providing detailed transcripts, verification services, and even fake accrediting agencies to legitimize fake schools. The only problem with using a phony degree to pad your résumé? In addition to your being uneducated and unqualified, there's the likelihood of getting caught and watching your career disappear like invisible ink on a fraudulent diploma.

Counterfeit Websites

Counterfeit websites are sites disguising themselves as legitimate sites for the purpose of disseminating misinformation. For example, *www.martinlutherking.org* disseminates hateful and false information about one of the greatest African American leaders of our era while pretending to be, on the surface, an "official" Martin Luther King, Jr. site. While the home page includes a photograph of King and links titled "Historical Writings," "The Death of the Dream," and "Suggested Books," subsequent pages include defamatory allegations and links to white power organizations and literature.

Thinking Activity 4.11

DETECTING AND ANALYZING FAULTY PERCEPTIONS ON THE WEB

1. Here's an opportunity to put your critical thinking skills to use as a detective. Surf the Web and identify at least one example of each of the following misleading or bogus sites or advertisements. Then critically evaluate them in terms of their accuracy, authenticity, reliability, and objectivity.

   - Phony journalism
   - Phony degrees
   - Counterfeit websites

2. Next, explore one or more "hoax-busting" websites (like www.snopes .com or www.hoaxbusters.org) and create your own personal guide to identifying and debunking false and misleading perceptions presented on the Web.

Thinking Passage

PERCEPTION AND REALITY IN THE SANDY HOOK ELEMENTARY SCHOOL SHOOTING

On the morning of December 14, 2012, Adam Lanza, age 20, shot and killed his mother as she lay sleeping. Then, armed with a Bushmaster XM-15 semi-automatic assault rifle and two handguns, he drove to Sandy Hook Elementary school. Wearing black clothes, earplugs, and a utility vest for carrying extra ammunition, he shot his way through a locked glass door and then proceeded to shoot and kill the principal, school counselor, 4 teachers, and 20 first grade students ranging in age from 6 to 7. With the police approaching, he fatally shot himself.

These are the basic facts of this horrific catastrophe about which there is fundamental agreement. However, in trying to understand *why* this event occurred and *how to prevent* events like this occurring in the future, there are many competing points of view that reflect different perceptions of reality. Some view this primarily as the act of a deeply emotionally disturbed individual who had been taught to shoot by his gun-loving mother. Others view this as the symptom of culture that is obsessed with guns and whose lenient laws make it possible for virtually anyone to secure virtually any kind of weapon. For example, on the day before the Sandy Hook massacre, lawmakers in Michigan passed a bill that would allow people to carry concealed weapons in schools, and Ohio lawmakers passed a bill that would allow concealed guns in the Statehouse. Still others view this as the product of a society in which gun violence is made to seem sexy and exciting in graphically violent movies, television shows, music, and hyperrealistic video games. Since the 1980s, firearms manufacturers have reacted to declines in demand for hunting rifles by increasingly focusing their production and marketing on pistols and "assault weapons." Those who view this as more than an isolated event point to similar events that have occurred on a regular basis in the United States, making schools the killing fields of our time:

- On July 20, 2012, the suspect James Egan Holmes killed 12 people and wounded 58 in a movie theatre in Aurora, Colorado, at a midnight screening of "The Dark Knight."

- On January 11, 2011, Jared Lee Loughner used a 9mm Glock semiautomatic pistol with a high capacity magazine and shot 19 people including U.S. Congressional Representative Gabrielle Giffords; 6 died.

- On April 16, 2007, Seung-Hui Cho, a student at Virginia Tech University, shot and killed 32 fellow students and wounded 17 others with a 9mm Glock semiautomatic pistol before committing suicide.

- On April 20, 1999, 2 high school students at Columbine High School in Colorado, using a Hi-Point 995 Carbine and a shotgun, killed 12 students and 1 teacher and injured 21 before committing suicide.

The world's perception of these events was framed, shaped, and communicated through the media's reporting. And this reporting influences the beliefs we form regarding our understanding of what occurred and what, if anything, can be done to diminish the likelihood of similar events occurring in the future. As you read the following accounts, reflect on the interpretations that they are presenting, the reasons and evidence that support their interpretations, and the perceptions that you are forming (and have formed) as a result of these and other responses. Then consider and respond to the questions that follow the articles.

Connecticut School Shooting 'An Attack On America'

by Ted Anthony

Pick a public elementary school somewhere in the continental United States and draw a half-mile circle around it. The odds are reasonable that you'll encounter some combination of the following:

A baseball field. A statue erected for war veterans. A municipal building. A community center. A polling place—probably the school itself. A library. A park. A basketball court crawling with kids playing pickup games.

In so many places, the school is the hub of civic life. Inside its walls, and around its grounds, are scattered the ideas and people and places that every day state the unspoken: When we talk of being American, this is what we mean.

It is for this reason that the excruciating saga of Newtown, Conn., has shaken the nation in a second way that is distinct from, yet of course related to, the actual death of so many young children.

Twenty-six lives ending so violently, so horrifyingly, is of course disruptive enough. But this event also disrupted the fundamental notion of what American community is. "Hurt a school and you hurt us all," The Chicago Tribune editorialized this week.

Americans have long had an unspoken social compact that says, hey—we build our lives around our schools because they're the bedrock of a society that makes sense. Without the sense of a strong school system—and, by extension, a safe school system—the whole grid buckles. Schools, where you pledge allegiance to the flag and gaze upon portraits of George Washington, have formed on a local level the civic contours of who we are as a nation.

"It's the place where you prepare to achieve the American dream—being president one day, going to outer space as an astronaut," says El Brown, a former teacher and the mother of a kindergartner in Fairfax, Va. "Classrooms are supposed to be where we build our tomorrows."

Schools are the field in which we farm our future. And when someone turfs that field so violently, leaving such chaos behind, it represents even more than the ugly notion of children dying violently. It feels, in some very visceral ways, like an act of war.

In remarks from the president on down during these jumbled days, the message comes through even when it's not said directly: In killing the children of Sandy Hook, Adam Lanza effectively attacked the American nest. He went after not only our young but two other precious commodities—our sense of what we might become, and the stories we tell about who we are. . . .

The Price of Gun Control

by Dan Baum

When you write about guns, as I do, and a shooting like the one in the Aurora movie theater happens an hour from your house, people call. I've already done an interview today with a Spanish newspaper and with Canadian radio. Americans and their guns: what a bunch of lunatics.

Among the many ways America differs from other countries when it comes to guns is that when a mass shooting happens in the United States, it's a gun story. How an obviously sick man could buy a gun; how terrible it is that guns are abundant; how we must ban particular types of guns that are especially dangerous. The Brady Campaign to Prevent Gun Violence responded to the news with a gun-control petition. Andrew Rosenthal of the *New York Times* has weighed in with an online column saying that "Politicians are far too cowardly to address gun violence . . . which keeps us from taking practical measures to avoid senseless shootings."

Compare that to the coverage and conversation after Anders Behring Breivik murdered sixty-nine people on the island of Utøya in Norway, a year ago next Sunday. Nobody focused on the gun. I had a hard time learning from the news reports what type of gun he used. Nobody asked, "How did he get a gun?" That seemed strange, because it's much harder to get a gun in Europe than it is here.

But everybody, even the American media, seemed to understand that the heart of the Utøya massacre story was a tragically deranged man, not the rifle he fired. Instead of wringing their hands over the gun Breivik used, Norwegians saw the tragedy as the opening to a conversation about the rise of right-wing extremism in their country.

Rosenthal is wrong, by the way, that politicians haven't addressed gun violence. They have done so brilliantly, in a million different ways, which helps explain why the rate of violent crime is about half what it was twenty years ago. They simply haven't used gun control to do it. Gun laws are far looser than they were twenty years ago, even while crime is plunging—a galling juxtaposition for those who place their faith in tougher gun laws. The drop in violence is one of our few unalloyed public-policy success stories, though perhaps not for those who bemoan an "epidemic of gun violence" that doesn't exist anymore in order to make a political point.

It's true that America's rate of violent crime remains higher than that in most European countries. But to focus on guns is to dodge a painful truth. America is more violent than other countries because Americans are more violent than other people. Our abundant guns surely make assaults more deadly. But by obsessing over inanimate pieces of metal, we avoid looking at what brings us more often than others to commit violent acts. Many liberal critics understand this when it comes to drug policy. The modern, sophisticated position is that demonizing chemicals is a reductive and ineffective way to address complicated social pathologies. When it comes to gun violence, though, the conversation often stops at the tool, because it is more comfortable to blame it than to examine ourselves. . . .

. . . 40 percent of Americans own guns, and like it or not, they identify with them, personally. Guns stand in for a whole range of values— individualism, strength, American exceptionalism—that many gun owners hold dear. Tell a gun owner that he cannot be trusted to own a firearm—particularly if you are an urban pundit with no experience around guns—and what he hears is an insult. Add to this that the bulk of the gun-buying public is made up of middle-aged white men with less than a college degree, and now you're insulting a population already rubbed raw by decades of stagnant wages.

The harm we've done by messing with law-abiding Americans' guns is significant. In 2010, I drove 11,000 miles around the United States talking to gun guys (for a book, to be published in the spring, that grew out of an article I wrote for this magazine), and I met many working guys, including plumbers, parks workers, nurses— natural Democrats in any other age—who wouldn't listen to anything the Democratic party has to say because of its institutional hostility to guns. I'd argue that we've sacrificed generations of progress on health care, women's and workers' rights, and climate change by reflexively returning, at times like these, to an ill-informed call to ban firearms, and we haven't gotten anything tangible in return. Aside from what it does to the progressive agenda, needlessly vilifying guns—and by extension, their owners—adds to the rancor that has us so politically frozen and culturally inflamed. Enough.

President Obama, to his credit, didn't mention gun control in his comments today. Maybe that was just a political calculation; maybe, during an election year, he didn't want to reopen a fight that has hurt his party so dearly in the past. But maybe it's a hint of progress, a sign that we're moving toward a more honest examination of who we are.

Response to Newtown, Connecticut Massacre by Wayne La Pierre, CEO of the National Rifle Association on December 21, 2012.

As reflected in the other articles in this section on the massacre of students and teachers of Newtown, Connecticut on December 14, 2012, many people believe that at least some of the responsibility for gun violence in this country is due to the absence of meaningful gun control laws. From this perspective, gun violence can be reduced by banning guns like military assault weapons, outlawing high capacity magazine clips, and instituting meaningful background checks for all people seeking to purchase guns. One of the most vocal opponents of any gun control restrictions is the leadership of the National Rifle Association (NRA) which cites Article 1 of the Constitution which grants citizens "the right to bear arms." (Contrary to the leadership of the NRA, the rank-and-file members of the NRA overwhelmingly support more restrictive background checks.)

Following the shootings at Sandyhook Elementary School, the leadership of the NRA did not issue a public statement until December 21, 2012. During those prepared remarks, the CEO of the NRA, Wayne La Pierre, did not make any reference to gun control initiatives or legislation. Instead, he advocated for having armed guards in every school, arguing that "The only thing that stops a bad guy with a gun is a good guy with a gun." From his perspective, the gun violence in this country is due to a number of factors unrelated to gun control restrictions, including the following:

- ". . .an unknown number of genuine monsters – people so deranged, so evil, so possessed by voices and driven by demons that no sane person can possibly comprehend them."

- ". . .a national media machine that rewards them (copycat killers) that rewards them with the wall-to-wall attention and sense of identity that they crave..."

- ". . .violent video games with names like Bulletstorm, Grand Theft Auto, Mortal Kombat , Splatterhouse, and...Kindergarten Killers."

- ". . .blood-soaked slasher films like 'American Psycho' and 'Natural Born Killers' that are aired like propaganda loops on 'Splatterdays'...

- ". . .a thousand music videos that portray life as a joke and murder as a way of life."

The answer of this gun violence, according to La Pierre, is to hire some of the "millions of qualified active and retired police; active reserve and retired military, security professionals" to be deployed, fully armed, in every school in the country in a "National School Shield Program." After all, La Pierre reasons, we protect other valued institutions in our country with armed protection, shouldn't we protect our most valuable institution, our schools?

Why Gun 'Control' Is Not Enough

by Jeff McMahan

Americans are finally beginning to have a serious discussion about guns. One argument we're hearing is the central pillar of the case for private gun ownership: that we are all safer when more individuals have guns because armed citizens deter crime and can defend themselves and others against it when deterrence fails. Those who don't have guns, it's said, are free riders on those who do, as the criminally disposed are less likely to engage in crime the more likely it is that their victim will be armed.

There's some sense to this argument, for even criminals don't like being shot. But the logic is faulty, and a close look at it leads to the conclusion that the United States should ban private gun ownership entirely, or almost entirely.

One would think that if widespread gun ownership had the robust deterrent effects that gun advocates claim it has, our country would be freer of crime than other developed societies. But it's not. When most citizens are armed, as they were in the Wild West, crime doesn't cease. Instead, criminals work to be better armed, more efficient in their use of guns ("quicker on the draw"), and readier to use them. When this happens, those who get guns may be safer than they would be without them, but those without them become progressively more vulnerable.

Source: © 2013 *The New York Times* (http://opinionator.blogs.nytimes.com/2012/12/19/why-gun-control-is-not-enough/).

Gun advocates have a solution to this: the unarmed must arm themselves. But when more citizens get guns, further problems arise: people who would once have got in a fistfight instead shoot the person who provoked them; people are shot by mistake or by accident.

And with guns so plentiful, any lunatic or criminally disposed person who has a sudden and perhaps only temporary urge to kill people can simply help himself to the contents of Mom's gun cabinet. Perhaps most important, the more people there are who have guns, the less effective the police become. The power of the citizens and that of the police approach parity. The police cease to have even a near-monopoly on the use of force.

To many devotees of the Second Amendment, this is precisely the point. As former Congressman Jay Dickey, Republican of Arkansas, said in January 2011, "We have a right to bear arms because of the threat of government taking over the freedoms we have." The more people there are with guns, the less able the government is to control them. But if arming the citizenry limits the power of the government, it does so by limiting the power of its agents, such as the police. Domestic defense becomes more a matter of private self-help and vigilantism and less a matter of democratically-controlled, public law enforcement. Domestic security becomes increasingly "privatized."

There is, of course, a large element of fantasy in Dickey's claim. Individuals with handguns are no match for a modern army. It's also a delusion to suppose that the government in a liberal democracy such as the United States could become so tyrannical that armed insurrection, rather than democratic procedures, would be the best means of constraining it. This is not Syria; nor will it ever be. Shortly after Dickey made his comment, people in Egypt rose against a government that had suppressed their freedom in ways far more serious than requiring them to pay for health care. Although a tiny minority of Egyptians do own guns, the protesters would not have succeeded if those guns had been brought to Tahrir Square. If the assembled citizens had been brandishing Glocks in accordance with the script favored by Second Amendment fantasists, the old regime would almost certainly still be in power and many Egyptians who're now alive would be dead. . . .

The logic is inexorable: as more private individuals acquire guns, the power of the police declines, personal security becomes more a matter of self-help, and the unarmed have an increasing incentive to get guns, until everyone is armed. When most citizens then have the ability to kill anyone in their vicinity in an instant, everyone is less secure than they would be if no one had guns other than the members of a democratically accountable police force.

The logic of private gun possession is thus similar to that of the nuclear arms race. When only one state gets nuclear weapons, it enhances its own security but reduces that of others, which have become more vulnerable. The other states then have an incentive to get nuclear weapons to try to restore their security. As more states get them, the incentives for others increase. If eventually all get them, the potential for catastrophe—whether through irrationality, misperception, or accident—is great. Each state's security is then much lower than it would be if none had nuclear weapons.

Gun advocates and criminals are allies in demanding that guns remain in private hands. They differ in how they want them distributed. Criminals want guns for themselves but not for their potential victims. Others want them for themselves but not for criminals. But while gun control can do a little to restrict access to guns by potential criminals, it can't do much when guns are to be found in every other household. Either criminals and non-criminals will have them or neither will. Gun advocates prefer for both rather than neither to have them.

But, as with nuclear weapons, we would all be safer if no one had guns—or, rather, no one other than trained and legally constrained police officers. Domestic defense would then be conducted the way we conduct national defense. We no longer accept, as the authors of the now obsolete Second Amendment did, that "a well-regulated militia" is "necessary to the security of a free state." Rather than leaving national defense to citizens' militias, we now, for a variety of compelling reasons, cede the right of national defense to certain state-authorized professional institutions: the Army, Navy, and so on. We rightly trust these forces to protect us from external threats and not to become instruments of domestic repression. We could have the same trust in a police force designed to protect us from domestic threats. . . .

Gun advocates will object that a prohibition of private gun ownership is an impossibility in the United States. But this is not an objection they can press in good faith, for the only reason that a legal prohibition could be impossible in a democratic state is that a majority oppose it. If gun advocates ceased to oppose it, a prohibition would be possible.

They will next argue that even if there were a legal prohibition, it could not be enforced with anything approaching complete effectiveness. This is true. As long as some people somewhere have guns, some people here can get them. Similarly, the legal prohibition of murder cannot eliminate murder. But the prohibition of murder is more effective than a policy of "murder control" would be.

Guns are not like alcohol and drugs, both of which we have tried unsuccessfully to prohibit. Many people have an intense desire for alcohol or drugs that is independent of what other people may do. But the need for a gun for self-defense depends on whether other people have them and how effective the protection and deterrence provided by the state are. Thus, in other Western countries in which there are fewer guns, there are correspondingly fewer instances in which people need guns for effective self-defense.

Gun advocates sometimes argue that a prohibition would violate individuals' rights of self-defense. Imposing a ban on guns, they argue, would be tantamount to taking a person's gun from her just as someone is about to kill her. But this is a defective analogy. Although a prohibition would deprive people of one effective means of self-defense, it would also ensure that there would be far fewer occasions on which a gun would be necessary or even useful for self-defense. For guns would be forbidden not just to those who would use them for defense but also to those who would use them for aggression. Guns are only one means of self-defense and self-defense is only one means of achieving security against attack. It is the right to security against attack that is fundamental. A policy that unavoidably deprives a person of one means of self-defense but on balance substantially reduces her vulnerability to attack is therefore respectful of the more fundamental right from which the right of self-defense is derived.

In other Western countries, per capita homicide rates, as well as rates of violent crime involving guns, are a fraction of what they are in the United States. The possible explanations of this are limited. Gun advocates claim it has nothing to do with our permissive gun laws or our customs and practices involving guns. If they are right, should we conclude that Americans are simply inherently more violent, more disposed to mental derangement, and less moral than people in other Western countries? If you resist that conclusion, you have little choice but to accept that our easy access to all manner of firearms is a large part of the explanation of why we kill each at a much higher rate than our counterparts elsewhere. Gun advocates must search their consciences to determine whether they really want to share responsibility for the perpetuation of policies that make our country the homicide capitol of the developed world.

The (Terrifying) Transformative Potential of Technology
by Lisa Wade

When Adam Lanza walked into Sandy Hook Elementary School, he was carrying a Bushmaster .223 caliber Remington semiautomatic. This is the frightening weapon he used to take the lives of 27 people:

Richard Green/Commercial/Alamy

Source: © 2013 Sociological Images (http://thesocietypages.org/socimages/2012/12/20/the-transformative-potential-of-technology-the-bushmaster-223/).

The refrain—"guns don't kill people, people kill people"—does an injustice to the complicated homotechnocultural phenomenon that we call a massacre. Evan Selinger, at *The Atlantic*, does a wonderful job taking apart this phrase. It assumes an *instrumentalist* view of technology, where we bend it to our will. In contrast, he argues in favor of a *transformative* view: when humans interact with objects, they are transformed by that interaction. A gun changes how a person sees the world. Selinger writes:

> To someone with a gun, the world readily takes on a distinct shape. It not only offers people, animals, and things to interact with, but also potential targets.

In other words, if you have a hammer, suddenly all the world's problems look like nails to you (see Law of the Instrument). The wonderful French philosopher Bruno Latour put it this way:

> You are different with a gun in your hand; the gun is different with you holding it. You are another subject because you hold the gun; the gun is another object because it has entered into a relationship with you.

So, that's the homotechnological part of the story. What of the cultural?

At Sociological Images, Michael Kimmel observes that the vast majority of mass killings in the U.S. are carried out by middle-class, white males. "From an early age," he writes, "boys learn that violence is not only an acceptable form of conflict resolution, but one that is admired." While the vast majority of men will never be violent, they are all exposed to lessons about what it means to be a real man:

> They learn that if they are crossed, they have the manly obligation to fight back. They learn that they are entitled to feel like a real man, and that they have the right to annihilate anyone who challenges that sense of entitlement. . . They learn that "aggrieved entitlement" is a legitimate justification for violent explosion.

Violence is *culturally* masculine. So, when the human picks up the object, it matters whether that person is a man or a woman.

Bushmaster, the manufacturer of the weapon used by Lanza, was explicit in tying their product to masculinity. Though it has now been taken down, before the shooting visitors to their website could engage in public shaming of men who were insufficiently masculine, revoking their man card and branding them with the image of a female stick figure.

Their man card is "revoked" and Bushmaster has just the solution, which is to "reissue" a man card once a weapon is purchased.

Manliness is tied to gun ownership (and, perhaps, gun use). Whatever it is that threatens his right to consider himself a man, a gun is an immediate cure.

Many people are calling on politicians to respond to this tragedy by instituting stricter gun control laws and trying to reduce the number or change the type of guns in American hands. That'll help with the homotechnological part. But, as Kimmel argues, we also need to address the cultural part of the equation. We need to change what it means to be a man in America.

This post was co-written with Gwen Sharp and originally posted at Sociological Images.

Morning Joe

Joe Scarborough began his show *Morning Joe* Monday, December 17, 2012 addressing the school shooting at Sandy Hook Elementary School in Newtown, Connecticut. Today, we as a nation grieve. Today, we as a people feel helpless. Helpless to stop these random acts of violence that seem to be getting less random by the day.

It may the geographic proximity of Newtown to my hometown, or the fact my children's ages average those of the 20 young children tragically killed on Friday, or the fact my second son has Aspergers, or the fact that too many other facts associated with Friday's nightmare strike so close to home. . . that for me, there is no escaping the horrors visited upon the children and teachers of Sandy Hook.

The events that occurred in a short, violent outburst on Friday, December 14, 2012, were so evil that no words that I know of have yet been invented to sufficiently describe the horror experienced by 20 precious first grade students, their heroic principal, their anguished parents or the shocked New England town that will never be the same.

There is no way to capture the final moments of these children's short lives or the loss and helplessness their parents must feel today. There is nothing they can do, there is nothing any of us can do, to ease their pain this morning, or to cause these little children to run back into the loving arms of their family members this Christmas season.

Soon, we will watch the burials of these babies. We will hold up their parents in prayer. And we will hold our own children tighter as we thank God every afternoon watching them walk off their school bus and into our arms.

But every American must know—from this day forward—that nothing can ever be the same again.

We have said this before: after Columbine, after Arizona, after Aurora, after so many other numbing hours of murder and of massacre.

But let this be our true landmark; let Newtown be the hour after which, in the words of the New Testament, we did all we could to make all things new.

Politicians can no longer be allowed to defend the status quo. They must instead be forced to protect our children.

Parents can no longer take "No" for an answer from Washington when the topic turns to protecting children.

The violence we see spreading from shopping malls in Oregon, to movie theaters in Colorado, to college campuses in Virginia, to elementary schools in Connecticut, is being spawned by the toxic brew of a violent pop culture, a growing mental health crisis and the proliferation of combat-styled guns.

Though entrenched special interests will try to muddy the issues, the cause of these sickening mass shootings is no longer a mystery to common-sense Americans. And blessedly, there are more common-sense Americans than there are special interests, even if it doesn't always seem that way. Good luck to the gun lobbyist or Hollywood

Thinking Critically About Visuals

The Aftermath of the Newtown Massacre

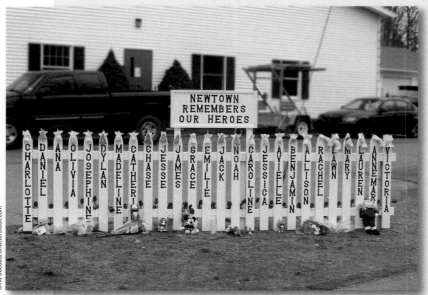

Gina Jacobs/Shutterstock.com

What are some of the elements of this simple memorial for those massacred at Newtown that make the photograph so profoundly heart-breaking?

lawyer who tries to blunt the righteous anger of ten million parents by hiding behind a twisted reading of our Bill of Rights.

Our government rightly obsesses day and night over how to prevent the next 9/11 from being launched from a cave in Afghanistan or a training base in Yemen. But perhaps now is the time to begin obsessing over how to stop the next attack on a movie theater, a shopping mall, a college campus or a first grade class.

The battle we now must fight, and the battle we must now win is for the safety and sanity of our children, and that is the war at home.

It's not all about guns, or all about violent movies and videogames. But we must no longer allow the perfect to be the enemy of the good. And we must not excuse total inaction by arguing that no single action can solve the problem and save our children.

I am a conservative Republican who received the NRA's highest ratings over 4 terms in Congress. I saw the debate over guns as a powerful, symbolic struggle between individual rights and government control. In the years after Waco and Ruby Ridge, the symbolism of that debate seemed even more powerful to my colleagues and me.

But the symbols of that ideological struggle have since been shattered by the harvest sown from violent, mind-numbing video games and gruesome Hollywood movies that dangerously desensitizes those who struggle with mental health challenges. Add military-styled weapons and high capacity magazines to that equation and tragedy can never be too far behind.

There is no easy ideological way forward. If it were only so simple as to blame Hollywood or the NRA, then our task could be completed in no time. But I come to you this morning with a heavy heart and no easy answers. Still, I have spent the past few days grasping for solutions and struggling for answers, while daring to question my long held beliefs on these subjects.

. . .

Abraham Lincoln once said of this great and powerful nation. . .

"From whence shall we expect the approach of danger? Shall some trans-Atlantic military giant step the earth and crush us at a blow? Never. All the armies of Europe and Asia. . . could not by force take a drink from the Ohio River or make a track on the Blue Ridge in the trial of a thousand years. No, if destruction be our lot we must ourselves be its author and finisher. As a nation of free men we will live forever or die by suicide."

For the sake of my four children, I choose life. And I choose change. It is time to turn over the tables inside the temple, for the sake of our children and for the sake of this great nation that we love.

QUESTIONS FOR ANALYSIS

1. In his article on the Sandy Hook massacre, Ted Anthony argues that the shooting was an attack on the American community and the values upon which it was built. "In killing the children of Sandy Hook, Adam Lanza effectively attacked the American nest. He went after not only our young but two other precious commodities—our sense of what we might become, and the stories we tell about who we are." What are the reasons that Anthony reaches this conclusion? Do you agree or disagree with his contention? Why or why not?

2. Dan Baum, in his article "The Price of Gun Control," contends that in our efforts to curb violence in America we are making a mistake by focusing on guns. He states: "It's true that America's rate of violent crime remains higher than in most European countries. But to focus on guns is to dodge a painful truth. America is more violent than other countries because Americans are more violent than other people. . . . by obsessing over inanimate pieces of metal, we avoid looking at what brings us more often than others to commit violent acts." Do you agree that "Americans are more violent than other people"? Should we not be focusing on gun control in our efforts to curb violence? Why or why not?

3. The CEO of the NRA, Wayne LaPierre, believes that the way to prevent massacres in schools is not by "demonizing lawful gun owners," but by placing armed officers in every school, contending that "The only thing that stops a bad guy with a gun is a good guy with a gun." He also argues that much of the blame rests on the producers of vicious, violent video games and slasher films. How would you critically evaluate his claims and the reasoning upon which they are based?

4. In his article "Why Gun 'Control' Is Not Enough," Jeff McMahan argues that introducing more guns into the culture will only increase violence, not diminish it. Describe the reasoning that leads him to this conclusion and then critically evaluate its soundness.

5. In their article on guns, Gwen Sharp and Lisa Wade contend that weapons transform the people using them, taking issue with the NRA slogan, "Guns don't kill people, people kill people." Why do the authors believe what they do? Be sure to include the ad for the Bushmaster assault weapon in your analysis.

6. In his passionate statement addressing the Sandy Hook shootings, the MSNBC host of *Morning Joe*, Joe Scarborough states, "But every American must know—from this day forward—that nothing can ever be the same again." What does Scarborough mean by this statement? What are the things that we as a society must do, and why must we do them?

CHAPTER 4   Reviewing and Viewing

Summary

- We construct our world by actively selecting, organizing, and interpreting our sensations.
- We view the world through our own unique "lenses," which shape and influence our perceptions, beliefs, and knowledge.
- The "prescription" of our lenses has been formed by our experiences and our reflection on those experiences.
- We construct beliefs based on our perceptions, and we construct knowledge based on our beliefs.
- Thinking critically involves understanding how perceiving lenses—ours and those of others—influence perceptions, beliefs, and knowledge.
- Different types of beliefs include *reports, inferences,* and *judgments*.

Assessing Your Strategies and Creating New Goals

How Aware Am I of My Perceiving Process?

Described below are key insights that are correlated with understanding the nature of the perceiving process. Evaluate your position regarding each of these insights, and use this self-evaluation to guide your choices as you seek to understand the nature of the way we perceive the world and construct beliefs based on this understanding.

Understand the Dynamic Nature of Your Perceiving Process

I am acutely aware of the extent to which I actively select, organize, and interpret my perceptions.	I tend to assume that I passively receive my perceptions of the world like a camera or tape recorder.
5 4 3 2 1	

All of us play an active role in the way we select, organize, and interpret our perceptions of the world. It's essential that we become aware of this active role because we too often assume that we are accurately experiencing the world and that if other people experience the world differently, they must be wrong. Critical thinkers are able to distinguish what we are "bringing" to our experience of the world from what is actually occurring in the world.

*Strategy: Become aware of your own perceiving process by becoming more critically aware of the way we actively **select** sensations to pay attention to, **organize** these sensations into meaningful relationships, and give the world meaning by actively **interpreting** the world that we have constructed.*

Become Aware of Your Personal "Lenses"

I am acutely aware of how my personal "lenses" shape and color what I experience.	I usually think that the way I see things is the way things are.
5 4 3 2 1	

All of us view the world through "lenses" that influence and "color" how we experience things, process information, and make decisions. Critical thinkers seek to become aware of their own personal lenses and the lenses of others so that they can understand the meanings people are projecting and discover the "truth."

Strategy: Become aware of your lenses by developing the habit of asking yourself: Are my perceptions accurate and complete? How are my biases influencing my perceptions? Are there other ways of viewing this situation that I am not acknowledging? Which ways of viewing the situation make the most sense?

Become Aware of How Your Personal "Lenses" Shape Your Beliefs

I am acutely aware of how my personal "lenses" shape my beliefs about the world.	I don't generally think about how my perceptions influence the beliefs I form.
5 4 3 2 1	

Our beliefs about the world are influenced by our perceiving "lenses," which in turn are shaped by our experiences. Since our perceiving lenses are typically subjective and biased, our beliefs about the world are often subjective and biased as well.

Strategy: As critical thinkers, we need to become aware of our perceiving lenses, so that we can compensate for their influence on our beliefs. A good way to do that is to carefully examine the beliefs and perceptions of others, analyze why they may be different from our own, and help those people become aware of their "perceiving lenses" as well.

Analyze Contrasting Points of View

I actively seek out other points of view and analyze why they are different from mine.	I generally assume that my point of view is correct and contrasting perspectives are wrong if they disagree with me.
5 4 3 2 1	

Because we cannot "remove" our perceiving lenses, everybody is biased all of the time, having perceptions and constructing beliefs that reflect our own subjective point of view. To complicate things, we are usually *unaware* of our perceiving lenses, assuming that our perceptions—and resulting beliefs—about the world are objectively true, and that people who disagree with us must be wrong.

Strategy: A very effective strategy in this regard is to carefully examine other points of view in order to compare and contrast them with our own, as we did with the different accounts of the assassination of Malcolm X in this chapter. This perspective-taking process enables us to identify the areas of common agreement and also better understand the areas of difference. Do these differences reflect factual differences, or do they reflect differences in our perceiving lenses?

Understand the Differences Between Reports, Inferences, and Judgments

I understand clearly the differences between reports, inferences, and judgments.	I am unclear about the differences between reports, inferences, and judgments.
5 4 3 2 1	

Reports, inferences, and judgments are three very different kinds of beliefs that play uniquely distinctive roles in our thinking, understanding, and communication with others. Failure to clearly understand—and make use of—the differences between them can result in unnecessary confusion and conflict.

Strategy: Working with others, describe in writing a scene or a situation. Then analyze your description: What statements are factual "reports"? Which are inductive

inferences? Which are evaluative judgments? Did your analysis agree with others'
analyses? Why or why not? Discuss how to resolve differences in contrasting reports,
inferences, and judgments.

Suggested Films

Babel (2006)

What role do the media play in shaping our perceptions? The stories of several families in different parts of the world are brought together by a single disaster. When a young woman traveling with her husband in Morocco is the victim of a shooting, the media immediately portray the event as a "terrorist attack." Meanwhile, the couple's children are taken by their nanny to Mexico. The story of a Japanese widower becomes a part of the intricate narrative web.

The Life of Pi (2013)

How do we discover truth? Is there an ultimate reality? Based on a book by the same name, the fantasy/adventure film tells the story of a sixteen-year-old Indian boy who, following a shipwreck, survives 227 days in a lifeboat with a Bengal tiger named Richard Parker. The film explores questions of survival and spirituality, and ultimately poses profound questions regarding what is truth and what is reality.

The Matrix (1999)

How can we distinguish reality from illusion? Is a life based on lies preferable to a challenging life of truth? In this futuristic film, a computer hacker discovers that his reality might be a false existence created by artificial intelligence machines, and is given the choice of remaining in this fantasy world or attempting to liberate himself and humankind from an artificial existence.

The Truman Show (1998)

Is there any way to tell the difference between reality and virtual reality? Truman Burbank is an apparently normal man with a normal life who does not realize that his entire existence is the artificial conception of a production studio. When Truman begins to suspect that this life is not what it appears to be, he attempts to defy the scripted fate and take his existence into his own hands.

When the Levees Broke: A Requiem in Four Acts (2006)

In this epic documentary, director Spike Lee explores the causes for the extensive destruction in New Orleans during Hurricane Katrina. As he critically examines the response to the disaster by media and relief and rescue crews, he gives voice to those people who witnessed and lived through the aftermath of the ordeal.

Why do you believe what you believe? Developing informed and well-reasoned beliefs is best accomplished through a process of vigorous discussion and debate, exploring all sides of an issue and the justifications that support these various viewpoints.

Constructing Knowledge

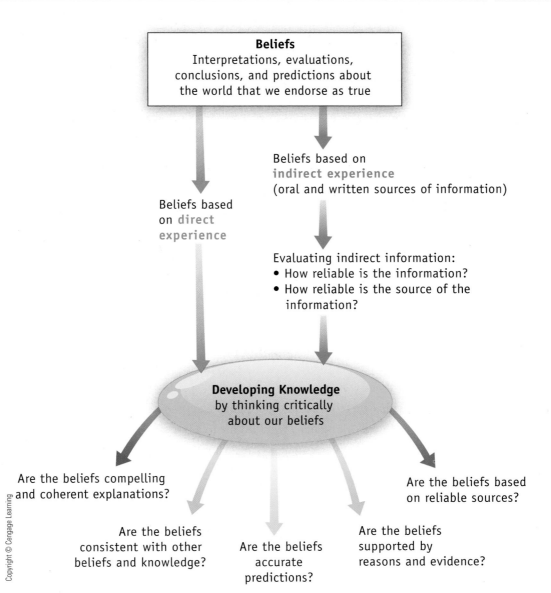

Beliefs
Interpretations, evaluations, conclusions, and predictions about the world that we endorse as true

Beliefs based on **indirect experience**
(oral and written sources of information)

Beliefs based on **direct experience**

Evaluating indirect information:
• How reliable is the information?
• How reliable is the source of the information?

Developing Knowledge
by thinking critically about our beliefs

Are the beliefs compelling and coherent explanations?

Are the beliefs consistent with other beliefs and knowledge?

Are the beliefs accurate predictions?

Are the beliefs supported by reasons and evidence?

Are the beliefs based on reliable sources?

As your mind develops through your experiences and your reflection on these experiences, your perceptions of the world should continue to develop as well. By thinking critically about your perceptions, by seeking to view the world from perspectives other than your own and to comprehend the reasons that support these perspectives, you should find that your understanding of the world becomes increasingly more accurate and complete. As you have seen in the previous chapter, much of your knowledge of the world begins with perceiving. But to develop knowledge and understanding, you must use your thinking abilities to examine this experience critically. Increased understanding of the way the world operates thus increases the accuracy and completeness of your perceptions and leads you to informed beliefs about what is happening.

Believing and Knowing

The beliefs you develop help you explain why the world is the way it is, and they guide you in making decisions. But all beliefs are not equal. Some beliefs are certain ("I believe that someday I will die") because they are supported by compelling reasons. Other beliefs are less certain ("I believe that life exists on other planets") because the support is not as solid. As you form and revise your beliefs, based on your experiences and your reflection on these experiences, it is important to make them as accurate as possible. The more accurate your beliefs are, the better you are able to understand what is taking place and to predict what will occur in the future.

The beliefs you form vary tremendously in accuracy. The idea of *knowing* is the ability to distinguish beliefs supported by strong reasons or evidence from beliefs for which there is less support, as well as from beliefs disproved by evidence to the contrary (such as the belief that the earth is flat). This distinction between "believing" and "knowing" can be illustrated by replacing the word *believe* with the word *know* in statements. For example:

1. I *know* that I will die.
2. I *know* that there is life on other planets.
3. I *know* that working hard will lead me to a happy life.
4. I *know* that the earth is flat.

The only statement with which most people would agree it clearly makes sense to use the word *know* is the first one because there is conclusive evidence that this belief is accurate. In the case of statement 2, we might say that although life on other planets is a possibility, there does not seem to be *conclusive* evidence at present that supports this view. In the case of statement 3, we might say that although for some people working hard leads to a happy life, this is not always the case. Statement 4 expresses a belief that we "know" is *not* true. In other words, when you say that you "know" something, you mean at least two different things:

1. I think this belief is completely accurate.
2. I can explain to you the reasons or evidence that support this belief.

If either of these standards is not met, we would usually say that you do not really "know." Or to state it another way, "You can *believe* what is not so, but you cannot *know* what is not so."

We work at evaluating the accuracy of our beliefs by examining the reasons or evidence that support them (known as the *justification* for the beliefs). As you learn more about the world and yourself, you try to form beliefs that are increasingly accurate and justified.

Determining the accuracy and justification of your beliefs is challenging. The key point is that as a critical thinker, you should continually try to form and revise your beliefs so that you can understand the world in increasingly effective ways. Even when you find that you maintain certain beliefs over a long period of time, your explorations will result in a deeper and fuller understanding of these beliefs.

Thinking Activity 5.1

EVALUATING THE ACCURACY OF BELIEFS

State whether you think that each of the following beliefs is

- *Completely accurate* (so that you would say, "I know this is the case")
- *Generally accurate* but not completely accurate (so that you would say, "This is often, but not always, the case")
- *Generally not accurate* but sometimes accurate (so that you would say, "This is usually not the case but is sometimes true")
- *Definitely not accurate* (so that you would say, "I know that this is not the case")

After determining the *degree of accuracy* in this way, explain why you have selected your answer.

- *Example:* I believe that if you study hard, you will achieve good grades.
- *Degree of accuracy:* Generally, but not completely, accurate.
- *Explanation:* Although many students who study hard achieve good grades, this is not always true. Sometimes students have difficulty understanding the work in a certain subject, no matter how hard they study. And sometimes they just don't know how to study effectively. In other cases, students may lack adequate background or experience in a certain subject area (e.g., English may be a second language), or they may have a personality conflict with the instructor.

1. I believe that essay exams are more difficult than multiple-choice exams.
2. I believe that longer prison sentences discourage people from committing crimes.
3. I believe that there are more people on the earth today than there were 100 years ago.
4. I believe fate plays an important role in determining life's events.
5. I believe that people have the freedom to change themselves and their circumstances if they really want to.

Now write some of your most important beliefs on the following subjects and evaluate them in the same way:

- love
- happiness
- physical health
- religion

Knowledge and Truth

Most people in our culture are socialized to believe that knowledge and truth are absolute and unchanging. One major goal of social institutions, including family, the school system, and religion, is to transfer the knowledge that has been developed over the ages. Under this model, the role of learners is to absorb this information passively, like sponges. As you have seen in this text, achieving knowledge and truth is a complicated process. Instead of simply relying on the testimony of authorities like parents, teachers, textbooks, and religious leaders, critical thinkers have a responsibility to engage *actively* in the learning process and participate in developing their own understanding of the world.

The need for this active approach to knowing is underscored by the fact that authorities often disagree about the true nature of a given situation or the best course of action. It is not uncommon, for example, for doctors to disagree about a diagnosis, for economists to differ on the state of the economy, for researchers to present contrasting views on the best approach to curing cancer, for psychiatrists to disagree on whether a convicted felon is a menace to society or a harmless victim of social forces, and for religions to present conflicting approaches to achieving eternal life.

What do we do when experts disagree? As a critical thinker, you must analyze and evaluate all the available information, develop your own well-reasoned beliefs, and recognize when you don't have sufficient information to arrive at well-reasoned beliefs. You must realize that these beliefs may evolve over time as you gain information or improve your insight.

Although there are compelling reasons to view knowledge and truth in this way, many people resist it. Either they take refuge in a belief in the absolute, unchanging nature of knowledge and truth, as presented by the appropriate authorities, or they conclude that there is no such thing as knowledge or truth and that trying to seek either is a futile enterprise. Some beliefs *are* better than others, not because an authority has proclaimed them so but because they can be analyzed in terms of the following criteria:

- How effectively do your beliefs *explain what is taking place*?
- To what extent are these beliefs *consistent with other beliefs* you have about the world?
- How effectively do your beliefs help you *predict what will happen* in the future?
- To what extent are your beliefs supported by *sound reasons and compelling evidence* derived from *reliable sources*?

Another important criterion for evaluating your beliefs is that the beliefs are *falsifiable*. This means that you can state conditions—tests—under which the beliefs could be disproved and the beliefs nevertheless pass those tests. For example, if you believe that you can create ice cubes by placing water-filled trays in a freezer, it is easy to see how you can conduct an experiment to determine if your belief is accurate. If you believe that your destiny is related to the positions of the planets and stars (as astrologers do), it is not clear how you can conduct an experiment to determine if your belief is accurate. Because a belief that is not falsifiable can never be proved, such a belief is of questionable accuracy.

A critical thinker sees knowledge and truth as goals that we are striving to achieve, processes that we are all actively involved in as we construct our understanding of the world. Developing accurate knowledge about the world is often a challenging process of exploration and analysis in which our understanding grows and evolves over a period of time.

STAGES OF KNOWING

The road to becoming a critical thinker is a challenging journey that involves passing through different stages of knowing in order to achieve an effective understanding of the world. These stages, ranging from simple to complex, characterize people's thinking and the way they understand their world. A critical thinker is a person who has progressed through all of the stages to achieve a sophisticated understanding of the nature of knowledge. This framework is based on the work of Harvard psychologist Dr. William Perry (*Forms of Intellectual and Ethical Development in the College Years: A Scheme*), who used in-depth research to create a developmental model of human thought. I use a condensed three-stage version of Perry's framework:

Stage 1: The Garden of Eden
Stage 2: Anything Goes
Stage 3: Thinking Critically

An individual may be at different stages simultaneously, depending on the subject or area of experience. For example, a person may be at an advanced stage in one area of life (academic work) but at a less sophisticated stage in another area (romantic relationships or conception of morality). In general, however, people tend to operate predominantly within one stage in most areas of their lives.

Stage 1: The Garden of Eden People in the Garden of Eden stage of thinking tend to see the world in terms of black and white, right and wrong. How do they determine what is right, what to believe? The "authorities" *tell* them. Just like in the biblical Garden of Eden, knowledge is absolute, unchanging, and in the sole possession of authorities. Ordinary people can never determine the truth for themselves; they must rely on the experts. If someone disagrees with what they have been told by the authorities, then that person *must* be wrong. There is no possibility of compromise or negotiation.

Who are the authorities? The first authorities we encounter are usually our parents. When parents are rooted in this stage of thinking, they expect children to do as they're told. Parents are the authorities, and the role of children is to benefit from their parents' years of experience, their store of knowledge, and their position of authority. Similarly, when children enter a school system built on the foundation of Stage 1 thinking (as most school systems are), they are likely to be told, "We have the questions and the answers; your role is to learn them, not ask questions of your own"—an approach that runs counter to children's natural curiosity.

People in this Garden of Eden stage of thinking become dissatisfied when they realize that they can't simply rely on authorities to tell them what to think and believe because in almost every arena—medicine, religion, economics, psychology, education, science, law, child rearing—authorities often disagree with each other. We explored this disturbing phenomenon earlier in the chapter, and it poses a mortal threat to Stage 1 thinking. If the authorities disagree with each other, then how do we figure out what (and whom) to believe? Stage 1 thinkers try to deal with this contradiction by maintaining that *my* authorities know more than *your* authorities. But if we are willing to think clearly and honestly, this explanation simply doesn't hold up: We have to explain *why* we choose to believe one authority over another. And as soon as that happens, we have transcended Stage 1 thinking. Just as Adam and Eve could not go back to blind, uncritical acceptance of authority once they had tasted the fruit of the Tree of the Knowledge of Good and Evil, so it is nearly impossible to return to Stage 1 after recognizing its oversimplifying inadequacies.

Why are some people able to go beyond Stage 1 thinking while others remain more or less stuck there throughout their lives? Part of the answer lies in how diverse their environment is. When people live in predominantly homogeneous environments, surrounded by people who think and believe the same way, it is much easier to maintain the artificially uniform worldview of the Garden of Eden thinking.

However, when people are exposed to diverse experiences that challenge them with competing perspectives, it is much more difficult to maintain the unquestioned faith in the authoritarian dictates of Stage 1 thinking. For example, in my philosophy of religion classes, the final term project is for students to visit five different places of religious worship selected from a list of thirty I provide; these range from Zen Buddhist to Pentecostal, Catholic to Southern Baptist, Jewish to Hindu. Students invariably report that this project transformed their thinking, stimulating them to view religion in a richer, more complex light. It gives them the opportunity to see other people who are just as serious and devout as themselves engage in very different religious practices.

However, simply providing people with diverse experiences does not guarantee that they will be stimulated to question and transcend the limiting confines of Stage 1 thinking. We need to have the emotional willingness to open ourselves to new possibilities and the intellectual ability to see issues from different perspectives. Very often people are so emotionally entangled in their point of view that they are simply unwilling to question its truth; the power of their emotional needs inhibits the potential illumination of their reasoning abilities. Additionally, many people have not developed the flexibility of thinking needed to extricate themselves from their own point of view and look at issues from different perspectives. To become a Stage 2 thinker, both of these conditions must be met: the emotional willingness *and* the cognitive ability to be open-minded.

Stage 2: Anything Goes Once one has rejected the dogmatic, authoritarian framework of Stage 1, the temptation in Stage 2 is to go to the opposite extreme and believe that anything goes. The reasoning is something like this: If authorities are not infallible and we can't trust their expertise, then no one point of view is ultimately any better than any other. In Stage 1 the authorities could resolve such disputes, but if their opinion is on the same level as yours and mine, then there is no rational way to resolve differences.

In the tradition of philosophy, such a view is known as *relativism*: the truth is relative to any individual or situation, and there is no standard we can use to decide which beliefs make the most sense. Take the example of fashion. You may believe that an attractive presentation includes loose-fitting clothing in muted colors, a natural hairstyle, and a minimum of makeup and jewelry. Someone else might prefer tight-fitting black clothing, gelled hair, tattoos, and body piercings. In Stage 2 thinking, there's no way to evaluate these or any other fashion preferences; they are simply "matters of taste." And, in fact, if you examine past photographs of yourself and what you considered to be "attractive" years ago, this relativistic point of view probably makes some sense.

Although we may be drawn to this seemingly open-minded attitude—anything goes—the reality is that we are often not so tolerant. We *do* believe that some appearances are more aesthetically pleasing than others. But there is an even more serious threat to Stage 2 thinking. Imagine the following scenario: As you are strolling down the street, you suddenly feel a gun pushed against your back accompanied by the demand for all your valuables. You protest, arguing with this would-be mugger that he has no right to your possessions. "On the contrary," your philosophically

Stages of Knowing

Stage 1: The Garden of Eden
Knowledge is clear, certain, and absolute and is provided by authorities. Our role is to learn and accept information from authorities without question or criticism. Anyone who disagrees with the authorities must be wrong.

Stage 2: Anything Goes
Because authorities often disagree with each other, no one really "knows" what is true or right. All beliefs are of equal value, and there is no way to determine whether one belief makes more sense than another belief.

Stage 3: Thinking Critically
Some viewpoints are better than other viewpoints, not because authorities say so but because there are compelling reasons to support these viewpoints. We have a responsibility to explore every perspective, evaluate the supporting reasons for each, and develop our own informed conclusions that we are prepared to modify or change based on new information or better insight.

inclined mugger responds, "I believe that 'might makes right,' and since I have a weapon, I am entitled to your valuables. You have your beliefs, I have my beliefs, and as Stage 2 thinkers, there's no way for you to prove me wrong!" Preposterous? Nevertheless, this is the logical conclusion of Anything Goes thinking. If we truly believe this, then we cannot condemn *any* belief or action, no matter how heinous, and we cannot praise *any* belief or action, no matter how laudatory.

When we think things through, it's obvious that the Anything Goes level of thinking simply doesn't work because it leads to absurd conclusions that run counter to our deeply felt conviction that some beliefs *are* better than other beliefs. So while Stage 2 may represent a slight advance over Stage 1 in sophistication and complexity, it's clear to a discerning thinker that a further advance to the next stage is necessary.

Stage 3: Thinking Critically The two opposing perspectives of Stages 1 and 2 find their synthesis in Stage 3, Thinking Critically. When people achieve this level of understanding, they recognize that some viewpoints *are* better than other viewpoints, not simply because authorities say so but because *there are compelling reasons to support these viewpoints.* At the same time, people in this stage are open-minded toward other viewpoints, especially those that disagree with theirs. They recognize that there are often a number of legitimate perspectives on complex issues, and they accept the validity of these perspectives to the extent that they are supported by persuasive reasons and evidence.

Consider a more complicated issue, like euthanasia. A Stage 3 thinker approaches this as she approaches all issues: trying to understand all of the different viewpoints on the issue, evaluating the reasons that support each of these viewpoints, and then coming to her own thoughtful conclusion. When asked, she can explain the rationale for her viewpoint, but she also respects differing viewpoints that are supported by legitimate reasons, even though she believes her viewpoint makes more sense. In addition, a Stage 3 thinker maintains an open mind, always willing to consider new evidence that might convince her to modify or even change her position.

Although people in the Thinking Critically stage are open to different perspectives, they *commit* themselves to definite points of view and are confident in explaining the reasons and evidence that have led them to their conclusions. Being open-minded is not the same thing as being intellectually wishy-washy. In addition to having clearly defined views, Stage 3 thinkers are always willing to listen to people who disagree with them. In fact, they actively seek out opposing viewpoints because they know that this is the only way to achieve the clearest, most insightful, most firmly grounded understanding. They recognize that their views may evolve over time as they learn more.

Becoming a Stage 3 thinker is a worthy goal, and it is the only way to adequately answer Socrates' challenge to examine our lives thoughtfully and honestly. To live a life of reflection and action, of open-mindedness and commitment, of purpose and fulfillment, requires the full development of our intellectual abilities and positive traits of character.

Thinking Activity 5.2

WHAT STAGE OF KNOWING AM I IN?

1. Create a diagram to illustrate the three stages of knowing.

2. We all know people who illustrate each of these three stages. Think about the people in your life—professionally and personally—and identify which stage you think they mainly fall into and why.

3. Consider carefully your beliefs in each of the following areas, and evaluate in which of the three stages of knowing you predominantly think.

education	human nature
professional area of expertise	social relationships
science	child rearing
moral issues	aesthetic areas (beauty)
religion	

Example: "My beliefs in the area of my academic classes tend to be Stage 1. I have always trusted the experts, whether they are my teachers or the textbooks we are reading. That's how I see the purpose of education: to learn the facts from those who know them." Or "My beliefs in my area of special interest, health, are Stage 3. When confronted with a set of symptoms, I consider all of the possible diagnoses, carefully evaluate the relevant evidence, get a second opinion if necessary, and then develop a plan that involves holistic and nutritional approaches as well as standard medical treatments."

Thinking Critically About Your Beliefs

The path to becoming a consistent Stage 3 thinker begins with evaluating the process you use to form beliefs and reach conclusions about the world. Some of your beliefs are deep and profound, with far-reaching implications, such as your belief (or disbelief) in a Supreme Being or your opinion on whether the Golden Rule should govern people's actions. Other beliefs are less significant, such as whether vitamin supplements improve your health or if requiring children to wear school uniforms is beneficial. Your total collection of beliefs constitutes your philosophy of life, the guiding beacon you use to chart the course of your personal existence. As you become a more accomplished critical thinker, you will develop beliefs that will enhance the quality of your life, beliefs that are clearly conceived, thoughtfully expressed, and solidly supported. This is the first step in constructing an enlightened philosophy, painting a portrait of yourself that you can present to the world with pride and satisfaction.

Everybody has a collection of beliefs that she or he uses to guide her or his actions. What differentiates people is the *quality* of their beliefs, the strength of the reasons and evidence that support their beliefs. As a critical thinker, you should be striving to develop beliefs constructed through a process of thoughtful reflection and analysis. For example, here is a brief survey of some beliefs that may contribute to your philosophy of life. Briefly answer the statements in the following activity and note how comfortable you would feel in justifying your answers as well as the paths you pursued to arrive at them.

Thinking Activity 5.3

SURVEYING YOUR BELIEFS

Answer the following questions, based on what you believe to be true:

1. Is there a God?

2. Should research on the cloning of humans be allowed?

3. Should women have the legal right to decide to have an abortion?

4. Should the government take all steps to keep our society safe from terrorism, even if this means curtailing some of our personal liberties?

5. Is the death penalty ever justified?

6. Should health care workers and potential patients be tested for AIDS and, if positive, be identified to each other?

7. Should the government provide public assistance to citizens who cannot support themselves and their families?

8. Should affirmative action programs be created to compensate for long-standing discrimination?

9. Have aliens visited the earth in some form?

10. Should parents be permitted to refuse conventional medical care for their children if their religious beliefs prohibit it?

11. Should certain "recreational" drugs, such as marijuana, be legalized?

12. Should people with terminal illnesses be permitted to end their lives with medical assistance?

Critical thinkers continually evaluate their beliefs by applying intellectual standards to assess the strength and accuracy of these beliefs. *Uncritical* thinkers generally adopt beliefs without thoughtful scrutiny or rigorous evaluation, letting these beliefs drift into their thinking for all sorts of superficial and illogical reasons. The most effective way for you to test the strength and accuracy of your beliefs is to evaluate evidence that supports them. There are four categories of evidence: authorities, written references, factual evidence, and personal experience.

Now you may be thinking, "Will I be called upon to apply this structure—these thinking tools—to every situation?" It may be overly optimistic to expect that we can take time out to step back and evaluate all our situations this way, especially because we already feel so overburdened and overextended. However, it is precisely because of this that we need to put on the brakes, or we risk losing ourselves in the frenetically accelerated flow of today's culture. What you are learning from these and additional exercises is a way of approaching both small and large questions differently from the way you did before. By recognizing the need to impose these intellectual standards, you will eventually use them habitually.

Thinking Critically About Evaluating Evidence

Authorities: Are the authorities knowledgeable in this area? Are they reliable? Have they ever given inaccurate information? Do other authorities disagree?

Written references: What are the credentials of the authors? Are there others who disagree with their opinions? On what evidence do the authors base their opinions?

Factual evidence: What are the source and foundation of the evidence? Can the evidence be interpreted differently? Does the evidence support the conclusion?

Personal experience: What were the circumstances under which the experience took place? Were distortions or mistakes in perception possible? Have other people had either similar or conflicting experiences? Are there other explanations for the experience?

Thinking Critically About Visuals

"Why Does a Salad Cost More Than a Big Mac?"

What people *say* they believe is often at odds with the choices they make. For example, the pyramid on the right depicts Federal Nutrition Recommendations, while the pyramid on the left presents what products the government actually supports in terms of farm subsidies. What is your reaction to this apparent contradiction between rhetoric and policy? Do you believe that the government should take a more active role in contributing to healthy eating and a less overweight population?

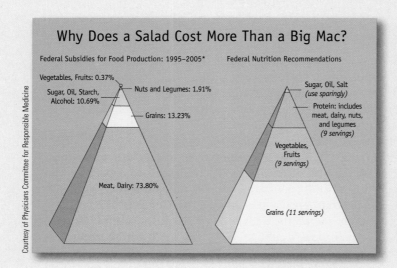

Why Does a Salad Cost More Than a Big Mac?

Federal Subsidies for Food Production: 1995–2005*

Vegetables, Fruits: 0.37%
Sugar, Oil, Starch, Alcohol: 10.69%
Nuts and Legumes: 1.91%
Grains: 13.23%
Meat, Dairy: 73.80%

Federal Nutrition Recommendations

Sugar, Oil, Salt *(use sparingly)*
Protein: includes meat, dairy, nuts, and legumes *(9 servings)*
Vegetables, Fruits *(9 servings)*
Grains *(11 servings)*

Courtesy of Physicians Committee for Responsible Medicine

Thinking Activity 5.4

EVALUATING MY BELIEFS

1. Select several of your responses to the Belief Survey (Thinking Activity 5.3 on pages 206–207), and explain the reasons, evidence, and experiences that led you to your conclusions. Be specific.

2. After you have recorded your evidence, use the questions under "Thinking Critically About Evaluating Evidence" to assess its accuracy and strength.

EXAMPLE: I believe that aliens have visited the earth in some form.

EXPLANATION: I have read a great deal about eyewitness sightings and evidence of a government cover-up, and I have met people who believe they have seen unidentified flying objects (UFOs).

Reasons/Evidence

- *Authorities:* Many reputable people have seen UFOs and had personal encounters with aliens. The government has documented these in secret files, which include the UFO crash at Roswell, New Mexico, in 1947. Government attempts at concealment and cover-up have been transparent.

- *References:* There are many books supporting alien visitations and alien abductions.
- *Factual evidence:* There are many photographs of UFOs and eyewitness accounts from people who have seen alien spacecraft. There have also been accounts of alien abductions. In addition, the movie *Alien Autopsy* purportedly shows an alien being dissected.
- *Personal experience:* I have personally spoken to several people who are convinced that they saw things in the sky that looked like flying saucers.

Thinking Critically About Visuals

"I Knew That Aliens Existed!"

Examine the faces and body language of people in the photo. Do you think they believe that this "alien" corpse is real? Do you think it might be real? Do you believe that alien life has visited earth? Why or why not?

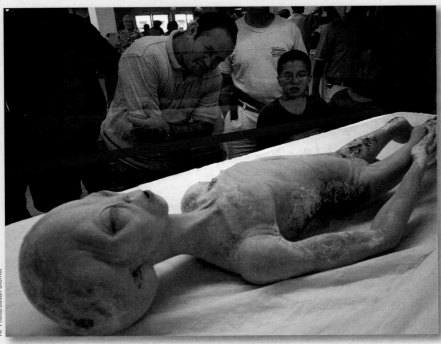

AP Photo/Susan Sterner

Let's examine the process of critical evaluation by thinking through a sample belief: "I believe that aliens have visited the earth in some form." A Gallup Poll found that 42 percent of American college graduates believe that flying saucers have visited the earth in some form.

Reasons/Evidence
Authorities

Many reputable people have seen UFOs and had personal encounters with aliens. The government has documented these in secret files, which include the UFO crash at Roswell, New Mexico, in 1947. Government attempts at concealment and cover-up have been transparent.

Thinking Critically About Authorities

Although many individuals have testified about alien encounters over the years, almost all scientific authorities have been extremely skeptical. They emphasize that all of the "evidence" is unsubstantiated, controversial, indirect, and murky—the markings of pseudoscientific fantasies. If aliens and UFOs exist, why haven't they announced their presence in an incontrovertible fashion? Some of the most intriguing evidence comes in the form of the government's belated and somewhat bizarre explanations for UFO sightings and the alleged Roswell incident. On June 25, 1997, the Air Force announced that the mysterious happenings in the New Mexico desert in the late 1940s and 1950s were in fact experiments involving crash dummies and weather balloons. Six weeks later, on August 3, 1997, the CIA "admitted" that the U.S. government had lied about alleged UFO sightings in the 1950s and 1960s to protect classified information regarding top-secret spy planes, the U-2 and SR-71. Why did the government suddenly attempt to explain these mysteries after all these years? And why does there appear to be contradictory testimony from different parts of the government? Why do the government explanations seem almost as fanciful and farfetched as the UFO stories?

References

There are many books supporting alien visitations and alien abductions.

Thinking Critically About References

Although many books regarding UFOs have been written, few have been more than unsubstantiated speculation. Philip J. Corso, who served on the National Security Council under President Dwight D. Eisenhower, contended in his book *The Day After Roswell* (Pocket Books, 1997) that he personally directed an army project that transferred to the military various types of technology recovered from the alien ship that crashed in the desert. To date, efforts to prove or disprove his account have been inconclusive. After reviewing written accounts and interviewing people claiming to be alien abductees, Dr. John Mack, a psychiatry professor at Harvard Medical School, came to the conclusion that many of these reports are true. Though he was harshly criticized by his colleagues, Dr. Mack became instantly popular on the UFO circuit, and he convened a conference at which 200 mental health professionals gathered to discuss alien abductions.

Factual Evidence

There are many photographs of UFOs and eyewitness accounts from people who have seen alien spacecraft. There have also been accounts of alien abductions. In addition, the movie *Alien Autopsy* purportedly shows an alien being dissected.

Thinking Critically About Factual Evidence

There have been innumerable UFO sightings, many of which can be explained by the presence of aircraft in the vicinity, meteors, or some other physical event. However, there is a core of sightings, sometimes by large groups of reputable people, that have not been satisfactorily explained. There are a number of photographs of "flying saucers" taken at a considerable distance, and though provocative in their possibilities, they are inconclusive. Most reports of alien abductions have been considered by the scientific establishment to be hoaxes or the result of mental illness or hallucinations—at least until Dr. Mack's analysis noted previously. Medical experts and moviemakers have derided *Alien Autopsy* as a crude hoax, although a small number of people knowledgeable about physiology and moviemaking techniques find it persuasive. There is no documented history of where the film came from, a fact that undermines its credibility.

Personal Experience

I have personally spoken to several people who are convinced that they saw things in the sky that looked like flying saucers.

Thinking Critically About Personal Experience

The perceptions of eyewitnesses are notoriously unreliable. People consistently mistake and misinterpret what they experience and often see what they want to see. In evaluating the testimony of personal experience, we must establish independent confirmation.

Thinking Critically About Visuals

Whose Truth Do You Believe?

Last Christmas season saw the advent of the "Battle of the Billboards." The very public skirmish began with the organization Atheist Americans placing a large billboard just outside the Lincoln Tunnel in New York City depicting the Nativity scene and the Three Wisemen along with the line, "You KNOW it's a Myth. This season, celebrate REASON."

Courtesy of American Atheists

Courtesy of Catholic League

The Catholic League rose swiftly to meet this challenge erecting its own billboard on the other side of the Lincoln Tunnel, again depicting the Nativity scene but with the very different message, "You Know it's Real. This Season, Celebrate Jesus."

Which billboard should you believe? Whose truth should you accept? As critical thinkers our responsibility is to explore deeply and carefully the foundation for all of our beliefs. In the final analysis, the truth we believe should be **our own**, not someone else's. How might you go about investigating these competing claims to the truth about Christmas?

Using Perspective-Taking to Achieve Knowledge

In Chapter 4, we examined contrasting media accounts of the assassination of Malcolm X. Each account, we found, viewed the event through its own perceiving lenses, which shaped and influenced the information the writer selected, the way the writer organized it, his or her interpretations of the event and the people involved, and the language used to describe it. We can see now that this type of organized evaluation of contrasting sources and opinions—perspective-taking—is an essential strategy of Stage 3 thinking and one of the most powerful ways to construct well-supported beliefs and genuine knowledge. The following activity, which centers on the events at Tiananmen Square in 1989 involving mainly Chinese college students, provides another opportunity to engage in perspective-taking as part of critical thinking.

Thinking Activity 5.5

ANALYZING DIFFERENT ACCOUNTS OF THE CONFRONTATION AT TIANANMEN SQUARE

In the spring of 1989, a vigorous prodemocracy movement erupted in Beijing, the capital of China. Protesting the authoritarian control of the Communist regime, thousands of students staged demonstrations, engaged in hunger strikes, and organized marches involving hundreds of thousands of people. The geographical heart of these activities was the historic Tiananmen Square, taken over by the demonstrators who had erected a symbolic "Statue of Liberty." On June 4, 1989, the fledgling prodemocracy movement came to a bloody end when the Chinese army entered Tiananmen Square and seized control of it. The following are various accounts of this event from different sources. After analyzing these accounts, construct your own version of what you believe took place on that day. Use these questions to guide your analysis of the varying accounts:

- Does the account provide a convincing description of what took place?
- What reasons and evidence support the account?
- How reliable is the source? What are the author's perceiving lenses, which might influence his or her account?
- Is the account consistent with other reliable descriptions of this event?

Several Accounts of Events at Tiananmen Square, 1989, as reported in the New York Times *(June 4, 1989)*

Tens of thousands of Chinese troops retook the center of the capital from prodemocracy protesters early this morning, killing scores of students and workers and wounding hundreds more as they fired submachine guns at crowds of people who tried to resist.

Source: Excerpts from "Square Is Cleared" and "Beijing Death Toll at Least 300; Army Tightens Control of City but Angry Resistance Goes On," by Nicholas D. Kristoff, *The New York Times*, June 4/June 5, 1989. Copyright © 1989 by The New York Times Co. Reprinted with permission.

Troops marched along the main roads surrounding central Tiananmen Square, sometimes firing in the air and sometimes firing directly at crowds who refused to move. Reports on the number of dead were sketchy. Students said, however, that at least 500 people may have been killed in the crackdown. Most of the dead had been shot, but some had been run over by personnel carriers that forced their way through the protesters' barricades.

A report on the state-run radio put the death toll in the thousands and denounced the government for the violence, the Associated Press reported. But the station later changed announcers and broadcast another report supporting the governing Communist party. The official news programs this morning reported that the People's Liberation Army had crushed a "counterrevolutionary rebellion." They said that more than 1,000 police officers and troops had been injured and some killed, and that civilians had been killed, but did not give details.

Deng Xiaoping, Chairman of the Central Military Commission, as Reported in *Beijing Review* (July 10–16, 1989)

In contrast to the accounts of students and independent reporters and eyewitness accounts, Deng Xiaoping had a very different perspective on the events that occurred at Tiananmen Square. According to Deng, it wasn't the Chinese military that was responsible for the lion's share of the violence, it was a small number of mysterious instigators who incited the students to act rebelliously, thus causing their own downfall. He states: "The main difficulty in handling this matter lay in that we had never experienced such a situation before, in which a small minority of bad people mixed with so many young students and onlookers. Actually, what we faced was not just some ordinary people who were misguided, but also a rebellious clique and a large number of the dregs of society. The key point is that they wanted to overthrow our state and the Party. They had two main slogans: to overthrow the Communist Party and topple the socialist system. Their goal is to establish a bourgeois republic entirely dependent on the West."

Consistent with this version of events, it wasn't the students who were assaulted, injured and killed by the Army—it was members of the Army who were assaulted, injured, and killed by the demonstrators. Deng explains: "During the course of quelling the rebellion, many comrades of ours were injured or even sacrificed their lives. Some of their weapons were also taken from them by the rioters. Why? Because bad people mingled with the good, which made it difficult for us to take the firm measures that were necessary. Handling this matter amounted to a severe political test for our army, and what happened shows that our People's Liberation Army passed muster. If tanks were used to roll over people, this would have created a confusion between right and wrong among the people nationwide."

Instead of being the aggressors, the Army is viewed from Deng's perspective as heroes who were trying to deal with the small number of rebellious demonstrators. "This shows that the people's army is truly a Great Wall of iron and steel of the Party and country. This shows that no matter how heavy the losses of with we suffer and no matter how generations change, this army of ours is forever an army under the leadership of the Party, forever the defender of the country, forever the defender of socialism, forever the defender of public interest, and they are the most beloved of the people. At the same time, we should never forget how cruel our enemies are. For them we should not have an iota of forgiveness."

Reporter (Eyewitness Account), as reported in the *New York Times* (June 4, 1989)

Changan Avenue, or the Avenue of Eternal Peace, Beijing's main east-west thoroughfare, echoed with screams this morning as young people carried the bodies of their friends away from the front lines. The dead or seriously wounded were heaped on the backs of bicycles or tricycle rickshaws and supported by friends who rushed through the crowds, sometimes sobbing as they ran.

The avenue was lit by the glow of several trucks and two armed personnel carriers that students and workers set afire, and bullets swooshed overhead or glanced off buildings. The air crackled almost constantly with gunfire and tear gas grenades.

Students and workers tried to resist the crackdown, and destroyed at least sixteen trucks and two armored personnel carriers. Scores of students and workers ran alongside the personnel carriers, hurling concrete blocks and wooden staves into the treads until they ground to a halt. They then threw firebombs at one until it caught fire, and set the other alight after first covering it with blankets soaked in gasoline. The drivers escaped the flames, but were beaten by students. A young American man, who could not be immediately identified, was also beaten by the crowd after he tried to intervene and protect one of the drivers.

Clutching iron pipes and stones, groups of students periodically advanced toward the soldiers. Some threw bricks and firebombs at the lines of soldiers, apparently wounding many of them. Many of those killed were throwing bricks at the soldiers, but others were simply watching passively or standing at barricades when soldiers fired directly at them.

It was unclear whether the violence would mark the extinction of the seven-week-old democracy movement, or would prompt a new phase in the uprising, like a general strike. The violence in the capital ended a period of remarkable restraint by both sides, and seemed certain to arouse new bitterness and antagonism among both ordinary people and Communist Party officials for the Government of Prime Minister Li Peng.

"Our Government is already done with," said a young worker who held a rock in his hand, as he gazed at the army forces across Tiananmen Square. "Nothing can show more clearly that it does not represent the people." Another young man, an art student, was nearly incoherent with grief and anger as he watched the body of a student being carted away, his head blown away by bullets. "Maybe we'll fail today," he said. "Maybe we'll fail tomorrow. But someday we'll succeed. It's a historical inevitability."

Official Chinese Government Accounts

"Comrades, thanks for your hard work. We hope you will continue with your fine efforts to safeguard security in the capital."

Prime Minister Li Peng (addressing a group
of soldiers after the Tiananmen Square event)

"It never happened that soldiers fired directly at the people."

General Li Zhiyun

"The People's Liberation Army crushed a counterrevolutionary rebellion. More than 1,000 police officers and troops were injured and killed, and some civilians were killed."

Official Chinese news program

"At most 300 people were killed in the operation, many of them soldiers."

Yuan Mu, official government spokesperson

"Not a single student was killed in Tiananmen Square."

Chinese army commander

"My government has stated that a mob led by a small number of people prevented the normal conduct of the affairs of state. There was, I regret to say, loss of life on both sides. I wonder whether any other government confronting such an unprecedented challenge would have handled the situation any better than mine did."

Han Xu, Chinese ambassador to the United States

The *New York Times* (June 5, 1989)

It was clear that at least 300 people had been killed since the troops first opened fire shortly after midnight on Sunday morning but the toll may be much higher. Word-of-mouth estimates continued to soar, some reaching far into the thousands. . . . The student organization that coordinated the long protests continued to function and announced today that 2,600 students were believed to have been killed. Several doctors said that, based on their discussions with ambulance drivers and colleagues who had been on Tiananmen Square, they estimated that at least 2,000 had died. Soldiers also beat and bayoneted students and workers after daybreak on Sunday, witnesses said, usually after some provocation but sometimes entirely at random. "I saw a young woman tell the soldiers that they are the people's army, and that they mustn't hurt the people," a young doctor said after returning from one clash Sunday. "Then the soldier shot her, and ran up and bayoneted her."

Xiao Bin (Eyewitness Account Immediately After the Event)

Tanks and armored personnel carriers rolled over students, squashing them into jam, and the soldiers shot at them and hit them with clubs. When students fainted, the troops killed them. After they died, the troops fired one more bullet into them. They also used bayonets. They were too cruel, I never saw such things before.

**Xiao Bin (Account After Being Taken into Custody
by Chinese Authorities)**
I never saw anything. I apologize for bringing great harm to the party and the
country.

Thinking Activity 5.6

ANALYZING DIFFERENT ACCOUNTS OF A CURRENT EVENT

Locate three different newspaper or magazine accounts of an important event—a
court decision, a crime, and a political demonstration are possible topics. Analyze
each of the accounts with the questions listed next, and then construct your own
version of what you believe took place.

- Does the account provide a convincing description of what took place?

- What reasons and evidence support the account?

- How reliable is the source? What are the author's perceiving lenses, which
  might influence his or her account?

- Is the account consistent with other reliable descriptions of this event?

Beliefs Based on Indirect Experience

Until now, we have been exploring the way we form and revise beliefs based on our
direct experiences. Yet no matter how much you have experienced in your life, the
fact is that no one person's direct experiences are enough to establish an adequate
set of accurate beliefs. We can only be in one place at one time—and with a limited
amount of time at that. As a result, we depend on the direct experience of *other
people* to provide us with beliefs and also to act as foundations for those beliefs.
Consider the following questions. How would you go about explaining the reasons
or evidence for your beliefs?

1. Were you really born on the day that you have been told you were?

2. Do germs really exist?

3. Do you have a brain in your head?

4. Does outer space extend infinitely in all directions?

In all probability, your responses to these questions reveal beliefs that are based
on reasons or evidence beyond your direct experience. Of all the beliefs each

one of us has, few are actually based on our direct experience. Instead, almost all are founded on the experiences of others, who then communicated to us these beliefs and the evidence for them in some shape or form. As you reach beyond your personal experience to form and revise beliefs, you find that the information provided by other people is available in two basic forms: written and spoken testimony.

It is crucial that you use all your critical-thinking abilities to examine what others suggest you believe. In critically examining the beliefs of others, you should pursue the same goals of accuracy and completeness that you seek when examining beliefs based on your personal experience. As a result, you should be interested in the reasons or evidence that support the information others are presenting. For example, when you ask directions from others, you try to evaluate how accurate the information is by examining the reasons or evidence that seems to support the information being given.

When you depend on information provided by others, however, there is a further question to be asked: How *reliable* is the person providing the information? For instance, what sort of people do you look for if you need to ask directions? Why do you look for these particular types of people? In most cases, when you need to ask directions, you try to locate someone who you think will be reliable—in other words, a person who you believe will give you *accurate* information.

During the remainder of this chapter, you will explore the various ways you depend on others to form and revise your beliefs. In each case you will try to evaluate the information being presented by asking the following questions:

1. How reliable (how accurate and justified) is the information?
2. How reliable is the *source* of the information?

HOW RELIABLE ARE THE INFORMATION AND THE SOURCE?

One of the main goals of your thinking is to make sense of information, and there are key questions that you should ask when evaluating information being presented to you. As you saw in Chapter 4, each of us views the world through our own unique "lenses," which shape how we view the world and influence how we select and present information. Comparing different sources helps to make us aware of these lenses and highlights the different interests and purposes involved.

There are a variety of standards or criteria you can use to evaluate the reliability of the sources of information. The following criteria are useful for evaluating both written and spoken testimony.

- Was the source of the information able to make *accurate* observations?
- What do you know about the past *reliability* of the source of the information?
- How *knowledgeable* or experienced is the source of the information?

Thinking Activity 5.7

EVALUATING DIFFERENT PERSPECTIVES

Locate two different passages concerning the same topic, and analyze each passage using the information evaluation questions in the box below. For example, you might choose two different reviews of a movie, a play, a book, an art exhibit, or a concert—or two different passages analyzing a topic of current interest, such as a criminal trial result or a U.S. foreign policy issue.

Information Evaluation Questions

1. How reliable is the information?

  a. What are the main ideas being presented?

  b. What reasons or evidence supports the information?

  c. Is the information accurate? Is there anything you believe to be false?

  d. Is there anything that you believe has been left out?

2. How reliable is the source of the information?

  a. What is the source of the information?

  b. What are the interests or purposes of the source of this information?

  c. How have the interests and purposes of the source of the information influenced the information selected for inclusion?

  d. How have these interests and purposes influenced the way this information is presented?

Was the Source of the Information Able to Make Accurate Observations? Imagine that you are serving as a juror at a trial in which two youths are accused of mugging an elderly person and stealing her Social Security check. During the trial the victim gives the following account of the experience:

> I was walking into the lobby of my building at about six o'clock. It was beginning to get dark. Suddenly these two young men rushed in behind me and tried to grab my pocketbook. However, my bag was wrapped around my arm, and I just didn't want to let go of it. They pushed me around, yelling at me to let go of the bag. They finally pulled the bag loose and went running out of the building. I saw them pretty well while we were fighting, and I'm sure that the two boys sitting over there are the ones who robbed me.

In evaluating the accuracy of this information, you have to try to determine how reliable the source of the information is. In doing this, you might ask yourself whether the person attacked was in a good position to make accurate observations. In the case of this person's testimony, what questions could you ask in order to evaluate the accuracy of the testimony?

> EXAMPLE: How sharp is the person's eyesight? (Does she wear glasses? Were the glasses knocked off in the struggle?)

When trying to determine the accuracy of testimony, you should try to use the same standards you would apply to yourself if you were in a similar situation. You would ask yourself questions: Was there enough light to see clearly? Did the excitement of the situation influence my perceptions? Were my senses operating at full capacity?

As you work toward evaluating the reliability of the source of the information, it is helpful to locate whatever additional sources of information are available. For instance, if you can locate others who can identify the muggers, or if stolen items were found in their possession, this will serve as evidence to support the testimony given by the witness.

Finally, accurate observations depend on more than how well your senses are functioning. Accurate observations also depend on how well you understand the personal factors (your "lenses") you or someone else brings to a situation. These personal feelings, expectations, and interests often influence what you are perceiving without your being aware of it. Once you become aware of these influencing factors, you can attempt to make allowances for them in order to get a more accurate view of what is taking place. For example, imagine that you and your friends have sponsored an antiracism rally on your college campus. The campus police estimate the crowd to be 250, while your friends who organized the rally claim it was more than 500. How could you determine the reliability of your friends' information? What questions could you ask them to help clarify the situation? How could you locate additional information to gain a more accurate understanding of the situation?

What Do You Know About the Past Reliability of the Source of the Information?
As you work at evaluating the reliability of sources, it is useful to consider how accurate and reliable their information has been in the past. If someone you know has consistently given you sound information over a period of time, you gradually develop confidence in the accuracy of that person's reports. Police officers and newspaper reporters must continually evaluate the reliability of information sources. Over time, people in these professions establish information sources who have consistently provided reliable information. Of course, this works the other way as well. When people consistently give you inaccurate or incomplete information, you gradually lose confidence in their reliability and in the reliability of their information.

Nevertheless, few people are either completely reliable or completely unreliable in the information they offer. You probably realize that your own reliability tends to vary, depending on the situation, the type of information you are providing, and the person you are giving the information to. Thus, in trying to evaluate the information offered by others, you have to explore each of these different factors before arriving at a provisional conclusion, which may then be revised in the light of additional information.

How Knowledgeable or Experienced Is the Source of the Information? A further step in evaluating information is to determine how knowledgeable or experienced the person is in that particular area. When you seek information from others, you try to locate people who you believe will have a special understanding of the area in which you are interested. When looking for directions, you look for a police officer, a cab driver, or a local resident. When your car begins making strange noises, you search for someone who has knowledge of car engines. In each case, you try to identify someone who has special experience or understanding of a particular area because you believe that this person will be reliable in giving you accurate information. Of course, there is no guarantee that the information will be accurate, even when you carefully select knowledgeable sources. By seeking people who are experienced or knowledgeable rather than those who are not, however, you increase your chances of gaining accurate information. For example, suppose you are interested in finding out more information about the career you are planning to pursue. Who are some of the people you would select to gain further information? What are the reasons you would select these people? Are these sound reasons?

In seeking information from others whom you believe to be experienced or knowledgeable, it is important to distinguish between the opinions of "average" sources, such as ourselves, and the opinions of experts. Experts are people who have specialized knowledge in a particular area, based on special training and experience. Who qualifies as an expert? Someone with professional expertise as certified by the appropriate standards qualifies as an expert. For instance, you do not want someone working on your teeth just because he or she has always enjoyed playing with drills or is fascinated with teeth. Instead, you insist on someone who has graduated from dental college and has been professionally certified.

It is also useful to find out how up-to-date the expert's credentials are. If practitioners have not been keeping abreast of developments in their field, they will have gradually lost their expertise, even though they may have an appropriate diploma. For example, identify some experts whose information and services you rely on. How could you learn if their expertise is still up-to-date and effective?

You should also make sure that the experts are giving you information and opinions in their field of expertise. It is certainly all right for people like George Clooney or Oprah Winfrey to give their views on a product, but you should remember that they are speaking simply as human beings (and ones who have been

THINKING CRITICALLY ABOUT NEW MEDIA

Evaluating Online Information

The Internet is an incredibly rich source of information on almost every subject. But it's important to remember that information is not knowledge. Information doesn't become *knowledge* until we think critically about it. As a critical thinker, you should never accept information at face value without first establishing its accuracy, evaluating the credibility of the source, and determining the point of view or bias of the source. These are issues that we will explore throughout this book, but for now you can use the checklist on pages 223–224 to evaluate information on the Internet—and from other sources as well.

Before You Search

The first stage of evaluating Web sources should happen *before* you search the Internet: Ask yourself what you are looking for. If you don't know what you're looking for, you probably won't find it! You might want

narratives   arguments
facts   statistics
opinions   eyewitness reports
photographs or graphics

Do you want new ideas, support for a position you already hold, or something entirely different? Once you decide, you will be better able to evaluate what you find on the Web.

Choose Sources Likely to Be Reliable

Ask yourself, "What sources (or what kinds of sources) would be most likely to give me the kind of reliable information I'm looking for?" Some sources are more likely than others to

be fair   lack hidden motives
be objective   show quality control

Sometimes a site's address—its uniform resource locator (URL)—suggests its reliability or its purpose. Sites ending in

- .edu indicate educational or research material.
- .gov indicate government resources.
- .com indicate commercial products or commercially sponsored sites.
- .org usually indicate nonprofit organizations.

"\ \ 7,126\ \ NAME" in a URL may indicate a personal home page without a recognized affiliation.

Keep these considerations in mind; don't just accept the opinion of the first sources you locate.

Checklist for Evaluating the Quality of Internet Resources

Criterion 1: Authority

❑ Is it clear who sponsors the page and what the sponsor's purpose is in maintaining the page? Is there a respected, well-known organizational affiliation?

❑ Is it clear who wrote the material and what the author's qualifications for writing on this topic are?

❑ Is there a way of verifying the legitimacy of the page's sponsor? In particular, is there a phone number or postal address to contact for more information? (An email address alone is not enough.)

❑ If the material is protected by copyright, is the name of the copyright holder given? Is there a date of page creation or version?

❑ *Beware!* Avoid anonymous sites and affiliations that you've never heard of or that can't be easily checked.

Criterion 2: Accuracy

❑ Are the sources for any factual information clearly listed so they can be verified by another source?

❑ Has the sponsor provided a link to outside sources (such as product reviews or reports filed with the Securities and Exchange Commission) that can be used to verify the sponsor's claims?

❑ Is the information free of grammatical, spelling, and other typographical errors? (These kinds of errors not only indicate a lack of quality control but can actually produce inaccuracies in information.)

❑ Are statistical data in graphs and charts clearly labeled and easy to read?

❑ Does anyone monitor the accuracy of the information being published?

❑ *Beware!* Avoid unverifiable statistics and claims not supported by reasons and evidence.

Criterion 3: Objectivity

❑ For any given piece of information, is it clear what the sponsor's motivation is for providing it?

❑ Is the purported factual information clearly separated from any advertising or opinion content?

(Continues)

THINKING CRITICALLY ABOUT NEW MEDIA (*CONTINUED*)

❑ Is the point of view of the sponsor presented in a clear manner, with his or her arguments well supported?

❑ *Beware!* Avoid sites offering "information" in an effort to sell a product or service, as well as sites containing conflicts of interest, bias and one-sidedness, emotional language, and slanted tone.

Criterion 4: Currentness

❑ Are there dates on the page to indicate when the page was written, first placed on the Web, and last revised?

❑ Are there any other indications that the material is kept current?

❑ If material is presented in graphs or charts, is there a clear statement about when the data were gathered?

❑ Is there an indication that the page has been completed and is not still in the process of being developed?

❑ *Beware!* Avoid sites that lack any dates, sources, or references.

Thinking Activity 5.8

EVALUATING THE QUALITY OF TWO WEBSITES WITH CONTRASTING PERSPECTIVES ON AN ISSUE

1. Select an issue that plays an important role in our world today, such as global warming, genetically modified foods, or the increasing use of drugs to treat children for attention deficit hyperactivity disorder (ADHD).

2. Locate two different websites that present contrasting views on the issue.

3. Evaluate each website using the preceding checklist.

4. Write a one-page summary of your informed view on the issue and explain the reasons and evidence that support your perspective.

Thinking Critically About Visuals

Is FactCheck.org a Reputable Source of Information?

Refer to the Checklist for Evaluating the Quality of Internet Resources. Which of the criteria do the circled items here represent?

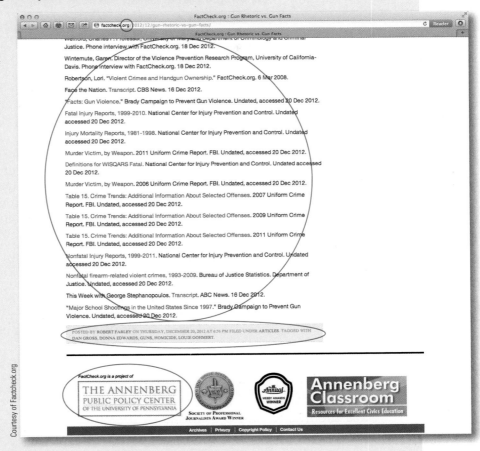

Courtesy of Factcheck.org

paid a large sum of money and told exactly what to say), not as scientific experts. This is exactly the type of mistaken perception encouraged by advertisers who want to sell their products. For example, identify two "experts" in television or magazine advertising who are giving testimony *outside* their fields of expertise. Why do you think they were chosen for the particular products they are endorsing? Do you trust such expertise in evaluating the products?

Finally, you should not accept expert opinion without question or critical examination, even if the experts meet all the criteria that you have been exploring.

Just because a mechanic assures you that your car needs a new transmission for $900 does not mean that you should accept that opinion at face value. Or simply because one doctor assures you that surgery is required for your ailment does not mean that you should stop investigating further. In both cases, seeking a second (or even third) expert opinion makes sense.

Thinking Activity 5.9

ANALYZING DIFFERENT ACCOUNTS OF THE DROPPING OF THE ATOM BOMB ON JAPAN

Chapter 4 emphasized the extent to which people's perceiving "lenses" shape and influence the way they see things, the conclusions they reach, and the decisions they make. Thinking critically involves becoming aware of these perceiving lenses and evaluating their validity when determining the accuracy of information and sources of information. One of the most powerful strategies for achieving this goal is to perform a comparative analysis of different perspectives. For example, one of the most controversial and still hotly debated events in U.S. history was our country's dropping of the atomic bomb on the Japanese cities of Hiroshima and Nagasaki. Although the bombings ended World War II, they killed more than 100,000 civilians and resulted in radiation poisoning that affected many thousands more at that time and in subsequent generations. In 1995, the Smithsonian Institution planned an exhibit to commemorate the fiftieth anniversary of the bombings, but controversy over whether the perspective of the exhibit was unbalanced led to its cancellation and the resignation of the Air and Space Museum's director.

The following activity, developed by historian Kevin O'Reilly, presents two contrasting analyses of this event, each supported by historical documentation.

Was the United States Justified in Dropping Atomic Bombs on Japan?

Background Information

For the United States, World War II began with a sneak attack by Japanese planes on American naval forces at Pearl Harbor. The war was fought in Europe against the Germans and their allies, and in the Pacific against the Japanese. During the war the secret Manhattan Project was commissioned to develop an atomic bomb for the United States. Germany surrendered (May 1945) before the bombs were completed, but on August 6, 1945, a single atomic bomb destroyed Hiroshima, and three days later, another atomic bomb destroyed Nagasaki.

Two viewpoints are presented here on the controversial use of the atomic bombs. Read and evaluate them according to the criteria of critical thinking. Consider the relevant information that follows the two viewpoints.

Thinking Critically About Visuals

After the Bomb

These Japanese schoolchildren are viewing photographs showing the aftereffects of dropping the atomic bomb on Japan. What impact might photos like these have on future generations?

© Yuriko Nakao/Reuters/Corbis

Historian A

Some historians argue that dropping atomic bombs on Japan was justified because it shortened the war, thus saving lives in the end. This view is wrong. The United States was not justified in dropping the bombs.

In the summer of 1945, the Japanese were almost totally defeated. American ships and planes pounded the island without any response by the Japanese. Leaders in Japan were trying to surrender and American leaders knew it. Several times the Japanese went to the Russians to ask them to mediate a peace settlement with the United States.[1] (It is not unusual for a country that wants to surrender to ask another country to speak for it at first and help negotiate a settlement.) There was only one

[1] Gar Alperovitz (a historian), *Atomic Diplomacy* (1965). (Direct quotations from *Foreign Relations Papers of the United States: Conference at Berlin,* Vol. II, pp. 1249, 1250, 1260, 1261.)

condition that the Japanese insisted on—they wanted to keep their emperor, the symbol of Japanese culture. The United States never even talked with the Japanese about surrender terms—American leaders kept demanding unconditional surrender. After we used the bombs and the Japanese surrendered, we let them keep their emperor anyway. We could have allowed the Japanese to surrender earlier and saved all those lives obliterated by the bombs by letting them have their one condition in the first place.

If the bombs were not used to bring about surrender, then why were they used? The plain truth is that they were used to scare Russia. In 1945 the United States disagreed with the Soviet Union in regard to Russia's actions in Europe. Our leaders felt that by showing the Russians we had a powerful weapon, we could get them to agree to our terms in Europe and Asia. As Secretary of War Stimson said in his diary, in diplomacy the bomb would be a "master card."[2]

President Truman had an important meeting scheduled with the Russian leader, Josef Stalin, at Potsdam, Germany, in July 1945. He wanted to have the bomb completed and successfully tested when he went into that meeting. Atomic scientist J. Robert Oppenheimer said, "We were under incredible pressure to get it [the bomb] done before the Potsdam meeting."[3] Truman hoped to have the bomb sticking out of his hip pocket, so to speak, when he negotiated with Stalin. Then he could make new demands of the Russians regarding eastern Europe. He told some of his friends at Potsdam before the final test, "If it explodes as I think it will, I'll certainly have a hammer on those boys."[4]

While Truman was negotiating in Potsdam, the bomb was successfully tested in New Mexico, and he became more demanding with Stalin. Secretary of War Stimson stated, "He [Truman] said it [the bomb] gave him an entirely new feeling of confidence. . . ."[5]

But the Russians had to see the power of the bomb before the United States could intimidate them with it. This was accomplished at Hiroshima. Truman remarked, "This is the greatest thing in history!"[6]

A second motive for dropping the bomb was to end the war in Asia before the Russians could get involved. The Japanese were talking of surrender, but the United States wanted surrender within days, not a negotiated surrender taking weeks to complete. The Russians had agreed at Yalta to enter the war against Japan three months after the end of the war in Europe. This would be three months after May 9, or somewhere around August 9. If the Russians got involved in the war in Asia, they could spread Communism to China and other countries and possibly to Japan itself. American leaders did not want to see this happen.[7]

If the United States could speed up the Japanese surrender, we could avoid all these problems. We dropped the first bomb on August 6; Russia entered the war on the eighth, and we dropped the second bomb on the ninth. Don't these dates look suspicious? No country could surrender in only three days—it takes longer than

[2]Stimson (Secretary of War) Diary, May 15.
[3]Atomic Energy Commission, Oppenheimer Hearings, p. 31.
[4]Jonathan Daniels (biographer), *The Man of Independence* (1950), p. 266.
[5]*Foreign Relations Papers of the United States: Conference at Berlin,* 1945, Vol. II, p. 1361.
[6]Harry S Truman, *Year of Decisions,* p. 421.
[7]Byrnes, *All in One Lifetime,* p. 300.

that to make such an important decision. We would not wait longer because we wanted Japan to surrender before the Russians could get involved.

Some scientists who worked on the bomb recommended that it not be dropped on people. They proposed that the United States demonstrate the bomb's power to Japanese leaders by dropping it on an uninhabited island. American political leaders rejected this idea. The devastating effect of the bomb had to be shown by destroying a city.

Even top military leaders opposed the use of the atomic bomb.[8] The bomb would have little effect on the war, they argued, since the Japanese were already trying to surrender.

All this evidence shows that the atomic bombs were not used to end the war and save lives, but rather to scare the Russians and speed up the end of the war before Russian influence spread further into Asia. The killing of over 100,000 civilians in one country in order to scare the leaders of another country was wrong. The United States was not justified in dropping the atomic bombs.

Endnotes for Historian A

"On July 17, the day of the first plenary session, another intercepted Japanese message showed that although the government felt that the unconditional surrender formula involved too great a dishonor, it was convinced that 'the demands of the times' made Soviet mediation to terminate the war absolutely essential. Further cables indicated that the one condition the Japanese asked was preservation of 'our form of government.' A message of July 25 revealed instructions to the [Japanese] Ambassador in Moscow to go anywhere to meet with [Soviet Foreign Minister] Molotov during the recess of the Potsdam meeting so as to 'impress them with the sincerity of our desire' to terminate the war. He was told to make it clear that 'we should like to communicate to the other party [the United States] through appropriate channels that we have no objection to a peace based on the Atlantic Charter.' The only 'difficult point is the . . . formality of unconditional surrender.'"

James F. Byrnes (Secretary of State), *All in One Lifetime*, 1958, p. 297:

"July 28: Secretary Forrestal arrived and told me in detail of the intercepted messages from the Japanese government to Ambassador Sato in Moscow, indicating Japan's willingness to surrender."

"The trouble is that the President has now promised apparently to meet Stalin and Churchill on the first of July [at Potsdam] and at that time these questions will become burning and it may become necessary to have it out with Russia on her relations to Manchuria and Port Arthur and various other parts of North China, and also the relations of China to us. Over any such tangled web of problems the S-1 secret [the atomic bomb] would be dominant and yet we will not know until after . . . that meeting, whether this is a weapon in our hands or not. We think it will be shortly afterwards, but it seems a terrible thing to gamble with such big stakes in diplomacy without having your master card in your hand."

[8]General Dwight Eisenhower, statement in "Ike on Ike," *Newsweek*, November 11, 1963, p. 107.

Leo Szilard (an atomic scientist who opposed use of the bombs on Japan), Conversation with Secretary of State Byrnes. Recorded on August 24, 1944, in Stewart to Bush, Atomic Energy Commission Document 200. Manhattan Engineering District—Top Secret, National Archives, Record Group 77, Box 7, folder 12; Box 14, folder 4:

> [Szilard argued that we should not use the bomb.]
>
> "Byrnes—Our possessing and demonstrating the bomb would make Russia more manageable in Europe."
>
> "Szilard—[The] interests of peace might best be served and an arms race avoided by not using the bomb against Japan, keeping it secret, and letting the Russians think that our work on it had not succeeded."
>
> "Byrnes—How would you get Congress to appropriate money for atomic energy research if you do not show results for the money which has been spent already?"

Stimson Diary, July 22:

> "Churchill read Grove's report [on the successful testing of the atomic bomb in New Mexico] in full. . . . He said, 'Now I know what happened to Truman yesterday. I couldn't understand it. When he got to the meeting after having read this report he was a changed man. He told the Russians just where they got on and off and generally bossed the whole meeting.'"
>
> "Though there was an understanding that the Soviets would enter the war three months after Germany surrendered, the President and I hoped that Japan would surrender before then."

Secretary of War Stimson stated in his diary on August 10, 1945, that he urged the President:

> "The thing to do was to get this surrender through as quickly as we can before Russia should get down in reach of the Japanese homeland. . . . It was of great importance to get the homeland into our hands before the Russians could put in any substantial claim to occupy and help rule it."
>
> "I voiced to him my grave misgivings, first on the basis of my belief that Japan was already defeated and that dropping the bomb was completely unnecessary and secondly, because I thought our country should avoid shocking world opinion by the use of a weapon whose employment was, I thought, no longer necessary as a measure to save American lives. It was my belief that Japan was, at the very moment, seeking some way to surrender with a minimum loss of 'face.' . . . It wasn't necessary to hit them with that awful thing."

Admiral W. D. Leahy, *I Was There* (1950), p. 441:

> "It was my opinion that the use of this barbarous weapon at Hiroshima and Nagasaki was of no material assistance in our war against Japan. The Japanese were already defeated and ready to surrender."

Air Force Chief of Staff LeMay, *New York Herald Tribune,* September 21, 1945:

> "The atomic bomb had nothing to do with the end of the war."

Historian B

Dropping atomic bombs on Hiroshima and Nagasaki helped the United States avoid a costly invasion of Japan. It therefore saved lives in the long run, which makes it a justifiable action.

It is true that the United States received some indication in the summer of 1945 that Japan was trying to surrender. Japan would not surrender unconditionally, however, and that was very important to the United States. The Germans had not surrendered unconditionally at the end of World War I and, as a result, they rose again to bring on World War II. The United States was not going to let that mistake happen again. As President Roosevelt said, "This time there will be no doubt about who defeated whom."[9]

Although the Japanese military situation in July 1945 was approaching total defeat, many Japanese leaders hoped for one last ditch victory in order to get softer peace terms.[10] One of their hopes was to divide the Grand Alliance by getting Russia (which was not at the time at war with Japan) to be the intermediary for peace negotiations. Maybe the Allies would begin to disagree, the Japanese militarists reasoned, and Japan would get off easy. Their other hope was that they could inflict enough casualties on the American troops, or hold out long enough, to get the American public to pressure their leaders to accept something less than unconditional surrender.[11]

Some historians argue that the only issue which prevented the Japanese from accepting unconditional surrender was their fear that the emperor would be removed by the Americans. American leaders, however, believed that allowing this one condition would encourage the militarists in Japan to further resistance. Americans also felt that it would weaken the war effort in the United States since we would be deviating from our well-publicized policy of unconditional surrender.[12]

Some Japanese leaders wanted much more, however, than just the one condition of keeping their emperor. They wanted their troops to surrender to them, and they wanted no occupation of Japan or war crimes trials of Japanese leaders. Even on August 9, after the bombing of Hiroshima and Nagasaki, and after the Russian declaration of war against them, the Japanese leaders still could not agree to surrender.[13] This shows that the bombs were necessary—anything less than the bombs or invasion would not have brought about unconditional surrender.

---

[9]President Roosevelt at a press conference, *F.D.R.: Public Papers of the Presidents,* Vol. XIII, p. 210.

[10]*Command Decisions* (a history of World War II), p. 504, quotes a study done by Brigadier General George A. Lincoln, June 4, 1945.

[11]*Command Decisions,* p. 517.

[12]*Command Decisions,* pp. 512–513, summarizing former Secretary of State Cordell Hull, *Memoirs,* Vol. II, p. 1593.

[13]Robert Butow (a historian), *Japan's Decision to Surrender* (1959), pp. 161, 163, 164. (Describing the debate among the six Japanese leaders about whether to surrender, August 9, 1945.)

Some people believe that the dates of dropping the bombs (August 6 and 9) show that the United States dropped them to stop Russian entry into the war (August 8). There are two problems with this line of reasoning. First, the United States did not know the exact date of Russian entry. Second, the bombs were to be dropped when a military officer decided that the weather was right.[14] If Truman wanted to beat the Russians, why didn't he order the bombs to be dropped sooner, or why didn't he give in on unconditional surrender?

The argument that the United States dropped the bombs in order to threaten the Russians is also weak. The fact that we were so unsuccessful in getting the Russians to agree to our policies in Europe shows that the bomb was not used for that reason. It must have been used to shorten the war. It certainly did not scare the Russians.

Some American scientists opposed using the bomb on civilian or military targets, preferring to demonstrate it on an uninhabited island. This recommendation was studied carefully by a committee (the Interim Committee) set up to consider how to use the bomb. The committee said that a demonstration could have had a lot of problems, which would have wasted one of the bombs and precious time. In light of the fact that it took two bombs dropped on cities to bring about a surrender, the demonstration idea does not seem like it would have been effective. The committee recommended the bombs be used against military targets.[15]

It is important to remember that on July 26, 1945, the United States warned the Japanese that we would use the atomic bomb against them unless they accepted unconditional surrender.[16] The fanatical Japanese leaders would not give in. They said they would ignore the warning.[17] Thus, the loss of life from atomic bombings was the responsibility of the Japanese leaders, not the Americans.

The United States was right in insisting on unconditional surrender. Since the Japanese would not surrender unconditionally, and since a demonstration bombing would not have been effective, the only alternative to using the atomic bombs was continuing the war. This would have cost hundreds of thousands more lives. In the long run, the use of the atomic bombs on Hiroshima and Nagasaki shortened the war and saved lives.

Endnotes for Historian B

(All are quotes from the sources cited except bracketed portions.)

"Practically all Germans deny the fact they surrendered in the last war, but this time they are going to know it. And so are the Japs."

[14]Memorandum to Major General I. R. Groves from Brigadier General T. F. Farrell.

[15]Interim Committee report, June 1, 1945, from Harry S. Truman, *Year of Decisions*, p. 419.

[16]Proclamation for Unconditional Surrender, July 26, 1945. *Foreign Relations Papers of the United States: Potsdam Papers*, Vol. II, p. 1258.

[17]*Foreign Relations Papers of the United States: Potsdam Papers*, Document 12518, July 28, 1945.

"In allied intelligence Japan was portrayed as a defeated nation whose military leaders were blind to defeat . . . Japan was still far from surrender. She had ample reserves of weapons and ammunition and an army of 5,000,000 troops, 2,000,000 of them in the home islands. . . . In the opinion of the intelligence experts, neither blockade nor bombing alone would produce unconditional surrender before the date set for invasion [November 1945]. And the invasion itself, they believed, would be costly and possibly prolonged."

"The militarists [in the Japanese government] could and did minimize the effects of the bomb, but they could not evade the obvious consequences of Soviet intervention, which ended all hope of dividing their enemies and securing softer peace terms."

"[Cordell] Hull's view . . . was the proposal [by Secretary of War Stimson to let the Japanese keep the Emperor] smacked of appeasement. . . .The proposal to retain the imperial system might well encourage resistance [by the Japanese] and have 'terrible political repercussions' in the United States."

"While Suzuki [Prime Minister], Togo [Foreign Minister] and Yonai [Navy Minister] were committed in varying degrees to an outright acceptance [of the Potsdam Declaration demanding unconditional surrender] on the basis of the sole reservation that the Imperial house would be maintained, Anami [War Minister], Umezu [Army Chief of Staff], and Toyoda [Navy Chief of Staff] felt quite differently. . . . What gagged these men—all true 'Samurai' bred in an uncompromising tradition—were the other points Yonai had mentioned. They wanted either to prevent a security occupation entirely or to exclude at least the metropolis of Tokyo . . . So far as war criminals were concerned, they felt it should be Japan and not the victorious enemy who must try such cases. In effect, they also wanted to accept the surrender of their own men. . . .

"From the standpoint of making postwar rationalizations and of 'opening up the future of the country' it was psychologically vital for the Japanese army and navy to make it appear as if they had voluntarily disbanded their military might in order to save the nation and the world at large from the continued ravages of war. If they could do this, they could very easily later plant an appealing suggestion to the effect that the imperial forces of Great Japan had not really suffered defeat at all. For this reason, too, a security occupation and war crimes trials conducted by Allied tribunals had to be avoided at all costs. . . .

"Togo pointedly asked whether Japan could win the war if a collapse of the type [of negotiations] occurred. To this the military heads could only reply that although they were not certain of ultimate victory, they were still capable of one more campaign 'decisive' battle in the homeland. . . . The Council was deadlocked."

Subject: Report on Overseas Operations—Atomic Bomb: 27 September 1945.

"After the Hiroshima strike we scheduled the second attack for 11 August [local time]. On learning that bad weather was predicted for that time, we reviewed the status of the assembly work for the Fat Man [the second atomic bomb], our uncompleted test program, and readiness of the planes and crews. It was determined that with an all-out effort, everything could be ready for takeoff on the early morning of 9 August [local time], provided our final test of the Fat Man proved satisfactory, which it did. The decision turned out to be fortunate in that several days of bad weather followed 9 August."

"Recommend unanimously:

"1. The bomb should be used against Japan as soon as possible.

"2. It should be used against a military target surrounded by other buildings.

"3. It should be used without prior warning of the nature of the weapon."

"Section 13: We call upon the government of Japan to proclaim now the unconditional surrender of the Japanese armed forces, and to provide proper and adequate assurance of their good faith in such action. The alternative for Japan is prompt and utter destruction."

Japanese Prime Minister Suzuki to reporters:

"I believe the Joint Proclamation [the Potsdam Proclamation—warning Japan to accept unconditional surrender] by the three countries is nothing but a rehash of the Cairo Declaration [which also called on Japan to surrender]. As for the [Japanese] Government, it does not find any important value in it, and there is no other recourse but to ignore it entirely and resolutely fight for the successful conclusion of the war."

QUESTIONS FOR ANALYSIS

1. Describe the main arguments, reasons, and evidence that support the perspective of Historian A.

2. Describe the main arguments, reasons, and evidence that support the perspective of Historian B.

3. Imagine that you were in the position of the U.S. president at the time, Harry Truman. Explain what action you would have taken with respect to the atomic bombs and explain the rationale for your decision.

Thinking Passages

GLOBAL WARMING

Global warming refers to the accelerating warming of the earth's climate that is the direct result of the burning of fossil fuels and the torching of rainforests. The emissions from these activities are adding to the atmosphere's invisible blanket of carbon dioxide and other heat-trapping "greenhouse" gases. Other factors that add to this greenhouse "blanket" include the release of methane gas, which emanates from landfills, livestock, and oil and gas facilities. A growing body of scientific evidence supports the conclusion that the cumulative result of these activities is causing the earth's climate to warm at an alarming rate. Since the early twentieth century, Earth's mean surface temperature has increased by about 1.4 degrees Fahrenheit. Scientists predict that at the present rate, global surface temperatures will rise between 2 degrees and a staggering 11 degrees during the twenty-first century.

What are the effects of global warming besides increased temperatures? (The year 2012 was the hottest on record for the United States since records first started being kept in 1895, breaking the previous record by a full degree!) Along with increased temperatures, global warming will bring devastating heat waves; extended droughts; decreasing crop yields; the loss of animal habitats; the melting of the polar ice caps, which will result in rising ocean levels and the flooding of coastal areas; more frequent occurrence of extreme weather events and storms; and other destructive consequences we cannot even imagine.

In order to deal with these frightening possibilities, there is scientific consensus that fossil fuel emissions must be reduced. Nevertheless, despite this realization, countries have been reluctant to limit emissions because of the economic consequences. In addition, there have been voices claiming that global warming and its connection to fossil fuel emissions are unproven, inaccurate, and overblown. It is the responsibility of individuals and countries to determine which of these competing claims represent accurate knowledge in order to guide the right course of action.

The articles that follow explore different perspectives on this complex and vitally important issue. Ken Caldeira's article, "The Great Climate Experiment," provides a comprehensive, in-depth analysis of this problem and the scientific research on which it rests. In the second article, "Global Warming: Hoax of the Century," Patrick Buchanan contends that the entire global warming issue is a myth propagated for other, nonscientific reasons. Finally, in "Why Media Tell Climate Story Poorly," Tyler Hamilton explains why, despite the compelling scientific evidence for global warming, nonscientific points of view have been permitted to gain traction and "muddy the waters" of this crucial issue. After reading the articles, respond to the critical-thinking questions that follow.

The Great Climate Experiment: How Far Can We Push the Planet?

by Ken Caldeira

Business, government or technology forecasts usually look five or 10 years out, 50 years at most. Among climate scientists, there is some talk of century's end. In reality, carbon dioxide dumped into the atmosphere today will affect Earth hundreds of thousands of years hence.

How will greenhouse gases change the far future? No one can say for sure exactly how Earth will respond, but climate scientists—using mathematical models built from knowledge of past climate systems, as well as the complex web of processes that impact climate and the laws of physics and chemistry—can make predictions about what Earth will look like.

Already we are witnessing the future envisioned by many of these models take shape. As predicted, there has been more warming over land than over the oceans, more at the poles than near the equator, more in winter than in summer and more at night than in the day. Extreme downpours have become more common. In the Arctic, ice and snow cover less area, and methane-rich permafrost soils are beginning to melt. Weather is getting weirder, with storms fueled by the additional heat.

What are the ultimate limits of the change that we are causing? The best historical example comes from the100-million-year-old climate of the Cretaceous period, when moist, hot air enveloped dinosaurs' leathery skin, crocodilelike creatures swam in the Arctic and teeming plant life flourished in the CO_2-rich air. The greenhouse that is forming now will have consequences that last for hundreds of thousands of years or more. But first, it will profoundly affect much of life on the planet—especially us.

A Desert in Italy

One of the greatest uncertainties in climate prediction is the amount of CO_2 that will ultimately be released into the atmosphere. In this article, I will assume industrial civilization will continue to do what it has been doing for the past 200 years—namely, burn fossil fuels at an accelerating rate until we can no longer afford to pull them out of the ground.

Just how much CO_2 could we put into the atmosphere? All told, there are about one quadrillion metric tons (10^{21} grams) of organic carbon locked up in Earth's sedimentary shell in one form or another. So far we have burned only one twentieth of 1 percent of this carbon, or roughly 2,000 billion metric tons of CO_2. With all the carbon locked in Earth's crust, we will never run out of fossil fuels. We are now extracting oil from tar sands and natural gas from water-fractured shale—both resources once thought to be technologically and economically inaccessible. No one can confidently predict just how far ingenuity can take us. Yet eventually the cost of extraction and processing will become so high that fossil fuels will become more expensive than alternative resources. In the scenario envisaged here, we ultimately burn about1 percent of the available organic carbon over the next few centuries. That is in the range of the amount of extraction most likely to become technologically feasible in the foreseeable future. We further assume that in the future humanity will learn to extract unconventional fossil fuels but will burn them at slower rates. Without any change in our habits, Earth may warm by about five degrees Celsius (nine degrees Fahrenheit) by 2100, although the actual warming could be half or even double this amount, depending primarily on how clouds respond. This change is about the difference between the average climate of Boston, Mass., and Huntsville, Ala.

In the northern midlatitudes between 30 degrees north and 60 degrees north—a band that includes the U.S., Europe, China, and most of Canada and Russia—the annual average temperature drops two thirds of a degree C with each degree of increasing latitude. With five degrees C of warming in a century, that translates into an average poleward movement of more than 800 kilometers in that period, for an average poleward movement of temperature bands exceeding 20 meters each day. Squirrels may be able to keep up with this rate, but oak trees and earthworms have difficulty moving that fast.

Then there will be the rains. Earth is a planetary-scale heat engine. The hot sun warms equatorial air, which then rises and cools. The cooling condenses water vapor in the air, which falls back to Earth as rain—hence, the belt of torrential rains that occur near the equator.

Thinking Critically About Visuals

Humans vs. Nature

Global warming, the phenomenon explored in these readings, is but one of the dire threats to the earth's ecosystem for which humans are responsible. What are some of the other destructive changes humans are visiting on our planet, including the air, the water, the land, and all of the other living creatures with which we share this global home? Why do you think our species is blindly pursuing such self-destructive courses of action?

67photo/Alamy

John Cancalosi/Peter Arnold/Getty Images

Yet this water condensation also heats the surrounding air, causing it to rise even more rapidly. This hot, dry air reaches as high as jets fly, then spreads laterally toward the poles. At this altitude, the hot air radiates heat to space and thus becomes cool, which causes it to sink back toward the planet's surface. The sun's rays pass through this dry, cloudless air, beating down to heat the arid surface. Today such dry air sinks occur at about 30 degrees north and south latitude, thus creating the great belts of desert that encircle the globe. With greenhouse warming, the rising air is hotter. Thus, it takes more time for this air to cool off and sink back to Earth. As a result, these desert bands move toward the poles.

The climate of the Sahara Desert may move northward. Already southern Europe has been experiencing more intense droughts despite overall increases in precipitation globally, and it may lose the Mediterranean climate that has long been considered one of the most desirable in the world. Future generations may say the same about the Scandinavian climate instead.

Up there in the northern midlatitudes, growing seasons are getting longer. Spring springs sooner: plants flower, lake ice melts and migratory birds return earlier than in the historical past.

That will not be the only benefit to croplands in Canada and Siberia. Plants make food by using the energy in sunlight to merge CO_2 and water. For the most part, plants absorb CO_2 via little pores in leaves known as stomata. When the stomata are open wide, the plants can get plenty of CO_2, but a lot of water evaporates through these gaping holes. Higher concentrations of atmospheric CO_2 mean a plant can get the CO_2 it needs by opening its stomata slightly or even building fewer stomata in leaves. In a high-CO_2 world, plants can grow more using the same amount of water. (This decrease in evaporation from plants also leads to a further decrease in precipitation, and because evaporation causes cooling, the decrease in evaporation causes further warming.)

Such gains will not be felt everywhere. In the tropics, high temperatures already compromise many crops; this heat stress will likely get worse with global warming. The outlook may be for increased crop productivity overall, with increases in the north exceeding the reductions near the equator. Global warming may not decrease overall food supply, but it may give more to the rich and less to the poor.

Oceans of Change

The vast oceans resist change, but change they will. At no time in Earth's past—with the possible exception of mass-extinction events—has ocean chemistry changed as much and as rapidly as scientists expect it to over the coming decades. When CO_2 enters the oceans, it reacts with seawater to become carbonic acid. In high enough concentrations, this carbonic acid can cause the shells and skeletons of many marine organisms to dissolve—particularly those made of a soluble form of calcium carbonate known as aragonite.

Scientists estimate that more than a quarter of all marine species spend part of their lives in coral reefs. Coral skeletons are made of aragonite. Even if chemical conditions do not deteriorate to the point where shells dissolve, acidification can make it more difficult for these organisms to build them. In just a few decades there will be no place left in the ocean with the kind of chemistry that has supported coral-reef growth in the geologic past. It is not known how many of these coral-dependent species will disappear along with the reefs.

Such chemical changes will most directly affect reef life, but the rest of us would be wise to consider the physical changes afoot. At the most basic level, water acts like mercury in a thermometer: add heat and watch it rise. The sea is also being fed by water now held in ice caps.

In high-CO_2 times in the ancient past, Earth warmed enough for crocodilelike animals to live north of the Arctic Circle. Roughly 100 million years ago annual average polar temperatures reached 14 degrees C, with summertime temperatures exceeding 25 degrees C. Over thousands of years temperatures of this magnitude would be sufficient to melt the great ice sheets of Greenland and Antarctica. With the ice sheets melted completely, sea level will be about 120 meters higher, flooding vast areas. That water's weight on low-lying continental regions will push those areas down farther into the mantle, causing the waters to lap even higher. The poles are expected to warm about 2.5 times faster than Earth as a whole. Already the Arctic has warmed faster than anywhere else, by about two degrees C compared with 0.8 degree C globally. At the end of the last ice age, when the climate warmed by about five degrees C over thousands of years, the ice sheets melted at a rate that caused sea level to rise about one meter per century. We hope and expect that ice sheets will not melt more rapidly this time, but we cannot be certain.

Chasing Venus

Over the past several million years Earth's climate has oscillated to cause the waxing and waning of great ice sheets. Our greenhouse gas emissions are hitting this complex system with a hammer. I have presented a scenario in which our climate evolves fairly smoothly, but jumps and starts that could shock biological, social and political systems beyond the limits of their resilience are also possible.

Consider that Arctic warming could cause hundreds of billions of metric tons of methane to rapidly bubble to the atmosphere from Arctic seabeds and soils. Molecule for molecule in the atmosphere, methane is about 37 times better at trapping heat than CO_2. Were this methane released suddenly, as may have occurred in a warming event 55 million years ago known as the Paleocene-Eocene Thermal Maximum, we could experience truly catastrophic warming. This risk is remote, however, according to most scientists. Some have also suggested that feedback effects such as melting permafrost could cause a runaway greenhouse scenario where the oceans become so hot they evaporate. Because water vapor is itself a greenhouse gas, such a stronger water cycle could cause Earth to get so hot that atmospheric water vapor would persist and never rain out. In this case, atmospheric CO_2 from volcanoes and other sources would continue to accumulate. Cosmic rays would break apart the water vapor at high altitudes; the resulting hydrogen would eventually escape to space. Earth's climate would then settle into a state reminiscent of its planetary neighbor Venus.

Fortunately, ocean vaporization is not even a remote risk from today's greenhouse gas emissions. Simply put, there is a limit to how much CO_2 can heat the planet. Once CO_2 and water vapor concentrations rise high enough, the molecules increasingly scatter the incoming sunlight, preventing it from getting any hotter. If we continue to burn fossil fuels, however, greenhouse gas concentrations in the atmosphere will reach levels last seen in the Cretaceous. Back then, inland seas flooded vast areas of the continents on a hot, moist Earth. Giant reptiles swam in the oceans. On land, dinosaurs grazed on luxuriant plant growth. If we burn just 1 percent of the organic carbon in Earth's crust over the next few centuries, humans will breathe the same CO_2 concentrations as the dinosaurs inhaled and experience similar temperatures.

Compared with the gradual warming of hothouse climates in the past, industrial climate change is occurring in fast-forward. In geologic history, transitions from low- to high-CO_2 atmospheres typically happened at rates of less than 0.00001 degree a year. We are re-creating the world of the dinosaurs 5,000 times faster. What will thrive in this hothouse? Some organisms, such as rats and cockroaches, are invasive generalists, which can take advantage of disrupted environments. Other organisms, such as corals and many tropical forest species, have evolved to thrive in a narrow range of conditions. Invasive species will likely transform such ecosystems as a result of global warming. Climate change may usher in a world of weeds. Human civilization is also at risk. Consider the Mayans. Even before Europeans arrived, the Mayan civilization had begun to collapse thanks to relatively minor climate changes. The Mayans had not developed enough resilience to weather small reductions in rainfall. The Mayans are not alone as examples of civilizations that failed to adapt to climate changes.

Crises provoked by climate change are likely to be regional. If the rich get richer and the poor get poorer, could this set in motion mass migrations that challenge political and economic stability? Some of the same countries that are most likely to suffer from the changes wrought by global warming also boast nuclear weapons. Could climate change exacerbate existing tensions and provoke nuclear or other apocalyptic conflict? The social response to climate change could produce bigger problems for humanity than the climate change itself.

Starting Over

The woody plants that flourished during the Cretaceous died, and some became coal over geologic time. The ocean's plankton ended up buried in sediments, and some became oil and gas. The climate cooled as sea life locked CO_2 in shells and skeletons.

The oceans will absorb most of our CO_2 over millennia. The resulting acidification will dissolve carbonate minerals, and the chemical effects of dissolution will allow yet more CO_2 to be absorbed. Nevertheless, atmospheric CO_2 concentrations will remain well above preindustrial levels of 280 parts per million for many tens of thousands of years. As a result, the ebb and flow of ice ages brought on by subtle variations in Earth's orbit will cease, and humanity's greenhouse gas emissions will keep the planet locked in a hothouse. Over time increased temperatures and precipitation will accelerate the rate at which bedrock and soils dissolve. Streams and rivers will bring these dissolved rocks and minerals, containing elements such as calcium and magnesium, to the oceans. Perhaps hundreds of thousands of years from now some marine organism will take the calcium and CO_2 and form a carbonate shell. That seashell and millions of others may eventually become limestone. Just as the White Cliffs of Dover in England are a remnant of the Cretaceous atmosphere, the majority of carbon in the fossil fuels burned today will become a layer in the rocks—a record, written in stone, of a world changed by a single species.

Global Warming: Hoax of the Century

by Patrick Buchanan

With publication of "On the Origin of Species" in 1859, the hunt was on for the "missing link." Fame and fortune awaited the scientist who found the link proving Darwin right: that man evolved from a monkey. In 1912, success! In a gravel pit near Piltdown in East Sussex, there was found the cranium of a man with the jaw of an ape. "Darwin Theory Proved True," ran the banner headline. Evolution skeptics were pilloried, and three English scientists were knighted for validating Piltdown Man.

It wasn't until 1953, after generations of biology students had been taught about Piltdown Man, that closer inspection discovered that the cranium belonged to a medieval Englishman, the bones had been dyed to look older and the jaw belonged to an orangutan whose teeth had been filed down to look human.

The scientific discovery of the century became the hoax of the century. But Piltdown Man was not alone. There was Nebraska Man. In 1922, Henry Fairfield Osborn, president of the American Museum of Natural History, identified a tooth fossil found in Nebraska to be that of an "anthropoid ape." He used his discovery to mock William Jennings Bryan, newly elected to Congress, as "the most distinguished primate which the State of Nebraska has yet produced." Invited to testify at the Scopes trial, however, Osborn begged off. For, by 1925, Nebraska Man's tooth had been traced to a wild pig, and Creationist Duane Gish, a biochemist, had remarked of Osborn's Nebraska Man, "I believe this is a case in which a scientist made a man out of a pig, and the pig made a monkey out of the scientist."

These stories are wonderfully told in Eugene Windchy's 2009 "The End of Darwinism." But if Piltdown Man and his American cousin Nebraska Man were the hoaxes of the

Source: © 1995–2013 Patrick J. Buchanan (http://buchanan.org/blog/hoax-of-the-century-3680).

20th century, global warming is the great hoax of the 21st. In a matter of months, we have we learned:

- In its 2007 report claiming that the Himalayan glaciers are melting, the U.N. Inter-governmental Panel on Climate Change relied on a 1999 news story in a popular science journal, based on one interview with a little-known Indian scientist who said this was pure "speculation" not supported by any research. The IPCC also misreported the supposed date of the glaciers' meltdown as 2035. The Indian had suggested 2350.

- The IPCC report that global warming is going to kill 40% of the Amazon rainforest and cut African crop yields 50% has been found to be alarmist propaganda.

- The IPCC 2007 report declared 55% of Holland to be below sea level, an exaggeration of over 100%.

- While endless keening is heard over the Arctic ice cap, we hear almost nothing of the 2009 report of the British Antarctica Survey that the sea ice cap of Antarctica has been expanding by 100,000 square kilometers a decade for 30 years. That translates into 3,800 square miles of new Antarctic ice every year.

- Though America endured one of the worst winters ever, while the 2009 hurricane season was among the mildest, the warmers say this proves nothing. But when our winters were mild and the 2005 hurricane season brought four major storms to the U.S. coast, Katrina among them, the warmers, said this validated their theory. You can't have it both ways.

- The Climate Research Unit at East Anglia University, which provides the scientific backup for the IPCC, apparently threw out the basic data on which it based claims of a rise in global temperatures for the century. And a hacker into its e-mail files found CRU "scientists" had squelched the publication of dissenting views.

What we learned in a year's time: Polar bears are not vanishing. Sea levels are not rising at anything like the 20-foot surge this century was to bring. Cities are not sinking. Beaches are not disappearing. Temperatures have not been rising since the late 1990s. And, in historic terms, our global warming is not at all unprecedented. How horrible was it?

"The Vikings discovered and settled Greenland around A.D. 950. Greenland was then so warm that thousands of colonists supported themselves by pasturing cattle on what is now frozen tundra. During this great global warming, Europe built the looming castles and soaring cathedrals that even today stun tourists with their size, beauty and engineering excellence. These colossal buildings required the investment of millions of man-hours—which could be spared from farming because of higher crop yields."

Today's global-warming hysteria is the hoax of the 21st century. H.L. Mencken had it right: "The whole aim of practical politics is to keep the populace alarmed—and hence clamorous to be led to safety—by menacing it with an endless series of hobgoblins, all of them imaginary."

Why Media Tell Climate Story Poorly

by Tyler Hamilton

I apologize on behalf of my profession.

If it's true that Canadians and Americans have become less concerned about the potential impact of climate change, and that more consider global warming a hoax, some blame can certainly be directed at the news media.

"The media (are) giving an equal seat at the table to a lot of non-qualified scientists," Julio Betancourt, a senior scientist at the U.S. Geological Survey, told a group of environment and energy reporters during a week-long learning retreat in New Mexico.

I was among them, listening to Betancourt and two of his colleagues describe the measurable impacts climate change is having on the U.S. southwest. Drought. More frequent and damaging forest fires. Northward migration of forest and animal species. Hotter, longer growing seasons. Less snow pack. Earlier snow melt.

"The scientific evidence reported in peer-reviewed journals is growing by the day, and it suggests the pace of climate change has surpassed the worst-case scenarios predicted just a few years ago.

Betancourt is the first to admit the science is constantly evolving and that the work at hand is highly complex. One challenge is separating the part of climate change caused by naturally occurring cyclical systems from the part caused by humans, who since the Industrial Revolution have dumped greenhouse gases into the atmosphere at an accelerating rate.

Clearly there is an interaction between the two. But can scientists explain it with bulletproof precision using predictive models everyone can agree on? No, of course not. That's not how science works. More difficult is that scientists such as Betancourt are realizing the climate changes observed are not happening in a gradual, predictable fashion but, instead, in sudden steps. Systems reach a certain threshold of environmental stress and then "pop," they act quickly to restabilize.

These changes also happen regionally, making it difficult for people in one region of the world to appreciate disruptive changes going on elsewhere.

Not surprisingly, those looking to stall action on climate change—or who altogether deny that humanity is contributing to global warming—are exploiting this complexity and lack of certainty.

A recent Pew Research Center poll of 1,500 Americans found that 57 per cent believed there was solid scientific evidence that the globe is warming, down from 77 per cent in 2007. The changing attitudes coincide with a growing effort to discredit climate science in the lead-up to the Copenhagen talks on Dec. 7 and efforts by U.S. legislators to cobble together climate legislation that would signal America's commitment to reducing its greenhouse-gas emissions.

It also coincides with an economic downturn, during which people are concerned most about their finances. There's also a strong likelihood that people want to hear that maybe this climate change stuff is all a bad dream.

It's much more difficult to have a story in the newspaper or a TV news segment, explaining the latest study in *Nature* or *Science*, than it is to have an unqualified scientist or "spokesman" offer a pithy, controversial quote or sound bite not necessarily grounded in fact.

This reality has given the fossil-fuel lobby a major leg up, writes James Hoggan, co-author of *A Climate Cover-Up* and founder of DeSmogBlog.com. Hoggan's must-read book describes in disturbing detail the well-oiled campaign to confuse the public and confound the science, creating enough doubt to thwart meaningful action and protect a world economic order built around the burning of oil, coal, and natural gas.

The Heartland Institute, Friends of Science, and Natural Resources Stewardship Project are among the groups that make their Rolodex of "experts" available to comment on climate issues.

But, as Hoggan points out, most of those experts are anything but. Lift their veil and they typically are funded by the fossil-fuel industry, long-retired climate scientists who have not published peer-reviewed papers for many years, or scientists who are experts but not necessarily in climate science. "If a doctor recommended that you undergo an innovative new surgical procedure, you might seek a second opinion, but you'd probably ask another surgeon," writes Hoggan, a public-relations veteran who is also chairman of the David Suzuki Foundation.

"You wouldn't check with your local carpenter, and you certainly wouldn't ask a representative of the drug company whose product would be rendered irrelevant if you had the operation."

Still, many journalists under deadline and without the time to verify credentials, journalists who do not follow climate science and the news around it, continue to give these so-called experts a soapbox to stand on. Even those with time to spare often offer up the soapbox out of some misplaced attempt at balance, giving the impression that the scientific community is deeply divided.

Once their comments are published, the blogs take over and public confusion grows deeper. Mark Twain said it best: "A lie travels halfway around the world while the truth is still putting on its boots." The Internet has only accelerated the speed of travel. It's why we've been seeing silly stories about "global cooling" appear in recent months, or articles about thickening Arctic ice, or the "Global Warming Conspiracy." On Friday, the latest conspiracy story began making its rounds. Hackers accessed email messages from some climate scientists on an Internet server at the University of East Anglia in Britain. The emails, from what I've read, do show that not all scientists agree, that some scientists don't like other scientists, and that some scientists are struggling with the complexity of their work. What these emails do not show is that there's any conspiracy or that consensus around the reality of human-influenced global warming is beginning to crack.

Still, that won't stop the skeptics from cherry picking what's in those emails and claiming this is some kind of smoking gun that will derail Copenhagen. The blogosphere is abuzz, and news media are never ones to turn down a juicy controversy. The timing of the hack makes it all the more suspicious, but no less dramatic.

It's a shame.

I asked Betancourt during his New Mexico talk why the scientific community has not done a better job of battling the misinformation campaign and speaking as a more united front.

The problem, he said, is working scientists don't tend to be communications specialists but are up against people who are. So, for honest, accurate describing of the science of climate, "it's more up to the media, and less up to us."

QUESTIONS FOR ANALYSIS

1. What exactly is "global warming"? What is the role of greenhouse gases like carbon dioxide in creating global warming? What are some of the devastating effects scientists believe that global warming will result in? What are the reasons and evidence that have convinced scientists that global warming poses a potentially catastrophic threat to the future of Earth?

2. According to Ken Caldeira in his article "The Great Climate Experiment," some of these global warming effects have already started occurring. "Already we are witnessing the future envisioned by many of these models take shape. As predicted, there has been more warming over land than over the oceans, more at the poles than near the equator, more in winter than in summer and more at night than in the day. Extreme downpours have become more common. In the Arctic, ice and snow cover less area, and methane-rich permafrost soils are beginning to melt. Weather is getting weirder, with storms fueled by the additional heat." Which of these unusual weather effects, like Hurricane Sandy in October of 2012, have you begun to witness?

3. In his article "Global Warming: Hoax of the Century," Patrick Buchanan argues that global warming is a hoax in the same way that Piltdown Man, the supposed "missing evolutionary link" between apes and homo sapiens, fooled scientists and laypeople for more than fifty years. What evidence does Buchanan present to support this belief? How do you think scientists who believe in the reality of global warming would respond to his evidence?

4. According to Tyler Hamilton's article "Why Media Tell Climate Story Poorly," only 57 percent of Americans believe that there is solid scientific evidence that the globe is warming, down from 77 percent in 2007. Why does the author believe that the media must shoulder much of the responsibility for this decline, and how can they correct it? What are some other factors that account for the public's confusion regarding the reality of global warming? Finally, what critical-thinking skills does the author believe should be used in responding to the "experts" who reject the threat of global warming?

Summary

- *Beliefs* are interpretations, evaluations, conclusions, and predictions about the world that we endorse as true.

- *Knowledge* is beliefs about the world that we believe are true and for which we can supply compelling reasons and evidence.

- Critical thinkers evaluate their beliefs by examining the evidence provided by authorities, references, factual evidence, and personal experience.

- Viewing situations and issues from a variety of perspectives is a very effective strategy for constructing an informed understanding.

- Because the Internet has become such a pervasive source of information, it is particularly important to critically evaluate the credibility and bias of the sources in determining the accuracy of the information being provided.

Assessing Your Strategies and Creating New Goals

How Accurate and Thoughtfully Reasoned Are My Beliefs?

There *is* a way to develop an accurate set of beliefs that you can use to guide you through life's treacherous currents. You need to develop and apply the *skills of critical thinking* in order to arrive at informed, intelligent opinions in every area of life. Described below are key elements of the process of developing accurate and thoughtfully reasoned beliefs. Evaluate your position regarding each of these elements, and use this self-evaluation to guide your choices as you seek to develop an informed and intelligent perspective on the world.

Develop Informed Beliefs

I am an insightful, powerful, confident critical thinker.	I'm not as strong a thinker as I feel I could be.
5 4 3 2 1	

How would you rate yourself on this scale? If it's more toward the right side than the left, you have plenty of company. One reason for this response is that we live in a complex, challenging world that is extremely demanding intellectually. Each day we are called on to solve difficult problems, analyze tangled issues, and sift through a tidal wave of information. We are expected to make intelligent decisions, negotiate our way through a jungle of relationships, and communicate our ideas clearly and persuasively. It's no wonder that we often feel overmatched, unable to marshal the thinking abilities needed to succeed in all of these demanding contexts.

Strategy: There is not one simple way to become an expert critical thinker. Instead, we need to learn and utilize all of the critical-thinking abilities included in this text. Becoming an expert critical thinker is a challenging, lifelong process, but it is well worth the effort because it enriches every single aspect of our lives.

Think Critically About Information

I think critically about media information by comparing different sources and asking analytical questions.	I usually depend on a limited number of sources for my information and rarely ask probing questions.
5 4 3 2 1	

The glut of information that we are subjected to serves to discourage us from thinking critically about the *truth* and *value* of this information. But this is the only way we can transform this information into knowledge that can be used and applied in our lives. Rather than blame the media for their biases and manipulation, we should instead take responsibility for analyzing various perspectives and coming to our own informed conclusions.

Strategy: When possible, develop the habit of comparing different sources, reading several news accounts and viewing various news shows. This comparative analysis is a powerful strategy for disclosing the inherent and inescapable bias of every presentation of information, no matter how reputable the source.

Evaluate the Accuracy of Information and the Credibility of Sources

I carefully evaluate the information that I receive and the sources that provide it.	I usually accept what I read and hear without much critical analysis.
5 4 3 2 1	

Intelligent beliefs are the product of active investigation and critical evaluation. Your responsibility as a critical thinker is to analyze each perspective carefully, evaluate the accuracy of the information and the credibility of the sources, take into account the bias that is an inescapable part of every viewpoint, and then reach your own thoughtful conclusions.

Strategy: When you are evaluating the validity of information and potential beliefs, ask yourself the questions included in this chapter in order to determine the accuracy of information and the credibility of sources.

Become a Stage 3 Critical Thinker in Every Area of Life

I am a Stage 3 thinker in most areas of life.	I am a Stage 1 or Stage 2 thinker in most areas of life.
5 4 3 2 1	

The three *stages of knowing* introduced in this chapter are a useful vehicle for assessing your overall development as a critical thinker. Stage 3: Thinking Critically represents the most advanced intellectual level, as people realize that some views *are* better than others, and it is *their* responsibility to develop informed beliefs by thinking for themselves.

Strategy: Once you recognize your own responsibility in constructing your understanding of the world, you can make meaningful progress in improving your sophistication as a thinker. Establish the habit of examining a variety of perspectives, critically evaluate the supporting reasons, develop your own well-reasoned conclusions, and remain open-minded to new insights.

Suggested Films

JFK (1991)

What is truth? How do we know? Based on fact and theory, this film addresses the causes of the assassination of President John F. Kennedy. The film follows the investigation of former New Orleans district attorney, Jim Garrison, into the events leading up to the assassination and explores the possible conspiracy involved.

Rashomon (1950)

Is there a single knowable reality? In twelfth-century Japan, a woman is raped and her husband is killed. In the trial that follows, four witnesses give four completely different accounts of what occurred. Which is the "true" account of what happened? Can we ever really know for sure?

The Thin Blue Line (1988)

Errol Morris's documentary recounts the story of an innocent man found guilty of murder and sentenced to death by a corrupt system. The film illustrates the different realities presented over the course of the investigation and conviction, and includes interviews with those involved. Morris explores the dangerous way in which perception and belief can be manipulated and altered.

Vanilla Sky (2001)

What is the value of our dream existence? A successful publisher and playboy, David Aames, survives a car crash orchestrated by a jilted lover and is left severely disfigured. After undergoing reconstructive surgery and gaining the support of a beautiful woman, David seems to be living his dream life. However, recurring hallucinations and strange occurrences cause him to question the reality and value of this dream existence.

What the Bleep Do We Know? (2004)

This film explores the limits of human knowledge through a combination of interviews with experts, narrative, documentary, and animation. When a young woman finds herself in an unfamiliar world, she needs to develop a new way of perceiving and responding to her surroundings.

Language is the extraordinary ability that enables us to think, to communicate, to say, "I am here, I am unique, I exist." In addition to graffiti, what are some other unique public uses of language that are designed to influence your thinking, feelings, and behavior?

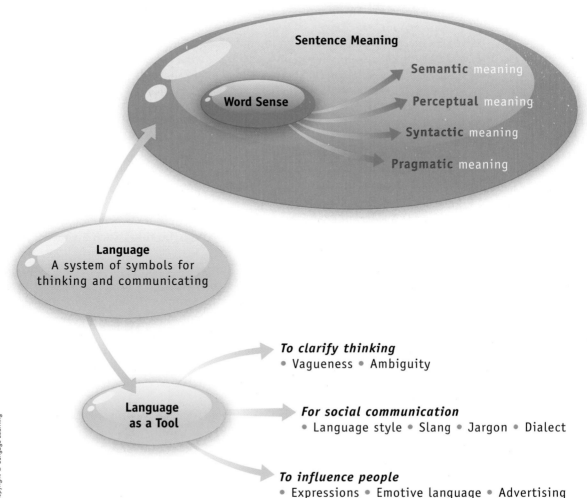

Sentence Meaning

Semantic meaning

Perceptual meaning

Word Sense

Syntactic meaning

Pragmatic meaning

Language
A system of symbols for thinking and communicating

Language as a Tool

To clarify thinking
• Vagueness • Ambiguity

For social communication
• Language style • Slang • Jargon • Dialect

To influence people
• Expressions • Emotive language • Advertising

Every time we use language, we send a message about our thinking. When we speak or write, we are conveying ideas, sharing feelings, and describing experiences. At the same time, language itself shapes and influences thinking. When language use is sloppy—vague, general, indistinct, imprecise, foolish, inaccurate—it leads to the same sort of thinking. The reverse is also true: Clear, precise language leads to clear, precise thinking, speaking, and writing. Thus, it is vital to use language with clarity and precision if other people are to understand the thoughts we are trying to communicate. And to use language effectively, we need to view language as a system, one with agreed-upon sets of rules and expectations.

To comprehend this essential tool more fully and use it more powerfully, we will consider both the development of languages and the symbolic nature of language. We will then examine strategies for using language effectively and for using language to clarify thinking. Finally, we will consider the social uses of language and how it can be used to influence thinking and behavior.

Throughout the chapter you will have opportunities to connect your ideas to these concepts. The various assignments place special emphasis on thinking and writing with precision: clearly conceptualizing what you want to say and discovering the best use of language to say it. You will also have the chance to explore the work of professional writers who have developed special expertise in thinking and communicating with language.

The Evolution of Language

Imagine a world without language. Imagine that you have suddenly lost your ability to speak, to write, to read. Imagine that your only means of expression are grunts, shrieks, and gestures. Finally imagine that everyone else in the world has also lost the ability to use language. What do you think such a world would be like?

As this exercise of the imagination illustrates, language forms the bedrock of your relations with others. It is the means you have to communicate your thoughts, feelings, and experiences to others, and they to you. This mutual sharing draws you together and leads to your forming relationships. Consider the social groups in your school, your neighborhood, or your community. Notice how language plays a central role in bringing people together into groups and in maintaining these groups. A loss of language would both limit the complexity of your individual relationships with others and drastically affect the entire way you live in society.

Linguists have ascertained that no single language was the parent of all languages. Rather, like people, languages belong to families. Languages in the same family share some characteristics with other members of their family, but they also demonstrate individual characteristics. We know that languages, like the human beings of whom they are a natural part, live, change, and die. Phrygian is no longer a living language, nor is Latin.

English—like Spanish, French, Chinese, Urdu, or any of the other languages that you may speak—is a living language, and it has changed over hundreds of years. The English language has gone through four major evolutionary stages: *Old English,* A.D. 700–1050; *Middle English,* A.D. 1050–1450; *Early Modern English,* A.D. 1450–1700; and *Modern English,* 1700 to the present. Because languages are systems based on sound, these evolutionary stages of English reflect variations in how the language sounds. It is difficult to represent these sounds accurately for the older periods of English because of the absence of recordings. The written symbols demonstrating early versions of the Lord's Prayer that follow are approximations based on the consensus of linguistic scholars.

The Lord's Prayer

Old English

Faeder ure
Thu the eart on heofonum,
Si thin name gehalgod.
Tobecume thin rice.
Gewurthe thin willa on eorthan swa swa on heofonum.
Urne gedaeghwamlican hlaf syle you to daeg.
And forgyf you urne gyltas, swa swa you forgyfath urum gyltendum.
And ne gelaed thu you on costnunge, ac alys you of yfele. Sothlice.

Middle English

Oure fadur
that art in hauenes,
halewid be thi name;
thi kyngdoom come to;
be thi wile don in erthe as in heuene;
zyue to vs this dai oure breed ouer othir substaunce;
and forzyue to vs oure dettis, as you forzyuen to oure dettouris;
and lede vs not in to temptacioun,
but delyuere vs from yeul. Amen.

Early Modern English

Our Father
which art in heaven,
hallowed be thy name.
Thy kingdom come.
Thy will be done, in earth, as it is in heaven.
Give us this day our daily bread.
And forgive us our debts, as we forgive our debtors.
And lead us not into temptation,
but deliver us from evil:
for Thine is the kingdom, and the power, and the glory for ever, Amen.

As you read these versions of the Lord's Prayer, think about the variations in sounds, words, and sentences. With the other members of your class, discuss variations in the language(s) you speak. Could any of these be considered evolutionary changes? Why or why not?

The Symbolic Nature of Language

As human beings, we are able to communicate with each other because of our ability to *symbolize*, or let one thing represent something else. Words are the most common symbols we use in our daily life. Although words are only sounds or written marks that have no meaning in and of themselves, they stand for objects, ideas, and other aspects of human experience. For example, the word *sailboat* is a symbol that represents a watergoing vessel with sails that is propelled by the wind. When you speak or write *sailboat*, you are able to communicate the sort of thing you are thinking about. Of course, if other people are to understand what you are referring to when you use this symbol, they must first agree that this symbol (*sailboat*) does in fact represent that wind-propelled vessel that floats on the water.

Language symbols (or words) can take two forms: They can be spoken sounds or written markings.* The symbol *sailboat* can be either written down or spoken aloud. Either way, it communicates the same idea. Because using language is so natural to us, we rarely stop to realize that our **language** is really a system of spoken sounds and written markings that we use to represent various aspects of our experience.

Language is like a set of symbolic building blocks. The basic blocks are sounds, which may be symbolized by letters. Sounds form the phonetic foundation of a language, and this process explains why different languages have distinctly different "sounds." Try having members of the class who speak other languages speak a word or a few sentences in the language they know. Listen to how the sound of each language differs from those of the others.

When humans are infants, they are able to make all the sounds of all languages. As they are continually exposed to the specific group of sounds of their society's language, they gradually concentrate on making only those sounds while discarding or never developing the others.

Sounds combine to form larger sets of blocks called *words*. Words are used to represent the various aspects of our experience—they symbolize objects, thoughts, feelings, actions, and concepts. When you read, hear, or think about a word, then it usually elicits in you a variety of ideas and feelings. Describe the ideas or feelings that the following words arouse in you: *college education, happiness, freedom, creative, love.*

The combination of all the ideas and feelings that a word arouses in your mind make up the "meaning" of that word to you. Although the meanings that these

language
A system of symbols for thinking and communicating.

---

*A unique language case is posed by American Sign Language (ASL), which is now regarded by linguists as a full-fledged language, possessing its own grammar and syntax.

words have for you are likely to be similar in many respects to the meanings they have for other people, there are likely also many differences. Consider the different meanings these words have for the two people in the following dialogue:

A: For me, a **college education** represents the most direct path to my dreams. It's the only way I can develop the knowledge and abilities required for my career.

B: I can't agree with you. I pursued a **college education** for a while, but it didn't work out. I found that most of my courses consisted of large classes with professors lecturing about subjects that had little relation to my life. The value of a college education is overblown. I know many people with college degrees who have not been able to find rewarding careers.

A: Don't you see? An important part of achieving **happiness** is learning about things you aren't familiar with, expanding your horizons about the world, developing new interests. That's what college can give you.

B: I have enough interests. As far as I'm concerned, **happiness** consists of having the opportunity to do the things that I enjoy doing with the people I enjoy doing them with. For me, happiness is **freedom**!

A: **Freedom** to do what? Freedom is meaningful only when you have worthwhile options to select and the wisdom to select the right ones. And a college education can help provide you both!

B: That sounds very idealistic, but it's also naive. Many of the college graduates I have met are neither wise nor happy. In order to be truly happy, you have to be involved in **creative** activities. Every day should be a surprise, something different to look forward to. Many careers pay well, but they don't provide creative opportunities.

A: Being **creative** means doing things you **love**. When you really love something you're doing, you are naturally creative. For example, I love to draw and paint, and these activities provide a creative outlet for me. I don't need to be creative at work—I have enough creative opportunities outside work.

B: You're wrong! **Creativity** doesn't simply mean being artistic. We should strive to be creative in every part of our lives, keep looking for new possibilities and unique experiences. And I think that you are misusing the word **love**. You can only really love things that are alive, like people and pets.

A: That's a very weird idea of **love** you have. As far as I'm concerned, **love** is a word that expresses a strong positive emotion that can be directed toward objects ("I love my car"), activities ("I love to dance"), or people. I don't see what's so complicated about that.

B: To be able to **love** in any meaningful sense, the object of your love has to be able to respond to you so that the two of you can develop a relationship together. When was the last time that your car responded to your love for it?

A: Very funny. I guess that we just have different ideas about the word **love**—as well as the words **happiness**, **freedom**, and **creative**.

As this dialogue suggests, words are not simple entities with one clear meaning that everyone agrees on. Instead, most words are complex, multidimensional carriers of meaning; their exact meaning often varies from person to person. These differences in meaning can lead to disagreements and confusion, as illustrated in the previous dialogue. To understand how words function in your language and your thinking, you have to examine the way words serve as vehicles to express meaning.

Words arouse in each of us a variety of ideas, feelings, and experiences. Taken together, these ideas, feelings, and experiences express the *total meaning* of the words for the individual. Linguists believe that this total meaning is actually composed of four different types of meaning:

- Semantic meaning
- Perceptual meaning
- Syntactic meaning
- Pragmatic meaning

Let us examine each of them in turn.

SEMANTIC MEANING (DENOTATION)

The *semantic meaning* of a word expresses the relationship between a linguistic event (speaking or writing) and a nonlinguistic event (an object, idea, or feeling). For example, saying "chair" relates to an object you sit in, while saying "college education" relates to the experience of earning an academic degree through post-secondary study. What events (ideas, feelings, objects) relate to the word *happiness*? *Freedom*? *Creative*? *Love*?

The semantic meaning of a word, also referred to as its *denotative meaning*, expresses the general properties of the word, and these properties determine how the word is used within its language system. How do you discover the general properties that determine word usage? Besides examining your own knowledge of the meaning and use of words, you can also check dictionary definitions. They tend to focus on the general properties that determine word usage. For example, a dictionary definition of *chair* might be "a piece of furniture consisting of a seat, legs, and back, and often arms, designed to accommodate one person."

However, to understand clearly the semantic meaning of a word, you often need to go beyond defining its general properties to identifying examples of the word that embody those properties. If you are sitting in a chair or can see one from where you are, examine its design. Does it embody all the properties identified in the definition? (Sometimes unusual examples embody most, but not all, of the properties of a dictionary definition—e.g., a "beanbag chair" lacks legs and arms.) If you are trying to communicate the semantic meaning of a word to someone, it is generally useful to provide both the general properties of the word and examples that embody those properties. Try identifying those properties and examples for the words *happiness, freedom, creative,* and *love.*

PERCEPTUAL MEANING (CONNOTATION)

The total meaning of a word also includes its *perceptual meaning*, which expresses the relationship between a linguistic event and an individual's consciousness. For each of us, words elicit unique and personal thoughts and feelings based on previous experiences and past associations. For example, I might relate saying "chair" to my favorite chair in my living room or the small chair that I built for my daughter. Perceptual meaning also includes an individual's positive and negative responses to a word. For this reason, perceptual meaning is sometimes called *connotative meaning*, the literal or basic meaning of a word plus all it suggests, or connotes, to you.

Think about the words you considered earlier and describe what personal perceptions, experiences, associations, and feelings they evoke in your mind: *college education, happiness, freedom, creative, love.*

SYNTACTIC MEANING

Another component of a word's total meaning is its *syntactic meaning*, which defines its relation to other words in a sentence. Syntactic relationships extend among all the words of a sentence that are spoken or written or that will be spoken or written. The syntactic meaning defines three relationships among words:

- Content: words that express the major message of the sentence
- Description: words that elaborate or modify the major message of the sentence
- Connection: words that join the major message of the sentence

For example, in the sentence "The two novice hikers crossed the ledge cautiously," *hikers* and *crossed* represent the content, or major message, of the sentence. *Two* and *novice* define a descriptive relationship to *hikers,* and *cautiously* elaborates *crossed.*

At first, you may think that this sort of relationship among words involves nothing more than semantic meaning. The following sentence, however, clearly demonstrates the importance of syntactic meaning in language: "Invisible fog rumbles in on lizard legs." Although *fog* does not *rumble,* and it is not *invisible,* and the concept of moving on *lizard legs* instinctively seems incompatible with *rumbling,* still the sentence "makes sense" at some level of meaning—namely, at the syntactic level. One reason it does is that in this sentence you still have three basic content words— *fog, rumbles,* and *legs*—and two descriptive words, namely, *invisible* and *lizard.*

A further major syntactic relationship is that of connection. You use connective words to join ideas, thoughts, or feelings being expressed. For example, you could connect content meaning to either of your two sentences in the following ways:

- "The two novice hikers crossed the ledge cautiously *after* one of them slipped."
- "Invisible fog rumbles in on lizard legs, *but* acid rain doesn't."

When you add content words such as *one slipped* and *rain doesn't,* you join the ideas, thoughts, or feelings they represent to the earlier expressed ideas, thoughts, or feelings (*hikers crossed* and *fog rumbles*) by using connective words like *after* and *but*, as in the previous sentences.

"Invisible fog rumbles in on lizard legs" also makes sense at the syntactic level of meaning because the words of that sentence obey the syntax, or order, of English. Most speakers of English would have trouble making sense of "Invisible rumbles legs lizard on fog in"—or "Barks big endlessly dog brown the," for that matter. Because of syntactic meaning, each word in the sentence derives part of its total meaning from its combination with the other words in that sentence.

Look at the following sentences and explain the difference in meaning between each pair of sentences:

1. a. The process of achieving an *education at college* changes a person's future possibilities.
   b. The process of achieving a *college education* changes a person's future possibilities.
2. a. She felt *happiness* for her long-lost brother.
   b. She felt the *happiness* of her long-lost brother.
3. a. The most important thing to me is *freedom from* the things that restrict my choices.
   b. The most important thing to me is *freedom to* make my choices without restrictions.
4. a. Michelangelo's painting of the Sistine Chapel represents his *creative* genius.
   b. The Sistine Chapel represents the *creative* genius of Michelangelo's greatest painting.
5. a. I *love* the person I have been involved with for the past year.
   b. I am *in love* with the person I have been involved with for the past year.

PRAGMATIC MEANING

The last element that contributes to the total meaning of a word is its *pragmatic meaning*, which involves the person who is speaking and the situation in which the word is spoken. For example, the sentence "That student likes to borrow books from the library" allows a number of pragmatic interpretations:

1. Was the speaker outside looking at *that student* carrying books out of the library?
2. Did the speaker have this information because he was a classmate of *that student* and saw her carrying books?
3. Was the speaker in the library watching *that student* check the books out?

The correct interpretation or meaning of the sentence depends on what was actually taking place in the situation—in other words, its pragmatic meaning, which is also called its *situational meaning*. For each of the following sentences, try describing a pragmatic context that identifies the person speaking and the situation in which the words are being spoken.

1. A *college education* is currently necessary for many careers that formerly required only high school preparation.
2. The utilitarian ethical system is based on the principle that the right course of action is that which brings the greatest *happiness* to the greatest number of people.
3. The laws of this country attempt to balance the *freedom* of the individual with the rights of society as a whole.
4. "You are all part of things, you are all part of *creation*, all kings, all poets, all musicians, you have only to open up, to discover what is already there." (Henry Miller)
5. "If music be the food of *love*, play on." (William Shakespeare)

After completing the activity, compare your answers with those of your classmates. In what ways are the answers similar or different? Analyze the way different pragmatic contexts (persons speaking and situations) affect the meanings of the italicized words.

The four meanings you just examined—*semantic, perceptual, syntactic, pragmatic*—create the total meaning of a word. That is to say, all the dimensions of any word—all the relationships that connect linguistic events with nonlinguistic events, your consciousness, other linguistic events, and situations in the world—make up the meaning *you* assign to a word.

Thinking Activity 6.1

THE LANGUAGE OF WAR*

During times of war and conflict, language takes on special significance, and political leaders take great care in selecting the key words related to the conflict. In the United States in late 2001, the significance of word meaning was thrust into the spotlight when words that were originally used to characterize the war against terrorism were found to be offensive to certain groups of people and were therefore replaced. Read the following texts by William Safire and Michael R. Gordon:

> "You are about to embark upon a great *crusade*," General Eisenhower told his troops on the eve of D-Day; he later titled his memoirs "*Crusade* in Europe." American presidents liked that word: Thomas Jefferson launched "a crusade against ignorance," Theodore Roosevelt exhorted compatriots to "spend and be spent in an endless *crusade*" and F.D.R., calling for a "new deal" in his acceptance speech at the

*Thanks to Nancy Erber for suggesting this activity.

1932 Democratic convention, issued "a call to arms," a "*crusade* to restore America to its own people."

But when George W. Bush ad-libbed that "this *crusade,* this war on terrorism, is going to take a while," his figure of speech was widely criticized. That's because the word has a religious root, meaning "taking the cross," and was coined in the eleventh century to describe the first military expedition of the Crusaders, European Christians sent to recover the Holy Land from the followers of Muhammad. The rallying-cry noun is offensive to many Muslims: three years ago, Osama bin Laden maligned U.S. forces in the Middle East as "*crusader* armies spreading like locusts. . . ."

In the same way, when the proposed Pentagon label for the antiterror campaign was floated out as "Operation Infinite Justice," a spokesman for the Council on American-Islamic Relations noted that such eternal retribution was "the prerogative of God." Informed of this, Defense Secretary Donald Rumsfeld quickly pulled the plug on the pretentious moniker.

Who coins these terms? Nobody will step forward; instead, software called "Code Word, Nickname and Exercise Term System" is employed to avoid responsibility; it spits out a list of random names from which commanders can choose. This avoidance of coinage responsibility leads to national embarrassment (which is finite justice). "Operations," said Winston Churchill, "ought not to be described by code words which imply a boastful and overconfident sentiment. . . ."

—William Safire, "Every Conflict Generates Its Own Lexicon"

LONDON, Oct. 26—Britain said today that it was prepared to join the United States in ground combat inside Afghanistan and would provide 600 Royal Marine commandos for the American-led military operation. The allies have their own lexicon. While the United States calls the operation Enduring Freedom, the British name for the operation is Veritas. The Canadians call the operation Apollo. The Australians call it Operation Slipper. An Australian official said the term was derived from Australian slang and alluded to the ability of forces to stealthily "slip in and slip out." The original name for the United States' operation was Infinite Justice, but this was changed recently.

—Michael R. Gordon, The *New York Times*

1. For each of the following terms, identify the *origin, definition,* and *related word forms*:

crusade	endure
infinite	apollo
justice	*veritas*

2. Next, find a quotation from an anthology (Bartlett's or another source) to illustrate the use and meaning of the word. Be sure to write down the entire quotation and any information about it, such as the author and date.

3. Finally, compare the word meanings in these quotations with the word meanings you identified in Question 1.

Thinking Activity 6.2

UNDERSTANDING NONSENSE WORDS

The importance of *syntactic meaning* is underscored in Lewis Carroll's famous poem "Jabberwocky," which appeared in *Through the Looking-Glass and What Alice Found There*. Although many of the words in the poem were creations of his own fertile imagination, the poem nevertheless has "meaning," due in large measure to the syntactic relationships between the words.

1. After reading the poem several times, write out your own "translation."

2. Compare your translation with that of the other students in the class. What similarities do you find? What differences? How do you account for the similarities and differences?

Jabberwocky

'Twas brillig, and the slithy toves
Did gyre and gimble in the wabe:
All mimsy were the borogoves,
And the mome raths outgrabe.
"Beware the Jabberwock, my son!
The jaws that bite, the claws that catch!
Beware the Jubjub bird, and shun
The frumious Bandersnatch!"
He took his vorpal sword in hand:
Long time the manxome foe he sought—
So rested he by the Tumtum tree,
And stood awhile in thought.
And, as in uffish thought he stood,
The Jabberwock, with eyes of flame,
Came whiffling through the tulgey wood,
And burbled as it came!
One, two! One, two! And through and through
The vorpal blade went snicker-snack!
He left it dead, and with its head
He went galumphing back.
"And hast thou slain the Jabberwock?
Come to my arm, my beamish boy!
O frabjous day! Callooh! Callay!"
He chortled in his joy.
'Twas brillig, and the slithy toves

Source: Lewis Carroll, *The Annotated Alice,* 191–197.

Did gyre and gimble in the wabe:
All mimsy were the borogoves,
And the mome raths outgrabe.

Thinking Passage

USING NONSENSE TO THINK MORE CLEARLY

Interestingly enough, modern research suggests that exposure to "nonsense" language, stories, and events can improve your critical thinking abilities and enhance your creativity. Some of these results are summarized in the following article by Benedict Carey, "How Nonsense Sharpens the Intellect."

How Nonsense Sharpens the Intellect

by Benedict Carey

In addition to assorted bad breaks and pleasant surprises, opportunities and insults, life serves up the occasional pink unicorn. The three-dollar bill; the nun with a beard; the sentence, to borrow from the Lewis Carroll poem, that gyres and gimbles in the wabe.

An experience, in short, that violates all logic and expectation. The philosopher Soren Kierkegaard wrote that such anomalies produced a profound "sensation of the absurd," and he wasn't the only one who took them seriously. Freud, in an essay called "The Uncanny," traced the sensation to a fear of death, of castration or of "something that ought to have remained hidden but has come to light."

At best, the feeling is disorienting. At worst, it's creepy.

Now a study suggests that, paradoxically, this same sensation may prime the brain to sense patterns it would otherwise miss—in mathematical equations, in language, in the world at large.

"We're so motivated to get rid of that feeling that we look for meaning and coherence elsewhere," said Travis Proulx, a postdoctoral researcher at the University of California, Santa Barbara, and lead author of the paper appearing in the journal Psychological Science. "We channel the feeling into some other project, and it appears to improve some kinds of learning."

Researchers have long known that people cling to their personal biases more tightly when feeling threatened. After thinking about their own inevitable death, they become more patriotic, more religious and less tolerant of outsiders, studies find. When insulted, they profess more loyalty to friends—and when told they've done poorly on a trivia test, they even identify more strongly with their school's winning teams.

In a series of new papers, Dr. Proulx and Steven J. Heine, a professor of psychology at the University of British Columbia, argue that these findings are variations on the same process: maintaining meaning, or coherence. The brain evolved to predict, and it does so by identifying patterns.

When those patterns break down—as when a hiker stumbles across an easy chair sitting deep in the woods, as if dropped from the sky—the brain gropes for something, anything that makes sense. It may retreat to a familiar ritual, like checking equipment. But it may also turn its attention outward, the researchers argue, and notice, say, a pattern in animal tracks that was previously hidden. The urge to find a coherent pattern makes it more likely that the brain will find one.

"There's more research to be done on the theory," said Michael Inzlicht, an assistant professor of psychology at the University of Toronto, because it may be that nervousness, not a search for meaning, leads to heightened vigilance. But he added that the new theory was "plausible, and it certainly affirms my own meaning system; I think they're onto something."

In the most recent paper, published last month, Dr. Proulx and Dr. Heine described having 20 college students read an absurd short story based on "The Country Doctor," by Franz Kafka. The doctor of the title has to make a house call on a boy with a terrible toothache. He makes the journey and finds that the boy has no teeth at all. The horses who have pulled his carriage begin to act up; the boy's family becomes annoyed; then the doctor discovers the boy has teeth after all. And so on. The story is urgent, vivid and nonsensical—Kafkaesque.

After the story, the students studied a series of 45 strings of 6 to 9 letters, like "X, M, X, R, T, V." They later took a test on the letter strings, choosing those they thought they had seen before from a list of 60 such strings. In fact the letters were related, in a very subtle way, with some more likely to appear before or after others.

The test is a standard measure of what researchers call implicit learning: knowledge gained without awareness. The students had no idea what patterns their brain was sensing or how well they were performing.

But perform they did. They chose about 30 percent more of the letter strings, and were almost twice as accurate in their choices, than a comparison group of 20 students who had read a different short story, a coherent one.

"The fact that the group who read the absurd story identified more letter strings suggests that they were more motivated to look for patterns than the others," Dr. Heine said. "And the fact that they were more accurate means, we think, that they're forming new patterns they wouldn't be able to form otherwise."

Brain-imaging studies of people evaluating anomalies, or working out unsettling dilemmas, show that activity in an area called the anterior cingulate cortex spikes significantly. The more activation is recorded, the greater the motivation or ability to seek and correct errors in the real world, a recent study suggests. "The idea that we may be able to increase that motivation," said Dr. Inzlicht, a co-author, "is very much worth investigating."

Researchers familiar with the new work say it would be premature to incorporate film shorts by David Lynch, say, or compositions by John Cage into school curriculums. For one thing, no one knows whether exposure to the absurd can help people with explicit learning, like memorizing French. For another, studies have found that people in the grip of the uncanny tend to see patterns where none exist—becoming more prone to conspiracy theories, for example. The urge for order satisfies itself, it seems, regardless of the quality of the evidence.

Still, the new research supports what many experimental artists, habitual travelers, and other novel seekers have always insisted: at least some of the time, disorientation begets creative thinking.

QUESTIONS FOR ANALYSIS

1. A pink unicorn, a three-dollar bill, a nun with a beard, the Lewis Carroll poem "Jabberwocky"—all these characterize unexpected events that create what the philosopher Soren Kierkegaard termed a "sensation of the absurd." According to research cited in the article, humans are motivated to try to make sense of nonsense and in so doing they are likely to think more creatively by looking for new patterns of meaning or explanations for the nonsense. Examine your thinking as you read "Jabberwocky"—how do you find your mind operating as you read it? Is your experience consistent with the thesis that nonsense can sharpen our thinking?

2. Recall a time when you encountered a situation that surprised you and initially made no sense. How did you deal with that situation? What does the way you dealt with the situation reveal about the way we think and use language?

Using Language Effectively

To develop your ability to use language effectively, you have to understand how language functions when it is used well. One way to do this is to read widely. By reading good writing, you get a "feel" for how language can be used effectively. You can get more specific ideas by analyzing the work of highly regarded writers, who use word meanings accurately. They also often use many action verbs, concrete nouns, and vivid adjectives to communicate effectively. By doing so, they appeal to your senses and help you understand clearly what is being communicated. Good writers may also vary sentence length to keep the reader's attention and create a variety of sentence styles to enrich meaning. Communicating your ideas effectively involves using the full range of words to express yourself. Writing is like painting a "word picture" of your thoughts: You need to use the full range of colors, not just a few basic ones. An equally important strategy is for you to write and then have others evaluate your writing and give you suggestions for improving it. You will be using both of these strategies in the pages that follow.

Thinking Passage

PAINTING A WORD PICTURE

The following selection is from *Blue Highways*, a book written by a young man of Native American heritage named William Least Heat-Moon. After losing his teaching job at a university and separating from his wife, he decided to explore America. He outfitted his van (named Ghost Dancing) and drove around the country using back roads (represented on the maps by blue lines) rather than superhighways. During his travels, he saw fascinating sights, met intriguing people, and developed some significant insights about himself.

From Blue Highways

by William Least Heat-Moon

A Place

Two Steller's jaybirds stirred an argy-bargy in the ponderosa. They shook their big beaks, squawked and hopped and swept down the sunlight toward Ghost Dancing and swooshed back into the pines. They didn't shut up until I left some orts from breakfast; then they dropped from the branches like ripe fruit, nabbed a gobful, and took off for the tops of the hundred-foot trees. The chipmunks got in on it too, letting loose a high peal of rodent chatter, picking up their share, spinning the bread like pinwheels, chewing fast.

It was May Day, and the warm air filled with the scent of pine and blooming manzanita. To the west I heard water over rock as Hot Creek came down from the snows of Lassen. I took towel and soap and walked through a field of volcanic ejections and broken chunks of lava to the stream bounding off boulders and slicing over bedrock; below one cascade, a pool the color of glacier ice circled the effervescence. On the bank at an upright stone with a basin-shaped concavity filled with rainwater, I bent to drink, then washed my face. Why not bathe from head to toe? I went down with rainwater and lathered up.

An Experience

Now, I am not unacquainted with mountain streams; a plunge into Hat Creek would be an experiment in deep-cold thermodynamics. I knew that, so I jumped in with bravado. It didn't help. Light violently flashed in my head. The water was worse than I thought possible. I came out, eyes the size of biscuits, metabolism running amuck and setting fire to the icy flesh. I buffed dry. Then I began to feel good, the way the old Navajos must have felt after a traditional sweat bath and roll in the snow. . . . I liked Hat Creek. It was reward enough for last night.

Another Person

Back at Ghost Dancing, I saw a camper had pulled up. On the rear end, by the strapped-on aluminum chairs, was something like "The Wandering Watkins." Time to go. I kneeled to check a tire. A smelly furry white thing darted from behind the wheel, and I flinched. Because of it, the journey would change.

"Harmless as a stuffed toy." The voice came from the other end of the leash the dog was on. "He's nearly blind and can't hear much better. Down just to the nose now." The man, with polished cowboy boots and a part measured out in the white hair, had a face so gullied even the Soil Conservation Commission couldn't have reclaimed it. But his eyes seemed lighted from within.

"Are you Mr. Watkins?" I asked.

"What's left of him. The pup's what's left of Bill. He's a Pekingese. Chinese dog. In dog years, he's even older than I am, and I respect him for that. We're two old men. What's your name?"

"Same as the dog's."

. . .

Watkins had worked in a sawmill for thirty years, then retired to Redding; now he spent time in his camper, sometimes in the company of Mrs. Watkins.

. . .

"What kind of work you in?" he asked.

That question again. "I'm out of work," I said to simplify.

"A man's never out of work if he's worth a damn. It's just sometimes he doesn't get paid. I've gone unpaid my share and I've pulled my share of pay. But that's got nothing to do with working. A man's work is doing what he's supposed to do, and that's why he needs a catastrophe now and again to show him a bad turn isn't the end, because a bad stroke never stops a good man's work. Let me show you my philosophy of life." From his pressed Levi's he took a billfold and handed me a limp business card. "Easy. It's very old."

The card advertised a cafe in Merced when telephone numbers were four digits. In quotation marks was a motto: "Good Home Cooked Meals."

"'Good Home Cooked Meals' is your philosophy?"

"Turn it over, peckerwood."

Imprinted on the back in tiny, faded letters was this:

I've been bawled out, balled up, held up, held down, hung up, bulldozed, blackjacked, walked on, cheated, squeezed and mooched; stuck for war tax, excess profits tax, sales tax, dog tax, and syntax, Liberty Bonds, baby bonds, and the bonds of matrimony, Red Cross, Blue Cross, and the double cross; I've worked like hell, worked others like hell, have got drunk and got others drunk, lost all I had, and now because I won't spend or lend what little I earn, beg, borrow or steal, I've been cussed, discussed, boycotted, talked to, talked about, lied to, lied about, worked over, pushed under, robbed, and damned near ruined. The only reason I'm sticking around now is to see WHAT THE HELL IS NEXT.

"I like it," I said.

"Any man's true work is to get his boots on each morning. Curiosity gets it done about as well as anything else."

1. After reading the passage from *Blue Highways*, analyze Least Heat-Moon's use of language. Make three columns on a page. Use these headings: Action Verbs, Concrete Nouns, and Vivid Adjectives. List at least six examples of each from the reading.

2. Describe how the author uses dialogue and analogies to introduce us to Mr. Watkins.

3. According to Mr. Watkins, "A man's never out of work if he's worth a damn. It's just sometimes he doesn't get paid. . . . Any man's true work is to get his boots on each morning. Curiosity gets it done about as well as anything else." What do you think he's trying to say about the challenges posed by life to both men and women?

Thinking Activity 6.3

COMMUNICATING AN EXPERIENCE

Create your own description of an experience you have had while traveling. Use language as effectively as possible to communicate the thoughts, feelings, and impressions you wish to share. Be conscious of your use of action verbs, concrete nouns, and vivid adjectives. Ask other students to read your description and identify examples of these words. Then ask for feedback on ways to improve your description.

Using Language to Clarify Thinking

Language reflects thinking, and thinking is shaped by language. Previous sections of this chapter examine the creature we call *language*. You have seen that it is composed of small cells, or units, pieces of sound that combine to form larger units called *words*. When words are combined into groups allowed by the rules of the language to form sentences, the creature grows by leaps and bounds. Various types of sentence structure not only provide multiple ways of expressing the same ideas, thoughts, and feelings, but also help to structure those thoughts, weaving into them nuances of focus. In turn, your patterns of thinking breathe life into language, giving both processes power.

Language is a tool powered by patterns of thinking. With its power to represent your thoughts, feelings, and experiences symbolically, language is the most important tool your thinking process has. Although research shows that thinking and communicating are two distinct processes, these two processes are so closely related that they are often difficult to separate or distinguish.*

*Seminal works on this topic are *Thought and Language*, by Lev Vygotsky, and *Cognitive Development: Its Cultural and Social Foundation*, by A. R. Luria.

Thinking Critically About Visuals

Reading the Unwritten

Graffiti have been used as a medium of communication for thousands of years. Here, an anonymous tagger in the Gaza Strip region of the Palestinian territories is responding to a lull in the continued violence between Israeli and Palestinian forces. The schoolchildren are Palestinian.

What is the message of this example, and to whom is it directed? How can you tell? What makes graffiti effective—or not—for conveying a specific kind of message to a particular audience?

Reuters/Ahmed Jadallah/CORBIS

Are citizens entitled to universal health care? In this mural, *The History of Medicine in Mexico, and the People Demanding Health*, which was created for a wall in the Hospital de la Raza in Mexico City, Mexico, Diego Rivera dramatizes the struggle of the poor for access to a health care system that favors the rich. Murals like this have a rich history as a visual language to express important ideas. Who might be the audience for this mural, and what message did the artist want to communicate? Can you describe other murals that you have seen and what you thought their audiences and messages were intended to be?

Thinking Critically About Visuals

Words Paint a Picture

Describe a time when you were able to "paint a picture" with words, as this professional storyteller is doing with his young audience. Why were you able to use language so effectively? How can we "paint" word pictures more frequently in our everyday lives?

Syracuse Newspapers/John Berry/The Image Works

Because language and thinking are so closely related, how well you perform one process is directly related to how well you perform the other. In most cases, when you are thinking clearly, you are able to express your ideas clearly in language. When you have unclear thoughts, it is usually because you lack a clear understanding of the situation, or you do not know the right language to give form to these thoughts. When your thoughts are truly clear and precise, this means that you know the words to give form to these thoughts and so are able to express them in language.

The relationship between thinking and language is *interactive*; both processes are continually influencing each other in many ways. This is particularly true in the case of language, as the writer George Orwell points out in the following passage from his classic essay "Politics and the English Language":

A man may take to drink because he feels himself to be a failure, and then fail all the more completely because he drinks. It is rather the same thing that is happening to the English language. It becomes ugly and inaccurate because our thoughts are foolish, but the slovenliness of our language makes it easier for us to have foolish thoughts. The point is that the process is reversible. Modern English, especially written English, is full of bad habits which spread by imitation and which can be avoided if one is willing to take the necessary trouble. If one gets rid of these habits one can think more clearly.

Just as a drinker falls into a vicious cycle that keeps getting worse, so too can language and thinking. When your use of language is sloppy—that is, vague, general, indistinct, imprecise, foolish, inaccurate, and so on—it leads to thinking of the same sort. And the reverse is also true: Clear and precise language leads to clear and precise thinking.

The opposite of clear, effective language is language that fails to help the reader (or listener) picture or understand what the writer (or speaker) means because it is vague or ambiguous. Most of us are guilty of using such ineffective language in speech ("It was a great party!"), but for college and work writing, we need to be as precise as possible. And our writing can gain clarity and power if we use our creative-thinking skills to develop fresh, striking figures of speech to illuminate our ideas.

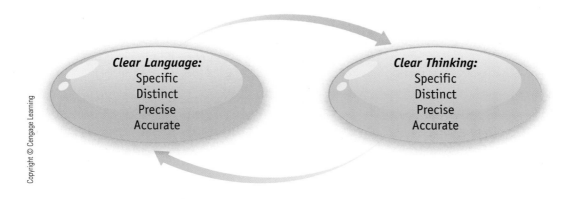

Clear Language:
Specific
Distinct
Precise
Accurate

Clear Thinking:
Specific
Distinct
Precise
Accurate

IMPROVING VAGUE LANGUAGE

Although our ability to name and identify gives us the power to describe the world in a precise way, often we tend to describe it using words that are imprecise and general. Such general and nonspecific words are called **vague words**. Consider the following sentences:

- I had a *nice* time yesterday.
- That is an *interesting* book.
- She is an *old* person.

In each of these cases, the italicized word is vague because it does not give a precise description of the thought, feeling, or experience that the writer or speaker is trying to communicate. A word (or group of words) is vague if its meaning is not clear

vague word
A word that lacks a clear and distinct meaning.

and distinct. That is, vagueness occurs when a word is used to represent an area of experience without clearly defining it.

Most words of general measurement—*short, tall, big, small, heavy, light,* and so on—are vague. The exact meanings of these words depend on the specific situation in which they are used and on the particular perspective of the person using them. For example, give specific definitions for the following words in italics by filling in the blanks. Then compare your responses with those of other members of the class. Can you account for the differences in meaning?

1. A *middle-aged* person is one who is _____ years old.

2. A *tall* person is one who is over _____ feet _____ inches tall.

3. It's *cold* outside when the temperature is _____ degrees.

4. A person is *wealthy* when he or she is worth _____ dollars.

Although the vagueness of general measurement terms can lead to confusion, other forms of vagueness are more widespread and often more problematic. Terms such as *nice* and *interesting*, for example, are imprecise and unclear. Vagueness of this sort permeates every level of human discourse, undermines clear thinking, and is extremely difficult to combat. To use language clearly and precisely, you must develop an understanding of the way language functions and commit yourself to breaking the entrenched habits of vague expression.

For example, read the following opinion of a movie and circle all the vague, general words that do not express a clear meaning.

> *Avatar* is a very good movie. It is a science fiction film that takes place on the planet Pandora where the Na'vi live. They get into a battle with an American corporation that wants to steal their natural resources and they are helped by an ex-marine who has taken their form. The plot is very interesting, and the main characters are great. I liked this movie a lot.

Because of the vague language in this passage, it expresses only general approval—it does not explain in exact or precise terms what the experience was like. Thus, the writer of the passage is not successful in communicating the experience.

Strong language users have the gift of symbolizing their experiences so clearly that you can actually relive those experiences with them. You can identify with them, sharing the same thoughts, feelings, and perceptions that they had when they underwent (or imagined) the experience. Consider how effectively the passages written by William Least Heat-Moon on pages 265–266 communicate the thoughts, feelings, and experiences of the author. Even if we don't give an elaborate version of our thinking, we can still communicate effectively by using language clearly and precisely. For example, contrast this review summary of *Avatar* by the professional film critic David Denby.

> As James Cameron, working in 3-D, thrusts us into the picture frame, brushing past tree branches, coursing alongside foaming-jawed creatures, we may be overcome by an uncanny sense of emerging, becoming, transcending—a sustained mood of elation produced by vaulting into space. This is the most physically

beautiful American film in years. It's set on Pandora, a verdant moon, a hundred and fifty years from now, where the long-waisted, translucent-blue Na'vi live on turf that contains an energy-rich mineral that an American corporation, armed to the teeth with military contractors, wants to harvest. An ex-marine (Sam Worthington) in the shape of a Na'vi—an avatar—is sent to spy, but he falls in love with a warrior princess (Zoe Saldana), and he winds up leading a defense of the Na'vi against the armed might of the military. It's the old story of Pocahontas and John Smith, mixed, perhaps, with "Dances with Wolves." The Na'vi, who are connected by neural networks to all living things, are meant to remind us of Native Americans; the military is meant to remind us of the shock-and-awe Bush Administration militarists. The story may be trite, but Cameron creates an entire world, including magnificent flying pterodactyls and a bright-red flying monster with jaws that could snap an oak. The movie is as much a vertical as a horizontal experience; its many parts cohere and flow together. With Sigourney Weaver as a high-minded biologist, Stephen Lang as a testosterone-pumped military leader, and Giovanni Ribisi as the cynical head of the corporate expedition.

"Avatar" by David Denby, newyorker.com, January 11, 2010.
Reprinted by permission of the author.

Thinking Activity 6.4

REVIEWING A MOVIE

Write a review of a movie that you saw recently, concentrating on expressing your ideas clearly and precisely. Share your review with other students in the class and exchange suggestions for making the reviews more effective.

Most people use vague language extensively in day-to-day conversations. In many cases, it is natural that your immediate reaction to an experience would be fairly general ("That's nice," "She's interesting," etc.). If you are truly concerned with sharp thinking and meaningful communication, however, you should follow up these initial general reactions by more precisely clarifying what you really mean.

- I think that she is a nice person *because* . . .
- I think that he is a good teacher *because* . . .
- I think that this is an interesting class *because* . . .

Vagueness is always a matter of degree. In fact, you can think of your descriptive/informative use of language as falling somewhere on a scale between extreme generality and extreme specificity. For example, the following statements move from the general to the specific.

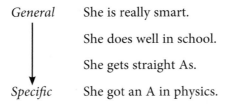

General   She is really smart.

                  She does well in school.

                  She gets straight As.

Specific   She got an A in physics.

Although different situations require various degrees of specificity, you should work at becoming increasingly more precise in your use of language.

Thinking Passage

THE DANGERS OF AMBIGUOUS LANGUAGE

Using language imprecisely can lead to miscommunication, sometimes with disastrous results. For example, on January 29, 1990, an Avianca Airlines flight from Colombia, South America, to New York City crashed, killing seventy-three persons. After circling Kennedy Airport for forty-five minutes, the plane ran out of fuel before it could land, apparently the result of imprecise communication between the plane's pilot and the air traffic controllers.

Malcolm Gladwell provides a riveting analysis of this catastrophe in his book *Outliers*.

The Crash of Avianca Airlines Flight 052

by Malcolm Gladwell

Consider, for example, the famous (in aviation circles, anyway) crash of the Colombian airliner Avianca flight 052 in January of 1990. The Avianca accident so perfectly illustrates the characteristics of the "modern" plane crash that it is studied in flight schools.

The captain of the plane was Laureano Caviedes. His first officer was Mauricio Klotz. They were en route from Medellin, Columbia, to New York City's Kennedy Airport. The weather that evening was poor. There was a nor'easter up and down the East Coast, bringing with it dense fog and high winds. Two hundred flights were delayed at LaGuardia Airport, 161 at Philadelphia, 53 at Boston's Logan Airport, and 99 at Kennedy. Because of the weather, Avianca was held up by Air Traffic Control three times on its way to New York. The plane circled over Norfolk, Virginia, for nineteen minutes, above Atlantic City for twenty-nine minutes, and forty miles south of Kennedy Airport for another twenty-nine minutes.

After an hour and a quarter of delay, Avianca was cleared for landing. As the plane came in on its final approach, the pilots encountered severe wind shear. One moment they were flying into a strong headwind, forcing them to add extra power to maintain their momentum, on the glide down. The next moment, without warning, the headwind dropped dramatically, and they were traveling much too fast to make the runway. Typically, the plane would have been flying on autopilot in that situation, reacting immediately and appropriately to wind shear. But the autopilot on the plane was malfunctioning, and it had been switched off. At the last moment, the pilot pulled up, and executed a "go-around." The plane did a wide circle over Long Island, and

Source: Excerpt from *Outliers*. The section on the Avianca is discussed on pages 185–202.

reapproached Kennedy Airport. Suddenly, one of the plane's engines failed. Seconds later, a second engine failed. "Show me the runway!" the pilot cried out, hoping desperately that he was close enough to Kennedy to somehow glide his crippled plane to a safe landing. But Kennedy was sixteen miles away.

The 707 slammed into the estate owned by the father of the tennis champion John McEnroe, in the posh Long Island town of Oyster Bay. Seventy-three of the 158 passengers aboard died. It took less than a day for the cause of the crash to be determined: "fuel exhaustion." There was nothing wrong with the aircraft. There was nothing wrong with the airport. The pilots weren't drunk or high. The plane had run out of gas. . . .

Here is the transcript from Avianca 052, as the plane is going in for its abortive first landing. The issue is the weather. The fog is so thick that Klotz and Caviedes cannot figure out where they are. Pay close attention, though, not to the content of their conversation but to the *form*. In particular, note the length of the silences between utterances and to the tone of Klotz's remarks.

CAVIEDES: The runway, where is it? I don't see it. I don't see it.

They take up the landing gear. The captain tells Klotz to ask for another traffic pattern. Ten seconds pass.

CAVIEDES (SEEMINGLY TO HIMSELF): We don't have fuel. . . .

Seventeen seconds pass as the pilots give technical instructions to each other.

CAVIEDES: I don't know what happened with the runway. I didn't see it.
KLOTZ: I didn't see it.

Air Traffic Control comes in and tells them to make a left turn.

CAVIEDES: Tell them we are in an emergency!
KLOTZ (TO ATC): That's right to one-eight-zero on the heading and, ah, we'll try once again. We're running out of fuel.

Imagine the scene in the cockpit. The plane is dangerously low on fuel. They have just blown their first shot at a landing. They have no idea how much longer the plane is capable of flying. The captain is desperate: "Tell them we are in an emergency!" And what does Klotz say? *That's right to one-eight-zero on the heading and, ah, we'll try once again. We're running out of fuel.*

To begin with, the phrase "running out of fuel" has no meaning in Air Traffic Control terminology. All planes, as they approach their destination, are by definition running out of fuel. Did Klotz mean that 052 no longer had enough fuel to make it to another, alternative airport? Did he mean that they were beginning to get worried about their fuel? Next, consider the structure of the critical sentence. Klotz begins with a routine acknowledgement of the instructions from ATC and doesn't mention his concern about fuel until the second half of the sentence. It's as if he were to say in a restaurant, "Yes, I'll have some more coffee and, ah, I'm choking on a chicken bone." How seriously would the waiter take him? The air traffic controller with whom Klotz was speaking testified later that he "just took it as a passing comment." On stormy nights, air traffic controllers hear pilots talking about running out of fuel all the time.

Even the "ah" that Klotz inserts between the two halves of his sentence serves to undercut the importance of what he is saying. According to another of the controllers who handled 052 that night, Klotz spoke "in a very nonchalant manner. . . . There was no urgency in the voice."

The term used by linguists to describe what Klotz was engaging in in that moment is "mitigated speech," which refers to any attempt to downplay or sugarcoat the meaning of what is being said. We mitigate when we're being polite, or when we're ashamed or embarrassed, or when we're being deferential to authority. If you want your boss to do you a favor, you don't say, "I'll need this by Monday." You mitigate. You say, "Don't bother, if it's too much trouble, but if you have a chance to look at this over the weekend, that would be wonderful." In a situation like that mitigation is entirely appropriate. In other situations, however,—like a cockpit on a stormy night— it's a problem.

The linguists Ute Fischer and Judith Orasanu once gave the following hypothetical scenario to a group of captains and first officers and asked them how they would respond:

You notice on the weather radar an area of heavy precipitation 25 miles ahead. (The pilot) is maintaining his present course at Mach .73, even though embedded thunderstorms have been reported in your area and you encounter moderate turbulence. You want to ensure that your aircraft will not penetrate this area. Question: what do you say to the pilot?

In Fischer's and Orasanu's minds, there were at least six ways to try to persuade the pilot to change course and avoid the bad weather, each with a different level of mitigation.

1. *Command:* "Turn thirty degrees right." That's the most direct and explicit way of making a point imaginable. It's zero mitigation.

2. *Crew Obligation Statement:* "I think we need to deviate right about now." Notice the use of "we" and the fact that the request is now much less specific. That's a little softer.

3. *Crew Suggestions:* "Let's go around the weather." Implicit in that statement is "we're in this together."

4. *Query:* "Which direction would you like to deviate?" That's even softer than crew suggestions, because the speaker is conceding that he's not in charge.

5. *Preference:* "I think it would be wise to turn left or right."

6. *Hint:* "That return at twenty-five miles looks mean." This is the most mitigated statement of all.

Fischer and Orasanu found that captains overwhelmingly said they would issue a command in that situation: "Turn thirty degrees right." They were talking to a subordinate. They had no fear of being blunt. The first officers, on the other hand, were talking to their boss, and so they overwhelmingly chose the most mitigated alternative. They hinted.

It's hard to read Fischer and Orasanu's study and not be just a little bit alarmed, because a hint is the hardest kind of request to decode and the easiest to refuse. . . .

Back to the cockpit of Avianca 052. The plane is now turning away from Kennedy, after the aborted first attempt at landing. Klotz has just been on the radio with ATC, trying to figure out when they can try to land again. Caviedes turns to him.

CAVIEDES: What did he say?

KLOTZ: I already advise him that we are going to attempt again because we now we can't . . .

Four seconds of silence pass.

CAVIEDES: Advise him we are in emergency.

Four more second of silence pass. The captain tries once again.

CAVIEDES: Did you tell him?

KLOTZ: Yes, sir. I already advise him.

Klotz starts talking to ATC—going over routine details.

KLOTZ: One-five-zero maintaining two thousand Avianca zero-five-two heavy.

The captain is clearly at the edge of panic.

CAVIEDES: Advise him we don't have fuel.

Klotz gets back on the radio with ATC.

KLOTZ: Climb and maintain three thousand and, ah, we're running out of fuel, sir.

There it is again. No mention of the magic word "emergency," which is what the traffic controllers are trained to listen for. Just "running out of fuel, sir" at the end of a sentence, preceded by the mitigating "ah." If you're counting errors, the Avianca crew is now in double digits.

CAVIEDES: Did you already advise that we don't have fuel?

KLOTZ: Yes, sir. I already advise him . . .

CAVIEDES: Bueno.

If it were not the prelude to a tragedy, their back-and-forth would resemble an Abbott and Costello comedy routine.

A little over a minute passes.

ATC: And Avianca zero-five-two heavy, ah, I'm gonna bring you about fifteen miles northeast and then turn you back onto the approach. Is that okay with you and your fuel?

KLOTZ: I guess so. Thank you very much.

I guess so. Thank you very much. They are about to crash! One of the flight attendants enters the cockpit to find out how serious the situation is. The flight engineer points to the empty fuel gauge, and makes a throat-cutting gesture with his finger. *(We know this because the flight attendant survived the crash and testified at the inquest.)*

But he says nothing. Nor does anyone else for the next five minutes. There's radio chatter and routine business, and then the fight engineer cries out, "Flameout on engine number four!"

Caviedes says, "Show me the runway," but the runway is sixteen miles away.

Thirty-six seconds of silence pass. The plane's air traffic controller calls out one last time.

ATC: You have, ah, you have enough fuel to make it to the airport?

The transcript ends.

QUESTIONS FOR ANALYSIS

1. The Avianca crew were confronting a number of challenges: bad weather conditions, long airport delays, an unexpected wind shear, malfunctioning autopilot. If you had to cite one reason for the plane crash, what would it be? Why?

2. Malcolm Gladwell believes the "mitigated speech" was the key factor in the crash.
   - What exactly is "mitigated speech"?
   - Describe some examples of when you have used mitigated speech.
   - Why does Gladwell believe that mitigated speech was the key element in the crash?

3. According to Suren Ratwatte, a veteran pilot who has been involved for years in "human factors" research:

   "All the guys had to do was tell the controller, 'We don't have the fuel to comply with what you are trying to do.' All they had to do was say, 'We can't do that. We have to land in the next ten minutes.' They weren't able to put that across to the controller."

   Why were the pilots of Avianca flight 052 not able to communicate that clear and direct message to air traffic control?

Using Language in Social Contexts

LANGUAGE STYLES

Language is always used in a context. That is, you always speak or write with an audience, whether a person or a group of people, in mind. The audience may consist of friends, coworkers, strangers, or only yourself! You also always use language in a particular situation. You may converse with your friends, meet with your boss, or carry out a business transaction at the bank or supermarket.

In each of these cases, you use the language style that is appropriate to the social situation. For example, describe how you usually greet the following people when you see them:

a good friend
a teacher
a parent
an employer
a waiter/waitress

Different social contexts call for different language responses. In a working environment, no matter how frequently you interact with coworkers or employers, your language style tends to be more formal and less abbreviated than it is in personal friendships. Conversely, the more familiar you are with someone and the better you know that person, the more abbreviated your style of language will be in that context, knowing that you already share a variety of ideas, opinions, and experiences. The language style identifies this shared thinking and consequently restricts the group of people who can communicate within this context.

We all belong to social groups in which we use styles that separate "insiders" from "outsiders." On the one hand, when you use an abbreviated style of language with your friend, you are identifying that person as a friend and sending a social message that says, "I know you pretty well, and I can assume many common perspectives between us." On the other hand, when you are speaking to someone at the office in a more elaborate language style, you are sending a different social message, namely, "I know you within a particular context [this workplace], and I can assume only certain common perspectives between us."

In this way we use language to identify the social context and to define the relationship between the people communicating. Language styles vary from informal, in which we abbreviate not only sentence structure but also the sounds that form words—as in "ya" for *you*—to increasingly formal, in which we use more complex sentence structure as well as complete words in terms of sound patterns.

STANDARD AMERICAN ENGLISH

The language style used in most academic and workplace writing is called *Standard American English (SAE)*. SAE follows the rules and conventions given in handbooks and taught in school. The ability to use SAE marks a person as part of an educated group that understands how and when to use it.

Unless otherwise specified, you should use SAE for college speaking and writing assignments, and your vocabulary should be appropriate for the intended audience. For example, social science students and instructors would immediately understand what *bell curve* means, but other audiences might need an explanation of this term. Again, if your literature teacher is the sole intended audience for your paper, you don't need to define a *literary symbol*. But if the assignment asks you to write for fourth-grade students to encourage them to enjoy poetry, then you

Thinking Critically About Visuals

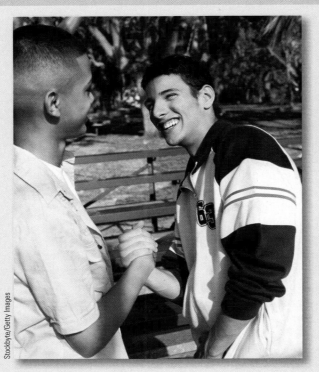

Stockbyte/Getty Images

"What Up?"

Using language effectively involves using the language style appropriate to the situation. What are some of the different language styles you use in your life? Which language styles do you feel least comfortable with? Why?

would want to define literary terms. Depending on your intended audience and purpose, you may or may not wish to employ slang, jargon, or dialect, but you should understand these forms of language.

SLANG

Read the following dialogue and then rewrite it in your own style:

GIRL 1: "Hey, did you see that new guy? He's a dime. I mean, really diesel."

GIRL 2: "All the guys in my class are busted. They are tore up from the floor up. Punks, crack-heads, low-lifes. Let's exit. There's a jam tonight that is going to be the bomb, really fierce. I've got to hit the books so that I'll still have time to chill."

How would you describe the style of the original dialogue? How would you describe the style of your version of the dialogue?

As linguists have long known, cultures create the most words for the things that preoccupy them the most. For example, Eskimos have more than seventy-six words for *ice* and *snow,* and Hawaiians can choose from scores of variations on the word *water.* Most teenage slang falls into one or two categories: words meaning "cool" and words meaning "out of it." A person who is really out of it could be described as a *nerd,* a *goober,* a *geek,* a *fade,* or a *pinhead,* to name just a few possibilities.

Thinking Activity 6.5

THINKING ABOUT SLANG

Review the slang terms and definitions in the following glossary. For each term, list a word that you use or have heard of to mean the same thing. How do your terms match up?

Word	Meaning	Your word
Hardcore	Serious	
Friend/defriend	To accept or reject a person on your Facebook site	
Sexting	Flirting via text messages	
Googling	Using the Google search engine to surf the Web	
Tweetup	Social gatherings arranged via messages posted on Twitter	
Fan of Larry the Cable Guy	Redneck, unsophisticated	
Carbon footprint	The amount of energy being used by an individual or society	
It's complicated	Couple in an ambiguous state between "friends" and "in a relationship"	
EUI	"Emailing under the influence," i.e., emailing when you're high	
Tap it/that	Hook up with someone	
What's good?	"What's going on?"	
Bling	Expensive jewelry; someone who has "bling" (is rich)	

If your meanings did not match those in the glossary or if you did not recognize some of the words, what do you think was the main reason for your lack of comprehension?

Slang is a restrictive style of language that limits its speakers to a particular group, and age is usually the determining factor in using slang. But there are special forms of slang that are not determined by age; rather, they are determined by profession or interest group. Let's look at this other type of language style.

JARGON

Jargon is made up of words, expressions, and technical terms that are intelligible to professional circles or interest groups but not to the general public. Consider the following interchanges:

1. A: Breaker 1-9. Com'on, Little Frog.

   B: Roger and back to you, Charley.

   A: You got to back down; you got a Smokey ahead.

   B: I can't afford to feed the bears this week. Better stay at 5-5 now.

   A: That's a big 10-4.

   B: I'm gonna cut the coax now.

2. OK A1, number six takes two eggs, wreck 'em, with a whiskey down and an Adam and Eve on a raft. Don't forget the Jack Tommy, express to California.

3. Please take further notice, that pursuant to and in accordance with Article II, Paragraph Second and Fifteen of the aforesaid Proprietary Lease Agreement, you are obligated to reimburse Lessor for any expense Lessor incurs including legal fees in instituting any action or proceeding due to a default of your obligations as contained in the Proprietary Lease Agreement.

Can you identify the groups that would understand the meaning of each of the previous examples?

THE SOCIAL BOUNDARIES OF LANGUAGE

Language is a system of communication, by sounds and markings, among given groups of people. Within each language community, members' thinking patterns are defined in many respects by the specific patterns of meaning that language imposes. Smaller groups within language communities display distinctive language patterns. When there are some differences from the norm, mainly in vocabulary and length of sentences, we say the speakers are using a specific language style. When the form of the language spoken by these smaller groups shows many differences from the "usual" or "regular" form in words and sentence structure, we call this language form a *dialect*. Often language style is determined by the context, but sometimes speakers who differ from each other in terms of age, sex, or social class also differ from each other in their speech—even in the same social context. This is called *social variation*.

We cannot ignore the way in which our thoughts about a social situation determine the variety of language we use. The connection between language and thought turns language into a powerful social force that separates us as well as binds us together. The language that you use and the way you use it serve as important clues to your social identity. For example, dialect identifies your geographical area or group, slang marks your age group and subculture, jargon often identifies your occupation, and accent typically suggests where you grew up and your socioeconomic class. Social dimensions of language are important influences in shaping your response to others. Sometimes they can trigger stereotypes you hold about someone's interests, social class, intelligence, personal attributes, and so on. The ability to think critically gives you the insight and the intellectual ability to distinguish people's language use from their individual qualities, to correct inaccurate beliefs about people, and to avoid stereotypical responses in the future.

Thinking Activity 6.6

ANALYZING LANGUAGE USES

1. Describe examples, drawn from individuals in your personal experience, of each of the following: accent, jargon, slang.

2. Describe your immediate responses to the examples you just provided. For example, what is your immediate response to someone speaking with a British accent? To someone speaking "computerese"? To someone speaking a slang that you don't understand?

3. Analyze your responses. How were they formed? Do they represent an accurate understanding of the person or a stereotyped belief?

4. Identify strategies for using critical-thinking abilities to overcome inaccurate and inappropriate responses to others based on their language usage.

Using Language to Influence

The intimate relationship between language and thinking makes it natural that people use language to influence the thinking of others. As you have seen, within the boundaries of social groups, people use a given language style or dialect to emphasize shared information and experience. Not only does this sharing socially identify the members of the group; it also provides a base for them to influence one another's thinking. The expression "Now you're speaking my language!" illustrates this point. Some people make a profession of using language to influence people's thinking. In other words, many individuals and groups are interested in influencing—and sometimes controlling—your thoughts, your feelings, and (as a result) your behavior. To avoid being unconsciously manipulated by these efforts, you must have an understanding and an awareness of how language functions. Such an understanding will help you distinguish actual arguments, information, and reasons from techniques of persuasion that others use to try to get you to accept their viewpoint without critical thought. Two types of language are often used to promote the uncritical acceptance of viewpoints:

- Euphemistic language
- Emotive language

By developing insight into these language strategies, you will strengthen your abilities to function as a critical thinker.

EUPHEMISTIC LANGUAGE

The term *euphemism* derives from a Greek word meaning "to speak with good words" and involves substituting a more pleasant, less objectionable way of saying something for a blunt or more direct way. For example, an entire collection of euphemisms exists to disguise the unpleasantness of death: "passed away," "went to her reward," "departed this life," and "blew out the candle."

Euphemisms can become dangerous when they are used to create misperceptions of important issues. For example, an alcoholic may describe himself as a "social drinker," thus ignoring the problem and the help he needs. Or a politician may indicate that one of his other statements was "somewhat at variance with the truth"—meaning that he lied. Even more serious examples include describing rotting slums as "substandard housing," making the deplorable conditions appear reasonable and the need for action less important. One of the most devastating examples of the destructive power of euphemisms was Nazi Germany's characterization of the slaughter of more than 12 million men, women, and children by such innocuous phrases as the "final solution" and the "purification of the race."

Euphemisms crop up in every part of our lives, but bureaucracies are particularly prolific and creative euphemizers. Every year the nation's English teachers present annual Doublespeak Awards to those institutions producing the most egregious euphemisms. Listed below are some past winners. Why do you think these organizations created these particular euphemisms? Can you add to the list euphemisms that you've heard or read recently?

Department of Defense

bombing	= "servicing the target"
people to be killed	= "soft targets"
buildings to be bombed	= "hard targets"

U.S. Senate

| voting a $23,200 raise for themselves | = "pay equalization concept" |

U.S. government economic report

| recession | = "meaningful downturn in aggregate output" |

Several foreign governments

assassinations	= "active self-defense," "interception"
terrorist	= "freedom fighter"
torture	= "moderate physical pressure"

Thinking Activity 6.7

ANALYZING EUPHEMISMS

Read the following essay by linguistics professor Robin Tolmach Lakoff about the use of euphemism to dehumanize the "enemy" in times of war. In what ways did George Orwell (see page 294) predict the use of euphemism to make the human costs of warfare more politically palatable? Can you think of other social policies with direct human consequences that are discussed, by politicians or the media, in euphemistic terms? Identify several euphemisms used to describe a policy or issue and explain how the euphemisms can lead to dangerous misperceptions and consequences. (For further discussion of how language can be used to influence, suppress, or direct behavior, see "Thinking Passages: Critical Thinking and Obedience to Authority" in Chapter 11.)

Ancient Greece to Iraq, the Power of Words in Wartime

by Robin Tolmach Lakoff

An American soldier refers to an Iraqi prisoner as "it." A general speaks not of "Iraqi fighters" but of "the enemy." A weapons manufacturer doesn't talk about people but about "targets."

Bullets and bombs are not the only tools of war. Words, too, play their part.

Human beings are social animals, genetically hard-wired to feel compassion toward others. Under normal conditions, most people find it very difficult to kill.

But in war, military recruits must be persuaded that killing other people is not only acceptable but even honorable.

The language of war is intended to bring about that change, and not only for soldiers in the field. In wartime, language must be created to enable combatants and noncombatants alike to see the other side as killable, to overcome the innate queasiness over the taking of human life. Soldiers, and those who remain at home, learn to call their enemies by names that make them seem not quite human—inferior, contemptible, and not like "us."

The specific words change from culture to culture and war to war. The names need not be obviously demeaning. Just the fact that we can name them gives us a sense of superiority and control. If, in addition, we give them nicknames, we can see them as smaller, weaker and childlike—not worth taking seriously as fully human.

The Greeks and Romans referred to everyone else as "barbarians"—etymologically those who only babble, only go "bar-bar." During the American Revolution, the British called the colonists "Yankees," a term with a history that is still in dispute. While the British intended it disparagingly, the Americans, in perhaps the first historical instance of reclamation, made the word their own and gave it a positive spin, turning the derisive song "Yankee Doodle" into our first, if unofficial, national anthem.

In World War I, the British gave the Germans the nickname "Jerries," from the first syllable of German. In World War II, Americans referred to the Japanese as "Japs."

The names may refer to real or imagined cultural and physical differences that emphasize the ridiculous or the repugnant. So in various wars, the British called the French "Frogs." Germans have been called "Krauts," a reference to weird and smelly food. The Vietnamese were called "slopes" and "slants." The Koreans were referred to simply as "gooks."

The war in Iraq has added new examples. Some American soldiers refer to the Iraqis as "hadjis," used in a derogatory way, apparently unaware that the word, which comes from the Arabic term for a pilgrimage to Mecca, is used as a term of respect for older Muslim men.

The Austrian ethologist Konrad Lorenz suggested that the more clearly we see other members of our own species as individuals, the harder we find it to kill them.

So some terms of war are collective nouns, encouraging us to see the enemy as an undifferentiated mass, rather than as individuals capable of suffering. Crusaders called their enemy "the Saracen," and in World War I, the British called Germans "the Hun."

American soldiers are trained to call those they are fighting against "the enemy." It is easier to kill an enemy than an Iraqi. The word "enemy" itself provides the facelessness of a collective noun. Its non-specificity also has a fear-inducing connotation; enemy means simply "those we are fighting," without reference to their identity.

The terrors and uncertainties of war make learning this kind of language especially compelling for soldiers on the front. But civilians back home also need to believe that what their country is doing is just and necessary, and that the killing they are supporting is in some way different from the killing in civilian life that is rightly punished by the criminal justice system. The use of the language developed for military purposes by civilians reassures them that war is not murder.

The linguistic habits that soldiers must absorb in order to fight make atrocities like those at Abu Ghraib virtually inevitable. The same language that creates a psychological chasm between "us" and "them" and enables American troops to kill in battle, makes enemy soldiers fit subjects for torture and humiliation. The reasoning is: They are not really human, so they will not feel the pain.

Once language draws that line, all kinds of mistreatment become imaginable, and then justifiable. To make the abuses at Abu Ghraib unthinkable, we would have to abolish war itself.

EMOTIVE LANGUAGE

What is your *immediate* reaction to the following words?

sexy	peaceful	disgusting	God
mouthwatering	bloodthirsty	whore	Nazi
		filthy	

Most of these words probably stimulate certain feelings in you. In fact, this ability to evoke feelings in people accounts for the extraordinary power of language. As a stark illustration of the way people (in this case, politicians) use language to manipulate emotions, several years ago a political action committee named GOPAC distributed a booklet titled "Language: A Key Mechanism of Control" to the candidates they supported. The booklet urged members of Congress to use words like "environment, peace, freedom, fair, flag, we-us-our, family, and humane" when speaking of themselves. When speaking of opponents, words like "betray, sick, pathetic, lie, liberal, hypocrisy, permissive attitude, and self-serving" were preferable. Think of a recent election: Do you recall candidates following these linguistic suggestions?

Emotive language often plays a double role—it not only symbolizes and expresses our feelings but also arouses or evokes feelings in others. When you say "I love you" to someone, you usually are not simply expressing your feelings toward that person— you also hope to inspire similar feelings in that person toward you. Even when you are communicating factual information, you make use of the emotive influence of language to interest other people in what you are saying. For example, compare the factually more objective account in the *New York Times* of Malcolm X's assassination with the more emotive/action account in *Life* magazine (pages 152–154). Which account do you find more engaging? Why?

Although an emotive statement may be an accurate description of how you feel, it is *not* the same as a factual statement because it is true only for you—not for others. For instance, even though you may feel that a movie is tasteless and repulsive, someone else may find it exciting and hilarious. By describing your feelings about the movie, you are giving your personal evaluation, which often differs from the personal evaluations of others (consider the case of conflicting reviews of the same movie). A factual statement, in contrast, is a statement with which all "rational" people will agree, providing that suitable evidence for its truth is available (e.g., the fact that mass transit uses less energy than automobiles).

In some ways, symbolizing your emotions is more difficult than representing factual information about the world. Expressing your feelings toward a person you know well often seems considerably more challenging than describing facts about that person.

When emotive words are used in larger groups (such as in sentences, paragraphs, compositions, poems, plays, novels), they become even more powerful. The pamphlets of Thomas Paine helped inspire American patriots during the Revolutionary War, and Abraham Lincoln's Gettysburg Address has endured as an expression of our most cherished values. In fact, it was the impassioned oratory of Adolf Hitler that helped influence the German people before and during World War II.

One way to think about the meaning and power of emotive words is to see them on a scale or continuum from mild to strong. For example: *plump, fat, obese.* Philosopher Bertrand Russell used this feature of emotive words to show how we perceive the same trait in various people:

- I am firm.
- You are stubborn.
- He or she is pigheaded.

Try this technique with two other emotive words:

1. I am. . . .   You are. . . .   He or she is. . . .
2. I am. . . .   You are. . . .   He or she is. . . .

Finally, emotive words can be used to confuse opinions with facts, a situation that commonly occurs when we combine emotive uses of language with informative uses. Although people may appear to be giving factual information, they actually may be adding personal evaluations that are not factual. These opinions are often emotional, biased, unfounded, or inflammatory. Consider the following statement: "New York City is a filthy and dangerous pigpen—only idiots would want to live there." Although the speaker is pretending to give factual information, he or she is really using emotive language to advance an opinion.

The presence of emotive words is usually a sign that a personal opinion or evaluation rather than a fact is being stated. Speakers occasionally do identify their opinions as opinions with such phrases as "In my opinion . . ." or "I feel that . . . ." Often, however, speakers do *not* identify their opinions as opinions because they want you to treat their *judgments* as *facts*. In these cases, the combination of the informative use of language with the emotive use can be misleading and even dangerous.

Thinking Activity 6.8

ANALYZING EMOTIVE LANGUAGE

Identify examples of emotive language in the following passages, and explain how it is used by the writers to influence people's thoughts and feelings:

> I draw the line in the dust and toss the gauntlet before the heel of tyranny, and I say segregation now, segregation tomorrow, segregation forever.
>
> —*Governor George C. Wallace, 1963*

> We dare not forget today that we are heirs of that first revolution. Let the word go forth from this time and place, to friend and foe alike, that the torch has been passed to a new generation of Americans—born in this century, tempered by war, disciplined by a hard and bitter peace, proud of our ancient heritage—and unwilling to witness or permit the slow undoing of those human rights to which this nation has always been committed, and to which we are committed today at home and around the world.
>
> —*President John F. Kennedy,*
> *Inaugural Address, 1961*

> Every criminal, every gambler, every thug, every libertine, every girl ruiner, every home wrecker, every wife beater, every dope peddler, every moonshiner, every crooked politician, every pagan Papist priest, every shyster lawyer, every white slaver, every brothel madam, every Rome-controlled newspaper, every black spider—is fighting the Klan. Think it over. Which side are you on?
>
> —*from a Ku Klux Klan circular*

Thinking Passages

PERSUADING WITH POLITICAL SPEECHES

The central purpose of political speeches has traditionally been to persuade listeners to a particular point of view, using language as the vehicle. This has never been more true than in times of war or national crisis. Visit www.youtube.com and search for the following speeches:

- President Franklin D. Roosevelt speaking after the attack on Pearl Harbor by the Japanese military
- Prime Minister Winston Churchill speaking after the invasion and defeat of most of the countries of Western Europe by Hitler's military
- President George W. Bush speaking ten days following the terrorist attacks on the World Trade Center and the Pentagon, on September 11, 2001
- Prime Minister Tony Blair speaking several weeks after the terrorist attacks on September 11, 2001
- Al Qaeda leader Osama bin Laden's videotaped comments released worldwide several days following the terrorist attacks on September 11, 2001

QUESTIONS FOR ANALYSIS

1. Identify the euphemisms and emotive words that tend to keep reappearing in these various speeches. Why do you think the authors/speakers chose the words that they did?
2. Identify the themes that keep reappearing in the various accounts. Why did the authors/speakers choose these particular themes?
3. Rank the speeches in order, from most persuasive to least persuasive, and explain your rationale for doing so.
4. How do our current president's persuasive abilities compare to those of his or her predecessor? Cite specific differences or similarities in their rhetorical style. Is one or the other style more effective—for certain audiences, or overall? If so, explain why.

Thinking Passages

WILL TWITTER MAKE US NIT-TWITS?

One of the forms of new media that is on the leading edge is Twitter, the online microblogging site that enables people to communicate instantly by smartphone or computer to a large number of people with "tweets," brief messages of no more

THINKING CRITICALLY ABOUT NEW MEDIA

How to Write for the New Media

Elsewhere in this text we have looked at the differences between expressing ourselves in writing and expressing ourselves orally. When we express ourselves in writing, our audience is not able to hear our vocal inflections or see our gestures and body language. The impression we make depends completely on what we write.

The same holds true for the use of email, which has changed the way many people communicate at work, in social settings, in the classroom, and at home. Consider the following questions:

- What are some of the differences between communicating via email, the spoken word, or another form of writing?
- Do you think an email is easier to misunderstand than other styles of writing? Why or why not? For example, have you ever
  - Received an email you thought was sarcastic, cruel, or too blunt?
  - Sent one that was misinterpreted?
  - Received "hoax" virus warnings?
  - Received chain letters promising unbelievable rewards?
  - Received jokes you didn't want?
- In your opinion, has the popularity of email changed the nature or frequency of these kinds of messages as compared to paper mail? If so, how has that happened?

The central point is that in order to be an effective communicator in any medium, we have to be continually aware of our audience, asking ourselves "How will my message be received or interpreted? What 'voice' will be most successful in communicating my intended message?" Writing is similar to speaking in this regard. Have you noticed that you speak differently to different groups of people in different situations? Depending on whether and where you work, you may notice that the words and even the grammatical constructions you use vary from those you use when speaking with, for example, family members. For that matter, how you speak to children is probably different from how you speak to siblings or to parents and other elders. You have a different "speaking personality" in different situations.

What different email personalities do you have? What steps can you take to ensure that you come across as you intend when you use email? These are "language landmines" that you want to keep in mind as you compose and send your emails, texts, and tweets. Writing for the new media effectively means developing a new set of writing strategies especially adapted to this new digital medium. In the following article by Neal Jansons, "How to Write for the New Media," he identifies some of the writing strategies to work at developing.

How to Write for the New Media

by Neal Jansons

Here are some tricks and tips for developing a new media writing style.

1. **Go Short**

   In school and literature, often we are taught that more is better. If you can slip in more detail, another source, or another idea, you should. Well, this is just plain wrong in the new media. Here we have to capture a reader who with the click of a mouse can be somewhere else. They are not a professor paid to read a paper or a book-reader sitting and relaxing in a nook. They are on a computer and working in a very "hot" (interactive) medium. **Keep your posts and articles between 400 and 700 words.** If you absolutely *must* go longer, consider splitting the post up into a series. DO NOT go for the "multi-pager". It does not work, nobody reads it and if you keep trying to write your *magnum opus* you will lose readers.

2. **Avoid Big Blocks of Texts**

   Break your articles up into multiple paragraphs. What seems like over-formatting in a book or magazine can be perfect for a post because of the difference in how they are read. People's eyes react differently to text on a screen. **Use pictures, changes in font size, and lists to break your content up into meaningful chunks.** The goal is that at any point a person could finish up a section in just a few seconds and easily come back for the next chunk later.

3. **Avoid the Passive Voice**

   In school we learn to speak in the passive voice to record facts. This makes things very "objective" and "neutral" sounding, but is not what people are looking for online. There are a billion other things they could be reading that can all be objective, but they will read *your* work because it is *yours*. **Make your writing drip with active verbs and your own personality.** Let your voice come through so strongly that the reader will hear you in their head.

4. **Lead the Reader**

   The formatting of online content is always a problem, but the best thing you can do is let your content guide the reader's eyes and mind. **Use lists, headings, and text styling to lead the reader's eyes to the important points.** This is what is sometimes called the "Command to Look" from a book by the same name.

Source: "How to Write for the New Media" by Neal Alan Spurlock. Reprinted by permission of the author.

THINKING CRITICALLY ABOUT NEW MEDIA (*CONTINUED*)

5. Make Your Content "Hot"

This is the internet, web 2.0 thank you very much, and we want our content to be dynamic. We want links, video, and the ability to converse. **Pepper your articles with interactivity**, even to the point of asking questions for your readers to answer. If you refer to something, link it (but only the first time!), if you say there was a video, include it in the post.

6. K.I.S.S.

Keep it simple. No, really. Really simple. Avoid clarifying clauses, complicated thoughts, and involved sentences. This is not to say you can't write difficult ideas . . . just break them down. **Tell them what you are going to tell them, tell them, then tell them what you told them.** The reason for this is (again) about how people read on the internet. Since people are always multi-tasking, being able to come back to an article and read it in little chunks without losing the thread of the thought is absolutely necessary.

Final Word

Following these simple steps you can increase your reader loyalty and the usefulness of your posts. People will be able to get what they need from your content easily and efficiently, which will make your posts and articles appealing and useful, which means people will come back to read more and pass on your work to other potential readers and clients. **Help your readers read and they will stay loyal, make them work too hard and they will just click something else.**

Thinking Activity 6.9

HOW WELL DO YOU COMMUNICATE?

How do you come across to your audience, and what can you do to improve the clarity of your message? One approach is to look through your sent email file and examine some of your older emails, asking yourself, "With the detachment of time, was this message written in a way that would best communicate my intended meaning, or were there possible misinterpretations? How could I revise the message to make it less vague or ambiguous?" Once you have revised some of these older emails, list some strategies to help make your future emails more successful in communicating the meaning you intend, such as "I should make more use of examples to illustrate my point."

than 140 characters, the maximum length that can be communicated via the platform used by most mobile phones. Twitter was originally created to allow individuals the opportunity to "follow" selected people as they broadcast their immediate thoughts or activities. For example, more than one million people "follow" celebrities like Rachel Maddow and Jay-Z by reading the "tweets" they send throughout the day, providing followers with ongoing updates of their lives. This new media phenomenon has spread like wildfire across the world, with more than 140 million "twitizens" occupying the "twitisphere." Despite its popularity (or perhaps because of it), Twitter has aroused impassioned consternation and critique. Why? To begin with, critics contend that its limit of 140 characters (roughly a sentence or two) encourages simplistic thinking and language use. It's unlikely that such restricted messages will ever communicate any complex ideas or intelligent analysis. Instead, tweets like "I'm now eating a chocolate cream-filled donut and drinking a double-latte with soy milk because I skipped breakfast for the umpteenth time!" (140 characters) are likely to be the more common message being broadcast live to an eager audience. Others have raised the concern that, along with the population's increasing preoccupation with phone calls, emails, and text messages, "tweeting" will simply expand the obsession with electronic communication, staying continually "connected" at the expense of normal social relationships and more productive activities. These electronic media create a false sense of urgency, encouraging people to be plugged in and overstimulated all the time.

Supporters of Twitter argue that these concerns are misdirected. They argue that the 140-character limit encourages people to be creatively succinct and focused; that the ease and flexibility of the medium create an infinite number of productive

Roz Chast/The New Yorker Collection/cartoonbank.com

social communities; and that by expanding to include "searching" and "reply" features, Twitter has become a powerful new technology that has changed in positive ways how we live our lives. To tweet or not to tweet? We will explore this timely question and the issues that it entails through the following three articles.

Twitter, Communication, and My Intermittent Inner Luddite
by Yves Smith

So why do I hate Twitter? Twitter is troubling reminiscent of Newspeak, the language being developed by Oceania in George Orwell's 1984 to control thought.

Orwell, in an appendix, describes the principles of Newspeak, and they are directed toward simplifying language so as to void it of inconvenient (for the power structure) propensities of thought:

> The purpose of Newspeak was not only to provide a medium of expression for the world-view and mental habits proper to the devotees of IngSoc, but to make all other modes of thought impossible. It was intended that when Newspeak had been adopted once and for all and Oldspeak forgotten, a heretical thought—that is, a thought diverging from the principles of IngSoc—should be literally unthinkable, at least so far as thought is dependent on words. Its vocabulary was so constructed as to give exact and often very subtle expression to every meaning that a Party member could properly wish to express, while excluding all other meaning and also the possibility of arriving at them by indirect methods.

Now what does that have to do with Twitter, one might ask? Well, while the main means by which Newspeak was implemented was simplifying and subtly changing the inference of words, another element was the extreme condensation of communication:

> Regularity of grammar was always sacrificed to it when it seemed necessary. And rightly so, since what was required, above all for political purposes, was short clipped words of unmistakable meaning which could be uttered rapidly and which roused the minimum of echoes in the speaker's mind. . . . . So did the fact of having very few words to choose from. Relative to our own, the Newspeak vocabulary was tiny, and new ways of reducing it were constantly being devised. Newspeak, indeed, differed from most all other languages in that its vocabulary grew smaller instead of larger every year. Each reduction was a gain, since the smaller the area of choice, the smaller the temptation to take thought. Ultimately it was hoped to make articulate speech issue from the larynx without involving the higher brain centers at all. . . .
>
> And it was to be foreseen that with the passage of time the distinguishing characteristics of Newspeak would become more and more pronounced—its words growing fewer and fewer, their meanings more and more rigid, and the chance of putting them to improper uses always diminishing.

Now the idea that have people communicate often within 140 characters and thought control seems awfully remote, no? Particularly since this is voluntary, customer driven, right?

Source: "Twitter, Communication, and My Inner Luddite" by Yves Smith from http://www
.nakedcapitalism.com/2009/02/twitter-communication-and-my.html. Reprinted by permission of the author.

I am not at all certain. I notice in reactions to my blog posts, which are often pretty lengthy, that readers sometimes miss important nuance in what I or readers I have cited say, or (just as bad) project onto what I have written something I never said.

. . .

Now this could just be normal comprehension issues. But I notice how the Internet has affected how I read. I have become impatient with longer stories (unless I am on an airplane). I spend most of my time on the Internet, and the vast majority of what I read fits within the browser window. I find that has conditioned my expectations. When confronted with a longer piece (say Sunday New York Times magazine feature or New Yorker length) I find after the first page wondering if it really had to be this long, and often not finishing the piece. Five years ago, I never would have responded this way.

. . .

You can't say anything complicated or nuanced in 140 characters. And Twitter encourages people to accept a medium that severely constrains communication, and calls a defect a virtue.

Marshall McLuhan was right.

I have a second issue with Twitter, and mobile communications generally, I can't control how they are used, but I see them as having a corrosive effect on interpersonal relations. It's one thing to take calls, check texts tweets, or the news when out and about by yourself. But it has become the norm to take them when meeting with others. That reduces the quality of the interaction and sends a message that the person you are with is merely an option, other options are ever present and must be assessed, maybe exercised.

For those in high urgency professions (doctors, traders) I can see this being acceptable. And everyone has occasions when they need to be on the alert for news, a call, or a text. But this has become routine.

Humans are a social species, with very big limbic brains (the emotional center) and smaller cerebral cortexes (the seat of higher reasoning). I cannot prove the connection, and doubtless many factors are in play, but the US is a society where enormous numbers of people take anti-depressants and brain chemistry altering chemicals, either to elevate their mood or improve performance in some way (and those are the legal drug users. BTW, the most recent data I could find was 2005, that anti-depressants are the most widely prescribed drugs in the US, with 118 million prescriptions written that year). That says something is deeply amiss.

We have a lot of other factors contributing to the erosion of social structures: high divorce rates, short job tenure (and now high unemployment), rising demands for on-the-job productivity (computers and the Internet are a double-edged sword: you can do more, but expectations have risen accordingly). These are clearly the big drivers, but I have to think that the degrading of routine interactions and the expectation (in at least some circles) that people multi-task, when the evidence is that it does not increase productivity, has to play a role.

Twitter feeds that addiction, that false sense of urgency. Most things can wait. Indeed, a lot of things are better off waiting. But we are encouraged to be plugged in, overstimulated all the time, at the expense of higher quality human relations.

I don't want to contribute to the problem by participating in this sort of thing, but I suspect I will give in to practical realities.

The Hidden Problem with Twitter

by Carin Ford

Oxford University Press has been studying the language of Twitter these past six months—take a look at what they've found.

Seems the most commonly tweeted word is (hold the drum roll) "the." And because Twitter thrives on users talking about themselves, the second most commonly tweeted word is "I." Interestingly, "I" ranks tenth in regular written communication.

Oxford University Press also found gerunds are heavily utilized by the Twitter crowd—among the most popular words are "going," "getting" and "watching." Tech terms such as "Google," "Facebook," "blog" and "Mac" also rank high with users. Here's more of what came from monitoring 1.5 million random tweets. There were:

- 2,098,630 total sentences
- 22,431,033 total words
- close to 15 words per tweet, and
- nearly 1.5 sentences per tweet.

And compared to formal writing, the casual lingo of Twitter includes a greater frequency of "OK" and "f***."

So here's the question: **Is Twitter—along with instant messaging and texting—contributing to the destruction of language skills among college students?**

Included below are summaries and paraphrases of points made by people who responded to this question. At the conclusion of this article, compose your own thoughtful response to this question. (You can use more than 140 characters!)

- Researchers should acknowledge the difference in spoken language, which is rarely grammatically correct, and written language. Twitter, texting, and social networking Web sites are generally cataloged by college students as an electronic conversation among their many means of communication. Spoken language is being captured in electronic written formats. While they are written down, that does not mean that researchers can confuse these "conversations" as the communicator's formal writing structure. You would never accuse an author of having poor language skills based on a casual conversation that you had with the author.

- I fully believe that Instant Messaging, texting, twittering, and social networking via the web are all contributing to a disintegration of English language skills. I text, IM, and socially network, and my friends and family actually tease me because I still utilize the skills I was taught in school.

- Yes, I believe the tech devices of today are destroying not only the language skills, but the social skills of our young people today. I have heard stories of young people in the same room that chose to text each other rather than talk. What a shame!

- Twitter is probably yet another sign of our grotesque self-centeredness, but it's not destroying our language skills. Contrarily, I propose that the brevity necessitated

Source: "The Hidden Problem With Twitter" by Carin Ford. www.higheredmorning.com.

by just 140 characters directly challenges users to compress their words/thoughts—a quality that is definitely lacking in the writing produced by college students. Tweeting might turn us all into poets.

- Twitter, instant messaging, and texting ARE contributing to, let's call it degraded language skills, by providing a set of forums in which these degraded skills are accepted and encouraged. I believe acceptance is primarily a function of the youth of the majority of contributors. They lack experience with more formal language and don't seem to grasp the subtly and nuance that come with its complexity. Degradation is encouraged by the fact that even the best texting phones or IM clients are poor writing instruments. 12 keys are inadequate as are one eighth scale, not quite QWERTY keyboards.

- Did the abbreviated wording used in telegrams destroy the English language? I don't think so. Neither will Twitter, or texting in general – as long as schools continue to stress good language skills in the classroom. As an English teacher and student of linguistics, I realize that English and all other living languages are constantly evolving, so Twitter and its "siblings" will affect English, but not to necessarily destroy or devalue it. As for spelling, well, English is a terrible model for spelling, so maybe these mediums will improve it!

- Just to be clear, shortening the word "right" to "rite" is not poetry! Nor is the use of the sentence, "wer can i fine sum mor info on ur school?" when addressing a university admissions officer. (Sadly, this is a true story.) If texting and tweeting do indeed aid the progression of a new dialect or language, then it should be recognized as such and given nomenclature to properly separate it from English, so that "English" teachers will stop accepting it in their classrooms.

- As a college teacher, I do not see a difference between my technology-dependent (even addicted) students and others in regard to writing skills. Some are excellent; some are awful; most are in-between. I will admit that good writing has become

© RypeArts/iStockphoto.com

increasingly rare, but I saw that decline way before Twitter and texting, so I have to conclude it has more to do with what students are taught earlier in school and the performance standards they are expected to meet. Students who text and twitter are very capable of shifting gears and writing excellent research papers, essays, and lab reports.

How Twitter Will Change the Way We Live

by Steven Johnson

The one thing you can say for certain about Twitter is that it makes a terrible first impression. You hear about this new service that lets you send 140-character updates to your "followers," and you think, Why does the world need this, exactly? It's not as if we were all sitting around four years ago scratching our heads and saying, "If only there were a technology that would allow me to send a message to my 50 friends, alerting them in real time about my choice of breakfast cereal."

I, too, was skeptical at first. I had met Evan Williams, Twitter's co-creator, a couple of times in the dotcom '90s when he was launching Blogger.com. Back then, what people worried about was the threat that blogging posed to our attention span, with telegraphic, two-paragraph blog posts replacing long-format articles and books. With Twitter, Williams was launching a communications platform that limited you to a couple of sentences at most. What was next? Software that let you send a single punctuation mark to describe your mood?

And yet as millions of devotees have discovered, Twitter turns out to have unsuspected depth. In part this is because hearing about what your friends had for breakfast is actually more interesting than it sounds. The technology writer Clive Thompson calls this "ambient awareness": by following these quick, abbreviated status reports from members of your extended social network, you get a strangely satisfying glimpse of their daily routines. We don't think it at all moronic to start a phone call with a friend by asking how her day is going. Twitter gives you the same information without your even having to ask.

The social warmth of all those stray details shouldn't be taken lightly. But I think there is something even more profound in what has happened to Twitter over the past two years, something that says more about the culture that has embraced and expanded Twitter at such extraordinary speed. Yes, the breakfast-status updates turned out to be more interesting than we thought. But the key development with Twitter is how we've jury-rigged the system to do things that its creators never dreamed of.

In short, the most fascinating thing about Twitter is not what it's doing to us. It's what we're doing to it.

The Open Conversation

Earlier this year I attended a daylong conference in Manhattan devoted to education reform. Called Hacking Education, it was a small, private affair: 40-odd educators, entrepreneurs, scholars, philanthropists, and venture capitalists, all engaged in a sprawling

---

six-hour conversation about the future of schools. Twenty years ago, the ideas exchanged in that conversation would have been confined to the minds of the participants. Ten years ago, a transcript might have been published weeks or months later on the Web. Five years ago, a handful of participants might have blogged about their experiences after the fact.

But this event was happening in 2009, so trailing behind the real-time, real-world conversation was an equally real-time conversation on Twitter. At the outset of the conference, our hosts announced that anyone who wanted to post live commentary about the event via Twitter should include the word *#hackedu* in his 140 characters. In the room, a large display screen showed a running feed of tweets.

· · ·

At first, all these tweets came from inside the room and were created exclusively by conference participants tapping away on their laptops or BlackBerrys. But within half an hour or so, word began to seep out into the Twittersphere that an interesting conversation about the future of schools was happening at #hackedu. A few tweets appeared on the screen from strangers announcing that they were following the #hackedu thread. Then others joined the conversation, adding their observations or proposing topics for further exploration. A few experts grumbled publicly about how they hadn't been invited to the conference. Back in the room, we pulled interesting ideas and questions from the screen and integrated them into our face-to-face conversation.

· · ·

Injecting Twitter into that conversation fundamentally changed the rules of engagement. It added a second layer of discussion and brought a wider audience into what would have been a private exchange. And it gave the event an afterlife on the Web. Yes, it was built entirely out of 140-character messages, but the sum total of those tweets added up to something truly substantive, like a suspension bridge made of pebbles.

The Super-Fresh Web

The basic mechanics of Twitter are remarkably simple. Users publish tweets—those 140-character messages—from a computer or mobile device. (The character limit allows tweets to be created and circulated via the SMS platform used by most mobile phones.) As a social network, Twitter revolves around the principle of followers. When you choose to follow another Twitter user, that user's tweets appear in reverse chronological order on your main Twitter page. If you follow 20 people, you'll see a mix of tweets scrolling down the page: breakfast-cereal updates, interesting new links, music recommendations, even musings on the future of education. Some celebrity Twitterers—most famously Ashton Kutcher—have crossed the million-follower mark, effectively giving them a broadcast-size audience. The average Twitter profile seems to be somewhere in the dozens: a collage of friends, colleagues, and a handful of celebrities. The mix creates a media experience quite unlike anything that has come before it, strangely intimate and at the same time celebrity-obsessed. You glance at your Twitter feed over that first cup of coffee, and in a few seconds you find out that your nephew got into med school and Shaquille O'Neal just finished a cardio workout in Phoenix.

· · ·

For as long as we've had the Internet in our homes, critics have bemoaned the demise of shared national experiences. . . . But watch a live mass-media event with Twitter open on your laptop and you'll see that the futurists had it wrong. We still have national events, but now when we have them, we're actually having a genuine, public conversation with a group that extends far beyond our nuclear family and our next-door neighbors. Some of that conversation is juvenile, of course, just as it was in our living room when we heckled Richard Nixon's Checkers speech. But some of it is moving, witty, observant, subversive.

Skeptics might wonder just how much subversion and wit is conveyable via 140-character updates. But in recent months Twitter users have begun to find a route around that limitation by employing Twitter as a pointing device instead of a communications channel: sharing links to longer articles, discussions, posts, videos—anything that lives behind a URL. Websites that once saw their traffic dominated by Google search queries are seeing a growing number of new visitors coming from "passed links" at social networks like Twitter and Facebook. This is what the naysayers fail to understand: it's just as easy to use Twitter to spread the word about a brilliant 10,000-word *New Yorker* article as it is to spread the word about your Lucky Charms habit.

Put those three elements together—social networks, live searching, and link-sharing—and you have a cocktail that poses what may amount to the most interesting alternative to Google's near monopoly in searching. At its heart, Google's system is built around the slow, anonymous accumulation of authority: pages rise to the top of Google's search results according to, in part, how many links point to them, which tends to favor older pages that have had time to build an audience. That's a fantastic solution for finding high-quality needles in the immense, spam-plagued haystack that is the contemporary Web. But it's not a particularly useful solution for finding out what people are saying *right now,* the in-the-moment conversation.

· · ·

From Toasters to Microwaves

Because Twitter's co-founders—Evan Williams, Biz Stone, and Jack Dorsey—are such a central-casting vision of start-up savvy, . . . much of the media interest in Twitter has focused on the company. . . . Focusing on it makes you lose sight of the much more significant point about the Twitter platform: the fact that many of its core features and applications have been developed by people who are not on the Twitter payroll.

This is not just a matter of people finding a new use for a tool designed to do something else. In Twitter's case, the users have been redesigning the tool itself. The convention of grouping a topic or event by the "hashtag"—#hackedu or #inauguration—was spontaneously invented by the Twitter user base (as was the convention of replying to another user with the @ symbol). The ability to search a live stream of tweets was developed by another start-up altogether, Summize, which Twitter purchased. . . . Thanks to these innovations, following a live feed of tweets about an event—political debates or *Lost* episodes—has become a central part of the Twitter experience. But just 12 months [earlier], that mode of interaction would have been technically impossible using Twitter.

One of the most telling facts about the Twitter platform is that the vast majority of its users interact with the service via software created by third parties. There are dozens of iPhone and BlackBerry applications—all created by enterprising amateur coders or small start-ups—that let you manage Twitter feeds. There are services that help you upload photos and link to them from your tweets, and programs that map other Twitizens who are near you geographically. Ironically, the tools you're offered if you visit Twitter.com have changed very little in the past two years. But there's an entire Home Depot of Twitter tools available everywhere else.

As the tools have multiplied, we're discovering extraordinary new things to do with them. [In 2009] an anticommunist uprising in Moldova was organized via Twitter.

Twitter has become so widely used among political activists in China that the government recently blocked access to it, in an attempt to censor discussion of the 20th anniversary of the Tiananmen Square massacre. A service called SickCity scans the Twitter feeds from multiple urban areas, tracking references to flu and fever. Celebrity Twitterers like Kutcher have directed their vast followings toward charitable causes (in Kutcher's case, the Malaria No More organization).

Social networks are notoriously vulnerable to the fickle tastes of teens and 20-somethings (remember Friendster?), so it's entirely possible that three or four years from now, we'll have moved on to some Twitter successor. But the key elements of the Twitter platform—the follower structure, link-sharing, real-time searching—will persevere regardless of Twitter's fortunes, just as Web conventions like links, posts, and feeds have endured over the past decade. In fact, every major channel of information will be Twitterfied in one way or another in the coming years:

"Last tweet?"

News and Opinion

Increasingly, the stories that come across our radar—news about a plane crash, a feisty Op-Ed, a gossip item—will arrive via the passed links of the people we follow. Instead of being built by some kind of artificially intelligent software algorithm, a customized newspaper will be compiled from all the articles being read that morning by your social network. This will lead to more news diversity and polarization at the same time: your networked front page will be more eclectic than any traditional-newspaper front page, but political partisans looking to enhance their own private echo chamber will be able to tune out opposing viewpoints more easily.

Searching

As the archive of links shared by Twitter users grows, the value of searching for information via your extended social network will start to rival Google's approach to the search. If you're looking for information on Benjamin Franklin, an essay shared by one of your favorite historians might well be more valuable than the top result on Google; if you're looking for advice on sibling rivalry, an article recommended by a friend of a friend might well be the best place to start.

Advertising

Today the language of advertising is dominated by the notion of impressions: how many times an advertiser can get its brand in front of a potential customer's eyeballs, whether on a billboard, a Web page, or a NASCAR hood. But impressions are fleeting things, especially compared with the enduring relationships of followers. Successful businesses will have millions of Twitter followers (and will pay good money to attract them), and a whole new language of tweet-based customer interaction will evolve to keep those followers engaged: early access to new products or deals, live customer service, customer involvement in brainstorming for new products.

Not all these developments will be entirely positive. Most of us have learned firsthand how addictive the micro-events of our personal e-mail inbox can be. But with the ambient awareness of status updates from Twitter and Facebook, an entire new empire of distraction has opened up. It used to be that you compulsively checked your BlackBerry to see if anything new had happened in your personal life or career: e-mail from the boss, a reply from last night's date. Now you're compulsively checking your BlackBerry for news from other people's lives. And because, on Twitter at least, some of those people happen to be celebrities, the Twitter platform is likely to expand that strangely delusional relationship that we have to fame.

· · ·

End-User Innovation

· · ·

Twitter serves as the best poster child for this new model of social creativity in part because these innovations have flowered at such breathtaking speed and in part because the platform is so simple. It's as if Twitter's creators dared us to do something interesting by giving us a platform with such draconian restrictions. And sure enough, we accepted the dare with relish. Just 140 characters? I wonder if I could use that to start a political uprising.

The speed with which users have extended Twitter's platform points to a larger truth about modern innovation. . . . Since the mid-'80s, a long progression of doomsayers have warned that our declining market share in the patents-and-Ph.D.s business augurs dark times for American innovation.

· · ·

But what actually happened to American innovation during that period? We came up with America Online, Netscape, Amazon, Google, Blogger, Wikipedia, Craigslist, TiVo, Netflix, eBay, the iPod and iPhone, Xbox, Facebook, and Twitter itself. Sure, we didn't build the Prius or the

Wii, but if you measure global innovation in terms of actual lifestyle-changing hit products and not just grad students, the U.S. has been lapping the field for the past 20 years.

. . .

If I go to grad school and invent a better mousetrap, I've created value, which I can protect with a patent and capitalize on by selling my invention to consumers. But if someone else figures out a way to use my mousetrap to replace his much more expensive washing machine, he's created value as well.

. . .

This is what I ultimately find most inspiring about the Twitter phenomenon. We are living through the worst economic crisis in generations, with apocalyptic headlines threatening the end of capitalism as we know it, and yet in the middle of this chaos, the engineers at Twitter headquarters are scrambling to keep the servers up, application developers are releasing their latest builds, and ordinary users are figuring out all the ingenious ways to put these tools to use. There's a kind of resilience here that is worth savoring. The weather reports keep announcing that the sky is falling, but here we are— millions of us—sitting around trying to invent new ways to talk to one another.

QUESTIONS FOR ANALYSIS

1. What factors account for the extraordinary growth and popularity of Twitter?

2. The author of "Why Do I Hate Twitter?" compares tweeting to Newspeak, the language being developed by the ruling authority in George Orwell's book *1984* for the purpose of influencing and controlling the thoughts of the citizenry. What are the specific points of comparison the author identifies between Newspeak and tweeting? Why does he consider these similar characteristics to be dangerous? What is your evaluation of the argument that he is making?

3. Some critics contend that Twitter has a corrosive effect on interpersonal relationships, with electronic communications replacing personal interactions between people. Do you think that this is a serious concern? Why or why not?

4. In the article "The Hidden Problem with Twitter," the author Carin Ford cites some Twitter language statistics and poses the question "Is Twitter— along with instant messaging and texting—contributing to the destruction of language skills among college students?" Many people responded to her query, and summaries and paraphrases of these responses were included above. In reviewing these responses, which points do you find most persuasive in arguing that these instant forms of communication are degrading language skills among students? Which responses do you find most persuasive that they are not?

5. In the article "How Twitter Will Change the Way We Live," the author Steven Johnson contends that critics of Twitter don't fully appreciate its power and potential, and so fail to understand how Twitter is destined to affect our lives in important and lasting ways. Identify what Johnson considers to be the unique qualities of Twitter and why he thinks this new medium is having and will have a profound impact on our culture.

Reviewing and Viewing

Summary

- *Language* is a system of symbols for thinking and communicating.
- Words and sentences can communicate a variety of different meanings: *semantic, perceptual, syntactic,* and *pragmatic.*
- Using language effectively involves using the full range of word sense and sentence meaning to communicate our thoughts in a rich, evocative way.
- Language and thought work together as partners: language that is clear and precise leads to thinking that is clear and precise, and vice versa. Becoming an articulate language user and thinker involves avoiding vagueness and ambiguity.
- Effective language use involves using the language style that is appropriate to the context, including Standard American English, slang, and jargon.
- Language is a powerful tool for influencing the thinking and behavior of others. *Emotive language* and *euphemisms* are two examples of effective language uses.
- New media has come to play such an important role in our lives that it makes using language clearly and effectively even more paramount.

Assessing Your Strategies and Creating New Goals

How Effective a Communicator Am I?

Described below are key thinking abilities and personal attributes that are correlated with communicating effectively. Evaluate your position regarding each of these abilities and attributes, and use this self-evaluation to guide your efforts to become an expert communicator.

Connect Your Thinking and Language

I actively connect my thinking and language.	I focus on my thinking and language separately.
5 4 3 2 1	

In most areas of life, becoming an expert thinker involves becoming an expert user of language, and vice versa. That's why it's important to express your thinking in *writing*, because the process of writing helps you generate ideas and clarify your thoughts. Similarly, *discussing* your thinking with others encourages you to articulate your ideas and test the quality of your beliefs. Even when you are thinking on your own, you should try to elaborate your thoughts fully, striving to give them form and clarity.

Strategy: Develop the habit of expressing yourself in writing. A good way is by keeping a **Thinking Notebook** *as previously suggested. Think critically about the ideas you have expressed, evaluate them for clarity and value, and reflect on how you can improve your thinking. In your conversations with others, pay particular attention to the language you are using to express your ideas, and work toward refining the quality of both your thinking and language.*

Communicate Your Ideas Precisely and Coherently

I express my thoughts precisely and coherently.	I express my thoughts in vague and disorganized ways.
5 4 3 2 1	

Precise and well-organized use of language contributes to clear and cogent thinking. It is much easier to communicate in vague and general terms because that doesn't require the rigor and articulation of careful thought. But this comes at a high cost, diluting the quality of our communication and our thinking.

Strategy: Work continually to refine the precision of both your language and thinking. When you express yourself in writing, always treat your initial effort as a first draft to be refined and improved, asking yourself "Could I say this more clearly?" When speaking with others, try to express exactly what you are thinking or feeling. Use examples and analogies to enrich your expression by developing the habit of saying "For example . . .," "In other words . . .," "It's analogous to . . . ."

Listen Carefully to Other Viewpoints

In discussions, I listen carefully to others.	I focus more on expressing my views than listening.
5 4 3 2 1	

A meaningful exchange of ideas requires that each party listen carefully to the other and try to fully appreciate the other person's position. This is the soul of thinking critically—striving to move outside of your own limited perspectives and think empathetically within other viewpoints.

Strategy: When you discuss issues that you feel passionate about, focus on your role as a listener. Give other people your complete attention and, instead of mentally evaluating or disagreeing with what they are saying, try to put yourself in their position in order to understand what they are proposing and why. Make a conscious effort not to speak until they have expressed themselves fully, and defer your response until you have reached an in-depth understanding of their point of view.

Respond Directly to the Views of Others

I respond directly to the views of others.	I focus on stating my views as strongly as possible and proving other views wrong.
5 4 3 2 1	

To sustain an effective discussion, listening is only half the job. Once you have understood what the other person is saying, you have to respond in a productive way. Although it may be tempting for you to express what you believe, it is important to respond directly to what others are saying.

Strategy: When you are discussing issues with others, make a special effort to respond directly to what they are saying in a way that encourages further discussion. Avoid responses that don't relate to their ideas or that undercut their points, and instead ask questions like "Why do you believe . . .?" or "Have you considered the point . . .?" As all parties begin to establish a sense of trust, respect, and mutual commitment to increase understanding, this will encourage them to forsake their aggressive and defensive postures. Discussions should be mutual explorations, not war.

Use the Appropriate Language Style

I adapt my language style to the social situation.	I am unaware of my use of language styles.
5 4 3 2 1	

Every communication situation is like a problem to be solved, and the language style that you use will have a significant impact on your success. You must analyze whether your communication should be formal or informal, and whether it is appropriate to use slang or jargon.

Strategy: Develop the habit of evaluating your communication situations from a critical-thinking perspective, asking yourself "What are my communication goals? Which language styles will help me accomplish these goals? If I use slang or jargon, will my audience understand me?" Monitor the effectiveness of your communication by asking "Does my audience seem to understand what I am trying to express?"

Suggested Films

A Beautiful Mind (2001)

Based on the life of John Forbes Nash Jr., this film follows the life of an economist with a brilliant understanding of the language of mathematics. In spite of his struggles with schizophrenia, he is able to use his incredible gift to create a life of meaning, ultimately winning a Nobel Prize.

A Clockwork Orange (1971)

How should a society treat its criminals? In the near future, an adolescent gang member accused of numerous rapes and violent attacks agrees to try a controversial aversion therapy in order to shorten his jail sentences. The results of the therapy are essentially brainwashing, and he emerges from the hospital a very different person from the one who entered. Also recommended is the novel by Anthony Burgess, which is written in the central character's distinctive language, evolved from current English.

Inherit the Wind (1960)

What happens when religion and science conflict, when the language of the Bible conflicts with the language of science? Based on the play of the same title, this film is a fictionalized account of the 1925 Scopes "Monkey" trial in which a science teacher, John Thomas Scopes, was arrested for teaching Darwin's theory of evolution because a Tennessee law disallowed the teaching of anything other than creationism.

The Diving Bell and the Butterfly (2007)

Who does one become when one is no longer physically oneself? How does language shape the way we think and our experience with the world? Based on the memoir of the same name, this film recounts the life of Jean-Dominique Bauby, a French journalist and author who was almost entirely paralyzed after suffering a stroke at age 42. The author was only able to blink his left eyelid, and used this to communicate and write his memoir.

The Hurt Locker (2008)

How does war affect language? How do we use or alter language to respond to and survive the experience of war? This dramatic film follows a squad of the U.S. Army responsible for identifying and dismantling explosive devices in Iraq as they deal with both internal and external conflict.

Who Is An American?

In contrast to many nationalities, Americans are not readily identifiable because of their inherent racial diversity, so the concept of an "American" is one that is particularly complex. How would you answer the question "Who is an American?" Why?

Forming and Applying Concepts

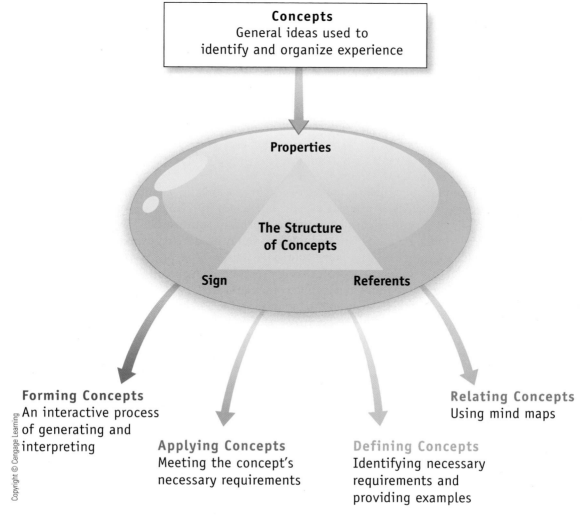

Concepts
General ideas used to
identify and organize experience

Properties

**The Structure
of Concepts**

Sign

Referents

Forming Concepts
An interactive process
of generating and
interpreting

Applying Concepts
Meeting the concept's
necessary requirements

Defining Concepts
Identifying necessary
requirements and
providing examples

Relating Concepts
Using mind maps

Developing your abilities as a thoughtful, clear-thinking, and articulate critical thinker entails becoming an expert in the use of "concepts." Why? Because *concepts* are the vocabulary of thought; they are the vehicles that we use to think about our world in organized ways and discuss our understanding with others. To become knowledgeable critical thinkers and effective users of language, we must necessarily become masters of concepts.

We live in a world filled with concepts. A large number of the words you use to represent your experience express concepts you have formed. *Internet, person, education, Facebook, sport, reality show, elated,* and *thinking* are only a few examples of concepts. Your academic study involves learning new concepts as well, and to be successful in college and your career, you need to master the conceptualizing process. For example, when you read textbooks or listen to lectures and take notes, you are required to grasp the key concepts and follow them as they are developed and supported. When you write papers or homework assignments, you are usually expected to focus on certain concepts, develop a thesis around them, present the thesis (itself a concept!) with carefully argued points, and back it up with specific examples. Many course examinations involve applying key concepts you have learned to new sets of circumstances.

What Are Concepts?

concepts
General ideas that we use to identify and organize our experience.

Concepts are general ideas you use to organize your experience and, in so doing, bring order and intelligibility to your life. In the same way that words are the vocabulary of language, concepts are the vocabulary of thought. As organizers of your experience, concepts work in conjunction with language to identify, describe, distinguish, and relate all the various aspects of your world.

To become a sophisticated thinker, you must develop expertise in the conceptualizing process, improving your ability to *form, apply, define,* and *relate* concepts. This complex conceptualizing process is going on all the time in your mind, enabling you to think in a distinctly human way.

How do you use concepts to organize and make sense of experience? Think back to the first day of the semester. For most students, this is a time to evaluate their courses by trying to determine which concepts apply.

- Will this course be interesting? Useful? A lot of work?
- Is the teacher stimulating? Demanding? Entertaining?
- Are the students friendly? Intelligent? Conscientious?

Each of these words or phrases represents a concept you are attempting to apply so that you can understand what is occurring at the moment and also anticipate what the course will be like in the future. As the course progresses, you gather further information from your actual experiences in the class. This information may support your initial concepts, or it may conflict with these initial concepts.

If the information you receive supports these concepts, you tend to maintain them ("Yes, I can see that this is going to be a difficult course"). But if the information you receive conflicts with these concepts, you tend to form new concepts to explain the situation ("No, I can see that I was wrong—this course isn't going to be as difficult as I thought at first"). A diagram of this process might look something like this:

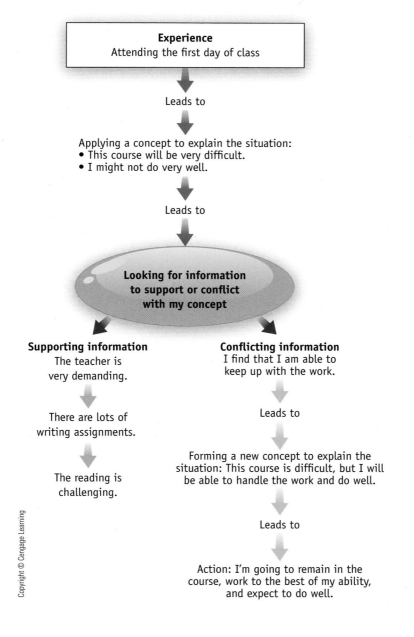

To take another example, imagine that you are a physician and that one of your patients comes to you complaining of shortness of breath and occasional pain in his left arm. After he describes his symptoms, you would ask a number of questions, examine him, and perhaps administer some tests. Your ability to *identify* the underlying problem would depend on your knowledge of various human diseases. Each disease is identified and described by a different concept. Identifying these various diseases means that you can *distinguish* different concepts and that you know in what situations to apply a given concept correctly. In addition, when the patient asks, "What's wrong with me, doctor?" you are able to describe the concept (e.g., heart disease) and explain how it is related to his symptoms. Fortunately, modern medicine has developed (and is continuing to develop) remarkably precise concepts to describe and explain the diseases that afflict us. In the patient's case, you may conclude that the problem is heart disease. Of course, there are different kinds of heart disease, represented by different concepts, and success in treating the patient will depend on figuring out exactly which type of heart disease is involved.

Thinking Activity 7.1

FORMING NEW CONCEPTS THROUGH EXPERIENCE

Identify an initial concept you had about an event in your life (starting a new job, attending college, and so on) that changed as a result of your experiences. After identifying your initial concept, describe the experiences that led you to change or modify the concept, and then explain the new concept you formed to explain the situation. Your response should include the following elements: *an initial concept, new information provided by additional experiences,* and *a new concept formed to explain the situation.*

Learning to master concepts will help you in every area of your life: academic, career, and personal. In college study, each academic discipline or subject is composed of many different concepts that are used to organize experience, give explanations, and solve problems. Here is a sampling of college-level concepts: *entropy, subtext, Gemeinschaft, cell, metaphysics, relativity, unconscious, transformational grammar, aesthetic, minor key, interface, health, quantum mechanics, schizophrenia.* To make sense of how disciplines function, you need to understand what the concepts of that discipline mean, how to apply them, and the way they relate to other concepts. You also need to learn the methods of investigation, patterns of thought, and forms of reasoning that various disciplines use to form larger conceptual theories and methods. We will be exploring these subjects in the next several chapters of the text.

Regardless of specific knowledge content, all careers require conceptual abilities, whether you are trying to apply a legal principle, develop a promotional theme, or devise a new computer program. Similarly, expertise in forming and applying concepts helps you make sense of your personal life, understand others, and make informed decisions. The Greek philosopher Aristotle once said that the intelligent person is a "master of concepts."

The Structure of Concepts

Concepts are general ideas you use to identify, distinguish, and relate the various aspects of your experience. Concepts allow you to organize your world into patterns that make sense to you. This is the process by which you discover and create meaning in your life.

In their role as organizers of experience, concepts act to group aspects of your experience based on their similarity to one another. Consider the thing that you usually write with: a pen. The concept *pen* represents a type of object that you use for writing. But look around the classroom at all the other instruments people are using to write with. You use the concept *pen* to identify these things as well, even though they may look very different from the one you are using.

Thus, the concept *pen* not only helps you make distinctions in your experience by indicating how pens differ from pencils, crayons, or markers, but also helps you determine which items are similar enough to each other to be called *pens*. When you put items into a group with a single description—like "pen"—you are focusing on the similarities among the items:

- They use ink.
- They are used for writing.
- They are held with a hand.

Being able to see and name the similarities among certain things in your experience is the way you form concepts and is crucial for making sense of your world. If you were not able to do this, then everything in the world would be different, with its own individual name.

The process by which you group things based on their similarities is known as *classifying*. The process of classifying is one of the main ways that you order, organize, and make sense of your world. Because no two things or experiences are exactly alike, your ability to classify things into various groups is what enables you to recognize things in your experience. When you perceive a pen, you recognize it as a *kind of thing* you have seen before. Even though you may not have seen this particular pen, you recognize that it belongs to a group of things that you are familiar with.

The best way to understand the structure of concepts is to visualize them by means of a model. Examine the following figure:

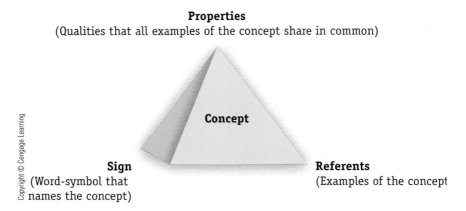

Properties
(Qualities that all examples of the concept share in common)

Concept

Sign
(Word-symbol that names the concept)

Referents
(Examples of the concept

Copyright © Cengage Learning

The *sign* is the word or symbol used to name or designate the concept; for example, the word *triangle* is a sign. The *referents* represent all the various examples of the concept; the three-sided figure we are using as our model is an example of the concept *triangle*. The *properties* of the concept are the features that all things named by the word or sign have in common; all examples of the concept *triangle* share the characteristics of being a polygon and having three sides. These are the properties that we refer to when we *define* concepts; thus, "a triangle is a three-sided polygon."

Let's take another example. Suppose you wanted to explore the structure of the concept *automobile*. The *sign* that names the concept is the word *automobile* or the symbol. *Referents* of the concept include the 1954 MG-TF currently residing in the garage as well as the Ford Explorer parked in front of the house. The *properties* that all things named by the sign *automobile* include are wheels, a chassis, an engine, and seats for passengers. The following figure is a conceptual model of the concept *automobile:*

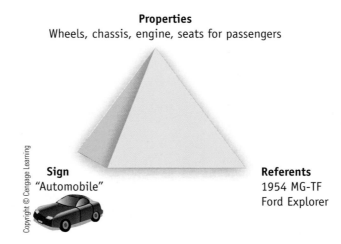

Properties
Wheels, chassis, engine, seats for passengers

Sign
"Automobile"

Referents
1954 MG-TF
Ford Explorer

Copyright © Cengage Learning

Thinking Activity 7.2

DIAGRAMMING THE STRUCTURE OF CONCEPTS

Using the model we have developed, diagram the structure of the following concepts, as well as two concepts of your own choosing: *table, dance, successful, student, religion, music, friend,* _____, _____ .

Forming Concepts

Throughout your life you are engaged in the process of forming—and applying—concepts to organize your experience, make sense of what is happening at the moment, and anticipate what may happen in the future. You form concepts by the interactive process of *generalizing* (focusing on the common properties shared by a group of things) and *interpreting* (finding examples of the concept). The common properties form the necessary requirements that must be met in order to apply the concept to your experience. If you examine the diagrams of concepts in the last section, you can see that the process of forming concepts involves moving back and forth between the *referents* (examples) of the concept and the *properties* (common features) shared by all examples of the concept. Let's explore further the way this interactive process of forming concepts operates.

Consider the following sample conversation between two people trying to form and clarify the concept *philosophy:*

A: What is your idea of what *philosophy* means?

B: Well, I think philosophy involves expressing important beliefs that you have—like discussing the meaning of life, assuming that there is a meaning.

A: Is explaining my belief about who's going to win the Super Bowl engaging in philosophy? After all, this is a belief that is very important to me—I've got a lot of money riding on the outcome!

B: I don't think so. A philosophical belief is usually a belief about something that is important to everyone—like what standards we should use to guide our moral choices.

A: What about the message that was in my fortune cookie last night: "Eat, drink, and be merry, for tomorrow we diet!"? This is certainly a belief that most people can relate to, especially during the holiday season! Is this philosophy?

B: I think that's what my grandmother used to call "foolosophy"! Philosophical beliefs are usually deeply felt views that we have given a great deal of thought to—not something plucked out of a cookie.

A: What about my belief in the Golden Rule: "Do unto others as you would have them do unto you"? After all, we all want to be treated well by others, and it's only fair—and reasonable—to conclude that we should treat other people the same way. Doesn't that have all of the qualities that you mentioned?

B: *Now* you've got it!

As we review this dialogue, we can see that *forming* the concept *philosophical belief* works hand in hand with *applying* the concept to different examples. When two or more things work together in this way, we say that they *interact*. In this case, there are two parts of this interactive process.

generalizing
Focusing on the common properties shared by a group of things.

We form concepts by **generalizing**, by focusing on the similar features among different things. In the dialogue just given, the things from which generalizations are being made are kinds of beliefs—beliefs about the meaning of life or standards we use to guide our moral choices. By focusing on the similar features among these beliefs, the two people in the dialogue develop a list of properties that philosophical beliefs share, including

- Beliefs that deal with important issues in life about which everyone is concerned
- Beliefs that reflect deeply felt views to which we have given a great deal of thought

These common properties act as the requirements an area must meet to be considered a philosophical belief.

interpreting
Looking for different examples of a concept in order to determine if they meet the requirements of that concept.

We apply concepts by **interpreting**, by looking for different examples of the concept and seeing if they meet the requirements of the concept we are developing. In the conversation, one of the participants attempts to apply the concept *philosophical belief* to the following examples:

- A belief about the outcome of the Super Bowl
- A fortune cookie message: "Eat, drink, and be merry, for tomorrow we diet!"

Both of these proposed examples are rejected as examples of the concept "philosophy," but they still are useful because they suggest the development of new requirements for the concept to help clarify how the concept can be applied. Applying a concept to different possible examples thus becomes the way we develop and gradually sharpen our idea of the concept. Even when a proposed example turns out *not* to be an example of the concept, our understanding of the concept is often clarified. For example, although the proposed example—a belief about the outcome of the Super Bowl—in the dialogue turns out not to be an example of the concept *philosophical belief*, examining it as a possible example helps clarify the concept and suggests other examples.

The process of developing concepts involves a constant back-and-forth movement between these two activities. As the back-and-forth movement progresses, we gradually develop a specific list of requirements that something must have to be considered an example of the concept and, at the same time, give ourselves a clearer idea of how it is defined. We are also developing a collection of examples that embodies the qualities of the concept and demonstrate situations in which the concept applies. This *interactive* process is illustrated in the following figure.

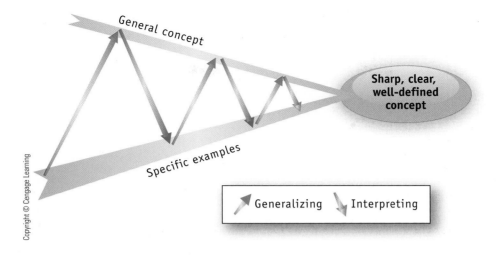

Thinking Activity 7.3

FORMING NEW CONCEPTS THROUGH GENERALIZING AND INTERPRETING

Select a type of music with which you are familiar (e.g., hip-hop) and write a dialogue similar to the one on page 315. In the course of the dialogue, be sure to include

1. Examples from which you are generalizing (e.g., West Coast rap, gangsta rap)
2. General properties shared by various types of this music (e.g., hip-hop has become an important theme in modern culture, influencing language, fashion, and creative media)
3. Examples to which you are trying to apply this developing concept (e.g., the music of Jay-Z, Eminem, 50 Cent, Foxy Brown, Queen Latifah)

Forming concepts involves performing both of these operations (*generalizing* and *interpreting*) together because

- You cannot form a concept unless you know how it might apply. If you have absolutely no idea what might be examples of *hip-hop* or *philosophy*, then you cannot begin to form the concept, even in vague or general terms.
- You cannot gather examples of the concept unless you know what they might be examples of. Until you begin to develop some idea of what the concept *hip-hop* or *philosophy* might be (based on certain similarities among various things), you will not know where to look for examples of the concept (or how to evaluate them).

Thinking Critically About Visuals

Fashion Statements as Concepts

There has always been a relationship between popular music and fashion, but this connection became even more prominent with the advent of music videos and MTV. For many performers today, fashion and dance choreography are an integral part of the overall music performance. For example, "Lady Gaga" (born Stefani Joanne Angelina Germanotta) uses elaborate costumes to frame her songs and has stated that "fashion is an inspiration for the song writing and her performances." We can contrast her "glam rock" (also exemplified by musicians like David Bowie, Freddy Mercury, Michael Jackson, and Madonna) with the fashion statements of other forms of music.

AP Photo/Peter Kramer

For example, in the mid-1970s, a grimmer countercultural youth movement was forming in New York City's underground music clubs and the streets of London. Punk, with its anarchic politics and shock-value fashion and music, had a bleak view of the potential for social change. However, just like the "glam rock" of Lady Gaga and others, punk's fashion statements soon became part of the mainstream. What are some of the fashion statements of the forms of music with which you are familiar?

Neil Marriott/Digital Vision/Getty Images

Playwright David Mamet has written: "The pursuit of Fashion is the attempt of the middle class to co-opt tragedy. In adopting the clothing, speech, and personal habits of those in straitened, dangerous, or pitiful circumstances, the middle class seeks to have what it feels to be the exigent and nonequivocal experiences had by those it emulates." In your own words, what is Mamet's argument about fashion? Can fashion choices that are meant to be political or social statements ever be frivolous, irresponsible, or counterproductive?

This interactive process is the way that you usually form all concepts, particularly the complicated ones. In school, much of your education is focused on carefully forming and exploring key concepts such as *democracy, dynamic equilibrium,* and *personality.* This book has also focused on certain key concepts, such as

- Thinking critically
- Solving problems
- Perceiving

- Believing
- Knowing
- Language

In each case, you have carefully explored these concepts through the interactive process of generalizing the properties/requirements of the concept and interpreting the concept by examining examples to which the concept applies.

Applying Concepts

Making sense of our experience means finding the right concept to explain what is going on. To determine whether the concept we have selected fits the situation, we have to determine whether the requirements that form the concept are being met. For example, the original television series *Superman* used to begin with the words "Look—up in the sky! It's a bird! It's a plane! No! It's Superman!"

To figure out which concept applies to the situation (so that we can figure out what is going on), we have to

1. Be aware of the properties that form the boundaries of the concept
2. Determine whether the experience meets those requirements, because only if it does can we apply the concept to it

In the opening lines from *Superman*, what are some of the requirements for using the concepts being identified?

- Bird:

- Plane:

- Superman: (Hint: He's wearing blue tights and a red cape.)

If we have the requirements of the concept clearly in mind, we can proceed to figure out which of these requirements are met by the experience—whether it is a bird, a plane, or the "man of steel" himself. This is the way we apply concepts, which is one of the most important ways we figure out what is going on in our experience.

In determining exactly what the requirements of the concept are, we can ask ourselves, *"Would something still be an example of this concept if it did not meet this requirement?"* If the answer to this question is *no*—that is, something would not be an example of this concept if it did not meet this requirement—then we can say the requirement is a necessary part of the concept.

Consider the concept *dog.* Which of the following descriptions are requirements of the concept that must be met to say that something is an example of the concept *dog*?

1. Is an animal

2. Normally has four legs and a tail

3. Bites the mail carrier

It is clear that descriptions 1 and 2 are requirements that must be met to apply the concept *dog* because if we apply our test question—"Would something still be an example of this concept if it did not meet this requirement?"—we can say that something would not be an example of the concept *dog* if it did not fit the first two descriptions: if it were not an animal and did not normally have four legs and a tail.

This does not seem to be the case, however, with description 3. If we ask ourselves the same test question, we can see that something might still be an example of the concept *dog* even if it did not bite the mail carrier. This is because even though some dogs do in fact bite, this is not a requirement for being a dog.

Of course, there may be other things that meet these requirements but are not dogs. For example, a cat is an animal (description 1) that normally has four legs and a tail (description 2). What this means is that the requirements of a concept tell us only what something *must* have to be an example of the concept. As a result, we often have to identify additional requirements that will define the concept more sharply. This point is clearly illustrated as children form concepts. Not identifying a sufficient number of the concept's requirements leads to such misconceptions as "All four-legged animals are doggies" or "All yellow-colored metal is gold."

This is why it is so important for us to have a very clear idea of the greatest possible number of specific requirements of each concept. These requirements determine when the concept can be applied and indicate those things that qualify as examples of it. When we are able to identify *all* of the requirements of the concept, we say these requirements are both *necessary* and *sufficient* for applying the concept.

Although dealing with concepts like *dog* and *cat* may seem straightforward, the situation quickly becomes more confusing when you start analyzing the more complex concepts that you encounter in your academic study. For example, consider the concepts *masculinity* and *femininity*, two of the more emotionally charged and politically contentious concepts in our culture. There are many different perspectives on what these concepts mean, what they should mean, or whether we should be using them at all. Identify what you consider to be the essential properties (specific requirements that must be met to apply the concept) for each of these concepts, as well as examples of people or behavior that illustrate these properties. For example, you might identify "physical strength" as a property of the concept *masculinity* and identify Dwayne Johnson (a.k.a. "The Rock") as a person who illustrates this quality. Or you might identify "intuition" as a property of the concept *femininity* and illustrate this with the behavior of "being able to predict what someone is going to do or say before it occurs." Then compare your responses with those of the other students in the class. What are the similarities and differences in your concepts? What factors might account for these similarities and differences?

Thinking Passages

THE EVOLVING CONCEPT OF "FAMILY"

The traditional concept of "family" in many parts of the world refers to a man and a woman (often married) with children. In Western culture this traditional concept of "family" has been referred to as the "nuclear family," in the sense that the family functions as a self-contained "atom" rather than the "extended families" in days gone by. After World War II, the gender roles of the nuclear family typically involved the man working as the "breadwinner" of the family while the woman took primary care of domestic responsibilities and child rearing. This idealized family was enshrined in the popular culture in television shows like *Leave it to Beaver*.

Our culture—and many cultures around the world—has changed dramatically, and the concept of "family" has changed with it. The idealized "nuclear family" with the working father and the housewife mother now represents less than 25 percent of the population. Many married women now have full-time careers, but more than that, we have entered an era of single parents, pairs of moms or dads, blended families, multigenerational households, grandparent caregivers, and countless other configurations as well. These "nontraditional" families are increasingly becoming the norm, the new "traditional" family.

The following passages explore the phenomenon of the evolving concept of "family," and also pose the provocative question of whether we are entering a post-family era in which families may become an endangered species. After reading of the articles, answer the Questions for Analysis that follow.

New 'Non-Traditional' American Families

by Kate Rice

Gina Smith and Heidi Norton of Northampton, Mass., have two sons. Norton is their biological mother, and Smith adopted them.

They live in a community in which there are several gay- or lesbian-headed households, but when they travel, they meet families with no experience with gay families and sometimes encounter clumsy questions.

While they may not fit the mold of what many Americans consider a typical family, they are a contemporary American family. There is no single typical American family anymore.

"We're in the midst of a major change in the way families and marriage are organized," says Stephanie Coontz, a college professor and author of The Way We Never Were, American Families and the Nostalgia Trap and The Way We Really Are, Coming to Terms With America's Changing Families. "It's distressing, because all of the rules we

Source: © 2013 ABC News (http://abcnews.go.com/Health/story?id=118267&page=1).

grew up with no longer work and so we're having to learn new ways of thinking about families."

Smith and Norton, both 39, head a family that helps others rethink their ideas of what a family is. When they're asked about themselves and their sons, Avery, 7, and Quinn, 3, they assume that questions are well-intended and that the clumsiness simply means that the questioner doesn't have the vocabulary to deal with the situation.

"What's worked for us is stepping into the void and giving people some language to use," says Smith. "We would say things like, 'Avery is a very lucky boy who has two moms who love him,' so we just give them that language."

The 1950s Myth

Most children these days have buddies whose families are very different from their parents'. In fact, they quite possibly are growing up in such a family.

Most people still believe in the two-biological-married-parents-with-kids model, says Alexis Walker, editor of the National Council on Family Relations' Journal of Marriage and the Family (www.ncfr.org).

"Family is both a belief and a practice," she says.

When she asks her students at Oregon State University, where she is a professor of human development and family sciences, if they think their family will be a mom, a dad, and children, most raise their hands.

But practice is far different. When she asks if they come from a family like that, only a few put their hands up.

Americans have to deal with the great myth of the 1950s, an era in which 60 percent of families consisted of a breadwinning father and a stay-at-home mother. But this model was actually a 15-year-aberration, fueled by post-World War II prosperity and a GI bill of unprecedented generosity that funded the education of returning war veterans, according to Coontz, a professor of family and history at Evergreen State College, Olympia, Wash., and co-chairman of the Council on Contemporary Families (www.contemporaryfamilies.org) The council's mission is to publicize the way the family is changing and to cover the consequences and implications of those changes.

Coontz says that for most of history, families have been co-provider families, with husband, wife and often children, all working to provide for the family.

"The fact is that families have always been diverse, and they've always been in flux and we've always been worried about it. As far back as colonial days people were complaining that the new generation of families was not like the old one," she says.

No Single Model

The 21st century child-rearing family can take any number of forms.

There's the 1950s model, one that is shrinking in number. An exact count is hard to come up with, but experts believe it's probably under 25 percent. Statistics show that today the majority of couples both earn income. Demographers estimate that only 50 percent of children will spend their entire childhood in a two-parent, married couple biological family, according to Coontz.

Increasingly common are blended families, couples with children from previous marriages as well as the current marriage. Then there are single parents, families with adopted children, gay families with adopted children or biological children, foster families, grandparents raising grandchildren, and so on.

Absent a single, cookie-cutter family model, the best definition of a healthy family is one that provides or performs certain core functions. These include basics such as food, shelter and economic support, according to Liz Gray, associate professor and family therapist in human development and family sciences at Oregon State University in Corvallis.

But a family does much more, providing love and affection, a sense of identity and a feeling of belonging. Families also provide a worldview or a spiritual belief that can help make sense of the world, as well as rules and boundaries for appropriate behavior and skills for dealing with the world.

More than a decade ago, Gray co-authored Nontraditional Families: A Guide For Parents (http://www.cyfernet.org/parent/nontradfam.html), which remains a highly useful piece for parents today. Looking back, Gray says she would never use the term "nontraditional," because today, those "nontraditional" families have become the norm.

Like any parents, Smith and Norton love to talk about how their family came to be, says Smith, and often handle curiosity by simply telling the story. Children had been part of each woman's life plan even before they met and fell in love 13 years ago, so it was only natural that they have children together. Smith says most people are accepting of their contemporary family.

"If you present yourself as comfortable with who you are as family, they'll take their cues from you," she says. She finds that the fact that she and Norton have such respect for themselves that others approach them and their sons with that same respect.

Tips: How to Deal

If you encounter a family that might once have been called nontraditional but aren't sure how to handle it, experts recommend first that you show respect no matter the others' family structure. Your children will closely follow your actions and their responses will mirror yours, as well. Some more of the experts' recommendations are below.

Look at your own family, your brothers, sisters, aunts, uncles, cousins, friends, neighbors. Odds are, you'll see a variety of family structures. That will give you an idea of what your children are encountering in school, and give you a way to discuss the issues with them.

Draw maps of families and extended families to help children understand family structure. Talk about it. Let children draw their own maps or pictures of families, then listen to what they have to say about it.

Your child has a friend whose family structure is one you're uncomfortable with. What do you do? Deal with it as though you were moving to a new neighborhood, suggests David Tseng, executive director of Parents, Families and Friends of Gays (www.pflag.org) in Washington, D.C. Be polite, respectful and curious to learn about others in a healthy and constructive way. It's important to recognize that your unspoken response influences your children as much as your spoken one.

Sometimes, you may disapprove of the family structure of one of your children's classmates. Mark Merrill, president of Family First, a non-profit research and communications organization (www.familyfirst.net) headquartered in Tampa, Fla., defines a family as any relationship of marriage, blood or adoption—but he limits that to heterosexuals. At the same time, he recognizes the reality of gay families. His response: "We are supposed to love everybody." And love, in Merrill's book, is not an emotion that leaps unsummoned from the heart. It is a decision to treat others, even those whose lifestyles you don't accept, with kindness and thoughtfulness and serve them in ways that are best for them.

Make a concerted effort within your own extended network of work colleagues and of friends to focus less on those who are like you and more on the diversity. "You want to be clear and deliberate about letting your kids know that this is America, this is the diversity of it and not to make a big deal of it," says James Morris, former president of the American Association for Marriage and Family Therapy (www.aamft.org) and assistant professor of marriage and family at Texas Tech University in Fredericksburg.

We Are Family

by Bob Morris

What's in a name?

On a recent Friday, Ira, my partner (or whatever you call him), and I were waiting at the Churchill School in Manhattan for a "Grandparents and Special Friends Day" concert to begin. My nephew, Ian, had invited both of us.

"How do I introduce myself?" Ira asked. "As Ian's Uncle Bobby's husband?"

Hard to say. Maybe significant other would be easier? Spouse? Domestic partner? Longtime companion? Special friend?

Eesh. The constant question of what to call one another in this nothing-is-normal age. Social fathers, birth mothers, donor dads and "Yes Donors" at sperm banks who let offspring contact them, creating "half sibling" relationships. Eight-grandparent families, civil unions, shacking-up seniors, co-parenting. It's all so confusing.

Jackie Woodson, a Brooklyn author, is raising a toddler with her lesbian partner—sired by a close friend who is himself married with a child.

"If people look confused when they see us all together," Ms. Woodson said, "then we explain he's the donor."

It makes the Royal Family's issue of what to call Camilla Parker Bowles (the Royal Consort and the Duchess of Cornwall, please) look like a cup of tea.

In her newly reissued "Miss Manners Guide to Excruciatingly Correct Behavior," Judith Martin addresses how to respond to a single sister deciding to have a child when you don't think she should or the proper greeting of someone's nontraditional partner. The simplest response—"Congratulations" or "How do you do?"—is all it takes, in her view. But "making others feel comfortable," she acknowledges, "can be a terrible burden."

Maybe the simplest way to deal with the nomenclature of newfangled family life is to take a cue from the Spanish and add a con (for with) to relationships to incorporate

Source: © 2013 The New York Times (http://www.nytimes.com/2005/05/22/fashion/sundaystyles/22age .html?pagewanted=print).

just about anyone. Or it may be useful to nationalize machetunim, the catch-all Yiddish word for in-laws and other relatives.

The advice in "Saving Face: Lie, Fake and Maneuver Your Way Out of Life's Most Awkward Situations," is never to label people before they have labeled themselves.

Andrew Cherlin, a sociologist at Johns Hopkins University, who has eight grandchildren, is careful not to take offense when the little ones confuse him with others.

"The language hasn't kept up," he said. "So you have to give people a lot of latitude these days to make mistakes."

You can also give them a lot of options to keep things inclusive.

That's what was behind the "special friends" phrasing at my nephew's school. Meryl Schwartz, the elementary principal, figured that with so many unconventional families, not every child has grandparents, aunts, uncles or siblings. But with "Grandparents and Special Friends Day," every child would have someone to invite.

"We even had a doorman once," she said.

Bring your doorman to school day? Why not?

"Never mind what you call people," Ms. Schwartz said. "When you ask children who is special to them and who's important to them, it becomes very simple and clear."

Maybe they know something we don't. When children tell Ms. Woodson's daughter that she has two mothers but no father, she bluntly tells them otherwise. "The child is the one who forces the nomenclature," her mother said.

At any rate, what seems to count in making a family is the effort you make to be a big part of one. In that way, Ira is as much an uncle now to my nephew as I am.

When the concert began, he and I cheered for Ian as he played the drums. One class played "Lean on Me," another "Respect." Two fitting titles for what family is and should always be, I think.

And what did Ian choose to call Ira, as he introduced him and gave him a hug to thank him for coming?

"My Ira," he said.

Simple as that.

Three Grown-Ups and a Baby

by Lisa Belkin

We only come to intimately know a handful of families in a lifetime. There's the one we were raised in, and the ones we form on our own. That's not a large sample size, which often leaves us wondering if the way we do things is "normal." When we get glimpses here and there of how other families work, we crane our necks toward those for hints of what happens behind doors that aren't ours.

A series starting in The Times today will offer a few such glimpses. It will be a periodic look into how "nontraditional" families are becoming a norm, and the first

Source: © 2013 The New York Times (http://parenting.blogs.nytimes.com/2011/06/19/three-grown-ups-and-a-baby/).

piece, which you can read here: http://www.nytimes.com/2011/06/19/nyregion/an-american-family-mom-sperm-donor-lover-child.html, was a reminder to me of how you don't always know about the lives that surround you. Sonny Kleinfeld's story is about a single mother, Carol Einhorn, who, as it happens, was a bridesmaid with me in my sister-in-law's wedding, and later sang hauntingly at my mother-in-law's funeral. I knew she'd had a son. But there is so much more I didn't know.

As Mr. Kleinfeld writes:

> The setup is complicated. Griffin's mother, Carol Einhorn, a fund-raiser for a non-profit group, is 48 and single. She conceived through in vitro fertilization with sperm from (George) Russell, 49, a chiropractor and close friend. Monday, Tuesday, Thursday and Sunday nights, Mr. Russell stays in the spare room of Ms. Einhorn's apartment. The other three days he lives a short walk away, on President Street, with his domestic partner, David Nimmons, 54, an administrator at a nonprofit. On Sunday evenings, they usually all have dinner together.

"It's not like Heather has two mommies," Mr. Russell said. "It's George has two families."

Two addresses, three adults, a winsome toddler and a mixed-breed dog officially named Buck the Dog. None of this was the familial configuration any of them had imagined, but it was, for the moment, their family. It was something they had stumbled into, yet had a certain revisionist logic.

Such is the hiccupping fluidity of the family in the modern world. Six years running now, according to census data, more households consist of the unmarried than the married. More people seem to be deciding that the contours of the traditional nuclear family do not work for them, spawning a profusion of cobbled-together networks in need of nomenclature. Unrelated parents living together, sharing chores and child-rearing. Friends who occupy separate homes but rely on each other for holidays, health care proxies, financial support.

"Some of the strictures that were used to organize society don't fit human change and growth," said Ann Schranz, chairwoman of the Alternatives to Marriage Project, a 10-year-old organization. "What matters to us is the health of relationships, not the form of relationships."

And so here on Plaza Street, four people are testing the fuzzy boundaries of an age-old institution, knowing there is no single answer to what defines family or what defines love.

The Rise of Post-Familialism: Humanity's Future?

by Joel Kotkin

For most of human history, the family—defined by parents, children and extended kin—has stood as the central unit of society. In Europe, Asia, Africa and, later, the Americas and Oceania, people lived, and frequently worked, as family units.

Source: http://www.joelkotkin.com/print/631.

Today, in the high-income world and even in some developing countries, we are witnessing a shift to a new social model. Increasingly, family no longer serves as the central organizing feature of society. An unprecedented number of individuals—approaching upwards of 30% in some Asian countries—are choosing to eschew child bearing altogether and, often, marriage as well.

The post-familial phenomena has been most evident in the high income world, notably in Europe, North America and, most particularly, wealthier parts of East Asia. Yet it has bloomed as well in many key emerging countries, including Brazil, Iran and a host of other Islamic countries.

The reasons for this shift are complex, and vary significantly in different countries and cultures. In some countries, particularly in East Asia, the nature of modern competitive capitalism often forces individuals to choose between career advancement and family formation. As a result, these economies are unwittingly setting into motion forces destructive to their future workforce, consumer base and long-term prosperity.

The widespread movement away from traditional values—Hindu, Muslim, Judeo-Christian, Buddhist or Confucian—has also undermined familialism. Traditional values have almost without exception been rooted in kinship relations. The new emerging social ethos endorses more secular values that prioritise individual personal socioeconomic success as well as the personal quest for greater fulfilment.

To be sure, many of the changes driving post-familialism also reflect positive aspects of human progress. The change in the role of women beyond sharply defined maternal roles represents one of the great accomplishments of modern times. Yet this trend also generates new pressures that have led some women to reject both child-bearing and marriage. Men are also adopting new attitudes that increasingly preclude marriage or fatherhood.

The great trek of people to cities represents one of the great triumphs of human progress, as fewer people are necessary to produce the basic necessities of food, fibre and energy. Yet the growth of urban density also tends to depress both fertility and marriage rates. The world's emerging postfamilial culture has been largely spawned in the crowded pool of the large urban centres of North America, Europe and, most particularly, East Asia. It is also increasingly evident in the fast growing cities of developing countries in south Asia, North Africa, Iran and parts of the Middle East.

The current weak global economy, now in its fifth year, also threatens to further slow family formation. Child-rearing requires a strong hope that life will be better for the next generation. The rising cost of urban living, the declining number of well-paying jobs, and the onset of the global financial crisis has engendered growing pessimism in most countries, particularly in Europe and Japan, but also in the United States and some developing countries.

This report will look into both the roots and the future implications of the post-familial trend. As Austrian demographer Wolfgang Lutz has pointed out, the shift to an increasingly childless society creates "self-reinforcing mechanisms" that make childlessness, singleness, or one-child families increasingly predominant.

Societal norms, which once almost mandated family formation, have begun to morph. The new norms are reinforced by cultural influences that tend to be concentrated in the very areas—dense urban centres—with the lowest percentages of married people and children. A majority of residences in Manhattan are for singles, while Washington D.C. has one of the highest percentages of women who do not live with children, some 70%. Similar trends can be seen in London, Paris, Tokyo and other cultural capitals.

A society that is increasingly single and childless is likely to be more concerned with serving current needs than addressing the future oriented requirements of children. Since older people vote more than younger ones, and children have no say at all, political power could shift towards nonchildbearing people, at least in the short and medium term. We could tilt more into a 'now' society, geared towards consuming or recreating today, as opposed to nurturing and sacrificing for tomorrow.

The most obvious impact from post-familialism lies with demographic decline. It is already having a profound impact on fiscal stability in, for example, Japan and across southern Europe. With fewer workers contributing to cover pension costs, even successful places like Singapore will face this same crisis in the coming decade.

A diminished labour force—and consumer base—also suggest slow economic growth and limit opportunities for business expansion. For one thing, younger people tend to drive technological change, and their absence from the workforce will slow innovation. And for many people, the basic motivation for hard work is underpinned by the need to support and nurture a family. Without a family to support, the very basis for the work ethos will have changed, perhaps irrevocably.

The team that composed this report—made up of people of various faiths, cultures, and outlooks—has concerns about the sustainability of a post-familial future. But we do not believe we can "turn back the clock" to the 1950s, as some social conservatives wish, or to some other imagined, idealised, time. Globalisation, urbanisation, the ascendancy of women, and changes in traditional sexual relations are with us, probably for the long run.

Seeking to secure a place for families requires us to move beyond nostalgia for a bygone era and focus on what is possible. Yet, in the end, we do not consider familialism to be doomed. Even in the midst of decreased fertility, we also see surprising, contradictory and hopeful trends. In Europe, Asia and America, most younger people still express the desire to have families, and often with more than one child. Amidst all the social change discussed above, there remains a basic desire for family that needs to be nurtured and supported by the wider society.

Our purpose here is not to judge people about their personal decision to forego marriage and children. Instead we seek to launch a discussion about how to carve out or maintain a place for families in the modern metropolis. In the process we must ask—with full comprehension of today's prevailing trends—tough questions about our basic values and the nature of the cities we are now creating.

QUESTIONS FOR ANALYSIS

1. What is your definition of a "family"? Describe your experiences as a family member growing up—what people comprised your family? Did the configuration of your family change over time?

2. The author of the first article on nontraditional families, Kate Rice, quotes Alexis Walker: "Family is both a belief and a practice." Professor Walker explains that her students tend to view a family in traditional terms, comprised of a mom, a dad, and children. Yet when she asks students if they come from a family like that, only a few put their hands up. How would you explain this discrepancy? Did you find the same "split perspective" in your response to the first question? Why or why not?

3. Again in the first article, Liz Gray is quoted as saying a healthy family is one that provides certain core functions such as food, shelter, and economic support. Does that capture your concept of "family"? Why or why not? Kate Rice contends that a family does much more than that, "providing love and affection, a sense of identity and a feeling of belonging. Families also provide a worldview or a spiritual belief that can help make sense of the world, as well as rules and boundaries for appropriate behavior and skill in dealing with the world." Do you believe that this more complex and elaborated definition does a better job of articulating the boundaries of the concept of "family"? Why or why not?

4. In this chapter we have described concepts as the "vocabulary" of thought, embodying the intersection of thought and language. Why does Bob Morris, in his article "We Are Family," begin by asking "What's in a name?" and then argue that we need to develop a new vocabulary to more clearly understand and communicate the evolving concept of "family"? What are some new terms you might recommend to aid in this challenge?

5. In her article "Three Grown-Ups and a Baby," Lisa Belkin provides an example of this modern concept of family, concluding "And so here on Plaza Street, four people are testing the fuzzy boundaries of an age-old institution, knowing there is no single answer to what defines family or what defines love." How does this statement illustrate the process of forming, applying, and defining concepts that we have explored in this chapter?

6. In the final article, Joel Kotkin observes: "For most of human history, the family—defined by parents, children and extended kin—has stood as the central unit of society. . . . Today, in the high-income world and even in some developing countries, we are witnessing a shift to a new social model. Increasingly, family no longer serves as the central organizing feature of society. An unprecedented number of individuals are choosing to eschew child bearing altogether and, often, marriage as well." What are the factors that Kotkin cites to explain this changing nature of the family? Do you think that the family is in danger of becoming obsolete and at some point extinct? Why or why not?

Thinking Critically About Visuals

"Pose!"

What's your reaction to the women in this photograph? Do you think that the concepts *masculinity* and *femininity* are outdated relics of earlier cultures? Or do you believe that these concepts reflect basic qualities of the human species that are still relevant today?

© Evan Hurd/Sygma/Corbis

USING CONCEPTS TO CLASSIFY

When you apply a concept to an object, idea, or experience, you are *classifying* the object, idea, or experience by placing it into the group of things defined by the properties/requirements of the concept. The individual objects, ideas, or experiences belong to no particular class until you classify them. In fact, the same things can often be classified in many different ways. For example, if someone handed you a tomato and asked, "Which class does this tomato belong in: fruit or vegetable?" how would you respond? The fact is a tomato can be classified as *both* a fruit and a vegetable, depending on your purposes.

Let us consider another example. Imagine that you are walking on undeveloped land with some other people when you come across an area of soggy ground with long grass and rotting trees. One person in your group surveys the parcel and announces: "That's a smelly marsh. All it does is breed mosquitoes. It ought to be covered with landfill and built on so that we can use it productively." Another member of your group disagrees with the classification "smelly marsh," stating: "This is a wetland of great ecological value. There are many plants and animals that need this area and other areas like it to survive. Wetland areas also help prevent the rivers from flooding by absorbing excess water during heavy rains." Which person is right? Should the wet area be classified as a "smelly marsh" or a "valuable wetland"? Actually, the wet area can be classified both ways. The classification that you select depends on your needs and your interests. Someone active in construction and land development may tend to view the parcel through perceptual lenses that reflect her interests and experience and classify it accordingly. Someone involved in preserving natural resources will tend to view the same parcel through different lenses and place it in a different category. The diagram on page 334 illustrates how a tree might be "seen" from a variety of perspectives, depending on the interest and experience of those involved.

These examples illustrate that the way you classify reflects and influences the way you see the world, the way you think about the world, and the way you behave in the world. This is true for almost all the classifications you make. Consider a vintage motorcycle like the 1939 Indian Four. Which classification should this motorcycle be placed into?

- Thrilling means of transformation
- Noise polluter
- Prized collectible
- Traffic circumventer
- Ride for an aspiring organ donor

You classify many of the things in your experience differently than others do because of your individual needs, interests, and values. For instance, smoking marijuana might be classified by some as "use of a dangerous drug" and by others as a "harmless good time." Some view large cars as "gas guzzlers"; others see the same cars as "safer, more comfortable vehicles." Some people categorize the latest music as "meaningless noise" while others think of it as "creative expression." The way you classify aspects of your experience reflects the kind of individual you are and the way you think and feel about the world.

You also place people into various classifications. The specific classifications you select depend on who you are and how you see the world. Similarly, each of us is placed into a variety of classifications by different people. For example, here are some of the classifications into which certain people placed me:

Classification	*People who classify me*
Firstborn son	My parents
Taxpayer	Internal Revenue Service
Tickler	My son/daughter
Bagel with cream cheese	Server where I pick up my breakfast

List some of the different ways that you can be classified, and identify the people who would classify you that way.

Thinking Critically About Visuals

Is Beauty "In the Eye of the Beholder"?

As with the concepts of "masculinity" and "femininity," the concept of "beauty" varies widely depending on the culture and time period. In the United States, the Barbie doll has been an influential standard of female beauty for over 50 years. A common criticism of Barbie is that she promotes an unrealistic idea of body image for young women, leading to health risks for girls who attempt to emulate her. A standard Barbie doll is 11.5 inches tall, giving a height of 5 feet 9 inches at <u>1/6 scale</u>, while her vital statistics have been estimated at 36 inches (chest), 18 inches (waist), and 33 inches (hips). This works out to an estimated weight of 110 lbs, which at 5' 9" in height meets the standard criteria of anorexia. In what ways is viewing a "real life" Barbie different than viewing a Barbie doll?

Whitehotpix/ZUMAPRESS/Newscom

Whitehotpix/ZUMAPRESS/Newscom

Finally, besides classifying the same thing or event in a variety of different ways, you can classify most collections of things in various ways. For example, consider the different ways the members of your class can be classified. You could group them according to their majors, their ages, their food preferences, and so on. The specific categories you would use would depend on the purposes of your classification. If you were trying to organize career counseling, then classifying according to majors makes sense. If you were trying to plan the menu for a class party, then food preferences would be the natural category for classification.

Thinking Critically About Visuals

"A Tree Is Just a Tree, Is Just a Tree . . ."

This cartoon illustrates the diverse ways in which a "tree" can be visualized by various individuals or agencies. Select a different thing—such as a "door" or a "car"—and illustrate how it might be seen from different perspectives.

Courtesy of Louis Hellman

Not only do you continually classify things and people into various groups based on the common properties you choose to focus on, you also classify ideas, feelings, actions, and experiences. Explain, for instance, why the killing of another person might be classified in different ways, depending on the circumstances.

Classification	Circumstance	Example
1. Manslaughter	Killing someone accidentally	Driving while intoxicated
2. Self-defense		
3. Premeditation		
4. Mercy killing		
5. Diminished capacity		

Each of these classifications represents a separate legal concept, with its own properties and referents (examples). Of course, even when you understand clearly what the concept means, the complexity of the circumstances often makes it difficult to determine which concept applies. For example, in Chapter 2, "Thinking Critically," you considered a court case that raised complex and disturbing issues. In circumstances like these, trying to identify the appropriate concepts and then to determine which of the further concepts, "guilty" or "innocent," also applies, is a challenging process. This is true of many of life's complex situations: You must work hard at identifying the appropriate concepts to apply to the situations you are trying to make sense of and then be prepared to change or modify these concepts based on new information or better insight.

Defining Concepts

When you define a concept, you usually identify the necessary properties/requirements that determine when the concept can be applied. In fact, the word *definition* is derived from the Latin word meaning "boundary" because that is exactly what a definition does: It gives the boundaries of the territory in your experience that can be described by the concept. For example, a definition of the concept *horse* might include the following requirements:

- Large, strong animal
- Four legs with solid hoofs
- Flowing mane and tail
- Domesticated long ago for drawing or carrying loads, carrying riders, and so on

By understanding the requirements of the concept *horse,* you understand what conditions must be met in order for something to qualify as an example of the concept. This lets you know in what situations you can apply the concept: to the animals running around the racetrack, the animals pulling wagons and carriages, the animals being ridden on the range, and so on. In addition, understanding the requirements lets you know to which things the concept can be applied. No matter how much a zebra looks like a horse, you won't apply the concept *horse* to it if you really understand the definition of the concept involved.

Definitions also often make strategic use of examples of the concept being defined. Consider the following definition by Ambrose Bierce:

An edible: Good to eat and wholesome to digest, as a worm to a toad, a toad to a snake, a snake to a pig, a pig to a man, and a man to a worm.

Contrast this definition with the one illustrated in the following passage from Charles Dickens's *Hard Times:*

> "Bitzer," said Thomas Gradgrind. "Your definition of a horse."
> "Quadruped. Graminivorous. Forty teeth, namely twenty-four grinders, four eye teeth, and twelve incisive. Sheds coat in the spring; in marshy countries sheds hoofs, too. Hoofs hard, but requiring to be shod with iron. Age known by marks in mouth." Thus (and much more) Bitzer.
> "Now girl number twenty," said Mr. Gradgrind, "you know what a horse is."

Although Bitzer has certainly done an admirable job of listing some of the necessary properties/requirements of the concept *horse,* it is unlikely that "girl number twenty" has any better idea of what a horse is than she had before because the definition relies exclusively on a technical listing of the properties characterizing the concept *horse* without giving any examples that might illustrate the concept more completely.

Definitions that rely exclusively on a technical description of the concept's properties are often not very helpful unless you already know what the concept means. A more concrete way of communicating the concept *horse* would be to point out various animals that qualify as horses and other animals that do not. You could also explain why they do not (e.g., "That can't be a horse because it has two humps and its legs are too long and skinny").

Although examples do not take the place of a clearly understood definition, they are often useful in clarifying, supplementing, and expanding such a definition. If someone asked you, "What is a horse?" and you replied by giving examples of different kinds of horses (thoroughbred racing horses, plow horses for farming, quarter horses for cowboys, hunter horses for fox hunting, circus horses), you certainly would be communicating a good portion of the meaning of *horse.* Giving examples of a concept complements and clarifies the necessary requirements for the correct use of that concept. For example, provide a dictionary definition for each of the following concepts, and describe ways you could supplement and expand each definition:

EXAMPLE: Smile

a. Definition: a facial expression characterized by an upward curving of the corners of the mouth and indicating pleasure, amusement, or derision.

b. Ways to expand the definition: smiling at someone or drawing a picture of a smiling face.

- ambivalent
- intelligent
- art
- thinking
- work
- create

The process of providing definitions of concepts is thus the same process you use to develop concepts. Of course, this process is often difficult and complex, and people don't always agree on how concepts should be defined.

Defining a Concept

Giving an effective definition of a concept means both

- ❑ Identifying the general qualities of the concept, which determine when it can be correctly applied
- ❑ Using appropriate examples to demonstrate actual applications of the concept—that is, examples that embody the general qualities of the concept

Thinking Activity 7.4

ANALYZING THE CONCEPT *RESPONSIBILITY*

Review the ideas we have explored in this chapter by analyzing the concept *responsibility*. "Responsibility" is a complex idea that has an entire network of meaning. The word comes from the Latin word *respondere,* which means "to pledge or promise."

Generalizing

1. Describe two important responsibilities you have in your life, and identify the qualities they embody that lead you to think of them as "responsibilities."

2. Describe a person in your life who you think is responsible, and then describe a person in your life who you think is irresponsible. In reflecting on these individuals, identify the qualities they embody that lead you to think of them as "responsible" or "irresponsible."

Interpreting

3. Consider the following situations. In each case, describe what you consider to be examples of responsible behavior and irresponsible behavior. Be sure to explain the reasons for your answers.

   a. You are a member of a group of three students who are assigned the task of writing a report on a certain topic. Your life is very hectic and, in addition, you find the topic dull. What is your response? Why?

   b. You are employed at a job in which you observe your supervisor and other employees engaged in activities that break the company rules. You are afraid that if you "blow the whistle," you might lose your job. What is your response? Why?

Defining

4. Using these activities of generalizing and interpreting as a foundation, define the concepts *responsible* and *irresponsible* by listing the qualities that make up the boundaries of each concept and identifying key examples that embody and illustrate the qualities of the concept.

Thinking Passage

DEFINING THE CONCEPT OF CULTURAL IDENTITY

To be "an American" is a complex, diverse concept that has had a variety of meanings at different points in America's history. Unlike most countries, where the majority populations tend to be more homogeneous and national identity is generally built around shared ancestry or common ethnic heritage, America is a country that has been built on diversity of every sort. How would you respond to the question "Who's American?" What are the qualities that you think form the structure of the concept "an American?"

Equally as interesting is the question "What are Americans like?" What are some of the general qualities that are thought to characterize most Americans, in contrast to other national identities? The following article, "Infographic: The American Identity According to Social Media" by Nicholas Jackson takes an ingenious approach to answering this question, utilizing social media as a tool for trying to get a handle on the American character.

Infographic: The American Identity According to Social Media

by Nicholas Jackson

Odds are that you're on at least one major social network. (There are about 150 million Facebook users in the United States alone.) And you've been on that network—or on those networks—for years, feeding in information about yourself, updating your status, posting pictures of your latest vacations and responding to events and messages from friends. Over time, those networks have learned a lot about you, about us. What do they know?

Social media strategy firm Hasai put together the infographic embedded below after deciding to find out. Not focused on the individual bits of information—phone numbers and movie preferences, email addresses and gender—Hasai took a step back to see what a bunch of data could tell us about the American people as a whole.

Infographics are always a bit of a hodgepodge of statistics culled from a variety of sources. Here, we sort through the clutter and pull out some of our favourite facts and figures:

Americans are followers: Nearly half of all Americans are now members of at least one social network, double the proportion of just two years ago.

Americans have a lot to say: Nearly half (48 percent) of all bloggers are based in the U.S.

Americans like to give advice: 28 percent of U.S. adults say that they give advice about purchases on social networking sites.

Americans are nostalgic: The average Facebook user has 229 friends. While less than 10 percent are college friends, more than 20 percent are friends from high school.

Americans want to be distracted from reality: The more than 63 million active users of FarmVille spend an average of 15 minutes a day pretending to run a farm. Over the

Thinking Critically About Visuals

Who Is an American?

This photo is of a section of the Ellis Island Museum's installation "American Flag of Faces." From one perspective, you can see just the American flag, but as you walk by the piece, you can see that each panel that makes up the flag also displays the picture of an American person. The Flag of Faces is meant to be a "living" interactive exhibit—the photo panels change and any American is welcome to submit his or her picture for inclusion.

Michael Matthews/Alamy

(To see "The Flag of Faces" online, visit www.flagoffaces.org.)

What concepts or ideals does this exhibit communicate with regard to what it means to be American? Does it imply anything about patriotism, equality, and inclusion? Would your answers be the same if you knew that, to get your photo in the exhibit, you would need to pay a $50 donation?

course of a year, that's 5,475 minutes—the equivalent of a full-time job for over two weeks.

Americans love routine: Of the more than 149 million Americans actively using Facebook, 70 percent of these active users in the U.S. log on to the social network daily.

Americans are obsessed with celebrities: The five most followed Twitter accounts are those of Lady Gaga, Justin Bieber, Barack Obama, Katy Perry, and Britney Spears.

Americans love television and they like others to know it: 77 percent of Americans report they use social media to share their love of a show, 65 percent use it as a platform to help save their favourite shows, and 35 percent use it to try to introduce new shows to their friends.

AMERICANS ARE FOLLOWERS

Nearly half of all Americans are now members of at least one social network, double the proportion of just two years ago.

OUT OF ALL AMERICAN ADULTS

79% USE THE INTERNET

47% USE AT LEAST ONE SOCIAL MEDIA SITE

In 2008, only 26 percent of adults were on online social networks.

AMERICANS HAVE A LOT TO SAY

48% of bloggers are US-based

48%

AMERICANS LIKE TO GIVE ADVICE

28% of U.S. adults say they give advice about purchases on social networking sites.

facebook

twitter

Linked in

TAGGED

Blogger

myspace

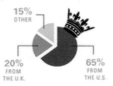

THE AMERICAN IDENTITY ACCORDING TO SOCIAL MEDIA

CAN A BUNCH OF DATA ABOUT SOCIAL NETWORKING HELP US UNDERSTAND THE AMERICAN PEOPLE?

AMERICANS LOVE TELEVISION AND THEY LIKE OTHERS TO KNOW IT

77% REPORT THAT THEY USE SOCIAL MEDIA TO SHARE THEIR LOVE OF A SHOW.

65% USE IT AS A PLATFORM TO HELP SAVE THEIR FAVORITE SHOWS.

35% USE IT TO TRY TO INTRODUCE NEW SHOWS TO THEIR FRIENDS

AMERICANS ARE INDUSTRIOUS

Just under 50% of LinkedIn's 120 million users are in the United States.

AMERICANS LIKE BRANDS

Four out of ten Americans on social media platforms (identified as frequent users) are following products, services and brands.

AMERICANS ARE NOSTALGIC

The average Facebook user has 229 friends.

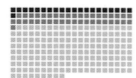

9% ARE COLLEGE FRIENDS

22% ARE PEOPLE FROM HIGH SCHOOL

AMERICANS ARE OBSESSED WITH ROYALTY

65% of all social media related to the royal wedding has come from the U.S. in the past month [April]. The U.K. has been responsible for just 20%.

15% OTHER

20% FROM THE U.K.

65% FROM THE U.S.

AMERICANS ARE OBSESSED WITH CELEBRITIES

The five most followed Twitter accounts are Lady Gaga, Justin Bieber, Barack Obama, Katy Perry and Britney Spears.

AMERICANS WANT TO BE DISTRACTED FROM REALITY

The more than 63 million active users of Farmville spend an average of 15 minutes a day pretending to run a farm. Over the course of a year, that's 5,475 minutes—the equivalent of a full-time job for over two weeks!

AMERICANS LOVE VIDEO GAMES

Video games are the second most heavily-used internet activity, accounting for 10% of all U.S. internet time.

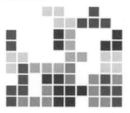

AMERICANS ARE HYPER-SOCIAL

Social media now reaches the majority of Americans 12+, with 52% having a profile on one or more social networks.

AMERICANS ARE CONNECTED

Six out of seven American homes have broadband internet access.

9 OUT OF 10 AMERICANS ARE ONLINE.

AMERICANS LOVE ROUTINE

Of the more than 149 million Americans actively using Facebook, 70% of these active users in the U.S. log on to the social network daily. Tagged comes in 2nd with the average user logging in every other day.

70% OF THESE ACTIVE USERS IN THE U.S. LOG ONTO THE SOCIAL NETWORK DAILY

AMERICANS ARE HIGHLY INFLUENCED BY OTHERS

The purchasing decisions of 38 million 13 to 80-year-olds in the U.S. are now influenced in various ways by social media—up 14% in just six months.

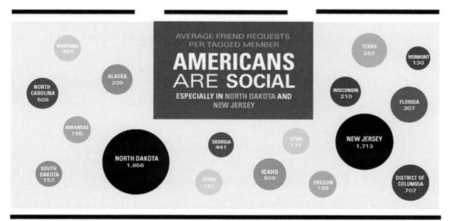

AVERAGE FRIEND REQUESTS PER TAGGED MEMBER

AMERICANS ARE SOCIAL

ESPECIALLY IN NORTH DAKOTA AND NEW JERSEY

MONTANA 401 · TEXAS 282 · VERMONT 130 · ALASKA 209 · NORTH CAROLINA 509 · WISCONSIN 210 · FLORIDA 307 · ARKANSAS 195 · GEORGIA 441 · UTAH 171 · NEW JERSEY 1,713 · NORTH DAKOTA 1,956 · SOUTH DAKOTA 157 · IOWA 161 · IDAHO 509 · OREGON 169 · DISTRICT OF COLUMBIA 707

SOURCES

http://www.pamorama.net/2010/03/07/social-media-everybodys-doing-it-but-for-different-reasons-charts/
http://www.mediapost.com/publications/?fa=Articles.showArticle&art_aid=125870&nid=113175
http://vator.tv/news/2011-06-16-wow-facebook-actually-makes-people-closer
http://blog.hubspot.com/blog/tabid/6307/bid/5965/The-Ultimate-List-300-Social-Media-Statistics.aspx?source=Webbiquity
http://blog.hubze.com/2011/eight-new-findings-on-how-americans-use-social-media/
http://vator.tv/news/2011-06-16-wow-facebook-actually-makes-people-closer
(TvGuide.com study via TVNewsCheck.com)
http://blog.hubze.com/2011/eight-new-findings-on-how-americans-use-social-media/
http://www.usatoday.com/life/people/2011-04-29-royal-wedding-social-media_N.htm
www.tagged.com
http://www.edisonresearch.com/home/archives/2011/05/the_social_habit_2011.php
http://www.techjournalsouth.com/2011/06/social-media-affects-purchase-decisions-of-38m-americans-influence-growing/
http://blog.nielsen.com/nielsenwire/online_mobile/what-americans-do-online-social-media-and-games-dominate-activity/
http://techcrunch.com/2011/02/10/facebook-now-has-149m-active-users-in-the-u-s-70-percent-log-on-daily
http://news.cnet.com/8301-27076_3-20014817-248.html#ixzz1TtWVHBLB/
http://twitaholic.com/top100/followers/
http://press.linkedin.com/about
http://venturebeat.files.wordpress.com/2011/03/final_520px.png?w=520&h=2370
http://www.marketwire.com/press-release/uff-da-and-hello-there-north-dakota-revealed-to-be-most-social-state-in-the-union-1540762.htm
http://about-tagged.com/company/facts

INFOGRAPHIC BROUGHT TO YOU BY

QUESTIONS FOR ANALYSIS

1. How would you answer the question "Who's American?" How did you develop this concept of being an American? If you or your parents were born in another country, how would you define the national identity of that country? (For example, what does it mean to be Dominican or Chinese?)

2. What are some of the central qualities that the author Nicholas Jackson believes are an essential part of the American character? Which of these qualities do you agree with? Why? Which of these qualities do you disagree with? Why not?

3. What do you think about the approach described in the article to determining the American character? Do you think it's a useful method of analysis? What are its strengths? Its limitations? What would be another way to try and describe the American character?

4. Different metaphors have been used to describe the unique composition of the American culture including "melting pot" and "garden salad." What metaphor do you think is best to describe the American culture? Why? How can metaphors like these be both helpful as well as potentially limiting and even destructive?

5. How can the concept of a national identity both unite and divide people?

6. After reflecting on these issues via this article, these questions, and class discussions, has your concept of what it means to be an American changed? If so, in what ways?

THINKING CRITICALLY ABOUT NEW MEDIA

Using New Media to Research a Concept

It's difficult to imagine, but it wasn't that long ago that if you wanted to research a subject, you had to physically go to the library and use the card catalog or periodical room to conduct your research. The creation of computers and the Internet has changed all of that, of course. Not only don't you have to go to a library, you don't even have to be sitting in front of a computer—through your smart phone or iPad you literally have the world at your fingertips.

In this new information universe, it's not simply our mobility that has been revolutionized, it's the *way* in which we're able to conduct research, roaming far and wide, with one link leading to another, and to another, and so on. It's very much

Relating Concepts with Mind Maps

A *mind map* is a visual presentation of the ways in which concepts can be related to one another. For example, each chapter in this book opens with a diagram—what we will call a "mind map" or "cognitive map"—that visually summarizes the chapter's basic concepts as well as the way in which these concepts are related to one another. These maps are a reference guide that reveals basic themes and chapter organization. Because they clearly articulate various patterns of thought, mind maps are effective tools for helping us understand complex bodies of information.

Mind mapping is a flexible and effective tool that can be used in nearly every part of the learning and thinking process. A mapping approach offers some clear advantages in organizing the information you receive from oral communication. For instance, when you as a student take notes of what a teacher is saying, it's difficult to write down whole sentences and quotations from the lecture or class discussion. Taking notes by mapping enables you to identify the key ideas and articulate the various relationships among them. Similarly, mapping is also an effective aid in preparing for oral presentations because by organizing the information you want to present in this way, you have all the key ideas and their relationships in a single whole.

Along with reading, listening, and speaking, mapping is also useful for writing. First, the organization grows naturally, reflecting the way your mind naturally makes associations and organizes information. Second, the organization can be easily revised on the basis of new information and your developing understanding of how this information should be organized. Third, you can express a range of relationships among the various ideas, and each idea can remain an active part of the overall pattern, suggesting new possible relationships. Fourth, you do not have to decide initially on a beginning, subpoints, sub-subpoints, and so on; you can do this after your pattern is complete, saving time and avoiding frustration.

the way in which our brain makes connections: spontaneously, dynamically, and at lightning speed.

Of course, as we've seen, with that boundless sea of information out there, it's essential that we keep our critical-thinking abilities dialed up to the maximum so that we can distinguish the true from false, objective from subjective, and fact from fiction. It's been said that in this new media age, "We're drowning in information but we're starved for knowledge." The reason for this is that "information" is *not* "knowledge." As we have seen in earlier chapters, information doesn't become knowledge until the human mind has *acted* upon it: analyzing, synthesizing, applying, evaluating, *thinking critically* about it.

Reviewing and Viewing

Summary

- *Concepts* are general ideas used to identify and organize experience and in so doing, bring order and intelligibility to our lives.

- The structure of concepts involves three qualities: *signs, referents,* and *properties.*

- Throughout our lives we are engaged in the process of *forming* and *applying* concepts through the interactive processes of *generalizing* and *interpreting.*

- Becoming an educated thinker involves learning to form and apply concepts in order to understand complex ideas, make sense of what is happening at the moment, and anticipate what may happen in the future.

- We *define concepts* by describing the necessary properties/requirements that determine when the concept can be applied, along with articulating legitimate examples of the concept.

- In the same way that words are the vocabulary of language, concepts are the vocabulary of thought. As organizers of our experience, concepts work in conjunction with language to help us understand the world, make informed decisions, think critically, and act intelligently.

Assessing Your Strategies and Creating New Goals

How Effective Am I in Forming and Applying Concepts?

Concepts are the general ideas that we use to organize our experience and, in so doing, to bring order and intelligibility to our lives. As organizers of our experience, concepts work in conjunction with language to identify, describe, distinguish, and relate all the various aspects of our world. To become sophisticated thinkers, we must develop expertise in the conceptualizing process. Described below are key aspects of the conceptualizing process. Evaluate your position regarding each of these conceptualizing abilities, and use this self-evaluation to guide your efforts to develop these crucial abilities.

Become Aware of the Structure of Concepts and How They Function in Our Lives

I am acutely aware of the structure of concepts and their central role in thinking, learning, and communication.	I don't have a great deal of understanding about the structure of concepts and how they function.
5 4 3 2 1	

In their role as the vocabulary of thought, concepts consist of *properties*—qualities that define the boundaries of the concept; a *sign*—which serves as a word symbol for the concept; and *referents*—which consist of examples of the concept.

Strategy: As critical thinkers, we need to become knowledgeable about the structure of concepts so that we can develop them and use them effectively in all areas of our lives.

Develop the Ability to Form and Apply Concepts Through the Interactive Processes of Generalizing and Interpreting

I understand the conceptualizing process and consciously use the processes of *generalizing* and *interpreting* to gain increased understanding of concepts.	I do not fully understand the way concepts are formed and applied.
5 4 3 2 1	

Throughout our lives we are engaged in the process of forming—and applying—concepts to organize our experience, make sense of what is happening in the present, and predict what will happen in the future. We form concepts through the interactive process of *generalizing* (focusing on the common properties shared by a group of things) and *interpreting* (finding examples of the concept). The common properties form the necessary requirements (the "boundaries") that must be met in order to apply the concept to our experience.

*Strategy: Focus on some of the new concepts you are learning in one of your academic courses. Write out the process of **generalizing** and **interpreting** you used to gain an understanding of the concepts and how they are applied.*

Develop the Ability to Define and Analyze Concepts by Identifying General Qualities ("Boundaries") and Relevant Examples

I am able to clearly define and analyze concepts by identifying the general qualities and relevant examples of the concept.	I am not able to clearly define and analyze concepts.
5 4 3 2 1	

Much of our education, and learning in general, is involved in trying to analyze, define, and understand concepts. That's what academic disciplines are—systems of concepts and methodologies designed to understand ourselves and our world. This is true in the rest of our lives as well: we are continually working to understand concepts like what is a "critical thinker," what is the "morally right" thing to do, what is a "family," what is "religion," and so on. Understanding the nature of concepts and how they develop and function is essential to becoming an expert critical thinker.

Strategy: *Take note of key concepts that you are thinking about or discussing with others and analyze them using the approaches explored in this chapter.*

Suggested Films

2001: A Space Odyssey (1968)

What distinguishes human beings from other animals? Humans from machines? In this science fiction film, a crew on a mission to uncover a mystery in space runs into complications when the machine they are using begins to make decisions for them.

The Atheism Tapes (2004)

In this documentary by Jonathan Miller, six leading intellectuals—playwright Arthur Miller, biologist Richard Dawkins, theologian Denys Turner, physicist Steven Weinberg, and philosophers Daniel Dennett and Colin McGinn—debate the existence of God.

Blade Runner (1982)

What does it mean to be human? In the future as depicted in this classic science fiction film, humans have developed the technology to create replicants, clones with fixed life spans that serve people in the colonies outside Earth. When the technology backfires and the clones rebel, a blade runner, Rick Decard (Harrison Ford) is hired to search out and terminate replicants in Los Angeles.

Crash (2005)

What happens when different value systems conflict? In Los Angeles, a collection of strangers is brought together by a single car crash. Issues of race, class, identity, and self-understanding emerge as the characters interact and react to the events.

The Namesake (2006)

This film explores the intersection between culture and identity. A young Indian American man finds himself caught between the traditions of his immigrant parents and his life in America. Based on the novel by Jhumpa Lahiri.

How Is Your World Related and Organized?

These four photos are stills from the OK GO music video "This Too Shall Pass," which displays an elaborate "Rube Goldberg machine" of causal sequences that are both surprising and entertaining. In this way the video is a metaphor for the way in which we work to make our world intelligible by relating and organizing all of its disparate parts into a coherent whole that we understand. When was the last time that you were totally mystified by something you experienced? What type of "relating" or "organizing" enabled you to ultimately make sense of it?

Relating and Organizing

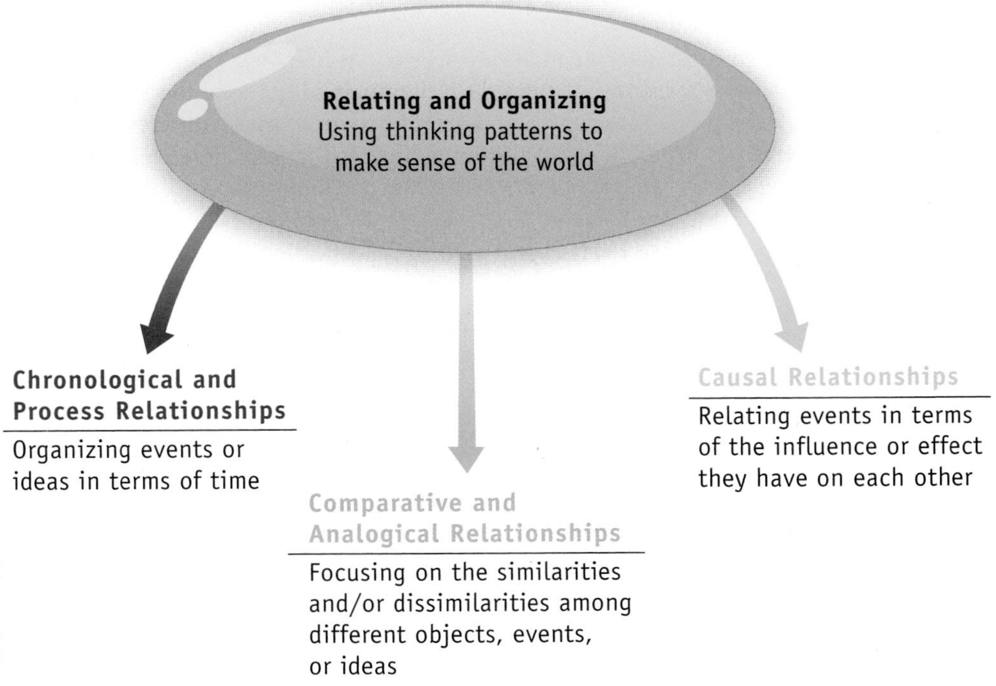

Relating and Organizing
Using thinking patterns to
make sense of the world

**Chronological and
Process Relationships**

Organizing events or
ideas in terms of time

**Comparative and
Analogical Relationships**

Focusing on the similarities
and/or dissimilarities among
different objects, events,
or ideas

Causal Relationships

Relating events in terms
of the influence or effect
they have on each other

Throughout this book we have been considering and experiencing the insight that each one of us is a "creator." Our world does not exist as a finished product, waiting for us to perceive it, think about it, and describe it with words and pictures. Instead, we are *active participants* in composing the world that seems so familiar to us.

The goal of this composing process is to organize your world into meaningful patterns that will help you figure out what is going on and what you ought to do. Composing your world involves all the activities that we have been exploring, including

perceiving	symbolizing	interpreting
believing	describing	conceptualizing
knowing	classifying	defining
solving problems	generalizing	analyzing

Your ability to think critically gives you the means to examine the different ways by which you are making sense of the world so that you can develop and sharpen your understanding. As you actively discover and compose various patterns, you are exploring the ways in which different aspects of your experience *relate* to each other.

Ideas, things, and events in the world can be related and organized in a variety of ways. For example, different individuals might take the same furniture and decorations in the same space and arrange them in many different ways, reflecting each person's needs, ways of thinking, and aesthetic preferences. To take another example, a class of students may write essays about the same subject and yet create widely differing results.

All these ways of relating and organizing reflect basic thinking patterns that you rely on constantly when you think, act, or use language. These basic thinking patterns are an essential part of your process of composing and making sense of the world. We will explore three basic ways of relating and organizing in this chapter.

Chronological and process relationships:
- Chronological—relating events in time sequence
- Process—relating aspects of the growth or development of an event or object

Comparative and analogical relationships:
- Comparative—relating things in the same general category in terms of similarities and dissimilarities
- Analogical—relating things belonging to different categories in terms of each other

Causal relationships:
- Causal—relating events in terms of the way some event(s) is/are responsible for bringing about some other event(s)

These basic thinking patterns (and others besides) play an active role in the way you perceive, shape, and organize your world to make it understandable to you. The specific patterns you use to organize your ideas in thinking, writing, and speaking depend on the subject you are exploring, the goals you are aiming for, the type of writing or speaking you are doing, and the audience who will be reading or listening to your work. In most cases, you will use a variety of basic patterns in thinking, writing, and speaking to organize and relate the ideas you are considering.

Chronological and Process Relationships

Chronological and process patterns of thinking organize events or ideas in terms of their occurrence in time, though the two patterns tend to differ in focus or emphasis. The *chronological* pattern of thinking organizes something into a series of events in the sequence in which they occurred. The *process* mode of thinking organizes an activity into a series of steps necessary for reaching a certain goal.

CHRONOLOGICAL RELATIONSHIPS

The simplest examples of chronological descriptions are logs or diaries, in which people record things that occurred at given points in time. The oldest and most universal form of chronological expression is the *narrative,* a way of thinking and communicating in which someone tells a story about experiences he or she has had. (Of course, the person telling the story can be a *fictional* character created by a writer who is using a narrative form.) Every human culture has used narratives to pass on values and traditions from one generation to the next, exemplified by such enduring works as the *Odyssey* and the Bible. The word *narrative* is derived from the Latin word for "to know." Narrators are people who "know" what happened because they were there to experience it firsthand (or spoke to people who were there) and who now share this experience with you.

One of America's great storytellers, Mark Twain, once said that a good story has to accomplish something and arrive somewhere. In other words, if a story is to be effective in engaging the interest of the audience, it has to have a purpose. The purpose may be to provide more information on a subject, to illustrate an idea, to lead us to a particular way of thinking, or to entertain us. An effective story does not merely record the complex, random, and often unrelated events of life. Instead, it has focus and purpose, possesses an ordered structure (a *plot*), and expresses a meaningful point of view.

Thinking Activity 8.1

CREATING A NARRATIVE DESCRIPTION

Write a narrative describing an event or experience that had special significance in your life. After completing your narrative, explain what you think is the most important point that you are trying to share with your audience. Read your narrative to the other members of the class, and then discuss it with them, comparing the meaning you intended with the meaning they derived. The following passage by Joseph Bruchac illustrates what such a narrative might look like.

Thinking Passage

NARRATING AN EXPERIENCE

Review the following narrative by Joseph Bruchac, which uses narrative examples of thinking and expression, and then answer the questions that follow.

Indian Renaissance

by Joseph Bruchac

From the top of Coffee Butte in the land of the Cheyenne River Sioux, you can see 50 miles in every direction. As I circled my gaze, I could see black dots on the wide, grassy plain below. Buffalo. I picked out one herd, then another, another and another. A herd in each of the four directions: good omen.

"Look," said Dennis Rousseau, of the tribe's Game, Fish, and Parks Department, "over there."

I followed his stare to a group of brown specks on a ridge, two miles to our east. "Wild horses," he said. "Coming our way."

I watched as perhaps a dozen animals flowed toward us down the slope, smooth as rushing water. They were half a mile away, led by a brown stallion, head up, alert to any danger. Sure enough, distant as we were, the stallion caught wind of us. He stopped abruptly on top of a hill, stared, then turned, driving the horses before him, out of sight as quick as the flash of a hawk's wing.

Wild horses are back on the reservation after an absence of 140 years, trucked in from Nevada, where they were being shot at and killed by poachers only a few years ago. Their return, like seeing buffalo in all directions, was enough to stir the blood of at least one old East Coast Indian: me. For the first time in generations, "the buffalo, the elk, and the mustang are all back on the reservation," said Dennis, lowering his binoculars. "One of our holy men told me that means something really good is going to happen."

I'd come to Cheyenne River looking for something good: the same spirit of revival and hope that I'd heard about in Indian communities across the United States, from the stone-cold canyons of Manhattan to the quietest hogan in the desert Southwest. In a thousand small ways, that revival—cultural, political, economic, spiritual—may wind up transforming the lives of 4.1 million Native Americans, the vast majority of whom today live somewhere besides a reservation.

And yet, as I'd driven across South Dakota to get here, I'd expected this place to be different. Confined to some of the driest, most unforgiving real estate in North America, Sioux reservations on the Great Plains are among the poorest in the country. Just south of Cheyenne River, people on the Pine Ridge Indian Reservation live on a third of what the average American earns and are three times as likely to be jobless. They also commit suicide twice as often. In this part of America, whole landscapes seem raw with the memory of

Source: Adapted from "Indian: Scenes from a Renaissance" by Joseph Bruchac: *National Geographic Magazine*, September 2004.

what went on here in the late 19th century. This is the land of the Custer campaigns and the Ghost Dance, where Lakota Sioux resisted the coming of the whites and the loss of their sacred lands with every beat of their hearts. Sitting Bull's grave is out here.

Approaching Cheyenne River after sundown, I hit the search button on the radio and landed on the biggest station around—KLND, Indian owned and operated—just in time to catch a dedication. "For all you lovebirds out there, whether you're snaggin', shackin', or married," said the deejay. "Here's Lil' Kim!" If nothing else, young Americans of all colors have music in common: 50 Cent and Eminem are just as popular with Indians as they are with other American kids. Short hair, tattoos, and baggy pants are everywhere you look. Even adult men who used to wear shoulder-length hair have gone to the buzz cut, in a quiet revolt against Indian stereotypes.

A while later, at my motel, I tuned in channel 30 on cable and saw an ad from Emmanuel Red Bear—who also goes by the Lakota name of Tatanka Iyotake, the same name as his great-great-grandfather, Sitting Bull—making it known that he is a certified Lakota language instructor, an experienced emcee for powwows, honorings, and giveaways, and is also available for suicide counseling and gang awareness workshops. It was a vision of hope that made me sit up in my chair.

The next day I caught another glimpse of hope, this time in black and white. On the wall of Dennis Rousseau's office hangs one of those reservation maps I've grown familiar with over the years, showing the checkerboard pattern of lands once reserved for Indians. Today about half of the original 2.8-million-acre Cheyenne River reservation is in tribal hands; the rest was expropriated by federal allotment acts between 1887 and 1934 and sold to whites. But the tribe is making a huge investment in its future by seeking a federal loan to buy back 22, 140 acres, including the grazing land where their buffalo herd now roams.

With more than 3,000 animals, the Cheyenne River herd is the largest tribally owned buffalo herd in America, and one of the best managed. Tribal biologists, for example, plant micro chips in young buffalo to identify and monitor each animal from a command post in Rousseau's office. Some of the animals are sold commercially, but most of the meat, which passes USDA inspection, goes to schools and other tribal programs such as the Elderly Nutrition Center, part of an effort to reintroduce buffalo meat, which is leaner than beef, as a staple of the reservation diet.

Long-term, says Dennis, the goal is to reestablish buffalo culture on the reservation, with benefits both practical and spiritual. "The buffalo, which is sacred, is still providing for us by giving us a paycheck and putting food on the table," said Dennis. "Nature put the buffalo on this Earth for a reason. So I guess it's come full circle."

QUESTIONS FOR ANALYSIS

Identify the key events in the author's life and their relationship to one another.

1. Explain the purpose(s) you think the narrator is trying to achieve in writing this essay.

2. Identify some of the specific experiences that the author cites to support the central theme of the narrative.

3. In the next section we are going to be examining process relationships which focus on relating aspects of the growth and development of an event or experience. One

of the themes this author is exploring is the way in which vibrant Native American cultures were nearly destroyed by the practices of the United States government and the ways in which these communities are beginning to evolve into vibrant cultures once again. After reading the following section, return to this reading and analyze it in terms of the evidence the author cites to support this perspective.

PROCESS RELATIONSHIPS

Another type of time-ordered thinking is the process relationship, which focuses on relating aspects of the growth and development of an event or experience. From birth onward, you are involved with processes in every facet of your life. These processes can be classified in various ways: natural (e.g., growing in height), mechanical (e.g., assembling a bicycle), physical (e.g., learning a sport), mental (e.g., developing your thinking), creative (e.g., writing a poem), and so on.

Performing a *process analysis* involves two basic steps. The first step is to divide the process or activity you are analyzing into parts or stages. The second step is to explain the movement of the process through these parts or stages from beginning to end. The stages you have identified should be separate and distinct and should involve no repetition or significant omissions.

In performing a process analysis, you are typically trying to achieve one or both of two goals. The first goal is to give people step-by-step instruction in how to perform an activity, such as taking a photograph, changing a tire, or writing an essay. The second goal is simply to give information about a process, not to teach someone how to perform it. For example, your biology teacher might explain the process of photosynthesis to help you understand how green plants function, not to teach you how to go about transforming sunlight into chlorophyll!

Thinking Activity 8.2

ANALYZING PROCESS RELATIONSHIPS

Review the following passages, which are examples of the process-analysis pattern of thinking. For each passage do the following:

1. Identify the purpose of the passage.
2. Describe the main stages in the process identified by the author.
3. List questions you still have about how the process operates.

Jacketing was a sleight-of-hand I watched with wonder each time, and I have discovered that my father was admired among sheepmen up and down the valley for his skill at it: *He was just pretty catty at that, the way he could get that ewe to take on a new lamb every time.* Put simply, jacketing was a ruse played on a ewe whose lamb had died. A substitute lamb quickly would be singled out, most likely from a set of twins. Sizing up the tottering newcomer, Dad would skin the dead lamb, and into the tiny pelt carefully snip four leg holes and a head hole. Then the stand-in lamb would have the skin fitted onto it like a snug jacket on a poodle. The next step of disguise was to cut out the dead lamb's liver and smear it several times across the jacket of pelt. In its borrowed and bedaubed skin, the new baby lamb then was presented to the ewe. She would sniff the baby impostor endlessly, distrustful but pulled by the blood-smell of her own. When in a few days she made up her dim sheep's mind to accept the lamb, Dad snipped away the jacket and recited his victory: *Mother him like hell now, don't ye? See what a hellava dandy lamb I got for ye, old sister? Who says I couldn't jacket day onto night if I wanted to, now-I-ask-ye?*

—Ivan Doig, *This House of Sky*

If you are inexperienced in relaxation techniques, begin by sitting in a comfortable chair with your feet on the floor and your hands resting easily in your lap. Close your eyes and breathe evenly, deeply, and gently. As you exhale each breath let your body become more relaxed. Starting with one hand direct your attention to one part of your body at a time. Close your fist and tighten the muscles of your forearm. Feel the sensation of tension in your muscles. Relax your hand and let your forearm and hand become completely limp. Direct all your attention to the sensation of relaxation as you continue to let all tension leave your hand and arm. Continue this practice once or several times each day, relaxing your other hand and arm, your legs, back, abdomen, chest, neck, face, and scalp. When you have this mastered and can relax completely, turn your thoughts to scenes of natural tranquility from your past. Stay with your inner self as long as you wish, whether thinking of nothing or visualizing only the loveliest of images. Often you will become completely unaware of your surroundings. When you open your eyes you will find yourself refreshed in mind and body.

—Laurence J. Peter, *The Peter Prescription*

The stages of mourning are universal and are experienced by people from all walks of life. Mourning occurs in response to an individual's own terminal illness or to the death of a valued being, human or animal. There are five stages of normal grief.

In our bereavement, we spend different lengths of time working through each step and express each stage more or less intensely. The five stages do not necessarily occur in order. We often move between stages before achieving a more peaceful acceptance of death. Many of us are not afforded the luxury of time required to achieve this final stage of grief. The death of a loved one might inspire you to evaluate your own feelings or mortality. Throughout each stage, a common thread of hope emerges. As long as there is life, there is hope. As long as there is hope, there is life.

1. *Denial and isolation:* The first reaction to learning of terminal illness or death of a cherished pet is to deny the reality of the situation. It is a normal reaction to rationalize overwhelming emotions. It is a defense mechanism that buffers the immediate shock. We block out the words and hide from the facts. This is a temporary response that carries us through the first wave of pain.

2. *Anger:* As the masking effects of denial and isolation begin to wear, reality and its pain re-emerge. We are not ready. The intense emotion is deflected from our vulnerable core, redirected and expressed instead as anger. The anger may be aimed at inanimate objects, complete strangers, friends or family. Anger may be directed at our dying or deceased loved one. Rationally, we

know the person is not to be blamed. Emotionally, however, we may resent it for causing us pain or for leaving us. We feel guilty for being angry, and this makes us more angry. The doctor who diagnosed the illness and was unable to cure the disease might become a convenient target.

3. *Bargaining:* The normal reaction to feelings of helplessness and vulnerability is often a need to regain control. If only we had sought medical attention sooner or secured a second opinion from another doctor. Secretly, we may make a deal with God or our higher power in an attempt to postpone the inevitable. This is a weaker line of defense to protect us from the painful reality.

4. *Depression:* Two types of depression are associated with mourning. The first one is a reaction to practical implications relating to the loss. Sadness and regret predominate. We worry that, in our grief, we have spent less time with others that depend on us. This phase may be eased by simple clarification and reassurance. We may need a bit of helpful cooperation and a few kind words. The second type of depression is more subtle and, in a sense, perhaps more private. It is our quiet preparation to separate and to bid our loved one farewell.

5. *Acceptance:* Reaching this stage of mourning is a gift not afforded to everyone. Death may be sudden and unexpected or we may never see beyond our anger or denial. It is not necessarily a mark of bravery to resist the inevitable and to deny ourselves the opportunity to make our peace. This phase is marked by withdrawal and calm. This is not a period of happiness and must be distinguished from depression.

Thinking Activity 8.3

CREATING A PROCESS DESCRIPTION

We tend to be most acutely aware of process analysis when we are learning a new activity for the first time, such as preparing formula for an infant or installing a new oil filter in a car. Identify such an occasion in your own life and then complete the following activities.

1. Describe the steps or stages in the process.
2. Write a passage explaining how the stages fit together in an overall sequence.
3. Describe any special problems you had to solve, the manner in which you went about solving them, and the feelings you experienced in learning this process.

Comparative and Analogical Relationships

Comparative and analogical patterns of thinking focus on the similarities and/or dissimilarities among different objects, events, or ideas. Comparative modes of thinking relate things in the *same* general category in terms of their similarities and differences. For example, when you shop for something important, like a car, you generally engage in a process of organized comparing (evaluating similarities and differences) as you examine the various makes and models. Analogical modes of thinking relate things in *different* categories in terms of their similarities. For example, on your shopping expedition for a car, you might say of a used car badly in need of repair, "That car is a real lemon." Obviously cars and lemons are in different categories, but the analogy brings out some similarities between the two (a sense of "sourness" or "bitterness").

COMPARATIVE RELATIONSHIPS

Think of an item you shopped for and bought in the past month. It might have been an article of clothing, a good book, or a smartphone. Identify the item you selected, noting as much specific information about it as you can remember—brand, color, size, cost, and so on. When you went shopping, you probably spent a fair amount of time examining other items of the same type, things that you looked at but did not buy. As you made your decision to purchase the item you did, you probably compared the various brands before making your selection. Identify some of the factors you took into consideration in comparing the different items. For example, if you were shopping for jeans:

Item purchased	Comparative factors	Item not purchased
Levi's jeans	Brand	True Religion
$69.00	Price	$185.00
Straight cut	Style	Skinny
Dark	Wash	Medium

You compare in this way all the time, usually without even realizing it. Whenever you select an item on a menu or in a store, or a seat in a theater or on a bus, you are automatically looking for similarities and differences among the various items from which you are selecting, and these similarities and differences guide you in making your decision.

Of course, you do not always engage in a systematic process of comparison. In many cases, the selections and decisions you make seem to be unconscious. This may be so because you have already performed an organized comparison at some time in the past and already know what you want and why you want it (e.g., "I always choose an aisle seat so that I don't have to climb over people").

Sometimes, however, you make decisions impulsively, without any thought or comparative examination. Maybe someone told you to, maybe you were influenced by a commercial you saw, or maybe you simply said, "What the heck, let's take a chance." Sometimes these impulsive decisions work out for you, but often they do not because they are simply a result of rolling the dice. In contrast, when you engage in a critical and comparative examination, you gain information that can help you make intelligent decisions.

Standards for Comparison Naturally, not all of the factors you use in comparing are equally important in your decision making. How do you determine which factors are more important than others and which information is more relevant than other information? Unfortunately, there is no simple formula for answering these questions.

For example, review the lists you completed previously and place a check next to the factors that played an important part in your decision to buy the item. These factors represent the comparative information you found to be most important and relevant and probably reflect your needs and purposes. If you are on a limited budget, price differences may play a key role in your decision. If money is no object, your decision may have been based solely on the quality of the item or on some other consideration.

Even though there is no hard-and-fast way to determine which areas of comparison are most important, it does help you to become aware of the factors that are influencing your perceptions and decisions. These areas of comparison represent the standards you use to come to conclusions, and a critical and reflective examination of these standards can help you sharpen, clarify, and improve them.

When making comparisons, you should try to avoid certain pitfalls:

- *Incomplete comparisons.* This difficulty arises when you focus on too few points of comparison. For example, in looking for a competent surgeon to operate on you, you might decide to focus only on the fee that each doctor charges. Even though this may be an important area for comparative analysis, you would be foolish to overlook other areas of comparison, such as medical training, experience, recommendations, and success rates.

- *Selective comparisons.* This problem occurs when you take a one-sided view of a comparative situation—when you concentrate on the points favoring one side of the things being compared but overlook the points favoring the other side. For example, in selecting a dependable friend to perform a favor for you, you may focus on Bob because he is your best friend and you have known him the longest, but you may overlook the fact that he let you down the last few times you asked him to do something for you.

Thinking Activity 8.4

ANALYZING COMPARATIVE RELATIONSHIPS

Review the following passages, which use comparative patterns of thinking to organize the ideas being presented. For each passage do the following:

1. Identify the key ideas being compared.
2. Analyze the points of similarity and dissimilarity between the ideas being presented.
3. Describe the conclusions to which the passage leads you.

The difference between an American cookbook and a French one is that the former is very accurate and the second exceedingly vague. American recipes look like doctors' prescriptions. Perfect cooking seems to depend on perfect dosage. You are told to take a teaspoon of this and a tablespoon of that, then to stir them together until thoroughly blended. A French recipe seldom tells you how many ounces of butter to use to make *crêpes suzette,* or how many spoonfuls of oil should go into a salad dressing. French cookbooks are full of unusual measurements such as a *pinch* of pepper, a *soupcon* of garlic, or a *generous sprinkling* of brandy. There are constant references to seasoning *to taste,* as if the recipe were merely intended to give a general direction, relying on the experience and art of the cook to make the dish turn out right.

—Raoul de Roussy de Sales, "American and French Cookbooks"

The rapidity of change and the speed with which new situations are created follow the impetuous and heedless pace of man rather than the deliberate pace of nature. Radiation is no longer merely the background radiation of rocks, the bombardment of cosmic rays, the ultraviolet rays of the sun that have existed before there was any life on earth; radiation is now the unnatural creation of man's tampering with the atom. The chemicals to which life is asked to make its adjustment are no longer merely the calcium and silica and copper and all the rest of the minerals washed out of the rocks and carried in rivers to the sea; they are the synthetic creations of man's inventive mind, brewed in his laboratories, and having no counterparts in nature. To adjust to these chemicals would require time on the scale that is nature's; it would require not merely the years of a man's life but the life of generations. And even this, were it by some miracle possible, would be futile, for the new chemicals come from our laboratories in an endless stream; almost five hundred annually find their way into actual use in the United States alone.

—Rachel Carson, *Silent Spring*

ANALOGICAL RELATIONSHIPS

We noted earlier that comparative relationships involve examining the similarities and differences of two items in the same general category, such as items on a menu or methods of birth control. There is another kind of comparison, however, that does not focus on things in the same category. Such comparisons are known as *analogies*, and their goal is to clarify or illuminate a concept from one category by saying that it is the same as a concept from a very different category.

The purpose of an analogy is not the same as the purpose of the comparison we considered in the last section. At that time, we noted that the goal of comparing similar things is usually to make a choice and that the process of comparing can provide you with information on which you can base an intelligent decision. The main goal of an **analogy**, however, is not to choose or decide; it is to illuminate our understanding. Identifying similarities between very different things can often stimulate you to see these things in a new light, from a different perspective than you are used to. This can result in a clearer and more complete understanding of the things being compared. Consider the following example:

> Life's but a walking shadow, a poor player
> That struts and frets his hour upon the stage
> And then is heard no more.

—William Shakespeare, *Macbeth*

analogy A comparison between things that are basically dissimilar made for the purpose of illuminating our understanding of the things being compared.

In this famous quotation, Shakespeare is comparing two things that at first glance don't seem to have anything in common at all: life and an actor. Yet as you look more closely at the comparison, you begin to see that even though these two things are unlike in many ways, there are also some very important similarities between them. What are some of these similarities?

We often use analogies to get a point across to someone else. Used appropriately, analogies can help you illustrate and explain what you are trying to communicate. This is particularly important when you have difficulty finding the right words to represent your experiences. Powerful or complex emotions can make you speechless or make you say things like "Words cannot describe what I feel." Imagine that you are trying to describe your feelings of love and caring for another person. To illustrate and clarify the feelings you are trying to communicate, you might compare your feelings of love to "the first rose of spring," noting the following similarities:

- Like the first rose, this is the first great love of my life.
- Like the fragile yet supple petals of the rose, my feelings are tender and sensitive.
- Like the beauty of the rose, the beauty of my love should grow with time.

What are some other comparisons of love to a rose?

- Like the color of the rose, . . .
- Like the fragrance of the rose, . . .
- Like the thorns of the rose, . . .

Another favorite subject for analogies is the idea of the meaning or purpose of life, which the simple word *life* does not communicate. You have just seen Shakespeare's comparison of life to an actor. Here are some other popular analogies involving life. What are some points of similarity in each of these comparisons?

- Life is just a bowl of cherries.
- Life is a football game.
- Life is like a box of chocolates.
- "Life is a tale told by an idiot, full of sound and fury, signifying nothing." (Shakespeare)

Create an analogy for life representing some of your feelings, and explain the points of similarity.

- Life is . . .

In addition to communicating experiences that resist simple characterization, analogies are useful when you are trying to explain a complicated concept. For instance, you might compare the eye to a camera lens or the immunological system of the body to the National Guard (corpuscles are called to active duty and rush to the scene of danger when undesirable elements threaten the well-being of the organism).

Analogies possess the power to bring things to life by evoking images that illuminate the points of comparison. Consider the following analogies and explain the points of comparison that each author is trying to make.

- "Laws are like cobwebs, which may catch small flies, but let wasps and hornets break through." (Jonathan Swift)
- "I am as pure as the driven slush." (Tallulah Bankhead)
- "He has all the qualities of a dog, except its devotion." (Gore Vidal)

Similes and Metaphors From the examples discussed so far, you can see that analogies have two parts: an *original subject* and a *compared subject* (what the original is being likened to). In comparing your love to the first rose of spring, the original subject is your feelings of love and caring for someone, whereas the compared subject is what you are comparing those feelings to in order to illuminate and express them—namely, the first rose of spring.

In analogies, the connection between the original subject and the compared subject can either be obvious (explicit) or implied (implicit). For example, you can echo the lament of the great pool hustler Minnesota Fats and say, "A pool player in a tuxedo is like a hot dog with whipped cream on it." This is an obvious analogy (known as a **simile**) because you have explicitly noted the connection between the original subject (pool player in a tuxedo) and the compared subject (hot dog with whipped cream) by using the comparative term *like*. (Sometimes the structure of the sentence calls for *as* in a similar position.) You could also have used another form of obvious comparison, such as "is similar to," "reminds me of," or "makes me think of."

Alternatively, you could say, "A pool player in a tuxedo is a hot dog with whipped cream on it." Here, you are making an implied analogy (known as a **metaphor**) because you have not included any words that point out that you are making a comparison. Instead, you are stating that the original subject *is* the compared subject. Naturally, you are assuming that most people will understand that you are making a comparison between two different things and not describing a biological transformation.

Create a *simile* (obvious analogy) for a subject of your own choosing, noting at least two points of comparison.

Subject

1.

2.

Create a *metaphor* (implied analogy) for a subject of your own choosing, noting at least two points of comparison.

Subject

1.

2.

> **simile** An explicit comparison between basically dissimilar things made for the purpose of illuminating our understanding of the things being compared.

> **metaphor** An implied comparison between basically dissimilar things made for the purpose of illuminating our understanding of the things being compared.

Thinking Activity 8.5

ANALYZING ANALOGICAL RELATIONSHIPS

Read the following passage, which uses an analogical pattern of thinking. Identify the major ideas being compared and describe the points of similarity between them. Explain how the analogy helps illuminate the subject being discussed.

> The mountain guide, like the true teacher, has a quiet authority. He or she engenders trust and confidence so that one is willing to join the endeavor. The guide accepts his leadership role, yet recognizes that success (measured by the heights that are scaled) depends upon the close cooperation and active participation of each member of the group. He has crossed the terrain before and is familiar with the landmarks, but each trip is new and generates its own anxiety and excitement. Essential skills must be mastered; if they are lacking, disaster looms. The situation demands keen focus and rapt attention; slackness, misjudgment, or laziness can abort the venture. The teacher is not a pleader, not a performer, not a huckster, but a confident, exuberant guide on expeditions of shared responsibility into the most exciting and least-understood terrain on earth—the mind itself.
>
> —Nancy K. Hill, "Scaling the Heights: The Teacher as Mountaineer"

Thinking Activity 8.6

CREATING ANALOGIES TO CAPTURE LIFE

Analogies are powerful tools to capture our thoughts and emotions about events in our lives that are profound or traumatic. The authors of articles describing the terrorist attacks on the World Trade Center towers and the Pentagon, for example, used a variety of analogies to communicate their intense feelings, including

- A hellish storm of ash, glass, smoke, and leaping victims
- The twisted, smoking, ash-choked carcasses of the twin towers
- The similarity to the special effects in the Hollywood film *Independence Day*
- The deeply scarred Pentagon, still on fire, suggesting the loss of America's collective sense of security
- The intense heat causing the seemingly invincible steel beams of the towers to melt like cotton candy
- The scenario of a Tom Clancy thriller or Spielberg blockbuster now unfolding live on the world's television screens
- In a grotesque parody of the tickertape parades that characterize New York celebrations, thousands of pieces of office paper being carried on the gusting wind

Select an event that you have personally experienced that has an intense and profound meaning to you. Compose a description of that experience that makes use of powerful analogies to communicate your thoughts and feelings.

USING ANALOGIES TO SHAPE OUR WORLD

As we have seen, analogies are often visually evocative and can stimulate us to think about things in fresh, creative ways. However, modern research is discovering that analogies play an even more fundamental role in the way we shape our world and give it meaning. Read carefully the following article, "Thinking Literally: The Surprising Ways That Metaphors Shape Your World," by Drake Bennett, and then answer the questions that follow.

Thinking Passage

USING METAPHORS

Thinking Literally: The Surprising Ways That Metaphors Shape Your World

by Drake Bennett

. . .

Metaphors are literary creations—good ones help us see the world anew, in fresh and interesting ways, the rest are simply cliches: a test is a piece of cake, a completed task is a load off one's back, a momentary difficulty is a speed bump.

But whether they're being deployed by poets, politicians, football coaches, or realtors, metaphors are primarily thought of as tools for talking and writing—out of inspiration or out of laziness, we distill emotions and thoughts into the language of the tangible world. We use metaphors to make sense to one another.

Now, however, a new group of people has started to take an intense interest in metaphors: psychologists. Drawing on philosophy and linguistics, cognitive scientists have begun to see the basic metaphors that we use all the time not just as turns of phrase, but as keys to the structure of thought. By taking these everyday metaphors as literally as possible, psychologists are upending traditional ideas of how we learn, reason, and make sense of the world around us. The result has been a torrent of research testing the links between metaphors and their physical roots, with many of the papers reading as if they were commissioned by Amelia Bedelia, the implacably literal-minded children's book hero. Researchers have sought to determine whether the temperature of an object in someone's hands determines how "warm" or "cold" he considers a person he meets, whether the heft of a held object affects how "weighty" people consider topics they are presented with, or whether people think of the powerful as physically more elevated than the less powerful.

What they have found is that, in fact, we do. Metaphors aren't just how we talk and write, they're how we think. At some level, we actually do seem to understand temperament as a form of temperature, and we expect people's personalities to behave accordingly. What's more, without our body's instinctive sense for temperature—or position, texture, size, shape, or weight—abstract concepts like kindness and power, difficulty and purpose, and intimacy and importance would simply not make any sense to us. Deep down, we are all Amelia Bedelia.

Metaphors like this "don't invite us to see the world in new and different ways," says Daniel Casasanto, a cognitive scientist and researcher at the Max Planck Institute for Psycholinguistics in the Netherlands. "They enable us to understand the world at all." Our instinctive, literal-minded metaphorizing can make us vulnerable to what seem like simple tweaks to our physical environment, with ramifications for everything from how we build polling booths to how we sell cereal. And at a broader level it reveals just how much the human body, in all its particularity, shapes the mind, suggesting that much of what we think of as abstract reasoning is in fact a sometimes awkward piggybacking onto the mental tools we have developed to govern our body's interactions with its physical environment. Put another way, metaphors reveal the extent to which we think with our bodies.

"The abstract way we think is really grounded in the concrete, bodily world much more than we thought," says John Bargh, a psychology professor at Yale and leading researcher in this realm.

. . .

George Lakoff, a professor of linguistics at the University of California at Berkeley, and Mark Johnson, a philosophy professor at the University of Oregon, see human thought as metaphor-driven. But, in the two greatly influential books they have co-written on the topic, "Metaphors We Live By" in 1980 and "Philosophy in the Flesh" in 1999, Lakoff and Johnson focus on the deadest of dead metaphors, the ones that don't even rise to the level of cliche. They call them "primary metaphors," and they group them into categories like "affection is warmth," "important is big," "difficulties are burdens," "similarity is closeness," "purposes are destinations," and even "categories are containers."

Rather than so much clutter standing in the way of true understanding, to Lakoff and Johnson these metaphors are markers of the roots of thought itself. Lakoff and Johnson's larger argument is that abstract thought would be meaningless without bodily experience. And primary metaphors, in their ubiquity (in English and other languages) and their physicality, are some of their most powerful evidence for this.

"What we've discovered in the last 30 years is—surprise, surprise—people think with their brains," says Lakoff. "And their brains are part of their bodies."

Inspired by this argument, psychologists have begun to make their way, experiment by experiment, through the catalog of primary metaphors, altering one side of the metaphorical equation to see how it changes the other.

Bargh at Yale, along with Lawrence Williams, now at the University of Colorado, did studies in which subjects were casually asked to hold a cup of either iced or hot coffee, not knowing it was part of the study, then a few minutes later asked to rate the personality of a person who was described to them. The hot coffee group, it turned out, consistently described a warmer person—rating them as happier, more generous, more sociable, good-natured, and more caring—than the iced coffee group. The effect seems to run the other way, too: In a paper published last year, Chen-Bo Zhong and Geoffrey J. Leonardelli of the University of Toronto found that people asked to recall a time when they were ostracized gave lower estimates of room temperature than those who recalled a social inclusion experience.

In a paper in the current issue of *Psychological Science*, researchers in the Netherlands and Portugal describe a series of studies in which subjects were given clipboards on which to fill out questionnaires—in one study subjects were asked to estimate the value of several foreign currencies, in another they were asked to rate the city of Amsterdam and its mayor. The clipboards, however, were two different weights, and the subjects who took the questionnaire on the heavier clipboards tended to ascribe more metaphorical weight to the questions they were asked—they not only judged the foreign currencies to be more valuable, they gave more careful, considered answers to the questions they were asked.

Similar results have proliferated in recent years. One of the authors of the weight paper, Thomas Schubert, has also done work suggesting that the fact that we associate power and elevation ("your highness," "friends in high places") means we actually unconsciously look upward when we think about power. Bargh and Josh Ackerman at MIT's Sloan School of Business, in work that has yet to be published, have done studies in which subjects, after handling sandpaper-covered puzzle pieces, were less likely to describe a social situation as having gone smoothly. Casasanto has done work in which people who were told to move marbles from a lower tray up to a higher one while recounting a story told happier stories than people moving them down.

Several studies have explored the metaphorical connection between cleanliness and moral purity. In one, subjects who were asked to recall an unethical act, then given the choice between a pencil and an antiseptic wipe, were far more likely to choose the cleansing wipe than people who had been asked to recall an ethical act. In a follow-up study, subjects who recalled an unethical act acted less guilty after washing their hands. The researchers dubbed it the "Macbeth effect," after the guilt-ridden, compulsive hand washing of Lady Macbeth.

To the extent that metaphors reveal how we think, they also suggest ways that physical manipulation might be used to shape our thought. In essence, that is what much metaphor research entails. And while psychologists have thus far been primarily interested in using such manipulations simply to tease out an observable effect, there's no reason that they couldn't be put to other uses as well, by marketers, architects, teachers, parents, and litigators, among others.

A few psychologists have begun to ponder applications. . . . How much of an effect these tweaks might have in a real-world setting, researchers emphasize, remains to be seen. Still, it probably couldn't hurt to try a few in your own life. When inviting a new friend over, suggest a cup of hot tea rather than a cold beer. Keep a supply of soft, smooth objects on hand at work—polished pebbles, maybe, or a silk handkerchief—in case things start to feel too daunting. And if you feel a sudden pang of guilt about some long-ago transgression, try taking a shower.

QUESTIONS FOR ANALYSIS

1. What does the author mean when he says, "Metaphors aren't just how we talk and write, they're how we think. At some level, we actually do seem to understand temperament as a form of temperature, and we expect people's personalities to behave accordingly"?

2. Explain what the author means when he says "we think with our bodies" and "abstract thought would be meaningless without bodily experience." What examples does he provide to support these statements? Can you think of examples of your own that illustrate this insight?

3. Reread the selection by William Least Heat-Moon on pages 265–266 and underline all of the analogies (both similes and metaphors) that you can find.

4. Review the traveling experience that you wrote for Thinking Activity 6.3 on page 267 and revise it by creating analogies to express the thoughts and feelings you are expressing.

5. Identify some of your favorite metaphors which you use in your communications with others and explain their effectiveness. For example, what's the difference between saying that "you were involved in a stimulating discussion" and saying that "you felt like your head was so filled with ideas it was threatening to explode"?

THINKING CRITICALLY ABOUT NEW MEDIA

New Media Metaphors for Our World

The previous article explores how the metaphors we use shape our world and the way we make sense of it. The advent of new media has given us a large number of new concepts that we can use as metaphors to better understand our world. Identify five concepts from new media—hardware, wired, twittering, tagging, etc.—and then explain how they are or might be used as metaphors to shape and understand our world.

Causal Relationships

Causal patterns of thinking involve relating events in terms of the influence or effect they have on one another. For example, if you were right now to pinch yourself hard enough to feel it, you would be demonstrating a cause-and-effect relationship. Stated very simply, a *cause* is anything that is responsible for bringing about something else—usually termed the *effect*. The cause (the pinch) brings about the effect (the feeling of pain). When you make a causal statement, you are merely stating that a causal relationship exists between two or more things: The pinch *caused* the pain in my arm.

Of course, when you make (or think) causal statements, you do not always use the word *cause*. For example, the following statements are all causal statements. In each case, underline the cause and circle the effect.

- Since I was the last person to leave, I turned off the lights.

- Taking lots of vitamin C really cured me of that terrible cold I had.

- I accidentally toasted my hand along with the marshmallows by getting too close to the fire.

In these statements, the words *turned off, cured,* and *toasted* all point to the fact that something has caused something else to take place. Our language contains thousands of these causal "cousins."

You make causal statements all the time, and you are always thinking in terms of causal relationships. In fact, the goal of much of your thinking is to figure out why something happened or how something came about, for if you can figure out how and why things occur, you can then try to predict what will happen in the future. These predictions of anticipated results form the basis of many of your decisions. For example, the experience of toasting your hand along with the marshmallows might lead you to choose a longer stick for toasting—simply because you are able to figure out the causal relationships involved and then make predictions based on your understanding (namely, a longer stick will keep your hand farther away from the fire, which will prevent it from getting toasted).

Consider the following activities, which you probably performed today. Each activity assumes that certain causal relationships exist, which influenced your decision to perform them. Explain one such causal relationship for each activity.

- Brushing your teeth. The *causal relationship* is _____.

- Locking the door. The *causal relationship* is _____.

- Studying for an exam. The *causal relationship* is _____.

Thinking Critically About Visuals

The Places We Think

Empty office cubicles await the start of another workday. Cubicles arranged in large windowless spaces (often sarcastically referred to as "cube farms") became part of the American workplace in the mid-1960s, as the economy moved away from manufacturing and toward service- and information-based industries.

Michael Prince/Corbis

CAUSAL CHAINS

Although you tend to think of causes and effects in isolation—*A* caused *B*—in reality causes and effects rarely appear by themselves. Causes and effects generally appear as parts of more complex patterns, including three that we will examine here:

- Causal chains
- Contributory causes
- Interactive causes

Consider the following scenario: Your paper on the topic "Is there life after death?" is due Monday morning. You have reserved the whole weekend to work

In Chapter 6, we explored different layers of meanings of words. Now, apply those different kinds of meaning to a place—specifically, an office space. How does the physical space and "look" of an average office shape the activities and interactions that happen within its walls? How does your understanding of the meaning of "office" affect your response to this photograph?

This type of office design is based on the assumption that we think better when we think collaboratively, working with others instead of being separated from them in separate cubicles. Based on your work experience, how did the physical space of your workplace convey particular messages to your customers or influence the way in which you performed your job? How are office spaces and classrooms analogous to each other, in both their physical appearances and their ultimate purposes?

on it and are just getting started when the phone rings—your best friend from childhood is in town and wants to stay with you for the weekend. You say yes. By Sunday night, you've had a great weekend but have made little progress on your paper. You begin writing, when suddenly you feel stomach cramps—it must have been those raw oysters you had for lunch! Three hours later, you are ready to continue work. You brew a pot of coffee and get started. At 3:00 A.M. you are too exhausted to continue. You decide to get a few hours of sleep and set the alarm clock for 6:00 A.M., giving you plenty of time to finish up. When you wake up, you find that it's 9:00 A.M.—the alarm failed to go off! Your class starts in forty minutes, and you have no chance of getting the paper done on time. As you ride to school, you go over the causes for this disaster in your mind. You are no longer worried about life after death—you are now worried about life after this class!

- What causes in this situation are responsible for your paper being late?
- What do you think is the single most important cause?
- What do you think your teacher will identify as the most important cause? Why?

A *causal chain*, as you can see from these examples, is a situation in which one thing leads to another, which then leads to another, and so on. There is not just *one* cause for the resulting effect; there is a whole string of causes. Which cause in the string is the "real" cause? Your answer often depends on your perspective. In the example of the unfinished paper, you might see the cause as a faulty alarm clock. The teacher, however, might see the cause as an overall lack of planning. Proper planning, she might say, does not involve leaving things until the last minute, when unexpected problems can prevent you from reaching your goal. You can illustrate this causal structure with the following diagram:

Causal Chain

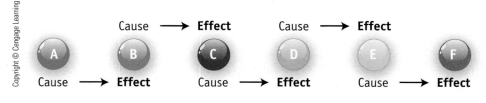

Copyright © Cengage Learning

Tatiana Popova/Shutterstock.com

Thinking Activity 8.7

CREATING A CAUSAL CHAIN

1. Create a similar scenario of your own, detailing a chain of causes that results in being late for class, standing someone up for a date, failing an exam, or producing another effect of your own choosing.
2. Review the scenario you have just created. Explain how the "real" cause of the final effect could vary, depending on your perspective.

CONTRIBUTORY CAUSES

In addition to operating in causal chains over a period of time (*A* leads to *B*, which leads to *C*, which leads to *D*, and so on), causes can act simultaneously to produce an effect. When this happens (as it often does), you have a situation in which a number of different causes are instrumental in bringing something about. Instead of working in isolation, each cause *contributes* to bringing about the final effect. In this situation, each cause serves to support and reinforce the action of the other causes, a structure illustrated in the following diagram:

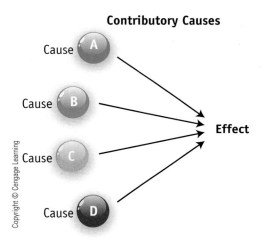

Contributory Causes

Cause **A**

Cause **B**

Cause **C**

Cause **D**

Effect

Copyright © Cengage Learning

Consider the following scenario: It is the end of the term, and you have been working incredibly hard at school—writing papers, preparing for exams, finishing up course projects. You haven't been getting enough sleep, and you haven't been eating regular or well-balanced meals. To make matters worse, you have been under intense pressure in your personal life, having serious arguments with the person you have been dating. You find that this situation is constantly on your mind. It is also the middle of the flu season, and many of the people you know have been sick with various bugs. Walking home from school one evening, you get soaked by an unexpected shower. By the time you get home, you are shivering. You soon find yourself in bed with a thermometer in your mouth—you are sick!

What was the "cause" of your getting sick? In this situation, you can see it probably was not just *one* thing that brought about your illness. It was probably a combination of different factors that led to your physical breakdown: having low resistance, getting wet and chilled, being exposed to various germs and viruses, being physically exhausted, not eating properly, and so on. Taken by itself, no one factor might have been enough to cause your illness. Working together, they all contributed to the final outcome.

Thinking Activity 8.8

CREATING A SCENARIO OF CONTRIBUTORY CAUSES

Create a similar scenario of your own, detailing the contributory causes that led to asking someone for a date, choosing a major, losing or winning a game you played in, or producing an effect of your own choosing.

INTERACTIVE CAUSES

Our examination of causal relationships has revealed that causes rarely operate in isolation but instead often influence (and are influenced by) other factors. Imagine that you are scheduled to give a speech to a large group of people. As the time for your moment in the spotlight approaches, you become anxious, with a dry mouth and throat, making your voice sound like a croak. The prospect of sounding like a bullfrog increases your anxiety, which in turn dries your mouth and constricts your throat further, reducing your croak to something much worse—silence.

This not uncommon scenario reveals the way different factors can relate to one another through reciprocal influences that flow back and forth from one to the other. This type of causal relationship, which involves an *interactive* pattern, is an extremely important way to organize and make sense of your experiences. For example, to understand social relationships, such as families, teams, or groups of friends, you have to understand the complex ways each individual influences—and is influenced by—all the other members of the group.

Understanding biological systems and other systems is similar to understanding social systems. To understand and explain how an organ like your heart, liver, or brain functions, you have to describe its complex, interactive relationships with all the other parts of your biological system.

Thinking Activity 8.9

ANALYZING CAUSAL RELATIONSHIPS

Read the following passage, which deals with the collapse of the World Trade Center. What are the causal relationships that resulted in the collapse?

· · ·

Since the collapse of the World Trade Center towers, on September 11th, structural engineers and their profession have received a great deal of public attention.

· · ·

Of course, you don't need an engineer to tell you why the towers fell down: two Boeing 767s, travelling at hundreds of miles an hour, and carrying more than ten thousand gallons of jet fuel each (if you converted the energy in the Oklahoma City bomb into jet fuel, it would amount to only fifty-one gallons), crashed into the north and south buildings at 8:45 A.M. and 9:06 A.M., respectively, causing them to fall—the south tower at 9:59 A.M. and the north tower at 10:28 A.M. Nor do we need a government panel to tell us that the best way to protect tall buildings is to keep airplanes out of them. Nevertheless, there is considerable debate among experts about precisely what order of events precipitated the collapse of each building, and whether the order was the same in both towers. Did the connections between the floors and the columns give way first or did the vertical supports that remained after the impact lose strength in the fire, and, if so, did the exterior columns or the core columns give way first?

· · ·

Was there any way for the structural engineers and architects involved in building the towers to know that they were going to collapse, and how quickly?

· · ·

Among the dozens of people I have spoken to recently who are experts in the construction of tall buildings (and many of whom witnessed the events of September 11th as they unfolded), only one said that he knew immediately, upon learning, from TV, of the planes' hitting the buildings, that the towers were going to fall. This was Mark Loizeaux, the president of Controlled Demolition Incorporated, a Maryland-based family business that specializes in reducing tall buildings to manageable pieces of rubble. "Within a nanosecond," he told me. "I said, 'It's coming down. And the second tower will fall first, because it was hit lower down.'"

· · ·

Loizeaux said he had an enhanced video of the collapses, and he talked about them in a way that indicated he had watched the video more than once. "First of all, you've got the obvious damage to the exterior frame from the airplane—if you count the number of external columns missing from the sides the planes hit, there are about two thirds of the total. And the buildings are still standing, which is amazing—even with all those columns missing, the gravity loads have found alternate pathways. O.K., but you've got fires—jet-fuel fires, which the building is not designed for, and you've also got lots of paper in there. Now, paper cooks. A paper fire is like a coal-mine fire: it keeps burning as long as oxygen gets to it. And you're high in the building, up in the wind, plenty of oxygen. So you've got a hot fire. And you've got these floor trusses, made of fairly thin metal, and fire protection has been knocked off most of them by the impact. And you have all this open space—clear span from perimeter to core—with no columns or partition walls, so the airplane is going to skid right through that space to the core, which doesn't have any reinforced concrete in it. Just sheetrock covering steel, and the fire is going to spread everywhere immediately, and no fire-protection systems are working—the sprinkler heads shorn off by the airplanes, the water pipes in the core are likely cut. So what's going to happen? Floor A is going to fall onto floor B, which falls onto floor C; the unsupported columns will buckle; and the weight of everything above the crash site falls onto what remains below—bringing loads of two thousand pounds per square foot, plus the force of the impact, onto floors designed to bear one hundred pounds per square foot. It has to fall."

· · ·

—John Seabrook, "The Tower Builder"

Thinking Critically About Visuals

Why . . .?

Mai/Time & Life Images/Time & Life Pictures/Getty Images

What is the emotional impact of this photograph on you? How does the juxtaposition of the World Trade Center wreckage with a New York City firefighter affect your perception? When you see photographs like this of the WTC remnant forked into the ground, do they have any special symbolic meaning for you?

Thinking Passage

GENETICALLY MODIFIED FOOD

The impact of human civilization on the environment has taken on increasing urgency as global warming, the razing of rain forests, the search for sustainable fuel sources, and our dependence on factory-farmed or genetically modified food are discussed and debated in the media. All these factors affect the most basic aspects of our lives, from the quality of our air to the safety of our next meal. In the following article, "GMO's: Fooling—Er, 'Feeding'—the World for 20 Years," the authors argue that we are threatening our health by ingesting GMO's (genetically modified organisms). And although proponents of GMO's claim that they represent an important weapon in attacking the problem of world hunger, the authors contend that GMO's are actually having the effect of *increasing* world hunger. And finally, to make things worse, it's almost impossible to avoid GMOs because, unlike in Europe, manufacturers are not required to label their products as being genetically modified. In counterpoint to this perspective is the article "*Eating the Genes*," in which Richard Manning argues that genetically modified food is an essential strategy in developing countries, the risks of which are of less consequence than the alternative of starvation and malnutrition. The final article, by the editors of *Scientific American*, bemoans the fact that seed companies control GMO crop research, making it nearly impossible to evaluate the claims and risks of having GMOs in our food supply. Once you have carefully read the articles, respond to the questions that follow.

GMOs: Fooling—Er, "Feeding"—The World for 20 Years

False in every case, and in this article we'll show how easy it is to debunk these myths. All it takes is a dispassionate, objective look at twenty years of commercial GE planting and the research that supposedly backs it up. The conclusion is clear: GMOs are part of the problem, not part of the solution.

MYTH: GE crops will end world hunger

FACT: GE crops have nothing to do with ending world hunger, no matter how much GE spokespeople like to expound on this topic. Three comments give the lie to their claim:

- FAO data clearly show that the *world produces plenty of food to feed everyone, year after year*. Yet hunger is still with us. That's because hunger is not primarily a question of productivity but of access to arable land and resources. Put bluntly: *Hunger is caused by poverty and exclusion*.

- Today's commercial GE crops weren't designed to fight hunger in the first place. They aren't even mainly for human consumption. Practically the entire area planted to GE crops

Source: GMOs: Fooling—Er, "Feeding"—The World for 20 Years (GRAIN, 15 May 2013).

consists of soybeans, corn, canola, and cotton. The first three of these are used almost exclusively to make cattle feed, car fuel, and industrial oils for the United States and Europe, while cotton goes into clothing.

- More damning, there appears to be an iniquitous causeandeffect relationship between GE crops and rural hunger. In countries like Brazil and Argentina, gigantic "green deserts" of corn and soybeans invade peasants' land, depriving them—or outright robbing them—of their means of subsistence. The consequence is hunger, abject poverty, and agrotoxin poisoning for rural people. *The truth is that GE crops are edging out food on millions of hectares of fertile farmland.*

In the year GMO seeds were first planted, 800 million people worldwide were hungry. Today, with millions of hectares of GMOs in production, 1 billion are hungry. When exactly do these crops start "feeding the world"?

MYTH: GE crops are more productive

FACT: Not true. Look at the data from the country with the longest experience of GMOs: the United States. In the most extensive and rigorous study, the Union of Concerned Scientists analyzed twenty years of GE crops and concluded that genetically engineered herbicide-tolerant soybeans and corn are no more productive than conventional plants and methods. Furthermore 86% of the corn productivity increases obtained in the past twenty years have been due to conventional methods and practices. Other studies have found GE productivity to be lower than conventional.

Crop plants are complex living beings, not Lego blocks. Their productivity is a function of multiple genetic and environmental factors, not some elusive "productivity gene." You can't just flip a genetic switch and turn on high productivity, nor would any responsible genetic engineer make such a claim. Even after all this time, GE methods are quite rudimentary. Proponents of the technology count it a success if they manage to transfer even two or three functional genes into one plant.

The bottom line is that twenty years and untold millions of dollars of research have resulted in a grand total of two marketable traits—herbicide tolerance and Bt pest resistance (see below). Neither has anything to do with productivity.

MYTH: GE crops will eliminate agrichemicals.

FACT: It's the reverse: GE crops increase the use of harmful agrichemicals. Industry people try to put this myth over by touting the "Bt gene" from the *Bacillus thuringiensis* bacteria, which produces a toxin lethal to some corn and cotton worms. The plants produce their own pesticide, supposedly obviating the need to spray. But with such large areas planted to Bt monocultures, the worms have quickly developed resistance to Bt worse, a host of formerly unknown secondary pests now have to be controlled with more chemicals.

The other innovation trumpeted by the "genetically modified corporations" consists of plants that can withstand high doses of herbicides. This allows vast monocultures to be sprayed from the air, year after year on the same site. It's a convenience for industrial farmers that has abetted the spectacular expansion of soybeans in recent years. Thirty years ago there were no soybeans in Argentina; now they take up half the country's arable land. Concurrently, the amount of the herbicide glyphosate sprayed in

Argentina has skyrocketed from 8 million litres in 1995 to 200 million litres today—a *twentyfold* increase, all for use in GE soy production.

The same thing is happening in the United States. Herbicide tolerant GMOs have opened the floodgates, and glyphosate and other herbicides are pouring through onto farmers' fields. In 2011, US farmers using this type of GMO sprayed 24% more herbicides than their colleagues planting conventional seeds. Why? For reasons any evolutionary biologist could have predicted: the weeds are evolving chemical resistance. In short, the GE "revolution" is an environmental problem, not a solution.

MYTH: Farmers can decide for themselves. After all, GMOs can peacefully coexist with other crops

It sure doesn't look that way. GE boosters may claim nobody's forcing farmers to use GMOs, but a pesky little fact of basic biology implicates non-GE farmers against their will. It's called cross-pollination: Plants of the same species interbreed, and sooner or later the genes artificially inserted in the GE crops cross into the conventional crops.

In Canada, the widespread growing of genetically engineered canola has contaminated nearly all the conventional canola and in so doing wiped out organic canola production. Similar contamination has been found in corn crops around the world. The introduction of GE seed is especially alarming when there is potential for contamination of local varieties. Mexico is the centre of origin and diversification of corn. For years now, Mexican indigenous communities have been noticing odd traits appearing in some of their varieties. Various studies confirm that this is because of contamination by GE corn imported from the United States. Now, the Mexican government is proposing to allow multinationals to plant up to 2.4 million ha of GE corn in the country. If this project goes ahead, it will not only be an attack on the food sovereignty of the Mexican people: it will be a threat to the biodiversity of one of the world's most important staple food crops.

In the Spanish state of Aragón, farm and environmental organizations have been complaining since 2005 that over 40% of organic grain has traces of GE content and can no longer be sold as organic or GMO-free.

What's really perverse about this fake "freedom to farm" argument is that certain transnationals have been forcing farmers to pay for seeds they never planted. In the United States, Monsanto has taken hundreds of farmers to court for supposedly infringing its intellectual-property rights. Monsanto detectives roam the countryside like debt collectors, looking for "their genes" in farmers' fields. In many cases, the genes got there because the farmers either purchased contaminated seed or had their own crops contaminated by a neighbour's field. Whatever the case, it's a lucrative strategy that has brought in millions of extra dollars for the corporation. And it has the added benefit of scaring farmers away from buying anything but Monsanto seeds. Sounds a lot more like the "freedom" to do exactly what the multinationals tell you to.

MYTH: GE crops pose no threat to health and the environment

At the very least, the biosafety of transgenic crops is an open question. Do we really want to entrust our health to an industrial agriculture system in which GE purveyors control food security offices and dictate their own standards? I don't think so. Food sovereignty requires that the people, not the companies, have control over what we eat.

Nevertheless, our plates are now filling up with food items from plants with altered DNA and heavy pesticide loads, and we are told to simply shut up and eat. Concerns have been heightened by a number of credible reports on GMOs and their attendant herbicides:

- The American Academy of Environmental Medicine (AAEM) stated in 2009 that genetically engineered foods"pose a serious health risk." Citing various studies, it concluded that "there is more than a casual association between GE foods and adverse health effects" and that these foods "pose a serious health risk in the areas of toxicology, allergy and immune function, reproductive health, and metabolic, physiologic and genetic health."

- The latest studies by Dr. Gilles-Éric Séralini looked at rats fed glyphosatetolerant GE maize for two years. These rats showed greater and earlier mortality in addition to hormonal effects, mammary tumors in females, and liver and kidney disease.

- A recent study at the University of Leipzig (Germany) found high concentrations of glyphosate, the main ingredient in Roundup, in urine samples from city dwellers— from 5 to 20 times greater than the limit for drinking water.

- Professor Andrés Carrasco of the CONICET-UBA Molecular Embryology Lab at the University of Buenos Aires medical school (Argentina) has unveiled a study showing that glyphosate herbicides cause malformations in frog and chicken embryos at doses much lower than those used in agriculture. The malformations were of a type similar to those observed in human embryos exposed to these herbicides.

Finally, there is the incontrovertible evidence that glyphosate can have a direct impact on human beings, causing abortions, illnesses, and even death in high enough doses, as explained by Sofía Gatica, the Argentine winner of the latest Goldman prize. Our health is ours to defend, and so are our farms, and so is the health of the food supply that will nourish the generations to come. Food sovereignty now!

Eating the Genes:
What the Green Revolution Did for Grain, Biotechnology May Do for Protein
by Richard Manning

Fears that genetically engineered foods will damage the environment have fueled controversy in the developed world. The debate looks very different when framed not by corporations and food activists but by three middle-aged women in saris working in a Spartan lab in Pune, India. The three, each with a doctoral degree and a full career in biological research, are studying the genes of chickpeas, but they begin their conversation by speaking of suicides.

The villain in their discussion is an insidious little worm, a pod borer, which makes its way unseen into the ripening chickpea pods and eats the peas. It comes every year, laying waste to some fields while sparing others. Subsistence farmers expecting a bumper crop instead find the fat pods hollow at harvest. Dozens will then kill themselves rather than face the looming hunger of their families. So while the battle wages over "frankenfood" in the well-fed countries of the world, here in this Pune lab the arguments quietly disappear.

Source: "Eating the Gene," by Richard Manning, July 2001, in *Technology*, published by MIT Review, http://www.technologyreview.com/Biotech/12499/. Copyright Technology Review 2001.

Thinking Critically About Visuals

"Are You What You Eat?"

Much of the food that we are ingesting has been treated with pesticides and genetically modified in ways that are unknown to us. Should we be concerned about the history of the food we are eating, the ways in which it has been treated and genetically altered before it arrives on our table?

Abid Katib/Getty Images

These two photos illustrate contrasting approaches to raising crops. The first photo depicts farmers spraying a crop with increasingly powerful pesticides, while the second illustrates an "organic" alternative to pesticides, in this case using lady bugs to devour destructive pests. Which food would you rather eat? Why?

ideeone/iStockphoto.com

A generation ago the world faced starvation, and India served as the poster child for the coming plague, occupying roughly the same position in international consciousness then that sub-Saharan Africa does today. The Green Revolution of the 1960s changed all that, with massive increases in grain production, especially in India, a country that now produces enough wheat, rice, sorghum, and maize to feed its people. Green Revolution methods, however, concentrated on grains, ignoring such crops as chickpeas and lentils, the primary sources of protein in the country's vegetarian diet. As a consequence, per capita production of carbohydrates from grain in India tripled. At the same time, largely because of population growth, per capita protein production halved.

The gains in grain yield came largely from breeding plants with shorter stems, which could support heavier and more bountiful seed heads. To realize this opportunity, farmers poured on nitrogen and water: globally, there was a sevenfold increase in fertilizer use between 1950 and 1990. Now, artificial sources of nitrogen, mostly from fertilizer, add more to the planet's nitrogen cycle than natural sources, contributing to global warming, ozone depletion, and smog. Add to this the massive loads of pesticides used against insects drawn to this bulging monoculture of grain, and one begins to see the rough outlines of environmental damage the globe cannot sustain.

During this same revolutionary period, India and other countries, including Mexico, Brazil, Chile, and Cuba, developed scientific communities capable of addressing many of their own food problems. High on their list is the promise of genetic engineering (see "New Markets for Biotech"). In India, researchers have found a natural resistance to pod borers in two other crops, the Asian bean and peanuts, and are trying to transfer the responsible gene to chickpeas. If they are successful, farmers will not only get more protein; they will also avoid insecticides. "The farmer has not to spray anything, has not to dust anything," D. R. Bapat, a retired plant breeder, told me. He need only plant a new seed.

This is the simple fact that makes genetic modification so attractive in the developing world. Seeds are packages of genes and genes are information—exceedingly valuable and powerful information. Biotech corporations can translate that information into profits. Yet when those same packets of power are developed by public-sector scientists in places like India, they become a tool, not for profit, but for quickly distributing important information. There is no more efficient means of spreading information than a seed.

The above argument built only slowly in my mind in the course of researching a book (*Food's Frontier: The Next Green Revolution*) that profiled nine food projects in the developing world, all of which were carried out largely by scientists native to the countries I visited. I expected to encounter low-technology projects appropriate for the primitive conditions of subsistence agriculture in the developing world—and I did. But I also found, in all nine cases, a sophisticated and equally appropriate use of genetic research or genetic engineering.

A lab in Uganda, for example, could not regularly flush its toilets for lack of running water, but could tag DNA. This tagging ability, used in six of the projects I studied, allows researchers to understand and accelerate the breeding of new strains. Typically, an effort to breed a disease- or pest-resistant strain of a crop can involve ten years of testing to verify the trait. Using genetic markers cuts that time in half—a difference that gains urgency in countries where test plots are surrounded by poor farmers whose crops are failing for want of that very trait.

In this manner, by allowing researchers to accelerate the development of new, pest-resistant sources of protein, genetic engineering can help fulfill the decades-old promise of the Green Revolution. Our last revolution created a world awash in grain. But if Uganda is to get better sweet potatoes, Peru better mashua, and India better chickpeas, then research on those orphan crops will have to catch up rapidly. Biotechnology can help.

Food researchers in developing countries are understandably worried they will be hampered by the controversy over genetically modified foods. Meanwhile, they have a hard time understanding why genetic engineering is the focus of such concern. The gains of the Green Revolution, after all—and for that matter the gains of 10,000 years of agriculture—have in many cases come from mating unrelated species of plants to create something new and better. Every new strain has brought with it the potential dangers now being ascribed with apparent exclusivity to genetic engineering, such as the creation of superresistant pests. Genetic engineering merely refines the tools.

When viewed from labs surrounded by subsistence farmers, where food research is a matter of life and death rather than an intellectual debate, genetic engineering is a qualified good—not without problems and dangers, but still of great promise. Genetic modification of foods becomes a natural extension of the millennia-old practice of plant breeding, less environmentally damaging than many modern alternatives. In the end, DNA is knowledge, which we can hope will build to wisdom, from which we may one day create an agriculture that both supports our population and coexists peacefully with our planet.

Do Seed Companies Control GM Crop Research?

by the Editors of *Scientific American*

Advances in agricultural technology—including, but not limited to, the genetic modification of food crops—have made fields more productive than ever. Farmers grow more crops and feed more people using less land. They are able to use fewer pesticides and to reduce the amount of tilling that leads to erosion. And within the next two years, agritech companies plan to introduce advanced crops that are designed to survive heat waves and droughts, resilient characteristics that will become increasingly important in a world marked by a changing climate.

Unfortunately, it is impossible to verify that genetically modified crops perform as advertised. That is because agritech companies have given themselves veto power over the work of independent researchers.

To purchase genetically modified seeds, a customer must sign an agreement that limits what can be done with them. (If you have installed software recently, you will recognize the concept of the end-user agreement.) Agreements are considered necessary to protect a company's intellectual property, and they justifiably preclude the replication of the genetic enhancements that make the seeds unique. But agritech companies such as Monsanto, Pioneer and Syngenta go further. For a decade their user agreements have explicitly forbidden the use of the seeds for any independent research. Under the threat of litigation, scientists cannot test a seed to explore the different conditions under which it thrives or fails. They cannot compare seeds from one company against those from another company. And perhaps most important, they cannot examine whether the genetically modified crops lead to unintended environmental side effects.

Research on genetically modified seeds is still published, of course. But only studies that the seed companies have approved ever see the light of a peer-reviewed journal. In a number of cases, experiments that had the implicit go-ahead from the seed company were later blocked from publication because the results were not flattering. "It is important to understand that it is not always simply a matter of blanket denial of all research requests, which is bad enough," wrote Elson J. Shields, an entomologist at Cornell University, in a letter to an official at the Environmental Protection Agency (the body tasked with regulating the environmental consequences of genetically modified crops), "but selective denials and permissions based on industry perceptions of how 'friendly' or 'hostile' a particular scientist may be toward [seed enhancement] technology."

Shields is the spokesperson for a group of 24 corn insect scientists that opposes these practices. Because the scientists rely on the cooperation of the companies for their research—they must, after all, gain access to the seeds for studies—most have chosen to remain anonymous for fear of reprisals. The group has submitted a statement to the EPA protesting that "as a result of restricted access, no truly independent research can be legally conducted on many critical questions regarding the technology."

It would be chilling enough if any other type of company were able to prevent independent researchers from testing its wares and reporting what they find—imagine car companies trying to quash head-to-head model comparisons done by *Consumer Reports*, for example. But when scientists are prevented from examining the raw ingredients in our nation's food supply or from testing the plant material that covers a large portion of the country's agricultural land, the restrictions on free inquiry become dangerous.

Although we appreciate the need to protect the intellectual property rights that have spurred the investments into research and development that have led to agritech's successes, we also believe food safety and environmental protection depend on making plant products available to regular scientific scrutiny. Agricultural technology companies should therefore immediately remove the restriction on research from their end-user agreements. Going forward, the EPA should also require, as a condition of approving the sale of new seeds, that independent researchers have unfettered access to all products currently on the market. The agricultural revolution is too important to keep locked behind closed doors.

QUESTIONS FOR ANALYSIS

1. What does it mean to say that a plant has been genetically "modified" or "engineered"? Seed companies contend that these genetically modified organisms (GMOs) increase crop yield and reduce the use of pesticides. Based on the reasons and evidence included in this article, has this proved to be the case? Why or why not?

2. The authors of the article make their case by debunking "myths" perpetrated by GMO seed companies. What are the reasons and evidence that they present to critically evaluate each of the following myths?
   - MYTH: GE crops will end world hunger.
   - MYTH: GE crops are more productive.
   - MYTH: GE crops will eliminate agrichemicals.
   - MYTH: Farmers can decide for themselves. After all, GMO's can peacefully coexist with other crops.
   - MYTH: GE crops pose no threat to health and the environment.

3. Unlike Europe where produce that is genetically modified is clearly indicated on the label, people in the United States have no idea whether the food they are eating has been genetically modified. Why are Europeans so concerned? Why isn't our produce clearly labeled? Should we be concerned?

4. Richard Manning, in his article "Eating the Genes," argues that in developing countries, the risks to the environment or people posed by genetically engineered foods is of much less consequence that the reality of starvation

and suicides by farmers whose crops are ruined by insects. Do you agree with the point he is making? Why or why not?

5. In contrast to developed countries like the United States and Europe, where biotechnology is controlled by large profit-oriented biotech corporations, in developing countries sophisticated native public-sector scientists are developing new disease-resistant and pest-resistant biotech crops for their countries. Which approach to biotechnology is better? Why?

6. In asking "Do Seed Companies Control GM Crop Research?" the editors of *Scientific American* are extremely concerned that companies that manufacture GM food control research on the efficacy and dangers of GMOs. They alone decide who can do the research, the nature of the research, and the publication of the research findings. Why do the authors believe this to be a practice of grave concern?

7. Most GMO research has been done on nonhuman animals such as rats and livestock, revealing serious health risks. Although these studies are suggestive, research on humans is obviously needed but blocked by the seed companies. Are you concerned about potential health risks associated with GMO's? If so, what steps might you take to address this risk?

CHAPTER 8   Reviewing and Viewing

Summary

- We use various *thinking patterns* to make sense of the world through the cognitive processes of "relating" and "organizing."
- Three important thinking patterns are *chronological* and *process* relationships; *comparative* and *analogical relationships;* and *causal* relationships.
- *Chronological* relationships relate events in time sequence. *Process* relationships relate aspects of the growth or development of an event or object.
- *Comparative* relationships relate things in the same general category in terms of similarities and dissimilarities.
- *Analogical* relationships relate things belonging to different categories in terms of each other for the purpose of illuminating our understanding.
- *Causal* relationships relate events in terms of the way some event(s) is/are responsible for bringing about some other event(s).
- There are different *types* of causal relationships, including *causal chains, contributory causes,* and *interactive causes.*
- As you refine your abilities to relate and organize the conceptual vocabulary of your mind, you are improving the power and creativity of your thinking processes while developing a more accurate understanding of the world.

Assessing Your Strategies and Creating New Goals

How Well Do I Understand Fundamental Thinking Relationships?

We construct an intelligible world by means of concepts, as we saw in the last chapter. But to fully develop a meaningful picture of our complex world, we also have to understand how we relate concepts one to the other by means of fundamental thinking relationships. Described below are some key thinking relationships: chronological and process; comparative and analogical; and causal. Evaluate your position regarding each of these thinking patterns and use this self-evaluation guide to help you become more competent in using and understanding them.

Develop a Clear Understanding of Chronological and Process Relationships

I have a clear understanding of the nature of chronological and process relationships.	I lack a clear understanding of the nature of chronological and process relationships.
5 4 3 2 1	

Chronology (relating events in terms of time) and process (relating events in terms of steps toward a goal) are two of the most basic ways we relate events in the world. It is important to know how to use these thinking patterns correctly, whether we are narrating an account or understanding the steps or stages in completing a process.

Strategy: Select a series of events that occurred over time and create an effective chronological account of them; then do the same for a process involving a number of steps and stages. Share these accounts with someone else to determine how effective your descriptions are and then make appropriate revisions.

Develop a Clear Understanding of Comparative and Analogical Relationships

I have a clear understanding of the nature of comparative and analogical relationships.	I lack a clear understanding of the nature of comparative and analogical relationships.
5 4 3 2 1	

Many of our decisions in the world are based on the ability to compare various possibilities in terms of relevant similarities, while much of our communication with others is enriched by using analogies between dissimilar things.

Strategy: Make a conscious effort in the next few days to use comparative relationships in the organized way described in the chapter, and do the same thing for analogical relationships. Record the effects of these projects, and consider how you might improve on your performance.

Develop a Clear Understanding of Causal Relationships

I have a clear understanding of the nature of causal relationships.	I lack a clear understanding of the nature of causal relationships.
5 4 3 2 1	

Causal relationships are the bedrock of science, and we depend on them in virtually every area of our lives. Yet people often misuse and misunderstand the logic of causal relationships.

Strategy: *Over the course of the next several days, make note of some of the more complex causal relationships you encounter in your courses and outside of school. Then evaluate these causal relationships in terms of the criteria described in this chapter.*

Suggested Films

The Future of Food (2004)

In this documentary, filmmaker Deborah Koons Garcia explores the ethical, environmental, political, legal, and health issues related to genetically modified foods. The film provides insight into the multitude of factors that are changing the food we eat and the effects of modified foods on individuals and our world.

Memento (2000)

How is memory connected to identity? In this neo-noir psychological thriller, a man who has lost the ability to create new memories and cannot recall his most recent memories attempts to reconstruct his identity and the events of his life in order to solve the murder of his wife. The film follows two narratives—one tracks his investigation while the second moves backward in time through a series of flashbacks.

Monsoon Wedding (2001)

How does one's culture influence personal choices in relationships? In modern-day India, a young woman from an upper-class family is about to marry a man she has never met, according to the traditions of arranged weddings. This film, which follows the celebrations and events leading up to the wedding, portrays five different romantic relationships that threaten the limits of class, nation, and morality.

No Impact Man: The Documentary (2009)

A family attempts to live for a year without making an impact on the environment by reexamining how and what they eat, how they use and dispose of resources, the types of transportation they use, and other aspects of daily life. Their yearlong journey provides insight into the direct effects that we all have on our environment.

Super Size Me (2004)

What are the responsibilities of business to the health of its customers? Director Morgan Spurlock documents thirty days in which he only eats McDonald's food. He explores the physical and psychological effects of his experiment and raises ethical questions regarding the role of America's commercial food industry in contributing to obesity.

In this photo, college volunteers work on renovating a house with the nonprofit group Habitat for Humanity in Silver Spring, Maryland. Do you think we have a moral responsibility to help others in need?

Thinking Critically About Moral Issues

Make morality a priority

Discover the "natural law"

Consider the ethic of care

Develop an informed intuition

The Thinker's Guide to Moral Decision Making
Your moral compass

Accept responsibility

Choose to be a moral person

Consider the ethic of justice

Promote happiness

Justify moral judgments

The abilities that you develop as a critical thinker are designed to help you think your way through all of life's situations. One of the most challenging and complex of life's areas is the realm of moral issues and decisions. Every day of your life you make moral choices, decisions that reflect your own internal moral compass. Often we are not aware of the deeper moral values that drive our choices, and we may even be oblivious to the fact that the choices we are making have a moral component. For example, consider the following situations:

- You consider purchasing a research paper from an online service, and you plan to customize and submit the paper as your own.
- As part of a mandatory biology course you are taking, you are required to dissect a fetal pig, something that you find morally offensive.
- A friend of yours has clearly had too much to drink at a party, yet he's insisting that he feels sober enough to drive home.
- The romantic partner of a friend of yours begins flirting with you.
- You find yourself in the middle of a conversation with people you admire in which mean-spirited things are being said about a friend of yours.
- Although you had plans to go away for the weekend, a friend of yours is extremely depressed and you're concerned about leaving her alone.
- A good friend asks you to provide some "hints" about an upcoming exam that you have already taken.
- You and several others were involved in a major mistake at work, and your supervisor asks you to name the people responsible.
- A homeless woman asks you for a donation, but you're not convinced that she will use your money constructively.
- Although you have a lot of studying to do, you had promised to participate in a charity walk-a-thon.

These and countless other situations like them are an integral part of the choices that we face each day as we shape our lives and create ourselves. In each case, the choices involved share the following characteristics:

- The choices involve your treatment of other people (or animals).
- There may not be one obvious "right" or "wrong" answer, and the dilemma can be discussed and debated.
- There are likely to be both positive and/or negative consequences to yourself or others, depending on the choices that you make.
- Your choices are likely to be guided by values to which you are committed and that reflect a moral reasoning process that leads to your decisions.
- The choices involve the concept of moral responsibility.

Critical thinking plays a uniquely central role in helping us to develop enlightened values, use informed moral reasoning, and make well-supported ethical conclusions. Most areas of human study are devoted to describing the world and how people behave, the way things *are*. Ethics and morality are concerned with helping people evaluate how the world *ought* to be and what courses of action people *should* take; to do this well, we need to fully apply our critical-thinking abilities. Thinking critically about moral issues will provide you with the opportunity to refine and enrich your own moral compass, so that you will be better equipped to successfully deal with the moral dilemmas that we all encounter in the course of living. As the Greek philosopher Aristotle observed:

> The ultimate purpose in studying ethics is not as it is in other inquiries, the attainment of theoretical knowledge; we are not conducting this inquiry in order to know what virtue is, but in order to become good, else there would be no advantage in studying it.

This was precisely how Socrates envisioned his central mission in life, to remind people of the moral imperative to attend to their souls and create upstanding character and enlightened values within themselves:

> For I do nothing but go about persuading you all, old and young alike, not to take thought for your persons or your properties, but first and chiefly to care about the greatest improvement of your soul. I tell you that virtue is not given by money, but that from virtue comes money and every other good of man, public as well as private. This is my teaching.

What Is Ethics?

Ethics and *morals* are terms that refer to the principles that govern our relationships with other people: the ways we *ought* to behave, the rules and standards that we *should* employ in the choices we make. The ethical and moral concepts that we use to evaluate these behaviors include right and wrong, good and bad, just and unjust, fair and unfair, responsible and irresponsible.

The study of **ethics** is derived from the ancient Greek word *ethos*, which refers to moral purpose or character—as in "a person of upstanding character." *Ethos* is also associated with the idea of "cultural customs or habits." In addition, the etymology of the word **moral** can be traced back to the Latin word *moralis*, which also means "custom." Thus, the origins of these key concepts reflect both the private and the public nature of the moral life: we strive to become morally enlightened people, but we do so within the social context of cultural customs.

ethical, morals of or concerned with the judgment of the goodness or badness of human action and character

Ethical and *moral* are essentially equivalent terms that can be used interchangeably, though there may be shadings in meaning that influence which term is used. For example, we generally speak about medical or business "ethics" rather than "morality," though there is not a significant difference in meaning. *Value* is the general term we use to characterize anything that possesses intrinsic worth, that we prize, esteem, and regard highly, based on clearly defined standards. Thus, you may value your devoted pet, your favorite jacket, and a cherished friendship, each based on different *standards* that establish and define their worth to you. One of the most important value domains includes your *moral values*, those personal qualities and rules of conduct that distinguish a person (and group of people) of upstanding character. Moral values are reflected in such questions as

- Who is a "good person" and what is a "good action"?
- What can we do to promote the happiness and well-being of others?
- What moral obligations do we have toward other people?
- When should we be held morally responsible?
- How do we determine which choice in a moral situation is right or wrong, just or unjust?

Although thinking critically about moral values certainly involves the moral customs and practices of various cultures, its true mandate goes beyond simple description to analyzing and evaluating the justification and logic of these moral beliefs. Are there universal values or principles that apply to all individuals in all cultures? If so, on what basis are these values or principles grounded? Are some ethical customs and practices more enlightened than others? If so, what are the reasons or principles upon which we can make these evaluations? Is there a "good life" to which all humans should aspire? If so, what are the elements of such a life, and on what foundation is such an ideal established? These are questions that we will be considering in this chapter, but they are questions of such complexity that you will likely be engaged in thinking about them throughout your life.

Who is a moral person? In the same way that you were able to define the key qualities of a critical thinker, you can describe the essential qualities of a moral person.

Thinking Activity 9.1

WHO IS A MORAL PERSON?

Think of someone you know whom you consider to be a person of outstanding moral character. This person doesn't have to be perfect—he or she doubtless has flaws. Nevertheless, this is a person you admire, someone you would like to emulate. After fixing this person in your mind, write down this person's qualities that, in your mind, qualify him or her as a morally upright individual. For each quality, try to think of an example of when the person displayed it. For example:

> **Moral Courage:** Edward is a person I know who possesses great moral courage. He is always willing to do what he believes to be the right thing, even if his point of view is unpopular with the other people involved. Although he may endure criticism for taking a principled stand, he never compromises and

instead calmly explains his point of view with compelling reasons and penetrating questions.

If you have an opportunity, ask some people you know to describe their idea of a moral person, and compare their responses to your own.

For millennia, philosophers and religious thinkers have endeavored to develop ethical systems to guide our conduct. But most people in our culture today have not been exposed to these teachings in depth. They have not challenged themselves to think deeply about ethical concepts, nor have they been guided to develop coherent, well-grounded ethical systems of their own. In many cases people attempt to navigate their passage through the turbulent and treacherous waters of contemporary life without an accurate moral compass, relying instead on a tangled mélange of childhood teachings, popular wisdom, and unreliable intuitions. These homegrown and unreflective ethical systems are simply not up to the task of sorting out the moral complexities in our bewildering and fast-paced world; thus, they end up contributing to the moral crisis described in the following passage by the writer M. Scott Peck:

> A century ago, the greatest dangers we faced arose from agents outside ourselves: microbes, flood and famine, wolves in the forest at night. Today the greatest dangers—war, pollution, starvation—have their source in our own motives and sentiments: greed and hostility, carelessness and arrogance, narcissism and nationalism. The study of values might once have been a matter of primarily individual concern and deliberation as to how best to lead the "good life." Today it is a matter of collective human survival. If we identify the study of values as a branch of philosophy, then the time has arrived for all women and men to become philosophers—or else.

How does one become a "philosopher of values"? By thinking deeply and clearly about these profound moral issues, studying the efforts of great thinkers through the ages who have wrestled with these timeless questions, discussing these concepts with others in a disciplined and open-minded way, and constructing a coherent ethical approach that is grounded on the bedrock of sound reasons and commitment to the truth. In other words, you become a philosopher by expanding your role as a critical thinker and extending your sophisticated thinking abilities to the domain of moral experience. This may be your most important personal quest. As Socrates emphasized, your values constitute the core of who you are. If you are to live a life of purpose, it is essential that you develop an enlightened code of ethics to guide you.

Thinking Activity 9.2

WHAT ARE MY MORAL VALUES?

You have many values—the guiding principles that you consider to be most important—that you have acquired over the course of your life. Your values deal with every aspect of your experience. The following questions are designed to elicit some of your values. Think carefully about each of the questions, and record your responses along with the reasons you have adopted that value. In addition, describe several of your moral values that are not addressed in these questions. A sample student response is included below.

- Do we have a moral responsibility toward less fortunate people?
- Is it wrong to divulge a secret that someone has confided in you?
- Should we eat meat? Should we wear animal skins?
- Should we try to keep people alive at all costs, no matter what their physical or mental condition?
- Is it wrong to kill someone in self-defense?
- Should people be given equal opportunities, regardless of race, religion, or gender?
- Is it wrong to ridicule someone, even if you believe it's in good fun?
- Should you "bend the rules" to advance your career?
- Is it all right to manipulate people into doing what you want if you believe it's for their own good?
- Is there anything wrong with pornography?
- Should we always try to take other people's needs into consideration when we act, or should we first make sure that our own needs are taken care of?
- Should we experiment with animals to improve the quality of our lives?

I do believe that we have a moral obligation to those less fortunate than us. Why can a homeless person evoke feelings of compassion in one person and complete disgust in another? Over time, observation, experience, and intuition have formed the cornerstones of my beliefs, morally and intellectually. As a result, compassion and respect for others are moral values that have come to characterize my responses in my dealings with others. As a volunteer in an international relief program in Dehra Dun, India, I was assigned to various hospitals and clinics through different regions of the country. In Delhi, I and the other volunteers were overwhelmed by the immense poverty—thousands of people, poor and deformed, lined the streets—homeless, hungry, and desperate. We learned that over 300 million people in India live in poverty. Compassion, as Buddhists describe it, is the spontaneous reaction of an open heart. Compassion for all sentient beings, acknowledging the suffering and difficulties in the world around us, connects us not only with others but with ourselves.

After you have completed this activity, examine your responses as a whole. Do they express a general, coherent, well-supported value system, or do they seem more like an unrelated collection of beliefs of varying degrees of clarity? This activity is a valuable investment of your time because you are creating a record of beliefs that you can return to and refine as you deepen your understanding of moral values.

Your Moral Compass

The purpose of the informal self-evaluation in Thinking Activity 9.2 is to illuminate your current moral code and initiate the process of critical reflection. Which of your moral values are clearly articulated and well grounded? Which are ill defined and tenuously rooted? Do your values form a coherent whole, consistent with one another, or do you detect fragmentation and inconsistency? Obviously, constructing a well-reasoned and clearly defined moral code is a challenging journey. But if we make a committed effort to think critically about the central moral questions, we can make significant progress toward this goal.

Your responses to the questions in Thinking Activity 9.2 reveal your current values. Where did these values come from? Parents, teachers, religious leaders, and other authority figures have sought to inculcate values in your thinking, but friends, acquaintances, and colleagues do as well. And in many cases they have undoubtedly been successful. Although much of your values education was likely the result of thoughtful teaching and serious discussions, in many other instances people may have bullied, bribed, threatened, and manipulated you into accepting their way of thinking. It's no wonder that our value systems typically evolve into a confusing patchwork of conflicting beliefs.

Margaret Bourke-White/Time & Life Pictures/Getty Images

In examining your values, you probably also discovered that, although you had a great deal of confidence in some of them ("I feel very strongly that animals should never be experimented on in ways that cause them pain because they are sentient creatures just like ourselves"), you felt less secure about other values ("I feel it's usually wrong to manipulate people, although I often try to influence their attitudes and behavior—I'm not sure of the difference"). These differences in confidence are likely related to how carefully you have examined and analyzed your values. For example, you may have been brought up in a family or religion with firmly fixed values that you have adopted but never really scrutinized or evaluated, wearing these values like a borrowed overcoat. When questioned, you might be at a loss to explain exactly why you believe what you do, other than to say, "This is what I was taught." In contrast, you may have other values that you consciously developed, the product of thoughtful reflection and the crucible of experience. For example, doing volunteer work with a disadvantaged group of people may have led to the conviction that "I believe we have a profound obligation to contribute to the welfare of people less fortunate than ourselves."

In short, most people's values are not systems at all: they are typically a collection of general principles ("Do unto others . . ."), practical conclusions ("Stealing is wrong because you might get caught"), and emotional pronouncements ("Euthanasia is wrong because it seems heartless"). This hodgepodge of values may reflect the serendipitous way they were acquired over the course of your life, and the current moral compass that you use to guide your decisions in moral situations likely comprise these values, even though you may not be consciously aware of it. Your challenge is to create a more refined and accurate compass, an enlightened system of values that you can use to confidently guide your moral decisions.

One research study that analyzed the moral compasses that young people use to guide their decision making in moral situations asked interviewees, "If you were unsure of what was right or wrong in a particular situation, how would you decide what to do?" (Think about how *you* would respond to this question.) According to the researcher, here's how the students responded:

- I would do what is best for everyone involved: 23 percent.
- I would follow the advice of an authority, such as a parent or teacher: 20 percent.
- I would do whatever made me happy: 18 percent.
- I would do what God or the Scriptures say is right: 16 percent.
- I would do whatever would improve my own situation: 10 percent.
- I do not know what I would do: 9 percent.
- I would follow my conscience: 3 percent.

Each of these guiding principles represents a different moral theory that describes the way people reason and make decisions about moral issues. However, moral values not only describe the way people behave; they also suggest that this is the way people ought to behave. For example, if I say, "Abusing children is morally wrong," I am not simply describing what *I* believe; I am also suggesting that abusing children is morally wrong for *everyone*. Let's briefly examine the moral theories represented by each of the responses just listed.

I WOULD FOLLOW MY CONSCIENCE

We could describe this as a *psychological* theory of morality because it holds that we should determine right and wrong based on our psychological moral sense. Our conscience is that part of our mind formed by internalizing the moral values we were raised with, generally from our parents but from other authority figures and peers as well. If that moral upbringing has been intelligent, empathic, and fair-minded, then our conscience can serve as a fairly sound moral compass to determine right and wrong. The problem with following our conscience occurs when the moral values we have internalized are *not* intelligent, empathic, or fair-minded. For example, if we were raised in an environment that encouraged racist beliefs or condoned child abuse, then our conscience might tell us that these are morally acceptable behaviors.

I DO NOT KNOW WHAT I WOULD DO

This statement expresses a morally *agnostic* theory of morality that holds there is no way to determine clearly what is right or wrong in moral situations. This view is a form of skepticism because it suggests that there is no universal common standard to determine how we ought to behave toward each other. Although we are often confused about the right course of action in complex moral situations, the moral agnostic theory is problematic because it does not permit us to evaluate the conduct of others. For example, if someone robs you and beats you up, you have no basis on which to say, "That was a morally wrong thing for that person to do." Instead, you have to tolerate such conduct because there is no ultimate right or wrong.

I WOULD DO WHATEVER WOULD IMPROVE MY OWN SITUATION

We could describe this viewpoint as a *ethical egoism* theory of morality because the right action is based on what works well for advancing the speaker's interests, while the wrong action is determined by what works against the speaker's interests. For example, if you are trying to decide whether you should volunteer at a local drug treatment center, you might conclude that this is the right thing to do because it will help you in your training as a psychologist and will look good on your résumé. The problem with this sort of moral reasoning is that you could also use it to justify cheating on an upcoming exam (if you were assured of not getting caught!) or hurting someone's reputation so that you could get ahead. At its heart, *the ethical egoist* theory of morality can be used to justify any actions that serve the individual interests of anyone.

I WOULD DO WHAT GOD OR THE SCRIPTURES SAY IS RIGHT

This statement expresses a *divine command* theory of morality that holds that right and wrong are determined by a supernatural supreme being ("God"). We determine what this supreme being wants us to do through divinely inspired writings (the Scriptures or holy books) or through divinely inspired messengers (priests, ministers, prophets, the pope). As an absolutist moral theory, this view holds that there are absolute moral principles that all humans should follow, and these principles are determined by the supreme being that created them. The strength of this moral theory lies in the fact that many religions embody values that are intelligent, empathic, and fair-minded, and the devotion of these religions' followers encourages them to act in these morally upright ways. The potential problem with this moral perspective is that all religions don't agree regarding moral values, and so we are left to determine which religion is the right one on which to base our moral views. In addition, there have been many historical instances in which religion has been used to justify actions that, by any standard, are cruel and inhuman, including torture, murder, and human sacrifice. There is always a danger when we surrender our critical-thinking faculties completely to another authority, as is shown by the actions of those who join cults.

Thinking Critically About Visuals

"Why Do You Believe?"

Many people's ethical beliefs are grounded on their religious beliefs: all religions present ways of behaving that will lead to a specific kind of spiritual enlightenment or transformation. However, there are many other people who develop strongly rooted ethical beliefs that are independent of any particular religion. What is the source and foundation for *your* ethical beliefs?

David Silverman/Getty Images News/Getty Images

Jeff Brass/Getty Images News/Getty Images

American Humanist Association

Why believe in a god?
Just be good for **goodness'** sake.
www.whybelieveinagod.org   1-800-837-3792

I WOULD DO WHATEVER MADE ME HAPPY

This statement reflects a slightly more refined version of the *hedonist* moral theory, which advises people to do whatever brings them pleasure. Although this is certainly an understandable goal in life—almost everybody wants to be happy—there are significant problems when we apply this way of thinking to the moral realm and our relationships with other people. For example, suppose you are contemplating an action that will make you very happy—stealing a new BMW convertible, for example—but will make someone else very unhappy, namely, the owner of the car. According to this moral theory, the right thing to do might be to steal the car, assuming that you didn't experience feelings of guilt or risk getting caught, feelings that would interfere with your happiness. In other words, the trouble with doing whatever makes you happy is the same difficulty we saw with doing whatever improves your situation. Neither moral theory takes into account the interests or rights of other people; thus, when your interests conflict with someone else's, your interests always prevail. If everyone thought this way, then our world would be an even more dangerous and unpleasant place to live!

I WOULD FOLLOW THE ADVICE OF AN AUTHORITY, SUCH AS A PARENT OR TEACHER

This *authoritarian* moral theory is analogous to the divine command moral theory ("I would do what God or the Scriptures say is right") in the sense that according to both theories, there are clear values of right and wrong and we should ask authorities to find out what these are. The difference is, of course, that in the divine command view, this authority is a supreme being, while the authoritarian view holds that the authority is human. The same difficulties we saw with the divine command view carry over to the authoritarian perspective because, although the values of parents and teachers often reflect wisdom and insight, many times they do not. How can we tell the difference between the appropriate and inappropriate values of these authorities? And what do we do when these authorities disagree with each other, as they often do? If we have deferred our critical judgment to the authorities, then we are at their mercy. But if we are prepared to evaluate critically the values of authorities, accepting what makes sense and discarding what doesn't, then we need another source for our moral values.

I WOULD DO WHAT IS BEST FOR EVERYONE INVOLVED

This response expresses an altruistic moral theory, a view in which the interests of other people are held to be as important as our own when we are trying to decide what to do. For example, if you are trapped with other students in a burning theater, the morally right course of action is to work for everyone's safe escape, not simply for your own. This moral perspective is an important part of many of the prominent world religions, and it is embodied in the Golden Rule: "Do unto others as you would have them do unto you." In other words, deciding on the morally right thing to do requires that we mentally and emotionally place ourselves in the positions of other people who might be affected by our action and then make our decision based on what will be best for their interests as well as for our own. By adopting this moral view, we eliminate many of the difficulties of other moral theories. For example, we will be reluctant to act in ways that harm other people because if we were in their position, we wouldn't want to be harmed that way ourselves. However, it is often difficult to determine what's best for everyone involved. Even more problematic is the question, What action should we take when the best interests of people conflict with one another? This is a very common moral dilemma. A variation of this moral view is known as the *utilitarian* moral theory, which holds that the morally right course of action is that which brings the greatest happiness for the greatest number of people.

Thinking Activity 9.3

ANALYZING MORAL DILEMMAS

The following dilemmas ask you to respond with decisions based on moral reasoning. After thinking carefully about each situation, do the following:

- Describe the decision that you would make in this situation and explain why.
- Identify the moral value(s) or principle(s) on which you based your decision.
- At the conclusion of the activity, compare the moral values that you used. Did you find that you consistently used the same values to make decisions, or did you use different values? If you used different ones, how did the various values relate to one another?
- Based on this analysis, describe your general conclusions about your own moral compass.

1. *The Lifeboat:* You are the captain, and your ship struck an iceberg and sank. There are thirty survivors, but they are crowded into a lifeboat designed to hold just seven. With the weather stormy and getting worse, it is obvious that many of the passengers will have to be thrown out of the lifeboat, or it will sink and everyone will drown. Will you have people thrown over the side? If so, on what basis will you decide who will go? Age? Health? Strength? Gender? Size?

2. *The Whistle-Blower:* You are employed by a large corporation that manufactures baby formula. You suspect that a flaw in the manufacturing process has resulted in contamination of the formula in a small number of cases. This contamination can result in serious illness, even death. You have been told by your supervisor that everything is under control and warned that if you blow the whistle by going public, you will be putting the entire company in jeopardy from multimillion-dollar lawsuits. You will naturally be fired and blackballed in the industry. As the sole provider in your household, your family depends on you. What do you do?

3. *The Mad Bomber:* You are a police lieutenant heading an investigation of a series of bombings that have resulted in extensive damage, injuries, and deaths. Your big break comes when you capture the person who you are certain is the so-called mad bomber. However, he tells you that he has placed a number of devices in public locations and that they will explode, at the cost of many innocent lives and injuries. You believe that your only chance of extracting the locations of these bombs is to torture this person until he tells. If you decide to do this, both your career and the legal case against the mad bomber will be placed in jeopardy. What do you do?

4. *The Patient:* As a clinical psychologist, you are committed to protecting the privacy of your patients. One afternoon, a patient tells you that her husband, who has been abusing her physically and mentally for years, has threatened to kill her, and she believes he will. You try to convince her to leave him, but she tells you that she has decided to kill *him.* She is certain that he would find her wherever she went, and she feels that she will be safe only when he is dead. What do you do?

5. *The Friend:* As the director of your department, you are in charge of filling an important vacancy. Many people have applied, including your best friend, who has been out of work for over a year and needs a job desperately. Although your friend would likely perform satisfactorily, there are several more experienced and talented candidates who would undoubtedly perform better. You have always prided yourself on hiring the best people, and you have earned a reputation as someone with high standards who will not compromise your striving for excellence. Whom do you hire?

As you think your way through the moral dilemmas in Thinking Activity 9.3, you will probably find yourself appealing to the basic moral principles that you typically use to guide your actions. Of course, what makes these examples moral dilemmas is the fact that they involve a conflict of traditional moral principles.

1. The Lifeboat involves a conflict between these moral beliefs:
   • It is wrong to take any innocent life.
   • It is right to save *some* lives rather than threaten *all* the lives on board.
2. The Whistle-Blower involves a conflict between these moral beliefs:
   • It is wrong to knowingly jeopardize the health of children.
   • It is right to protect the welfare of your family and your career.
3. The Mad Bomber involves a conflict between these moral beliefs:
   • It is wrong to harm a human being.
   • It is right to save the lives of many innocent people.
4. The Patient involves a conflict between these moral beliefs:
   • It is wrong to violate the confidentiality of a professional relationship.
   • It is right to prevent someone from committing murder.

5. The Friend involves a conflict between these moral beliefs:
   - It is wrong to hire someone who is not the best-qualified candidate for the job.
   - It is right to try to help and support your friend.

A moral dilemma is a situation in which at least two different moral principles to which you are appealing seem ethically sound and appropriate; the problem is that they contradict each other. What should you do when this happens? How do you decide which principle is more right? There is no simple answer to this question, just as there is no easy answer to the question, What do you do when experts disagree? In both cases, you need to think critically to arrive at intelligent and informed conclusions.

Moral dilemmas can provoke intense angst and vigorous debate. For example, you might be faced with the decision of which employees to fire to keep your company afloat. Employees working for companies that manufacture baby formula, contraceptives, and tobacco products have often found themselves in a moral dilemma: Do they risk their own job and those of their coworkers by alerting the public to the dangers of a product? You yourself may have been in a job situation in which telling the truth or objecting to an unethical practice would have jeopardized your position or opportunity for advancement. Many therapists, clergy members, lawyers, and doctors wrestle daily with issues of confidentiality. We all have to decide when it is morally appropriate to break our promises to avoid a greater evil or achieve a greater good. There are countless instances in which we are forced to balance our feelings of personal obligation with our objective or professional analysis.

In addition to these kinds of ethical situations, you will undoubtedly confront other types of moral dilemmas that are at least as problematic. It is possible that at some point in your life you will have to make a right-to-die decision regarding a loved one nearing the end of life. You might also find yourself in a situation in which you are torn between ending a difficult marriage or remaining as a full-time parent of young children. Or you might be tempted to take advantage of an investment opportunity that, while not illegal, is clearly unethical. Dealing with complicated, ambiguous moral challenges is an inescapable part of the human condition. Because these situations can't be avoided, you need to develop the insight and conceptual tools to deal with them effectively.

The Thinker's Guide to Moral Decision Making

After wrestling with the moral dilemmas presented in the previous section, you might be wondering exactly how people develop a clear sense of right and wrong to guide them through complex moral situations. The answer is found by applying to moral issues the same critical-thinking abilities we have been developing in the activities presented throughout this book to create "The Thinker's Guide to Moral Decision Making." Consider the following guide a moral blueprint for constructing your own personal moral code. Using the concepts and principles provided by this guide, you can create a moral philosophy to analyze successfully almost any moral situation and to make informed decisions that you can justify with confidence.

MAKE MORALITY A PRIORITY

To live a life that achieves your moral potential, you must work to become aware of the moral issues that you face and strive to make choices that are grounded in thoughtful reflection and supported by persuasive reasoning. By living a morally enlightened life, you are defining yourself as a person of substance, a person with a vision that informs the quality of your relationships with others.

Thinking Critically About Visuals

"Who Is Homeless?"

Andrew Holbrooke/Corbis News/Corbis

How is the woman in this photo behaving in relation to the homeless person on the sidewalk? Why? What kinds of moral judgments do people make about homeless people? Do you think these judgments are justified? Why or why not?

STRATEGY: During the next week, identify the moral issues that you encounter in your daily life and that involve other people—choices related to right and wrong, good and evil, just and unjust. Select several of these moral choices, and think about the approach that you used in making each decision: What was the issue? What choices could you have made? Why did you make the choice that you did? If you had it to do over again, would you make the same choice? Why or why not?

During the recent economic downturn, the concept of "homeless" has taken on a new meaning as many people of all economic levels lost their homes because they could not keep up with their mortgage payments. How would you describe the differences between these two different concepts of "homeless"?

AP Photo/Eric Gay, file

RECOGNIZE THAT A CRITICAL-THINKING APPROACH TO ETHICS IS BASED ON REASON

Some ethical viewpoints are "better"—more enlightened—than other viewpoints, based on the supporting reasons and evidence. The logic of ethical statements demands that they be supported by reasons. Ethical viewpoints are not a matter of taste, like your preferred hairstyle or your favorite kind of pizza. Unlike moral judgments, it *does* make sense to say, "I like pepperoni pizza, but I can't give you a reason why. I just like it!" But it would *not* make sense for someone to say, "Your taste in pizza is wrong." Ethical judgments are very different from expressions of taste. They are independent of personal preferences and are evaluated in the public arena. When someone says, "I think that child abuse is immoral," they are not expressing a personal preference that applies only to them. They are making a pronouncement that they believe applies to everyone: child abuse is immoral for all people. And they should be prepared to justify their conclusion with a rationale that others can discuss and evaluate. Unlike matters of taste, it *does* make sense to disagree with someone's ethical judgment: "I don't agree that legalized gambling is immoral because. . . ." Ethical statements are usually intended to be universally true.

As a result, ethical views are primarily statements of reason, *not* expressions of emotion. When you express your moral disapproval toward child abuse, you are communicating what you think about this issue based presumably on a thoughtful analysis. If someone asks, "Why do you think this?" you should be able to provide persuasive reasons that support your conclusion. Of course, there may be strong feelings that accompany your moral belief about child abuse, but you are primarily making a statement based on reason. When you express feelings, you may be accurately describing your emotional state ("I *feel* angry when I hear stories about child abuse"), but you are not expressing a moral point of view that you believe applies to everyone.

> STRATEGY: Whenever you express your moral judgments, develop the habit of explaining why you believe that this is a moral perspective that others should support. Similarly, when others offer their moral judgments—as many people are eager to do—be sure to ask them *why* they believe what they do (even if you agree with their conclusion).

INCLUDE THE ETHIC OF JUSTICE IN YOUR MORAL COMPASS

We are all different from one another, and unless these differences pose some threat to other people, our individuality should be respected. A critical-thinking approach to ethics is founded on the principle of impartiality: it is our moral obligation to treat everyone equally, with the same degree of consideration and respect, unless there is some persuasive reason not to. This is the basic principle of the ethic of justice. For example, differences among people based on race, religion, gender, or sexual orientation pose no threat to society, and so the people involved deserve to be treated with the same respect everyone is entitled to. However, if a person threatens the rights of others—assaulting, stealing, raping, killing—then that person is not entitled to be treated like everyone else. He or she needs to be segregated from the rest of society and possibly rehabilitated.

The ethic of justice emphasizes the intentions or motivations behind an action, not the consequences. It expresses the conviction that you experience when, confronted by a moral decision, you respond, "I have to do my duty. It's the principle of the thing. Regardless of the consequences, it's important for me to do what's right." This emphasis on moral duty through reason was perhaps best articulated by the German philosopher Immanuel Kant: through reasoning, we can analyze moral situations, evaluate possible choices, and then choose the one we believe is best. Kant based his approach to ethics on a universal rational principle (the "categorical imperative") that every virtuous person should obey: "Act only according to that maxim by which you can at the same time will that it should become a universal law." Should you spread unflattering gossip about an unpopular coworker, even if you think the person deserves it? Applying this principle, you should do it only if you believe that all people in all situations should spread unflattering gossip. Most people would be reluctant to sign on for this sort of universal rule.

But why should you go along with this categorical imperative in the first place? Because, as first and foremost a rational creature, you are necessarily committed to a belief in logical consistency. How could you defend doing something that you would condemn other people for doing? What qualities make you so unique, so superior to everyone else, that you are not bound by the same rules and requirements? Your intrinsic value is no greater and no worse than that of any other rational person. Reason dictates that everyone's interests must be treated the same, without special consideration. We should be willing to make every personal choice a universal law.

> STRATEGY: As you deliberate the various moral choices in your life, both small (Should I cut ahead in line?) and large (Should I pursue my own self-interest at the risk of hurting someone else?), make a conscious effort to universalize your anticipated actions. Would you be willing to have everyone take this same action in similar circumstances? If not, evaluate whether the action is truly morally justified and consistent with the other moral values you hold.

Kant also formulated a second version of the categorical imperative: "Act so that you treat humanity, whether in your own person or in that of another, always as an end and never as a means only." Because all people possess the same intrinsic value, a value that is defined by an ability to understand their options and make free choices, we should always act in a way that respects their inherent dignity as rational agents.

Imagine, for example, that you want to sell something. Is it all right to manipulate people's feelings so that they will buy it? Or suppose that your child or friend is planning to do something that you don't think is in his or her best interests. Is it permissible to manipulate this person's thinking indirectly so that he or she will make a different choice? According to Kant, both of these actions are morally wrong because you are not treating the people involved as "ends," rational agents who are entitled to make their own choices. Instead, you are treating them as a "means" to an end, even though you may believe that your manipulation is in their best interests. The morally right thing to do is to tell them exactly what you are thinking and then give them the opportunity to reason through the situation and make their own choices.

> STRATEGY: Think about some recent instances in which you attempted to influence someone's thoughts, feelings, or behavior. Did you make a clear case for your recommendation, respecting the person's right to make a free choice? Or did you try to manipulate him or her by using techniques designed to influence the person without his or her knowledge or to coerce the person against his or her wishes? If you discover examples of such manipulation, try to imagine how things would have turned out if you had taken a more forthright approach.

Thinking Activity 9.4

EVALUATING MY MORAL BELIEFS WITH REASON

Apply Kant's two formulations of the categorical imperative to the ethical beliefs that you expressed in Thinking Activity 9.2 on page 391.

1. Act only according to that maxim by which you can at the same time will that it should become a universal law.
2. Act so that you treat humanity, whether in your own person or in that of another, always as an end and never as a means only.

How do your ethical beliefs measure up? Are they consistent with Kant's formulations? Think about a moral dilemma that you recently agonized over. Does either formulation of the categorical imperative point you in a clearer direction?

INCLUDE THE ETHIC OF CARE IN YOUR MORAL COMPASS

The ethic of care is built on empathy, a critical-thinking commitment to view issues and situations from multiple perspectives. According to an empathetic point of view, achieving happiness and fulfillment in life does not mean pursuing your own narrow desires; instead it involves pursuing your aspirations in a context of genuine understanding of and concern for other people. When you actively work to transcend your own perspective and think within other points of view, particularly those with which you disagree, you are gaining a deeper and richer understanding. You need to listen carefully to people who disagree with you and try to appreciate how their thinking brought them to their conclusion. Perspective-taking is the cornerstone of many of the world's ethical systems such as the Golden Rule: "Do unto others as you would have them do unto you." In other words, strive to place yourself in the position of the object of your moral judgment and see how that affects your evaluation. For instance, if you are trying to evaluate the morality of racism, imagine that you are the target of the evaluation. You didn't choose your racial heritage; it's just who you are. From this vantage point, do you think that you should be treated differently, discriminated against, and condemned as being alien and inferior?

> STRATEGY: Increase your ability to empathize by making a special effort to transcend your own perspective and to place yourself in other people's shoes. In your dealings with others, use your imagination to experience what you believe they are thinking and feeling, and observe whether this viewpoint influences your attitudes and actions toward them.

ACCEPT RESPONSIBILITY FOR YOUR MORAL CHOICES

From a critical-thinking perspective, morality makes sense only if we assume that people are able to make free choices for which they are responsible. When people choose courses of action that we consider to be "right," we judge them as morally "good." On the other hand, when they choose courses of action that we consider to be "wrong," we condemn them as morally "evil." For example, when Princess Diana was the victim of a fatal car crash, it was widely reported that the photographers who were pursuing her (the *paparazzi*) were preoccupied with taking photographs of the carnage rather than helping the victims. In France, not actively aiding a person in distress actually violates the law, but in most countries the photographers' actions would not be considered illegal. Nevertheless, most people would judge their failure to help and their efforts to profit from this tragedy to be *ethically* wrong. They were judged this way because they had a choice to make; they were aware of their options, their motivations, and the consequences of their actions. By choosing to take photographs rather than assist, they were motivated by greed and were diminishing the chances of survival for the occupants of the car.

Now imagine that you are driving down a street in your neighborhood, within the speed limit and stone sober, when a child darts out from between two parked cars. Though you brake instantly, you nevertheless hit the child. Is your action wrong—immoral, unethical? Most people would say no. This was an accident that was unavoidable, not the result of a free choice, so you should not be held responsible for the tragedy. You were not faced with clear options from which to choose,

Thinking Critically About Visuals

Ethics and Emotions

People for the Ethical Treatment of Animals (PETA) is an animal-rights advocacy group that supports modern alternatives to the use of animals for medical and other experiments and other compassionate choices for clothing and entertainment.

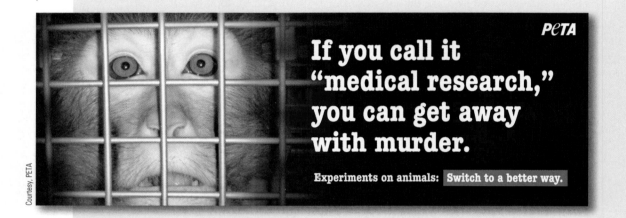

How does the PETA poster argue against the use of animal experimentation? What do you think PETA means when they say "switch to a better way"?

you were not motivated by evil intentions, and you had no way of foreseeing the consequences of your action.

To be held morally accountable, for good or ill, your actions need to be the result of *free choices*. And to exercise your freedom, you need to have insight into your options, your motivations, and the consequences of your actions. This is the uniquely human gift: we have the intelligence, the imagination, and the reflective insight to consider a range of options and make choices. Sometimes we choose

Americans for Medical Progress is a nonprofit advocacy group of physicians, researchers, veterinarians, and others that works to promote awareness of the benefits of animal research as well as the need to support humane treatment of research animals.

How would you characterize the ethical position of Americans for Medical Progress on animal research? In your own words, describe the four key arguments about animal research that this advertisement anticipates and addresses. Finally, compare the visual used in this advertisement with that used by PETA. Which visual makes a stronger ethical argument, in your opinion, the one for or against animal research?

wisely, sometimes we choose poorly, but in all instances we are responsible for the choices that we make.

STRATEGY: Strengthen your moral integrity by actively seeking to acknowledge your moral failings and then by committing yourself to improve. Self-honesty will build your inner strength and moral fiber, and you will find that moral integrity of this sort is both rewarding and habit forming.

SEEK TO PROMOTE HAPPINESS FOR ONESELF AND OTHERS

Evaluating moral choices involves examining the intent or motivation behind the choice as well as the consequences of the action. In the case of the photographers at the scene of Princess Diana's fatal crash, their intent—to secure photographs that they could sell for a great deal of money rather than aid the victims—was certainly morally reprehensible. Their actions represented an inversion of common moral values because they placed money higher than human life. But in addition to the immorality of their intent, the consequences of their actions were also catastrophic because three of the four passengers died. We'll never know if their assistance could have made a difference to the victims. Had Princess Diana and the others survived the accident, the actions of the photographers, while still immoral in intent, might not have been judged so harshly. But with fatal consequences, their choices were evaluated even more gravely: they contributed to the accident by pursuing the car, they took photographs instead of helping the victims, and those who were able to went on to sell their photos for large sums of money. In the minds of many people, it doesn't get much worse than that.

Promoting human happiness—along with its corollary, diminishing human suffering—has been a mainstay of many ethical systems through the ages. Most people are perfectly willing to pursue their own happiness; it's the way we're genetically programmed and taught as well. However, you don't receive moral accolades for pursuing your own interests only. Moral recognition is typically earned by devoting your time and resources to enhancing the happiness of others, sometimes at the expense of your own interests. This moral value is founded on the principle of perspective-taking, which we explored earlier. Identifying with another's situation can generate the desire to assist the person, who could just as easily have been you ("There but for the grace of God. . ."). Perspective-taking is the wellspring of charitable acts toward others.

But this moral concept is relevant in our ordinary dealings with people also. All things being equal, it makes sense to promote the happiness of others through your words and actions. Being friendly, generous, supportive, understanding, sympathetic, helpful—these and other similar traits enhance the quality of others' lives, usually at a minimal cost to yourself. This is not to suggest that you should devote yourself to promoting the interests of others to the exclusion of your own. In fact, if you don't take care of your own interests, you probably won't be able to sustain the inner resources needed to help others. Self-interest and selfishness are not the same thing. Pursuing your self-interest is ethically appropriate and necessary for your own physical and emotional health. But if you are devoted exclusively to pursuing your interests, then you run the risk of your life being morally empty. And if you are intent on pursuing your interests at the expense of other people, then you are being selfish. When you take more than your share of dessert, diminishing the portions of others, or you step on other people to advance your career, you are exhibiting selfishness.

Promoting human happiness is the foundation of the ethical approach developed by Jeremy Bentham, a philosopher who was concerned with British social problems in the late eighteenth and early nineteenth centuries. From his perspective, good and right are defined in terms of what brings about the greatest pleasure for the greatest number of people, a moral theory that became known as *utilitarianism*. Another British philosopher, John Stuart Mill, argued that we need to distinguish the "higher pleasures" (intellectual stimulation, aesthetic appreciation, education, healthfulness) from the "lower pleasures" (animal appetites, laziness, selfishness). Otherwise, he declared mischievously, it would seem preferable to be a contented pig rather than a discontented human, a conclusion that is surely absurd:

> It is better to be a human being dissatisfied than a pig satisfied; better to be Socrates dissatisfied than a fool satisfied. And if the fool, or the pig, are of a different opinion, it is because they only know their own side of the question. The other party to the comparison knows both sides.

But even this more refined notion of higher pleasures seems too limited. We need to expand the concept of pleasure to the more general idea of human happiness in a deep and rich sense. It *does* make sense for us to promote human happiness if this means helping other people secure shelter, food, and health care; providing education and creating opportunities for career success; protecting their freedom and supporting their quest for personal fulfillment. If we view human happiness within this larger framework, then helping the greatest number of people achieve it is surely a morally good and ethically right goal to pursue.

> STRATEGY: Think about specific ways in which you can increase the happiness of the people in your life. These may involve bestowing a small kindness on someone you know casually or making a more significant commitment to someone to whom you are very close. Create and implement a plan for doing this during the next few days and then evaluate the results of your efforts. How did applying the extra effort to make others happy make you feel? How did they respond? Doesn't it make sense to continue this effort and even to increase it?

Thinking Activity 9.5

WHAT IS MY IDEA OF HUMAN HAPPINESS?

The ancient Greeks defined "happiness" as *eudaemonia*, which translates as "the full exercise of the soul's powers." What do you consider to be the ingredients of human happiness? What things do you believe most people need to achieve genuine happiness? Review the moral values that you identified in Thinking Activity 9.2 on page 391 and identify which ones promote human happiness as you have defined it. Can you think of other moral values that might contribute to the happiness of yourself and others?

SEEK TO DEVELOP AN INFORMED INTUITION

When you find yourself in the throes of a moral decision, there may come a point when you have a clear intuition about what course of action you should take. Is this your conscience speaking to you? Is this your moral compass pointing you in the right direction? Can you trust your intuition?

To answer these questions, it's necessary to understand how the human mind operates. One dominant aspect of your thinking process is its synthesizing quality: It is continually trying to construct a picture of the world that is intelligible, and this picture is updated on an instantaneous basis as circumstances change. Your mind does this by taking into account all available information, utilizing appropriate concepts, and integrating all of this into a pattern that makes sense. When this pattern clicks into place, like fitting the final piece into a jigsaw puzzle, you experience an intuition. Although some of these processes are conscious, others are unconscious, sometimes giving your intuition a mysterious aura. Many of your intuitions are commonplace: deciding on an ingredient when creating a new recipe or having the clear sense that someone you just met is not entirely trustworthy. Although these intuitions may seem to be coming out of the blue, they are generally the result of your accumulated experience, insight, and the information you are picking up at the moment. When you taste the sauce of your new dish, your accumulated expertise tells you what the recipe needs. When you meet a person for the first time, you are picking up a great deal of information about him or her on subtle and even subliminal levels communicated not just by words and appearance, but by facial expressions, gestures, voice tone, eye contact, and so on. As you absorb this information at a dizzying rate, it is fed into your mental computer, programmed with lessons about people learned through years of experience. A pattern emerges, and . . . presto, an intuition!

These sorts of informed intuitions are often quite reliable because they are based on a great deal of experience, reflection, knowledge, insight, and expertise. But there are many uninformed intuitions as well, and these are not reliable. In fact, they can be catastrophic because they are *not* based on sufficient experience, reflection, knowledge, insight, and expertise. For example, imagine that you have just learned how to play chess, and suddenly you are struck with the intuitive certainty that you should sacrifice your queen. Because this intuition is not the product of accumulated knowledge and insight, it may very well lose you the game. If you think back on your own life, you can doubtless identify intuitions that seemed certain at the time but turned out to be tragically—or comically—wrong. You may have experienced the thunderbolt of true love, and several months later wondered what you were thinking at the time. The point is that an intuition is only as sound as the foundation of experience, knowledge, insight, and expertise on which it is based.

This is precisely the same situation with moral intuition. If your moral intuition is informed, the product of a great deal of thought and reflection, then it has a high degree of credibility. But if your moral intuition is uninformed, the product of inaccurate information or inadequate experience, then your intuition is not credible. People with depraved and underdeveloped moral sensibilities will have instincts and intuitions that reflect their diminished moral understanding. There is nothing magical or infallible about your conscience or moral intuition: If you have consciously worked at becoming a moral person, a person of character and integrity, then your intuitions will be largely trustworthy. But if you have not consciously striven to develop and refine your moral sensibilities, or if you have been raised in an environment saturated with destructive values like prejudice and violence, then you should be very suspicious of your moral intuitions.

Though your intuitions may seem initially certain, further reflection can plant seeds of doubt that eventually threaten that initial certainty. Moral judgments are not factual statements that we can easily prove or disprove through observation and experimentation. In most moral situations, the facts are known—it's the interpretation of the facts and what to do about the situation that poses the moral problem. When a woman discovers that the fetus developing inside her is severely malformed and disabled, the facts of the situation are fairly straightforward. What is not clear is what moral choice she and the father of the fetus should make: whether to have an abortion or confront the challenge of raising a severely retarded and physically disabled child. While it makes sense to gather as much accurate information as possible to anticipate what this child's life will be like and the impact it will have on the lives of the other family members, no amount of information will add up to making the moral decision. It's an entirely different category of reasoning, a deliberative process that often involves moral uncertainty and a profound sense of responsibility. Each one of us confronts this same anguish when we struggle with difficult moral questions for which there aren't any clear, unambiguous answers. In these circumstances, appealing to one's moral intuition simply doesn't seem adequate.

> STRATEGY: Imagine an ideal, perfect human being. What personal qualities would such a person possess? How would such a person treat other people? What moral vision and specific moral values would such a person display? Using these explorations, construct a composite portrait of an ideal person that you can use to guide your own moral intuitions.

Thinking Activity 9.6

THINKING ABOUT MY MORAL INTUITION

Think about the way you arrive at moral decisions. How do you know when you are doing the right thing? Where does your sense of moral certainty come from? Do you experience moral intuitions about good and evil, right and wrong? Consider the values that you identified in Thinking Activity 9.2 on page 391 and others of your values as well. To what extent are they based on your moral intuition of right and wrong? How would you justify these values to a skeptical acquaintance? What does it feel like when you have a moral intuition?

DISCOVER THE "NATURAL LAW" OF HUMAN NATURE

There have been centuries of energetic efforts to provide a foundation for moral intuition, a grounding that will remove it from the grip of social conditioning and the shadows of inscrutable mystery. Once again, it was the ancient Greeks who first elaborated this approach by making a distinction between "nature" (*physis*) and "convention" (*nomos*). The social conventions of a society are the human-made customs, beliefs, laws, and tastes that are peculiar to that society. That's why when you examine the numerous cultures in the world, past and present, you find a spectacular diversity in the social fabric of each society: You are observing the social conventions that are relative to each individual society.

Nature, however, embodies the vast realm of truth that exists on a deeper level than social conventions. These natural truths are *not* relative to each society; they are constant from culture to culture, and from age to age. These truths are rooted in the fundamental nature of what it means to be human. According to this view, there is a natural law based on the essential nature of human beings that is universal and binding on all people. We can discover these natural moral truths through reason and reflection, and they have been articulated in the greatest legal and moral philosophies and theological systems of Western culture. The challenge for each individual and culture is to discover this immutable natural law that underlies the specific conventions of any society. It is an effort that the religious thinker St. Thomas Aquinas devoted his life to, and that America's founding fathers sought to articulate in the Declaration of Independence and Constitution.

> We hold these truths to be self-evident that all men are created equal, that they are endowed by their Creator with certain inalienable rights. . . .

To discover the specifics of the natural law, we need to develop an in-depth understanding of the essential nature of human beings, not simply as they currently are, but as they could be if they were fully morally developed. What are the basic requirements of human fulfillment? What are the most enlightened values that humans can aspire to? What are the norms of conduct that foster the most meaningful and productive society? What are the conditions that maximize the exercise of individual freedom and personal growth? What are the moral responsibilities that we have to each other as members of an interdependent human community?

To answer these difficult questions, some people turn to religion. After all, if we are indeed God's creations (whatever your religion's conception of God), designed in God's image, then it makes sense that, by understanding our true nature, we will be following the path of both moral and spiritual enlightenment. In fact, it would be shocking if there was *not* an essential identity between the ethics of our religion and our natural moral intuitions. By following what Thomas Aquinas described as the dictates of reason, we are able to discover God's ethic encoded in our human nature, in the same way that we are able to display the mysteries of the physical universe through the study of science. In other words, we can use our critical-thinking abilities to reveal the essential moral nature of people—the ideal image of fulfilled human potential—and then use this image to inform our moral choices and guide our personal development.

CHOOSE TO BE A MORAL PERSON

An individual can possess a comprehensive understanding of moral concepts and approaches and *not* be a moral person. How is that possible? Just as people can possess an array of critical-thinking abilities and yet choose not to use them, so people can be a walking compendium of moral theory and yet not choose to apply it to their lives. To achieve an enlightened moral existence in your own life, you need to *choose* to be a moral person struggling to live a moral life. You need to value morality, to aspire to an enhanced moral awareness, to exert the motivation and commitment required to reach this lofty but reachable goal.

Once you have developed a clear understanding of your moral code, the struggle has just begun. Becoming a morally enlightened person—a person of character, compassion, and integrity—is a hard-won series of accomplishments, not a one-time award like winning an Oscar. Every day confronts you with new choices and unexpected challenges, many of which you cannot possibly anticipate. With your moral code in hand to guide you, you need to commit yourself to making the choices that best express your moral philosophy of life. As a reflective critical thinker, you will be conscious of the choices you are making and the reasons you are making them, and you will learn from experience, refining your code of ethics and improving your moral choices through self-exploration. Achieving moral enlightenment is an ongoing process, and it is a struggle that is not for the faint-hearted. But it is a struggle that cannot be avoided if you are to live a life of purpose and meaning, created by a self that is authentic and, as Aristotle would have said, "great souled."

The psychologist Abraham Maslow conducted a comprehensive study of the qualities of what he considered to be self-actualized people, and he found that people with healthy human personalities also had strong moral characters. Morally mature, psychologically healthy people think, decide, and act in accordance with thoughtfully developed moral standards, are open-minded about their moral beliefs, defend them with reasoned argument when they are challenged, and change or modify them when they are shown to be false or unjustified. Their conclusions are based on their own reflective analysis, rather than on being unquestioning "children of their culture." And they are fully committed to living their values, recognizing that ethics is not an intellectual game; it's a light that guides their moral growth and personal evolution.

Thinking Critically About Visuals

"Should I Volunteer?"

People who volunteer often find that there is a special gratification that comes from helping other people in need, whether it's residents recovering from a hurricane, kids in need of tutoring, elderly citizens who are benefiting from meals brought to them, and so on. What volunteering activities have you been involved in? How did volunteering your time and talents make you feel? If you're not sure how to go about finding places to volunteer, websites like the one pictured, "New York Cares," provides you with many structured opportunities to donate your services and help make the world a better place to live.

Courtesy of New York Cares

These considerations provide a convincing answer to the question "Why be moral?" As it turns out, becoming a moral person helps you become a psychologically healthy person; promoting the happiness of others frequently enhances your own happiness. Often adages are clichéd and empty of meaning, but in this case, "Virtue is its own reward" contains a substantial measure of truth, a point noted by Socrates in his observation that doing wrong "will harm and corrupt that part of ourselves that is improved by just actions and destroyed by unjust actions." As a free individual, you create yourself through the choices that you make, much as a sculptor gradually forms a figure through countless cuts of the chisel. If you create yourself as a moral person, you create a person of character and worth, with an acute sense of right and wrong and the power to choose appropriately. But if you don't choose to create yourself as a moral person, you gradually become corrupted. You lose your moral sensitivity, developing a moral blindness that handicaps your ability to see yourself or the world clearly. It is no wonder that Socrates believed "It is better to suffer wickedness than to commit it." You gain true power when you possess the unfettered and unrestrained ability to choose freely. Choosing immorality binds your hands, one loop of thread at a time, until your freedom of movement disappears. In the same way that substance abusers gradually surrender their freedom of choice to their destructive cravings, so immoral people have only the illusion of genuine freedom in their lives. While moral people enjoy healthy personalities and psychological wholeness, immoral people are corrupted at their core, progressively ravaged by a disease of the spirit.

> STRATEGY: Develop the habit of conducting a regular appraisal of your self and your life. Ask—and answer—questions such as these: Am I achieving my goals as a moral person? As a critical thinker? As a creative individual? Then use this evaluation regularly to maintain a much-needed perspective on your life, reminding yourself of the big picture and applying it to guide your evolution into the most worthy person you can become.

Thinking Activity 9.7

NURTURING MY MORAL GROWTH

No matter how highly evolved you are as a moral person, you can achieve a more enlightened state by choosing to nurture your moral growth. Your critical-thinking abilities will give you the means to explore the moral dimensions of your experience with insight, and your personal dedication to moral improvement will provide you with the ongoing motivation. Remember that becoming a moral person is both a daily and a lifetime project. Nurture your continued moral growth by cultivating the qualities that we have been exploring in this section.

- Make morality a priority.
- Recognize that ethics is based on reason.
- Include the ethic of justice in your moral compass.
- Include the ethic of care in your moral compass.
- Accept responsibility for your moral choices.
- Seek to promote human happiness.
- Develop an informed moral intuition.
- Discover the natural law of human nature.
- Choose to be a moral person.

THINKING CRITICALLY ABOUT NEW MEDIA

Ethical Issues with the Internet

In the same way that medical technology has created an entire new universe of moral issues, such as those involving the beginning and end of life, so the creation of the Internet and digital technology has confronted people with moral choices that didn't exist before this age of new media. That is because the Internet and its related digital technologies allow information to be easily and cheaply manipulated, duplicated, and shared. In this new environment, what happens to the concept of "ownership" of information, music, text, films, or other online material? What are the ethics of using such material for one's personal enjoyment or enrichment? And what is the morality of duplicating material from other sources and incorporating it into our own writing without appropriate attribution? These are complex and challenging questions, and our responses to them typically reflect the perspective from which we are coming.

For example, imagine yourself in the position of Jammie Thomas-Rasset, a Minnesota woman who was found guilty of stealing and illegally distributing twenty-four songs for the sole purpose of obtaining free music. Her penalty? A $2 million dollar fine! (The fine was reduced to $54,000 on appeal.) Is she a culprit or a victim?

Living in a culture in which the sharing of songs is commonplace, many people would consider such a judgment to be unfair. The reasons why the sharing of music files is so popular are obvious: sharing files is as easy as snapping your fingers, and the cost—$0—is considerably less than the $15–$20 you would have to spend for a CD.

However, from the perspective of the music industry—including the recording artists and the record companies—the sharing of music files is stealing, pure and simple. People may not be walking out of a music store with a CD concealed on their body, but sharing and playing the music without paying amounts to the same thing. Music sharers are illegally taking something that does not belong to them and using it for their own enjoyment, in the process cutting out of the money equation those who created and produced the product.

Defenders of file sharing—which includes not just music but books and movies—argue that these companies have been charging too much for their products for too long, and this is just "balancing the scales," making it possible for many people to enjoy things they otherwise wouldn't be able to afford. What's the ethically correct thing to do in this case?

One of the principles we explored in "The Thinker's Guide to Moral Decision Making" was "Include the ethic of justice in your moral compass." Applying this perspective, imagine yourself as a musician who has invested much of your life in creating music. Finally, all of your talent and hard work pay off: you get a recording contract! After a year spent producing your album, your CD is released, and it initially turns out to be extremely popular. However, after a few months, sales drop off dramatically, even though your songs have only grown in popularity. What happened? File sharing by a large number of people. Rather than buy your CD, people can simply link up to file-sharing sites or individuals and select the songs from the CD that they want for no charge. As someone who is now having others enjoy your work without compensating you, how do you feel? How would you respond to the arguments they might present for why they should be able to enjoy your music for free? Seen from this perspective, might you not feel that the product of your talent, creativity, and hard work was being stolen from you?

An additional implication of the *ethic of justice* involves the philosopher Immanuel Kant's suggestion that when trying to decide what to do in moral situations, we should apply the categorical imperative, asking ourselves "Is it rational for me to will that my choice become a universal law of nature?" In other words, in deciding whether file sharing of music, books, or movies is ethically appropriate, we should ask ourselves, "Is it rational for this choice—sharing files—to become a universal law of nature, meaning that people *should* share files whenever they have the opportunity?" If we apply this standard, we can see that the answer must be "File sharing is ethically wrong." Why? Because if everyone were encouraged to share files at every opportunity, it would spell the end to the music business (already the music business has been severely damaged by file sharing), and books and movies wouldn't be far behind. It's not reasonable to expect individuals to create, and companies to produce, products for which they will receive minimal compensation. To the defense "I'm not saying *everyone* should share files, just *me*" the ethic of justice says that you cannot exclude yourself from being a member of the human race with the same basic rights and responsibilities.

The ease of locating, copying, and sharing information that the Internet provides has also expanded the possibilities for *plagiarism*—the copying of text and ideas written by someone else and passing them off as material that you created by not giving credit to the original source. Before the advent of the Internet, plagiarism was a much more explicit process. Someone had to go to the library or some similar place, physically locate text(s) or periodicals, copy down or photocopy passages, and then type these into the research paper or other document without attributing them to their original source. Today, however, it's simply a matter of surfing around the Internet, guided by any number of search engines, highlighting and copying the material you intend to take, and then pasting it into the document you are presenting as your own.

(Continues)

THINKING CRITICALLY ABOUT NEW MEDIA (*CONTINUED*)

Because plagiarism—both intentional and accidental—has become so much easier, it's also become more prevalent. In fact, even highly respected, award-winning writers—such as the historians Stephen Ambrose and Doris Kearns Goodwin—have been found to have plagiarized material that turned up in their best-selling books. But simply because plagiarism is easier or more widespread doesn't make it "right." It's still stealing, because you're taking the ideas and writing produced by someone else and presenting them to the world as something you created. In general, there is no problem with using the ideas and writing of others; we simply have to give them the credit they deserve.

In addition to the ethical wrongness of plagiarizing, there are other reasons to avoid it as well. First, there is an increasing likelihood that you will be found out and suffer severe consequences. Most professors can tell immediately when passages are not consistent with other written work that you—or any college student—typically does. Plus, there is increasingly sophisticated software that enables someone to determine instantly exactly where the questionable passages originated from. Second, plagiarizers end up cheating themselves, because they are not developing the abilities and knowledge that the assignment—and college as a whole—are designed to teach them. To sum up, plagiarizing is ethically wrong, self-defeating, and extremely risky—three good reasons why an accomplished critical thinker would avoid it like the plague!

Thinking Activity 9.8

WALK A MILE IN MY SHOES

1. Imagine yourself as a college student who is operating on a limited budget—which might not be too far from the truth! Make the strongest case you can for illegally sharing music and movie files and downloading pirated copies of your textbook.

2. Now imagine yourself as a successful musician/filmmaker/author who is being ripped off by people illegally sharing what you have created. Make the strongest case you can for doing what it takes to end the illegal sharing of music, movies, and books.

3. Now imagine yourself as yourself—this shouldn't be too difficult. Explain your conclusion about the morally right thing to do in terms of illegally sharing music and films and downloading books.

Thinking Passages

THINKING AND ACTING MORALLY

In this chapter we have examined the process of thinking critically about ethics and moral behavior. But is this merely an academic exercise, or can you make the connection between theory and the choices you make on a daily basis? The following essay, "The Disparity Between Intellect and Character," is by Robert Coles, a professor of psychiatry and medical humanities at Harvard University, who has focused much of his work on the moral development of people, especially children. In this essay he explores the question of how someone can be intellectually knowledgeable about ethics and yet not act ethically or be an ethical person, as well as what responsibility the college community has to encourage students to become more ethically enlightened.

The Disparity Between Intellect and Character

by Robert Coles

Over 150 years ago, Ralph Waldo Emerson gave a lecture at Harvard University, which he ended with the terse assertion: "Character is higher than intellect." Even then, this prominent man of letters was worried (as many other writers and thinkers of succeeding generations would be) about the limits of knowledge and the nature of a college's mission. The intellect can grow and grow, he knew, in a person who is smug, ungenerous, even cruel. Institutions originally founded to teach their students how to become good and decent, as well as broadly and deeply literate, may abandon the first mission to concentrate on a driven, narrow book learning course of study in no way intent on making a connection between ideas and theories on one hand and, on the other, our lives as we actually live them.

Students have their own way of realizing and trying to come to terms with the split that Emerson addressed. A few years ago, a sophomore student of mine came to see me in great anguish. She had arrived at Harvard from a Midwestern, working-class background. She was trying hard to work her way through college, and, in doing so, cleaned the rooms of some of her fellow students. Again and again, she encountered classmates who apparently had forgotten the meaning of *please*, or *thank you*—no matter how high their Scholastic Assessment Test scores—students who did not hesitate to be rude, even crude toward her.

One day she was not so subtly propositioned by a young man she knew to be a very bright, successful premed student and already an accomplished journalist. This was not the first time he had made such an overture, but now she had reached a breaking point. She had quit her job and was preparing to quit college in what she called "fancy, phony Cambridge."

The student had been part of a seminar I teach, which links Raymond Carver's fiction and poetry with Edward Hopper's paintings and drawings—the thematic convergence of literary and artistic sensibility in exploring American loneliness, both its social and its personal aspects. As she expressed her anxiety and anger to me, she soon was sobbing hard. After her sobs quieted, we began to remember the old days of that class. But she had some weightier matter on her mind and began to give me a detailed, sardonic account of college life, as viewed by someone vulnerable and hardpressed by it. At one point, she observed of the student who had propositioned her: "That guy gets all A's. He tells people he's in Group I (the top academic category). I've taken two moral-reasoning courses with him, and I'm sure he's gotten A's in both of them—and look at how he behaves with me, and I'm sure with others."

She stopped for a moment to let me take that in. I happened to know the young man and could only acknowledge the irony of his behavior, even as I wasn't totally surprised by what she'd experienced. But I was at a loss to know what to say to her. A philosophy major, with a strong interest in literature, she had taken a course on the Holocaust and described for me the ironies she also saw in that tragedy—mass murder of unparalleled historical proportion in a nation hitherto known as one of the most civilized in the world, with a citizenry as well educated as that of any country at the time.

Drawing on her education, the student put before me names such as Martin Heidegger, Carl Jung, Paul De Man, Ezra Pound—brilliant and accomplished men (a philosopher, a psychoanalyst, a literary critic, a poet) who nonetheless had linked themselves with the hate that was Nazism and Fascism during the 1930s. She reminded me of the willingness of the leaders of German and Italian universities to embrace Nazi and Fascist ideas, of the countless doctors and lawyers and judges and journalists and schoolteachers, and, yes, even members of the clergy—who were able to accommodate themselves to murderous thugs because the thugs had political power. She pointedly mentioned, too, the Soviet Gulag, that expanse of prisons to which millions of honorable people were sent by Stalin and his brutish accomplices—prisons commonly staffed by psychiatrists quite eager to label those victims of a vicious totalitarian state with an assortment of psychiatric names, then shoot them up with drugs meant to reduce them to zombies.

I tried hard, toward the end of a conversation that lasted almost two hours, to salvage something for her, for myself, and, not least, for a university that I much respect, even as I know its failings. I suggested that if she had learned what she had just shared with me at Harvard—why, *that* was itself a valuable education acquired. She smiled, gave me credit for a "nice try," but remained unconvinced. Then she put this tough, pointed, unnerving question to me: "I've been taking all these philosophy courses, and we talk about what's true, what's important, what's *good*. Well, how do you teach people to *be* good?" And she added: "What's the point of *knowing* good, if you don't keep trying to *become* a good person?"

I suddenly found myself on the defensive, although all along I had been sympathetic to her, to the indignation she had been directing toward some of her fellow students, and to her critical examination of the limits of abstract knowledge. Schools are schools, colleges are colleges, I averred, a complaisant and smug accommodation in my voice. Thereby I meant to say that our schools and colleges these days don't take major responsibility for the moral values of their students, but, rather, assume that their students acquire those values at home. I topped off my surrender to the *status quo* with a shrug of my shoulders, to which she responded with an unspoken but barely concealed anger. This she expressed through a knowing look that announced that she'd taken the full moral measure of me.

Suddenly, she was on her feet preparing to leave. I realized that I'd stumbled badly. I wanted to pursue the discussion, applaud her for taking on a large subject in a forthright, incisive manner, and tell her she was right in understanding that moral reasoning is not to be equated with moral conduct. I wanted, really, to explain my shrug—point out that there is only so much that any of us can do to affect others' behavior, that institutional life has its own momentum. But she had no interest in that kind of self-justification—as she let me know in an unforgettable aside as she was departing my office: "I wonder whether Emerson was just being 'smart' in that lecture he gave here. I wonder if he ever had any ideas about what to *do* about what was worrying him—or did he think he'd done enough because he'd spelled the problem out to those Harvard professors?"

She was demonstrating that she understood two levels of irony: One was that the study of philosophy—even moral philosophy or moral reasoning—doesn't necessarily prompt in either the teacher or the student a determination to act in accordance with moral principles. And, further, a discussion of that very irony can prove equally sterile—again carrying no apparent consequences as far as one's everyday actions go.

When that student left my office (she would soon leave Harvard for good), I was exhausted and saddened—and brought up short. All too often those of us who read books or teach don't think to pose for ourselves the kind of ironic dilemma she had posed to me. How might we teachers encourage our students (encourage *ourselves*) to take that big step from thought to action, from moral analysis to fulfilled moral commitments? Rather obviously, community service offers us all a chance to put our money where our mouths are; and, of course, such service can enrich our understanding of the disciplines we study. A reading of *Invisible Man* (literature), *Tally's Corner* (sociology and anthropology), or *Childhood and Society* (psychology and psychoanalysis) takes on new meaning after some time spent in a ghetto school or a clinic. By the same token, such books can prompt us to think pragmatically about, say, how the wisdom that Ralph Ellison worked into his fiction might shape the way we get along with the children we're tutoring—affect our attitudes toward them, the things we say and do with them.

Yet I wonder whether classroom discussion, *per se*, can't also be of help, the skepticism of my student notwithstanding. She had pushed me hard, and I started referring again and again in my classes on moral introspection to what she had observed and learned, and my students more than got the message. Her moral righteousness, her shrewd eye and ear for hypocrisy hovered over us, made us uneasy, goaded us.

She challenged us to prove that what we think intellectually can be connected to our daily deeds. For some of us, the connection was established through community service. But that is not the only possible way. I asked students to write papers that told of particular efforts to honor through action the high thoughts we were discussing. Thus goaded to a certain self-consciousness, I suppose, students made various efforts. I felt that the best of them were small victories, brief epiphanies that might otherwise have been overlooked, but had great significance for the students in question.

"I thanked someone serving me food in the college cafeteria, and then we got to talking, the first time," one student wrote. For her, this was a decisive break with her former indifference to others she abstractly regarded as "the people who work on the serving line." She felt that she had learned something about another's life and had tried to show respect for that life.

The student who challenged me with her angry, melancholy story had pushed me to teach differently. Now, I make an explicit issue of the more than occasional disparity between thinking and doing, and I ask my students to consider how we all might bridge that disparity. To be sure, the task of connecting intellect to character is daunting, as Emerson and others well knew. And any of us can lapse into cynicism, turn the moral challenge of a seminar into yet another moment of opportunism: I'll get an A this time, by writing a paper cannily extolling myself as a doer of this or that "good deed"!

Still, I know that college administrators and faculty members everywhere are struggling with the same issues that I was faced with, and I can testify that many students will respond seriously, in at least small ways, if we make clear that we really believe that the link between moral reasoning and action is important to us. My experience has given me at least a measure of hope that moral reasoning and reflection can somehow be integrated into students'—and teachers'—lives as they actually live them.

QUESTIONS FOR ANALYSIS

1. The following quote appears near the beginning of the chapter:

   The ultimate purpose in studying ethics is not as it is in other inquiries, the attainment of theoretical knowledge; we are not conducting this inquiry in order to know what virtue is, but in order to become good, else there would be no advantage in studying it.

   —Aristotle

2. How would Robert Coles respond to this quote? How do you respond to it?

3. How do you explain the fact that morally evil people can be highly educated in terms of ethics and religion? In other words, how do you account for the gap that sometimes occurs between knowledge of ethics and being an ethical person?

4. If you were in Coles's position, what would have been your response to the student's concerns regarding the disconnect between ethics and education?

5. Do you think that colleges have a moral obligation to help students become more ethical individuals? Why or why not?

6. If you were teaching a course in ethics, what would be your major goals for the course? For example, in addition to exposing students to the major ethical theories in philosophy, would you also want to encourage students to become more thoughtful and enlightened moral individuals?

SOLVING THE PROBLEM OF WORLD HUNGER

Two thousand years ago, the Roman philosopher Cicero observed that Socrates, the founder of Western philosophy, had brought philosophy "out of the clouds and into the marketplace," into the homes and lives of people. In this same spirit,

Peter Singer is a philosopher who has brought ideas out of the abstract realm of conjecture and into the vibrant immediacy of our lives. Combining moral passion with compelling logic, Singer forces us to confront the significance and implications of the choices we make every day of our lives. As we evaluate our reflections in the moral mirror he provides, we may find the resulting image to be profoundly disturbing. For example, consider this passage from his book *Practical Ethics,* in which Dr. Singer argues that by allowing people in poor countries to die because we have chosen not to share our resources with them, we are guilty of the moral equivalent of murder.

> The path from the library at my university to the humanities lecture theater passes a shallow ornamental pond. Suppose that on my way to give a lecture I notice that a small child has fallen in and is in danger of drowning. Would anyone deny that I ought to wade in and pull the child out? This will mean getting my clothes muddy and either canceling my lecture or delaying it until I can find something dry to change into; but compared to the avoidable death of a child this is insignificant. A plausible principle that would support the judgment that I ought to pull the child out is this: if it is in our power to prevent something very bad from happening, without thereby sacrificing anything of comparable moral significance, we ought to do it. This principle seems uncontroversial. . . . Nevertheless the uncontroversial appearance of the principle is deceptive. If it were taken seriously and acted upon, our lives and our world would be fundamentally changed. For the principle applies, not just to rare situations in which one can save a child from a pond, but to the everyday situation in which we can assist those living in absolute poverty. In saying this I assume that absolute poverty, with its hunger and malnutrition, lack of shelter, illiteracy, disease, high infant mortality, and low life expectancy, is a bad thing. And I assume that it is within the power of the affluent to reduce absolute poverty, without sacrificing anything of comparable moral significance. If these two assumptions and the principle we have been discussing are correct, we have an obligation to help those in absolute poverty that is no less strong than our obligation to rescue a drowning child from a pond. Not to help would be wrong, whether or not it is intrinsically equivalent to killing. Helping is not, as conventionally thought, a charitable act that it is praiseworthy to do, but not wrong to omit; it is something that everyone ought to do.

The Singer Solution to World Poverty

by Peter Singer

The Australian philosopher Peter Singer, who [teaches] at Princeton University, is perhaps the world's most controversial ethicist. Many readers of his book "Animal Liberation" were moved to embrace vegetarianism, while others recoiled at Singer's attempt to place humans and animals on an even moral plane. Similarly, his argument that severely disabled infants should, in some cases, receive euthanasia has been praised as courageous by some—and denounced by others, including anti-abortion activists, who have protested Singer's Princeton appointment.

Source: "The Singer Solution to World Poverty," by Peter Singer, *The New York Times* on the Web, September 5, 1999. http://people.brandeis.edu/~teuber/singermag.html. Reprinted by permission of the author.

Singer's penchant for provocation extends to more mundane matters, like everyday charity. A recent article about Singer in The New York Times revealed that the philosopher gives one-fifth of his income to famine-relief agencies. "From when I first saw pictures in newspapers of people starving, from when people asked you to donate some of your pocket money for collections at school," he mused, "I always thought, 'Why that much—why not more?'"

Is it possible to quantify our charitable burden? In the following essay, Singer offers some unconventional thoughts about the ordinary American's obligations to the world's poor and suggests that even his own one-fifth standard may not be enough.

. . .

In the Brazilian film "Central Station," Dora is a retired schoolteacher who makes ends meet by sitting at the station writing letters for illiterate people. Suddenly she has an opportunity to pocket $1,000. All she has to do is persuade a homeless 9-year-old boy to follow her to an address she has been given. (She is told he will be adopted by wealthy foreigners.) She delivers the boy, gets the money, spends some of it on a television set and settles down to enjoy her new acquisition. Her neighbor spoils the fun, however, by telling her that the boy was too old to be adopted—he will be killed and his organs sold for transplantation. Perhaps Dora knew this all along, but after her neighbor's plain speaking, she spends a troubled night. In the morning Dora resolves to take the boy back.

Suppose Dora had told her neighbor that it is a tough world, other people have nice new TV's too, and if selling the kid is the only way she can get one, well, he was only a street kid. She would then have become, in the eyes of the audience, a monster. She redeems herself only by being prepared to bear considerable risks to save the boy.

At the end of the movie, in cinemas in the affluent nations of the world, people who would have been quick to condemn Dora if she had not rescued the boy go home to places far more comfortable than her apartment. In fact, the average family in the United States spends almost one-third of its income on things that are no more necessary to them than Dora's new TV was to her. Going out to nice restaurants, buying new clothes because the old ones are no longer stylish, vacationing at beach resorts—so much of our income is spent on things not essential to the preservation of our lives and health. Donated to one of a number of charitable agencies, that money could mean the difference between life and death for children in need.

All of which raises a question: In the end, what is the ethical distinction between a Brazilian who sells a homeless child to organ peddlers and an American who already has a TV and upgrades to a better one—knowing that the money could be donated to an organization that would use it to save the lives of kids in need?

Of course, there are several differences between the two situations that could support different moral judgments about them. For one thing, to be able to consign a child to death when he is standing right in front of you takes a chilling kind of heartlessness; it is much easier to ignore an appeal for money to help children you will never meet. Yet for a utilitarian philosopher like myself—that is, one who judges whether acts are right or wrong by their consequences—if the upshot of the American's failure to donate the money is that one more kid dies on the streets of a Brazilian city, then it is, in some sense, just as bad as selling the kid to the organ peddlers. But one doesn't need to embrace my utilitarian ethic to see that, at the very least, there is a troubling incongruity in being so quick to condemn Dora for taking the child to the organ peddlers while, at the same time, not regarding the American consumer's behavior as raising a serious moral issue.

In his 1996 book, "Living High and Letting Die," the New York University philosopher Peter Unger presented an ingenious series of imaginary examples designed to probe our intuitions about whether it is wrong to live well without giving substantial amounts of money to help people who are hungry, malnourished or dying from easily treatable illnesses like diarrhea. Here's my paraphrase of one of these examples:

Bob is close to retirement. He has invested most of his savings in a very rare and valuable old car, a Bugatti, which he has not been able to insure. The Bugatti is his pride and joy. In addition to the pleasure he gets from driving and caring for his car, Bob knows that its rising market value means that he will always be able to sell it and live comfortably after retirement.

One day when Bob is out for a drive, he parks the Bugatti near the end of a railway siding and goes for a walk up the track. As he does so, he sees that a runaway train, with no one aboard, is running down the railway track. Looking farther down the track, he sees the small figure of a child very likely to be killed by the runaway train. He can't stop the train and the child is too far away to warn of the danger, but he can throw a switch that will divert the train down the siding where his Bugatti is parked. Then nobody will be killed—but the train will destroy his Bugatti. Thinking of his joy in owning the car and the financial security it represents, Bob decides not to throw the switch. The child is killed. For many years to come, Bob enjoys owning his Bugatti and the financial security it represents.

Bob's conduct, most of us will immediately respond, was gravely wrong. Unger agrees. But then he reminds us that we, too, have opportunities to save the lives of children. We can give to organizations like Unicef or Oxfam America. How much would we have to give one of these organizations to have a high probability of saving the life of a child threatened by easily preventable diseases? (I do not believe that children are more worth saving than adults, but since no one can argue that children have brought their poverty on themselves, focusing on them simplifies the issues.) Unger called up some experts and used the information they provided to offer some plausible estimates that include the cost of raising money, administrative expenses and the cost of delivering aid where it is most needed. By his calculation, $200 in donations would help a sickly 2-year-old transform into a healthy 6-year-old—offering safe passage through childhood's most dangerous years. To show how practical philosophical argument can be, Unger even tells his readers that they can easily donate funds by using their credit card and calling one of these toll-free numbers: (800) 367-5437 for Unicef; (800) 693-2687 for Oxfam America.

Now you, too, have the information you need to save a child's life. How should you judge yourself if you don't do it? Think again about Bob and his Bugatti. Unlike Dora, Bob did not have to look into the eyes of the child he was sacrificing for his own material comfort. The child was a complete stranger to him and too far away to relate to in an intimate, personal way. Unlike Dora, too, he did not mislead the child or initiate the chain of events imperiling him. In all these respects, Bob's situation resembles that of people able but unwilling to donate to overseas aid and differs from Dora's situation.

If you still think that it was very wrong of Bob not to throw the switch that would have diverted the train and saved the child's life, then it is hard to see how you could deny that it is also very wrong not to send money to one of the organizations listed above. Unless, that is, there is some morally important difference between the two situations that I have overlooked.

Is it the practical uncertainties about whether aid will really reach the people who need it? Nobody who knows the world of overseas aid can doubt that such uncertainties exist. But Unger's figure of $200 to save a child's life was reached after he had made conservative assumptions about the proportion of the money donated that will actually reach its target.

One genuine difference between Bob and those who can afford to donate to overseas aid organizations but don't is that only Bob can save the child on the tracks, whereas there are hundreds of millions of people who can give $200 to overseas aid organizations. The problem is that most of them aren't doing it. Does this mean that it is all right for you not to do it?

Suppose that there were more owners of priceless vintage cars—Carol, Dave, Emma, Fred and so on, down to Ziggy—all in exactly the same situation as Bob, with their own siding and their own switch, all sacrificing the child in order to preserve their own cherished car. Would that make it all right for Bob to do the same? To answer this question affirmatively is to endorse follow-the-crowd ethics—the kind of ethics that led many Germans to look away when the Nazi atrocities were being committed. We do not excuse them because others were behaving no better.

We seem to lack a sound basis for drawing a clear moral line between Bob's situation and that of any reader of this article with $200 to spare who does not donate it to an overseas aid agency. These readers seem to be acting at least as badly as Bob was acting when he chose to let the runaway train hurtle toward the unsuspecting child. In the light of this conclusion, I trust that many readers will reach for the phone and donate that $200. Perhaps you should do it before reading further.

Now that you have distinguished yourself morally from people who put their vintage cars ahead of a child's life, how about treating yourself and your partner to dinner at your favorite restaurant? But wait. The money you will spend at the restaurant could also help save the lives of children overseas! True, you weren't planning to blow $200 tonight, but if you were to give up dining out just for one month, you would easily save that amount. And what is one month's dining out, compared to a child's life? There's the rub. Since there are a lot of desperately needy children in the world, there will always be another child whose life you could save for another $200. Are you therefore obliged to keep giving until you have nothing left? At what point can you stop?

Hypothetical examples can easily become farcical. Consider Bob. How far past losing the Bugatti should he go? Imagine that Bob had got his foot stuck in the track of the siding, and if he diverted the train, then before it rammed the car it would also amputate his big toe. Should he still throw the switch? What if it would amputate his foot? His entire leg?

As absurd as the Bugatti scenario gets when pushed to extremes, the point it raises is a serious one: only when the sacrifices become very significant indeed would most people be prepared to say that Bob does nothing wrong when he decides not to throw the switch. Of course, most people could be wrong; we can't decide moral issues by taking opinion polls. But consider for yourself the level of sacrifice that you would demand of Bob, and then think about how much money you would have to give away in order to make a sacrifice that is roughly equal to that. It's almost certainly much, much more than $200. For most middle-class Americans, it could easily be more like $200,000.

Isn't it counterproductive to ask people to do so much? Don't we run the risk that many will shrug their shoulders and say that morality, so conceived, is fine for saints but not for them? I accept that we are unlikely to see, in the near or even medium-term future, a world in which it is normal for wealthy Americans to give the bulk of their wealth to strangers. When it comes to praising or blaming people for what they do, we tend to use a standard that is relative to some conception of normal behavior. Comfortably off Americans who give, say, 10 percent of their income to overseas aid organizations are so far ahead of most of their equally comfortable fellow citizens that I wouldn't go out of my way to chastise them for not doing more. Nevertheless, they should be doing much more, and they are in no position to criticize Bob for failing to make the much greater sacrifice of his Bugatti.

At this point various objections may crop up. Someone may say: "If every citizen living in the affluent nations contributed his or her share I wouldn't have to make such a drastic sacrifice, because long before such levels were reached, the resources would have been there to save the lives of all those children dying from lack of food or medical care. So why should I give more than my fair share?" Another, related, objection is that the Government ought to increase its overseas aid allocations, since that would spread the burden more equitably across all taxpayers.

Yet the question of how much we ought to give is a matter to be decided in the real world—and that, sadly, is a world in which we know that most people do not, and in the immediate future will not, give substantial amounts to overseas aid agencies. We know, too, that at least in the next year, the United States Government is not going to meet even the very modest United Nations-recommended target of 0.7 percent of gross national product; at the moment it lags far below that, at 0.09 percent, not even half of Japan's 0.22 percent or a tenth of Denmark's 0.97 percent. Thus, we know that the money we can give beyond that theoretical "fair share" is still going to save lives that would otherwise be lost. While the idea that no one need do more than his or her fair share is a powerful one, should it prevail if we know that others are not doing their fair share and that children will die preventable deaths unless we do more than our fair share? That would be taking fairness too far.

Thus, this ground for limiting how much we ought to give also fails. In the world as it is now, I can see no escape from the conclusion that each one of us with wealth surplus to his or her essential needs should be giving most of it to help people suffering from poverty so dire as to be life-threatening. That's right: I'm saying that you shouldn't buy that new car, take that cruise, redecorate the house or get that pricey new suit. After all, a $1,000 suit could save five children's lives.

So how does my philosophy break down in dollars and cents? An American household with an income of $50,000 spends around $30,000 annually on necessities, according to the Conference Board, a nonprofit economic research organization.

Therefore, for a household bringing in $50,000 a year, donations to help the world's poor should be as close as possible to $20,000. The $30,000 required for necessities holds for higher incomes as well. So a household making $100,000 could cut a yearly check for $70,000. Again, the formula is simple: whatever money you're spending on luxuries, not necessities, should be given away.

Now, evolutionary psychologists tell us that human nature just isn't sufficiently altruistic to make it plausible that many people will sacrifice so much for strangers. On the facts of human nature, they might be right, but they would be wrong to draw a moral conclusion from those facts. If it is the case that we ought to do things that, predictably, most of us won't do, then let's face that fact head-on. Then, if we value the life of a child more than going to fancy restaurants, the next time we dine out we will know that we could have done something better with our money. If that makes living a morally decent life extremely arduous, well, then that is the way things are. If we don't do it, then we should at least know that we are failing to live a morally decent life—not because it is good to wallow in guilt but because knowing where we should be going is the first step toward heading in that direction.

When Bob first grasped the dilemma that faced him as he stood by that railway switch, he must have thought how extraordinarily unlucky he was to be placed in a situation in which he must choose between the life of an innocent child and the sacrifice of most of his savings. But he was not unlucky at all. We are all in that situation.

QUESTIONS FOR ANALYSIS

1. Singer uses multiple examples to dramatize our moral responsibility in reducing world hunger: a child drowning in a pond, a child imperiled on a railroad track. In what way are these examples similar with respect to the central argument that he is making? Do you agree with Singer's point that it is our moral obligation to save a child's life if we are able to do so without great sacrifice on our part? Why or why not?

2. Stated in even stronger terms, Singer believes that if we *don't* take the initiative to donate a significant portion of our income to help alleviate world hunger, then we are guilty of the moral equivalent of murder. Do you agree or disagree with this conclusion? Why or why not? If not, what counterarguments would you propose to Singer? How do you think he would respond?

3. If you put yourself in the situation that Singer describes, what would you be willing to sacrifice in order to save the life of a child with whom you had no personal connection? Whatever your level of sacrifice, would it be fair to say that this reflects the value you place on a human life?

4. Even if people are persuaded by the powerful logic of Singer's reasoning, why do you think they might be reluctant to take the next logical step of contributing much of their income to save the lives of starving children? Do you think their actions are justified?

Summary

- Ethics and morality are concerned with the judgment of the goodness or badness of human action and character.
- Each of us has a "moral compass"—our set of moral beliefs that we use to guide our choices in moral situations. By studying ethics and engaging in critical reflection, we can improve our moral compass to make it as ethically enlightened as possible.
- The Thinker's Guide to Moral Decision Making includes the following points:
  - Make morality a priority.
  - Recognize that ethics is based on reason.
  - Include the ethic of justice.
  - Include the ethic of care.
  - Accept responsibility.
  - Seek to promote happiness.
  - Develop an informed moral intuition.
  - Discover the natural law of human nature.
  - Choose to be a moral person.

Assessing Your Strategies and Creating New Goals

How Moral Am I?

Described next are key personal attributes that are correlated with having an enlightened sense of morality. Evaluate your position regarding each of these attributes, and use this self-evaluation to guide your choices as you shape the moral person that you want to become.

Develop a Clear Moral Code

I have a clear moral code I use to guide my choices.	I am often confused and uncertain about my moral choices.
5 4 3 2 1	

The key to living a moral life is developing a clear, intelligent moral code to guide your choices. Such a moral code should be *coherent* (your values fit together with consistency); *comprehensive* (your code can be applied effectively to many different kinds of moral situations); and *well-grounded* (your beliefs are supported by cogent reasons).

Strategy: *Using your responses to the **Thinking Activities** as a springboard, record in your **Thinking Notebook** the moral principles that you use to guide your choices. After writing down your moral principles, evaluate them for consistency and try to organize them into coherent patterns. Keep developing and refining your moral code as you learn through experience and increase your moral maturity over time.*

Adopt the Ethic of Justice

The ethic of justice is an important part of my moral code.	The ethic of justice is not something I have consciously applied to my moral code.
5 4 3 2 1	

The ethic of justice is built on the concept of *impartiality*, which is our moral obligation to treat everyone equally, with the same degree of consideration and respect we accord ourselves, unless there is some persuasive reason not to. It is both illogical and, according to thinker's like Immanuel Kant, immoral to discriminate against other people.

Strategy: *Think about your own biases toward others, and begin working to treat these people with the respect they are due.*

Adopt the Ethic of Care

The ethic of care is an important part of my moral code.	The ethic of care is not an important part of my moral code.
5 4 3 2 1	

The ethic of care expresses a moral responsibility to others that is based on your ability to *empathize*—to imaginatively put yourself in other people's situations and view the world from their perspectives. This ability to empathize enables you to feel compassion and sympathy toward others, and serves as the foundation of all your healthy relationships.

Strategy: *Increase your ability to empathize by making a special effort to transcend your own perspective and place yourself in other people's "shoes." In your dealings with others, use your imagination to experience what you believe they are thinking and feeling, and observe whether this influences your attitudes and actions toward them.*

Universalize Your Moral Choices

I often universalize my choices in deciding what to do.	I rarely universalize my choices in making moral decisions.
5 4 3 2 1	

An effective strategy, proposed by Immanuel Kant, during your moral deliberations is to ask yourself if it would be logical for everyone, in situations similar to your own, to make the same choice that you are making.

Strategy: As you deliberate the various moral choices in your life, both small ("Should I cut ahead in line?") and large ("Should I pursue my own self-interest at the risk of hurting someone else?"), make a conscious effort to universalize your anticipated action. Would you be willing for everyone to take this same action in similar circumstances? If not, evaluate whether the action is truly morally justified and consistent with other moral values you hold.

Treat People as Ends, Not Means

I usually treat people with respect for their autonomy.	I often treat people as a means to achieving my own interests.
5 4 3 2 1	

Although Kant's admonition to treat people *always* as ends and *never* as means to our own ends may seem extreme, we should perhaps take his recommendation more seriously than we normally do. By respecting someone else's right to make free choices—even a child's—we are bringing out the best in them as we enhance our own moral stature.

*Strategy: Think about some recent instances in which you attempted to influence people's thoughts, feelings, or behavior. Did you make a clear case for your recommendation, respecting their right to make a free choice? Or did you try to manipulate them by using techniques designed to influence them without their knowledge or coerce them against their wishes? If you discover examples of manipulation, try to imagine how things would have turned out if you had taken a more forthright approach, and record your reflections in your **Thinking Notebook**.*

Choose to Be a Moral Person

I am determined to create myself as a moral person.	Becoming a moral person is not a conscious priority.
5 4 3 2 1	

Becoming a morally enlightened person—a person of character, compassion, and integrity—is a daily struggle that requires true grit and determination. You must consciously choose to achieve your moral potential, reflecting on the moral choices you make and working to clarify and refine your moral code.

*Strategy: Develop the habit of conducting a regular appraisal of yourself and your life, written in your **Thinking Notebook**. Ask—and answer—questions like: Am I achieving my goals as a moral person? As a critical thinker? As a creative individual? Use this evaluation regularly to maintain a much-needed perspective on your life, remind yourself of the "big picture," and guide your evolution into the most worthy person you can become.*

Suggested Films

A Dry White Season (1989)

What is the moral responsibility of an individual in addressing injustice? Ben Du Toit is a schoolteacher in South Africa during apartheid who witnesses the results of a murder committed by the corrupt government police. Du Toit puts himself at risk when he stands up to an oppressive government in an attempt to reveal their inhumane actions. Based on the novel by Andre Brink.

The Insider (1999)

Does the public have a right to be informed about products that could potentially harm them? Based on true events, this film recounts the story of former tobacco executive, Jeffrey Wigand, who agrees to appear on *60 Minutes* to discuss unethical behavior and malpractice in the tobacco industry. On advice from lawyers and pressure from higher-ups, the show opts not to air the interview.

Peter Singer: A Dangerous Mind (2003)

Dr. Peter Singer has been called the most influential living philosopher. He has also been called a monster. In this thought-provoking program, he faces his critics and discusses his ideas on euthanasia, abortion, and infanticide. The program follows his worldwide tour of lectures and encounters, including case conferences and a trip to Austria, where most of his family was killed in the Holocaust. A range of commentators consider his utilitarian stance and its impact on public policy.

Schindler's List (1993)

How does one find a purpose in life? This film is based on the true story of Oskar Schindler, a businessman who intended to exploit Jewish labor to amass a personal fortune. Witnessing the horrors of the Holocaust profoundly affects his perspective, and he then uses his business to save 1,100 Jews from extermination in the gas chambers at Auschwitz. It is a story of personal transformation, self-sacrifice, and the ability of a single person to influence the lives of many.

A Simple Plan (1998)

Three men are confronted with a series of moral dilemmas when they find millions of dollars in a crashed plane. They devise a plan to keep the money, but tension rises as concealing the secret becomes more complex, leading to increasingly disastrous consequences.

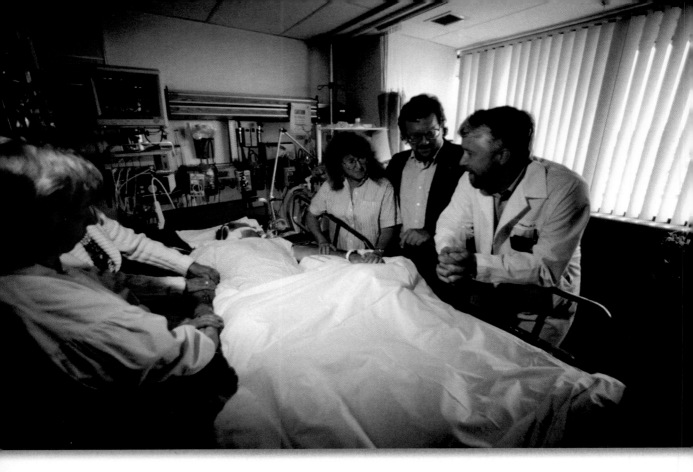

Should We Prolong Life at All Costs?

Ethical dilemmas are an unavoidable part of life. What is your reaction to this photograph of a comatose patient on life-support equipment surrounded by his family? Do you believe that medical technology should be used to extend people's lives in all cases? Why or why not?

Constructing Arguments

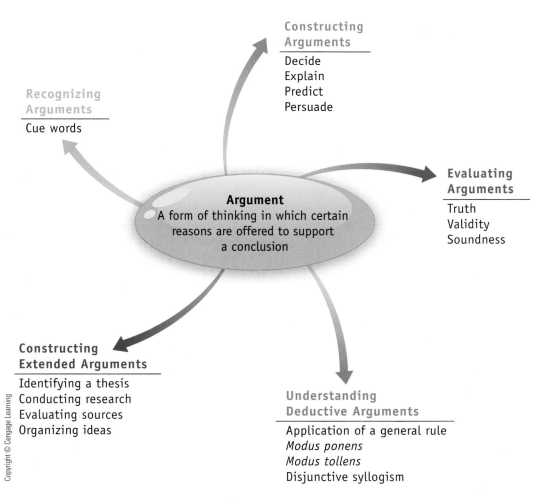

Recognizing Arguments

Cue words

Constructing Arguments

Decide
Explain
Predict
Persuade

Argument
A form of thinking in which certain reasons are offered to support a conclusion

Evaluating Arguments

Truth
Validity
Soundness

Constructing Extended Arguments

Identifying a thesis
Conducting research
Evaluating sources
Organizing ideas

Understanding Deductive Arguments

Application of a general rule
Modus ponens
Modus tollens
Disjunctive syllogism

Consider carefully the following dialogue about whether marijuana should be legalized:

DENNIS: Did you hear about the person who was sentenced to fifteen years in prison for possessing marijuana? I think this is one of the most outrageously unjust punishments I've ever heard of! In most states, people who are convicted of armed robbery, rape, or even murder don't receive fifteen-year sentences. And unlike the possession of marijuana, these crimes violate the rights of other people.

CAROLINE: I agree that this is one case in which the punishment doesn't seem to fit the crime. But you have to realize that drugs pose a serious threat to the young people of our country. Look at all the people who are addicted to drugs, who have their lives ruined, and who often die at an early age of overdoses. And think of all the crimes committed by people to support their drug habits. As a result, sometimes society has to make an example of someone—like the person you mentioned—to convince people of the seriousness of the situation.

DENNIS: That's ridiculous. In the first place, it's not right to punish someone unfairly just to provide an example. At least not in a society that believes in justice. And in the second place, smoking marijuana is nothing like using drugs such as heroin or even cocaine. It follows that smoking marijuana should not be against the law.

CAROLINE: I don't agree. Although marijuana might not be as dangerous as some other drugs, smoking it surely isn't good for you. And I don't think that anything that is a threat to your health should be legal.

DENNIS: What about cigarettes and alcohol? We *know* that they are dangerous. Medical research has linked smoking cigarettes to lung cancer, emphysema, and heart disease, and alcohol damages the liver. No one has proved that marijuana is a threat to our health. And even if it does turn out to be somewhat unhealthy, it's certainly not as dangerous as cigarettes and alcohol.

CAROLINE: That's a good point. But to tell you the truth, I'm not so sure that cigarettes and alcohol should be legal. And in any case, they are already legal. Just because cigarettes and alcohol are bad for your health is no reason to legalize another drug that can cause health problems.

DENNIS: Look—life is full of risks. We take chances every time we cross the street or climb into our car. In fact, with all of these loonies on the road, driving is a lot more hazardous to our health than any of the drugs around. And many of the foods we eat can kill. For example, red meat contributes to heart disease, and artificial sweeteners can cause cancer. The point is if people want to take chances with their health, that's up to them. And many people in our society like to mellow out with marijuana. I read somewhere that over 70 percent of the people in the United States think that marijuana should be legalized.

Thinking Critically About Visuals

"Let Herbs Grow Free!"

Would you be inclined to join a "Legalize Marijuana" protest like this one? Why do some people believe that marijuana should be legalized? Why do others believe that it shouldn't?

LondonPhotos-Homer Sykes/Alamy

CAROLINE: There's a big difference between letting people drive cars and letting them use dangerous drugs. Society has a responsibility to protect people from themselves. People often do things that are foolish if they are encouraged or given the opportunity to. Legalizing something like marijuana encourages people to use it, especially young people. It follows that many more people would use marijuana if it were legalized. It's like society saying, "This is all right—go ahead and use it."

DENNIS: I still maintain that marijuana isn't dangerous. It's not addictive—like heroin is—and there is no evidence that it harms you. Consequently, anything that is harmless should be legal.

CAROLINE: Marijuana may not be physically addictive like heroin, but I think that it can be psychologically addictive because people tend to use more and more of it over time. I know a number of people who spend a lot of their time getting high. What about Carl? All he does is lie around and get high. This shows that smoking it over a period of time definitely affects your mind. Think about the people you know who smoke a lot—don't they seem to be floating in a dream world? How are they ever going to make anything of their lives? As far as I'm concerned, a pothead is like a zombie—living but dead.

DENNIS: Since you have had so little experience with marijuana, I don't think that you can offer an informed opinion on the subject. And anyway, if you do too much of anything, it can hurt you. Even something as healthy as exercise can cause problems if you do too much of it. But I sure don't see anything wrong with toking up with some friends at a party or even getting into a relaxed state by yourself. In fact, I find that I can even concentrate better on my schoolwork after taking a little smoke.

CAROLINE: If you believe that, then marijuana really *has* damaged your brain. You're just trying to rationalize your drug habit. Smoking marijuana doesn't help you concentrate—it takes you away from reality. And I don't think that people can control it. Either you smoke and surrender control of your life, or you don't smoke because you want to retain control. There's nothing in between.

DENNIS: Let me point out something to you: Because marijuana is illegal, organized crime controls its distribution and makes all the money from it. If marijuana were legalized, the government could tax the sale of it—like cigarettes and alcohol—and then use the money for some worthwhile purpose. For example, many states have legalized gambling and use the money to support education. In fact, the major tobacco companies have already copyrighted names for different marijuana brands—like "Acapulco Gold." Obviously, they believe that marijuana will soon become legal.

CAROLINE: Just because the government can make money out of something doesn't mean that they should legalize it. We could also legalize prostitution or muggings and then tax the proceeds. Also, simply because the cigarette companies are prepared to sell marijuana doesn't mean that it makes sense to. After all, they're the ones who are selling us cigarettes.

Continue this dialogue, incorporating other views on the subject of legalizing marijuana.

Recognizing Arguments

argument
A form of thinking in which certain statements (reasons) are offered in support of another statement (a conclusion).

The preceding discussion is an illustration of two people engaging in *dialogue*, which we have defined (in Chapter 2) as the systematic exchange of ideas. Participating in this sort of dialogue with others is one of the keys to thinking critically because it stimulates you to develop your mind by carefully examining the way you make sense of the world. Discussing issues with others encourages you to be mentally active, to ask questions, to view issues from different perspectives, and to develop reasons to support conclusions. It is this last quality of thinking critically—supporting conclusions with reasons—that we will focus on in this chapter and the next.

When we offer reasons to support a conclusion, we are considered to be presenting an **argument**.

At the beginning of the dialogue, Dennis presents the following argument against imposing a fifteen-year sentence for possession of marijuana (argument 1):

REASON: Possessing marijuana is not a serious offense because it hurts no one.

REASON: There are many other more serious offenses in which victims' basic rights are violated—such as armed robbery, rape, and murder—for which the offenders don't receive such stiff sentences.

CONCLUSION: Therefore, a fifteen-year sentence is an unjust punishment for possessing marijuana.

Can you identify an additional reason that supports this conclusion?

REASON:

The definition of *argument* given here is somewhat different from the meaning of the concept in our ordinary language. In common speech, "argument" usually refers to a dispute or quarrel between people, often involving intense feelings (e.g., "I got into a terrible argument with the idiot who hit the back of my car"). Very often these quarrels involve people presenting arguments in the sense in which we have defined the concept, although the arguments are usually not carefully reasoned or clearly stated because the people are so angry. Instead of this common usage, in this chapter we will use the word's more technical meaning.

Using our definition of *argument*, we can define, in turn, the main ideas that make up an argument: **reasons** that are presented to support an argument's **conclusion**.

The type of thinking that uses argument—reasons in support of conclusions—is known as *reasoning*, and it is a type of thinking you have been doing throughout this book, as well as in much of your life. We are continually trying to explain, justify, and predict things through the process of reasoning.

Of course, our reasoning—and the reasoning of others—is not always correct. For example, the reasons someone offers may not really support the conclusion they are supposed to support. Or the conclusion may not really follow from the reasons stated. These difficulties are illustrated in a number of the arguments contained in the dialogue on marijuana. Nevertheless, whenever we accept a conclusion as likely or true based on certain reasons, or whenever we offer reasons to support a conclusion, we are using arguments to engage in reasoning—even if our reasoning is weak or faulty. In this chapter and the next, we will be exploring both the way we construct effective arguments and the way we evaluate arguments to develop and sharpen our reasoning ability.

Let us return to the dialogue on marijuana. After Dennis presents the argument with the conclusion that the fifteen-year prison sentence is an unjust punishment, Caroline considers that argument. Although she acknowledges that in this case "the punishment doesn't seem to fit the crime," she goes on to offer another argument (argument 2), giving reasons that lead to a conclusion that conflicts with the one Dennis drew.

reasons Statements that support another statement (known as a conclusion), justify it, or make it more probable.

conclusion A statement that explains, asserts, or predicts on the basis of statements (known as reasons) that are offered as evidence for it.

REASON: Drugs pose a very serious threat to the young people of our country.

REASON: Many crimes are committed to support drug habits.

CONCLUSION: As a result, sometimes society has to make an example of someone to convince people of the seriousness of the situation.

Can you identify an additional reason that supports this conclusion?

REASON:

CUE WORDS FOR ARGUMENTS

Our language provides guidance in our efforts to identify reasons and conclusions. Certain key words, known as *cue words*, signal that a reason is being offered in support of a conclusion or that a conclusion is being announced on the basis of certain reasons. For example, in response to Caroline's conclusion that society sometimes has to make an example of someone to convince people of the seriousness of the situation, Dennis gives the following argument (argument 3):

REASON: In the first place, it's not right to punish someone unfairly just to provide an example.

REASON: In the second place, smoking marijuana is nothing like using drugs such as heroin or even cocaine.

CONCLUSION: It follows that smoking marijuana should not be against the law.

In this argument, the phrases *in the first place* and *in the second place* signal that reasons are being offered in support of a conclusion. Similarly, the phrase *it follows that* signals that a conclusion is being announced on the basis of certain reasons. Here is a list of the most commonly used cue words for reasons and conclusions.

Cue words signaling reasons

since	in view of
for	first, second
because	in the first (second) place
as shown by	may be inferred from
as indicated by	may be deduced from
given that	may be derived from
assuming that	for the reason that

Cue words signaling conclusions

therefore	then
thus	it follows that
hence	thereby showing
so	demonstrates that
(which) shows that	allows us to infer that
(which) proves that	suggests very strongly that
implies that	you see that

points to	leads me to believe that
as a result	allows us to deduce that
consequently	

Of course, identifying reasons, conclusions, and arguments involves more than looking for cue words. The words and phrases listed here do not always signal reasons and conclusions, and in many cases arguments are made without the use of cue words. However, cue words do help alert us that an argument is being made.

Thinking Activity 10.1

IDENTIFYING ARGUMENTS WITH CUE WORDS

1. Review the dialogue on marijuana and underline any cue words signaling that reasons are being offered or that conclusions are being announced.

2. With the aid of cue words, identify the various arguments contained in the dialogue on marijuana. For each argument, describe
   a. The *reasons* offered in support of a conclusion
   b. The *conclusion* announced on the basis of the reasons

   Before you start, review the three arguments we have examined thus far in this chapter.

3. Go back to the additional arguments you wrote on page 440. Reorganize and add cue words if necessary to clearly identify your reasons as well as the conclusion you drew from those reasons.

Thinking Passages

LEGALIZING DRUGS

Two essays that discuss the issue of whether drugs should be legalized are reproduced below. The first passage, "Drugs," was written by Gore Vidal, a well-known essayist and novelist. The second, "The Case for Slavery," was authored by *New York Times* editor and columnist A. M. Rosenthal. After carefully reading the essays, answer the questions that follow.

Drugs

by Gore Vidal

It is possible to stop most drug addiction in the United States within a very short time. Simply make all drugs available and sell them at cost. Label each drug with a precise description of what effect—good and bad—the drug will have on the taker. This will require heroic honesty. Don't say that marijuana is addictive or dangerous when it is neither, as millions of people know—unlike "speed," which kills most unpleasantly, or heroin, which is addictive and difficult to kick.

For the record, I have tried—once—almost every drug and liked none, disproving the popular Fu Manchu theory that a single whiff of opium will enslave the mind. Nevertheless many drugs are bad for certain people to take and they should be told why in a sensible way.

Along with exhortation and warning, it might be good for our citizens to recall (or learn for the first time) that the United States was the creation of men who believed that each man has the right to do what he wants with his own life as long as he does not interfere with his neighbor's pursuit of happiness. (That his neighbor's idea of happiness is persecuting others does confuse matters a bit.)

This is a startling notion to the current generation of Americans. They reflect a system of public education which has made the Bill of Rights, literally, unacceptable to a majority of high school graduates who now form the "silent majority"—a phrase which that underestimated wit Richard Nixon took from Homer who used it to describe the dead.

Now one can hear the warning rumble begin: If everyone is allowed to take drugs everyone will and the GNP will decrease, the Commies will stop us from making everyone free, and we shall end up a race of zombies, passively murmuring "groovy" to one another. Alarming thought. Yet it seems most unlikely that any reasonably sane person will become a drug addict if he knows in advance what addiction is going to be like.

Is everyone reasonably sane? No. Some people will always become drug addicts just as some people will always become alcoholics, and it is just too bad. Every man, however, has the power (and should have the legal right) to kill himself if he chooses. But since most men don't, they won't be mainliners either. Nevertheless, forbidding people things they like or think they might enjoy only makes them want those things all the more. This psychological insight is, for some mysterious reason, perennially denied our governors.

It is a lucky thing for the American moralist that our country has always existed in a kind of time-vacuum: We have no public memory of anything that happened before last Tuesday. No one in Washington today recalls what happened during the years alcohol was forbidden to the people by a Congress that thought it had a divine mission to stamp out Demon Rum—launching, in the process, the greatest crime wave in the country's history, causing thousands of deaths from bad alcohol, and creating a general (and persisting) contempt among the citizenry for the laws of the United States.

The same thing is happening today. But the government has learned nothing from past attempts at prohibition, not to mention repression.

Last year when the supply of Mexican marijuana was slightly curtailed by the Feds, the pushers got the kids hooked on heroin and deaths increased dramatically, particularly in New York. Whose fault? Evil men like the Mafiosi? Permissive Dr. Spock? Wild-eyed Dr. Leary? No.

The Government of the United States was responsible for those deaths. The bureaucratic machine has a vested interest in playing cops and robbers. Both the Bureau of Narcotics and the Mafia want strong laws against the sale and use of drugs because if drugs are sold at cost there would be no money in it for anyone.

If there was no money in it for the Mafia, there would be no friendly playground pushers, and addicts would not commit crimes to pay for the next fix. Finally, if there was no money in it, the Bureau of Narcotics would wither away, something they are not about to do without a struggle.

Will anything sensible be done? Of course not. The American people are as devoted to the idea of sin and its punishment as they are to making money—and fighting drugs is nearly as big a business as pushing them. Since the combination of sin and money is irresistible (particularly to the professional politician), the situation will only grow worse.

The Case for Slavery

by A. M. Rosenthal

Across the country, a scattered but influential collection of intellectuals is intensely engaged in making the case for slavery.

With considerable passion, these Americans are repeatedly expounding the benefits of not only tolerating slavery but legalizing it:

It would make life less dangerous for the free. It would save a great deal of money. And since the economies could be used to improve the lot of the slaves, in the end they would be better off.

The new antiabolitionists, like their predecessors in the nineteenth century, concede that those now in bondage do not themselves see the benefits of legalizing their status.

But in time they will, we are assured, because the beautiful part of legalization is that slavery would be designed so as to keep slaves pacified with the very thing that enslaves them!

The form of slavery under discussion is drug addiction. It does not have every characteristic of more traditional forms of bondage. But they have enough in common to make the comparison morally valid—and the campaign for drug legalization morally disgusting.

Like the plantation slavery that was a foundation of American society for so long, drug addiction largely involves specifiable groups of people. Most of the enchained are children and adolescents of all colors and black and Hispanic adults.

Like plantation slavery, drug addiction is passed on from generation to generation. And this may be the most important similarity: Like plantation slavery, addiction can destroy among its victims the social resources most valuable to free people for their own betterment—family life, family traditions, family values.

In plantation-time America, mothers were taken from their children. In drug-time America, mothers abandon their children. Do the children suffer less, or the mothers?

Antiabolitionists argue that legalization would make drugs so cheap and available that the profit for crime would be removed. Well-supplied addicts would be peaceful addicts. We would not waste billions for jails and could spend some of the savings helping the addicted become drug-free.

That would happen at the very time that new millions of Americans were being enticed into addiction by legalization—somehow.

Are we really foolish enough to believe that tens of thousands of drug gang members would meekly steal away, foiled by the marvels of the free market?

Not likely. The pushers would cut prices, making more money than ever from the evergrowing mass market. They would immediately increase the potency and variety beyond anything available at any government-approved narcotics counters.

Crime would increase. Crack produces paranoid violence. More permissiveness equals more use equals more violence.

And what will legalization do to the brains of Americans drawn into drug slavery by easy availability?

Earlier this year, an expert drug pediatrician told me that after only a few months babies born with crack addiction seemed to recover. Now we learn that stultifying behavioral effects last at least through early childhood. Will they last forever?

How long will crack affect neurological patterns in the brains of adult crack users? Dr. Gabriel G. Nahas of Columbia University argues in his new book, *Cocaine: The Great White Plague,* that the damage may be irreversible. Would it not be an act of simple intelligence to drop the legalization campaign until we find out?

Then why do a number of writers and academicians, left to right, support it? I have discussed this with antidrug leaders like Jesse Jackson, Dr. Mitchell Rosenthal of Phoenix House, and William J. Bennett, who search for answers themselves.

Perhaps the answer is that the legalizers are not dealing with reality in America. I think the reason has to do with class.

Crack is beginning to move into the white middle and upper classes. That is a tragedy for those addicted.

However, it has not yet destroyed the communities around which their lives revolve, not taken over every street and doorway. It has not passed generation to generation among them, killing the continuity of family.

But in ghetto communities poverty and drugs come together in a catalytic reaction that is reducing them to social rubble.

The antiabolitionists, virtually all white and well-to-do, do not see or do not care. Either way they show symptoms of the callousness of class. That can be a particularly dangerous social disorder.

QUESTIONS FOR ANALYSIS

1. Identify and rewrite the arguments that each of the authors uses to support his position regarding the legalization of drugs, using the following format:

   Reason:

   Reason:

   Conclusion:

   Use cue words to help you identify arguments.

2. Construct one new argument to support each side of this issue, using the form shown in question 1.

3. State whether or not you believe drugs should be legalized, and provide reasons to support your conclusion.

ARGUMENTS ARE INFERENCES

When you construct arguments, you are composing and relating to the world by means of your ability to infer. As you saw in Chapter 4, *inferring* is a thinking process that you use to reason from what you already know (or believe to be the case) to form new knowledge or beliefs. This is usually what you do when you construct arguments. You work from reasons you know or believe in to form conclusions based on these reasons.

Just as you can use inferences to make sense of different types of situations, so you can also construct arguments for different purposes. In a variety of situations, you construct arguments to do the following:

- decide
- explain
- predict
- persuade

An example of each of these different types of arguments follows. After examining each example, construct an argument of the same type related to issues in your own life.

We Construct Arguments to Decide

REASON: Throughout my life, I've always been interested in all different kinds of electricity.

REASON: There are many attractive job opportunities in the field of electrical engineering.

CONCLUSION: I will work toward becoming an electrical engineer.

REASON:

REASON:

CONCLUSION:

We Construct Arguments to Explain

REASON: I was delayed in leaving my house because my dog needed an emergency walking.

REASON: There was an unexpected traffic jam caused by motorists slowing down to view an overturned chicken truck.

CONCLUSION: Therefore, I was late for our appointment.

REASON:

REASON:

CONCLUSION:

We Construct Arguments to Predict

REASON: Some people will always drive faster than the speed limit allows, whether the limit is 55 or 65 mph.

REASON: Car accidents are more likely to occur at higher speeds.

CONCLUSION: It follows that the newly reinstated 65-mph speed limit will result in more accidents.

REASON:

REASON:

CONCLUSION:

We Construct Arguments to Persuade

REASON: Chewing tobacco can lead to cancer of the mouth and throat.

REASON: Boys sometimes are led to begin chewing tobacco by ads for the product that feature sports heroes they admire.

CONCLUSION: Therefore, ads for chewing tobacco should be banned.

REASON:

REASON:

CONCLUSION:

Evaluating Arguments

To construct an effective argument, you must be skilled in evaluating the effectiveness, or soundness, of arguments that have already been constructed. You must investigate two aspects of each argument independently to determine the soundness of the argument as a whole:

1. How true are the reasons being offered to support the conclusion?

2. To what extent do the reasons support the conclusion, or to what extent does the conclusion follow from the reasons offered?

We will first examine each of these ways of evaluating arguments separately and then see how they work together.

TRUTH: HOW TRUE ARE THE SUPPORTING REASONS?

The first aspect of the argument you must evaluate is the truth of the reasons that are being used to support a conclusion. Does each reason make sense? What evidence is being offered as part of each reason? Do you know each reason to be true based on your experience? Is each reason based on a source that can be trusted? You use these questions and others like them to analyze the reasons offered and to determine how true they are. As you saw in Chapter 5, evaluating the sort of beliefs usually found as reasons in arguments is a complex and ongoing challenge. Let us evaluate the truth of the reasons presented in the dialogue at the beginning of this chapter about whether marijuana should be legalized.

Argument 1

REASON: Possessing marijuana is not a serious offense.

EVALUATION: As it stands, this reason needs further evidence to support it. The major issue of the discussion is whether possessing (and using) marijuana is in fact a serious offense or no offense at all. This reason would be strengthened by stating: "Possessing marijuana is not as serious an offense as armed robbery, rape, and murder, according to the overwhelming majority of legal statutes and judicial decisions."

REASON: There are many other more serious offenses—such as armed robbery, rape, and murder—for which criminals don't receive such stiff sentences.

EVALUATION: The accuracy of this reason is highly doubtful. It is true that there is wide variation in the sentences handed down for the same offense. The sentences vary from state to state and also vary within states and even within the same court. Nevertheless, on the whole, serious offenses like armed robbery, rape, and murder do receive long prison sentences.

The real point here is that a fifteen-year sentence for possessing marijuana is extremely unusual when compared with other sentences for marijuana possession.

Argument 2

REASON: Drugs pose a very serious threat to the young people of our country.

EVALUATION: As the later discussion points out, this statement is much too vague. "Drugs" cannot be treated as being all the same. Some drugs (such as aspirin) are beneficial, while other drugs (such as heroin) are highly dangerous. To strengthen this reason, we would have to be more specific, stating, "Drugs like heroin, amphetamines, and cocaine pose a very serious threat to the young people of our country." We could increase the accuracy of the reason even more by adding the qualification "*some* of the young people of our country" because many young people are not involved with dangerous drugs.

REASON: Many crimes are committed to support drug habits.

EVALUATION:

Argument 3

REASON: It's not right to punish someone unfairly just to provide an example.

EVALUATION: This reason raises an interesting and complex ethical question that has been debated for centuries. The political theorist Machiavelli stated that "the ends justify the means," which implies that if we bring about desirable results, it does not matter how we go about doing so. He would therefore probably disagree with this reason because using someone as an example might bring about desirable results, even though it might be personally unfair to the person being used as an example. In our society, however, which is based on the idea of fairness under the law, most people would probably agree with this reason.

REASON: Smoking marijuana is nothing like using drugs such as heroin or even cocaine.

EVALUATION:

Thinking Activity 10.2

EVALUATING THE TRUTH OF REASONS

Review the other arguments from the dialogue on marijuana that you identified in Thinking Activity 10.1 (page 443). Evaluate the truth of each of the reasons contained in the arguments.

VALIDITY: DO THE REASONS SUPPORT THE CONCLUSION?

In addition to determining whether the reasons are true, evaluating arguments involves investigating the relationship between the reasons and the conclusion. When the reasons support the conclusion so that the conclusion follows from the reasons being offered, the argument is **valid**.* If, however, the reasons do *not* support the conclusion so that the conclusion does *not* follow from the reasons being offered, the argument is **invalid**.

One way to focus on the concept of validity is to *assume* that all the reasons in the argument are true and then try to determine how probable they make the conclusion. The following is an example of one type of valid argument:

valid argument An argument in which the reasons support the conclusion so that the conclusion follows from the reasons offered.

REASON: Anything that is a threat to our health should not be legal.

REASON: Marijuana is a threat to our health.

CONCLUSION: Therefore, marijuana should not be legal.

This is a valid argument because if we assume that the reasons are true, then the conclusion necessarily follows. Of course, we may not agree that either or both of the reasons are true and thus not agree with the conclusion. Nevertheless, the structure of the argument is valid. This particular form of thinking is known as *deduction*; we will examine deductive reasoning more closely in the pages ahead.

Now let's turn our attention to a different kind of argument.

invalid argument An argument in which the reasons do not support the conclusion so that the conclusion does not follow from the reasons offered.

REASON: As part of a project in my social science class, we selected 100 students in the school to be interviewed. We took special steps to ensure that these students were representative of the student body as a whole (total students: 4,386).

*In formal logic, the term *validity* is reserved for deductively valid arguments in which the conclusions follow necessarily from the premises. (See the discussion of deductive arguments later in this chapter.)

We asked the selected students whether they thought the United States should actively try to overthrow foreign governments that the United States disapproves of. Of the 100 students interviewed, 88 students said the United States should definitely *not* be involved in such activities.

CONCLUSION: We can conclude that most students in the school believe the United States should not be engaged in attempts to actively overthrow foreign governments that the United States disapproves of.

This is a persuasive argument because if we assume that the reason is true, then it provides strong support for the conclusion. In this case, the key part of the reason is the statement that the 100 students selected were representative of the entire 4,386 students at the school. To evaluate the truth of the reason, we might want to investigate the procedure used to select the 100 students to determine whether this sample was in fact representative of all the students. This particular form of thinking is an example of *induction*; we will explore inductive reasoning more fully in Chapter 11.

The following argument is an example of an invalid argument:

REASON: Barrack Obama believes that it is vital for our national security that we develop alternative sources of energy.

REASON: Barrack Obama is the president of the United States.

CONCLUSION: Therefore, we should develop alternative sources of energy.

This argument is *not* valid because even if we assume that the reasons are true, the conclusion does not follow. Although Barrack Obama is the president of the United States, that fact does not give him any special expertise on the subject of alternative sources of energy. Indeed, this is a subject of such complexity and global significance that it should not be based on any one person's opinion, no matter who that person is. This form of invalid thinking is a type of *fallacy*; we will investigate fallacious reasoning in Chapter 11.

THE SOUNDNESS OF ARGUMENTS

When an argument includes both true reasons and a valid structure, the argument is considered to be *sound*. When an argument has either false reasons or an invalid structure, however, the argument is considered to be *unsound*.

True reasons Valid structure	}	⟶	Sound argument
False reasons Valid structure	}	⟶	Unsound argument
True reasons Invalid structure	}	⟶	Unsound argument
False reasons Invalid structure	}	⟶	Unsound argument

Thinking Critically About Visuals

The Changing Rules of Love

Many states and municipalities are changing their laws in order to allow same-sex couples to marry, or at least to claim a formal "civil union" that guarantees such couples the same civic rights as heterosexual married people.

Do you believe that same-sex marriage is a personal issue, a civic concern, or something in between? This cartoon is a takeoff on a famous painting, *American Gothic*, by Grant Wood, from 1930. The original painting shows a farmer standing beside a woman: the couple represent the traditional roles of men and women, with the man's pitchfork symbolizing hard labor and the flowers over the woman's right shoulder suggesting domesticity. What point do you think the cartoonist was trying to make with this updated image featuring two women?

David Fitzsimmons, The Arizona Star/Cagle Cartoons

From the diagram on the previous page, we can see that in terms of arguments, "truth" and "validity" are not the same concepts. An argument can have true reasons and an invalid structure or false reasons and a valid structure. In both cases the argument is *unsound*. To be sound, an argument must have both true reasons and a valid structure. For example, consider the following argument:

The Saturday Evening Post, first published in 1821, is the oldest continuously published magazine in America. In the early to mid-twentieth century, its cover illustrations depicted a sunny, mythic America.

The issue of same-sex marriage is just one of many challenges to traditional concepts of family in contemporary American culture. Were you to make an argument about marriage in America today, what kinds of illustrations would you use to support your claims? Are there similarities or differences between these two images that would support your argument about the changing nature of American marriage?

REASON: For a democracy to function most effectively, its citizens should be able to think critically about the important social and political issues.

REASON: Education plays a key role in developing critical-thinking abilities.

CONCLUSION: Therefore, education plays a key role in ensuring that a democracy is functioning most effectively.

A good case could be made for the soundness of this argument because the reasons are persuasive, and the argument structure is valid. Of course, someone might contend that one or both of the reasons are not completely true, which illustrates an important point about the arguments we construct and evaluate. Many of the arguments we encounter in life fall somewhere between complete soundness and complete unsoundness because we are often not sure if our reasons are completely true. Throughout this book we have found that developing accurate beliefs is an ongoing process and that our beliefs are subject to clarification and revision. As a result, the conclusion of any argument can be only as certain as the reasons supporting the conclusion.

To sum up, evaluating arguments effectively involves both the truth of the reasons and the validity of the argument's structure. The degree of soundness an argument has depends on how accurate our reasons turn out to be and how valid the argument's structure is.

Understanding Deductive Arguments

deductive argument An argument form in which one reasons from premises that are known or assumed to be true to a conclusion that follows necessarily from these premises.

We use a number of basic argument forms to organize, relate to, and make sense of the world. As already noted, two of the major types of argument forms are **deductive arguments** and *inductive arguments*. In the remainder of this chapter, we will explore various types of deductive arguments, reserving our analysis of inductive arguments for Chapter 11.

The deductive argument is the one most commonly associated with the study of logic. Though it has a variety of valid forms, they all share one characteristic: If you accept the supporting reasons (also called *premises*) as true, then you must necessarily accept the conclusion as true.

For example, consider the following famous deductive argument:

REASON/PREMISE: All men are mortal.

REASON/PREMISE: Socrates is a man.

CONCLUSION: Therefore, Socrates is mortal.

In this example of deductive thinking, accepting the premises of the argument as true means that the conclusion necessarily follows; it cannot be false. Many deductive arguments, like the one just given, are structured as *syllogisms*, an argument form that consists of two supporting premises and a conclusion. There are also, however, a large number of *invalid* deductive forms, one of which is illustrated in the following syllogism:

REASON/PREMISE: All men are mortal.

REASON/PREMISE: Socrates is a man.

CONCLUSION: Therefore, all men are Socrates.

In the next several pages, we will briefly examine some common valid deductive forms.

APPLICATION OF A GENERAL RULE

Whenever we reason with the form illustrated by the valid Socrates syllogism, we are using the following argument structure:

PREMISE: All *A* (men) are *B* (mortal).

PREMISE: *S* is an *A* (Socrates is a man).

CONCLUSION: Therefore, *S* is *B* (Socrates is mortal).

This basic argument form is valid no matter what terms are included. For example:

PREMISE: All politicians are untrustworthy.

PREMISE: Bill White is a politician.

CONCLUSION: Therefore, Bill White is untrustworthy.

Notice again that with any valid deductive form, *if* we assume that the premises are true, then we must accept the conclusion. Of course, in this case there is considerable doubt that the first premise is actually true.

When we diagram this argument form, it becomes clear why it is a valid way of thinking:

The *first premise* states that classification *A* (men) falls within classification *B* (mortal).

The *second premise* states that *S* (Socrates) is a member of classification *A* (men).

The *conclusion* simply states what has now become obvious—namely, that *S* (Socrates) must fall within classification *B* (mortal).

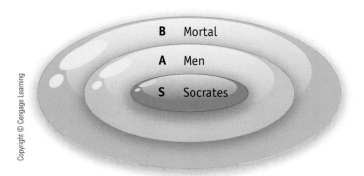

Although we are usually not aware of it, we use this basic type of reasoning whenever we apply a general rule in the form *All A is B*. For instance:

PREMISE: All children eight years old should be in bed by 9:30 P.M.

PREMISE: You are an eight-year-old child.

CONCLUSION: Therefore, you should be in bed by 9:30 P.M.

Review the dialogue at the beginning of this chapter and see if you can identify a deductive argument that uses this form.

PREMISE:

PREMISE:

CONCLUSION:

Describe an example from your own experience in which you use this deductive form.

MODUS PONENS

A second valid deductive form that we commonly use in our thinking goes by the name *modus ponens*—that is, "affirming the antecedent"—and is illustrated in the following example:

PREMISE: If I have prepared thoroughly for the final exam, then I will do well.

PREMISE: I prepared thoroughly for the exam.

CONCLUSION: Therefore, I will do well on the exam.

When we reason like this, we are using the following argument structure:

PREMISE: If *A* (I have prepared thoroughly), then *B* (I will do well).

PREMISE: *A* (I have prepared thoroughly).

CONCLUSION: Therefore, *B* (I will do well).

Like all valid deductive forms, this form is valid no matter what specific terms are included. For example:

PREMISE: If the Democrats are able to register 20 million new voters, then they will win the presidential election.

PREMISE: The Democrats were able to register more than 20 million new voters.

CONCLUSION: Therefore, the Democrats will win the presidential election.

As with other valid argument forms, the conclusion will be true *if* the reasons are true. Although the second premise in this argument expresses information that can be verified, the first premise would be more difficult to establish.

Review the dialogue at the beginning of this chapter and see if you can identify any deductive arguments that use this form.

MODUS TOLLENS

A third commonly used valid deductive form has the name *modus tollens*—that is, "denying the consequence"—and is illustrated in the following example:

PREMISE: If Michael were a really good friend, he would lend me his car for the weekend.

Thinking Critically About Visuals

Is "Socialist" a Dirty Word?

One of President Barack Obama's major legislative accomplishments was passage of the Patient Protection and Affordable Care Act, nicknamed "Obamacare." Some critics of "Obamacare" claimed that the Act represented a "Socialist" agenda, and some even accused Obama of being a "Communist" and likened him to Mao Zedong. What these critics often failed to acknowledge was that extremely popular programs like Medicare and Medicaid are every bit examples of "socialism" as Obamacare. Why is it that people are frequently able to fervently advocate for beliefs that are self-contradictory?

Michael Reynolds/EPA/Newscom

PREMISE: Michael refuses to lend me his car for the weekend.

CONCLUSION: Therefore, Michael is not a really good friend.

When we reason in this fashion, we are using the following argument structure:

PREMISE: If *A* (Michael is a really good friend), then *B* (he will lend me his car).

PREMISE: Not *B* (he won't lend me his car).

CONCLUSION: Therefore, not *A* (he's not a really good friend).

Again, like other valid reasoning forms, this form is valid no matter what subject is being considered. For instance:

PREMISE: If Iraq were genuinely interested in world peace, it would not have invaded Kuwait.

PREMISE: Iraq did invade Kuwait (i.e., Iraq did not "not invade" Kuwait).

CONCLUSION: Therefore, Iraq is not genuinely interested in world peace.

This conclusion—and any other conclusion produced by this form of reasoning—can be considered accurate if the reasons are true. In this case, the second premise would be easier to verify than the first.

Review the dialogue at the beginning of this chapter and see if you can identify any deductive arguments that use this reasoning form.

DISJUNCTIVE SYLLOGISM

A fourth common form of a valid deductive argument is known as a *disjunctive syllogism*. The term *disjunctive* means presenting several alternatives. This form is illustrated in the following example:

PREMISE: Either I left my wallet on my dresser, or I have lost it.

PREMISE: The wallet is not on my dresser.

CONCLUSION: Therefore, I must have lost it.

When we reason in this way, we are using the following argument structure:

PREMISE: Either *A* (I left my wallet on my dresser) or *B* (I have lost it).

PREMISE: Not *A* (I didn't leave it on my dresser).

CONCLUSION: Therefore, *B* (I have lost it).

This valid reasoning form can be applied to any number of situations and still yield valid results. For example:

PREMISE: Either your stomach trouble is caused by what you are eating, or it is caused by nervous tension.

PREMISE: You tell me that you have been taking special care with your diet.

CONCLUSION: Therefore, your stomach trouble is caused by nervous tension.

To determine the accuracy of the conclusion, we must determine the accuracy of the premises. If they are true, then the conclusion must be true.

Review the dialogue at the beginning of this chapter and see if you can identify any deductive arguments that use this reasoning form.

All these basic argument forms—application of a general rule, *modus ponens*, *modus tollens*, and disjunctive syllogism—are found not only in informal, everyday conversations but also at more formal levels of thinking. They appear in academic disciplines, in scientific inquiry, in debates on social issues, and elsewhere. Many other argument forms—both deductive and inductive—also constitute human reasoning. By sharpening your understanding of these ways of thinking, you will be better able to make sense of the world by constructing and evaluating effective arguments.

Thinking Activity 10.3

EVALUATING ARGUMENTS

Analyze each of the following arguments by completing these steps:

1. Summarize the reasons and conclusion given.

2. Identify which, if any, of the following deductive argument forms is used:
   - application of a general rule
   - *modus ponens* (affirming the antecedent)
   - *modus tollens* (denying the consequence)
   - disjunctive syllogism

3. Evaluate the truth of the reasons that support the conclusion.

> For if the brain is a machine of ten billion nerve cells and the mind can somehow be explained as the summed activity of a finite number of chemical and electrical reactions, [then] boundaries limit the human prospect—we are biological and our souls cannot fly free.
>
> —Edward O. Wilson, *On Human Nature*

> The state is by nature clearly prior to the family and to the individual, since the whole is of necessity prior to the part.
>
> —Aristotle, *Politics*

> There now is sophisticated research that strongly suggests a deterrent effect [of capital punishment]. Furthermore, the principal argument against the deterrent effect is weak. The argument is that in most jurisdictions where capital punishment has been abolished there has been no immediate, sharp increase in what had been capital crimes. But in those jurisdictions, the actual act of abolition was an insignificant event because for years the death penalty had been imposed rarely, if at all. Common sense—which deserves deference until it is refuted—suggests that the fear of death can deter some premeditated crimes, including some murders.
>
> —George F. Will, *Cleveland Plain-Dealer, March 13, 1981*

> If the increased power which science has conferred upon human volitions is to be a boon and not a curse, the ends to which these volitions are directed must grow commensurately with the growth of power to carry them out. Hitherto, although we have been told on Sundays to love our neighbor, we have been told on weekdays to hate him, and there are six times as many weekdays as Sundays. Hitherto, the harm that we could do to our neighbor by hating him was limited by our incompetence, but in the new world upon which we are entering there will be no such limit, and the indulgence of hatred can lead only to ultimate and complete disaster.
>
> —Bertrand Russell, *"The Expanding Mental Universe"*

THINKING CRITICALLY ABOUT NEW MEDIA

Freedom of Speech on the Internet

The dramatic growth of the new media has created new issues with respect to freedom of speech. Of course, even before the Internet, the guarantee of freedom of speech under the Constitution never meant that people could say *anything*. For example, you have never been permitted to yell "Fire" in a crowded theater because of the panic that might ensue. Nor is it legal to use wildly inflammatory language toward other people—"fighting words"—that could precipitate an altercation. And if you make false and unflattering allegations about a person or organization that are demonstrably false you can be sued for *libel* (written defamation) or *slander* (spoken defamation), or both. And, of course, there have been bans on content dealing with child pornography and other taboo subjects.

But the development of new media has introduced new battlegrounds where freedom of speech is being debated. For example, the Center for Democracy & Technology (CDT) (**www.cdt.org**) is an organization devoted to maximizing freedom of speech and minimizing censorship on the Internet to the greatest extent possible, as they explain in the following passage:

Free speech has long been a hallmark of a healthy democracy and a free society. The Internet and new communications technologies have become unprecedented tools for expanding the ability for individuals to speak and receive information, participate in political and democratic processes, and share knowledge and ideas. Recognizing the potential of these technologies, courts have extended the highest level of First Amendment protection to the Internet medium. Online free expression also requires that private online service providers be protected from legal liability for content posted by users, so they will be willing to host that speech.

CDT works to keep the Internet and communications technologies free of government censorship and content gatekeepers alike, and to extend the highest level of free speech protection afforded the Internet to all converged media. User choice and control over access to information are the key to protecting core First Amendment values while still addressing important social ills in the digital age. Through our advocacy, CDT seeks to maximize the ability of individuals to decide for themselves what they say, hear, publish, and access online. (**www.cdt.org/issue/free-expression**)

There are others who believe that although freedom of expression is of paramount importance in a free democracy, this right must be balanced against threats to personal safety. For example, should sexual predators be permitted to create false Internet identities and try to lure children into inappropriate correspondence or even dangerous encounters in the real world? Should advertisers be allowed to use deceptive advertising to sell prescription drugs to both minors and adults? What about information related to your personal health: should insurance companies be able to gain access to this material, which they might then use to raise your rates or deny you health coverage? The entire issue of consumer privacy is an issue also, as detailed profiles about each one of us—our demographics, the websites we visit, our buying patterns, our financial data—are available and often shared among organizations and businesses without our knowledge. One recent court judgment has ruled that Internet organizations like Craigslist. com on which people post advertisements cannot be held responsible for the content of the ads. For example, if people want to use these online venues to solicit sexual business or sell illegal pharmaceuticals, it is not up to the owners of the site to "police" these ads and prohibit or report them.

In addition to the Center for Democracy & Technology, which provides frequent updates on challenges to free speech online and elsewhere in society, there are other sites devoted to this complex issue, including:

- Electronic Frontier Foundation (**www.eff.org**) is a site that advocates for freedom of speech online and offers legal resources and information for people interested in pursuing these issues.
- *PCWorld.com* (**www.pcworld.com**) and *Wired* (**www.wired.com**) are consumer magazines about computing that frequently publish articles that go beyond the *content* of "free speech" online to the *technology* that allows for—and complicates—freedom of speech.

Thinking Activity 10.4

FREEDOM OF SPEECH ON THE INTERNET

After exploring some websites devoted to freedom of speech on the Internet, including those noted above, respond to the following questions:

1. Do you believe that existing laws concerning consumer rights, freedom of speech, and intellectual property (copyrights, performance licensing, etc.) are sufficient to cover what occurs on the Internet, or do we need stricter regulations to protect children, the elderly, consumers, and others? Explain the reasoning supporting your perspective.

(Continues)

THINKING CRITICALLY ABOUT NEW MEDIA (*CONTINUED*)

2. Which, if any, of these Internet activities should be prohibited or regulated? In each case, construct an argument (with a conclusion and supporting reasons) that supports your position.
   - Emailed chain letters and petitions
   - Unsolicited email "spam" (bulk mail messages from people trying to sell products)
   - False "virus alerts" and other hoaxes
   - The creation and dissemination of computer viruses
   - Programs that defeat advertising and "pop-up banners" on web pages
   - *Your example . . .*
   - *Your example . . .*

The extreme vulnerability of a complex industrial society to intelligent, targeted terrorism by a very small number of people may prove the fatal challenge to which Western states have no adequate response. Counterforce alone will never suffice. The real challenge of the true terrorist is to the basic values of a society. If there is no commitment to shared values in Western society—and if none are imparted in our amoral institutions of higher learning—no increase in police and burglar alarms will suffice to preserve our society from the specter that haunts us—not a bomb from above but a gun from within.

—James Billington, *"The Gun Within"*

To fully believe in something, to truly understand something, one must be intimately acquainted with its opposite. One should not adopt a creed by default, because no alternative is known. Education should prepare students for the "real world" not by segregating them from evil but by urging full confrontation to test and modify the validity of the good.

—Robert Baron, *"In Defense of 'Teaching' Racism, Sexism, and Fascism"*

The inescapable conclusion is that society secretly *wants* crime, *needs* crime, and gains definite satisfactions from the present mishandling of it! We condemn crime; we punish offenders for it; but we need it. The crime and punishment ritual is a part of our lives. We need crimes to wonder at, to enjoy vicariously, to discuss and speculate about, and to publicly deplore. We need criminals to identify ourselves with, to envy secretly, and to punish stoutly. They do for us the forbidden, illegal things we *wish* to do and, like scapegoats of old, they bear the burdens of our displaced guilt and punishment—"the iniquities of us all."

—Karl Menninger, *"The Crime of Punishment"*

Constructing Extended Arguments

The purpose of mastering the forms of argument is to become a sophisticated critical thinker who can present her or his ideas to others effectively. The art of discussing and debating ideas with others was explored in Chapter 2. We saw then that effective discussion involves

- Listening carefully to other points of view
- Supporting views with reasons and evidence
- Responding to the points being made
- Asking—and trying to answer—appropriate questions
- Working to increase understanding, not simply to "win the argument"

Although learning to discuss ideas with others in an organized, productive fashion is crucial for thinking critically, it is equally important to be able to present your ideas in written form. Term papers, interoffice memos, research analyses, grant proposals, legal briefs, evaluation reports, and countless other documents that you are likely to encounter require that you develop the skills of clear, persuasive writing. Composing your ideas develops your mind in distinctive, high-level ways. When you express your ideas in writing, you tend to organize them into more complex relationships, select your terms with more care, and revise your work after an initial draft. As a result, your writing is often a more articulate and comprehensive expression of your ideas than you could achieve in verbal discussions. And the process of expressing your ideas in such a clear and coherent fashion has the simultaneous effect of sharpening your thinking. As you saw in Chapter 6, language and thinking are partners that work together to create meaning and communicate ideas. How well you perform one of these activities is directly related to how well you perform the other.

WRITING AN EXTENDED ARGUMENT

Learning to construct extended arguments is one of the most important writing skills that you need to develop. Since an argument is a form of thinking in which you are trying to present reasons to support a conclusion, it is likely that much of your writing will fall into this category. Composing thoughtfully reasoned and clearly written arguments is very challenging, and few people are able to do it well. In the same way that many discussions are illogical, disorganized, and overly emotional, much of argumentative writing is also ineffective.

Thinking Passage

SHOULD SOCIAL NETWORKING BE GOVERNED?

Imagine living in a society in which important decisions affecting your life were made by a central authority completely independent of your wishes or input: would you resent living in a society so lacking in personal freedom? If you are one of the 900 million members of the social network Facebook, that's precisely the situation in which you find yourself. As the following article explains, in a society of that many people, conflicts and disputes are inevitable: in the case of Facebook, 2 million such disputes a week. For example, here are some of the recent disputes and how they were adjudicated:

- A complaint about a photograph of two men kissing: the photograph was removed.
- A copyright complaint against an information-providing service: the site was closed down without explanation.
- A professional photographer whose fan base listing was removed without explanation.
- A complaint against a women's group by an antipornography group: the group's site was taken down.

Who makes these decisions and on what basis are they made? It's a team of individuals working for Facebook using a collection of sophisticated technological tools and guided by Facebook's guiding principle of getting people more open and connected with a minimum of negative experiences. After reading the following article, "The Perfect Technocracy: Facebook's Attempt to Create Good Government for 900 Million People," answer the questions that follow.

The Perfect Technocracy: Facebook's Attempt to Create Good Government for 900 Million People
by Alexis C. Madrigal

Let's stipulate that Facebook is not a country, that real governments fulfill many more functions, and that people are not citizens of their social networks.

Nonetheless, 900 million human beings do something like live in the blue-and-white virtual space of the world's largest structured web of people. And those people get into disputes that they expect to be adjudicated. They have this expectation in part because Facebook has long said it wants to create a safe environment for connecting with other people. (How else can you get people to be "more open and connected"?) But people also want someone to be in charge, they want an authority to whom they can appeal if some other person is being a jerk.

Except in this case, the someone really is a corporate person. So when you report something or someone reports something of yours, it is Facebook that makes the decision about what's been posted, even if we know that somewhere down the line, some human being has to embody the corporate we, if only for long enough to click a button.

Any individual decision made by Facebook's team—like taking down this photo of a gay couple kissing—is easy to question. Ars Technica's Ken Fisher detailed a whole bunch of one-off problems that people have encountered with Facebook's reporting system. In each, there is an aggrieved party, but we're only hearing one side of the conflict when these problems bubble up. Across many single events, you have two people (or entities like businesses) with conflicting desires. This is a classic case where you need some sort of government.

It's not hard to imagine making one or 20 or even 200 decisions about photographs or status updates in a week, but it's mindboggling to consider that Facebook has to process *2 million reports per week*, and that's not including simple "mark as spam" messages.

How do you design a system to deal with that workload? I spoke with James Mitchell, who helms what Facebook calls "site integrity" within its user-operations department, and Jud Hoffman, the company's global policy manager about the reporting process. They are the architects of Facebook's technocracy.

"The amount of thought and debate that goes into the process of creating and managing these rules is not that different from a legislative and judicial process all rolled up into one," Hoffman, a lawyer, told me. "And James has the executive/judicial element. I don't think it is a stretch to think about this in a governance context, but it's a different form and we take it really, really seriously."

The key step, Mitchell told me, was to put some structure into the reporting process. Back when he started in 2006, there wasn't any form to complaints from users. That meant there was a massive queue of undifferentiated problems. So, he and his team started to think about what kinds of problems they received and created categories of problems, which they refined over time.

That allows the reports to be channeled through a complex set of processes and teams so that they arrive in front of human beings or computers that know what to do with them.

Facebook has revealed this infrastructure for the first time today. It's the product of more than five years of work by several teams within Facebook, who have worked to make the process of handling this flood of user inquiries as efficient as possible.

At the end of many of these reporting lines, there's a person who has to make a decision about the user's message. Some of these decisions are binary—Does this photograph contain nudity?—and those are generally outsourced to teams that can apply

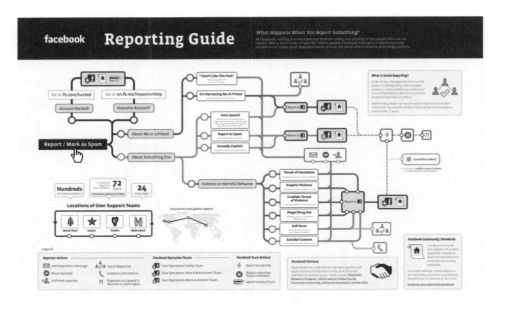

simple and rigorous formulas such as asking, "Is this person naked?" Other decisions are complex in ways that make machines very good at dealing with them. (For example, there are more than 50 signals that Facebook's algorithms look at to determine whether a profile is spam, and the automated responses are more accurate than human ones would be.)

But the bulk of the reports are fielded by a faceless team of several hundred Facebook employees in Mountain View, Austin, Dublin, and Hyderabad. These people and the tools they've built have become the de facto legislators, bureaucrats, police, and judges of the quasi-nation of Facebook. Some decisions they make impact hundreds of millions of people in some small way; other decisions will change some small number of people's lives in a big way.

What's fascinating to me is that Facebook has essentially recreated a government bureaucracy complete with regulators and law enforcement, but optimized for totally different values than traditional governments. Instead of a constitution, Facebook has the dual missions of making "the world more open and connected" and keeping users on its site by minimizing their negative experiences. Above all, Facebook's solution to all governance problems have to be designed for extreme efficiency at scale.

As stipulated above, real-world governments have to fulfill all kinds of functions aside from disputes between citizens, but just look at the difference in scale between Facebook's government and Palo Alto's government. Palo Alto has roughly 65,000 residents and 617 full-time employees. Facebook has 900 million "residents" and a few hundred bureaucrats who make all the content decisions.

Facebook's desire for efficiency means democracy is out and technocratic, developer-king rule is in. People don't get to vote on the rules, and even when Facebook offered its users the opportunity to vote on a new privacy policy last week, voter turnout was 0.038 percent. People know that Facebook controls a large slice of their digital lives,

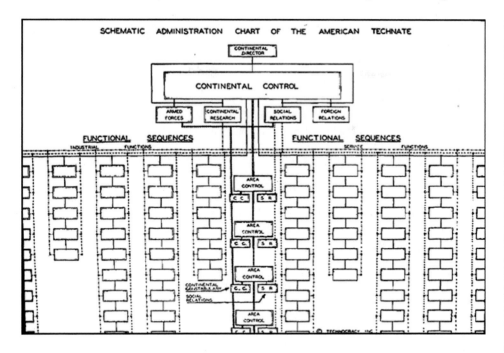

but they don't have a sense of digital citizenship. And that apathy gives Facebook's technocracy a chance to succeed where its historical antecedents did not.

The original technocrats were a group of thinkers and engineers in the 1930s who revived Plato's dream of the philosopher-king, but with a machine-age spin. Led by Thorstein Veblen, Howard Scott and M. King Hubbert, they advocated not rule by the people or the monarchy or the dictator, but by the engineers. The engineers and scientists would rule rationally and impartially. They would create a Technocracy that functioned like clockwork and ensured the productivity of all was efficiently distributed. They worked out a whole system by which the North American continent would be ruled with functional sequences that would allow the Continental Director to get things done.

Technocracy, as originally conceived, was explicitly not democratic. Its proponents did not want popular rule; they wanted rule by a knowledgeable elite who would make good decisions. And maybe they would have, but there was one big problem. Few people found the general vision of surrendering their political power to engineers all that appealing.

With Facebook, people seem to care much more about individual decisions that Facebook makes than the existence of the ultraefficient technocratic system. They are not challenging the principles or values of the system, so much as wanting them to be applied quickly to resolve their particular dispute. And desire for speed, of course, drives the efficiency-first mindset that makes it hard to deal with nuanced problems. None of the accusations leveled at Facebook's administrative system read to me like criticisms of its core structure.

I mean, of course Facebook's governance isn't perfect. Of course the people who run it make mistakes, mistakes that they use every bit of data to squeeze out of the system. These problems are a consequence of running our social lives through a centralized, corporate social network with a set of rather staid goals: openness, connectedness, and the minimization of negative experiences. Given these goals, Facebook has come to a rational set of structures for dealing with social problems within its walled garden. It is a gated community with some CCRs and if you don't like it . . . Well, there's always Brooklyn!

That is to say, the real question is whether Facebook's goals—and the systems it uses to promote them—reflect one's own desires. Do you want a clean, well-lighted place that works without any effort on your part? If so, Facebook has the governance structure for you. You want a more permissive place with fewer rules? Allow me to introduce you to 4chan.

QUESTIONS FOR ANALYSIS

1. Are you a member of Facebook? If so, were you aware of their policy for resolving disputes? What is your reaction to the system that they have instituted for answering complaints and resolving disputes?

2. Review the infrastructure model that Facebook has developed (included on page 466): what is their goal in developing such a model? What is your analysis of it: does it make sense to you? Do you have any suggestions for improvement?

3. The prospect of reviewing 2 million complaints per week is a daunting challenge. If you were in charge of developing a system to respond in a timely and informed way to this volume of complaints, how would you go about doing it?

4. Facebook's guiding principles are getting people more open and connected with a minimum of negative experiences. Do you think these principles are appropriate? Are there other principles that you think Facebook should be using to guide their decisions? Why or why not

---

CHAPTER 10 | **Reviewing and Viewing**

Summary

- *Argument* is a form of thinking in which certain reasons are offered to support a conclusion.

- *Cue words* for arguments help us identify reasons and conclusions.

- Arguments are *inferences* that we use to help us *decide, explain, predict,* and *persuade*.

- We *evaluate* arguments by asking "How true are the supporting reasons?" and "Do the reasons support the conclusion?"

- A *valid argument* is one in which the reasons support the conclusion so that the conclusion follows from the reasons offered.

- *Deductive argument* is an argument form in which one reasons from premises that are known or assumed to be true to a conclusion that follows necessarily from these premises.

- Some common deductive argument forms include *modus ponens, modus tollens, disjunctive syllogism,* and *application of a general rule.*

Assessing Your Strategies and Creating New Goals

How Well Do I Construct and Evaluate Arguments?

Arguments are a form of thinking in which certain reasons are offered to support a conclusion, and they are at the heart of the reasoning process. Described below are key thinking abilities that are correlated with analyzing complex issues by recognizing, constructing, and evaluating arguments. Evaluate your position regarding each of these abilities and attributes, and use this self-evaluation to guide your efforts to become a more effective reasoner.

Make Analytic Reasoning a Priority

I analyze complex issues in a thoughtful, well-reasoned way.	I usually make quick decisions on issues without careful analysis.
5 4 3 2 1	

Becoming a sophisticated reasoner means developing certain habits of mind that you use on a daily basis. As a critical thinker, you need to resist the trend toward thoughtlessness, analyzing issues carefully and encouraging others to do the same.

*Strategy: Make a special effort to analyze issues thoughtfully before reaching a conclusion. Avoid making quick decisions based on incomplete information. Instead, ask questions, think carefully, and develop well-supported conclusions. Encourage others to become more thoughtful by asking them **why** they think what they do, and helping them to clarify their analyses.*

Recognize Arguments and Understand Their Structure

I am able to recognize arguments and understand their structure whenever I encounter them.	I am generally unaware of arguments and do not understand their structure very well.
5 4 3 2 1	

One of the core elements of our ability to reason is our ability to construct and evaluate arguments, which are forms of thinking in which certain reasons are offered to support a conclusion. The first step in this process is to be able to recognize arguments, which turn up in many contexts in various guises. Cue words can provide hints, but recognizing the logical form is the only sure way to identify them.

*Strategy: For the next several days, pay particular attention to arguments that you encounter in various contexts: in your classes, with friends, watching television, at work. Record these arguments in your **Thinker's Notebook**, and identify the structure of each (reasons and conclusions).*

Construct Sound Arguments

I am skilled at constructing valid arguments with true reasons and logical conclusions.	I usually don't take time to use logical arguments to organize and support my thinking.
5 4 3 2 1	

Constructing sound arguments is the heart of the reasoning process—that's why so many people are poor reasoners. By developing your skills at constructing and evaluating arguments, you will gain a powerful reasoning tool that you can use in every area of your life.

*Strategy: Develop the habit of analyzing the key arguments in articles that you read, information from television, and conversations with others. Use your **Thinking Notebook** to outline the arguments: What are the reasons? What is the conclusion? Then evaluate the soundness of the argument: Are the reasons true? Is the reasoning valid? Is the conclusion supported by the premises? This may seem time-consuming at first, but it is an invaluable activity, and before long you will find yourself arguing in a much more accomplished fashion.*

Evaluate Arguments Effectively

I am skilled at evaluating arguments in terms of their soundness.	I am not particularly skilled at evaluating arguments in terms of their soundness.
5 4 3 2 1	

Just because arguments are constructed doesn't mean that they are logically sound. Many arguments are illogical and unsound, and we need to be able to distinguish the valuable from the worthless. Evaluating arguments is a two-step process conducted by posing the following questions: Are the reasons accurate and relevant? Does the conclusion follow logically from the reasons?

Strategy: Look again at the arguments you identified and recorded in the previous activity, and evaluate them in terms of their logical soundness. The more you evaluate arguments in this way, the more this will become an automatic habit when you encounter or construct arguments (much to the consternation of others!).

Suggested Films

An Inconvenient Truth (2006)

Al Gore's documentary addresses the scientific causes of global warming as well as the social and political factors that support and/or inhibit its decrease.

Do the Right Thing (1989)

Produced, written, directed by, and starring Spike Lee, this film deals with issues of race conflict and prejudice in Brooklyn, New York. During one of the hottest days of summer, the tensions in the neighborhood explode into violence.

Maria, Full of Grace (2004)

Are the women hired by traffickers to act as drug mules ethically culpable for the lives that drugs destroy? What are the various social and political causes and effects? This film follows a young Colombian girl who becomes involved in the trade in an attempt to escape the desperate circumstances of her life.

Million Dollar Baby (2004)

A 31-year-old female amateur boxer convinces a veteran boxing coach to train her in spite of his initial prejudices. Through their collaboration, she develops into a talented fighter. The coach eventually finds himself grappling with the question of euthanasia. This film raises questions about what it means to be fully alive, and where the line is between murder and mercy.

Paradise Now (2005)

Two Palestinian childhood friends spend their final days together after being recruited as suicide bombers to launch an attack in Israel. After a series of complications, both men reflect on their reasons for participating in the attack, and each must decide whether or not he will go through with it.

"Is Seeing Believing?"

How do we know what we know? How do we know what we don't know? We certainly can't depend entirely on our senses to achieve knowledge, for if we did we would "know" that the woman in this photo is levitating without any means of support. So how exactly do our minds go about constructing trustworthy and accurate knowledge of the world? And how do we avoid all of the deceptive traps that are eager to ensnare our thinking efforts?

Reasoning Critically

Inductive Reasoning
Reasoning from premises assumed
to be true to a conclusion
supported (but not logically)
by the premises

Empirical Generalization

Drawing conclusions about
a target population based
on observing a sample
population

Is the sample known?
Is the sample sufficient?
Is the sample representative?

Fallacies

Unsound arguments
that can appear logical

Causal Reasoning

Concluding that an event
is the result of another
event

Scientific Method

1. Identify an event
   for investigation
2. Gather information
3. Develop a theory/hypothesis
4. Test/experiment
5. Evaluate results

Fallacies of False Generalization

Hasty generalization
Sweeping generalization
False dilemma

Causal Fallacies

Questionable cause
Misidentification of the cause
Post hoc ergo propter hoc
Slippery slope

Fallacies of Relevance

Appeal to authority
Appeal to tradition
Bandwagon
Appeal to pity
Appeal to fear
Appeal to flattery
Special pleading
Appeal to ignorance
Begging the question
Straw man
Red herring
Appeal to personal attack
Two wrongs make a right

R easoning is the type of thinking that uses arguments—reasons in support of conclusions—to decide, explain, predict, and persuade. Effective reasoning involves using all of the intellectual skills and critical attitudes we have been developing in this book. In this chapter we will further explore various dimensions of the reasoning process.

Inductive Reasoning

inductive reasoning An argument form in which one reasons from premises that are known or assumed to be true to a conclusion that is supported by the premises but does not necessarily follow from them.

Chapter 10 focused primarily on *deductive reasoning*, an argument form in which one reasons from premises that are known or assumed to be true to a conclusion that follows necessarily from the premises. In this chapter we will examine **inductive reasoning**, an argument form in which one reasons from premises that are known or assumed to be true to a conclusion that is supported by the premises but does not follow logically from them.

When you reason inductively, your premises provide evidence that makes it more or less probable (but not certain) that the conclusion is true. The following statements are examples of conclusions reached through inductive reasoning:

1. A recent Gallup Poll reported that 74 percent of the American public believes that abortion should remain legal.

2. On the average, a person with a college degree will earn over $1,000,000 more in his or her lifetime than a person with just a high school diploma.

3. In a recent survey, twice as many doctors interviewed stated that if they were stranded on a desert island, they would prefer Bayer aspirin to Extra Strength Tylenol.

4. The outbreak of food poisoning at the end-of-year school party was probably caused by the squid salad.

5. The devastating disease AIDS is caused by a particularly complex virus that may not be curable.

6. The solar system is probably the result of an enormous explosion—a "big bang"—that occurred billions of years ago.

fallacies
Unsound arguments that appear to be logical and are often persuasive because they usually appeal to our emotions and prejudices and often support conclusions that we want to believe are accurate.

The first three statements are forms of inductive reasoning known as *empirical generalization*, a general statement about an entire group made on the basis of observing some members of the group. The final three statements are examples of *causal reasoning*, a form of inductive reasoning in which it is claimed that an event (or events) is the result of the occurrence of another event (or events). We will be exploring the ways each of these forms of inductive reasoning functions in our lives and in various fields of study.

In addition to examining various ways of reasoning logically and effectively, we will also explore certain forms of reasoning that are not logical and, as a result, are usually not effective. These ways of pseudo-reasoning (false reasoning) are often termed **fallacies**—arguments that are not sound because of various errors in reasoning. Fallacious reasoning is typically used to influence others. It seeks to persuade not on the basis of sound arguments and critical thinking but rather on the basis of emotional and illogical factors.

Empirical Generalization

One of the most important tools used by both natural and social scientists is empirical generalization. Have you ever wondered how the major television and radio networks can accurately predict election results hours before the polls close? These predictions are made possible by the power of **empirical generalization**, a major type of inductive reasoning that is defined as reasoning from a limited sample to a general conclusion based on this sample.

Network election predictions, as well as public opinion polls that occur throughout a political campaign, are based on interviews with a select number of people. Ideally, pollsters would interview everyone in the *target population* (in this case, voters), but this, of course, is hardly practical. Instead, they select a relatively small group of individuals from the target population, known as a *sample*, who they have determined will adequately represent the group as a whole. Pollsters believe that they can then generalize the opinions of this smaller group to the target population. And with a few notable exceptions (such as in the 1948 presidential election, when New York governor Thomas Dewey went to bed believing he had been elected president and woke up a loser to Harry Truman, and the 2000 election, when Al Gore was briefly declared the presidential winner over George W. Bush), these results are highly accurate.

There are three key criteria for evaluating inductive arguments:

- Is the sample known?
- Is the sample sufficient?
- Is the sample representative?

empirical generalization A form of inductive reasoning in which a general statement is made about an entire group (the target population) based on observing some members of the group (the sample population).

IS THE SAMPLE KNOWN?

An inductive argument is only as strong as the sample on which it is based. For example, sample populations described in vague and unclear terms—"highly placed sources" or "many young people interviewed," for example—provide a treacherously weak foundation for generalizing to larger populations. In order for an inductive argument to be persuasive, the sample population should be explicitly known and clearly identified. Natural and social scientists take great care in selecting the members of sample groups, and this is an important part of the data made available to outside investigators who may wish to evaluate and verify the results.

IS THE SAMPLE SUFFICIENT?

The second criterion for evaluating inductive reasoning is to consider the size of the sample. It should be sufficiently large to give an accurate sense of the group as a whole. In the polling example discussed earlier, we would be concerned if only a few registered voters had been interviewed, and the results of these interviews were then generalized to a much larger population. Overall, the larger the sample, the more reliable the inductive conclusions. Natural and social scientists have developed precise guidelines for determining the size of the sample needed to achieve reliable results. For example, poll results are often accompanied by a qualification such as "These results are subject to an error factor of 63 percentage points." This means that if the sample reveals that 47 percent of those interviewed prefer candidate X, then we can reliably state that 44 to 50 percent of the target population prefer candidate X. Because a sample is usually a small portion of the target population, we can rarely state that the two match each other exactly—there must always be some room for variation. The exceptions to this are situations in which the target population is completely homogeneous. For example, tasting one cookie from a bag of cookies is usually enough to tell us whether or not the entire bag is stale.

IS THE SAMPLE REPRESENTATIVE?

The third crucial element in effective inductive reasoning is the *representativeness* of the sample. If we are to generalize with confidence from the sample to the target population, then we have to be sure the sample is similar to the larger group from which it is drawn in all relevant aspects. For instance, in the polling example the sample population should reflect the same percentage of men and women, of Democrats and Republicans, of young and old, and so on, as the target population. It is obvious that many characteristics, such as hair color, favorite food, and shoe size, are not relevant to the comparison. The better the sample reflects the target population in terms of *relevant* qualities, the better the accuracy of the generalizations. However, when the sample is *not* representative of the target population—for example, if the election pollsters interviewed only females between the ages of thirty and thirty-five—then the sample is termed *biased*, and any generalizations about the target population will be highly suspect.

How do we ensure that the sample is representative of the target population? One important device is *random selection*, a selection strategy in which every member of the target population has an equal chance of being included in the sample. For example, the various techniques used to select winning lottery tickets are supposed to be random—each ticket is supposed to have an equal chance of winning. In complex cases of inductive reasoning—such as polling—random selection is often combined with the confirmation that all of the important categories in the population are adequately represented. For example, an election pollster would want to be certain that all significant geographical areas are included and then would randomly select individuals from within those areas to compose the sample.

Understanding the principles of empirical generalization is of crucial importance to effective thinking because we are continually challenged to construct and evaluate this form of inductive argument in our lives.

Thinking Activity 11.1

EVALUATING INDUCTIVE ARGUMENTS

Review the following examples of inductive arguments. For each argument, evaluate the quality of the thinking by answering the following questions:

1. Is the sample known?
2. Is the sample sufficient?
3. Is the sample representative?
4. Do you believe the conclusions are likely to be accurate? Why or why not?

Link Between Pornography and Antisocial Behavior?

In a study of a possible relationship between pornography and antisocial behavior, questionnaires went out to 7,500 psychiatrists and psychoanalysts whose listing in the directory of the American Psychological Association indicated clinical experience. More than 3,400 of these professionals responded. The result: 7.4 percent of the psychiatrists and psychologists had cases in which they were convinced that pornography was a causal factor in antisocial behavior; an additional 9.4 percent were suspicious; 3.2 percent did not commit themselves; and 80 percent said they had no cases in which a causal connection was suspected.

To Sleep, Perchance to Die?

A survey by the Sleep Disorder Clinic of the VA hospital in La Jolla, California, involving more than one million people, found that people who sleep more than ten hours a night have a death rate 80 percent higher than those who sleep only seven or eight hours. Men who sleep less than four hours a night have a death rate 180 percent higher, and women with less than four hours sleep have a rate 40 percent higher. This might be taken as indicating that too much or too little sleep causes death.

"Slow Down, Multitaskers"

Think you can juggle phone calls, email, instant messages, and computer work to get more done in a time-starved world? Several research reports provide evidence of the limits of multitasking. "Multitasking is going to slow you down, increasing the chances of mistakes," according to David E. Meyer, a cognitive scientist at the University of Michigan. The human brain, with its hundred billion neurons and hundreds of trillions of synaptic connections, is a cognitive powerhouse in many ways. "But a core limitation is an inability to concentrate on two things at once," according to Rene Marois, a neuroscientist at Vanderbilt University. In a recent study, a group of Microsoft workers took, on average, 15 minutes to return to serious mental tasks, like writing reports or computer code, after responding to incoming email or instant messages. They strayed off to reply to other messages or to browse news, sports, or entertainment websites.

Thinking Activity 11.2

DESIGNING A POLL

Select an issue about which you would like to poll a group of people—for example, the population of your school or your neighborhood. Describe in specific terms how you would go about constructing a sample both large enough and representative enough for you to generalize the results to the target population accurately.

Fallacies of False Generalization

In Chapter 7 we explored the way that we form concepts through the interactive process of generalizing (identifying the common qualities that define the boundaries of the concept) and interpreting (identifying examples of the concept). This generalizing and interpreting process is similar to the process involved in constructing empirical generalizations, in which we seek to reach a general conclusion based on a limited number of examples and then apply this conclusion to other examples. Although generalizing and interpreting are useful in forming concepts, they also can give rise to fallacious ways of thinking, including

- Hasty generalization
- Sweeping generalization
- False dilemma

HASTY GENERALIZATION

Consider the following examples of reasoning. Do you think that the arguments are sound? Why or why not?

> My boyfriends have never shown any real concern for my feelings. My conclusion is that men are insensitive, selfish, and emotionally superficial.

> My mother always gets upset over insignificant things. This leads me to believe that women are very emotional.

In both of these cases, a general conclusion has been reached that is based on a very small sample. As a result, the reasons provide very weak support for the conclusions that are being developed. It just does not make good sense to generalize from a few individuals to all men or all women. The conclusions are *hasty* because the samples are not large enough and/or not representative enough to provide adequate justification for the generalization.

Of course, many generalizations are more warranted than the two given here because the conclusion is based on a sample that is larger and more representative of the group as a whole. For example:

> I have done a lot of research in a variety of automotive publications on the relationship between the size of cars and the gas mileage they get. In general, I think it makes sense to conclude that large cars tend to get fewer miles per gallon than smaller cars.

In this case, the conclusion is generalized from a larger and more representative sample than those in the preceding two arguments. As a result, the reason in the last argument provides much stronger support for the conclusion.

SWEEPING GENERALIZATION

Whereas the fallacy of hasty generalization deals with errors in the process of generalizing, the fallacy of *sweeping generalization* focuses on difficulties in the process of interpreting. Consider the following examples of reasoning. Do you think that the arguments are sound? Why or why not?

> Vigorous exercise contributes to overall good health. Therefore, vigorous exercise should be practiced by recent heart attack victims, people who are out of shape, and women who are about to give birth.

> People should be allowed to make their own decisions, providing that their actions do not harm other people. Therefore, people who are trying to commit suicide should be left alone to do what they want.

In both of these cases, generalizations that are true in most cases have been deliberately applied to instances that are clearly intended to be exceptions to the generalizations because of special features that the exceptions possess. Of course, the use of sweeping generalizations stimulates us to clarify the generalization, rephrasing it to exclude instances, like those given here, that have special features. For example, the first generalization could be reformulated as "Vigorous exercise contributes to overall good health, *except for* recent heart attack victims, people out of shape, and women who are about to give birth." Sweeping generalizations become dangerous only when they are accepted without critical analysis and reformulation.

Review the following examples of sweeping generalizations, and in each case (a) explain *why* it is a sweeping generalization and (b) reformulate the statement so that it becomes a legitimate generalization.

1. A college education stimulates you to develop as a person and prepares you for many professions. Therefore, all persons should attend college, no matter what career they are interested in.

2. Drugs such as heroin and morphine are addictive and therefore qualify as dangerous drugs. This means that they should never be used, even as painkillers in medical situations.

3. Once criminals have served time for the crimes they have committed, they have paid their debt to society and should be permitted to work at any job they choose.

FALSE DILEMMA

The fallacy of the *false dilemma*—also known as the "either/or" fallacy or the "black-or-white" fallacy—occurs when we are asked to choose between two extreme alternatives without being able to consider additional options. For example, we may say, "Either you're for me or against me," meaning that a choice has to be made between these alternatives. Sometimes giving people only two choices on an issue makes sense ("If you decide to swim the English Channel, you'll either make it or you won't"). At other times, however, viewing situations in such extreme terms may be a serious oversimplification—for it would mean viewing a complicated situation in terms that are too simple.

The following statements are examples of false dilemmas. After analyzing the fallacy in each case, suggest different alternatives than those being presented.

EXAMPLE: "Everyone in Germany is a National Socialist—the few outside the party are either lunatics or idiots." (Adolf Hitler, quoted by the *New York Times*, April 5, 1938)

ANALYSIS: This is an oversimplification. Hitler is saying that if you are not a Nazi, then you are a lunatic or an idiot. By limiting the population to these groups, Hitler was simply ignoring all the people who did not qualify as Nazis, lunatics, or idiots.

1. America—love it or leave it!

2. She loves me; she loves me not.

3. Live free or die.

4. If you're not part of the solution, then you're part of the problem. (Eldridge Cleaver)

5. If you know about BMWs, you either own one or you want to.

causal reasoning A form of inductive reasoning in which an event (or events) is claimed to be the result of another event (or events).

Causal Reasoning

A second major type of inductive reasoning is **causal reasoning**, a form in which an event (or events) is claimed to be the result of the occurrence of another event (or events).

As you use your thinking abilities to try to understand the world you live in, you often ask the question "Why did that happen?" For example, if the engine of your car is running roughly, your natural question is "What's wrong?" If you wake up one morning with an upset stomach, you usually ask yourself, "What's the cause?" Or maybe the softball team you belong to has been losing recently. You typically wonder, "What's going on?" In each of these cases you assume that there is some factor (or factors) responsible for what is occurring, some *cause* (or causes) that results in the *effect* (or effects) you are observing (the rough engine, the upset stomach, the losing team).

As you saw in Chapter 8, causality is one of the basic patterns of thinking we use to organize and make sense of our experience. For instance, imagine how bewildered you would feel if a mechanic looked at your car and told you there was no explanation for the poorly running engine. Or suppose you take your upset stomach to the doctor, who examines you and then concludes that there is no possible causal explanation for the malady. In each case you would be understandably skeptical of the diagnosis and would probably seek another opinion.

THE SCIENTIFIC METHOD

Causal reasoning is also the backbone of the natural and social sciences; it is responsible for the remarkable understanding of our world that has been achieved. The *scientific method* works on the assumption that the world is constructed in a complex web of causal relationships that can be discovered through systematic investigation. Scientists have devised an organized approach for discovering causal relationships and testing the accuracy of conclusions. The sequence of steps is as follows:

1. Identify an event or a relationship between events to be investigated.
2. Gather information about the event (or events).
3. Develop a hypothesis or theory to explain what is happening.
4. Test the hypothesis or theory through experimentation.
5. Evaluate the hypothesis or theory based on experimental results.

How does this sequence work when applied to the situation of the rough-running engine mentioned earlier?

1. ***Identify an event or a relationship between events to be investigated.*** In this case, the event is obvious—your car's engine is running poorly, and you want to discover the cause of the problem so that you can fix it.

2. ***Gather information about the event (or events).*** This step involves locating any relevant information about the situation that will help solve the problem. You initiate this step by asking and trying to answer a variety of questions: When did the engine begin running poorly? Was this change abrupt or gradual? When did the car last have a tune-up? Are there other mechanical difficulties that might be related? Has anything unusual occurred with the car recently?

3. ***Develop a hypothesis or theory to explain what is happening.*** After reviewing the relevant information, you will want to identify the most likely explanation

hypothesis
A possible explanation that is introduced to account for a set of facts and that can be used as a basis for further investigation.

of what has happened. This possible explanation is known as a **hypothesis**. (A *theory* is normally a more complex model that involves a number of interconnected hypotheses, such as the theory of quantum mechanics in physics.)

Although your hypothesis may be suggested by the information you have, it goes beyond the information as well and so must be tested before you commit yourself to it. In this case the hypothesis you might settle on is "water in the gas." This hypothesis was suggested by your recollection that the engine troubles began right after you bought gas in the pouring rain. This hypothesis may be correct or it may be incorrect—you have to test it to find out.

When you devise a plausible hypothesis to be tested, you should keep three general guidelines in mind:

- *Explanatory power:* The hypothesis should effectively explain the event you are investigating. The hypothesis that damaged windshield wipers are causing the engine problem doesn't seem to provide an adequate explanation of the difficulties.

- *Economy:* The hypothesis should not be unnecessarily complex. The explanation that your engine difficulty is the result of sabotage by an unfriendly neighbor is possible but unlikely. There are simpler and more direct explanations you should test first.

- *Predictive power:* The hypothesis should allow you to make various predictions to test its accuracy. If the "water in the gas" hypothesis is accurate, you can predict that removing the water from the gas tank and gas line should clear up the difficulty.

4. *Test the hypothesis or theory through experimentation.* Once you identify a hypothesis that meets these three guidelines, the next task is to devise an experiment to test its accuracy. In the case of your troubled car, you would test your hypothesis by pouring several containers of "dry gas" into the tank, blowing out the gas line, and cleaning the fuel injection valve. By removing the moisture in the gas system, you should be able to determine whether your hypothesis is correct.

5. *Evaluate the hypothesis or theory based on experimental results.* After reviewing the results of your experiment, you usually can assess the accuracy of your hypothesis. If the engine runs smoothly after you remove moisture from the gas line, then this strong evidence supports your hypothesis. If the engine does *not* run smoothly after your efforts, then this persuasive evidence suggests that your hypothesis is not correct. There is, however, a third possibility. Removing the moisture from the gas system might improve the engine's performance somewhat but not entirely. In that case you might want to construct a *revised* hypothesis along the lines of "Water in the gas system is partially responsible for my rough-running engine, but another cause (or causes) might be involved as well."

If the evidence does not support your hypothesis or supports a revised version of it, you then begin the entire process again by identifying and testing a new hypothesis.

The natural and social sciences engage in an ongoing process of developing theories and hypotheses and testing them through experimental design. Many theories and hypotheses are much more complex than our "moisture in the gas" example and take years of generating, revising, and testing. Determining the subatomic structure of the universe and finding cures for various kinds of cancers, for example, have been the subjects of countless theories and hypotheses, as well as experiments to test their accuracy. We might diagram this operation of the scientific process as follows:

Acceptance, rejection, or revison of a theory/hypothesis

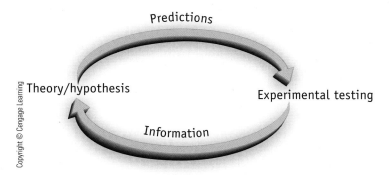

Thinking Activity 11.3

APPLYING THE SCIENTIFIC METHOD

Select one of the following situations or a situation of your own choosing. Then analyze the situation by working through the steps of the scientific method listed here.

- Situation 1: You wake up in the morning with an upset stomach.
- Situation 2: Your grades have been declining all semester.
- Situation 3: (Your own choosing)

1. *Identify an event or a relationship between events to be investigated.* Describe the situation you have selected.

2. *Gather information about the event (or events).* Elaborate the situation by providing additional details. Be sure to include a variety of possible causes for the event (e.g., an upset stomach might be the result of food poisoning, flu, anxiety, etc.).

3. *Develop a hypothesis or theory to explain what is happening.* Based on the information you have described, identify a plausible hypothesis or theory that (a) explains what occurred, (b) is clear and direct, and (c) leads to predictions that can be tested.

4. ***Test the hypothesis or theory through experimentation.*** Design a way of testing your hypothesis that results in evidence proving or disproving it.

5. ***Evaluate the hypothesis or theory based on experimental results.*** Describe the results of your experiment and explain whether the results lead you to accept, reject, or revise your hypothesis.

In designing the experiment in Thinking Activity 11.3, you may have used one of two common reasoning patterns.

REASONING PATTERN 1: *A* caused *B* because *A* is the only relevant common element shared by more than one occurrence of *B*.

For example, imagine that you are investigating your upset stomach, and you decide to call two friends who had dinner with you the previous evening to see if they have similar symptoms. You discover they also have upset stomachs. Because dining at "Sam's Seafood" was the only experience shared by the three of you that might explain the three stomach problems, you conclude that food poisoning may in fact be the cause. Further, although each of you ordered a different entrée, you all shared an appetizer, "Sam's Special Squid," which suggests that you may have identified the cause. As you can see, this pattern of reasoning looks for the common thread linking different occurrences of the same event to identify the cause; stated more simply, "The cause is the common thread."

REASONING PATTERN 2: *A* caused *B* because *A* is the only relevant difference between this situation and other situations in which *B* did not take place.

For example, imagine that you are investigating the reasons that your team, which has been winning all year, has suddenly begun to lose. One way of approaching this situation is to look for circumstances that might have changed at the time your team's fortunes began to decline. Your investigation yields two possible explanations. First, your team started wearing new uniforms about the time it started losing. Second, one of your regular players was sidelined with a foot injury. You decide to test the first hypothesis by having the team begin wearing the old uniforms again. When this doesn't change your fortunes, you conclude that the missing player may be the cause of the difficulties, and you anxiously await the player's return to see if your reasoning is accurate. As you can see, this pattern of reasoning looks for relevant differences linked to the situation you are trying to explain; stated more simply, "The cause is the difference."

CONTROLLED EXPERIMENTS

Although our analysis of causal reasoning has focused on causal relationships between specific events, much of scientific research concerns causal factors influencing populations composed of many individuals. In these cases the causal relationships tend to be much more complex than the simple formulation *A causes B*.

For example, on every package of cigarettes sold in the United States appears a message such as "Surgeon General's Warning: Smoking Causes Lung Cancer, Heart Disease, Emphysema, and May Complicate Pregnancy." This does not mean that every cigarette smoked has a direct impact on one's health, nor does it mean that everyone who smokes moderately, or even heavily, will die prematurely of cancer, heart disease, or emphysema. Instead, the statement means that if you habitually smoke, your chances of developing one of the diseases normally associated with smoking are significantly higher than are those of someone who does not smoke or who smokes only occasionally. How were scientists able to arrive at this conclusion?

The reasoning strategy scientists use to reach conclusions like this one is the *controlled experiment*, and it is one of the most powerful reasoning strategies ever developed. There are three different kinds of controlled experiment designs:

1. Cause-to-effect experiments (with intervention)
2. Cause-to-effect experiments (without intervention)
3. Effect-to-cause experiments

Cause-to-Effect Experiments (with Intervention) The first of these forms of reasoning, known as *cause-to-effect experiments (with intervention)*, is illustrated by the following example. Imagine that you have developed a new cream you believe will help cure baldness in men and women and you want to evaluate its effectiveness. What do you do? To begin with, you have to identify a group of people who accurately represent all of the balding men and women in the United States because testing the cream on all balding people simply isn't feasible. This involves following the guidelines for inductive reasoning described in the last section. It is important that the group you select to test be *representative* of all balding people (known as the *target population*) because you hope your product will grow hair on all types of heads. For example, if you select only men between the ages of twenty and thirty to test, the experiment will establish only whether the product works for men of these ages. Additional experiments will have to be conducted for women and other age groups. This representative group is known as a *sample*. Scientists have developed strategies for selecting sample groups to ensure that they fairly mirror the larger group from which they are drawn.

Once you have selected your sample of balding men and women—say, you have identified 200 people—the next step is to divide the sample into two groups of 100 people that are alike in all relevant respects. The best way to ensure that the groups are essentially alike is through the technique we examined earlier called *random selection*, which means that each individual selected has the same chance of being chosen as everyone else. You then designate one group as the experimental group and the other group as the control group. You next give the individuals in the experimental group treatments of your hair-growing cream, and you give either no treatments or a harmless, non-hair-growing cream to the control group. At the conclusion of the testing period, you compare the experimental group with the control group to evaluate hair gain and hair loss.

Suppose that a number of individuals in the experimental group do indeed show evidence of more new hair growth than the control group. How can you be sure this is because of the cream and not simply a chance occurrence? Scientists have developed a formula for statistical significance based on the size of the sample and the frequency of the observed effects. For example, imagine that thirteen persons in your experimental group show evidence of new hair growth, whereas no one in the control group shows any such evidence. Statisticians have determined that we can say with 95 percent certainty that the new hair growth was caused by your new cream—that the results were not merely the result of chance. This type of experimental result is usually expressed by saying that the experimental results were significant at the 0.05 level, a standard criterion in experimental research. The diagram below shows the cause-to-effect experiment (with intervention).

Cause-to-Effect Experiments (with Intervention)

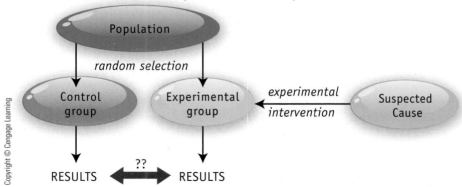

Cause-to-Effect Experiments (Without Intervention) A second form of controlled experiment is known as the *cause-to-effect experiment (without intervention)*. This form of experimental design is similar to the one just described except that the experimenter does not intervene to expose the experimental group to a proposed cause (like the hair-growing cream). Instead, the experimenter identifies a cause that a population is already exposed to and then constructs the experiment. For example, suppose you suspect that the asbestos panels and insulation in some old buildings cause cancer. Because it would not be ethical to expose people intentionally to something that might damage their health, you would search for already existing conditions in which people are being exposed to the asbestos. Once located, these individuals (or a representative sample) could be used as the experimental group. You could then form a control group of individuals who are not exposed to asbestos but who match the experimental group in all other relevant respects. You could then investigate the health experiences of both groups over time, thereby evaluating the possible relationship between asbestos and cancer. The following diagram illustrates the procedure used in cause-to-effect experiments (without intervention).

Cause-to-Effect Experiments (without Intervention)

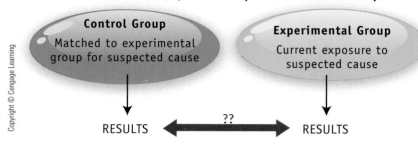

Effect-to-Cause Experiments A third form of reasoning employing the controlled experimental design is known as the *effect-to-cause experiment*. In this case the experimenter works backward from an existing effect to a suspected cause. For example, imagine that you are investigating the claim by many Vietnam veterans that exposure to the chemical defoliant Agent Orange has resulted in significant health problems for them and for children born to them. Once again, you would not want to expose people to a potentially harmful substance just to test a hypothesis. And unlike the asbestos case we just examined, people are no longer being exposed to Agent Orange as they were during the Vietnam War. As a result, investigating the claim involves beginning with the effect (health problems) and working back to the suspected cause (Agent Orange). In this case the target population would be Vietnam veterans who were exposed to Agent Orange, so you would draw a representative sample from this group. You would form a matching control group from the population of Vietnam veterans who were not exposed to Agent Orange. Next, you would compare the incidence of illnesses claimed to have been caused by Agent Orange in the two groups and evaluate the proposed causal relation. The following diagram illustrates the procedure used in effect-to-cause experiments.

Effect-to-Cause Experiments

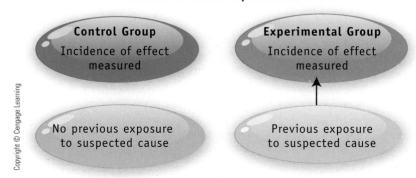

Thinking Activity 11.4

EVALUATING EXPERIMENTAL RESULTS

Read the following experimental situations. For each situation:

1. Describe the proposed causal relationship (the theory or hypothesis).
2. Identify which kind of experimental design was used.
3. Evaluate
   a. The representativeness of the sample.
   b. The randomness of the division into experimental and control groups.
4. Explain how well the experimental results support the proposed theory or hypothesis.

Mortality Shown to Center Around Birthdays

A study, based on 2,745,149 deaths from natural causes, has found that men tend to die just before their birthdays, whereas women tend to die just after their birthdays. Thus an approaching birthday seems to prolong the life of women and precipitate death in men. The study, published in the journal *Psychosomatic Medicine*, found 3 percent more deaths than expected among women in the week after a birthday and a slight decline the week before. For men, deaths peaked just before birthdays and showed no rise above normal afterward.

A Shorter Life for Lefties

A survey of 5,000 people by Stanley Coren found that although 15 percent of the population at age ten was left-handed, there was a pronounced drop-off as people grew older, leaving 5 percent among fifty-year-olds and less than 1 percent for those age eighty and above. Where have all the lefties gone? They seem to have died. Lefties have a shorter life expectancy than righties, by an average of nine years in the general population, apparently due to the ills and accidents they are more likely to suffer by having to live in a right-handed world.

Nuns Offer Clues to Alzheimer's and Aging

Experts on aging consider the famous "Nun Study" to be one of the most innovative efforts to answer questions about who gets Alzheimer's disease and why. Studying 678 nuns at seven convents has shown that folic acid may help stave off Alzheimer's disease. Early language ability may also be linked to lower risk of Alzheimer's because nuns who packed more ideas into the sentences of their early autobiographies were less likely to get Alzheimer's disease six decades later. Also, nuns who expressed more positive emotions in their autobiographies lived significantly longer—in some cases ten years longer—than those expressing fewer positive emotions.

Thinking Activity 11.5

DESIGNING A SCIENTIFIC EXPERIMENT

Construct an experimental design to investigate a potential causal relationship of your own choosing. Be sure that your experimental design follows the guidelines established.

- A clearly defined theory or hypothesis expressing a proposed relationship between a cause and an effect in a population of individuals
- Representative samples
- Selection into experimental and control groups
- A clear standard for evaluating the evidence for or against the theory or hypothesis

Thinking Passage

TREATING BREAST CANCER

Scientific discovery is rarely a straightforward, uninterrupted line of progress. Rather, it typically involves confusing and often contradictory results, false starts and missteps, and results that are complex and ambiguous. It is only in retrospect that we are able to fit all of the pieces of the scientific puzzle into their proper places.

The race to discover increasingly effective treatments for breast cancer is a compelling example of the twisted path of scientific exploration. One American woman in eight develops breast cancer, and it is the health threat women fear most, although heart disease is by far the leading cause of death (ten times more lethal than breast cancer). But women have been receiving conflicting advice on the prevention and cure of breast cancer, based on scientific studies that have yielded seemingly confusing results. For example, one study concluded that support groups for women with advanced breast cancer extended their lives an average of eighteen months, whereas another found that such groups had no impact on life expectancy.

But it is a recent study on the efficacy of mammograms that is causing the widest and most disturbing confusion. This study, reported in a British medical journal, asserts that the promise of regular mammograms is an illusion: Mammograms have no measurable impact on reducing the risk of death or avoiding mastectomies! And in November 2009, the U.S. Preventative Services Task Force—with members appointed by the U.S. Department of Health and Human Services—said women do not need routine screenings until they're 50. The independent panel also discouraged breast self-examinations, saying they don't significantly reduce breast cancer deaths. The new study has sparked a great deal of controversy and confusion among patients and physicians. The article titled "Understanding the New Mammogram Guidelines" provides an analysis of this bewildering situation and provides a window into the complex process of scientific discovery.

Listen to the radio broadcast available at http://www.npr.org/templates/story/story.php?storyId=120537928 on NPR.org. As you do so, use the transcript of the show provided on the same page to read along.

QUESTIONS FOR ANALYSIS

1. Why have the U.S. Preventative Services Task Force's new guidelines for breast cancer screening cast doubt on previous, long-standing recommendations that women over the age of 40 get routine mammograms and that all women should perform regular breast self-exams? On what evidence did the Task Force base their guidelines?

2. In this radio program, at least one caller as well as one of the guests (Constance Lehman, the medical director of radiology and director of breast imaging at Seattle Cancer Care Alliance) criticize the Task Force's new guidelines. What reasoning do they offer in their objections?

3. If you were a physician, would you recommend that women over 50 get annual mammograms? Why or why not?

Causal Fallacies

Because causality plays such a dominant role in the way we make sense of the world, it is not surprising that people make many mistakes and errors in judgment in trying to determine causal relationships. The following are some of the most common fallacies associated with causality:

- Questionable cause
- Misidentification of the cause
- *Post hoc ergo propter hoc*
- Slippery slope

QUESTIONABLE CAUSE

The fallacy of *questionable cause* occurs when someone presents a causal relationship for which no real evidence exists. Superstitious beliefs, such as "If you break a mirror, you will have seven years of bad luck," usually fall into this category. Some people feel that astrology, a system of beliefs tying one's personality and fortunes in life to the position of the planets at the moment of birth, also falls into this category.

Consider the following passage from St. Augustine's *Confessions*. Does it seem to support or deny the causal assertions of astrology? Why or why not?

> Firminus had heard from his father that when his mother had been pregnant with him, a slave belonging to a friend of his father's was also about to bear. It happened that since the two women had their babies at the same instant, the men were forced to cast exactly the same horoscope for each newborn child down to the last detail, one for his son, the other for the little slave. Yet Firminus, born to wealth in his parents' house, had one of the more illustrious careers in life whereas the slave had no alleviation of his life's burden.

Other examples of this fallacy include explanations like those given by fourteenth-century sufferers of the bubonic plague who claimed that "the Jews are poisoning the Christians' wells." This was particularly nonsensical since an equal percentage of Jews were dying of the plague as well. The evidence did not support the explanation.

MISIDENTIFICATION OF THE CAUSE

In causal situations we are not always certain about what is causing what—in other words, what is the cause and what is the effect. *Misidentifying the cause* is easy to do. For example, which are the causes and which are the effects in the following pairs of items? Why?

- Poverty and alcoholism
- Headaches and tension
- Failure in school and personal problems
- Shyness and lack of confidence
- Drug dependency and emotional difficulties

Of course, sometimes a third factor is responsible for both of the effects we are examining. For example, the headaches and tension we are experiencing may both be the result of a third element—such as some new medication we are taking. When this occurs, we are said to commit the fallacy of *ignoring a common cause*. There also exists the fallacy of *assuming a common cause*—for example, assuming that both a sore toe and an earache stem from the same cause.

POST HOC ERGO PROPTER HOC

The translation of the Latin phrase *post hoc ergo propter hoc* is "After it, therefore because of it." It refers to those situations in which, because two things occur close together in time, we assume that one caused the other. For example, if your team wins the game each time you wear your favorite shirt, you might be tempted to conclude that the one event (wearing your favorite shirt) has some influence on the other event (winning the game). As a result, you might continue to wear this shirt "for good luck." It is easy to see how this sort of mistaken thinking can lead to all sorts of superstitious beliefs.

Consider the causal conclusion arrived at by Mark Twain's fictional character Huckleberry Finn in the following passage. How would you analyze the conclusion that he comes to?

> I've always reckoned that looking at the new moon over your left shoulder is one of the carelessest and foolishest things a body can do. Old Hank Bunker done it once, and bragged about it; and in less than two years he got drunk and fell off a shot tower and spread himself out so that he was just a kind of layer. . . . But anyway, it all come of looking at the moon that way, like a fool.

Can you identify any of your own superstitious beliefs or practices that might have been the result of *post hoc* thinking?

SLIPPERY SLOPE

The causal fallacy of *slippery slope* is illustrated in the following advice:

> Don't miss that first deadline, because if you do, it won't be long before you're missing all your deadlines. This will spread to the rest of your life, as you will be late for every appointment. This terminal procrastination will ruin your career, and friends and relatives will abandon you. You will end up a lonely failure who is unable to ever do anything on time.

Slippery slope thinking asserts that one undesirable action will inevitably lead to a worse action, which will necessarily lead to a worse one still, all the way down the "slippery slope" to some terrible disaster at the bottom. Although this progression may indeed happen, there is certainly no causal guarantee that it will. Create slippery slope scenarios for one of the following warnings:

- If you get behind on one credit card payment . . .
- If you fail that first test . . .
- If you eat that first fudge square . . .

Review the causal fallacies just described and then identify and explain the reasoning pitfalls illustrated in the following examples:

- The person who won the lottery says that she dreamed the winning numbers. I'm going to start writing down the numbers in my dreams.
- Yesterday I forgot to take my vitamins, and I immediately got sick. That mistake won't happen again!
- I'm warning you—if you start missing classes, it won't be long before you flunk out of school and ruin your future.

- I always take the first seat in the bus. Today I took another seat, and the bus broke down. And you accuse me of being superstitious!

- I think the reason I'm not doing well in school is that I'm just not interested. Also, I simply don't have enough time to study.

Many people want us to see the cause-and-effect relationships that they believe exist, and they often use questionable or outright fallacious reasoning. Consider the following examples:

- Advertisers tell us that using this detergent will leave our wash "cleaner than clean, whiter than white."

- Doctors tell us that eating a balanced diet will result in better health.

- Educators tell us that a college degree is worth an average of $1,140,000 additional income over an individual's life.

- Scientists inform us that nuclear energy will result in a better life for all.

In an effort to persuade us to adopt a certain point of view, each of these examples makes certain causal claims about how the world operates. As critical thinkers, it is our duty to evaluate these various causal claims in an effort to figure out whether they are sensible ways of organizing the world.

Explain how you might go about evaluating whether each of the following causal claims makes sense:

EXAMPLE: Taking the right vitamins will improve health.

EVALUATION: Review the medical research that examines the effect of taking vitamins on health; speak to a nutritionist; speak to a doctor.

- Sweet Smell deodorant will keep you drier all day long.

- Allure perfume will cause people to be attracted to you.

- Natural childbirth will result in a more fulfilling birth experience.

- Aspirin Plus will give you faster, longer-lasting relief from headaches.

- Listening to loud music will damage your hearing.

Fallacies of Relevance

Many fallacious arguments appeal for support to factors that have little or nothing to do with the argument being offered. In these cases, false appeals substitute for sound reasoning and a critical examination of the issues. Such appeals, known as *fallacies of relevance*, include the following kinds of fallacious thinking, which are grouped by similarity into "fallacy families":

- Appeal to authority
- Appeal to tradition

- Bandwagon
- Appeal to pity
- Appeal to fear
- Appeal to flattery
- Special pleading
- Appeal to ignorance
- Begging the question
- Straw man
- Red herring
- Appeal to personal attack
- Two wrongs make a right

APPEAL TO AUTHORITY

In Chapter 5, we explored the ways in which we sometimes *appeal to authorities* to establish our beliefs or prove our points. At that time, we noted that to serve as a basis for beliefs, authorities must have legitimate expertise in the area in which they are advising—like an experienced mechanic diagnosing a problem with your car. People, however, often appeal to authorities who are not qualified to give an expert opinion. Consider the reasoning in the following advertisements. Do you think the arguments are sound? Why or why not?

> Hi. You've probably seen me out on the football field. After a hard day's work crushing halfbacks and sacking quarterbacks, I like to settle down with a cold, smooth Maltz beer.
> SONY. Ask anyone.
> Over 11 million women will read this ad. Only 16 will own the coat.

Each of these arguments is intended to persuade us of the value of a product through appeal to various authorities. In the first case, the authority is a well-known sports figure; in the second, the authority is large numbers of people; and in the third, the authority is a select few, appealing to our desire to be exclusive ("snob appeal"). Unfortunately, none of these authorities offers legitimate expertise about the product. Football players are not beer experts; large numbers of people are often misled; exclusive groups of people are frequently mistaken in their beliefs. To evaluate authorities properly, we have to ask:

- What are the professional credentials on which the authorities' expertise is based?
- Is their expertise in the area they are commenting on?

APPEAL TO TRADITION

A member of the same fallacy family as appeal to authority, *appeal to tradition* argues that a practice or way of thinking is "better" or "right" simply because it is older, it is traditional, or it has "always been done that way." Although traditional beliefs often express some truth or wisdom—for example, "Good nutrition, exercise, and regular medical check-ups are the foundation of good health"—traditional beliefs are often misguided or outright false. Consider, for example, the belief that "intentional bleeding is a source of good health because it lets loose evil vapors in the body" or traditional practices like Victorian rib-crushing corsets, Chinese footbinding, or female circumcision. How do we tell which traditional beliefs or practices have merit? We need to think critically, evaluating the value based on informed reasons and compelling evidence. Critically evaluate the following traditional beliefs:

- Spare the rod and spoil the child.
- Children should be seen and not heard.
- Never take "no" for an answer.
- I was always taught that a woman's place was in the home, so pursuing a career is out of the question for me.
- Real men don't cry—that's the way I was brought up.

BANDWAGON

Joining the illogical appeals to authority and tradition, the fallacy *bandwagon* relies on the uncritical acceptance of others' opinions, in this case because "everyone believes it." People experience this all the time through "peer pressure," when an unpopular view is squelched and modified by the group opinion. For example, you may change your opinion when confronted with the threat of ridicule or rejection from your friends. Or you may modify your point of view at work or in your religious organization in order to conform to the prevailing opinion. In all of these cases your views are being influenced by a desire to "jump on the bandwagon" and avoid getting left by yourself on the side of the road. The bandwagon mentality also extends to media appeals based on views of select groups such as celebrities or public opinion polls. Again, critical thinking is the tool that you have to distinguish an informed belief from a popular but uninformed belief. Critically evaluate the following bandwagon appeals:

- I used to think that _____ was my favorite kind of music. But my friends convinced me that only losers enjoy this music. So I've stopped listening to it.
- Hollywood celebrities and supermodels agree: Tattoos in unusual places are very cool. That's good enough for me!
- In the latest Gallup Poll, 86 percent of those polled believe that economic recovery will happen in the next six months, so I must be wrong.

APPEAL TO PITY

Consider the reasoning in the following arguments. Do you think that the arguments are sound? Why or why not?

I know that I haven't completed my term paper, but I really think that I should be excused. This has been a very difficult semester for me. I caught every kind of flu that came around. In addition, my brother has a drinking problem, and this has been very upsetting to me. Also, my dog died.

I admit that my client embezzled money from the company, your honor. However, I would like to bring several facts to your attention. He is a family man, with a wonderful wife and two terrific children. He is an important member of the community. He is active in the church, coaches a Little League baseball team, and has worked very hard to be a good person who cares about people. I think that you should take these things into consideration in handing down your sentence.

In each of these *appeal to pity* arguments, the reasons offered to support the conclusions may indeed be true. They are not, however, relevant to the conclusion. Instead of providing evidence that supports the conclusion, the reasons are designed to make us feel sorry for the person involved and therefore agree with the conclusion out of sympathy. Although these appeals are often effective, the arguments are not sound. The probability of a conclusion can be established only by reasons that support and are relevant to the conclusion.

Of course, not every appeal to pity is fallacious. There *are* instances in which pity may be deserved, relevant, and decisive. For example, if you are soliciting a charitable donation, or asking a friend for a favor, an honest and straightforward appeal to pity may be appropriate.

APPEAL TO FEAR

Consider the reasoning in the following arguments. Do you think that the arguments are sound? Why or why not?

I'm afraid I don't think you deserve a raise. After all, there are many people who would be happy to have your job at the salary you are currently receiving. I would be happy to interview some of these people if you really think that you are underpaid.

If you continue to disagree with my interpretation of *The Catcher in the Rye*, I'm afraid you won't get a very good grade on your term paper.

In both of these arguments, the conclusions being suggested are supported by an *appeal to fear*, not by reasons that provide evidence for the conclusions. In the first case, the threat is that if you do not forgo your salary demands, your job may be in jeopardy. In the second case, the threat is that if you do not agree with the teacher's interpretation, you will fail the course. In neither instance are the real issues—Is a salary increase deserved? Is the student's interpretation legitimate?—being discussed. People who appeal to fear to support their conclusions are interested only in prevailing, regardless of which position might be more justified.

APPEAL TO FLATTERY

Flattery joins the emotions of pity and fear as a popular source of fallacious reasoning. This kind of apple polishing is designed to influence the thinking of others by appealing to their vanity as a substitute for providing relevant evidence to support your point of view. Of course, flattery is often a harmless lubricant for social relationships, and it can also be used in conjunction with compelling reasoning. But *appeal to flattery* enters the territory of fallacy when it is the main or sole support of your claim, such as "This is absolutely the best course I've ever taken. And I'm really hoping for an A to serve as an emblem of your excellent teaching." Think critically about the following examples:

- You have a great sense of humor, boss, and I'm particularly fond of your racial and homosexual jokes. They crack me up! And while we're talking, I'd like to remind you how much I'm hoping for the opportunity to work with you if I receive the promotion that you're planning to give to one of us.
- You are a beautiful human being, inside and out. Why don't you stay the night?
- You are *so* smart. I wish I had a brain like yours. Can you give me any hints about the chemistry test you took today? I'm taking it tomorrow.

SPECIAL PLEADING

This fallacy occurs when someone makes him- or herself a special exception, without sound justification, to the reasonable application of standards, principles, or expectations. For example, consider the following exchange:

"Hey, hon, could you get me a beer? I'm pooped from work today."

"Well, I'm exhausted from working all day, too! Why don't you get it yourself?"

"I need you to get it because I'm really thirsty."

As we saw in Chapter 4, we view the world through our own lenses, and these lenses tend to let us see the world as tilted toward our interests. That's why *special pleading* is such a popular fallacy: We're used to treating our circumstances as unique and deserving of special consideration when compared to the circumstances of others. Of course, other people tend to see things from a very different perspective. Critically evaluate the following examples:

- I know that the deadline for the paper was announced several weeks ago and that you made clear there would be no exceptions, but I'm asking you to make an exception because I experienced some very bad breaks.
- I really don't like it when you check out other men and comment on their physiques. I know that I do that toward other women, but it's a "guy thing."
- Yes, I would like to play basketball with you guys, but I want to warn you: As a woman, I don't like getting bumped around, so keep your distance.
- I probably shouldn't have used funds from the treasury for my own personal use, but after all I *am* the president of the organization.

Thinking Critically About Visuals

Stop and Think

This poster was created by the Do It Now Foundation, formed in 1968 to provide education and outreach about drug abuse but which now addresses a wide range of health and social issues such as sexuality, eating disorders, and alcoholism.

Courtesy, Do It Now Foundation

Many school districts and private groups promote an "abstinence-only" approach to sex education, or encourage young people to remain virgins until marriage. Reasons given for abstinence education range from moral and religious principles (including "purity pledges" and "secondary virginity") to avoidance of pregnancy and sexually transmitted diseases. Do a web search using terms such as *abstinence education* and *secondary virginity* to find sites with information on such programs and organizations. What kinds of appeals—or fallacies—do these websites use to promote their message? Examine the origins and assumptions behind each site's message.

The Campaign to End AIDS was founded in 2005 as a coalition of diverse people living with HIV/AIDS, their families and caretakers, and others. The group advocates accessible and affordable health care for people with HIV/AIDS, research into treatments and cures, and HIV education and prevention.

Both of these images use the universally understood sign for STOP, but to convey very different messages. Are either or both of these messages effective examples of inductive reasoning? What are the causal relationships implied by each message, and how clearly does each message use causal reasoning to support its claim?

Matthias Kulka/Bridge/Corbis

APPEAL TO IGNORANCE

Consider the reasoning in the following arguments. Do you think that the arguments are sound? Why or why not?

> You say that you don't believe in God. But can you prove that He doesn't exist? If not, then you have to accept the conclusion that He does in fact exist.
>
> Greco tires are the best. No others have been proved better.
>
> With me, abortion is not a problem of religion. It's a problem of the Constitution. I believe that until and unless someone can establish that the unborn child is not a living human being, then that child is already protected by the Constitution, which guarantees life, liberty, and the pursuit of happiness to all of us.

When the *appeal to ignorance* argument form is used, the person offering the conclusion is asking his or her opponent to *disprove* the conclusion. If the opponent is unable to do so, then the conclusion is asserted to be true. This argument form is not valid because it is the job of the person proposing the argument to prove the conclusion. Simply because an opponent cannot *dis*prove the conclusion offers no evidence that the conclusion is in fact justified. In the first example, for instance, the fact that someone cannot prove that God does not exist provides no persuasive reason for believing that he does.

BEGGING THE QUESTION

This fallacy is also known as *circular reasoning* because the premises of the argument assume or include the claim that the conclusion is true. For example:

> "How do I know that I can trust you?"
> "Just ask Adrian; she'll tell you."
> "How do I know that I can trust Adrian?"
> "Don't worry; I'll vouch for her."

Begging the question is often found in self-contained systems of belief, such as politics or religion. For example:

> "My religion worships the one true God."
> "How can you be so sure?"
> "Because our Holy Book says so."
> "Why should I believe this Holy Book?"
> "Because it was written by the one true God."

In other words, the problem with this sort of reasoning is that instead of providing relevant evidence in support of a conclusion, it simply goes in a circle by assuming the truth of what it is supposedly proving. Critically evaluate the following examples:

- Smoking marijuana has got to be illegal. Otherwise, it wouldn't be against the law.
- Of course, I'm telling you the truth. Otherwise, I'd be lying.

Thinking Critically About Visuals

Fallacies in Action

These two images illustrate two different forms of fallacies in action. The first one portrays a church sign with the statement "If evolution were true then moms would have 3 arms." What is the implicit argument being made here? Why might someone find this argument to be appealing? Why is this claim illogical?

The cartoon in the second image depicts an accused man using flattery to plead his case to the judge. What is the man hoping to accomplish with this approach? Why is an instance like this considered to be a fallacy? Can you cite an example from your own experience in which you engaged in a similar form of fallacious reasoning? Was it effective? Why or why not?

Mark Lehigh/Shutterstock.com

Baloo/www.CartoonStock.com

"Before I sum up, Your Honor, I'd just like to say that you're beautiful when you're mad."

STRAW MAN

This fallacy is best understood by visualizing its name: You attack someone's point of view by creating an exaggerated *straw man* version of the position, and then you knock down the straw man you just created. For example, consider the following exchange:

"I'm opposed to the missile defense shield because I think it's a waste of money."

"So you want to undermine the security of our nation and leave the country defenseless. Are you serious?"

The best way to combat this fallacy is to point out that the straw man does not reflect an accurate representation of your position. For instance:

> "On the contrary, I'm very concerned about national security. The money that would be spent on a nearly useless defense shield can be used to combat terrorist threats, a much more credible threat than a missile attack. Take your straw man somewhere else!"

How would you respond to the following arguments?

- You're saying that the budget for our university has to be reduced by 15 percent to meet state guidelines. That means reducing the size of the faculty and student population by 15 percent, and that's crazy.
- I think we should work at keeping the apartment clean; it's a mess.
- So you're suggesting that we discontinue our lives and become full-time maids so that we can live in a pristine, spotless, antiseptic apartment. That's no way to live!

RED HERRING

Also known as "smoke screen" and "wild goose chase," the *red herring* fallacy is committed by introducing an irrelevant topic in order to divert attention from the original issue being discussed. So, for example:

> I'm definitely in favor of the death penalty. After all, overpopulation is a big problem in our world today.

Although this is certainly a novel approach to addressing the problem of overpopulation, it's not really relevant to the issue of capital punishment. Critically evaluate the following examples:

- I think all references to sex should be eliminated from films and music. Premarital sex and out-of-wedlock childbirths are creating moral decay in our society.
- I really don't believe that grade inflation is a significant problem in higher education. Everybody wants to be liked, and teachers are just trying to get students to like them.

APPEAL TO PERSONAL ATTACK

Consider the reasoning in the following arguments. Do you think that the arguments are valid? Why or why not?

> Your opinion on this issue is false. It's impossible to believe anything you say.

> How can you have an intelligent opinion about abortion? You're not a woman, so this is a decision that you'll never have to make.

Appeal to personal attack has been one of the most frequently used fallacies through the ages. Its effectiveness results from ignoring the issues of the argument and focusing instead on the personal qualities of the person making the argument. By trying to discredit the other person, this argument form tries to discredit the argument—no matter what reasons are offered. This fallacy is also referred to as the *ad hominem* argument, which means "to the man" rather than to the issue, and *poisoning the well* because we are trying to ensure that any water drawn from our opponent's well will be treated as undrinkable.

The effort to discredit can take two forms, as illustrated in the preceding examples. The fallacy can be abusive in the sense that we are directly attacking the credibility of our opponent (as in the first example). The fallacy can be *circumstantial* in the sense that we are claiming that the person's circumstances, not character, render his or her opinion so biased or uninformed that it cannot be treated seriously (as in the second example). Other examples of the circumstantial form of the fallacy would include disregarding the views on nuclear plant safety given by an owner of one of the plants or ignoring the views of a company comparing a product it manufactures with competing products.

TWO WRONGS MAKE A RIGHT

This fallacy attempts to justify a morally questionable action by arguing that it is a response to another wrong action, either real or imagined—in effect, that *two wrongs make a right*. For example, someone undercharged at a store might justify keeping the extra money by reasoning that "I've probably been overcharged many times in the past, and this simply equals things out." Or he or she might even speculate, "I am likely to be overcharged in the future, so I'm keeping this in anticipation of being cheated." This is a fallacious way of thinking because each action is independent and must be evaluated on its own merits. If you're overcharged and knowingly keep the money, that's stealing. If the store knowingly overcharges you, that's stealing as well. If the store inadvertently overcharges you, that's a mistake. Or as expressed in a common saying, "Two wrongs *don't* make a right." Critically evaluate the following examples:

- Terrorists are justified in killing innocent people because they and their people have been the victims of political repression and discriminatory policies.
- Capital punishment is wrong because killing murderers is just as bad as the killings they committed.

Thinking Activity 11.6

IDENTIFYING FALLACIES

Locate (or develop) an example of each of the following kinds of false appeals. For each example, explain why you think that the appeal is not warranted.

1. Appeal to authority
2. Appeal to pity
3. Appeal to fear
4. Appeal to ignorance
5. Appeal to personal attack

THINKING CRITICALLY ABOUT NEW MEDIA

Internet Hoaxes, Scams, and Urban Legends

As we have seen in this chapter, *fallacies* are unsound arguments that are often persuasive and appear to be logical because they usually appeal to our emotions and prejudices, and because they often support conclusions that we want to believe are accurate. One expression of fallacious thinking in new media can be found in the existence of *Internet hoaxes:* messages, offers, solicitations, advice, or threats that are often seductive in their appeal but false and sometimes dangerous. The hoaxes come in all shapes and sizes: "helping" someone from an African country transfer 20 million dollars; receiving birthday greetings from a secret admirer; verifying your credit card information with an alleged bank; passing along a message to ten friends with the hope of receiving special blessings or cash; helping to provide medical care for an ill or injured child; and many, many more. Often these hoaxes are harmless, resulting in nothing more than our wasting time and bandwidth by forwarding phony chain letters. Other times, however, we risk donating money to scam artists, divulging credit or bank information to financial predators, or introducing destructive viruses into our computer by opening attached files from Internet anarchists.

Most virus warnings are hoaxes and can be spotted by the following signs:

- They falsely claim to describe an extremely dangerous virus.
- They use pseudo-technical language to make impressive-sounding claims.
- They falsely claim that the report was issued or confirmed by a well-known company.
- They ask you to forward it to all your friends and colleagues.

You should avoid passing on warnings of this kind, as the continued re-forwarding of these hoaxes wastes time and email bandwidth. Sometimes you may receive hoaxes with an attached file that may be infected with a virus. A good principle is to delete all hoaxes and *never* open an attached file from a source that you don't know personally.

There are a number of sites devoted to uncovering these Internet hoaxes, including:

www.snopes.com (Urban Legends Reference Pages)
www.hoaxbusters.org
urbanlegends.about.com

Hoaxbusters.org offers a guide to help detect whether an email is a hoax or the real deal. Listed below are their "Top Five Signs That an E-mail Is a Hoax." After reading through their warning signs, conduct some independent research of your own by locating three possible Internet hoaxes and then analyzing their authenticity by applying the "Five Top Signs."

Top Five Signs That an E-mail Is a Hoax

The next time that you receive an alarming e-mail calling you to action, look for one or more of these five telltale characteristics before even thinking about sending it along to anybody else.

Urgent

The e-mail will have a great sense of urgency! You'll usually see a lot of exclamation points and capitalization. The subject line will typically be something like:

URGENT!!!!!!
WARNING!!!!!!
IMPORTANT!!!!!!
VIRUS ALERT!!!!!!
THIS IS NOT A JOKE!!!!!!

Tell All Your Friends

There will always be a request that you share this "important information" by forwarding the message to everybody in your e-mail address book or to as many people as you possibly can. This is a surefire sign that the message is a hoax.

This Isn't a Hoax

The body of the e-mail may contain some form of corroboration, such as a pseudoquote from an executive of a major corporation or government official. The message may include a sincere-sounding premise, such as this, for example: *My neighbor, who works for Microsoft, just received this warning so I know it's true. He asked me to pass this along to as many people as I can.*

Sometimes the message will contain a link to Snopes to further confuse people. The references to Snopes are just red herrings, though, meant only to give a sense of

(Continues)

THINKING CRITICALLY ABOUT NEW MEDIA (*CONTINUED*)

legitimacy to the hoax. The author knows that lots of folks will believe it because they see it in print and won't bother to really check it for themselves. Anyone actually bothering to check the story with Snopes would, of course, discover that it was not true. Hoax writers count on folks being too lazy to verify those stories before they hit the forward button.

It's all a bunch of baloney. Don't believe it for a second.

Watch for e-mails containing a subtle form of self-corroboration. Statements such as "This is serious!" or "This is not a hoax!" can be deceiving. Just because somebody says it's not a hoax doesn't make it so.

Dire Consequences

The e-mail text will predict dire consequences if you don't act immediately. You are led to believe that a missing child will never be found unless the e-mail is forwarded immediately. It may infer that someone won't die happy unless they receive a bazillion business cards. Or it may state that a virus will destroy your hard drive and cause green fuzzy things to grow in your refrigerator.

History

Look for a lot of >>>> marks in the left margin. These marks indicate that people suckered by the hoax have forwarded the message countless times before it has reached you.

In her book, *Cyberliteracy*, Laura Gurak identified three things that are common to all hoax and urban legend e-mail chain letters. They are the **hook**, the **threat**, and the **request**. To hook you in, a hoax will play on your sympathy, your greed, or your fears. It will threaten you with bad luck, play on your guilt, or label you a fool for not participating. And, of course, it will request that you forward the e-mail to all of your friends and family.

The hook catches your interest to make you read the whole e-mail. The hook may be a sad story about a missing or sick child, or about the latest computer virus. Once you're hooked, the threat warns you about the terrible things that will happen if you don't keep the chain going. The threat may be that someone will die if you don't respond, or that your computer will suffer a melt-down from the latest virus. Last is the request. It will implore you to send the message to as many others as possible. It may even promise a small donation to a group with a legitimate-sounding name because they are able to track every forwarded e-mail (also a hoax).

Source: "Top Five Signs That an E-mail Is a Hoax" from www.hoaxbusters.org/hoax10.html. Reprinted by permission.

Thinking Activity 11.7

IDENTIFYING INTERNET HOAXES

Use the guidelines you have just read to identify the telltale signs of a hoax in these examples:

Read Immediately and Pass On!

Someone is sending out a very cute screensaver of the Budweiser Frogs. If you download it, you will lose everything! Your hard drive will crash and someone from the Internet will get your screen name and password! DO NOT DOWNLOAD IT UNDER ANY CIRCUMSTANCES! It just went into circulation yesterday. Please distribute this message. This is a new, very malicious virus and not many people know about it. This information was announced yesterday morning from Microsoft. Please share it with everyone that might access the Internet. Once again, pass this along to EVERYONE in your address book so that this may be stopped. AOL has said that this is a very dangerous virus and that there is NO remedy for it at this time.

Bonzai Kittens

To anyone with love and respect for life: In New York there is a Japanese who sells "bonsai-kittens." Sounds like fun huh? NOT! These animals are squeezed into a bottle. Their urine and feces are removed through probes.

(Continues)

THINKING CRITICALLY ABOUT NEW MEDIA (*CONTINUED*)

They feed them with a kind of tube. They feed them chemicals to keep their bones soft and flexible so the kittens grow into the shape of the bottle. The animals will stay there . . . as long as they live. They can't walk or move or wash themselves. Bonsai-kittens are becoming a fashion in New York and Asia. See this horror at: **http://www.bonsaikitten.com** Please sign this email in protest against these tortures. If you receive an email with over 500 names, please send a copy to: anacheca@hotmail.com. From there this protest will be sent to USA and Mexican animal protection organizations.

Missing Child Picture

I am asking you all, begging you to please forward this email onto anyone and everyone you know, PLEASE. My 9 year old girl, Penny Brown, is missing. She has been missing for now two weeks. It is still not too late. Please help us. If anyone anywhere knows anything, sees anything, please contact me at **zicozicozico@hotmail.com** I am including a picture of her. All prayers are appreciated!! In only takes 2 seconds to forward this on, if it was your child, you would want all the help you could get. Please. Thank you for your kindness, hopefully you can help us.

Virus Warning

Just to let you know a new virus was started in New York last night. This virus acts in the following manner: It sends itself automatically to all contacts on your list with the title "A Virtual Card for You." As soon as the supposed virtual card is opened, the computer freezes so that the user has to reboot. When the ctrl+alt+del keys or the reset button are pressed, the virus destroys Sector Zero, thus permanently destroying the hard disk. Yesterday in just a few hours this virus caused panic in New York, according to news broadcast by CNN **www.cnn.com**. This alert was received by an employee of Microsoft itself. So don't open any mails with subject "A Virtual Card for You." As soon as you get the mail, delete it. Please pass on this email to all your friends. Forward this to everyone in your address book. I would rather receive this 25 times than not at all.

Thinking Critically About Visuals

It's a Jungle Out There!

And there are many predators roaming around, eager to influence your thoughts and choices, often with the goal of separating you from your money. How does one combat these "hoax sites"? Hoax-busting websites like this one can help, but in the final analysis, it's your ability to think critically that will determine your success.

The Critical Thinker's Guide to Reasoning

This book has provided you with the opportunity to explore and develop many of your critical thinking and reasoning abilities. As you have seen, these abilities are complex and difficult to master. The process of becoming an accomplished critical thinker and effective reasoner is a challenging quest that requires ongoing practice and reflection. This section presents a critical thinking/reasoning model that will help you pull together the important themes of this book into an integrated perspective. This model is illustrated on page 511. To become familiar with the model, you will be thinking through an important issue that confronts every human being: Are people capable of choosing freely?

WHAT IS MY INITIAL POINT OF VIEW?

Reasoning always begins with a point of view. As a critical thinker, it is important for you to take thoughtful positions and express your views with confidence. Using this statement as a starting point, respond as specifically as you can:

I believe (or don't believe) that people can choose freely because . . .

Here is a sample response:

I believe that people are capable of choosing freely because when I am faced with choosing among a number of possibilities, I really have the feeling that it is up to me to make the choice that I want to.

HOW CAN I DEFINE MY POINT OF VIEW MORE CLEARLY?

After you state your initial point of view, the next step is to define the issues more clearly and specifically. As you have seen, the language that we use has multiple levels of meaning, and it is often not clear precisely what meaning(s) people are expressing. To avoid misunderstandings and sharpen your own thinking, it is essential that you clarify the key concepts as early as possible. In this case the central concept is "choosing freely." Respond by beginning with the following statement:

From my point of view, the concept of "choosing freely" means . . .

Here is a sample response:

From my point of view, the concept of "choosing freely" means that when you are faced with a number of alternatives, you are able to make your selection based solely on what you decide, not on force applied by other influences.

WHAT IS AN EXAMPLE OF MY POINT OF VIEW?

Once your point of view is clarified, it's useful to provide an example that illustrates your meaning. As you saw in Chapter 7, the process of forming and defining

The Critical Thinker's Guide to Reasoning

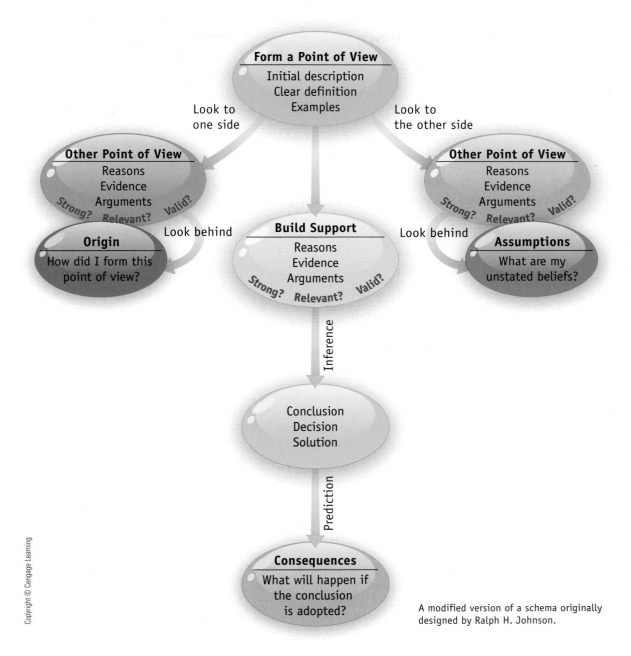

A modified version of a schema originally designed by Ralph H. Johnson.

concepts involves the process of generalizing (identifying general qualities) and the process of interpreting (locating specific examples). Respond to the issue we have been considering by beginning with the following statement:

An example of a free choice I made (or was unable to make) is . . .

Here is a sample response:

An example of a free choice I made was deciding what area to major in. There are a number of career directions I could have chosen to go out with, but I chose my major entirely on my own, without being forced by other influences.

WHAT IS THE ORIGIN OF MY POINT OF VIEW?

To fully understand and critically evaluate your point of view, it's important to review its history. How did this point of view develop? Have you always held this view, or did it develop over time? This sort of analysis will help you understand how your perceiving "lenses" regarding this issue were formed. Respond to the issue of free choice by beginning with the following statement:

I formed my belief regarding free choice . . .

Here is a sample response:

I formed my belief regarding free choice when I was in high school. I used to believe that everything happened because it had to, because it was determined. Then when I was in high school, I got involved with the "wrong crowd" and developed some bad habits. I stopped doing schoolwork and even stopped attending most classes. I was on the brink of failing when I suddenly came to my senses and said to myself, "This isn't what I want for my life." Through sheer willpower, I turned everything around. I changed my friends, improved my habits, and ultimately graduated with flying colors. From that time on, I knew that I had the power of free choice and that it was up to me to make the right choices.

WHAT ARE MY ASSUMPTIONS?

Assumptions are beliefs, often unstated, that underlie your point of view. Many disputes occur and remain unresolved because the people involved do not recognize or express their assumptions. For example, in the very emotional debate over abortion, when people who oppose abortion call their opponents "murderers," they are assuming the fetus, at *any* stage of development from fertilized egg onward, is a "human life," because murder refers to the taking of a human life. When people who support abortion rights call their opponents "moral fascists," they are assuming that antiabortionists are trying to impose their own narrow moral views on others.

Thus, it's important for all parties to identify clearly the assumptions that form the foundation of their points of view. They may still end up disagreeing, but at least they will know what they are arguing about. Thinking about the issue that we have been exploring, respond by beginning with the following statement:

> When I say that I believe (or don't believe) in free choice, I am assuming . . .

Here is a sample response:

> When I say that I believe in free choice, I am assuming that people are often presented with different alternatives to choose from, and I am also assuming that there is at least the possibility that they are able to select one or more of these alternatives independently of any influences.

WHAT ARE THE REASONS, EVIDENCE, AND ARGUMENTS THAT SUPPORT MY POINT OF VIEW?

Everybody has opinions. What distinguishes informed opinions from uninformed opinions is the quality of the reasons, evidence, and arguments that support the opinions. Respond to the issue of free choice by beginning with the following statement:

> There are several reasons, pieces of evidence, and arguments that support my belief (or disbelief) in free choice. First, . . . Second, . . . Third, . . .

Here is a sample response:

> There are several reasons, pieces of evidence, and arguments that support my belief in free choice. First, I have a very strong and convincing personal intuition when I am making choices that my choices are free. Second, freedom is tied to responsibility. If people make free choices, then they are responsible for the consequences of their choices. Since we often hold people responsible, that means we believe that their choices are free. Third, if people are not free, and all of their choices are determined by external forces, then life would have little purpose and there would be no point in trying to improve ourselves. But we do believe that life has purpose, and we do try to improve ourselves, suggesting that we also believe that our choices are free.

WHAT ARE OTHER POINTS OF VIEW ON THIS ISSUE?

One of the hallmarks of critical thinkers is that they strive to view situations from perspectives other than their own, to "think empathically" within other viewpoints, particularly those of people whose views disagree with their own. If we stay entrenched in our own narrow ways of viewing the world, the development of our minds will be severely limited. This is the only way to achieve a deep and full understanding of life's complexities. In working to understand other points of view, we need to identify the reasons, evidence, and arguments that have brought people to these conclusions. Respond to the issue we have been analyzing by beginning with the following statement:

> A second point of view on this issue might be . . . A third point of view on this issue might be . . .

Here is a sample response:

> A second point of view on this issue might be that many of our choices are conditioned by experiences that we have had in ways that we are not even aware of. For example, you might choose a career because of someone you admire or because of the expectations of others, although you may be unaware of these influences on your decision. Or you might choose to date someone because he or she reminds you of someone from your past, although you believe you are making a totally free decision. A third point of view on this issue might be that our choices are influenced by people around us, although we may not be fully aware of it. For example, we may go along with a group decision of our friends, mistakenly thinking that we are making an independent choice.

WHAT IS MY CONCLUSION, DECISION, SOLUTION, OR PREDICTION?

The ultimate purpose of reasoning is to reach an informed and successful conclusion, decision, solution, or prediction. Chapters 1 and 3 described reasoning approaches for making decisions and solving problems; Chapters 2 and 5 analyzed reaching conclusions; Chapter 4 explored the inferences we use to make predictions. With respect to the sample issue we have been considering—determining whether we can make free choices—the goal is to achieve a thoughtful conclusion. This is a complex process of analysis and synthesis in which we consider all points of view; evaluate the supporting reasons, evidence, and arguments; and then construct our most informed conclusion. Respond to our sample issue by using the following statement as a starting point:

> After examining different points of view and critically evaluating the reasons, evidence, and arguments that support the various perspectives, my conclusion about free choice is . . .

Here is a sample response:

> After examining different points of view and critically evaluating the reasons, evidence, and arguments that support the various perspectives, my conclusion about free choice is that we are capable of making free choices but that our freedom is sometimes limited. For example, many of our actions are conditioned by our past experience, and we are often influenced by other people without being aware of it. In order to make free choices, we need to become aware of these influences and then decide what course of action we want to choose. As long as we are unaware of these influences, they can limit our ability to make free, independent choices.

WHAT ARE THE CONSEQUENCES?

The final step in the reasoning process is to determine the *consequences* of our conclusion, decision, solution, or prediction. The consequences refer to what is likely to happen if our conclusion is adopted. Looking ahead in this fashion is helpful not simply for anticipating the future but also for evaluating the present. Identify the consequences of your conclusion regarding free choice by beginning with the following statement:

> The consequences of believing (or disbelieving) in free choice are . . .

Here is a sample response:

> The consequences of believing in free choice are taking increasing personal responsibility and showing people how to increase their freedom. The first consequence is that if people are able to make free choices, then they are responsible for the results of their choices. They can't blame other people, bad luck, or events "beyond their control." They have to accept responsibility. The second consequence is that, although our freedom can be limited by influences of which we are unaware, we can increase our freedom by becoming aware of these influences and then deciding what we want to do. If people are not able to make free choices, then they are not responsible for what they do, nor are they able to increase their freedom. This could lead people to adopt an attitude of resignation and apathy.

Thinking Activity 11.8

APPLYING THE "GUIDE TO REASONING"

Identify an important issue in which you are interested, and apply "The Critical Thinker's Guide to Reasoning" to analyze it.

- What is my initial point of view?
- How can I define my point of view more clearly?
- What is an example of my point of view?
- What is the origin of my point of view?
- What are my assumptions?
- What are the reasons, evidence, and arguments that support my point of view?
- What are other points of view on this issue?
- What is my conclusion, decision, solution, or prediction?
- What are the consequences?

Thinking Passages

THINKING CRITICALLY ABOUT AUTHORITY

The following reading selections demonstrate graphically the destructive effects of failing to think critically and suggest ways to avoid these failures.

Critical Thinking and Obedience to Authority

by John Sabini and Maury Silver

In his 1974 book, *Obedience to Authority*, Stanley Milgram reports experiments on destructive obedience. In these experiments the subjects are faced with a dramatic choice, one apparently involving extreme pain and perhaps injury to someone else. When the subject arrives at the laboratory, the experimenter tells him (or her) and another subject—a pleasant, avuncular, middle-aged gentleman (actually an actor)—that the study concerns the effects of punishment on learning. Through a rigged drawing, the lucky subject wins the role of teacher and the experimenter's confederate becomes the "learner."

In the next stage of the experiment, the teacher and learner are taken to an adjacent room; the learner is strapped into a chair and electrodes are attached to his arm. It appears impossible for the learner to escape. While strapped in the chair, the learner diffidently mentions that he has a heart condition. The experimenter replies that while the shocks may be painful, they cause no permanent tissue damage. The teacher is instructed to read to the learner a list of word pairs, to test him on the list, and to administer punishment—an electric shock—whenever the learner errs. The teacher is given a sample shock of 45 volts (the only real shock administered in the course of the experiment). The experimenter instructs the teacher to increase the level of shock one step on the shock generator for each mistake. The generator has thirty switches labeled from 15 to 450 volts. Beneath these voltage readings are labels ranging from "SLIGHT SHOCK" to "DANGER: SEVERE SHOCK," and finally "XX."

The experiment starts routinely. At the fifth shock level, however, the confederate grunts in annoyance, and by the time the eighth shock level is reached, he shouts that the shocks are becoming painful. Upon reaching the tenth level (150 volts), he cries out, "Experimenter, get me out of here! I won't be in the experiment any more! I refuse to go on!" This response makes plain the intensity of the pain and underscores the learner's right to be released. At the 270-volt level, the learner's response becomes an agonized scream, and at 300 volts the learner refuses to answer further. When the voltage is increased from 300 volts to 330 volts, the confederate shrieks in pain at each shock and gives no answer. From 330 volts on, the learner is heard from no more, and the teacher has no way of knowing whether the learner is still conscious or, for that matter, alive (the teacher also knows that the experimenter cannot tell the condition of the victim since the experimenter is in the same room as the teacher).

Typically the teacher attempts to break off the experiment many times during the session. When he tries to do so, the experimenter instructs him to continue. If he refuses, the experimenter insists, finally telling him, "You must continue. You have no other choice." If the subject still refuses, the experimenter ends the experiment.

We would expect that at most only a small minority of the subjects, a cross section of New Haven residents, would continue to shock beyond the point where the victim screams in pain and demands to be released. We certainly would expect that very, very few people would continue to the point of administering shocks of 450 volts. Indeed, Milgram asked

Source: From "Critical Thinking and Obedience to Authority" by John Sabini and Maury Silver, reprinted from *National Forum: The Phi Kappa Phi Journal, Winter 1985*, pp. 13–17, by permission.

Thinking Critically About Visuals

Milgram's Experiment

In this actual photo from Milgram's obedience study, the man being strapped into the chair for the experiment is one of Milgram's research assistants and will receive no shock, although the subjects in the experiment believe that they are administering painful shocks because they are instructed to by the "experimenter." Why do you think the majority of people went along with these instructions? What do you think the research assistant thought of the experiment? In his place, would you have been surprised by the findings?

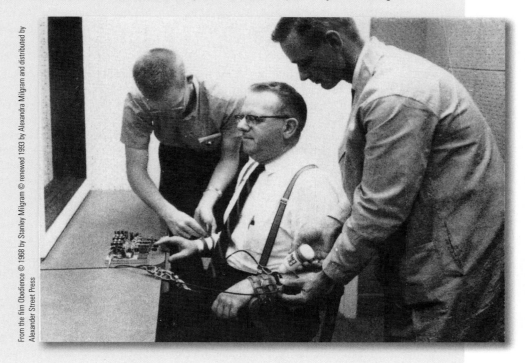

From the film Obedience © 1968 by Stanley Milgram © renewed 1993 by Alexandra Milgram and distributed by Alexander Street Press

a sample of psychiatrists and a sample of adults with various occupations to predict whether they would obey the orders of the experimenter. All of the people asked claimed that they would disobey at some point. Aware that people would be unwilling to admit that they themselves would obey such an unreasonable and unconscionable order, Milgram asked another sample of middle-class adults to predict how far other people would go in such a procedure. The average prediction was that perhaps one person in a thousand would continue to the end. The prediction was wrong. In fact, 65 percent (26/40) of the subjects obeyed to the end.

It is clear to people who are not in the experiment what they should do. The question is, *What features of the experimental situation make this clear issue opaque to subjects?*

Our aim is to suggest some reasons for such a failure of thinking and action and to suggest ways that people might be trained to avoid such failures—not only in the experiment, of course, but in our practical, moral lives as well. What are some of the sources of the failure?

The experimental conditions involve entrapment, and gradual entrapment affects critical thought. One important feature inducing obedience is the gradual escalation of the shock. Although subjects in the end administered 450-volt shocks, which is clearly beyond the limits of common morality and, indeed, common sense, they began by administering 15-volt shocks, which is neither. Not only did they begin with an innocuous shock, but it increased in innocuous steps of 15 volts. This gradualness clouds clear thinking: we are prepared by our moral training to expect moral problems to present themselves categorically, with good and evil clearly distinguished. But here they were not. By administering the first shock, subjects did two things at once—one salient, the other implicit. They administered a trivial shock, a morally untroublesome act, and they in that same act committed themselves to a policy and procedure which ended in clear evil.

Surely in everyday life, becoming entrapped by gradual increases in commitment is among the most common ways for us to find ourselves engaging in immoral acts, not to mention simple folly. The corrective cannot be, of course, refusing to begin on any path which *might* lead to immorality, but rather to foresee where paths are likely to lead, and to arrange for ourselves points beyond which we will not go. One suspects that had the subjects committed themselves—publicly—to some shock level they would not exceed, they would not have found themselves pushing the 450-volt lever. We cannot expect to lead, or expect our young to lead, lives without walking on slopes: our only hope is to reduce their slipperiness.

Distance makes obedience easier. Another force sustaining obedience was the *distance* between the victim and the subject. Indeed, in one condition of the experiment, subjects were moved physically closer to the victim; in one condition they had to hold his hand on the shock plate (through Mylar insulation to protect the teachers from shock). Here twelve out of forty subjects continued to the end, roughly half the number that did so when the subjects were farther from their victim.

Being closer to the victim did not have its effect by making subjects think more critically or by giving them more information. Rather it intensified their *discomfort* at the victim's pain. Still, being face to face with someone they were hurting probably caused them at least to focus on their victim, which might well be a first step in their taking seriously the pain they were causing him.

Both the experimenter's presence and the objective requirements of the situation influenced decisions to obey authority. The experimenter's *presence* is crucial to the subjects' obedience. In one version of the experiment he issued his commands at a distance, over the phone, and obedience was significantly reduced—to nine out of forty cases. The experimenter, then, exerts powerful *social influence* over the subjects.

One way to think about the experimenter's influence is to suppose that subjects uncritically cede control of their behavior to him. But this is too simple. We suggest that if the experimenter were to have told the subjects, for example, to shine his shoes, every subject would have refused. They would have refused because shining shoes is not a sensible command within the experimental context. Thus, the experimenter's ability to confuse and control subjects follows from his issuing commands which make sense given the ostensible purpose of the experiment; he was a guide, for them, to the experiment's objective requirements.

This interpretation of the experimenter's *role* is reinforced by details of his behavior. For example, his language and demeanor were cold—bureaucratic rather than emotional or personal. The subjects were led to see his commands to them as his dispassionate interpretations of something beyond them all: the requirements of the experiment.

Embarrassment plays a key role in decisions to obey authority. The experimenter entrapped subjects in another way. Subjects could not get out of the experiment without having to explain and justify their abandoning their duty to the experiment and to him. And how were they to do this?

Some subjects attempted to justify their leaving by claiming that they could not bear to go on, but such appeals to "personal reasons" were rebutted by the experimenter's reminding them of their duty to stay. If the subjects could not escape the experiment by such claims, then how could they escape? *They could fully escape his power only by confronting him on moral grounds*. It is worth noting that this is something that virtually none of the hundreds of subjects who took part in one condition or another fully did. Failing to address the experimenter in moral terms, even "disobedient" subjects just passively resisted; they stayed in their seats refusing to continue until the experimenter declared the experiment over. They did *not* do things we might expect them to: leave, tell the experimenter off, release the victim from his seat, and so on. Why did even the disobedient subjects not confront the experimenter?

One reason seems too trivial to mention: confronting the experimenter would be embarrassing. This trivial fact may have much to do with the subjects' obedience. To confront the experimenter directly, on moral grounds, would be to disrupt in a profound way implicit expectations that grounded this particular, and indeed most, social interaction: namely, that the subject and experimenter would behave as competent moral actors. Questioning these expectations is on some accounts, at least, the source of embarrassment.

Subjects in Milgram's experiment probably did not realize that it was in part embarrassment that [was] keeping them in line. Had they realized that—had they realized that they were torturing someone to spare themselves embarrassment—they might well have chosen to withstand the embarrassment to secure the victim's release. But rather we suspect that subjects experience their anticipation of embarrassment as a nameless force, a distressing emotion they were not able to articulate. Thus the subjects found themselves unable to confront the experimenter on moral grounds and unable to comprehend why they could not confront the experimenter.

Emotional states affect critical thought. Obviously the emotions the subjects experienced because of the embarrassment they were avoiding and the discomfort produced by hearing the cries of the victim affected their ability to reason critically. We do not know much about the effects of emotion on cognition, but it is plausible that it has at least one effect—a focusing of attention. Subjects seem to suffer from what Milgram has called "Tunnel Vision": they restricted their focus to the technical requirements of the experimental task, for these, at least, were clear. This restriction of attention is both a consequence of being in an emotional state more generally, and it is a strategy subjects used to avoid unwanted emotional intrusions. This response to emotion is, no doubt, a formidable obstacle to critical thought. To reject the experimenter's commands, subjects had to view their situation in a perspective different from the technical one the experimenter offered them. But their immediate emotional state made it particularly difficult for them to do just that: to look at their own situation from a broader, moral perspective.

How can we train individuals to avoid destructive obedience? Our analysis leads to the view that obedience in the Milgram experiment is not primarily a result of a failure of knowledge, or at least knowledge of the crucial issue of what is right or wrong to do in this circumstance. People do not need to be told that torturing an innocent person is something they should not do—even in the context of the experiment. Indeed, when the experimenter turns his back, most subjects are able to apply their moral principles and disobey. The subjects' problem instead is not knowing how to break off, how to make the moral response without social stickiness. If the subjects' defect is not primarily one of thinking correctly, then how is education, even education in critical thinking, to repair the defect? We have three suggestions.

First, we must teach people how to confront authority. We should note as a corollary to this effort that teaching has a wide compass: we teach people how to ride bikes, how to play the piano, how to make a sauce. Some teaching of how to do things we call education: we teach students how to do long division, how to parse sentences, how to solve physics problems. We inculcate these skills in students not by, or not only by, giving them facts or even strategies to remember, but also by giving them certain sorts of experiences, by correcting them when they err, and so on. An analogy would be useful here. Subjects in the Milgram experiment suffered not so much from a failure to remember that as center fielders they should catch fly balls as they did from an inability to do so playing under lights at night, with a great deal of wind, and when there is ambiguity about whether time-out has been called. To improve the players' ability to shag fly balls, in game conditions, we recommend practice rather than lectures, and the closer the circumstances of practice to the conditions of the actual game, the more effective the practice is likely to be.

Good teachers from Socrates on have known that the intellect must be trained; one kind of training is in criticizing authority. We teachers are authorities and hence can provide practice. Of course, we can only do that if we *remain* authorities. Practice at criticizing us if we do not respect our own authority is of little use. We do not have a recipe for being an authority who at the same time encourages criticism, but we do know that is what is important. And sometimes we can tell when we are either not encouraging criticism or when we have ceased being an authority. Both are equally damaging.

Practice with the Milgram situation might help too; it might help for students to "role play" the subjects' plight. If nothing else, doing this might bring home in a forcible way the embarrassment that subjects faced in confronting authority. It might help them develop ways of dealing with this embarrassment. Certainly, it would at least teach them that doing the morally right thing does not always "feel" right, comfortable, natural. There is no evidence about whether such experiences generalize, but perhaps they do.

If they are to confront authority assertively, individuals must also be taught to use social pressure in the service of personal values. Much of current psychology and education sees thought, even critical thought, as something that goes on within individuals. But we know better than this. Whether it be in science, law, or the humanities, scholarship is and must be a public, social process. To train subjects to think critically is to train them to expose their thinking to others, to open *themselves* to criticism, from their peers as well as from authority. We insist on this in scholarship because we know that individual thinking, even the best of it, is prey to distortions of all kinds, from mere ignorance to "bad faith."

Further, the support of others is important in another way. We know that subjects who saw what they took to be two other naive subjects disobey, and thus implicitly criticize the action of continuing, were very likely to do so themselves. A subject's sense that the experimenter had the correct reading was undermined by the counter reading offered by the "other subjects." Public reinforcement of our beliefs can liberate us from illegitimate pressure. The reason for this is twofold.

Agreement with others clarifies the cognitive issue and helps us see the morally or empirically right answer to questions. But it also can have another effect—a nonrational one.

We have claimed that part of the pressure subjects faced in disobeying was produced by having to deal with the embarrassment that might emerge from confrontation. Social support provides a counter-pressure. Had the subjects committed themselves publicly to disobedience before entering the experiment then they could have countered pressures produced by disobedience (during the experiment) by considering the embarrassment of admitting to others (after the experiment) that they had obeyed. Various self-help groups like Alcoholics Anonymous and Weight Watchers teach individuals to manage social pressures to serve good ends.

Social pressures are forces in our lives whether we concede them or not. The rational person, the person who would keep his action in accord with his values, must learn to face or avoid those pressures when they act to degrade his action, but equally important he ought to learn to *employ* the pressure of public commitment, the pressure implicit in making clear to others what he values, in the service of his values.

Students should know about the social pressures that operate on them. They should also learn how to use those pressures to support their own values. One reason we teach people to think critically is so that they may take charge of their own creations. We do not withhold from engineers who would create buildings knowledge about gravity or vectors or stresses. Rather we teach them to enlist this knowledge in their support.

A second area requires our attention. We need to eliminate intellectual illusions fostering nonintellectual obedience. These are illusions about human nature which the Milgram experiment renders transparent. None of these illusions is newly discovered; others have noticed them before. But the Milgram experiment casts them in sharp relief.

The most pernicious of these illusions is the belief, perhaps implicit, that only evil people do evil things and that evil announces itself. This belief, in different guises, bewildered the subjects in several ways.

First, the experimenter looks and acts like the most reasonable and rational of people: a person of authority in an important institution. All of this is, of course, irrelevant to the question of whether his commands are evil, but it does not seem so to subjects. The experimenter had no personally corrupt motive in ordering subjects to continue, for he wanted nothing more of them than to fulfill the requirements of the experiment. So the experimenter was not seen as an evil man, as a man with corrupt desires. He was a man, like Karl Adolf Eichmann, who ordered them to do evil because he saw that evil as something required of him (and of them) by the requirements of the situation they faced together. Because we expect our morality plays to have temptation and illicit desire arrayed against conscience, our ability to criticize morally is subverted when we find evil instructions issued by someone moved by, of all things, duty. [For a fuller discussion of this point, see Hannah Arendt's *Eichmann in Jerusalem* (1965), where the issue is placed in the context of the Holocaust.]

And just as the experimenter escaped the subjects' moral criticism because he was innocent of evil desire, the subjects escaped their own moral criticism because *they too* were free of evil intent: they did not *want* to hurt the victim; they really did not. Further, some subjects, at least, took action to relieve the victim's plight—many protested the experimenter's commands, many tried to give the victim hints about the right answers—thus further dramatizing their purity of heart. And because they acted out of duty rather than desire, the force of their conscience against their own actions was reduced. But, of course, none of this matters in the face of the evil done.

The "good-heartedness" of people, their general moral quality, is something very important to us, something to which we, perhaps rightly, typically pay attention. But if we are to think critically about the morality of our own and others' acts, we must see through this general fact about people to assess the real moral quality of the acts they do or are considering doing.

A second illusion from which the subjects suffered was a confusion about the notion of responsibility. Some subjects asked the experimenter who was responsible for the victim's plight. And the experimenter replied that he was. We, and people asked to predict what they would do in the experiment, see that this is nonsense. We see that the experimenter cannot discharge the subjects' responsibility—no more than the leader of a bank-robbing gang can tell his cohorts, "Don't worry. If we're caught, I'll take full responsibility." We are all conspirators when we participate in planning and executing crimes.

Those in charge have the right to assign *technical* responsibility to others, responsibility for executing parts of a plan, but moral responsibility cannot be given, taken away, or transferred. Still, these words—mere words—on the part of the experimenter eased subjects' "sense of responsibility." So long as the institutions of which we are a part are moral, the need to distinguish technical from moral responsibility need not arise. When those institutions involve wanton torture, we are obliged to think critically about this distinction.

There is a third illusion illustrated in the Milgram experiment. When subjects threatened to disobey, the experimenter kept them in line with prods, the last of which was, "You have no choice; you must go on." Some subjects fell for this, believed that they had no choice. But this is also nonsense. There may be cases in life when we *feel* that we have no choice, but we know we always do. Often feeling we have no choice is really a matter of believing that the cost of moral action is greater than we are willing to bear—in the extreme we may not be willing to offer our lives, and sometimes properly so. Sometimes we use what others have done to support the claim that we have no choice; indeed, some students interpret the levels of obedience in the Milgram experiment as proof that the subjects had no choice. But we all know they did. Even in extreme situations, we have a choice, whether we choose to exercise it or not. The belief that our role, our desires, our past, or the actions of others preclude our acting morally is a convenient but illusory way of distancing ourselves from the evil that surrounds us. It is an illusion from which we should choose to disabuse our students.

Thinking Critically About Visuals

Resisting the Pressure to Go Along with Authority

The discovery in 2004 of the events at the Abu Ghraib prison in Iraq focused on the shameful abuse of prisoners that took place. Yet there were other examples of soldiers who resisted the pressure to "go along." Why do you think that some individuals went along with the abuse and others refused to? How does this relate to the findings in Milgram's experiment?

AP Photo

Pressure to Go Along with Abuse Is Strong, but Some Soldiers Find Strength to Refuse

by Anahad O'Connor

The images of prisoner abuse still trickling out of Iraq show a side of human behavior that psychologists have sought to understand for decades. But the murky reports of a handful of soldiers who refused to take part bring to light a behavior psychologists find even more puzzling: disobedience.

Buried in his report earlier this year on Abu Ghraib prison in Iraq, Maj. Gen. Antonio M. Taguba praised the actions of three men who tried to stop the mistreatment of Iraqi detainees. They are nowhere to be seen in the portraits of brutality that have touched off outrage around the world.

Although details of their actions are sketchy, it is known that one soldier, Lt. David O. Sutton, put an end to one incident and alerted his commanders. William J. Kimbro, a Navy dog handler, "refused to participate in improper interrogations despite significant pressure" from military intelligence, according to the report. And Specialist Joseph M. Darby gave military police the evidence that sounded the alarm.

In numerous studies over the past few decades, psychologists have found that a certain percentage of people simply refuse to give in to pressure—by authorities or by peers—if they feel certain actions are wrong.

The soldiers have been reluctant to elaborate on what they saw and why they came forward. In an interview with *The Virginian-Pilot* in Norfolk, [VA], Lieutenant Sutton, a Newport News police sergeant, said, "I don't want to judge, but yes, I witnessed something inappropriate and I reported it."

The public will assume that there was widespread corruption, he told another local paper, "when in reality, it's just one bad apple."

In the noted experiment 40 years ago when Dr. Stanley Milgram showed that most people will deliver a lethal dose of electricity to another subject if instructed to do so by a scientist in a white lab coat, a minority still said no.

"These people are rare," said Dr. Elliot Aronson, a professor of psychology at the University of California, Santa Cruz, who studies social influence. "It's really hard for us to predict in advance who is going to resist by looking at things like demographic data or religious background."

The men singled out by General Taguba dissented despite the threat of being ridiculed or even court-martialed for not following orders. Psychologists believe they may have been guided by a strong moral compass and past experiences with conformity.

"It is sometimes the case that they themselves have been scapegoated or turned on by the crowd," said Dr. John Darley, a professor of psychology and public affairs at Princeton. "If you go back into the lives of these people you can often find some incident that has made very vivid to them the pressures of conformity working on the others in the group."

People who break from the crowd to blow the whistle, history shows, are often the most psychologically distanced from the situation. In 1968, Hugh Thompson, a helicopter pilot, was flying over Vietnam as G.I.'s were killing civilians. The soldiers on the ground had been told that the village, My Lai, was a Vietcong stronghold. But from above Mr. Thompson could see there was no enemy fire. He landed his helicopter, rescued some villagers, and told his commanders about the massacre.

What happened there, and what occurred at Abu Ghraib, Dr. Darley said, was a slow escalation.

Referring to reports that the guards were told to "soften up" the prisoners for interrogation, he said that it apparently "drifted more and more toward humiliation."

"Perhaps they thought they were doing the right thing," he said. "But someone who didn't get caught up at the start, someone who walks in and hasn't been involved in the escalation, like the pilot Thompson, can see the process for what it really is."

Mr. Thompson was supported by his gunner, Larry Colburn, who helped him round up civilians and radioed for help.

It is not clear when the three men cited in General Taguba's report tried to interfere with the interrogations or whether they had contact with one another. But a transcript of a court-martial hearing on May 1 suggests that additional officers who knew one another also tried to pass reports of the scandal up the chain of command.

Dr. Solomon E. Asch showed in experiments on compliance half a century ago that people are more likely to break from a group if they have an ally. Subjects in his experiment were asked to look at different lines on a card and judge their lengths. Each subject was unknowingly placed in a group of "confederates" who deliberately chose a line that was obviously wrong. About a third of the time, the subjects would give in and go along with the majority.

But if one confederate broke from the group and gave another answer, even a wrong answer, the subjects were more likely to give the response they knew was correct.

"The more you feel support for your dissent, the more likely you are to do it," said Dr. Danny Axsom, an associate professor of psychology at Virginia Tech.

A lack of supervision, which General Taguba pointed out in his report, and confusion over the chain of command, Dr. Axsom said, may have also emboldened the three soldiers.

"There was less perceived legitimacy," he said. "If it's clear who the authority is, then you're more likely to obey. If it's not, then the legitimacy of the whole undertaking is undermined."

The power to resist coercion reflects what psychologists call internal locus of control, or the ability to determine one's own destiny. People at the other end of the scale, with external locus of control, are more heavily influenced by authority figures. They prefer to put their fate in the hands of others.

"If they fail a test, it's the teacher's fault; if they do poorly at a job, it's the boss's fault," said Dr. Thomas Ollendick, a professor of psychology at Virginia Tech. "They put the blame for everything outside of themselves. They are high in conformity because they believe someone else [is] in charge."

The average person, research shows, falls somewhere in the middle of the scale. People who voluntarily enlist in the military, knowing they will take orders, Dr. Ollendick suggested, may be more likely to conform. "These are people who are being told what to do," he said. "The ones who are conforming from the outset feel they can't change the system they're in. Those who blow the whistle can go above the situation and survive. They can basically endure whatever negative consequences might come from their actions."

QUESTIONS FOR ANALYSIS

1. Sabini and Silver describe the reasons they believe that the majority of subjects in the Stanley Milgram experiment were willing to inflict apparent pain and injury on an innocent person. Explain what you believe were the most significant reasons for the absence of critical thinking and moral responsibility by many individuals.

2. O'Connor's article focuses on three individuals who were able to resist the pressures to inflict pain on Iraqi prisoners at Abu Ghraib prison. Why were these individuals able to retain their critical-thinking abilities and sense of moral responsibility in the face of powerful pressures to do otherwise, including the obedience to authority?

3. Sabini and Silver argue that the ability to think critically must be developed within a social context, that we must expose our thinking to the criticism of others because "individual thinking, even the best of it, is prey to distortions of all kinds, from mere ignorance to 'bad faith.'" Explain how "allies" were helpful in enabling those at Abu Ghraib prison to resist the pressure to conform to the prevailing norm of prisoner abuse.

4. Sabini and Silver contend that in order to act with critical thinking and moral courage, people must be taught to confront authority, and the individuals highlighted in O'Connor's article demonstrated precisely this ability. Explain how you think people can be taught and encouraged to confront authority in a constructive way.

5. "Even in extreme situations, we have a choice, whether we choose to exercise it or not. The belief that our role, our desires, our past, or the actions of others preclude our acting morally is a convenient but illusory way of distancing ourselves from the evil that surrounds us." Evaluate this claim in light of the behavior of the military and intelligence personnel at Abu Ghraib prison, both those who participated in prisoner abuse and those who resisted such participation.

CHAPTER 11 | Reviewing and Viewing

Summary

- *Inductive argument* is an argument form in which one reasons from premises assumed to be true to a conclusion supported (but not logically) by the premises.

- *Fallacies* are unsound arguments that appear to be logical are often persuasive because they usually appeal to our emotions and prejudices.

- *Empirical generalization* is a form of inductive reasoning in which a general statement is made about an entire group (the target population) based on observing some members of the group (the sample population).

- *Causal reasoning* is a form of inductive reasoning in which an event (or events) is claimed to be the result of another event (or events).

- The *scientific method* works on the assumption that the world is constructed in a complex web of causal relationships that can be discovered through systematic investigation.

- A *hypothesis* is a possible explanation that is introduced to account for a set of facts and that can be used as a basis for further investigation.

- "The Critical Thinker's Guide to Reasoning" is an organized approach for exploring complex issues.

Assessing Your Strategies and Creating New Goals

How Well Do I Reason Critically?

Expert critical thinkers are able to use all of the forms of reasoning effectively, including *deductive reasoning*, which we explored in the last chapter, and *inductive reasoning*, which we examined in this chapter. Inductive arguments involve reasoning from premises assumed to be true to a conclusion supported (but not logically) by the premises. Many of the arguments to which we are exposed in our daily lives are of this order, including scientific studies, polls on various topics, and generalizations about large populations of people. Evaluate your ability on the following dimensions of inductive reasoning.

Think Critically About Opinion Surveys and Polls

I have a sophisticated understanding of surveys and opinion polls.	I rarely think critically about surveys and opinion polls.
5 4 3 2 1	

People in our society are besieged with surveys and polls on every imaginable topic. Yet the overwhelming majority of these polls and surveys are unscientific and unreliable: the questions are phrased *ambiguously*, the sample is usually *biased*, and the results are consistently *misinterpreted*. To be an informed citizen in today's world, it is essential to be able to evaluate critically the design and validity of these new cultural icons.

Strategy: Make a point of applying the knowledge and skills from this chapter to the surveys and opinion polls that you encounter. Determine whether the sample is known, sufficient, and representative. Also evaluate whether the questions are constructed in a way that is likely to lead to intelligent results, or whether the findings are destined to be oversimplified and misleading.

Think Critically About Scientific Studies

I have a sophisticated understanding of scientific studies.	I rarely think critically about the scientific studies I read and hear about.
5 4 3 2 1	

Another influential form of cultural thinking are the "scientific studies" that are reported to us regularly, offering both disturbing and promising information. Many of the conclusions, if true, have direct implications for our lives.

Strategy: Seek out the details of scientific studies that are reported in newspapers and magazines, and critically evaluate them using the skills and knowledge you have developed in this chapter. The results reported on television and some newspapers are virtually useless because they are so brief; find more detailed descriptions in other publications including, if you have a special interest in the topic, the original scientific journal in which the study was published.

Thinking Critically About Fallacies

I have an incisive understanding of arguments that are fallacies and can respond to them effectively.	I am not very adept at identifying and responding to arguments that are fallacies.
5 4 3 2 1	

Fallacies are arguments that can appear to be logical and persuasive but are actually illogical and unsound. There are many different kinds of fallacious arguments, and we encounter them every day.

Strategy: *Using your* **Thinking Notebook**, *spend several days recording all of the fallacies you encounter: in your classes, with your friends, on television, and on the Internet. Then explain why the arguments are unsound fallacies.*

Use The Thinker's Way to Analyze Complex Issues

I use a systematic approach to analyze complex issues.	My approach to analyzing complex issues is more disorganized than I'd like.
5 4 3 2 1	

"The Critical Thinker's Guide to Reasoning" (page 511) provides you with a versatile and flexible approach for analyzing any complex issue, a skill that most people sorely need. By *defining the issue* clearly, examining *different points of view*, evaluating the *arguments*, assessing the *consequences*, and reaching an informed *conclusion*, you will impress both yourself and others with your insightful understanding.

Strategy: *Select an article from a newspaper or magazine each day and use "The Critical Thinker's Guide to Reasoning" to explore it, recording your results in your* **Thinking Notebook**. *Then bring the issue up in a conversation with someone else, using your written analysis to guide your discussion. You will immediately begin to notice a significant improvement in your ability to discuss these issues with insight and understanding.*

Suggested Films

Agnes of God (1985)

What is the relation of religious faith to moral truth? An infant is found dead in a convent. The mother, a young nun, claims to have had a virgin birth. When a psychiatrist is brought in to determine whether the nun is capable of standing trial for the child's murder, she also attempts to uncover the truth of the infant's conception and death.

Dead Man Walking (1995)

What are the ethical arguments for and against the death penalty? After receiving a letter from a convicted murderer on death row, a nun agrees to be his spiritual adviser. Her experience prompts her both to protest capital punishment and to start an organization to give support to victims' families.

Gattaca (1997)

Are we defined by our DNA? In the future envisioned by this science fiction film, generic engineering and DNA determine people's social classes and life possibilities. One of the few naturally-born humans, Vincent faces prejudice and genetic discrimination due to his congenital heart disease. Vincent refuses to accept the lot he is dealt with and attempts to defy society's laws in order to achieve the life he wants.

Thank You for Smoking (2005)

A Big Tobacco spokesman defends the cigarette industry through spin tactics such as media promotion and censorship of information about the dangers of smoking. He simultaneously attempts to act as role model for his adolescent son. This satire provides insight into the forces shaping our perceptions and the importance of critical reasoning in making sound choices.

The Fog of War (2004)

This Errol Morris documentary, which focuses on former secretary of defense Robert McNamara, brings critical reasoning to the events of American history and raises questions about the ethical implications of obeying authority as well as the responsibility of holding that position of power. Throughout, Morris attempts to reveal the perspectives behind controversial moments in history, including the U.S. commitment to the Vietnam War.

Are You the Master of Your Fate?

Life does not come with a set of instructions. It's up to each one of us to deal as best we can with the challenges and opportunities with which we are presented. As critical thinkers we need to develop our understanding of the world and ourselves so that we can make the most enlightened choices possible.

Thinking Critically, Living Creatively

Living Creatively
Developing ideas that are unique, useful, and worthy of further elaboration

Thinking Critically
Carefully examining our thinking in order to clarify and improve understanding

Creating a Life Philosophy
- Establishing harmonious relationships
- Choosing freely
- Choosing a meaningful life
- Choosing a satisfying career

Living a Life Philosophy

As the artist of your own life, your brush strokes express your philosophy of life, a vision that incorporates your most deeply held values, aspirations, and convictions. The challenge you face is to create a coherent view of the world that expresses who you are as well as the person you want to become. It should be a vision that not only guides your actions but also enables you to understand the value of your experiences, the significance of your relationships, and the meaning of your life.

The quality of your life philosophy is a direct result of your abilities to think critically and think creatively, abilities that you have been developing while working on activities presented throughout this book. But a life philosophy is incomplete until it is acted upon through the decisions you make, decisions made possible by your ability to choose freely. These are the three life principles of human transformation upon which this book is based: *thinking critically, living creatively, choosing freely.* These three principles are interlocking pieces of the puzzle of your life. Working together as a unified force, these principles can illuminate your existence: answering questions, clarifying confusion, creating meaning, and providing fulfillment.

- *Think critically:* When used properly, your thinking process acts like a powerful beacon of light, illuminating the depths of your personality and the breadth of your experience. Clear thinking is a tool that helps you disentangle the often confused jumble of thoughts and feelings that compose much of your waking consciousness. By becoming a more powerful critical thinker, you are acquiring the abilities you need to achieve your goals, solve problems, and make intelligent decisions. Critical thinkers are people who have developed thoughtful and well-founded beliefs to guide their choices in every area of their lives. In order to develop the strongest and most accurate beliefs possible, you need to become aware of your own biases, explore situations from many different perspectives, and develop sound reasons to support your points of view.

- *Live creatively:* Creativity is a powerful life force that can infuse your existence with meaning. Working in partnership with critical thinking, creative thinking helps you transform your life into a rich tapestry of productivity and success. When you approach your life with a mindful sense of discovery and invention, you can continually create yourself in ways limited only by your imagination. A creative lens changes everything for the better: Problems become opportunities for growth, mundane routines become challenges for inventive approaches, relationships become intriguing adventures. When you give free rein to your creative impulses, every aspect of your life takes on a special glow. You are able to break out of unthinking habitual responses and live fully in every minute, responding naturally and spontaneously. It sounds magical, and it is.

- **Choose freely:** People can transform themselves only if they choose to take different paths in their lives—and only if their choices are truly free. To exercise genuine freedom, you must have the insight to understand all of your options and the wisdom to make informed choices. When you fully accept your freedom, you redefine your daily life and view your future in a new light. By working to neutralize the constraints on your autonomy and guide your life in positive directions, you see alternatives that were not previously visible, having been concealed by the limitations of your previous vision. Your future becomes open, a field of rich possibilities that you can explore and choose among. A life that is free is one that is vital and exciting, suffused with unexpected opportunities and the personal fulfillment that comes from a life well lived.

Your "self" is, in its essence, a dynamic life force that is capable of thinking critically, creating, and choosing freely. These three essential dimensions of your self exist optimally when they work together in harmonious unity. When working together, these three basic elements create a person who is intelligent, creative, and determined—the ingredients for success in any endeavor.

Consider the unfortunate consequences of subtracting any of these elements from the dynamic equation. If you lack the ability to think critically, you won't be able to function very well in most challenging careers because you will have difficulty thinking clearly, solving complex problems, and making intelligent decisions. What's more, whatever creative ideas you come up with will be rootless, lacking an intelligible framework or practical strategies for implementing them. You will be an impractical dreamer, condemned to a life of frustrated underachieving. Without insight into yourself, your freedom will be imprisoned because you won't be able to see your choices clearly or to liberate yourself from the influences that are constraining you.

If you lack the ability to think creatively, then your thinking abilities may enable you to perform in a solid, workmanlike fashion, but your work will lack imagination, you will be afraid to try original approaches because of the risk of failure, and your personality will be lacking the spontaneous sparkle that people admire and are drawn to. You will in time become a competent but unimaginative "worker bee," performing your duties with predictable adequacy but never rising to the lofty heights that you are capable of attaining. Your choices will be as limited as your imagination, and your habitual choices of safe and secure paths will eventually create a very small canvas for your personal portrait.

If you lack the ability to choose freely, then your abilities to think critically or creatively cannot save you from a life of disappointment. Though you may be able to clearly analyze and understand, you will lack the will to make the difficult choices and stay the course when you encounter obstacles and adversities. And though you may develop unique and valuable ideas, your inability to focus your energies and make things happen will doom these ideas to anonymity. Because you lack the will to create yourself as a strong individual of character and integrity, the people you encounter will come to view you as a shallow-rooted reed that bends with the wind of superficial trends, not as someone deserving of authority and responsibility.

Think of what you aspire to have: a life of purpose and meaning, the respect and devotion of those around you, success and fulfillment in your chosen endeavors, and a secure sense of who you are, a person with the courage and vision to accomplish great things. These aspirations are within your grasp, but only if you develop all of these fundamental dimensions of your self to their fullest potential: the abilities to think critically, think creatively, and choose freely.

Choose Freely

You have the power to create yourself through the choices that you make, but only if your choices are truly free. To exercise genuine freedom you must possess the insight to understand all of your options and the wisdom to make informed choices. In many instances passive, illogical, and superficial thinking inhibits people's abilities to make intelligent choices and erodes their motivation to persevere when obstacles are encountered. This section is designed to provide you with a general framework for understanding the nature of free choice and the practical thinking strategies needed to translate this understanding into transformed behaviors and attitudes. You can redefine your daily life in a new light and enhance its value through free choices derived from thinking critically and creatively.

CONDEMNED TO BE FREE

> Man is condemned to be *free*. Condemned, because he did not create himself, yet is nevertheless at liberty, and from the moment that he is thrown into this world, he is responsible for everything he does.
>
> —Jean-Paul Sartre

This book is based on the conviction, articulated here by the philosopher Jean-Paul Sartre, that we create ourselves through the choices that we make, and that we are capable of choosing different courses of action. But often we get so caught up in routine, so mired in the day-to-day demands of reality and the pressures of conformity that we don't even *see* alternatives to our condition, much less act on them. Our complaints often far outnumber our shining moments, as we tend to focus on the forces and people that have thwarted our intentions.

> "If only I got the breaks now and then . . ."
> "If only I could get rid of my habitual tendency to _____, I would . . ."

These complaints, and millions of others like them, bitterly betray W. E. Hanley's notion that "I am the master of my fate, I am the captain of my soul." It is much more common for people to believe that fate mastered them and that they never had sufficient opportunity to live life "their way." Instead of feeling free, we often feel beleaguered, trying desperately to prevent our small dinghy from getting swamped in life's giant swells, rather than serenely charting a straight course in our sleek sailboat.

The end result is that when people think of "being free," they often conjure up a romantic notion of "getting away" from their concerns and responsibilities, imagining a world where anything is possible and there is plenty of money to pay for it. However appealing this fantasy may be, it is a misconceived and unrealistic notion of freedom. Genuine freedom consists of making thoughtful choices from among the available options, choices that reflect your genuine desires and deepest values, resisting the pressures to surrender your autonomy to external pressures *or* internal forces.

The most important and disturbing element of personal freedom is that it necessarily involves *personal responsibility*. And personal responsibility is the main reason why people are reluctant to embrace their freedom and in fact actively seek to "escape" from it. If you acknowledge that your choices are *free*, then you must accept that you are *responsible* for the outcome of your choices. When you are successful, it is easy to take full responsibility for your success. But when failure occurs, people tend to dive for cover, blaming others or forces outside of their control. This is exactly what's going on in all the preceding "If only" statements and many others like them: they each express the belief that if only some *outside force* had not intervened, people would have achieved the goals they set for themselves. However, in many instances, these explanations are bogus, and these efforts to escape from freedom are illegitimate. They represent weak and inauthentic attempts to deny freedom *and* responsibility.

FREE CHOICE: THE MAINSPRING OF HUMAN ACTION

Every day we are confronted with the mystery of human action. One person commits an armed robbery, killing a guard in the process. Another person is found to have embezzled large sums of money from the charitable organization he directed. A firefighter risks his life to save the life of an infant trapped in a burning building. A peaceful protest gets out of control and turns into a violent and destructive altercation. A respected member of the community is accused of abusing the children on the teams that he coached. Two teenagers are accused of murdering their newborn infant and dumping the body in a garbage container. An 84-year-old woman who spent her life cleaning the homes of others donates her life savings—$186,000—to a local college with which she had no previous relationship. In each of these instances, and countless others, we struggle to understand "why" people acted the way they did. Our answers typically depend on our deepest beliefs about the nature of the human self. For example:

Human nature: "I believe in human nature; people are born with certain basic instincts that influence and determine how they behave." Based on this view, the actions described previously, whether "good" or "evil," are no more than the natural expression of a *universal nature* that is genetically hardwired into every person.

From this perspective, we should no more hold people responsible for their destructive actions than we would an animal in the wild that kills in order to survive. There is no possibility of free choice because our actions necessarily follow from our inborn nature, and we cannot be other than who we are. Whether you act virtuously or destructively in your life is really beyond your control, and you cannot alter your fundamental character.

The environment: "I believe that people are shaped by their environment, conditioned by their experiences to be the kind of people they are." From this vantage point, the actions described previously are the direct products of the *life experiences* that the individuals had. If the environment in which a person developed was deprived or abusive, then these forces shaped a violent individual with little regard for the rights or lives of others. On the other hand, if you were fortunate enough to grow up in a loving and nurturing environment in which kindness and empathy were considered paramount values, then this upbringing shaped who you are. But once again, you cannot be held responsible for how you turned out because you didn't choose your environment; you were a *passive agent* molded by forces beyond your control. And, of course, you are incapable of making free choices. We should no more condemn the embezzler than we should reward the firefighter who risks his life, since they are each merely products of environments that are ultimately responsible for their behavior.

Psychological forces: "I believe that people are governed by psychological forces, many of them unconscious, that cause them to think, feel, and act in certain ways." Based on this point of view, the actions described previously are the direct result of deep psychological impulses that have been formed by people's earliest relationships and experiences. Although these people may *think* they are choosing to do the things, in reality, they are puppets manipulated by unseen psychological strings. The same is true for you. So when the coach sexually abused the children on his teams, he was not actually *choosing* this reprehensible course of action, he was impelled by *psychological forces* over which he had no control. Similarly, your behavior results from psychological motivations, often repressed, that form the basic structure of your personality. Your feelings of freedom are illusory.

Social dynamics: "I believe that we are social creatures that are greatly influenced by the people around us." From this perspective, people's behavior results in large measure from the forces exerted by those around them. The need to conform to the prevailing norms, to be accepted by the groups to which you belong, to please those who are close to you, to obey those in positions of authority—these and other social needs determine your behavior and define who you are as an individual. For example, the violent actions of the initially peaceful demonstrators can be understood only by examining the dynamics of *social interaction.* Since the group as a whole is to blame, responsibility is removed from the individuals. In the same way, individuals who act illegally (or immorally) within an organization often seek to be exonerated on the grounds that they were merely acting as cogs in the machine, not independent agents. An extreme version of this occurred after World

War II at the Nuremberg trials when many people accused of wartime atrocities explained that they were "only following orders."

Thinking Activity 12.1

YOUR THEORY OF HUMAN BEHAVIOR

Think about some of the actions described at the beginning of this section. How would *you* explain why those people acted in the ways that they did? Which of the above theories make the most sense to you? Do you have your own theory to explain why people behave the way they do?

CREATING YOURSELF THROUGH FREE CHOICES

If we examine all of these beliefs regarding the nature of human beings, we can see that they have several significant things in common:

- These beliefs represent attempts to explain human behavior in terms of factors that *precede* the action: a universal human nature, past experiences, psychological forces, and social dynamics. In other words, all of these beliefs assume that the "essence" of a person, as defined by the factors identified previously, comes *before* the human actions and in fact *causes* these actions to take place. As a result, all of these beliefs about the human self have the effect of *removing responsibility* from the individual for his actions. If what you did was the direct result of human nature, past experiences, psychological forces, or social dynamics, then *you cannot be held accountable.* You didn't have a choice, your behavior was outside of your control. As a final consequence, these beliefs about the self *limit future possibilities.* If your thoughts, feelings, and actions are caused by forces beyond your control, then you do not have it in your power to change, to alter direction, to improve—any more than a puppet can decide to act independently and contrary to the wishes of the puppeteer.

From a framework rooted in human freedom, these traditional perspectives regarding the nature of people can be dangerous and destructive. One of the most passionate and articulate modern exponents of individual freedom was Jean-Paul Sartre. His position is extreme—you are *completely* free. *You create yourself* entirely through the free choices that you make every day of your life. Though you may try to pretend otherwise, the reality is that you are the originator of your actions, the master of your fate and the captain of your soul, for better or for worse. You may choose to surrender control of your life to other individuals or organizations, but this is ultimately a free choice that *you make* and for which you are completely responsible. Let's revisit the examples identified previously and analyze them from this perspective.

Free choice: "I believe that people are free to choose their courses of action, and that they should be held responsible for the choices they make."

- The person who committed the armed robbery and murdered the guard *freely chose* to steal money and he is completely *responsible.* He was not compelled to act in this fashion; he could have chosen not to.

- The person who embezzled money from the charitable organization which he headed *freely chose* to betray his trusted position out of greed and should be held fully accountable.

- The heroic firefighter *freely chose* to overcome his natural fear of death and risk his life to save someone else's, and he should be awarded full credit for his heroism.

- The child abuser *freely chose* to surrender to his destructive sexual impulses, and he deserves to be condemned and fully punished.

- The infant-murdering teenagers *freely chose* to deal with their fear of having an unwanted child by killing it and trying to hide the body (despite having many other alternatives available), and they should be held fully responsible for their choice.

- The philanthropic senior citizen *freely chose* to donate her money to improve educational opportunities for underprivileged young people rather than spending the money on herself, and she deserves to be praised for her altruism.

Each of these people had other alternatives available to them, and they could have made different choices—but they didn't. Therefore, they must be held responsible for the choices that they *did* make.

But surely, you might be thinking, I can't be held *completely* responsible for my life. After all, there are many factors outside of my control, people and forces that *do* create obstacles and undermine my efforts. And we are subject to pressures and influences from *within* ourselves: feelings of greed, fear of death, altruistic impulses, sexual compulsions, need for social acceptance, and so on. Still, it is up to us to freely choose *which* impulses, motivations, fears, and desires we want to act in accordance with. In other words, it is up to you, your "self." You make the ultimate choice regarding who you want to become and the direction of your life. When you look in the mirror, the person that you see reflected is the person you have created. If you are pleased with who you are and the state of your life, then you have every right to feel proud. On the other hand, if you are dissatisfied with the person you have become and disappointed with the course of your life, then you have to look no further than yourself to determine who is responsible. You must have the courage to accept full responsibility for your situation, but it is within your power to change, to improve yourself and your life through the free choices that you are able to make.

Sartre characterizes humans as the one living creature whose "existence" precedes its "essence." In other words, *you* create your "essence" (your self, soul, personality) through the free choices that you make in your daily "existence." He explains:

> Man first of all exists, encounters himself, surges up in the world—and defines himself afterwards. Man simply **is**—he is what he **wills** to be after that leap towards existence. Man is nothing else but that which he makes of himself.

This is exactly what distinguishes human consciousness from the rest of the animal kingdom: when confronted with a decision situation, we are able to *think about the options* available to us and then *make a free choice* based on our evaluation. And that makes us responsible for our actions, as Sartre explains:

> If existence is prior to essence, then man is **responsible** for what he is, it puts every person in possession of himself as he is, and places the entire responsibility for his existence squarely on his shoulders.

In today's culture, personal freedom and responsibility are in danger of extinction, threatened by an array of psychological, sociological, and genetic explanations that have the cumulative effect of robbing people of their autonomy and dignity. It is refreshing and enlightening to view people through the lens of personal freedom, awarding them the power to make free choices for which they are responsible, rather than viewing them as victims of circumstance with little control over their destinies. George Bernard Shaw dismissed this "victimized" view of life when he stated, "I don't believe in circumstances. Rather than blaming their circumstances, the people who get on in this world create their own."

BECAUSE YOU ARE FREE . . .

This discussion of freedom may seem abstract and theoretical to you, and you might be asking yourself: What difference do my beliefs about personal freedom make in my life? The truth is that along with your beliefs about morality and religion, there is perhaps no other belief that has a greater impact on your life. Here are a few examples.

Self-improvement: If you are a person who is constantly striving to improve yourself and the quality of your life, then it is essential that you possess the freedom to make different choices from those you have previously made. *Personal freedom is the lifeblood of human change.* By using your critical-thinking abilities, you can identify appropriate goals and intelligent alternatives; by exercising your freedom, you can choose the goals and alternatives that best meet your needs and fulfill your ideals. On the other hand, an exclusive belief in one of the "non-freedom" theories (human nature, environmental determinism, etc.) undermines and even eliminates the possibility of changing yourself. The die has been cast, and whatever the future has in store for you, you cannot influence it in any meaningful way.

Morality: Morality deals with the way we relate to people around us. Societies have developed moral ideals and prohibitions to help their citizens live together in a

Thinking Critically About Visuals

Why Do People Make the Choices That They Do?

There are many theories to explain why people do what they do: human nature, environmental influences, social pressures, unconscious motivation, chemical imbalances, and so on. Yet many people believe that humans are capable of making free choices and ought to be held responsible for their actions. What do you believe are the mainsprings of human action?

AP Photo/Peter R. Barber/The Daily Gazette

Flying Colours Ltd/Digital Vision/Jupiter Images

harmonious and productive fashion. As a result, most societies consider things like murder, robbery, cheating, stealing, and raping to be "wrong," and they have enacted laws and punishments to discourage antisocial behavior. On the other hand, most societies consider things like compassion, altruism, sharing in communal responsibilities, and working for the good of everyone as well as yourself to be "right," and this sort of behavior is encouraged through teaching, exhortation, and example. But none of this makes any sense if you don't believe that people are free to choose among different alternatives. If you believe that people are *not free,* that their actions are caused by genes, past conditioning, or uncontrollable impulses, then they cannot be held responsible for what they do, and there is little point in trying to encourage them to act differently. *Without freedom, morality becomes irrelevant.* People act the way they are programmed or compelled to act, and that's all there is.

Religion: Most of the world's religions offer a path to an ultimate, spiritual transformation. And this spiritual transformation requires devotion to religious principles and practices so that people can achieve a higher spiritual state on earth and in life after death. But if an individual is *not free* to choose—or not to choose—a spiritual path, then most religions lose their logic and rationale. If your religious actions are completely conditioned by your upbringing or determined by other factors beyond your conscious control, then you can never achieve any spiritual enlightenment through your own efforts. Because enlightenment through self-choice is the main purpose of most religions, they require that individuals have the ability to choose freely in determining their spiritual destiny. *In the absence of freedom, religion becomes irrelevant.*

Social improvement: It doesn't take a Nobel prize winner to see that we live in an imperfect world, saturated with poverty, discrimination, crime, substance abuse, addictions, war and strife, political repression, environmental pollution, child and spousal abuse, and so on. Many people want to create a better world, but to do so requires the ability to change the past and present by freely choosing to alter the future. *But if freedom doesn't exist, then there is no point in even trying to solve social problems and improve society as a whole.* Without the possibility of free choice, these problems are destined to take their own course, and all we can do is watch as passive spectators. On the other hand, if freedom *does* exist, then it is our responsibility to envision a better future and to make choices that will help make this future a reality.

Raising children: Whether or not you believe people are capable of free choice can make a dramatic difference in how you approach raising your children. If you believe that people are the product of their circumstances, then you will emphasize external forms of motivation like rewards and punishments; and if you believe that personalities are genetically constructed, you may minimize your involvement in the natural unfolding of who they are. However, if you believe that your children *are* capable of making free, independent choices, then you will work to educate them regarding the responsibility they have for directing their lives and the importance of thinking critically about their alternatives. *With free choice as a framework, you will seek to help them become reflective and principled individuals* who make thoughtful decisions and accept responsibility for their choices. In other words, you will want them to understand the nature of their freedom and to exercise its power wisely.

Crime and punishment: In recent years we have been subjected to a number of high-profile criminal trials, including those of the kidnappers of Elizabeth Smart and Jaycee Dugard, the 9/11 terrorists, Bernard Madoff (pled guilty before going to trial), and others. Every trial attempts to answer two basic questions: Did the accused person commit the crime he (or she) is charged with? Did he know what he was doing and make a free choice to do it? If the first question is answered "yes," then the second question becomes pivotal in evaluating a person's guilt and responsibility. *But in order to hold people responsible for what they do, we have to believe that they are capable of making free choices.* If people's behavior is caused by other factors, then they couldn't help what they did and it makes no sense to hold them responsible, any more than we should hold a rabid raccoon or a trained pit bull personally responsible for their attacks. These types of defenses are becoming increasingly prevalent. It used to be that the "insanity defense" was reserved for the most obviously deranged criminal defendants. More recently, however, this type of defense has spread like a virus.

To sum up, whether or not you believe that people are capable of making free choices—independent of habit, past conditioning, genetic heritage, social pressure, psychological compulsions, and so on—will have a significant and far-reaching impact on the way you think and act toward yourself, others, and the world as a whole. The way you live your life is a direct reflection of your most deeply held beliefs, and your understanding of freedom is one of the cornerstones of your philosophy of life. Having a clear and accurate understanding about your freedom of choice will enable you to create yourself as the kind of person you want to be, and to inspire the best in others as well. The German poet Rainer Maria Rilke wrote, "We are always becoming the self that we are." Your freedom gives you the power to discover and become your true, authentic self.

USING YOUR FREEDOM TO SHAPE YOUR LIFE

Clearly, you are capable of making free choices. But how can you be sure? You are born with a *genetic heritage* that determines not just your gender, race, and physical characteristics, but influences your personality as well. For example, studies of identical twins (who possess identical genetic "fingerprints") who were separated at birth and reared in different environments have revealed provocative (although complex) results. Years later, despite great differences in their experiences since birth, some twins have exhibited remarkable similarities: identical gestures and sense of humor, the same number (and even names) of children, similar careers and hobbies—all underscoring the influence of genetic factors.

We know that the *environment* also plays a significant role in shaping people's characters and personalities. Young children are indeed like sponges, absorbing all of the information and influences around them and incorporating these elements into their thinking and behavior. Our attitudes, values, beliefs, interests, ways of relating to others—these and many other qualities are influenced by family, friends, and culture. This is the process by which positive values like empathy and commitment get transmitted from generation to generation, and it is also how negative beliefs like racism and violence are perpetuated.

If our genetic heritage and environmental background are such powerful forces in molding who we are, how is it possible to think that we are capable of making free choices in any meaningful sense? The answer to this enigma lies in the nature of *thinking critically,* which we have explored throughout this book—an approach that recognizes that, despite the early influences on our development, our mind and our thinking continue to mature. Not only do you have ongoing experiences, but you *reflect* on these experiences and *learn* from them. Instead of simply accepting the views of others, you gradually develop the ability to *examine* this thinking and to *decide* whether it makes sense to you and whether you should accept it. Although you may share many beliefs with your parents or the prevailing culture in which you were raised, there are likely many other areas of disagreement. Although your parents might believe that sex should begin with marriage or that the most important thing about a career is job security, you might have gradually developed very different perspectives on these issues.

The same is true of your personality. Although your genetic background and early experiences might have *contributed* to shaping the framework of your personality, it is up to you to *decide* what your future self will be. For example, your personality may incorporate many positive qualities from your parents as well as some that you dislike—such as a quick temper. But you can decide not to let this temper dominate your personality or be expressed inappropriately. With sufficient determination, you can be successful in controlling and redirecting this temper, though there may be occasional lapses. In other words, you can take a personality tendency formed early in your development and reshape it according to your own personal goals. In the same way, if your early history created qualities of insecurity, shyness, pessimism, insensitivity, passivity, or other qualities that you are unhappy about, realize that these traits do not represent a life sentence! You have it within your power to *remold* yourself, creating yourself to be the kind of person that you wish and choose to be. *This is the essence of freedom.* Free choice means dealing with an existing situation, selecting from a limited number of options, and working to reshape the present into the future.

Freedom *does not,* however, involve limitless and unconstrained options—this idea of freedom is a fantasy, not a realistic perspective. Freedom doesn't occur in a vacuum; it always involves concrete options and limited possibilities. In analyzing your personality, you may feel that you too often lack confidence and are beset with feelings of insecurity. In reviewing your personal history you may discover that these feelings stem in part from the fact that your parents were excessively critical and did not provide the kind of personal support that leads to a solid sense of security and self-worth. You might discover other factors in your history that contributed to these feelings as well: painful disappointments such as having a meaningful romantic relationship break apart or being fired from a job. All of these experiences will have influenced who you are, and these historical events cannot now be changed. But the significant question is: *What are you going to do now?* How are you going to respond to the results of these events as embodied in your current thinking and behavior? *This is where free choice enters in.* While you can't change what has previously happened, you can control *how you respond* to what happened. You can choose to let these historical influences continue to control your personality, like specters long dead reaching from the grave to influence and entangle the present and future. Or you can *choose to move beyond* these historical influences, to choose a different path for yourself that transcends their influence and liberates your future. The psychiatrist Victor Frankl explains:

> Man is not fully conditioned and determined but rather determines himself whether he gives in to conditions or stands up to them. In other words, man is ultimately self-determining. Man does not simply exist but always decides what his existence will be, what he will become in the next moment. No matter what the circumstances we find ourselves, we always retain the last of human freedoms—the ability to choose one's attitude in a given set of circumstances.

Of course change doesn't occur immediately. It took a long time for your personality to evolve into its present state, and it's going to take a while for you to reconceptualize and redirect it. It's like changing the course of a large ship: you need to turn the rudder to change course, but the past momentum of the ship makes the turn a gradual process, not a radical change of direction. The same is true with the human personality: meaningful change is a complex process, but by choosing to set the rudder on a new course and maintaining its position, *you will change*.

ESCAPING FROM FREEDOM

Given the power of freedom to create and transform people's lives, it would be logical to think that they would enthusiastically embrace their power to make free choices. Unfortunately, people are often not very logical. In fact, they often spend an extraordinary amount of time, thought, and energy actively trying to *deny* and *escape from* their freedom. Why?

The short answer is *responsibility*, summed up in the clever Chinese proverb, "Success has a thousand fathers, but failure is an orphan." In other words, people are generally delighted to acknowledge their freedom when the results of their choices are successful, but shrink from responsibility when the result is failure.

This panicked flight from responsibility is evident in every area of life. Think about life at your workplace. The credit for success generally moves up the hierarchy, with people in the upper echelons congratulating themselves and enjoying the fruits of success. Although the people on the lower rungs might deserve the lion's share of the credit, their role is usually progressively diminished and eventually forgotten. In the case of failure, the process is exactly the reverse—blame tends to move down the hierarchy, ending up with the lowest possible fall guy.

There has been an increasing trend in our society to evade responsibility by becoming a *victim*. Becoming members of this "new culture of victimization" is attractive for many people because it confers on them the moral superiority of innocence and enables them to avoid taking responsibility for their own behavior—not to mention the possibility of gaining financial awards through the legal system. One woman sued Disney World for the "emotional trauma" her daughter endured when she inadvertently saw Mickey Mouse without his costume head. After spilling a cup of hot coffee from McDonald's on her lap while driving a car, another person brought suit for the "psychological scars" that resulted—and received an award of $650,000. People are grasping for their tickets to fame and fortune, without regard to whether their behavior is ethically "right."

Focusing attention on "deserving" victims such as battered wives, abused children, and casualties of crime is certainly commendable, but as the journalist John Taylor pointed out in his article "Don't Blame Me!" the trend toward universal "victimology" (a new academic discipline!) has snowballed out of control. Thus, lifelong smokers are blaming cigarette companies for their own choice to smoke; vicious criminals blame their actions on oppressive social forces; the parade of social misfits on the morbidly voyeuristic afternoon talk shows blame everything and everyone except themselves for their plight; even participants in "refrigerator races" have sued manufacturers because the warning labels did not specifically warn against the dangers of racing with the mammoth appliances strapped to one's back! Fear of liability suits has resulted in the elimination of diving boards at public pools, the outlawing of sports like pole-vaulting at many schools, the exorbitant prices of equipment like football helmets, and the withdrawal of sponsors for Little League teams. Lawyers actively solicit and encourage such suits, buying police logs of accident and crime victims, and acquiring access to the registries of handicapped children in order to locate potential victims. In perhaps the last word on victimology, a New York man was mutilated after jumping in front of a subway, then sued the city because the train had not stopped in time to avoid hitting him. He received an award of $650,000.

All of this stems from the increasing sense of entitlement that people have developed. People have come to assume that they *deserve* to be personally fulfilled, financially prosperous, and successful in their careers—and if they aren't, then they are being *victimized* by someone else who must be held accountable. They have become convinced that they are entitled not only to the right to "life, liberty, and the pursuit of happiness," but to happiness itself. In fact, they have come to believe that they are entitled to a steadily increasing list of "rights"—but without the *responsibilities* that typically accompany these rights. Roger Connor, director of the American Alliance for Rights & Responsibilities, explains: "If you try to think where we went wrong, it was in delinking rights and responsibilities. People are fixated on their rights but have a shriveled sense of responsibility, so if they don't have what they want, they assume it must be someone else's fault."

Looking outside one's self for explanations of misfortune is understandably seductive, but this attitude is ultimately *dis*empowering, having the cumulative effect of stealing one's dignity, self-respect, and freedom. It is analogous to a pact with the devil, in which one's soul is progressively exchanged for the fleeting satisfaction of holding others responsible for the disappointments and mistakes in your life. But the converse is also true: fully accepting your personal responsibility is *personally empowering,* for you are seizing the freedom to shape your destiny through the choices that you make.

Thinking Activity 12.2

ESCAPING FROM MY FREEDOM

Identify areas in your life in which you consistently *accept your freedom*. Provide several specific examples. For example, describe situations in which you have sufficient confidence in yourself to say "I made a free choice and I am responsible for what happened." Identify areas in your life in which you seek to *escape from your freedom* and provide some examples. You can use your reluctance to fully accept responsibility for your choices (and their consequences) as a clue to "escape attempts."

INCREASE YOUR FREEDOM BY ELIMINATING CONSTRAINTS

Freedom consists of making thoughtful choices that reflect your authentic self—your genuine desires and deepest values. But many forces threaten to limit your freedom and even repress it altogether. The limits to your freedom can come from outside yourself (*external constraints*), or they can come from within yourself (*internal constraints*). Although external factors may limit your freedom—for example, being incarcerated or working in a dead-end job—the more challenging limits are the ones you impose on *yourself* through internal constraints. For instance, people don't generally procrastinate, smoke, suffer anxiety attacks, feel depressed, or engage in destructive relationships because someone is coercing them. Instead, they are *victimizing themselves* in ways that they are often unaware of.

In order to remove constraints, you first have to *become aware* that they exist. For example, if someone is manipulating you to think or feel a certain way, you can't begin to deal with the manipulation until you become aware that it exists. Similarly, you can't solve a personal problem like insecurity or emotional immaturity without first acknowledging that it *is* a problem and then developing insight into the internal forces that are driving your behavior. Once you have achieved this deeper level of understanding, you are then in a position to *choose* a different path for yourself, using appropriate decision-making and problem-solving approaches. But there is a great deal of ignorance and confusion regarding the nature of free choice. Let's examine some of the major myths.

Myth #1: Freedom Means Simply Making a Choice Many times we make choices that are not free because the choices are compelled by others. For example, if you are threatened with bodily harm by a mugger or an abusive spouse, your choices are made in response to these threats and are clearly not free. Similarly, if you are being subjected to unreasonable pressure on the job by someone who has the power to fire you, the choices that you make are obviously constrained by the circumstances. These kinds of limitations on your freedom are known as **external constraints**, because they are external influences that force you to choose under duress. While

external constraints Limits to one's freedom that come from outside oneself.

hostage tapes, ransom payments, and blackmail threats are extreme examples of this sort of coercion, there are many incipient forms of it as well. The appeal to fear used by political leaders, the subtle manipulations of an acquaintance, the implied threat by a panhandler, the sexual harassment perpetrated by someone in authority—these and other instances are testimony to the prevalence of external constraints on your freedom.

The way to free yourself from external constraints is to *neutralize* or *remove* them, so that you can make choices that reflect your genuine desires. For example, if your choices are constrained by an abusive spouse or an unreasonable boss, you either have to change their coercive behavior or you have to remove yourself from the situation in order to achieve genuine freedom. If you believe that your choices are excessively limited by the geographical location in which you live, you might have to move in order to increase your possibilities.

Myth #2: Freedom Is Limited to Choosing from Available Options This second myth about freedom interferes with people's capacity to make free choices because it encourages them to passively accept the alternatives presented to them. However, the most vigorous exercise of freedom involves *actively creating* alternatives that may not be on the original menu of options. This talent involves both thinking critically—by taking active initiatives—and thinking creatively—by generating unique possibilities. For example, if you are presented with a project at work, you should not restrict yourself to considering the conventional alternatives for meeting the goals, but should instead actively seek improved possibilities. If you are enmeshed in a problem situation with someone else, you should not permit that person to establish the alternatives from which to choose, but you should instead work to formulate new or modified ways of solving the problem. Too often people are content to sit back and let the situation define their choices instead of taking the initiative to shape the situation in their own way. Critical and creative thinkers view the world as a malleable environment that they have a responsibility to form and shape. This liberates them to exercise their freedom of choice to the fullest extent possible.

Myth #3: Freedom Means Simply "Doing What You Want" "No man is free who is a slave to himself." This saying captures the insight that while you may believe that you are making a free choice because you are not the victim of visible *external constraints*, your choice may indeed be *unfree*. How is this possible? Because your choice can be the result of **internal constraints**, irrational impulses that enslave you. Even though you may on one level be choosing what you "want," the "want" itself does not express your truest self, your deepest desires and values. Consider the following examples:

internal constraints Limits to one's freedom that come from within oneself.

- You are addicted to cigarettes and have been unable to quit despite many attempts.
- You are consumed by jealousy and find yourself unable to break free of your obsession.

- You can't go to bed without checking all of the locks three times.
- Whenever you think about speaking in front of a group of people, you are paralyzed by anxiety and perform miserably.
- You have frequent and lasting episodes of depression from which you are unable to rouse yourself and that sap your interest in doing anything.

This is just a small sampling of common behaviors that are clearly "unfree," even though there are no external threats that are compelling people to make their choices. Instead, in these instances and countless others like them, the compulsions come from *within* people, inhibiting them from making choices that originate from their *genuine* self. How can you tell if your choice originates from your genuine self or is the result of an internal constraint? There is no simple answer. You have to think critically about your situation in order to understand it fully, but here are some questions to guide your reflective inquiry:

- Do you feel that you are making a *free, unconstrained choice* and that you could easily "do otherwise" if you wanted to? Or do you feel that your choice is in some sense beyond your conscious control, that you are "in the grip of" a force that does not reflect your genuine self, a compulsion that has in some way "taken possession" of you?
- Does your choice *add positive qualities* to your life: richness of experience, success, happiness? Or does your choice have negative results that undermine many of the positive goals that you are striving for?
- If you are asked "why" you are making the choice, are you able to provide a persuasive, *rational explanation*? Or are you at a loss to explain why you are behaving this way, other than to say "I can't help myself."

Let's apply these criteria to an example like smoking cigarettes.

- When people are addicted to cigarettes, they usually feel that they are *not* making a free, unconstrained choice to smoke because it is very difficult for them to stop smoking. Instead, they generally feel that they are enslaved by the habit, despite numerous and determined attempts to quit.
- Smoking cigarettes adds many negative elements to a person's life, including health risks to themselves and others near them, stained teeth, and bad breath. On the positive side, people cite reduced anxiety, suppressed appetite, and lessened social awkwardness. But smoking deals with only the symptoms of these problems, not the causes. On balance, the bottom line on smoking is clearly negative.
- Most people who want to stop are at a loss to explain why they smoke, other than to say "I can't help myself."

Using these criteria, habitual smoking seems to be a clear example of an internal constraint. Although smoking might not be your concern, it is likely that there are other elements of your life that are. You might find it easy to advise "Just say no!" to cigarettes but have great difficulty accepting this same simple advice when confronted with an urge for a chocolate eclair, a panicked feeling of insecurity, or a paralyzing fear of public speaking.

Some internal constraints originate from the expectations of others that we have unconsciously "adopted" as our own. For example, someone in your life may demand exaggerated deference from you, and over time you may have internalized this expectation to the point that you actually believe you are freely choosing to exhibit this self-denying subjugation. But although you may have convinced yourself on a surface level, on a deeper level it is clear that you have *surrendered your psychological freedom* to the demands of someone else. That's one reason why people have difficulty in breaking out of abusive and destructive relationships: they don't view the relationships as abusive or destructive and instead may believe that they have freely chosen to be where they are.

This same psychological pattern repeats itself throughout your social life. It is in people's nature to want to be loved, accepted, and respected by others, to fit in with the larger social whole, and to secure the rewards that others can provide. But though you may try to convince yourself otherwise, your choices in response to these pressures and needs are often not truly free because the impetus for these actions does not originate with you, it originates from outside yourself. The key variable is the extent of your *self-awareness*. Free choice demands that you are consciously aware of social pressures and expectations and that you *consciously choose* how to respond to them. Because this crucial awareness is often lacking, our behavior is the result of external manipulation rather than self-originated choice. The psychologist Erich Fromm provides penetrating insight into this complex phenomenon in his seminal work, *Escape from Freedom*:

> Most people are convinced that as long as they are not overtly forced to do something by an outside power, their decisions are theirs, and that if they want something, it is they who want it. But this is one of the great illusions we have about ourselves. A great number of our decisions are not really our own but are suggested to us from the outside; we have succeeded in persuading ourselves that it is we who have made the decision, whereas we have actually conformed with expectations of others, driven by the fear of isolation and by more direct threats to our life, freedom, and comfort.

Even though you may believe that you are making a genuinely free choice, the reality may be that you are making a "pseudo-choice" in response to internal or external constraints. And because you are *unaware* of the influences that are acting upon your behavior, you are living the illusion of the puppet who does not see the strings controlling his every movement.

While everybody engages in some pseudo-thinking and pseudo-choosing, the crucial question is to what extent. If you are a person who reflects, reasons, and thinks critically about your beliefs and your choices, then you will be a predominantly "inner-directed" person, the author of the majority of your thinking and choosing. On the other hand, if you are a person who spends comparatively little time thinking critically about your beliefs and choices, then you will be a much more "other-directed" person, defined in terms of the expectations of others or inner demons over which you have little control. Genuine freedom requires the will and the capacity to reflect, reason, and think critically about our "self"; in the absence of these abilities, we are in danger of becoming a "pseudo-self."

Thinking Activity 12.3

WHAT ARE THE LIMITATIONS TO MY FREEDOM?

Making full use of your freedom involves first eliminating the constraints that limit your freedom. Here's a useful approach to beginning this process:

1. Identify some of the important *external constraints*, limitations on your options that are imposed by people or circumstances outside of you. Are there people in your life who actively seek to limit your freedom? Are you locked into situations that present limited opportunities? After identifying some of the significant external constraints, identify ways to diminish their impact on your freedom by either modifying or eliminating them.

2. Evaluate the extent to which you are *passively content* to choose from a *limited selection of alternatives* that are presented to you. Identify several situations to begin actively creating your own possibilities.

3. Identify some of the important *internal constraints* in your life by identifying behaviors that

   - you feel are out of your conscious control.
   - add negative results to your life.
   - you cannot provide a rational explanation for.

It would be natural to think that if your freedom is so often limited by internal and external constraints, this diminishes your responsibility, because these seem to be factors beyond your control. However, this is not the case. *You are still responsible.* Why? Because the constraints you find yourself burdened with are typically the result of choices that you *previously* made. For example, although you may now feel under the spell of some drug or in an emotionally and/or physically abusive relationship, the fact is that your enslavement took place *over time*. You may now feel that you are trapped and can't even envision different possibilities. Yet your situation didn't happen overnight; it is the result of a long *series of choices* that you have made. It's similar to a thread being slowly wrapped around your hands, binding them together. In the early stages, it is easy for you to break free, but if no action is taken, it gradually reaches the point at which you cannot extricate yourself without outside help. Still, it is within your power to choose to seek such assistance. And so you are responsible for what occurs.

But what about situations like recurring depression, phobias, emotional insecurity, and other paralyzing and debilitating psychological problems? Should people be held responsible for these circumstances as well? Although we have "progressed" to medicating almost every symptom, especially in the psychological realm, we need to step back and view the role of *thinking* in these emotional disturbances, as we are often unwittingly complicitous in perpetuating and even strengthening them through our thinking and choices. Of course, in the case of serious, chronic, long-term emotional disturbances, professional therapeutic help is essential. But in the case of the more common disturbances that keep us from fulfilling our human potential, we can often work our way out of the thickets of these kinds of difficulties if we *think clearly* and *choose freely*.

Deciding on a Career

Work is a search for daily meaning as well as daily bread, for recognition as well as cash . . . in short, for a life rather than a Monday through Friday sort of dying.

—Studs Terkel, *Working*

"What are you going to be when you grow up?" In childhood this question is fun to contemplate because life is an adventure and the future is unlimited. However, now that you are "grown up," this question may elicit more anxiety than enjoyment. "What am I going to be?" "Who am I going to be?" Enrolling in college is certainly an intelligent beginning. The majority of professional careers require a college education, and the investment is certainly worthwhile in monetary terms. But having entered college, many students react by asking, "Now what?"

Perhaps you entered college right out of high school, or perhaps you are returning to college after raising a family, working in a variety of jobs, or serving in the armed forces. The question is the same: What is the right decision to make about your career future? Some people have no idea how to answer this question; others have a general idea about a possible career (or careers) but aren't sure exactly which career they want or precisely how to achieve their career goals. Even if you feel sure about your choice, it makes sense to engage in some serious career exploration to ensure that you fully understand your interests and abilities as well as the full range of career choices that match your talents.

Most college students will change their majors a number of times before graduating. Although many students are concerned that these changes reveal instability and confusion, in most cases they are a healthy sign. They suggest that the students are actively engaged in the process of career exploration: considering possible choices, trying them out, and revising their thinking to try another possibility. Often we learn as much from discovering what we don't want as from what we do want. The student who plans to become a veterinarian may end up concluding,

"I never want to see a sick animal the rest of my life," as one of my students confided after completing a three-month internship at a veterinary hospital.

The best place to begin an intelligent analysis of your career future is by completing a review of what you already know about your career orientation. Your personal history contains clues regarding which career directions are most appropriate for you. By examining the careers you have considered in your life, and by analyzing the reasons that have motivated your career choices, you can begin creating a picture of yourself that will help you define a fulfilling future. With these considerations in mind, complete the following activity as a way to begin creating your own individual "career portrait." Start by describing two careers that you have considered for yourself in the past few years along with the reason(s) for your choices, and then complete Thinking Activity 12.4.

Thinking Activity 12.4

THINKING ABOUT YOUR CAREER PLANS

Describe in a two-page paper your current thoughts and feelings about your career plans. Be very honest, and include the following:

1. A specific description of the career(s) you think you might enjoy
2. A description of the history of this choice(s) and the reasons why you think you would enjoy it (them)
3. The doubts, fears, and uncertainties you have concerning your choice(s)
4. The problems you will have to solve and the challenges you will have to overcome in order to achieve your career goal

THINKING ERRORS IN CAREER DECISIONS

Too often, people choose careers for the wrong reasons, including the following:

- They consider only those job opportunities with which they are familiar and fail to discover countless other career possibilities.
- They focus on certain elements, such as salary or job security, while ignoring others like job satisfaction or opportunities for advancement.
- They choose careers because of pressure from family or peers rather than selecting careers that they really want.
- They drift into jobs by accident or circumstance and never reevaluate their options.
- They fail to understand fully their abilities and long-term interests, and what careers will match these.
- They don't pursue their "dream jobs" because they are afraid that they will not succeed.
- They are reluctant to give up their current unsatisfactory job for more promising possibilities because of the risk and sacrifice involved.

Whatever the reasons, the sad fact is that too many people wind up with dead-end, unsatisfying jobs that seem more like lifetime prison sentences than their "field of dreams." However, such depressing outcomes are not inevitable. This text is designed to help you develop the thinking abilities, knowledge, and insight you will need to achieve the appropriate career.

CREATING YOUR DREAM JOB

One of the powerful thinking abilities you possess is the capacity to think imaginatively. In order to discover the career that is right for you, it makes sense to use your imagination to create an image of the job that you believe would make you feel most fulfilled. Too often people settle for less than they have to because they don't believe they have any realistic chance to achieve their dreams. Using this self-defeating way of thinking almost guarantees failure in a career quest. Another thinking error occurs when people decide to pursue a career simply because it pays well, even though they have little interest in the work itself. This approach overlooks the fact that in order to be successful over a long period of time, you must be continually motivated—otherwise you may "run out of gas" when you most need it. Interestingly enough, when people pursue careers that reflect their true interests, their success often results in financial reward because of their talents and accomplishments, even though money wasn't their main goal!

So the place to begin your career quest is with your dreams, not with your fears. To get started, it's best to imagine an ideal job in as much detail as possible. Of course, any particular job is only one possibility within the field of your career choice. It is likely that you will have a number of different jobs as you pursue your career. However, your imagination works more effectively when conjuring up specific images, rather than images in general. You can begin this exploratory process by completing Thinking Activity 12.5.

Thinking Activity 12.5

DESCRIBING YOUR DREAM JOB

Write a two-page description of your ideal job. Spend time letting your imagination conjure up a specific picture of your job, and don't let negative impulses ("I could never get a job like that!") interfere with your creative vision. Be sure to address each of the four dimensions of your ideal job:

1. Physical setting and environment in which you would like to spend your working hours

2. Types of activities and responsibilities you would like to spend your time performing

3. Kinds of people you would like to be working with

4. Personal goals and accomplishments you would like to achieve as part of your work

DISCOVERING WHO YOU ARE

What career should you pursue? This is a daunting question and, as we have noted, one to which many people have difficulty finding the right answer. The best approach to discovering the "right" career depends on developing an in-depth understanding of who you are: your deep and abiding interests, and your unique talents. Each of us possesses an original combination of interests, abilities, and values that characterizes our personality. Discovering the appropriate goals for yourself involves becoming familiar with your unique qualities: the activities that interest you, the special abilities and potentials you have, and the values that define the things you consider to be most important. Once you have a reasonably clear sense of who you are and what you are capable of, you can then begin exploring those goals, from career paths to personal relationships, that are a good match for you. However, developing a clear sense of who you are is a challenging project and is one of the key goals of this text. Many people are still in the early stages of self-understanding, and this situation makes identifying the appropriate career particularly difficult.

WHAT ARE YOUR INTERESTS?

To live a life that will be stimulating and rewarding to you over the course of many years, you must choose a path that involves activities that you have a deep and abiding interest in performing. If you want to be a teacher, you should find helping people learn to be an inspiring and fulfilling activity. If you want to be an architect, you should find the process of creating designs, working with others, and solving construction problems to be personally challenging activities. When people achieve a close match between their natural interests and the activities that constitute a career, they are assured of living a life that will bring them joy and satisfaction.

Although there is not necessarily a direct connection between interests and eventual career choice, carefully examining your interests should nevertheless provide you with valuable clues in discovering a major and a career that will bring lifelong satisfaction. In addition, thinking critically about your interests will help you to seek relationships that support and complement your goals and to select course work and a major that you will genuinely enjoy.

Thinking Activity 12.6

IDENTIFYING YOUR INTERESTS

1. Create a list of the interests in your life, describing each one as specifically as possible. Begin with the present and work backward as far as you can remember, covering your areas of employment, education, and general activities. Make the list as comprehensive as you can, including as many interests as you can think of. (Don't worry about duplication.) Ask people who know you how they would describe your interests.

2. Once you have created your list, classify the items into groups based on similarity. Don't worry if the same interest fits into more than one group.

3. For each group you have created, identify possible careers that might be related to the interests described in the group.

A student example follows:

Interest Group #1

- I enjoy helping people solve their problems.
- I am interested in subjects like hypnotism and mental therapy.
- I have always been interested in the behavior of people.
- I enjoy reading books on psychology.

Possible careers: clinical psychologist, occupational therapist, social worker, gerontologist, behavioral scientist, community mental health worker, industrial psychologist

Interest Group #2

- I am interested in developing websites, for myself and my friends.
- I love blogging and have created a blog for the Honor Society at school.
- I have always enjoyed playing virtual reality games like World of Warcraft.
- I have built a number of applications for my iPhone that I have shared with others.

Possible careers: e-business consultant, website designer, blogger, programmer, applications analyst, technical support specialist

Interest Group #3

- I am interested in the sciences, especially chemistry and anatomy.
- I like going to hospitals and observing doctors and nurses at work.
- When I was in high school, I always enjoyed biology and anatomy labs.
- I am interested in hearing about people's illnesses and injuries.

Possible careers: doctor, nurse, physical therapist, paramedic, biomedical worker, chemical technician, mortician, medical laboratory technician

Interest Group #4

- I enjoy going to museums and theaters.
- I enjoy painting and drawing in my free time.
- I enjoy listening to music: classical, jazz, and romantic.
- I enjoy reading magazines like *Vogue, Vanity Fair,* and *Vanidades.*

Possible careers: actor, publicist, advertising executive, interior designer, fashion designer

WHAT ARE YOUR ABILITIES?

In general, the activities that you have a sustained interest in over a period of time are activities that you are good at. This is another key question for you to address as you pursue your career explorations: "What are the special abilities and talents that I possess?" Each of us has a unique combination of special talents, and it is to our advantage to select majors and careers that utilize these natural abilities. Otherwise, we will find ourselves competing against people who do have natural abilities in that particular area. Think of those courses you have taken that seemed extremely difficult to you despite your strenuous efforts, while other students were successful with apparently much less effort—or, conversely, those courses that seemed easy for you while other students were struggling. There is a great deal of competition for desirable careers, and if we are to be successful, we need to be able to use our natural strengths.

How do you identify your natural abilities? One productive approach to begin identifying your abilities is to examine important accomplishments in your life, a strategy described in Thinking Activity 12.7. In addition, there are career counselors, books, and computer software programs that can help you zero in on your areas of interest and strength. We sometimes possess unknown abilities that we simply haven't had the opportunity to discover and use. With this in mind, it makes sense for you to explore unfamiliar areas of experience to become aware of your full range of potential.

Thinking Activity 12.7

IDENTIFYING YOUR ABILITIES

1. Identify the ten most important accomplishments in your life. From this list of ten, select three accomplishments of which you are most proud. Typically, these will be experiences in which you faced a difficult challenge or a complex problem that you were able to overcome with commitment and talent.

2. Compose a specific and detailed description (one to two pages) of each of these three accomplishments, paying particular attention to the skills and strategies you used to meet the challenge or solve the problem.

3. After completing the descriptions, identify the abilities that you displayed in achieving your accomplishments. Then place them into groups, based on their similarity to one another. Here is how one student completed this activity:

Accomplishments

1. Graduating from high school
2. Getting my real estate license
3. Succeeding at college
4. Owning a dog
5. Winning a swim team championship
6. Moving into my own apartment
7. Finding a job
8. Getting my driver's license
9. Buying a car
10. Learning to speak another language

Accomplishment #1: Graduating from High School

The first accomplishment I would like to describe was graduating from high school. I never thought I would do it. In the eleventh grade I became a truant. I only attended classes I liked, after which I would go home or hang out with friends. I was having a lot of problems with my parents and the guy I was dating, and I fell into a deep depression in the middle of the term. I decided to commit suicide by taking pills. I confided this to a friend, who went and told the principal. I was called out of class to the principal's office. He said he wanted to talk to me, and it seemed like we talked for hours. Suddenly my parents walked in with my guidance counselor, and they joined the discussion. We came to the conclusion that I would live with my aunt for two weeks, and I would also speak with the counselor once a day. If I didn't follow these rules, they would place me in a group home. During those two weeks I did a lot of thinking. I didn't talk to anyone from my neighborhood. Through counseling I learned that no problems are worth taking your life. I joined a peer group in my school, which helped me a lot as well. I learned to express my feelings. It was very difficult to get back into my schedule in school, but my teachers' help made it easier. I committed myself to school and did very well, graduating the following year.

Abilities/Skills from Accomplishment #1:

- I learned how to analyze and solve difficult problems in my life.
- I learned how to understand and express my feelings.
- I learned how to work with other people in order to help solve each other's problems.
- I learned how to focus my attention and work with determination toward a goal.
- I learned how to deal with feelings of depression and think positively about myself and my future.

FINDING THE RIGHT MATCH

In Chapter 1 you learned how to use your thinking abilities to begin identifying your interests, abilities, and values. Discovering who you are is one part of identifying an appropriate career. The second part involves researching the careers that are available to determine which ones match your interests, abilities, and values. There are literally thousands of different careers, most of which you probably have only a vague notion about. How do you find out about them? There are a number of tools at your disposal. To begin with, your college probably has a career resource center that likely contains many reference books, periodicals, DVDs, CDs, and software programs describing various occupations. Career counselors are also available either at your school or in your community. Speaking to people working in various careers is another valuable way to learn about what is really involved in a particular career. Work internships, summer jobs, and volunteer work are other avenues for learning about career possibilities and whether they might be right for you.

THINKING CRITICALLY ABOUT NEW MEDIA

Searching Online for the Right Career

You can harness the power of the Internet as you search for the ideal position for yourself. Websites like **CareerBuilder.com** and **Monster.com** are devoted to facilitating the employment matchmaking process. You can browse the job postings at these sites and/or you can post your résumé for potential employers to see. The Internet can also be extremely helpful in researching potential careers, giving you the means to explore various dimensions of different careers—information you can use to make informed choices about your future. Finally, once you have secured a job in your career, you can use professional networking sites like **LinkedIn.com** to keep in touch with your network of colleagues. Of course, as with anything on the Internet, you have to be careful about divulging important information about yourself, even on official job and career websites. The following brief passage, written by a member of **CareerBuilder.com**, provides six practical tips for ensuring your privacy online.

Seeking Employment Online—Is Fear a Factor?

6 Tips to Protect Your Privacy
Kate Lorenz

Does the thought of posting your resume online and exposing yourself to hundreds of thousands of Internet users give you white knuckles? If so, your fears are founded. According to the FBI, identity theft is the number one fraud perpetrated on the Internet. So how do job seekers protect themselves while continuing to circulate their resumes online? The key to a successful online job search is learning to manage the risks. Here are some tips for staying safe while conducting a job search on the Internet.

1. **Check for a privacy policy.** If you are considering posting your resume online, make sure the job search site you are considering has a privacy policy, like **CareerBuilder.com**. The policy should spell out how your information will be used, stored, and whether or not it will be shared. You may want to think twice about posting your resume on a site that automatically shares your information with others. You could be opening yourself up for unwanted calls from solicitors.

   When reviewing the site's privacy policy, you'll be able to delete your resume just as easily as you posted it. You won't necessarily want your resume to remain out there on the Internet once you land a job. Remember, the longer your resume remains posted on a job board, the more exposure, both positive and not-so-positive, it will receive.

2. **Take advantage of site features.** Legitimate job search sites offer levels of privacy protection. Before posting your resume, carefully consider your job search objectives and the level of risk you are willing to assume.

CareerBuilder.com, for example, offers three levels of privacy from which job seekers can choose. The first is standard posting. This option gives job seekers who post their resumes the most visibility to the broadest employer audience possible.

The second is anonymous posting. This allows job seekers the same visibility as those in the standard posting category without any of their contact information being displayed. Job seekers who wish to remain anonymous but want to share some other information may choose which pieces of contact information to display.

The third is private posting. This option allows job seekers to post their resumes without having it searched by employers. Private posting allows job seekers to quickly and easily apply for jobs that appear on **CareerBuilder.com** without retyping their information.

3. **Safeguard your identity.** Career experts say that one of the ways job seekers can stay safe while using the Internet to search out jobs is to conceal their identities. Replace your name on your resume with a generic identifier such as:

Confidential Candidate

Intranet Developer Candidate

Confidential Resume: Experienced Marketing Representative

You should also consider eliminating the name and location of your current employer. Depending on your title, it may not be all that difficult to determine who you are once the name of your company is provided. Use a general description of the company such as:

Major auto manufacturer

International packaged goods supplier

Confidential employer

If your job title is unique, consider using the generic equivalent instead of the exact title assigned by your employer.

4. **Establish an email address for your search.** Another way to protect your privacy while seeking employment online is to open up a mail account specifically for your online job search. This will safeguard your existing email box in the event someone you don't know gets a hold of your email address and shares it with others. Using a dedicated email address specifically for your job search also eliminates the possibility that you will receive unwelcome email solicitations in your primary mailbox. When naming your new email address, be sure it is nondescript and that it doesn't contain references to your name or other information that will give

(Continues)

THINKING CRITICALLY ABOUT NEW MEDIA (*CONTINUED*)

away your identity. The best solution is an email address that is relevant to the job you are seeking such as **salesmgr2004@provider.com**.

5. **Protect your references.** If your resume contains a section with the names and contact information for your references, take it out. There's no sense in safeguarding your information while sharing private contact information for your references.

6. **Keep confidential information confidential.** Do not, under any circumstances, share your social security, driver's license, and bank account numbers or other personal information, such as marital status or eye color. Credible employers do not need this information with an initial application. Don't provide this even if they say they need it in order to conduct a background check. This is one of the oldest tricks in the book—don't fall for it. Most legitimate employers don't do background checks until they have met with you, conducted an extensive interview process, and decided you're the ideal candidate. Even then, you need only provide limited information. Contact an attorney if you still have concerns.

Source: Copyright 2008 CareerBuilder, LLC. Reprinted with permission. http://www.careerbuilder.com.

Thinking Activity 12.8

RESEARCHING CAREERS ONLINE

1. Identify two possible careers in which you might be interested.
2. Use the Internet to research these careers, answering questions like:
   - What are the educational qualifications needed? What is the salary range?
   - How difficult is it to secure a job? What is the job security?
   - What are the different types of positions available in this career?
   - What do the actual work and responsibilities consist of?
   - What are the opportunities for growth and advancement?
3. Visit sites like **CareerBuilder.com** and **monster.com** and research some of the specific positions being advertised within each of these careers. How does your research relate to the questions in #2?

Thinking Critically About Visuals

A Bad Hair Day?

There are countless careers that people don't consider because they are unfamiliar. What unusual occupation do you think is depicted in this photo? What would you expect to be the educational background and training of this person? What are three of the most unusual careers you can think of? After sharing with the class, were you surprised at some of the unusual careers other students identified? Are any of interest to you?

Michael Newman/PhotoEdit

As you begin your career explorations, don't lose sight of the fact that your career decisions will likely evolve over time, reflecting your growth as a person and the changing job market. Many people alter their career paths often, so you should avoid focusing too narrowly. Instead, concentrate on preparing for broad career areas and developing your general knowledge and abilities. For example, by learning to think critically, solve problems, make intelligent decisions, and communicate effectively, you are developing the basic abilities needed in almost any career. As an "educated thinker," you will be able to respond quickly and successfully to the unplanned changes and unexpected opportunities that you will encounter as you follow—and create—the unfolding path of your life.

Choosing the "Good Life"

What is the ultimate purpose of your life? What is the "good life" that you are trying to achieve?

Psychologist Carl Rogers, who has given a great deal of thought to these issues, has concluded that the good life is

- *not* a fixed state like virtue, contentment, nirvana, or happiness
- *not* a condition like being adjusted, fulfilled, or actualized
- *not* a psychological state like drive or tension reduction

Instead, the good life is a process rather than a state of being, a direction rather than a destination. But what direction? According to Rogers, "The direction which constitutes the Good Life is that which is selected by the total organism when there is psychological freedom to move in any direction." In other words, the heart of the good life is creating yourself through genuinely free choices once you have liberated yourself from external and internal constraints. When you are living such a life, you are able to fulfill your true potential in every area of your existence. You are able to be completely open to your experience, becoming better able to listen to yourself, to experience what is going on within yourself. You are more aware and accepting of feelings of fear, discouragement, and pain, but also more open to feelings of courage, tenderness, and awe. You are more able to live your experiences fully instead of shutting them out through defensiveness and denial.

How do you know what choices you should make, what choices will best create the self you want to be and help you achieve your good life? As you achieve psychological freedom, your *intuitions* become increasingly more trustworthy, because they reflect your deepest values, your genuine desires, your authentic self. It is when we are hobbled by constraints on ourselves that our intuitions are distorted and often self-destructive. As previously noted, you need to think clearly about yourself, to have an optimistic, self-explanatory style that enables you to approach life in the most productive way possible. When you have achieved this clarity of vision and harmony of spirit, what "feels right"—the testimony of your reflective consciousness and common sense—will serve as a competent and trustworthy guide to the choices you ought to make. The choices that emerge from this enlightened state will help you create a life that is enriching, exciting, challenging, stimulating, meaningful, and fulfilling. It will enable you to stretch and grow, to become more and to attain more of your potentialities. As author Albert Camus noted, "Freedom is nothing else but a chance to be better, whereas enslavement is a certainty of the worst."

The good life is different for each person, and there is no single path or formula for achieving it. It is the daily process of creating yourself in ways that express your deepest desires and highest values—your authentic self. Thinking critically and thinking creatively provide you with the insight to clearly see the person you want

Thinking Critically About Visuals

Envisioning the Good Life

How do you exercise your critical-thinking abilities to determine your own path in a world full of choices, obstacles, and possibilities?

How might this image illustrate the quote from Fyodor Dostoyevsky: "Without a firm idea of himself and the purpose of life, man cannot live, and would sooner destroy himself than remain on earth, even if he was surrounded with bread"? How do your experiences with work, learning, and personal relationships work as lenses through which you perceive the story of this photograph? Compare your responses with those of a few classmates.

Cliff Leight/Aurora/Getty Images

to become, while choosing freely gives you the power actually to create the person you have envisioned.

> STRATEGY: Describe your ideal "good life." Make full use of your imagination, and be specific regarding the details of the life you are envisioning for yourself. Compare this imagined good life with the life you have now. What different choices do you have to make in order to achieve your good life?

MEANING OF YOUR LIFE

According to psychiatrist and concentration camp survivor Victor Frankl, "Man's search for meaning is the primary motivation in his life." A well-known Viennese psychiatrist in the 1930s, Dr. Frankl and his family were arrested by the Nazis, and he spent three years in the Auschwitz concentration camp. Every member of his family, including his parents, siblings, and pregnant wife, was killed. He himself miraculously survived, enduring the most unimaginably abusive and degrading conditions. Following his liberation by the Allied troops, he wrote *Man's Search for Meaning*, an enduring and influential work, which he began on scraps of paper during his internment. Since its publication in 1945, it has become an extraordinary best seller, read by millions of people and translated into twenty languages. Its success reflects the profound hunger for meaning that people have continually been experiencing, trying to answer a question that, in the author's words, "burns under their fingernails." This hunger expresses the pervasive meaninglessness of our age, the "existential vacuum" in which many people exist.

Dr. Frankl discovered that even under the most inhumane conditions, it is possible to live a life of purpose and meaning. But for the majority of prisoners at Auschwitz, a meaningful life did not seem possible. Immersed in a world that no longer recognized the value of human life and human dignity, that robbed prisoners of their will and made them objects to be exterminated, most people suffered a loss of their values. If a prisoner did not struggle against this spiritual destruction with a determined effort to save his or her self-respect, the person lost the feeling of being an individual, a being with a mind, with inner freedom and personal value. The prisoner's existence descended to the level of animal life, plunging him or her into a depression so deep that he or she became incapable of action. No entreaties, no blows, no threats would have any effect on the person's apathetic paralysis, and he or she soon died, underscoring Russian novelist Fyodor Dostoyevsky's observation, "Without a firm idea of himself and the purpose of life, man cannot live, and would sooner destroy himself than remain on earth, even if he was surrounded with bread."

Dr. Frankl found that the meaning of his life in this situation was to try to help his fellow prisoners restore their psychological health. He had to find ways for them to look forward to the future: a loved one waiting for the person's return, a talent to be used, or perhaps work yet to be completed. These were the threads he tried to weave back into the patterns of meaning in these devastated lives. His efforts led him to the following insight:

> We had to learn ourselves, and furthermore we had to teach the despairing men, that it did not matter what we expected from life, but rather *what life expected from us*. We needed to stop asking about the meaning of life but instead to think of ourselves as those who were being questioned by life, daily and hourly. Our answer must consist not in talk and meditation, but in right action and in right conduct. Life ultimately means taking the responsibility to find the right answer to its problems and to fulfill the tasks which it constantly sets for each individual.

We each long for a life of significance, to feel that in some important way our life has made a unique contribution to the world and to the lives of others. We each strive to create our self as a person of unique quality, someone who is admired by others as extraordinary. We hope for lives characterized by unique accomplishments and lasting relationships that will distinguish us as memorable individuals both during and after our time on earth.

FINAL THOUGHTS

The purpose of this book has been to help provide you with the thinking abilities you will need to guide you on your personal journey of self-discovery and self-transformation. Its intention has *not* been to provide you with answers but to equip you with the thinking abilities, conceptual tools, and personal insights to find your own answers. Each chapter has addressed an essential dimension of the thinking process, and the issues raised form a comprehensive blueprint for your life, a life that you wish to be clear in purpose and rich in meaning. For you to discover the meaning of your life, you need to seek meaning actively, to commit yourself to challenging projects, to meet with courage and dignity the challenges that life throws at you. You will have little chance of achieving meaning in your life if you simply wait for meaning to present itself to you or if you persist in viewing yourself as a victim of life.

But how do you determine the "right" way to respond and select the path that will infuse your life with meaning and fulfillment? You need to think critically, think creatively, and make enlightened choices—all of the thinking abilities and life attitudes that you have been cultivating throughout your work with this book. They will provide you with the clear vision and strength of character that will enable you to create yourself as a worthy individual living a life of purpose and meaning. Your explorations of issues presented throughout this book have given you the opportunity to become acquainted with yourself and with the potential that resides within you: your unique intellectual gifts, imaginative dreams, and creative talents. As psychologist Abraham Maslow notes, you are so constructed that you naturally press toward fuller and fuller being, realizing your potentialities, becoming fully human, everything that you can become. But you alone can determine what choices you will make among all of the possibilities: which will be condemned to nonbeing and which will be actualized, creating your immortal portrait, the monument to your existence.

Clearly, the ultimate meaning of your life can never be fully realized within the confines of your own self. Meaning is encountered and created through your efforts to *go beyond* yourself. In the same way that "happiness" and "success" are the outgrowths of purposeful and productive living rather than ends in themselves, so your life's meaning is a natural by-product of reaching beyond yourself to touch the lives of others. This self-transcendence may take the form of a creative work or a heroic action that you display to the human community. It may also be expressed through your loving and intimate relationships with other people, your contribution to individual members of your human community.

What is the meaning of your life? It is the truth that you will discover as you strive, through your daily choices, to create yourself as an authentic individual, committed to enhancing the lives of others, fulfilling your own unique potential, and attuning yourself to your essential nature and the mysteries of the universe. It is the reality you will find as you choose to respond to both the blessings and the suffering in your life with courage and dignity. Joy and suffering, fulfillment and despair, birth and death—these are the raw materials that life provides you. Your challenge and responsibility are to shape these experiences into a meaningful whole—guided by a philosophy of life that you have constructed with your abilities to think critically, think creatively, and choose freely. This is the path you must take in order to live a life that is rich with meaning, lived by a person who is noble and heroic—a life led as an enlightened thinker.

CHAPTER 12 | Reviewing and Viewing

Summary

- The challenge to an enlightened *critical thinker* is to develop a philosophy of life that expresses who you are as well as the person you want to become.

- The quality of our life philosophy is a direct result of our ability to think critically, think creatively, and choose freely.

- Choosing freely means that we possess the insight to understand all of our options and the wisdom to make informed choices. Passive, illogical, and superficial thinking inhibits our ability to make intelligent choices and erodes our motivation to persevere when obstacles are encountered.

- Exercising genuine freedom involves recognizing and then liberating ourselves from both *external constraints* and *internal constraints*, and accepting responsibility for the choices we make.

- Discovering the "right" career for us involves finding the best match between our abilities and interests and the careers that are available.

- In order to envision and achieve "the good life" for ourselves, we must continually exercise our critical thinking abilities to determine our own path in a world full of choices, obstacles, and possibilities.

Assessing Your Strategies and Creating New Goals

How Free Am I?

Described next are key personal attributes that are correlated with choosing freely. Evaluate your position regarding each of these attributes, and use this self-evaluation to guide your choices as you shape the free person you want to become.

Accept Your Freedom and Responsibility

I willingly accept my freedom and my responsibility.	I often try to escape from my freedom and evade personal responsibility.
5 4 3 2 1	

Your reaction to responsibility is an effective barometer of your attitude toward freedom. If you are comfortable with your personal responsibility, able openly to admit your mistakes as well as take pleasure in your successes, this is an indication that you accept your freedom. Similarly, if you take pride in your independence, welcoming the opportunity to make choices for which you are solely responsible, this also reveals a willing embracing of your freedom.

Strategy: Create a "responsibility chart" that evaluates your acceptance of responsibility (and freedom) in various areas of your life. On one side of the page describe common activities in which you are engaged ("Decisions at work," "Conflicts with my partner") and on the other side list typical judgments that you make ("I am solely responsible for that mistaken analysis," "You made me do that embarrassing thing and I can't forgive you"). After several days of record-keeping and reflection, you should begin to get an increasingly clear picture of the extent to which you accept (or reject) your personal freedom.

Emphasize Your Ability to Create Yourself

I believe that I create myself through my free choices.	I believe that I am created by forces over which I have little control.
5 4 3 2 1	

Although you may not be fully aware of it, you have your own psychological theory of human nature, which is expressed in how you view yourself and deal with other people. Do you believe that your personality is determined by your genetic history or the environmental circumstances that have shaped you? Or do you believe that people are able to transcend their histories and choose freely?

*Strategy: Instead of explaining your (and others') behavior entirely in terms of genes and environmental conditioning, develop the habit of analyzing your behavior in terms of the **choices** you make. I have personally witnessed many people who have triumphed over daunting odds, and I have seen others who have failed miserably despite having every advantage in life. The key ingredient? An unshakable belief in the ability to choose one's destiny.*

Become Aware of Constraints on Your Freedom

I am aware of the constraints on my freedom	I am generally unaware of the constraints on my freedom.
5 4 3 2 1	

The key to unlocking your freedom is becoming aware of the external and internal forces that are influencing you. As long as you remain oblivious to external manipulations and internal compulsions, you are powerless to escape from their hold. However, by using your critical-thinking abilities, you are able to identify these influences and then neutralize their effect.

*Strategy: In your **Thinking Notebook**, identify the **external** limitations (people or circumstances) on your freedom and think about ways to remove these constraints. Then identify—as best you can—the **internal** compulsions that are influencing you to act in ways at variance with your genuine desires. Use the indicators on page 548 to help in your identification.*

Create New Options to Choose From

I usually try to create additional options to those presented.	I usually accept the options that are presented.
5 4 3 2 1	

Active thinking, like passive thinking, is habit forming. Once you develop the habit of looking beyond the information given, consistently transcending the framework within which you are operating, you will be increasingly unwilling to be limited by the alternatives determined by others. Instead, you will seek to create new possibilities and actively shape situations to fit your needs.

*Strategy: When you find yourself in a situation with different choices, make a conscious effort to identify alternatives other than those explicitly presented. You don't have to choose the new options you have created if they are not superior to others, but you **do** want to start developing the habit of using your imagination to look beyond the circumstances as presented.*

Work Purposefully to Achieve the "Good Life" for Yourself and Others

I have a clear idea of the "good life" that I want to create for myself.	I am confused about what the "good life" is and how to achieve it for myself.
5 4 3 2 1	

The good life is different for each person, and there is no single path or formula for achieving it. It is the daily process of creating yourself in ways that express your deepest desires and highest values—your authentic self. *Thinking critically* and *thinking creatively* provide you with the insight to see clearly the person you want to become, while *choosing freely* gives you the power actually to create the person you have envisioned.

Strategy: *Describe your ideal "good life" in your* **Thinking Notebook**. *Make full use of your imagination, and be specific regarding the details of the life you are envisioning for yourself. Compare this imagined good life with the life you have now. What different choices do you have to make in order to achieve your good life?*

Suggested Films

Billy Elliot (2000)

Set in northern England during the 1984 miners' strike, an 11-year-old boy from a community in conflict discovers his interest and talent for dance. He overcomes social pressures to follow his creative passion and create a fulfilled life, encouraging others around him to think differently in the process.

Cool Hand Luke (1967)

How can the spirit be free while the body is imprisoned? When Luke Jackson is sent to prison camp, he refused to submit to the tyrannical authority of the camp's captain. His repeated escapes and attempts to bring meaning and fraternity to the other prisoners only provoke the anger of the captain, who makes it his mission to break Luke's spirit.

One Flew Over the Cuckoo's Nest (1975)

What does it mean to be sane? A criminal, Randle Patrick McMurphy, pretends to be insane to avoid a prison sentence. He is sent to a mental institution, where a tyrannical nurse uses any means necessary to force the patients into numbed submission. Based on the book of the same name, the film follows McMurphy's attempts to save himself and his fellow inmates from the oppressive authority of the mental hospital.

Shine (1996)

Based on a true story, this film recounts the life of an Australian piano virtuoso who overcame childhood trauma and a mental breakdown by using his art to live a passionate and meaningful life.

Waking Life (2001)

In this innovative and dynamic animated film, a young man who is unsure if he is dreaming or awake discusses the meaning and purpose of the universe with a variety of intellectuals, artists, and vibrant thinkers. The conversations inspire questions that get to the core of the mysteries of human existence.

Glossary

accomplishment Something completed successfully; an achievement. Also, an acquired skill or expertise.

accurate Conforming exactly to fact; errorless; deviating only slightly or within acceptable limits from a standard.

active learner One who takes initiative in exploring one's world, thinks independently and creatively, and takes responsibility for the consequences of one's decisions.

active participant One who is always trying to understand the sensations one encounters instead of being a passive receiver of information, a "container" into which sense experience is poured.

alternative A choice between two mutually exclusive possibilities, a situation presenting such a choice, or either of these possibilities.

altruistic Showing unselfish concern for the welfare of others.

ambiguous Open to more than one interpretation; doubtful or uncertain.

analogical relationships Relationships that relate things belonging to different categories in terms of each other.

analogy A comparison between things that are basically dissimilar made for the purpose of illuminating our understanding of the things being compared.

analysis The study of the parts of an intellectual or material whole and their interrelationships in making up a whole.

appeal to authority A type of fallacious thinking in which the argument is intended to persuade through the appeal to various authorities with legitimate expertise in the area in which they are advising.

appeal to fear An argument in which the conclusion being suggested is supported by a reason invoking fear and not by a reason that provides evidence for the conclusion.

appeal to flattery A source of fallacious reasoning designed to influence the thinking of others by appealing to their vanity as a substitute for providing relevant evidence to support a point of view.

appeal to ignorance An argument in which the person offering the conclusion calls upon his or her opponent to disprove the conclusion. If the opponent is unable to do so, then the conclusion is asserted to be true.

appeal to personal attack A fallacy that occurs when the issues of the argument are ignored and the focus is instead directed to the personal qualities of the person making the argument in an attempt to discredit the argument. Also referred to as the *ad hominem* ("to the man" rather than to the issue) argument or "poisoning the well."

appeal to pity An argument in which the reasons offered to support the conclusions are designed to invoke sympathy toward the person involved.

appeal to tradition A misguided way of reasoning that argues that a practice or way of thinking is "better" or "right" simply because it is older, is traditional, or has "always been done that way."

application The act of putting something to a special use or purpose.

argument A form of thinking in which certain statements (reasons) are offered in support of another statement (a conclusion).

assumption Something taken for granted or accepted as true without proof.

authoritarian moral theory A moral theory in which there are clear values of "right" and "wrong," with authorities determining what these are.

authority An accepted source of expert information or advice.

bandwagon A fallacy that relies on the uncritical acceptance of others' opinions because "everyone believes it."

begging the question A circular fallacy that assumes in the premises of the argument that the conclusion about to be made is already true. Also known as "circular reasoning."

beliefs Interpretations, evaluations, conclusions, or predictions about the world that we endorse as true.

bias A preference or an inclination, especially one that inhibits impartial judgment.

blueprint A detailed plan of action, model, or prototype.

Boolean logic A system of symbolic logic devised by George Boole; commonly used in computer languages and Internet searches.

brainstorming A method of shared problem solving in which all members of a group spontaneously contribute ideas.

causal chain A situation in which one thing leads to another, which then leads to another, and so on.

causal fallacies Mistakes and errors made in judgment in trying to determine causal relationships.

causal reasoning A form of inductive reasoning in which it is claimed that an event (or events) is the result of the occurrence of another event (or events).

causal relationship A relationship that involves relating events in terms of the influence or effect they have on one another.

Glossary definitions have been adapted and reproduced by permission of *The American Heritage Dictionary of the English Language*, Fourth Edition. Copyright © 2006 by Houghton Mifflin Company.

cause Anything that is responsible for bringing about something else, which is usually termed the *effect*.

cause-to-effect experiment (with intervention) A form of controlled experiment in which the conditions of one designated "experimental group" are altered, while those of a distinct "control group" (both within a target population) remain constant.

cause-to-effect experiment (without intervention) A form of experimental design similar to cause-to-effect experiment (with intervention), except that the experimenter does not intervene to expose the experimental group to a proposed cause.

certain Established beyond doubt or question; indisputable.

challenge A test of one's abilities or resources in a demanding but stimulating undertaking.

choose freely To choose to take different paths in life by exercising genuine freedom.

chronological Arranged in order of time of occurrence.

chronological relationship A relationship that relates events in time sequence.

circumstantial Of, relating to, or dependent on the conditions or details accompanying or surrounding an event.

classify To arrange or organize according to class or category.

cognition The thinking process of constructing beliefs that forms the basis of one's understanding of the world.

commit To pledge or obligate one's own self.

comparative/contrastive relationship A relationship that relates things in the same general category in terms of similarities and dissimilarities.

compared subject In an analogy, the object or idea that the original subject is being likened to.

comparing Evaluating similarities and differences.

concepts General ideas that we use to identify and organize our experience.

conclusion A statement that explains, asserts, or predicts on the basis of statements (known as reasons) that are offered as evidence for it.

conflict To be in or come into opposition; differ.

consequence Something that logically or naturally follows from an action or condition.

constructive criticism Analysis that serves to develop a better understanding of what is going on.

context The circumstances in which an event occurs; a setting.

contradict To be contrary to; be inconsistent with.

contribute To give or supply in common with others; give to a common fund or for a common purpose.

controlled experiment A powerful reasoning strategy used by scientists.

creative Able to break out of established patterns of thinking and approach situations from innovative directions.

creative thinking The act or habit of using our thinking process to develop ideas that are unique, useful, and worthy of further elaboration.

criteria A set of standards, rules, or tests on which a judgment or decision can be based.

critical analysis Analysis characterized by careful, exact evaluation and judgment.

critical thinking The act or habit of carefully exploring the thinking process to clarify our understanding and make more intelligent decisions.

cue words Key words that signal that a reason is being offered in support of a conclusion or that a conclusion is being announced on the basis of certain reasons.

curious Willing to explore situations with probing questions that penetrate beneath the surface of issues, instead of being satisfied with superficial explanations.

database A collection of data arranged for ease and speed of search and retrieval.

deductive argument An argument form in which one reasons from premises that are known or assumed to be true to a conclusion that follows necessarily from these premises.

define To describe the nature or basic qualities of; explain.

desirability The degree to which something is worth having, seeking, doing, or achieving, as by being useful, advantageous, or pleasing.

dialect A regional or social variety of a language distinguished by pronunciation, grammar, or vocabulary, especially a variety of speech differing from the standard literary language or speech pattern of the culture in which it exists.

dialogue A systematic exchange of ideas or opinions.

dilemma A situation that requires a choice between options that are or seem equally unfavorable or mutually exclusive.

disadvantage Something that places one in an unfavorable condition or circumstance.

disjunctive Presenting several alternatives.

disprove To prove to be false, invalid, or in error; refute.

distinguish To perceive as being different or distinct.

effect Something brought about by a cause or agent; a result.

effectiveness The degree to which something produces an intended or expected effect.

effect-to-cause experiment A form of reasoning employing the controlled experimental design in which the experimenter works backward from an existing effect to a suspected cause.

email A system for sending and receiving messages electronically over a computer network, as between personal computers; a message sent or received by an email system.

empirical generalization A form of inductive reasoning in which a general statement is made about an entire group (the target population) based on observing some members of the group (the sample population).

endorsement The act of giving approval or support.

ethical Of or concerned with the judgment of the goodness or badness of human action or character.

euphemism The act or an example of substituting a mild, indirect, or vague term for one considered harsh, blunt, or offensive.

evaluate To examine and judge carefully, based on specified criteria.

evidence A thing or things helpful in forming a conclusion or judgment.

external constraints Limits to one's freedom that come from outside oneself.

fact Knowledge or information based on real-world occurrences.

factual beliefs Beliefs based on observations.

factual evidence Evidence derived from a concrete, reliable source or foundation.

fallacies Unsound arguments that can appear to be logical and are often persuasive because they usually appeal to our emotions and prejudices and often support conclusions that we want to believe are accurate.

fallacy of relevance A fallacious argument that appeals for support to factors that have little or nothing to do with the argument being offered.

false dilemma A fallacy that occurs when we are asked to choose between two extreme alternatives without being able to consider additional options. Also known as the "either/or fallacy" or the "black-or-white fallacy."

falsifiable beliefs Beliefs that pass a set of tests or stated conditions formulated to test the beliefs.

fictional Relating to or characterized by an imaginative creation or a pretense that does not represent actuality but has been invented.

flexible Responsive to change; adaptable.

form To develop in the mind; conceive.

generalize To focus on the common properties shared by a group of things.

genuine Honestly felt or experienced.

hasty generalization A general conclusion that is based on a very small sample.

hedonism A moral theory that advises people to do whatever brings them pleasure.

home page The opening or main page of a website, intended chiefly to greet visitors and provide information about the site or its owner.

hypertext A computer-based text retrieval system that enables a user to access particular locations in web pages or other electronic documents by clicking on links within specific web pages or documents.

hypothesis A possible explanation that is introduced to account for a set of facts and that can be used as a basis for further investigation.

identify To ascertain the origin, nature, or definitive characteristics.

illumination Spiritual or intellectual enlightenment; clarification; elucidation.

incomplete comparison A comparison in which focus is placed on too few points of comparison.

independent thinkers Those who are not afraid to disagree with the group opinion and who develop well-supported beliefs through thoughtful analysis, instead of uncritically "borrowing" the beliefs of others.

inductive reasoning An argument form in which one reasons from premises that are known or assumed to be true to a conclusion that is supported by the premises but does not necessarily follow from them.

infer To conclude from evidence or premises.

inference The act or process of deriving logical conclusions from premises known or assumed to be true; the act of reasoning from factual knowledge or evidence.

inferential beliefs Beliefs that are based on inferences, that go beyond what can be directly observed.

inferring Describing the world in ways that are based on factual information yet going beyond this information to make statements about what is not currently known.

informed Well acquainted with knowledge of a subject.

insightful Displaying an incisive understanding of a complex event.

interactive Acting or capable of acting on each other.

internal constraints Limits to one's freedom that come from within oneself.

Internet An interconnected system of networks that links computers around the world via the TCP/IP protocol.

interpret To explain the meaning of; to conceive the significance of, construe; to look for different examples of a concept in order to determine if they meet the requirements of that concept.

interpretation The result of conceiving or explaining the meaning of.

intuition A sense of something not evident or deducible; an impression.

invalid argument An argument in which the reasons do not support the conclusion so that the conclusion does not follow from the reasons offered.

jargon A style of language made up of words, expressions, and technical terms that are intelligible to professional circles or interest groups but not to the general public.

judging Describing the world in ways that express an evaluation based on certain criteria.

justification The act of demonstrating or proving to be just, right, or valid.

key questions Questions that can be used to explore situations and issues systematically.

knowledge Familiarity, awareness, or understanding gained through experience or study. Information doesn't become knowledge until it has been thought about critically.

knowledgeable Perceptive or well-informed.

language A system of symbols for thinking and communicating.

link A segment of text or a graphical item that serves as a cross-reference between parts of a hypertext document or between files or hypertext documents. Also called "hotlink," "hyperlink." By clicking on a link, one can directly access a website or home page.

live creatively To approach life with a mindful sense of discovery and invention, enabling one to continually create oneself in ways limited only by the imagination.

mentally active Taking initiative and actively using intelligence to confront problems and meet challenges, instead of responding passively to events.

metaphor An implied comparison between basically dissimilar things for the purpose of illuminating our understanding of the things being compared.

mindful Making use of our responsive, perceptive faculties, thus avoiding rigid, reflexive behavior in favor of a more improvisational and intuitive response to life.

mind map A visual presentation of the ways concepts can be related to one another.

misidentification of the cause An error that occurs in causal situations when identification of the cause and the effect are unclear.

modus ponens "Affirming the antecedent"; a valid deductive form commonly used in our logical thinking.

modus tollens "Denying the consequence"; a commonly used valid deductive form.

moral Of or concerned with the judgment of the goodness or badness of human action and character.

moral agnosticism A theory of morality that holds there is no way to determine clearly what is "right" or "wrong" in moral situations.

moral values Personal qualities and rules of conduct that distinguish a person (and group of people) of upstanding character.

narrative A way of thinking and communicating in which someone tells a story about experiences he or she has had.

necessary Needed to achieve a certain result or effect; requisite.

open-minded Listening carefully to every viewpoint, evaluating each perspective carefully and fairly.

organize To put together into an orderly, functional, structured whole.

original subject In an analogy, the primary object or idea being described or compared.

paradox A seemingly contradictory statement that may nonetheless be true.

passionate Having a passion for understanding; always striving to see issues and problems with more clarity.

perceiving Actively selecting, organizing, and interpreting what is experienced by your senses.

perceptual meaning A component of a word's total meaning that expresses the relationship between a linguistic event and an individual's consciousness. Also known as "connotative meaning."

personal experience Examples from one's own life; one of the four categories of evidence.

perspective Point of view.

post hoc ergo propter hoc "After it, therefore because of it"; refers to situations in which, because two things occur close together in time, an assumption is made that one causes the other.

practice A habitual or customary way of doing something.

pragmatic Dealing or concerned with facts or actual occurrences; practical.

pragmatic meaning A component of a word's total meaning that involves the person who is speaking and the situation in which the word is spoken. Also known as "situational meaning."

precision The state or quality of being specific, detailed, and exact.

prediction The act of stating, telling about, or making known in advance, especially on the basis of special knowledge.

premise A proposition on which an argument is based or from which a conclusion is drawn.

principle A plausible or coherent scenario that has yet to be applied to experience.

prioritize To organize things in order of importance.

process analysis A method of analysis involving two steps: (1) to divide the process or activity being analyzed into parts or stages, and (2) to explain the movement of the process through these parts or stages from beginning to end.

process relationships Relationships based on the relation of aspects of the growth or development of an event or object.

procrastinate To put off doing something, especially out of habitual carelessness or laziness; to postpone or delay needlessly.

properties Qualities or features that all things named by a word or sign share in common.

psychological Of, relating to, or arising from the mind or emotions.

quality An inherent or distinguishing characteristic; property; essential character or nature.

questionable cause A causal fallacy that occurs when someone presents a causal relationship for which no real evidence exists.

random selection A selection strategy in which every member of the target population has an equal chance of being included in the sample.

reasoning The type of thinking that uses argument—reasons in support of conclusions.

reasons Statements that support another statement (known as a conclusion), justify it, or make it more probable.

receptive Open to new ideas and experiences.

red herring A fallacy that is committed by introducing an irrelevant topic in order to divert attention from the original issue being discussed. Also known as "smoke screen" and "wild goose chase."

referents All the various examples of a concept.

relate To bring into or link in logical or natural association; to establish or demonstrate a connection between.

relativism A philosophical view that says that truth is relative to the individual or situation, that there is no standard we can use to decide which beliefs make most sense.

relevant Having a bearing on or connection with the matter at hand.

reliable Offering dependable information.

report A description of something experienced that is communicated as accurately and as completely as possible.

reporting factual information Describing the world in ways that can be verified through investigation.

representative In statistical sampling, when the sample is considered to accurately reflect the larger whole, or target population, from which the sample is taken.

revise To reconsider and change or modify.

role The characteristic and expected social behavior of an individual.

sample A portion, piece, or segment that is intended to be representative of a whole.

scientific method An organized approach devised by scientists for discovering causal relationships and testing the accuracy of conclusions.

select To choose from among several; to pick out.

selective comparison A problem that occurs in making comparisons when a one-sided view of a comparative situation is taken.

self-aware Being conscious of one's own biases and being quick to point them out and take them into consideration when analyzing a situation.

semantic meaning A component of a word's total meaning that expresses the relationship between a linguistic event and a nonlinguistic event. Also known as "denotative meaning."

senses Sight, hearing, smell, touch, and taste; means through which you experience your world and are aware of what occurs outside you.

sign The word or symbol used to name or designate a concept.

simile An explicit comparison between basically dissimilar things made for the purpose of illuminating our understanding of the things being compared.

skilled discussants Those who are able to discuss ideas in an organized and intelligent way. Even when the issues are controversial, they listen carefully to opposing viewpoints and respond thoughtfully.

slang A kind of language occurring chiefly in casual and playful speech, made up typically of short-lived coinages

and figures of speech that are deliberately used in place of standard terms for added raciness, humor, irreverence, or other effect.

slippery slope A causal fallacy that asserts that one undesirable action will inevitably lead to a worse action, which will necessarily lead to a worse one still, all the way down the "slippery slope" to some terrible disaster at the bottom.

social variation Variation of language style due to differences in the age, sex, or social class of the speakers.

Socratic method A method of inquiry that uses a dynamic approach of questioning and intellectual analysis to explore the essential nature of concepts.

solution The answer to or disposition of a problem.

sound argument A deductive argument in which the premises are true and the logical structure is valid.

source A person or document that supplies information.

special pleading A fallacy that occurs when someone makes him- or herself a special exception, without sound justification, to the reasonable application of standards, principles, or expectations.

Standard American English (SAE) The style of the English language used in most academic and workplace writing, following the rules and conventions given in handbooks and taught in school.

standards Degrees or levels of requirement, excellence, or attainment.

stereotype A conventional, formulaic, and oversimplified conception, opinion, or image.

stimulus Something causing or regarded as causing a response.

straw man A fallacy in which a point of view is attacked by first creating a "straw man" version of the position and then "knocking down" the straw man created. The fallacy lies in that the straw man does not reflect an accurate representation of the position being challenged.

subject directory Created by universities, libraries, companies, organizations, and even volunteers, consisting of links to Internet resources.

sufficient Being as much as is needed; enough.

surfing the Web Following a chain of links from web pages to other related pages.

sweeping generalization A general conclusion that overlooks exceptions that should be excluded because of their special features.

syllogism A form of deductive reasoning consisting of a major premise, a minor premise, and a conclusion.

symbolize To represent something else.

syntactic meaning A component of a word's total meaning that defines its relation to other words in the sentence.

synthesis The combining of separate elements or substances to form a coherent whole.

target population The entire group regarding which conclusions are drawn through statistical sampling and inductive reasoning.

testimony A declaration by a witness under oath, as that given before a court or deliberative body.

theist moral theory A theory of morality that holds that "right" and "wrong" are determined by a supernatural Supreme Being ("God").

theory A plausible or coherent scenario that has yet to be applied to experience; a set of statements or principles devised to explain a group of facts or phenomena, normally involving a number of interconnected hypotheses.

thesis A proposition that is maintained by argument; the issue on which an argument takes position.

thinking A purposeful, organized cognitive process that we use to understand the world and make informed decisions.

thinking creatively Using our thinking process to develop ideas that are unique, useful, and worthy of further elaboration.

thinking critically The cognitive process we use to carefully explore our thinking (and the thinking of others) to clarify and improve our understanding and to make more intelligent decisions.

total meaning The meaning of a word believed by linguists to be composed of the semantic meaning, perceptual meaning, syntactic meaning, and pragmatic meaning.

two wrongs make a right A fallacy that attempts to justify a morally questionable action by arguing that it is a response to another wrong action, either real or imagined.

uniform resource locator (URL) An Internet address (e.g., http://www.cengage.com/english), usually consisting of the access protocol (*http*), the domain name (*www.cengage.com*), and optionally the path to a file or resource residing on that server (*/english/*).

uninformed decision A decision that is the product of inaccurate information or inadequate experience.

unsound argument A deductive argument in which the premises are false, the logical structure is invalid, or both.

vague word A word that lacks a clear and distinct meaning.

valid argument An argument in which the reasons support the conclusion so that the conclusion follows from the reasons offered.

values Beliefs regarding what is most important to us.

vocation A calling; an occupation for which a person is particularly suited.

Web Shortened reference to the World Wide Web.

web browser A program such as Microsoft Internet Explorer or Safari that uses a URL to identify and retrieve files from the host computer on which they reside, displaying web pages in a convenient manner to the user.

web search engine A program such as Yahoo! or Google that retrieves information about Internet sites containing user-entered keywords.

website A set of interconnected web pages, usually including a home page, generally located on the same server, and prepared and maintained as a collection of information by a person, group, or organization.

word A sound or a combination of sounds that symbolizes and communicates a meaning.

written references Evidence derived from the written opinions of another person; one of the four categories of evidence.

Index

THINKING CRITICALLY ABOUT NEW MEDIA